REBEL

GIBRALTAR

Fort Fisher
and
Wilmington, C.S.A.

By James L. Walker, Jr.

Dram Tree Books
Books
A JEF Publications Company

First Edition 2005

Published in the United States of America by Dram Tree Books, a JEF Publications company.

Publisher's Cataloging-in-Publication Data
(Provided by DRT Press)

Walker, James Laurence
    Rebel Gibraltar: Fort Fisher and Wilmington, C.S.A. / by James L. Walker, Jr.
    p. cm.
    Includes bibliographical references and index.
    ISBN 0-9723240-7-0

1. Fort Fisher Region (N.C.)--History--Civil War, 1861-1865. 2. Fort Fisher (N.C. : Fort)--Siege, 1864-1865. 3. Fort Fisher (N.C. : Fort)--Capture, 1865. 4. Wilmington Region (N.C.)--History--Civil War, 1861-1865. 5. North Carolina--History--Civil War, 1861-1865. 6. North Carolina--History--Civil War, 1861-1865--Blockades. 7. Confederate States of America--History. 8. United States--History--Civil War, 1861-1865. I. Title.

E524 .W35 2005
973.737--dc22

10 9 8 7 6 5 4 3 2

Dram Tree Books
2801 Lyndon Avenue
Wilmington, N.C. 28405-3045
(910) 538-4076
dramtreebooks@ec.rr.com

Discounts available
for educators.
Call or e-mail for terms.

This Volume is Affectionately

Dedicated to my Loving Wife of 34 years,

Janice,

Without whose enduring patience and steadfast love,

It would have never seen

The light of day.

Acknowledgements

Anyone who writes history will readily confess to having had tremendous help from many people. My experience has been no exception. Those with knowledge and resources far beyond mine have graciously offered their assistance for years. First in the ranks of those who encouraged me in this project nearly twenty years ago is my dear friend and mentor, Mr. Selby Daniels. Selby is widely known and much esteemed in history circles in North Carolina. A walking encyclopedia of knowledge of all eras of North Carolina's history, particularly related to the American Revolution or the Confederacy, those who know Selby could liken him to a current-day Samuel Ashe. Ashe was a Confederate officer and acclaimed post-war historian. He wrote a massive, some would say definitive, two-volume study of the State's history in the 1920's called, *History of North Carolina*. There is probably little in Ashe's history about which Selby could not expound.

As soon as Selby heard of my research in the late 1980's, he began loaning or giving me from his own collection, books, diaries, letters, orders, etc., without which this volume would be far less in scope than it is. He has inquired about the project constantly, dug up additional material to help, and in every way been a major contributor to the study. I will never be able to thank this true Southern gentleman and World War II combat veteran enough. He is an inspiration for all who know him and aspire to study history.

Very close to Selby must come my good friend, Dan Barefoot, author of the invaluable biography directly related to the last chapters of this study, *General Robert F. Hoke, Lee's Modest Warrior*. Dan, also, is a gifted and widely known historian, as well as an excellent speaker, with nine volumes of history and historical tour guides under his belt. Dan generously offered to read and critique the manuscript. Critique it he did, pointing out ways to significantly improve certain aspects of the work. I am most grateful for Dan's detailed comments and suggestions, which have been of much value in improving the study.

I am equally appreciative of Dan's kind words in the forward, and hope that the work comes close to meeting the endorsement he has graciously given. Dan and I have discussed for years the roles of Robert Hoke, Braxton Bragg, Chase Whiting, William Lamb, Ben Butler and others who were at Fort Fisher. With the expert knowledge he possesses of General Hoke's performance on the Cape Fear, it seemed appropriate that he would be the one to examine this study. For his help and endorsement, I am extremely grateful.

Mr. Gehrig Spencer, retired now from his duties as site specialist at Fort Fisher State Historic Site, was very giving of his time and help in the 1980's and early 1990's. He helped with information related to Colonel Lamb, the fight for the *Hebe* in 1863, and discussed details of the infantry battle of January 15, 1865. Fifteen years ago, he took my battlefield buddies and me on a personal guided tour at dusk of the area north of the landface. We walked down the old River Road for a while, and then cut across the ground over which Martin Curtis' Brigade attacked before they crossed the marsh slough to hit Shepherd's Battery. It was truly a memorable hike we took that evening, listening to him describe the battle as we walked. Mr. Spencer encouraged me to continue the research, stating that there was much that could be written about Fort Fisher, that some of the most important history of the entire war was right there in the Wilmington area. How true it is, and for his kind help and encouragement, I am most appreciative.

Miss Margaret C. Cook, Curator of Manuscripts and Rare Books Emerita of the Earl Gregg Swem Library, College of William and Mary in Williamsburg, Virginia, was most gracious 14 years ago. She not only helped with diary copies and information related to Colonel Lamb, where his papers are carefully preserved, but permitted me to visit and handle some of the Colonel's diaries and other documents. For her kindness, and that of her staff, I am most grateful.

I wish to express my appreciation to the staffs of the following institutions: the Sargeant Memorial Room of the Norfolk Public Library, Norfolk, Virginia, the Carolina Room of the Public Library, Charlotte, North Carolina, the William R. Perkins Library, Duke University, Durham, the Southern Historical Collection, Chapel Hill, North Carolina, the North Carolina Department of Archives and History, Raleigh, and the Manuscript Department of Yale University Library, New Haven, Connecticut.

For having faith in the value of this manuscript, I thank Mr. Jack Fryar, publisher and owner of Dram Tree Books. For introducing me to Jack Fryar, I thank Mr. Ray Flowers, historian at Fort Fisher State Historic Site. I thank Mr. Danny Barbie, who works at the fort in the summers, for introducing me to Ray Flowers.

Thanks go to two of my good friends for loaning some of their collections. Doug Proctor loaned a letter from his ancestor, George Moffett, to be used in the narrative. Rusty Lewis, great-great grandson of George W. Benson, last survivor of Fort Fisher, kindly loaned newspaper articles. His mother, Doris Lewis, generously loaned a picture of her great-grandfather for publication.

My daughter, Kelly Burton, and her husband Anthony, as well as my wife Janice and son, Shawn, were most patient and helpful when old Dad was about to pull his hair out dealing with the computer. Thanks to all four of you for rescuing me from technology jams. Thanks must also go to my dear mother, Lib Walker, a Wilmington gal born and raised, who has reminded me not to lose faith, and to see the job through. Thanks also to my aunt, Annell Brown, for the picture of her grandfather, Joe King.

I wish also to thank my good friends who have been with me on trips over the years to visit Colonel Lamb's home and grave in Norfolk, or to visit Fort Fisher and Wilmington, or just to patiently listen while I bored them with stories. All of them have accompanied me on trips to those places or other battlefield sites for many years, part of the time being spent discussing Fort

Fisher and Wilmington. All have encouraged me to stay the course and finish the job. Those compatriots of many fine history trips are: Jim Richardson, Steve Suther, Brad Bush, Dan Stroupe, Doug Proctor, Mike Ridge, and my brother-in-law Ronnie Cranford. Another good friend who is an author of conscription history during the war, Walt Hilderman, has also encouraged me. Likewise, so has another friend, Hugh Harkey, a historian of four volumes of his own, urged me to complete the task. John Ellis, another good friend, has also offered encouragement and suggestions over the years.

Finally, I would be remiss if I did not express thanks to five wonderful ladies, two of them deceased now, who provided inspiration over the years. They have all been, or were, for years, members of the United Daughters of the Confederacy. All worked diligently and tirelessly to preserve Southern history, and had a profound influence on my interest to write history. They are Mrs. Betty Terwilliger and Mrs. Ann Fleming, of the Stonewall Jackson Chapter, Mrs. Helen Chappell of the Henry Severs Chapter, Mrs. Hazel Robinson (deceased) of the Henry Severs Chapter, and Mrs. Martha Washam (deceased) of the Stonewall Jackson Chapter. Mrs. Terwilliger, Mrs. Fleming, and Mrs. Chappell have been staunch promoters of Southern history for decades, and encouraged me to keep pushing. Mrs. Washam, who lived to be 100 years old, and gave her last public talk on the War when she was 99, was truly an icon of Confederate history and knowledge in this area. As a 12-year-old girl in 1915, she saw the funeral of Mrs. Stonewall Jackson here in Charlotte. Her love for reading and learning Southern history was infectious, and all of us who knew her consider ourselves blessed for the experience. Mrs. Hazel Robinson was an energetic worker, as well, playing a prominent role in 1977, in the erection of Charlotte's first Confederate monument to be erected in many years. She and Mrs. Washam are sorely missed. I hope they would consider this manuscript a project that does justice to the memory of the Confederate soldiers of Fort Fisher.

James L. Walker, Jr.

A Special Acknowledgement

I particularly want to extend special thanks and acknowledgement to Mr. Mark A. Moore for permission to publish in this study many of the maps from his excellent work, *The Wilmington Campaign and the Battles for Fort Fisher*. Mark is the premiere Civil War cartographer in the country today. Mr. Edwin Bearss, Historian Emeritus of the National Park Service, and one of the most esteemed and knowledgeable of battlefield historians, has compared Mark Moore to Stonewall Jackson's mapmaker during the war. Mr. Bearss has said that Mark Moore is the "Jedediah Hotchkiss of the twentieth century." Quite a strong and lauditory comparison, considering the fame that Jedediah Hotchkiss earned making maps for one of the greatest American generals!

Mark Moore's maps have graced the pages and enhanced the study of Mark Bradley's ground-breaking work, *Last Stand in the Carolinas: The Battle of Bentonville*. So, too, has Chris Fonvielle, Jr.'s *Last Rays of Departing Hope: The Wilmington Campaign*, benefited from Moore's excellent campaign and battle maps, some of which are reproduced in this work.

The understanding of this manuscript as well, then, is tremendously enhanced by Mr. Moore's incomparable maps. His precise attention to detail and accuracy comes from intense study and knowledge of the geography and fortifications of the Lower Cape Fear, and the movements of regiments and brigades in the battles of December 1864 through February 1865. No historical work today concerned with the Fort Fisher and Wilmington Campaigns would be complete without Mark Moore's maps. I am deeply grateful for his permission to reprint them in this study.

James L. Walker, Jr.

Chapters

Foreword

In the pages that follow, you will read the gripping account of the vital role
that Fort Fisher and the port city of Wilmington played in the Civil War.
Larry Walker has meticulously crafted a worthwhile, detailed story of the
coastal area in southeastern North Carolina which ultimately grew to such
importance and prominence that General Robert E. Lee proclaimed, "If
Wilmington falls, I shall have to evacuate Richmond."

Larry Walker and I quickly became friends soon after our paths first
crossed some fifteen years ago at a historical meeting related to the events in
the Cape Fear area of North Carolina during the titanic struggle from 1861 to
1865. Our common interests in Confederate history, and particularly in the
Civil War history of North Carolina, had led us to begin work on separate, but
somewhat related, books. At the time, I was engaged in researching and writing
General Robert F. Hoke: Lee's Modest Warrior (the first and only biography of
the division commander assigned to the defense of the Cape Fear in December
1864), and Larry was at work on this volume. *General Robert F. Hoke* was
released by John F. Blair, Publisher, in 1996 and remains in print. In the
meantime, Larry continued to perfect the in-depth study now embodied in
Rebel Gibraltar.

Larry Walker is very passionate about his subject, and that great passion has enabled him to deliver a volume unlike any other in the annals of Civil War literature. During the course of the twenty-year period that he spent researching and writing this engrossing story, two fine volumes, devoted specifically to the battles fought at Fort Fisher and the subsequent struggle for Wilmington from December 1864 to February 1865, have been published. Rod Gragg's *Confederate Goliath: The Battle for Fort Fisher* (1991) and Dr. Chris Fonvielle's *The Wilmington Campaign: Last Rays of Departing Hope* (1997) are both excellent studies of the military operations in the Cape Fear during the climactic days of late 1864 and early 1865. But unlike the books by Gragg and Fonvielle, *Rebel Gibraltar* chronicles the full story of Fort Fisher and the upriver port city of Wilmington during the entire span of the war.

Through his years of dedicated research and study, Larry Walker has produced a work that brings life to the places, the people, and the events in the Cape Fear during the turbulent times from 1860 to 1865. From the planning stages of Fort Fisher to the bloody battles fought on its ramparts, the complete story of the magnificent, sturdy fortification known as "the Gibraltar of the South" is told for the first time. And likewise, the crucial place of Wilmington in Confederate military history, long neglected by many scholars, is thoroughly examined and explained. To complete the study, Larry carefully weaves a detailed account of the blockade runners that frequently plied the Atlantic to reach the Cape Fear. Laden with badly-needed supplies for the Southern war effort, these ships were called "the lifeline of the Confederacy."

My great-great-great-grandfather was taken prisoner while manning the Confederate artillery at Fort Fisher when the fort was captured on January 15, 1865. He subsequently died as a prisoner of war in the Union prison at Elmira, New York. Larry Walker has written an account that helps me to better understand the events that led to the capture and death of my grandfather. You, too, will be captivated by the story that is told here: it is a story of political and military intrigue, of swashbuckling naval action, of massive land and sea battles, of hand-to-hand combat, of the dramatic, desperate struggle to keep the hopes of Southern independence alive. It is a story well told by Larry Walker.

Daniel W. Barefoot
Author of
General Robert F. Hoke: Lee's Modest Warrior
and
Let Us Die Like Brave Men:
Behind the Dying Words of Confederate Warriors

Preface

My earliest recollections are of the dark gray sand of Wilmington. It was October 1949, and my father, Jimmy Walker, had accepted a new job in Charlotte, a much larger North Carolina city 200 miles west of Wilmington. We were leaving our home off Princess Place Drive, across Burnt Mill Creek from old Bellevue Cemetery. Three years old at the time, I remember standing in the soft, rich soil my people have called home for 250 years, and talking to our neighbor. I was explaining to the lady next door, as a small child would do, about the big move to a big town that Mamma and Daddy and I were making.

Many years later, I would learn that our house stood no more than 300 yards from the Bellevue Cemetery graves of my grandfather, Harry Lee Walker, and his parents, William and Sallie Walker. Not far from them, lies the grave of another great-grandfather, Joseph Piram King, who as a teenager butchered cattle for the garrison of Fort Fisher, and had died in 1948, the year before we moved. Buried almost beside Joe lies his brother, Isaac Watts King, who was wounded in 1862 fighting for Robert E. Lee, and near them both, my great-great grandfather Owen Kennedy, who had also fought for Lee and later served in the trenches outside Wilmington.

Mamma's family, the Hewletts, had a major creek named for them long ago that empties into Masonboro Sound, an area where they have lived for over 200 years. Another of Lib Hewlett Walker's great-grandfathers, John Savage, who rests in Oakdale Cemetery, manned an artillery piece in 1865 in trenches that still stand on either side of 17th Street Extension. And Daddy, a combat pilot in World War II, now rests in the National Cemetery on Market Street, which opened in 1865 as a burial site for Union troops killed at Fort Fisher and during fighting over the following month. Some years ago, I learned that my father's name, and thereby mine, were derived from that of James Sprunt, the premier chronicler of Cape Fear history. It seems that Sprunt's son, James Laurence, was best friend of my grandfather Harry Lee, who gave Daddy his friend's name. In Wilmington, one's heritage is often close by.

My interest in Wilmington's history began over 50 years ago, when Granny Grace King Walker, Harry Lee's wife, told us grandchildren stories about her "Papa", Joe King, riding horseback and driving cattle down the old River Road from town to Fort Fisher. She also told us of his founding the Advent Christian Church in the 1870's after the war, and becoming a self-taught doctor who treated folks and delivered hundreds of babies, white and black, for many years. Daddy and his eight brothers and sisters, who were all close to their grandfather, frequently discussed Grandpa King's interesting and long life (he was six months shy of 100 when he died). They told of his driving and butchering cattle for the Confederate soldiers at the fort as if it occurred the previous week, of Grandpa's brothers fighting for General Lee in the army in Virginia, and of their playing on Confederate earthworks as children on their Grandpa's property in the 1920's. Not knowing it at the time, I internalized as a child what the great Mississippi novelist William Faulkner alluded to when he wrote, "In the South the past is not dead; it isn't even past."

Those many stories about my people fascinated and pulled at me as a boy, generating an abiding love for learning and reading all I could find on the War Between the States. By the time I reached adulthood, I had learned much about Grandpa King's life, the service of his brothers in the Army of Northern Virginia, and had become a serious student of that conflict. Most students of the war are keenly aware that the majority of battles and campaigns have not been given their fair share of historical study. Gettysburg, the most universally recognized engagement in Civil War history, is the only campaign that has been accorded a massive amount of study, and there are still several volumes each year that are published on this bloody and significant battle. Campaigns in the western theater of equal or nearly equal decisiveness as Gettysburg, such as Elkhorn Tavern (Pea Ridge), Arkansas, Vicksburg, Mississippi, Chickamauga, Georgia, or the Atlanta Campaign, have had very few volumes written on the combat and consequences of each. So too it is with Wilmington's Confederate history.

After the contribution North Carolina's 127,000 troops made on the battlefields of the war, the next most important was the preservation of Robert E. Lee's line of supply. That line of supply was a regular, predictable, and continuous flow of goods of every manner and description to sustain the Confederacy's most successful army in the field. Those goods arrived on blockade-runners, fast, low-slung, all steel, propeller or paddlewheel driven, camouflaged commerce runners. Those swift and most modern ships of the day were able to arrive at Wilmington's docks because of Fort Fisher. The captains of those vessels knew they would usually be safe running past the Union blockading fleet, once they got within range of Fort Fisher's guns, or her outlying batteries up and down the beach.

Fort Fisher was the largest and most successful fortification in the Confederate States, and was the site of one of the most vicious battles of the war. Without Fort Fisher, Lee's army would have starved or been forced to evacuate Richmond many months before the end finally came. The fight that occurred at this massive sand Gibraltar on Federal Point (Confederate Point during the war), twenty miles south of Wilmington on the peninsula between the Atlantic and the Cape Fear River, was first given long-overdue recognition in Rod Gragg's ground-breaking study, *Confederate Goliath: The Battle of Fort Fisher*, published in 1991. His is a detailed and graphically written account of the battles for the fort that occurred in December 1864 and January 1865, and is highly valued by those who seek an excellent narrative of the battles and personalities involved.

So, too, is Chris Fonvielle's 1997 volume, *The Wilmington Campaign: Last Rays of Departing Hope.* The massive amount of detail Chris has incorporated in his first-rate, well written study of the battles of December 1864 and January 1865, as well as the month long campaign to secure Wilmington in February, a month after Fisher fell, is truly impressive. His superb book, also, is much prized by students of Fort Fisher.

Mark Moore's 1999 study, *Moore's Historical Guide to The Wilmington Campaign and the Battles for Fort Fisher*, is another fine volume dealing with the battles for the fort and the campaign to take Wilmington the following month. Replete with excellent battle maps, detailed maps of the many different forts that surrounded the entrance to the Cape Fear River, and directions to guide one around the entire Wilmington area to see what remains from the war days, Mark's book is a goldmine for those who enjoy battlefield tramping.

In addition to these three fine volumes, there is much more that can, and likely will be written in the coming years. This volume, *Rebel Gibraltar: Fort Fisher and Wilmington, C.S.A.*, seeks to add to that overlooked history of the war on the Cape Fear. The story of Fort Fisher and Wilmington is more than the story of the December 1864 through February 1865 campaigns. Those last three months of the war on the Cape Fear certainly witnessed one of the greatest and bloodiest battles on North Carolina soil, and merits extensive scholarly study. However, the story of the three-year success of Fort Fisher, from late 1861 to late 1864, has not been told, until now.

Fort Fisher's success was in its vigilant, violent protection of the blockade-running fleet, which employed Wilmington as its primary port for at least two years before the town fell. The blockade-runners sustained an army and a people with their cargo of every description, much as the "Hump" pilots of the U.S. Army Air Force, flying C-46 and other transport planes over the Himalayas, sustained the Nationalist Chinese Army and General Claire Chennault's fighters and bombers against the Japanese, 80 years later.

From late 1861, and particularly from 1862, after William Lamb took command at Fort Fisher, the artillerists manning the big seacoast guns there and in other area forts, as well as at detached batteries, fought the Yankee gunboats frequently to protect the swift commerce vessels. Mainly British owned, these ships ran in almost every day from Nassau and Bermuda (the primary transshipment points) with weapons, ammunition, food and clothing, bound for Wilmington's docks. As the Federal blockaders chased and fired on them, the Rebel forts fired back to protect them. Vicious fights occurred often, with both Northern and Southern blood being spilled. Usually the Confederates were victorious and the blockade-runners saved, the sometimes-battered gunboats withdrawing to keep from being sunk. Some, in fact, were sunk, and ships' crews wound up in Confederate prisons. Sometimes the runners were lost, but the fights were fierce and the Yankees were driven off.

The emphasis of this book is that story. Battles, for example, over the blockade-runners *Kate* in July 1863 off Bald Head Island, the *Hebe* in August 1863 off Myrtle Sound, and the *Fanny and Jenny* off Wrightsville Beach in February 1864, were all hot fights and are given their fair share of narrative. The destruction of the *U.S.S. Columbia* off Masonboro Sound in January 1863, and the sinking of the *U.S.S. Peterhoff* in March 1864 off Bald Head Island, are examples of Union vessels that paid the ultimate price for blockade duty off the Cape Fear.

The centerpiece of *Rebel Gibraltar*, then, relates to those battles for the protection of the Confederacy's lifeline, the success of which motivated the Federal attacks to secure the fort and town. Some chapters are devoted to Wilmington at the beginning of and during the war. Detailed coverage is given to the terrible yellow fever epidemic of 1862, the horrific scourge that killed approximately one-fifth of Wilmington's wartime population in four months. The last few chapters, of course, do cover the battles for Fisher and those that resulted in the fall of Wilmington.

It is my sincere wish that this volume helps to further historical understanding and promote additional study of Wilmington's Confederate history.

James L. Walker Jr.
Charlotte, N.C.
March, 2005

The Chase

(from Chronicles of the Cape Fear River: 1660 - 1916)

Freed from the lingering chase, in devious ways
Upon the swelling tides
Swiftly the "Lilian" glides
Through hostile shells and eager foemen past;
The lynx-eyed pilot gazing through the haze,
And engines straining, "far hope dawns at last."

Now falls in billows deep the welcome night
Upon white sands below;
While signal lamps aglow
Seek out Fort Fisher's distant answering gleams,
The blockade runner's keen, supreme delight, -
Dear Dixie Land, the haven of our dreams!

- James Sprunt

Chapter 1

"The young men wore secession rosettes..."

N orth Carolinians were a worried people as the year 1860 drew to a close. The most dramatic political decision in the nation's history since 1776 was being determined on Tuesday, November the 6th. The election of the President of the United States was at hand, and the results would determine whether some Southern states would secede if the Illinoisan Abraham Lincoln were sent to the White House by a Northern majority.

The *Wilmington Daily Journal* told its readers on the day before the election that the 6th of November would "be among the most momentous days in the history of the American people, and all ought to feel that upon those vested with the right of suffrage is also imposed the responsibility of exercising that right honestly, after reflection and consideration." The editors of the paper, James Fulton and A.L. Price, felt the South had a chance to carry the election, and for the good of the nation, urged all Wilmington Democrats to cast their votes for Kentuckian John C. Breckinridge, the current Vice President under James Buchanan, for President, and his running mate, General Joseph Lane of Oregon, for Vice President. [1]

"Can Lincoln be defeated? is the question most frequently and most earnestly asked," voiced the *Daily Journal*. "We think he can – at least there appears to be a chance, a fair chance for doing so...Let us do our duty here, by voting for those men and that party whose firm position alone has brought the North to pause and ponder in the midst of its wild career. If Lincoln is defeated, and sectionalism rebuked, the country will owe it to the firm attitude of the National Democracy, and the party of Breckinridge and Lane." [2]

November 6 came, and when the day ended, the worst fear of most Southerners had been realized. Lincoln was elected. "A new era is to be entered upon", voiced the *Daily Journal* in its November 7 edition, "one which ought to unite every Southern man in defence of the right of the South, for they are threatened, menaced and actually in danger. This election of Lincoln is a serious thing. It means all the insult for the present and all the injury for the future that such an act can do. We doubt if too gloomy or too serious a view can be taken of this event." [3]

Reverend John L. Prichard of the First Baptist Church in Wilmington noted in his diary on November 7, "The telegraph says that Lincoln is elected President! The deepest feeling is manifested by all. Secession is talked of. O God, undertake for us, we beseech Thee." [4]

Several days later, the *Daily Journal* echoed the sentiments of many Wilmingtonians, saying that "the great step has been taken which must end either in the disruption of the government, or the annihilation of the rights of the Southern States and the citizens thereof." [5]

Lincoln's accession to the White House had sounded a tocsin that reverberated through every corner of the Southern States. Here now was a sectionally elected President of a sectional party, one of whose prime purposes, it was perceived, was to not only prevent the spread of slavery into the territories, but eventually to legislate it out of existence altogether. The dire consequences of a bloodbath of racial insurrection that might follow such action was more than most southerners could bear to contemplate. They recalled the 1790's slave uprisings in San Domingo, where the blacks had perpetrated "wholesale massacres of the white population of that French colony." [6]

Nat Turner's Rebellion, in which about sixty people, mostly women and children, had been brutally murdered in Southampton County, Virginia, was only thirty years in the past, and the whole of the Yankee nation, it seemed, had eulogized John Brown into sainthood, ignoring the fact that he was a murderer from "Bleeding Kansas" and a lunatic to boot. [7]

Now here the Yankees were, bringing into the White House and the halls of Congress those Republican fanatics, whose sole purpose was to extinguish slavery and the whole of Southern civilization for the political gain of power hungry Northern industrialists. Lincoln was elected because he was "put forth at this time as the representative of the Northern sentiment of hostility to the South and to her institutions." [8]

Slavery, Southerners believed, was just an emotional rallying cry and vote-getter to sway the Northern electorate the way of the rising industrialists, whose attempts at securing government subsidies had been frustrated for years by Southern political dominance in Washington. So when Lincoln was elected, it was believed he and his party, through restriction of the political force of the South by limiting the spread of slavery, would attempt to remake Southerners in the mold of the North, one way or the other. And that, too, as well as just the issue of slavery, was something the South would not stand for. [9]

"The more Southerners viewed their own civilization the more they feared the dangers of its disintegration by the infiltration of Northern radicalism and its actual overthrow by continued Northern agitation and outright attack." They despised the notion that they should be forced to adopt Yankee ways. "The deluge of European immigrants with their strange and dangerous ideas made of Northerners another race...In the North there was corruption in state and municipal government; the rulers were King numbers, agrarian mobs, lawless democracies, black and red Republicans. There were overgrown grimy cities filled with crime and poverty...There were freesoilism, abolitionism, freeloveism, Fourierism, Mormonism, a fanatical press 'without honor or modesty,' free thought and infidelism, 'intemperance and violence and indecorum' of the clergy...Capital and labor were in perpetual conflict..." Violent social upheaval akin to the French Revolution was likely to occur at any time, and the South didn't care to be a part of the country that would experience it. [10]

Southerners were also fed up with the constant insults and holier-than-thou attitudes displayed by Yankees. One New York newspaper, for instance, flailed Southern medical students attending classes there. A Southerner, the paper said, was brought up "in the semi-savage solitude of a remote plantation, and deriving his ideas of morals, grammar, and behavior from his Negro nurse and piccaninny playmates, he becomes in New York a puzzle to professors, a terror to landladies, and a munificent patron of grog-shops...Next to his love for tobacco and grog comes his taste for Disunion." [11]

Less than two weeks after the Presidential election, Wilmington was seething with notions of impending secession. That South Carolina would go out soon was a foregone conclusion, as evidenced by actions and discussions in Charleston immediately after Lincoln's election. One visitor to that town observed speakers addressing the crowds, military companies filling up and drilling nightly, and new Palmetto flags with a "a Palmetto in the center, with a single star in the corner where the stars usually are upon the U. S. flag," hanging throughout the city. Those who had lived through the nullification crisis of the early 1830's said that "the present state of feeling far exceeds in its intensity that then existing." [12]

Rev. John Lamb Prichard

Reverend John Prichard heard the ominous rumblings coming out of South Carolina, and noted in his diary on Friday, November 16, that "Men's hearts tremble for fear; deep mutterings are heard from the South. It does seem that a dissolution of the glorious Union is inevitable!" [13]

Three days after Rev. Pritchard's concerns were penned in his journal, a large and "enthusiastic" crowd filled the New Hanover County Court House to overflowing, and called on the state to secede. "In this crisis," the *Daily Journal* stated, "the people are decidedly in advance of the politicians – the country is in advance of the town...Those who have usually occupied the position of leaders must now be content to follow a sentiment which appears to move faster than they do." [14]

In a series of resolutions that were all unanimously adopted, the citizens of New Hanover said that the election of the Republicans to the White House made it "the imperative duty of the State of North Carolina to prepare for assuming her position as an Independent Sovereignty." A law should be enacted to see to the organization and proper arming of the State militia, but until that time a corps of Minute Men would be organized for temporarily protecting the Cape Fear region from possible hostile intervention. [15]

One disgusted Wilmington merchant, expressing the opinion of many Southern businessmen, wrote several days later that the South had become an economic vassal of the North, and would be better off once it seceded and formed its own nation. High protective tariffs and unfair appropriations by the Federal government on the South, he said, "has had the tendency to centralize capital at the North, draining the South to an extent which would long since have impoverished her, but for her immense agricultural products. Upon these, Northerners have grown fat, and have gained the power to 'crush' us. Trade has placed the South under a commercial vassalage to the North, which nothing but a dissolution can remedy. Change this, establish manufactories, do your trading among your friends, and in a very short time capital will stay at home and be rewarded." [16]

Samuel Day, an English visitor to the South during the secession crisis, echoed something of the same opinion, noting that the upheaval going on in the land was "but a war of alien races, distinct nationalities, and antagonistic governments." The North and the South were really two identifiable nations, "whose separate foundations...were laid on Plymouth Rock and the banks of the James River. Whoever would rightly understand the causes of the present convulsion in America must find their explanation in the irreconcilable character of the Cavalier and Puritan, the antagonisms of agricultural and commercial communities, and the conflicts between free and slave labor, when the manufacturing and navigating interests attempt to wrest the scepter from agriculture by unfriendly legislation." [17]

As the full impact of Lincoln's election began to weigh on peoples' minds, so concerns for the future grew daily. On Tuesday evening, the 11th of December, the "largest meeting ever held in the town of Wilmington" took place at Town Hall, as a densely packed crowd met to discuss the future of the Union and North Carolina's part in or out of it. Unlike the meeting of nearly a month before, when the call first went out advocating secession and organizing the Minute Men, this meeting was supposed to be a "Union" meeting. Reverend John Prichard opened the meeting with a "most appropriate and impressive prayer," and a committee of five of the city's most prominent merchants and political leaders drafted a series of resolutions that were unanimously adopted by the large crowd.

While affirming their love for the Union and desire to see it perpetuated, the Union men also stated they knew the time was close at hand when secession of other Southern states would place North Carolina at "the feet of a Black Republican majority in Congress, and thus secession may be made a question of practical necessity, and it is the part of prudent men deliberately and firmly to prepare for so great an emergency." [18]

The resolutions called for a convention of the people to determine the State's course of action, "a conference of all Southern States, to establish unity of feeling and concert of action, and to consult for the common safety and welfare," and large appropriations to organize and arm the military of the State. Union meeting it may have been billed, but the resolutions demonstrated the realistic attitudes of even conservative non-secessionists in light of the current crisis. [19]

The next night, Wednesday, December 12, an even larger crowd jammed into the city's theater, Thalian Hall, to hear speeches and discussions sponsored by the secessionist Cape Fear Minute Men, the local militia group organized the month before. Attendance was so great, in fact, it would have been impossible for the Town Hall to contain all the people who came.

Mr. Robert H. Cowan, a native Wilmingtonian respected for his role in state and local politics, and admired for his "charming personality and graceful manners," summed up the feelings of most in the theater. He contended with much force and persuasion for an hour and a half, that "the honor, the interests, the safety of North Carolina and the South, demanded a severance of the ties that now unite them with the States of the North...Our only choice was whether we would take and exercise this right on our own terms, or wait until forced to do so by our enemies, and on their terms." [20]

The next speaker, Mr. John Dickson, told the multitude that it was ridiculous now to talk of remaining in the Union to fight for Southern rights. "All peaceable means in the Union had been exhausted," he said. "We must now treat with the North separately and independently." [21]

Against this same backdrop of fear and hatred for Yankees and Republicans, South Carolinians passed the Ordinance of Secession eight days after the Cape Fear secessionists met in Thalian Hall. On Thursday, December 20, 1860, exercising to the fullest the notion of states' rights first broached by the Virginia Rebel, Thomas Jefferson, and emulating the example of their fathers of 1776 who seceded from the British Empire, they quit the Union.

For some Wilmingtonians, the news was cause for celebration. On December 21, commencing at noontime, the Cape Fear Minute Men fired a one hundred gun salute in honor of South Carolina, that thundered throughout the town, and which startled Reverend John Prichard as he worked in his church that afternoon. They were responded to and seconded gun for gun by the Schooner *Marine*, anchored in the river. One Wilmingtonian wrote that North Carolinians could "truly rejoice that one Southern State has been prompt in declaring her independence." Down at Smithville (later renamed Southport), at a Southern Rights meeting held in the Brunswick County Court House, a large and enthusiastic crowd declared that "the cause of Charleston is the cause of all," and pledged their lives and honor to secure Southern independence. [22]

Other residents received the news with grave concern and foreboding. All around town, "at street corners and elsewhere, earnest groups of earnest men stood engaged in serious converse upon the one topic of the day. Sometimes the conversation became discussional, sometimes speculative or deliberative, but never noisy or demonstrative." Some believed that if the Federal government attempted to coerce South Carolina back into the Union, and Southern blood was shed in the process, "all hope for any cordial Union being ever again formed or maintained would be out of the question." Reverend Prichard wondered if the authorities in Washington would permit South Carolina to remain out of the Union. "If not, what then?" he noted in his diary. "War? I suppose so. Lord, undertake for us." [23]

War or no war, South Carolina looked for the rest of her Southern sisters to follow suit in rapid order. In less than a month, she would be more

Major John J. Hedrick

than pleased with the response from the Deep South. There, tempers and disdain for the Yankees waxed hot, slaves were more numerous than in the Upper South, and heavier dependence on the agricultural economy than in the more diversified Southern states brought greater dread for anything that promised to alter the way of life.

In the Upper South, though, in North Carolina, Virginia, Tennessee, Arkansas, Missouri, Kentucky and Maryland, more conservative political attitudes, closer proximity to the North and therefore closer trade ties, more industry and fewer slaves, all contributed to more of a wait and see attitude about what Lincoln and his kind might try in Washington. For a few days in early January, however, it looked as though North Carolina might become one of the first states to join her southern neighbor in secession.

While the State at large was generally Unionist in attitude at this time, the lower Cape Fear burned with secession fever, as evidenced by the meetings and activities in November and December. On Thursday, January 3, 1861, a red secession flag "with a large white star in the center" was raised on a pole in the "vicinity of Front and Market streets." A large crowd was in attendance, and fiery speeches were given. Several days later, an announcement was made in the *Daily Journal* for the formation of a rifle company, and the newspaper itself endorsed the need for a company of artillery and cavalry. [24]

Many Cape Fear people regarded delays in action "as dangerous, and anticipated with foreboding the occupation of the forts by the Union forces." The forts near Smithville, Forts Johnston and Caswell, were felt to be likely targets for takeover by Federal troops in large numbers, as had Fort Sumter in Charleston harbor. Major John J. Hedrick and the Cape Fear Minute Men, in company with Captain S.D. Thruston and his Smithville Guards, as well as other citizens of Smithville, set out to insure that the Yankees would not establish a fortified post on their very doorstep in North Carolina. [25]

In the dead of night, about 4 a.m. on Wednesday, January 9, Ordnance Sergeant James Reilly of the United States Army, in charge of the small outpost known as Fort Johnston, which dated from Colonial times, was rudely awakened by knocking at his door. He was met, he reported, by a "party of the citizens of Smithville." They had come to demand of him the keys to the magazine. Reilly at first told them he wouldn't give them up.

Maj. James Reilly, C.S.A.
(formerly Sergeant Reilly, U.S. Army)

"They replied that it was no use to be obstinate, for they had the magazine already in their possession, and that they had a party of twenty men around it, and were determined to keep it; if not by fair means, they would break it open. I considered a while and seen it was no use to persevere, for they were determined to have what ordnance stores there was at the post. I then told them that if they would sign receipts to me for the ordnance and ordnance stores at the post, I would give it up to them. (There was no alternative left me but to act as I did.) They replied that they would do so. The receipt was signed, and they left fifteen men in charge of the post; the remainder proceeded to take Fort Caswell, which is in their possession by this time. I do not know what arrangement Ordnance Sergeant Dardingkiller made with them." [26]

Sergeant Frederick Dardingkiller was in the same unenviable position a few miles further down the Cape Fear at Fort Caswell. The sergeant reported that a party of citizens of Wilmington and Smithville had occupied the fort on the 10th of January (it was actually the 9th), and that they were under the command of a Mr. Hedrick of Wilmington. Hedrick had, Dardingkiller said, signed receipts "for all the ordnance stores at the post, and is using such of them as he needs." [27]

The primary reason for the seizure of Forts Johnston and Caswell at this time was fear that the two were on the verge of being reinforced by Federal troops. Major Hedrick and his Cape Fear Minute Men had received a dispatch on January 8 that stated a revenue cutter, the *U.S.S. Forward*, "was on her way with troops, destined for Fort Caswell." Despite having previously been ordered by Governor John Ellis not to take such precipitate action, on the basis that North Carolina was still very much part of the Union, the Wilmingtonians and their Smithville allies were not to be dissuaded. [28]

If the State had not yet seceded, most North Carolinians, with the exception of some of the old Whig persuasion, embraced the theory of states' rights and the legality of secession. They would fiercely resist any Federal invasion of Southern soil to coerce a seceded state back into the Union, or prevent one from going out. As one man stated shortly after South Carolina seceded, "I am a Union man but when they send men South it will change my notions. I can do nothing against my own people." [29]

This same attitude was the source of the commotion over Caswell and Johnston. Many Cape Fear citizens believed the Yankees were sending troops down to seize and secure the arms and munitions at each place to suppress the secession movement in the lower Cape Fear region, and possibly employ the troops in helping to intimidate South Carolina, now already out of the Union. The Wilmingtonians and Smithvillians seized the positions, then, setting up headquarters at Caswell, and patrolled the beach and guarded the ramparts with their personal arms, mostly shotguns. [30]

"There were only two 24-pounder guns mounted, one on the sea face and one on the inner face, both carriages being too decayed to withstand their own recoil, but such as they were, with them they determined to defy the army and navy of the United States. The smoke of an approaching steamer being once descried below the horizon the alarm was signaled, and believing it to be a man-of-war, the brave men of Smithville flew to arms, and soon the bay was alive with boats hurrying them to the aid of their comrades within the fort. Women, as in the old days, armed sons and fathers, and urged them to the front. But the steamer proved to be a friendly one." [31]

Hedrick's occupation of these positions was to be short lived. Governor Ellis, on learning of the action taken by the secessionists, ordered Colonel John Cantwell of the Thirtieth North Carolina Militia to proceed to Smithville and restore the forts to Federal authority. Never for a moment doubting the sincerity and patriotic motives of the Cape Fear men, Ellis nevertheless believed their action was not legally justified. Such takeover of military positions could only properly take place at such time as North Carolina left the Union. The forts must be vacated. [32]

From Fort Caswell, Major Hedrick wrote to Colonel Cantwell that, "we, as North Carolinians will obey his command. This post will be evacuated tomorrow (January 14) at 9 o'clock a.m." [33] And from Raleigh, Governor Ellis wrote President James Buchanan on January 12, "that on the 9th instant Forts Johnston and Caswell were taken possession of by State troops and persons resident in that vicinity, in an irregular manner. Upon receipt of this information I immediately issued a military order requiring the forts to be restored to the authorities of the United States, which order will be executed this day." [34]

Sergeant Dardingkiller, writing to Washington on the 14th, stated "the party of citizens who occupied this post (Caswell) has left this day. Mr. Hedrick, who signed receipts to me for the ordnance stores, has returned them to me in good order, except what he expended." [35]

Though the forts were vacated for the time being, and secession and war were averted, the people in the lower Cape Fear, unlike most of the State, were as militant and defiant as ever. On the day the forts were returned to

United States authority, the people of Smithville held a meeting at their courthouse "for the purpose of giving public expression of the deep sense of obligation under which the gallant conduct of a portion of the C.F. Minute Men of Wilmington had placed them, by reinforcing the Smithville volunteers." Major Hedrick and some of his subordinate officers were asked to speak to the assembled citizens, and they cheerfully did so amid "frequent bursts of applause." [36]

The Smithville folks adopted resolutions that praised Hedrick and his men. They resolved that a "portion of the Cape Fear Minute Men of Wilmington gallantly came to the assistance of our fellow citizens, who had taken possession of the forts in our harbor immediately on receiving intelligence that they were about to be garrisoned by Federal troops; and whereas, we, the people of Smithville, believe that the circumstances under which this step was taken fully justified it, and that those who took the forts, and those who reinforced them, were actuated by the noblest patriotism, and by a laudable fidelity to the interests, the institutions and rights of North Carolina." [37]

The people of Smithville owed the Cape Fear Minute Men their "warmest thanks," which was "cheerfully tendered." And speaking to the non-secessionist attitudes of many in the state, they felt that "however much their course may be now deprecated by some, yet we believe the day is not distant when it will be properly appreciated, and they will receive the plaudits of all true-hearted North Carolinians." [38]

On January 26, in response to the evacuation of the two forts, and information in the *Daily Journal* of correspondence between Governor Ellis and Secretary of War Holt, a citizen of the lower Cape Fear wrote to the editors of the paper to give his opinion of the situation. "It was in case war should be declared against South Carolina by the Federal Government, that these forts, located within a short distance of the South Carolina line, would serve as appropriate debut's from whence military inroads could be readily made upon her soil. Would it have been consistent with the policy or honor of our State that these forts should have been used for any such purpose? One branch of our Legislature (the House of Commons) has nobly answered this question by a vote of 63 to 20, virtually declaring that such an occupation for such a purpose, would be considered as a cause of war, to be resisted at all hazards." If the government tried to occupy any of the forts in North Carolina, the writer continued, they would find "that the fires which in '75 and '76 burned so brightly, have not yet been extinguished." [39]

Emotions and anxieties continued to build in Wilmington. At the same time as the seizure of the forts, a group of mechanics and other working men organized themselves into a new military organization called the Cape Fear Riflemen. There were initially about sixty men in the unit, and prominent merchants and townsmen came forward to contribute to the furnishing of uniforms and equipment. They were privileged to help the volunteers, they said, since these men were giving of their time, services and lives, if need be "for the honor and welfare of their country." [40]

On the same day Caswell and Johnston had been taken, January 9, Mississippi had seceded. In the intervening days and weeks up to February 1, she was followed by Florida, Alabama, Georgia, Louisiana, and Texas in that order. By mutual agreement, delegates from the seceded states met in Montgomery, Alabama in early February, and the 8th of that month adopted a provisional constitution for the new Confederate States of America. Jefferson Davis of Mississippi, former U.S. Senator, Secretary of War under Franklin Pierce, West Point graduate and Mexican War hero, was elected provisional President of the Confederacy.

Many North Carolinians obviously felt a deep swell of Southern pride at the establishment of the new nation, albeit not yet a member of it. And they surely sensed what would come of all this when they read in the papers Davis' inaugural address, which made perfectly clear the South's willingness to fight, if need be, to secure independence. The Confederate States would seek harmony and peace with her former Northern brethren still in the Union, Davis said, but if "the integrity of our territory and jurisdiction be assailed, it will but remain for us with firm resolve to appeal to arms and invoke the blessing of Providence on a just cause." [41]

At least until James Buchanan left office, the Federal government would make no moves to assail the territory or jurisdiction of the new nation. While denying the legality of secession, he nonetheless believed the government had no legal right to coerce a state back into the Union. So the status quo was maintained for a while, no more states going out of the Union, and no Federal troops coming South to force the already departed sisters back in.

For the leaders of the Confederate States and the secessionists in the Upper South, though, the status quo was not at all what they wanted. To be successful in her bid for independence, the Confederacy needed all the members she could get. And the secessionists in places like North Carolina were convinced their state's only hope for salvation from northern dominance lay in becoming one of those members.

In a meeting held at Thalian Hall in Wilmington even before Davis' inauguration, various prominent citizens of the town were called upon to express their opinions on secession. Mr. O.P. Meares stated that "the time had come in which it behooved all Southern men to look the circumstances fairly in the face, and to let no sentimental devotion to a Union which was once the source of so many blessings, blind him to the fact that that Union no longer exists - that the constitutional guarantees upon which it alone could exist, had been violated - that all demands for our right, all proposals for arrangement had been scoffed and scouted by the Republicans, until not one hope remained," and "secession had become a practical necessity. He therefore felt it his duty to take a position in favour of the secession of North Carolina from the Northern States and her union with a Southern Confederacy." Mr. Meares further stated that he did not believe there was any real threat of coercion from the North, and that if it ever should materialize, it "should be sternly repelled." [42]

Mr. Joshua Wright, a prominent Wilmington attorney, was the next gentleman to step to the podium. After reviewing the history of the political arguments and "complications, brought about by persons and sections animated by a lust of power or stimulated by an unreasoning fanaticism," persons who had continued to agitate and march onward in their aggression toward the Southern states, Mr. Wright asked of the gathering, "Ought the South now to stop or falter when called upon to take up arms in her own defence?" Mr. Wright had nothing but the highest praise for the actions of South Carolina, and called on all Southern men to remain united, avoid criticism of each other, and be ready to secure peace or "defy a world in arms." The meeting saw a quite large and enthusiastic turnout of citizens. [43]

Less than a week later, Mr. George Davis, one of the most noted political leaders of the lower Cape Fear, was in Washington attending the so-called Peace Commission, which was a last ditch effort to save the country from the threatened scourge of fratricidal war. The Peace Congress failed, and representatives from the upper Southern states, such as North Carolina, Virginia, and Tennessee, went back home convinced that the Yankees were going to do everything possible to secure domination of the government to the

Thalian Hall, where Wilmington leaders met to consider seccesion.

eternal detriment of the South. When George Davis returned to Wilmington from the conference, he was sought after by some of his prominent friends in town in order to hear from him "with reference to the proceeding of the Peace Congress, and to have your opinion as to their probable effect in settling the distracting questions of the day." [44]

Davis addressed his friends and fellow Wilmingtonians on March 2 at Thalian Hall. The pro-secession oratory of this old line Whig and former Unionist alleviated no anxieties for those who still hoped for maintenance of the Union. "Mr. Davis was obliged to close before he had finished his address. The people were profoundly moved, and the hearts of all were deeply stirred. Many left the hall while he was speaking, for they could not restrain their emotion." Davis stated that he had gone to the Peace Conference with the idea of helping to affect a solution for "final settlement of existing difficulties." He had done all he could to help preserve North Carolina's rights, honor, and economic interests within the Union, which was consistent with the preferences of most North Carolinians, who were still not in favor of secession. [45]

Davis concluded his speech by stating unequivocally that the South would never secure better terms as long as she remained in the Union, that the terms of the Peace Congress were not acceptable to the South, and he could never assent to them himself. The *Wilmington Daily Journal* reported "Mr. Davis, in old party times, was an ardent and consistent member of the opposition, and was opposed to a severance from the North until he felt satisfied by the result of the Peace Conference that all peaceful means had been exhausted." [46]

As in the Wilmington area, the failure of the so-called Peace Congress in Washington put a damper on Unionist support in the rest of the State, and Lincoln's inaugural address in early March, in which he vowed to "hold, occupy and possess the property and places belonging to the government, and to collect the duties and imposts," gave further impetus to the drive for secession. On March 22 and 23, over 1,000 delegates met in Goldsboro for the first state convention of the Southern Rights or States' Rights Party. In a set of resolutions, North Carolinians were urged to quit the Union and ally themselves with the new Confederate States. "A final resolution declared that any additional forces placed in the United States forts in North Carolina would be regarded as a menace and would be resisted at all hazards." [48]

A Southern Rights meeting was also held in Raleigh on April 3, with Senators Bragg and Clingman, and Representative Laurence O'Brien Branch calling for secession. (A year and a half later Branch would prove the sincerity of his convictions by giving his life for them at an obscure little town in western Maryland called Sharpsburg.) "All these speakers pointed out there were other causes for apprehension besides slavery. The Morrill Tariff, the Pacific Railroad Bill, and the Homestead Bill were pointed to as measures which were inimical to the interests of the South." [49]

Union sentiment, even among ardent Unionists, was fast collapsing in North Carolina as March wore into April 1861. Cabarrus County Unionist Rufus Barringer, who would one day command a brigade of cavalry for another staunch Unionist named Robert E. Lee, a Virginian, in March told the people of his community that it was now apparent the Lincoln government intended to put the border states "between the upper and nether millstone, and grind us to an impalpable powder." Barringer called for the immediate withdrawal of North Carolina from the Union. [50]

With even former Unionists clamoring for independence, it was axiomatic that any act by Lincoln's government that smacked of coercion would be automatically countered with secession, and the appeal to arms that Jefferson Davis had prophesied.

On April 12, 1861, a Friday, the first clap of thunder that foretold of the awesome storm to descend on the land, came rolling up out of Charleston, South Carolina. The Confederate authorities in Montgomery and Charleston were putting the rest of the country and the world on notice, that they had meant what they said about protecting "the integrity of our territory and jurisdiction." Fort Sumter, in Charleston harbor, had been occupied in December 1860, shortly after South Carolina seceded, by Kentuckian Robert Anderson. Major Anderson had moved over from Fort Moultrie, across the harbor, feeling it was untenable against possible hostile action by South Carolina, after she had left the Union. By April, Sumter had become a symbol to both Abraham Lincoln and Jefferson Davis, as it was to their respective countries.

To Lincoln, it was the place to take a stand to uphold the laws of the United States, and prevent subordination of the government to a band of hotheaded insurgents bent on destroying the Union. To Davis and the South, Sumter represented one of the last nests of the despotic government from which they had recently chosen to separate. Fort Sumter was in Confederate territory, and yet was still occupied by foreign troops. Those troops must get out, if not willingly, then by force.

Major Anderson had reported to Washington that his provisions were nearly exhausted, and without additional supplies, he would be forced to surrender the fort soon. Lincoln decided to make the attempt to resupply him, aware that if the Confederates resisted the attempt, the whole venture would likely fail, but bearing in mind that he would at least provoke Davis into firing the first gun.

So when Governor Pickens of South Carolina was notified that Fort Sumter was to be reprovisioned, the Confederate authorities concluded the time for talk had finally come to an end. Independence would be put to the test.

On April 13, 1861, the *Wilmington Daily Journal* reported the "Exciting News!" In bold print the Journal reported that hostilities had begun;

"War! War! War! War!" it proclaimed. A dispatch had been received at Wilmington on the evening of April 12 from one of its correspondents in Charleston. "The Ball has opened," read the dispatch. "War is inaugurated. The batteries on Sullivan's Island, Morris Island and other points, opened on Fort Sumter at 4 1/2 o'clock this morning. Fort Sumter returned the fire, and a brisk cannonade has been kept up. No information has been received from seaward yet.

"The militia are under arms, and the whole of our people are in the streets. Every available space facing our harbor is filled with anxious spectators." A second dispatch of the same evening from Charleston stated that two of Sumter's guns had been silenced, and that no casualties had occurred among the Confederate troops firing on the brick bastion. Of nineteen Rebel batteries surrounding Fort Sumter, only seven had been opened on the fort. The other twelve were being "held in reserve for the expected fleet." [51]

Alfred M. Waddell was a Wilmingtonian who had gone to Charleston upon hearing that a bombardment of Sumter was imminent. Arriving at his hotel in town just as the cannonade was getting underway, he rushed up the stairs to the top to get a panoramic

Alfred Moore Waddell

view. "As I...looked out upon that splendid harbor, there in the center of its gateway to the sea, half wrapped in the morning mist, lay Sumter, and high above its parapets, fluttering in the morning breeze floated proudly and defiantly the stars and stripes. In a moment afterwards just above it there was a sudden red flash, and a column of smoke, followed by an explosion, and opposite on James Island, a corresponding puff floated away on the breeze, and I realized with emotions indescribable that I was looking upon a civil war among my countrymen." [52]

Pastor John Prichard confided his anxieties to his diary again, noting on April 13, "Fort Sumter bombarded all night! Everybody is excited. War has commenced; when will it end? Sumter surrendered unconditionally, by Major Anderson, commander! Great rejoicing in Wilmington, flag raising, etc." [53]

The April 15 edition of the *Daily Journal* echoed Prichard's entry concerning the capture of Sumter. The news had been received on Saturday afternoon, the 13th, creating "the wildest excitement. We need hardly attempt a description. It may be enough to say that the tone of feeling was unmistakable and the effect was evidently to convince even the most skeptical that the time for resistance had come. Men who had before clung to the hope however feeble of being able to preserve or re-construct the Union, were at last forced to confess they could cling to that hope no longer. No doubt they will now be as strong Southern Rights men as the strongest." [54]

On April 15, Lincoln issued a call for 75,000 volunteers to suppress the Southern "insurrection," and Secretary of War Simon Cameron wired Governor Ellis to furnish North Carolina's quota of two militia regiments. There was no doubt about the response, and Ellis wired Cameron immediately: "Your dispatch is received, and if genuine, which its extraordinary character leads me to doubt, I have to say in reply that I regard the levy of troops made by the administration for the purpose of subjugating the States of the South as in violation of the Constitution and a gross usurpation of power. I can be no party to this wicked violation of the laws of the country, and to this war upon the liberties of a free people. You can get no troops from North Carolina." [56]

Straightway, the governor "telegraphed orders to Colonel J.L. Cantwell, at Wilmington, 'to take Forts Caswell and Johnston without delay, and hold them until further orders against all comers' " [57] The *Daily Journal* vouched for Colonel Cantwell's speedy obedience of the governor, as on the 15th, the newspaper ran in bold headlines an announcement from the "Headquarters 30th Reg't. N.C.M.," of which Cantwell was commanding officer, that "The officers in command of the Wilmington Light Infantry, German Volunteers, and Wilmington Rifle Guards, are hereby ordered to notify their respective Commands to assemble in front of the Carolina Hotel at – o'clock, fully armed and equipped, THIS AFTERNOON." In addition to these units, the recently formed Wilmington Horse Artillery and the Cape Fear Light Artillery were also ordered by their respective captains to assemble that afternoon, due to "Business of great importance." [58]

Next day, April 16, Cantwell moved downriver to the mouth of the Cape Fear with his forces, numbering in all fewer than 150 men, and took possession of Fort Johnston from U.S. Sergeant James Reilly (who would later become a Major of Confederate artillery on the lower Cape Fear), and then took Fort Caswell from Sergeant Walker. Walker was placed in "close confinement in his quarters, 'in consequence of the discovery of repeated attempts to communicate with his government.' " Cantwell stated that officers, as well as the men, worked with much energy to "mount guns and prepare for defence." [59]

The Wilmington Light Infantry soon were dispatched to Federal Point, quickly renamed Confederate Point, where under direction of Captain Charles

P. Bolles, engineer, and Captain William L. DeRosset, commanding the
infantry, the erection of sand batteries commenced that would in the months
ahead grow to tremendous size, and prove of vast significance to the Southern
war effort. [60]

Wilmingtonians were obviously not waiting for formal separation from
the Union to put defenses in order. About the time of Colonel Cantwell's
seizure of Caswell, Major William H.C. Whiting had been asked by Governor
Ellis to come from Charleston, where he was serving with General Beauregard,
and take charge of military affairs in the Wilmington vicinity. He went right to
work, being an excellent engineer and West Pointer, and a Wilmingtonian by
choice, having married a Miss Kate Walker of Wilmington. [61]

Very soon after assuming command, Whiting wrote to Beauregard of
his preparations and problems in carrying out his assignment. "I find myself
installed here in command of the defenses of Cape Fear; to be sure, by
commission from the governor, but in a babel of confusion, to which Morris
Island and Charleston Harbor were child's play. Without having had the
advantage of you for my exemplar during the past six trying weeks, I would be
utterly at a loss. The worst is I have nothing to work with. Can you not cause to
be sent me a few hundred fuses for the 8 inch shells? We have shells enough
here at the railroad depot; also some boxes of friction tubes with lanyards.
Besides, I desire very much the sponge staves and various implements
belonging to the guns you have lent us. This would be a great favor.

"I have started all the ladies to making cartridge bags and sand bags,
and that keeps their little hearts quiet...Please to examine whether it is possible
to spare us one hundred pounds of 24-grape. We have the arsenal today. (This
was the Federal arsenal in Fayetteville.)

"I try to be as cool and patient as you are, but it is awful hard work.
They are military in South Carolina. Here they are willing enough, but the
military has yet to grow." [62] Whiting would make it one of his prime goals in
the coming conflict to insure that the military defenses of the lower Cape Fear
did grow and strengthen. In this, he and his assistants would be most
successful.

The drama of events in mid-April had extinguished all Union
sentiment in North Carolina. Former Unionists and secessionists were now all
for resistance, with Lincoln and the Republicans looked on as symbols of
tyranny and despotism as the British were in 1776. "No matter where any of
our citizens was born," theorized the *Daily Journal*, "whether North or South,
whether on this side of the Atlantic or on the other side, we are all in the same
boat, and every loyal North Carolina citizen will rally to the standard of
resistance to sectional aggression." [63]

Mrs. William Parsley, a Wilmingtonian, wrote that the whole Cape
Fear area was "fired" at this time, and "looked upon secession and war as the

inevitable outcome. The young men wore secession rosettes and badges made of small pine burs. The military companies already organized greatly increased their ranks, and drilled vigorously. Other companies were organized and men of Northern birth who did not join some military organization were regarded with suspicion." Many of the former Yankees would return to the North in the months to come. [64]

Men too elderly for field service formed themselves into a home defense cavalry company under a Captain William C. Howard. There was also a company of "quite elderly gentlemen," that was "known popularly as the 'Horse-and-Buggy Company,' and though they did not drill, they held themselves in readiness to do what they could when called upon." These old

fellows assisted in equipping companies in the field, as well as helping out families of soldiers who left to go to the front. [65]

"School boys," Mrs. Parsley continued, "drilled constantly in the streets with wooden guns and tin swords, and those owning a real gun or a good imitation were sure of being officers, no matter about their other qualifications, though to do them justice they did strive like men." [66]

The secession of North Carolina from the Union, like that of Virginia, Tennessee, and Arkansas, was only a matter of formality and paperwork. The convention that assembled in Raleigh on Monday, May 20, was very likely the "ablest group of men who had ever met in North Carolina. The gravity of the situation had made the people turn to their best and most trusted leaders, without regard

Judah P. Benjamin

to political differences." There was actually a preponderance of former Unionists in the convention, though by this time, "all were agreed upon separation and all were conscious that separation meant war." [67]

In a harmonious atmosphere, the Secession Convention unanimously adopted an ordinance written by the brilliant Louisiana Jew, Judah P. Benjamin. The document got quickly to the point. It reads boldly:

"AN ORDINANCE DISSOLVING THE UNION BETWEEN THE STATE OF NORTH CAROLINA AND THE OTHER STATES UNITED WITH HER UNDER THE COMPACT OF GOVERNMENT ENTITLED 'THE CONSTITUTION OF THE UNITED STATES'

"We, the people of the state of North Carolina, in convention assembled, do declare and ordain, and it is hereby declared and ordained, that the ordinance adopted by the state of North Carolina in the convention of 1789,

whereby the Constitution of the United States was ratified and adopted, and also all acts and parts of acts of the General Assembly, ratifying and adopting amendments to the said Constitution, are hereby repealed, rescinded, and abrogated.

"We do further declare and ordain that the union now subsisting between the state of North Carolina and the other states, under the title of 'The United States of America', is hereby dissolved, and the state of North Carolina is in full possession and exercise of all those rights of sovereignty which belong and appertain to a free and independent state." [68]

In Raleigh, amid the "ringing of bells and the booming cannon, mingled with the deafening shouts of thousands of loyal voices issuing from the stentorian lungs of as many true freemen," people went wild. [69] In Wilmington, just hours after the State had left the Union, the *Daily Journal* reported "SECESSION OF NORTH CAROLINA! GREAT ENTHUSIASM!!...The ordinance of secession passed at 6 o'clock last evening. The Convention is now voting on the adoption of the Confederate Constitution. The wildest enthusiasm prevails here. SECOND DISPATCH Raleigh, May 21st, 1861 Received 12:20 AM We are now in the Southern Confederacy UNANIMOUSLY. The act of secession is FINAL." [70]

In Wilmington, there was little real excitement on receipt of the news, much of which had already been expended following Fort Sumter and the occupation of Caswell and Johnston, with secession looked on as inevitable and a "foregone conclusion." On the morning of the 21st though, the Wilmington Horse Artillery did fire a salute in honor of the independence of the State. [71]

May 20 was to have been the day of another celebration in New Hanover County. Besides the anniversary of the Mecklenburg Declaration of Independence in 1775, as well as the State's secession from the Union, this day was also the anniversary of the organization of the Wilmington Light Infantry, having been formed in 1853. Encamped at Battery Bolles, just north of New Inlet on Confederate Point, the company had undergone the usual routine of camp duty for nearly three weeks now, drilling, erecting sand fortifications, and mounting guns. On this day, as North Carolina dissolved her allegiance to the Federal Union, the boys under Captain William L. DeRosset had planned on having fun. As it turned out, though, the day was "too windy and unpleasant for the purposes intended, and on that account nothing was done until the 21st." [72]

Despite having to wait until the next day for their real celebration, the young soldiers did have some fun on the 20th by singing a song written in their honor, by none other than the prominent Wilmingtonian, George Davis. He had titled the piece "Carolina's Sons are Ready," and it was sung to the tune of "Dixie's Land." It was full of Southern attachment to home, defiance for the Yankees, and patriotism, and went as follows:

"Our gallant boys are going to battle,
Seeking fame where the cannon rattle,
    Look away, look away, look away, cheer the boys!
Oh cheer them on in the path of duty,
To fight for home, and love, and beauty,
    Look away, look away, look away, cheer the boys!
        Carolina's sons are ready,
        Hurrah! Hurrah!
        With heart and hand,
        They'll by her stand,
        With a courage true and steady,
        Hurrah! Hurrah!
        Our own brave boys are ready.
          II.
Oh, Mecklenburg! Thy proud old story,
Never shall they dim its glory,
    Look away, look away, look away, cheer the boys!
Their fathers gave them freedom's blessing,
They will ne'er forget the lesson,
    Look away, look away, look away, cheer the boys!
        Carolina's sons are ready, &c.
          III.
Let Lincoln's trait'rous hordes pursue them,
They will meet, but not subdue them,
    Look away, look away, look away, cheer the boys!
In the last ditch, where the last flag's flying,
They will victors be, or dying,
    Look away, look away, look away, cheer the boys!
        Carolina's sons are ready, &c.
          IV.
Oh, gallant boys, God's arms enfold you!
Mothers, sisters, wives behold you,
    Look away, look away, look away, cheer the boys!
In the din of strife, in the war's delaying,
Mothers, sisters, wives are praying,
    Look away, look away, look away, cheer the boys!
        Carolina's sons are ready, &c.
          V.
To freedom's battle on we send them,
God of battles, Thy help lend them!
    Look away, look away, look away, cheer the boys!
We send 'our boys', our best and bravest,

> *Guard, protect them, Thou who savest!*
> *Look away, look away, look away, cheer the boys!*
> *Carolina's sons are ready, &c."* [73]

The Wilmington Confederates sang the tune with a rousing chorus, after which they gave "repeated cheers for the author, Mecklenburg and 'Dixie's Land'." [74]

For their company's anniversary, which did come off the next day, Captain DeRosset's boys had asked some of their friends to come down from Wilmington, especially girls. The young ladies, "in the fresh bloom of maidenhood, with buoyant hearts and bright eyes entering into the spirit of a celebration," enjoyed the soft sea breezes, wandered through their soldiers' tents, and some even played at handling the rifles. The soldiers spent most of the morning with target practice. Later, they "partook of the refreshments kindly provided by their lady friends – differing somewhat in quality from their ordinary fare, to judge from their gratified faces. After dinner the Company formed at the drum roll for the presentation of the prizes shot for." Election of officers was held next, and Captain DeRosset was gratified to be re-elected company commander. He then had them perform skirmish drill for the guests, and they did so with "the steadiness for which this Company is justly noted." [75]

Now the party was over. Carriages came to pick up the guests and drive back the roughly twenty miles to Wilmington, hugs and handshakes were given, goodbyes said, and here and there a tear rolled down the cheek of a young soldier or his belle. One of the soldiers pondered, "who may note the emotions of these young hearts as they bid farewell. In the uncertain events of war who can say that they will ever meet again?" [76]

The day after the party at Battery Bolles, Wilmingtonians learned that Governor Ellis was calling for 30,000 volunteers for North Carolina regiments. One announcement in the *Daily Journal* for May 22 trumpeted, "Come out young men, now is the time to serve your country." Another noted that D.R. Murchison, Recruiting Sergeant for the Wilmington Light infantry, the Captain being away at Confederate Point, was still receiving recruits for the company, and applicants should come to E. Murray & Company store, on North Water Street. Still another notice advised that William H. Lippitt, a druggist in town, had adopted the "cash system" in his store, to enable him to continue doing business during the present unsettled times. "I hope," he said, "my friends will not ask for credit." [77]

Wilmingtonians had been Confederates just two weeks when Reverend John Prichard noted in his diary some of the changed attitudes and daily doings in the life of the people, even people of the Gospel. "June 4th – Lord, bless me and all thy people today. Guide our rulers, our officers and soldiers. Be our God. Let not our enemies have dominion over us, I pray thee. Enjoyed the day much in my study. Drilled several hours this afternoon – was quite tired but enjoyed it. Everything is warlike." A few days later he appealed to his maker, "Lord be with the Southern people today." [78]

Endnotes to Chapter 1

1. *Wilmington Daily Journal*, November 5, 1860 (hereinafter Daily Journal); Wood, Richard E., *Port Town at War: Wilmington, North Carolina 1860-1865*, p.34, Unpublished dissertation at Florida State University, (hereinafter cited as Port Town at War)
2. Daily Journal, November 5, 1860
3. Ibid, November 7, 1860
4. Hufham, Rev. J.D., *Memoir of Rev. John L. Prichard, Late Pastor of the First Baptist Church, Wilmington, N.C.*, p.120, Hufham and Hughes Publishers, Raleigh, N.C., 1867 (hereinafter cited as Prichard Memoir)
5. Daily Journal, November 13, 1860
6. Abernathy, Thomas P., *The South in the New Nation, 1789-1819,Volume IV of A History of the South*, p.127, Louisiana State University Press, Baton Rouge, 1961; Phillips, Ulrich B., *American Negro Slavery*, p.467-469, Louisiana State University Press, 1966, Reprint of 1918 edition
7. Dowdey, Clifford, *The Land They Fought For,The Story of the South as the Confederacy, 1832-1865*, p.14-22, Doubleday & Company, Garden City, New York, 1955; Craven, Avery, *The Growth of Southern Nationalism, 1848-1861,Volume VI of A History of the South*, p.305-311, LSU Press, 1953
8. Daily Journal, November 13, 1860
9. Coulter, E. Merton, *The Confederate States of America, Volume VII of A History of the South*, p.13, LSU Press, 1950, (hereinafter Coulter, Confederate States)
10. Ibid, p.11-12
11. Daily Journal, November 15, 1860
12. Ibid, November 10,1860
13. Prichard Memoir, p.120
14. Daily Journal, November 20, 1860
15. Ibid, November 20, 1860
16. Ibid, November 28, 1860
17. Osterweis, Rollin G., "The Idea of Southern Nationalism", from *The Causes of the American Civil War*, p.145, D.C. Heath and Company, Lexington, Massachusetts, 1961
18. Daily Journal, December 12, 1860

19. Ibid, December 12, 1860
20. Ibid, December 13, 1860; Sprunt, James, *Chronicles of the Cape Fear River 1660-1916*, p.299-300, Edwards & Broughton Printing Co., Raleigh, N.C., 1916 (hereinafter cited as Chronicles)
21. Daily Journal, December 13, 1860
22. Ibid, December 21, 1860, December 24, 1860, January 2, 1861; Prichard Memoir, p.121
23. Ibid, December 21, 1860; Prichard Memoir, p.121
24. Ibid, January 5 and January 9, 1861; Ashe, Samuel A., *History of North Carolina, Volume II, From 1783 to 1925*, p.544, Edwards & Broughton Printing Co., Raleigh, 1925 (hereinafter cited as Ashe)
25. Clark, Walter, *Histories of the Several Regiments and Battalions from North Carolina in the Great War, 1861-1865*, Volume V, p.23-24, Nash Brothers Book and Job Printers, Goldsboro, North Carolina, 1901 (hereinafter cited as Clark)
26. *War of the Rebellion, A Compilation of the Official Records of the Union and Confederate Armies, Series I, Volume I*, p.474-475, 70 volumes in 128 parts. United States War Department, Government Printing Office, Washington, D.C., 1880-1901, (hereinafter cited as OR, with future citing considered Series I volumes unless otherwise specified); Chronicles, p.52-55
27. OR, Volume I, p.476
28. Daily Journal, January 10, 1861; Barrett, John G., *The Civil War in North Carolina*, p.6-7, University of North Carolina Press, Chapel Hill, 1963 (hereinafter cited as Barrett)
29. Barrett, p.6; Ashe, Volume II, p. 544
30. Clark, Volume V, p.23-24
31. Ibid, p.24-25
32. Ibid, p.24-25
33. Ibid, p.26
34. OR, Volume I, p.484
35. Ibid, p.476
36. Daily Journal, January 28, 1861
37. Ibid, January 28, 1861
38. Ibid, January 28, 1861
39. Ibid, January 28, 1861
40. Ibid, January 28, 1861; Port Town at War, p.50-51
41. Davis, Jefferson, *The Rise and Fall of the Confederate Government*, Volume I, p.234, Thomas Yoseloff, Publisher, Cranbury, New Jersey, 1958 (hereinafter cited as Rise and Fall)
42. Daily Journal, January 30, 1861
43. Ibid, January 30, 1861

44. Chronicles, p.269
45. Ibid, p.269-270
46. Ibid, p.270-271
47. Foote, Shelby, *The Civil War, A Narrative, Fort Sumter to Perryville*, p.39, Random House, New York, 1958
48. Sitterson, J.C., *The Secession Movement in North Carolina*, p.235-237, University of North Carolina Press, Chapel Hill, 1939 (hereinafter cited as Secession Movement)
49. Secession Movement, p.237
50. Ibid, p.232
51. Daily Journal, April 13, 1861
52. Waddell, Alfred M., *Some Memories of My Life*, p.54, Edwards & Broughton Printing, Raleigh, 1908
53. Prichard Memoir, p.122
54. Daily Journal, April 15, 1861
55. Ibid, April 15, 1861
56. OR, Volume I, p.486
57. Clark, Volume V, p.27
58. Daily Journal, April 15, 1861 and February 2, 1861; Manarin, Louis, *North Carolina Troops 1861-1865, A Roster,* Volume I Artillery, p. 218, North Carolina Division of Archives and History, Raleigh, 1966 (hereinafter cited as NC Troops)
59. Clark, Volume V, p.27-28; Port Town at War, p.56-57; NC Troops, Volume I, p.40
60. DeRosset, Colonel William L. to "Wilmington Messenger", October, 1906, in North Carolina Department of Archives & History; "Colonel William Lamb Day Booklet", p.3, Carolina Printing Company, Wilmington, N.C., 1962
61. Chronicles, p.295; Port Town at War, p.58
62. OR, Volume I, p.486-487
63. Daily Journal, April 15, 1861
64. Chronicles, p.271-272
65. Ibid, p.272
66. Ibid, p.272
67. Hill, Daniel H, *Bethel to Sharpsburg – A History of North Carolina in the War Between the States*, Volume I, p.39, The North Carolina Historical Commission, Edwards & Broughton Company, Raleigh, 1926 (hereinafter Bethel to Sharpsburg)
68. Bethel to Sharpsburg, Volume I, p.43
69. Daily Journal, May 22, 1861
70. Ibid, May 22, 1861
71. Ibid, May 22, 1861

72. Russell, Anne, *Wilmington - A Pictorial History*, The Donning Company Publishers, Norfolk, Virginia, 1981, p.31; Daily Journal, May 24, 1861; DeRosset to Messenger, October, 1906
73. Daily Journal, May 23, 1861
74. Ibid, May 23, 1861
75. Ibid, May 24, 1861
76. Ibid, May 24, 1861
77. Ibid, May 22, 1861
78. Prichard Memoir, p.124

Fort Fisher, C.S.A.

The mighty Fort Fisher and the other forts and installations guarded the Cape Fear River, and protected the daring little blockade runners that brought the vital cargoes the South needed into the port at Wilmington.

Chapter 2

Blockade Runners in the Misty Dawn

O n August 16, 1861, a Mr. Thomas Warren of Edenton, North Carolina wrote to Confederate Secretary of War Leroy P. Walker in Richmond. He pointed out to him the numerous inlets and sounds that marked the North Carolina coast, and the difficulty to a Union fleet of trying to blockade and seal them off. "I think it would be no difficult task," he wrote, "to get arms, etc., from Europe, provided the arms can be sent to one of the West India Islands and there met by small-class vessels sent from our waters to receive and continue the transportation." Warren was prepared to render what assistance he could without compensation. "I have three steamers which, at any time that such an enterprise might demand, could be commanded, and at any time I have it in my power to engage schooners of light draft that might, under skillful navigators, reach, I think, in safety one of the West India islands, and return, bringing arms, etc." [1]

This idea took immediate hold, and just four days later the Honorable Secretary wrote to his commissioners, Captain Caleb Huse and Major Edward Anderson, who were then in London, charged with procuring munitions in Europe for transshipment to the Confederacy. "With the view of affording you every possible facility for the accomplishment of your difficult and precarious mission, this Department has from time to time communicated to you such suggestions with regard to the means of importing arms, etc., as had come within its possession and were likely to be of use to you in the formation of your plans. A suggestion of this character has just been communicated by Dr. Thomas D. Warren," adding that it was a guide for "your consideration, not as instructions." These official communications were an excellent forecast of what was to transpire on the Carolina coast. [2]

One unfortunate Yankee master of a vessel captured by Confederates off the coast of Cape Hatteras, revealed in a statement to the New York Board of Underwriters, that the Rebels in North Carolina were busy at work in blockade running and privateering in this first summer of the war. While a prisoner at New Bern he was permitted to visit any area of the town he chose. During his tenure there, he observed four ships depart that were "loaded with rice" brought from Charleston by the railroad. Almost as if they were following Mr. Warren's suggestions to Secretary Walker, the vessels were reportedly headed for the West Indies. "Two other vessels, loaded with spirits of turpentine, sailed for Halifax. There were three more vessels loading when he left. While he was at New Bern four vessels were brought there as prizes, two schooners loaded with fruit and two brigs loaded with sugar and molasses. He was present at an auction sale of about six hundred hogsheads of sugar, which had been taken from prizes previously brought there. When he left there were twelve vessels lying in the river at anchor, all of which were prizes." [3]

North Carolina's coast, as the gentleman from Edenton had pointed out, was well suited for blockade running, as well as the equally enterprising business of privateering. Most of the mainland does not touch the ocean. Starting at the Virginia line and going all the way down to the Cape Fear River below Wilmington, sand bars "run parallel to the mainland and separate it from the Atlantic Ocean. Enclosed between the sand bars, or banks, as the natives call them, and the mainland are the placid waters of Currituck, Albemarle, Roanoke, Croatan, Pamlico, Bogue, and Core sounds." [4]

Major towns of the eastern section of the state are located on navigable rivers that empty into these generally calm sounds, which vary in size from one to forty miles in width. The Pasquotank River runs past Elizabeth City into Albemarle Sound; the Roanoke River runs past Plymouth into Albemarle as well. The Pamlico River in Washington gives into the Pamlico Sound; from Washington to the interior the Pamlico River is the Tar River to Tarboro and beyond. The Neuse runs past Goldsboro, Kinston, and New Bern to empty into Pamlico Sound also. Beaufort and Morehead City, as well, are guarded by outer banks and are accessible from Pamlico Sound. These are the major cities and protecting sounds north of Wilmington. [5]

Wilmington itself was accessible by way of the Cape Fear River through either New Inlet or Old Inlet, below Smithville. There were also outer banks east of Wilmington and the mainland, with the sounds of Middle,

Wrightsville, Masonboro, and Myrtle from north to south, protecting the land. None of the sounds, however, were any closer to Wilmington than five or six miles, which would mean that any supplies brought in by way of them would have to be off-loaded from a blockade runner and transported by wagon over sandy roads into town. River access, then, was the most direct way for supplies to get to Wilmington. As long as the major sound inlets and the Cape Fear River were held by Southern troops, North Carolina would be secure from Yankee invasion by sea. [6]

Immediately upon secession, the state began to see to the protection of its long coastline by the building of forts at the various inlets, as well as the seizure of such pre-existing ones as Johnston and Caswell. Also, a fleet of small vessels was created to "defend the water of the sounds." [7] A small side-wheel steamboat, the *Winslow*, was fitted out and sallied forth outside Hatteras "to annoy and destroy the commerce of the United States." The little steamer was quite successful in her sojourns off the coast, capturing among other prizes, "the bark *Lenwood*, with 6000 bags of coffee; the schooner *Lydia French*, the brig *Gilvery*, with 315 tierces of molasses...the schooner *Gordon*, with fruit; the schooner *Priscilla*, with 600 bushels of salt...The outcry that went up from commercial circles at the North may have had no little to do in influencing the naval authorities to block the outlet from which the little *Winslow* inflicted such damages." Other converted steamboats soon joined the *Winslow* in her efforts, and harassment of United States commerce off the Outer Banks became commonplace. [8]

The Federals saw early on that they would have to take and hold Hatteras and the sounds. As well demonstrated by such actions as those of the *Winslow*, the sounds would serve as military and naval bases for gunboats to be fitted out, to roam and assail the "whole coast of Virginia and North Carolina from Norfolk to Cape Lookout. The position was deemed second in importance only to Norfolk." [9]

Lieutenant Thomas O. Selfridge, U.S. Navy, recognized the importance of North Carolina's Outer Banks and sounds, and seems to have been the first to suggest an expedition to secure those vital areas. On August 10, 1861, the lieutenant wrote to Lincoln's Secretary of the Navy, Gideon Welles, expounding on some of the reasons for his suggestion. "It seems the coast of Carolina is infested with a nest of privateers that have thus far escaped capture, and in the ingenious manner of cruising are probably likely to avoid the clutches of our cruisers. Hatteras Inlet, a little south of Cape Hatteras light, seems their principal rendezvous. Here they have a fortification that protects them from assault. A lookout at the lighthouse proclaims the coast clear and a merchantman in sight; they dash out and are back again in a day with their prize. So long as these remain it will be impossible to entirely prevent their depredations, for they do not venture out when men-of-war are in sight; and in the bad weather of the coming season, cruisers cannot always keep their stations off these inlets without great risk of going ashore." [10]

On August 27, 1861, just three months following secession, North Carolina troops saw the powerful expedition put together by the United States Navy and Army round the point of Cape Hatteras. Their purpose was to break up the commerce and privateering that was so aggravating and costly to Yankee shipping merchants, and to set up permanent occupation on North Carolina soil. It was a formidable force of seven warships with 149 guns and crews totaling 1,972 men, and was accompanied by 880 Federal infantry under General Benjamin Butler (later to be reviled by Southerners as "Beast Butler"), all of whom had set sail from Fortress Monroe, Virginia on August 26. [11]

Hatteras was defended by Forts Hatteras and Clark, garrisoned by a total of about 700 men of the Seventh North Carolina Volunteers, and detachments of the Tenth North Carolina Artillery. The Rebels had less than twenty heavy guns with which to reply to the Union fleet. To say the Confederates were ill prepared is an understatement. The Seventh North Carolina had just been organized when the fleet hove to off the cape, "and the lieutenant-colonel and major received their commissions after the battle began." [12]

On August 28 the Federal gunboats opened up with heavy barrages on Fort Clark, which by midday had exhausted its ammunition to no effect against the powerful fleet, and had been abandoned, its men heading for Fort Hatteras. But the guns of Fort Hatteras did not have sufficient range to reach the Yankee fleet with any effect, either. Captain Samuel Barron, C.S. Navy, a sailor since the War of 1812, and highest ranking officer in the area, expressed the degree of confidence the Rebels had in their position when he wrote, "In assuming this grave responsibility (the command of the post) I was not unaware that we could be shelled out of the fort." [13]

Captain Barron, in his report of the fall of Hatteras, explained that the Yankee warships pounded the small fort, while the Confederate projectiles would not reach the vessels. The Southern troops were ordered to "take shelter under the parapet and traverses, and I called a council of officers, at which it was unanimously agreed that holding out any longer could only result in a greater loss of life...The personnel of the command are now prisoners of war on board this ship where everything is done to make them as comfortable as possible under the circumstances, Flag Officer Stringham, Captain Van Brunt, and Commander Case extending to us characteristic courtesy and kindness." [14]

The capture of Hatteras was the first real Union victory of the war, and resulted in a genuine uplifting of spirits in the North, which had recently suffered humiliating defeats at Manassas, Virginia and Wilson's Creek, Missouri. "This was our first naval victory, indeed our first victory of any kind," said Admiral David Dixon Porter. "The Union cause was then in a depressed condition, owing to the reverses it had experienced. The moral effect of this affair was very great, as it gave us a foothold on Southern soil and possession of the Sounds of North Carolina, if we chose to occupy them. It was a death-blow to blockade running in that vicinity, and ultimately proved one of the most important events of the war." [15]

In the South, and North Carolina particularly, the blow produced depression and indignation at the obvious lack of preparation and almost impotence on the part of the Confederate authorities to resist such attacks. The Southern people were fast learning that there just were not enough of them to go around to repel every blow the Yankees could throw at a point of their own choosing.

The best sea entrance to the North Carolina sounds was now in Union control. The "back door" to Norfolk was about to be opened, and a favorite channel for Confederate blockade-runners and Rebel commerce raiders, was not to serve the Southern Cause again.

Just three months after secession, much anxiety was already felt by the people on the coast, as well as by Governor Henry Clark, successor to Governor Ellis, who had died from disease in July. He wrote to the Secretary of War in Richmond. "We feel very defenseless here without arms...We see just over our lines in Virginia, near Suffolk, two or three North Carolina regiments, well armed and well drilled, who are not allowed to come to the defense of their homes...We are threatened with an expedition of 15,000 men. That is the amount of our seaboard army, extending along four hundred miles of territory." The governor went on to say that the only arms officials had been able to gather lately were shotguns and hunting rifles, but even those were difficult to come by, because the people were hanging on to them for their own defense. [16]

In Wilmington, the *Daily Journal* told its readers that no one should have been surprised that the Yankees hit them at Hatteras, considering their power to control the sea with their strongest arm, the navy. The newspaper predicted that "this will be the course of events for some time we may feel certain." With the enemy having a lodgment at Hatteras, they could "threaten the whole coast of the mainland, as, in the calm waters of the Sound a landing may easily be made at any point." [17]

The effect of the loss of Hatteras on Wilmington was soon evident in the amount of ocean traffic that appeared off Cape Fear. On Sunday, September 22, 1861, Acting Master Edward Cavendy, Commanding U.S. Ship *Gemsbok*, filed a report with Commodore S.H. Stringham, Flag Officer Atlantic Blockading Squadron, in which he wrote that on September 16, an English brig had arrived and "gone into New Inlet. There have been a good many vessels of light draft popping in and out New Inlet, and it is important that both sides of the shoals should be blockaded." [18]

Master Cavendy also related his capture that morning of a schooner called the *Mary E. Pindar* of Edenton, twelve miles off New Inlet. The vessel carried sixty casks of lime on board, and Cavendy had placed a prize master and crew aboard the ship and sent them off to the United States authorities at Hampton Roads. He had also learned of a British vessel, purportedly a man-of-war, at anchor off New Inlet, but by the time he got there, the ship had left. From two men who came aboard his vessel about six miles north of the inlet, ostensibly for the purpose of serving as pilots to bring his ship into the harbor, he learned there were 900 troops stationed at a camp in the vicinity from which the men had left shore. [19]

There would be many more "vessels of light draft popping in and out New Inlet," as well as running past Fort Caswell, in the months to follow. There were good reasons for this, in addition to the loss of Hatteras, and Yankee control of the sounds to the west of Hatteras that soon would follow. One of the primary reasons was geographic. Though less than kind to mariners for centuries, the natural advantages of the approaches to Wilmington made it an ideal haven for blockade-runners. There are two entrances to the Cape Fear River, New Inlet on the north, and Old Inlet or the Western Inlet on the south of Cape Fear. The cape is the most southern projection of Smith's Island (modern Bald Head Island), "a naked, bleak elbow of sand, jutting far out into the ocean. Immediately in its front are the Frying Pan Shoals," non-navigable sand bar ridges barely beneath the surface, jutting straight out from the cape at least twenty miles to sea.

Mr. George Davis, the former Unionist who had sorrowfully advised his friends in the March meeting at Thalian Hall that the South could no longer expect security in the Union, wrote graphically of what Cape Fear and Frying Pan Shoals meant to those familiar with those dangerous features of nature. "Together they stand for warning and for woe; and together they catch the long, majestic roll of the Atlantic, as it sweeps through a thousand miles of grandeur and power from the Arctic towards the Gulf. It is the playground of billows and tempests, the kingdom of silence and awe, disturbed by no sound save the seagull's shriek and the breaker's roar. Its whole aspect is suggestive, not of repose and beauty, but of desolation and terror. Imagination cannot adorn it. Romance cannot hallow it. Local pride cannot soften it. There it stands today, bleak and threatening, and pitiless, as it stood three hundred years ago, when Greenville and White came near unto death upon its sands. And there it will stand, bleak, and threatening, and pitiless, until the earth and the sea shall give up their dead. And, as its nature, so its name, is now, always has been, and always will be, the Cape of Fear." [20]

In addition to the Union Navy's difficulty of having to contend with two entrances to the Cape Fear River, widely separated by Smith Island and the extension of Frying Pan Shoals, and in some of the most treacherous waters of the Atlantic, the beach in this area and for miles around slopes very gradually to deep water. "The soundings along the coast are regular, and the floor of the ocean is remarkably even. A steamer hard pressed by the enemy could run along the outer edge of the breakers without great risk of grounding; the pursuer, being usually of deeper draft, was obliged to keep further off shore."[21]

Another significant reason blockade-runners would begin using Wilmington as a major port was due to the present forts and rising installations at the mouth of the Cape Fear. Two of the existing ones at the time of secession were Fort Caswell and Fort Johnston, the same ones seized in January against the orders of the governor, which had been returned to the United States by more stringent orders of the governor. Those installations were taken possession of on April 16, the day after Lincoln's call for troops, by the Thirtieth North Carolina Militia, under Colonel John Cantwell. The men immediately went to work to "mount guns and prepare for defence." It was a proud boast of Colonel Cantwell, "that the news of the act dissolving its (North Carolina's) connection with the Union, and the call upon her sons to arms themselves was first made known to the pioneer troops of the Cape Fear on the parade ground at Fort Caswell." [22]

The troop strength was beefed up, and substantial bodies of men were used in the mounting of guns, erection of company quarters on the terre-pleins

The geographic obstacle posed by Cape Fear's two inlets, separated by Frying Pan Shoals off Bald Head Island, made it almost impossible for Union blockaders to close the port at Wilmington. Map courtesy of Mark A. Moore from his book, **The Wilmington Campaign and the Battles for Fort Fisher.**

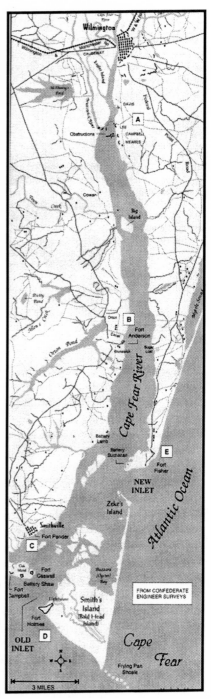

Col. John Cantwell, C.S.A.

(top horizontal surface of the rampart), and the building of a rail line from the wharf up to the fort. Caswell's moat was deepened around the fort, and about a half mile from the fort out on the beach, a battery of earth and sand was erected. This battery would become known as Battery Shaw. [23]

There were eighteen guns inside Caswell when it was seized, and these were soon mounted on carriages, while four others were brought in and mounted as well. In addition to the twenty-two guns around the walls, there were two others at the main gates. "A considerable quantity of provisions and many boxes of rifles were landed and stored in the forts. The lights in lighthouses and beacons are put out, and the Frying Pan Shoal light-ship removed." [24]

One soldier at Caswell reported that the mounting of guns there, with the inexperience of the troops and lack of proper tools, proved to be a tremendous job. The first time a gun was fired, "the recoil that always follows firing caused the gun carriage to tilt up and the infernal thing went end over end to the foot of the embankment." Despite such initial mishaps, enough artillery got mounted and properly in place at Caswell to keep Yankee blockaders at a respectable distance. [25]

In April, about the same time as Colonel Cantwell's occupation of Caswell, Captain Charles P. Bolles, a native of Wilmington, was ordered by Major William H.C. Whiting to Confederate Point, which overlooked New Inlet about six miles northeast of Fort Caswell, to commence the building of two sand batteries. One of the batteries was situated to have a direct line "of fire toward the end of the inlet and the other battery to the westward of it to have a direct and ricochet fire toward the main part of the channel. These two sand batteries were connected by a covered way or curtain for infantry which ran eastwardly toward a line of natural sand dunes extending across the peninsula from the Cape Fear River to the Atlantic Ocean." This line of sand dunes was later to be incorporated into part of the land face of what would become Fort Fisher. [26]

On May 4, 1861, Captain Bolles was transferred to Oak Island, to supervise the erection of a sand battery to the west of Fort Caswell, the one to

Captain Charles P. Bolles, C.S.A.

become known as Battery Shaw. He was later relocated to the Fayetteville Arsenal. The same day he left for Oak Island, Captain William L. DeRossett, commanding the Wilmington Light Infantry, assumed command on Confederate Point. His men were native to the area, and had drilled for years before the war. They had mustered for duty April 15, 1861, the very day Fort Sumter was formally surrendered to the Confederates, in company with the German Volunteers and the Wilmington Rifle Guards, and they were all part of the Thirtieth North Carolina Militia, ready and willing to defend their soil from invasion. [27]

The Wilmington Light Infantry was privileged to have on its muster roll a rather distinguished gentleman, who also happened to be President of the Confederate States of America. It seems that when Jefferson Davis was Secretary of War under Franklin Pierce, the Wilmington Light Infantry was in need of more modernized rifle-muskets. Davis saw to it that they got them. The Wilmington men, anticipating his help beforehand, made him an honorary member of the unit. Davis was in good company, for these infantry represented some of the best families of the Lower Cape Fear, and sixty-five of them were destined to become commissioned officers in the Confederate Army. [28]

The Wilmington Light Infantry worked on and finished the earthworks Captain Bolles had begun, and named the most southern of the battery works "Battery Bolles" in his honor. Soon after he arrived, Captain DeRosset received and mounted two 24-pounder cannon. "His men rolled the cannon on skids at least a quarter of a mile up on to the parapet, and mounted the guns with no implements

Col. Charles Fisher, C.S.A.

whatever except a bit of seine rope and four 4 x 4 scantlings." [29]

In less than a month, DeRosset was gone, having been reassigned as commander of a recruit camp at Garysburg, North Carolina. His position was assumed by Captain John J. Hedrick, the Wilmingtonian of the January fort seizures, who would remain at this post until early summer of 1862. Under Hedrick's supervision, more sand batteries were erected on Confederate Point. He was also assisted by two very qualified engineers. Captain John Winder "designed a casemate battery of railroad iron and palmetto logs," while Colonel S.L. Fremont had a casemate built that was "riveted at the portholes by palmetto logs." [30]

By early summer, the rest of the Thirtieth North Carolina Militia, the German Volunteers and the Wilmington Rifle Guards, had joined the Wilmington Light Infantry on Confederate Point. These three companies, along with six others from the counties of Bladen, Robeson, Richmond and Columbus, as well as one other from New Hanover, elected field officers in July, and were designated the Eighth North Carolina Regiment Volunteers. [31]

Nine of the companies were assigned to Camp Wyatt, "named in honor of Henry L. Wyatt, the first soldier killed in regular battle in the Southern army." Wyatt was a North Carolinian, and the camp in his honor had been built on the western side of Confederate Point near the river, slightly over one mile north of the sand batteries being erected near New Inlet. Commanding officer of the Eighth North Carolina was Colonel James D. Radcliff, a former principal of a Wilmington military school, who was "an excellent drill master and disciplinarian, and soon had the regiment in good shape." [32]

One company, The Scotch Boys, from Richmond County, must have been strong, stout workers, able to perform the labor required in building large batteries and mounting heavy guns, judging by the observations of the regimental adjutant, First Lieutenant William H. McLaurin. Lieutenant McLaurin observed, "Sixty of them were 6 feet to 6 feet 4 inches high, 24 over 5 feet 10 inches, 7 over 5 feet 8 inches, and 3 under 5 feet 8 inches, making an average height for the whole company of 6 feet 1 3/8 inches, believed to be unprecedented for so large a company, in the Confederate or Federal armies, if it does not challenge the armies of the world, for a company not especially selected." [33]

In mid-September, Company K of the Eighth was ferried "across New Inlet channel to a battery on Zeke's Island." At the same time, Companies F and I were assigned the task of helping to build a large sand battery about four hundred yards in from the beach, and about one and a half miles north of New Inlet, known as Fort Fisher. The work was named for Colonel Charles Frederick Fisher of Salisbury, who had died at First Manassas while leading the Sixth North Carolina Infantry on July 21, 1861. "A few weeks later the other seven companies joined F and I and engaged in laying the foundation of Fort Fisher." [34]

In company with the Eighth Volunteers, which in the spring of 1862 would be designated the Eighteenth North Carolina Troops, the New Inlet batteries and the Western Bar at Caswell, as well as other positions around Wilmington and along the Cape Fear, were defended by the Thirty Sixth Regiment North Carolina Troops in the fall of 1861. First Company A, also known as the Wilmington Horse Artillery, and later as Bunting's Battery, was mustered into state service at Wilmington on June 18, 1861. In August, it became part of the Thirty Sixth Regiment, and was mustered into the Confederate Army. The unit was originally assigned to Camp Davis, along the Middle South, some twenty miles north of New Inlet, and about eight miles northeast of Wilmington. In the fall, the battery was assigned to duty at Camp Anderson in Wilmington, the camp being named for Brigadier General Joseph R. Anderson, a Virginian, who in September became commander of the Cape Fear District. [35]

The Bladen Guards served as 1st Company B of the Thirty Sixth Regiment for four months, from November 1861 through February 1862, pulling its duty on Zeke Island, across New Inlet from Confederate Point. It was returned in the winter to the Eighteenth North Carolina, from which it had been detached. In company with the Bladen Guards on Zeke Island was the Cape Fear Light Artillery. This outfit was first known as Hedrick's Company Artillery, North Carolina Volunteers, and had participated in the capture of Fort Johnston on April 16, when Governor Ellis had ordered that post seized along with Caswell. These Rebels were now officially designated as 1st Company C of the Thirty Sixth, and served the pieces at Zeke Island until December 12, 1861, when the artillerists were ordered to Confederate Point to serve the big guns at Fort Fisher. [36]

The result of Captain Hedrick's efforts at New Inlet, assisted by the troops of the Eighth Volunteers and the Thirty Sixth Regiment, became apparent to the Yankees on November 18, 1861. The Federal warship *U.S.S. Monticello* was fired upon from a masked battery, "while reconnoitering near New Inlet," reported Lieutenant D.L. Braine, the ship's commander. "After firing three shots the battery ceased firing," Braine wrote Flag Officer L.M. Goldsborough, commanding officer of the Atlantic Blockading Squadron. "Knowing it was not the object of the blockading vessels to engage land batteries, I also ceased firing and drew off." Braine said he subsequently learned from some "contrabands" who visited the ship, that the Federal guns had dismounted one of the Confederate pieces. [37]

J. And D. MacRae & Company of Wilmington hoped that blockading officers such as Lieutenant Braine would develop a healthy respect for and an abiding fear of engaging batteries on the Lower Cape Fear, so vessels could run the blockade with their wares. On November 21, MacRae & Company wrote its agent in Bristol, England, a Mr. William Gough, that they had loaded the blockade runner *Bruce* with a shipment of pale rosin. "We leave you to effect insurance, and have filled up our invoice and bill of lading as your property, so that in case of capture you can treat it as such. We have drawn against this on you at three days, favor of Alex. McRae, payable in London, for 250 pounds sterling, being about one half the cost, and bill disbursements, which latter goes by vessel, with samples rosin, etc. Captain Muir thinks he will have a chance to get safely to sea in a few days, as the blockade is very irregular and ineffectual. A vessel came in safely this week." The Wilmington shipping agent told Mr. Gough that salt, shoes, gray cloths, blankets, iron, kerseys, blocks of tin and military stores, were "all very scarce and command extreme prices." The Wilmington company was interested "in a shipment including any of the above articles," and would welcome a joint venture with the English gentleman. [38]

Such business deals between Southerners and Englishmen were destined to grow tremendously as the war on the Carolina coast progressed, and as defensive positions below Wilmington grew stronger. By December, seven months after secession, fortifications on Confederate Point had taken on a dangerous look, at least from the perspective of Federal naval officers. Lieutenant D.L. Braine wrote that fortifications at New Inlet in December consisted of one battery of twelve guns, a casemate earthwork of six guns, a small battery armed with three guns, and a battery on Zeke's Island with four guns. Braine had also been informed that there were 1400 troops at New Inlet, that all the battery positions were armed with "short 32-pounders," and that there was also stationed here a battery of horse artillery with four guns. [39]

As for Wilmington itself, Braine's informant advised him that there were not many soldiers around the city environs. On December 27, Braine said, a blockade running steamer called the *Gordon* or *Theodora* had arrived at Wilmington "from Cuba with a cargo of coffee and fruit, and that she was partially disabled, having been struck by a shot passing through the wheelhouse." The steamer had sailed from the West Indies under the British flag. [40]

In mid-December, the Confederates towed down the river four heavy, large wooden cribs, forty to fifty feet in width, and twelve feet in depth, that "they moored on the shoal and in the channel way close together at the northwestern end of Zeke's Island." The large cribs were filled with rocks and sunk at this position, in order to block the channel of New Inlet at that point. Lieutenant Braine felt it was impossible for any vessel to navigate this part of the channel off Zeke's Island that had a draft of nine feet of water or more. [41]

Captain John N. Maffitt, a Carolinian whose mother gave birth to him at sea, and who was destined to be one of the South's great sea captains, would steam many times past the big rock obstructions near Zeke's Island. In January 1862, however, he decided to exit the Cape Fear by way of Old Inlet past Fort Caswell. His vessel was the *Cecile*, and she had been offered for use of the Confederate government by Fraser, Trenholm & Company, the Liverpool branch of John Fraser & Company of Charleston.[42] Captain Maffitt said she was an "unusually fast" vessel, one capable of stowing about seven hundred bales of cotton, which was the prime medium of exchange from the Confederacy for purchase of European goods. With the cargo loaded, they left Wilmington, and anchored off the town of Smithville before nightfall. From here they could observe the Yankee vessels lying off this western mouth of the river, and wait for the most opportune moment to exit for the high sea. [43]

It was essential that they wait for the moon to go down, said Captain Maffitt, and "her sluggishness in retiring for the night was regarded with considerable impatience. At last her royal majesty, over the margin of the western horizon, tips us a knowing wink and disappears. We improve the hint and get under way. In silence Caswell is passed, and a dim glimpse of Fort Campbell affords a farewell view of Dixie, as the steamer's head is turned seaward through the channel. The swelling greetings of the Atlantic billows announce that the bar is passed; over the cresting waves the good craft swiftly dashes, as if impatient to promptly face her trials of the night. Through the settled darkness all eyes on board are peering, eagerly straining to catch a view of the dreaded sentinels who sternly guard the tabooed channel. Nothing white is exposed to view;

Captain John Newland Maffitt

every light is extinguished, save those that are hooded in the binnacle and engine-room. No sound disturbs the solemn silence of the moment but the dismal moaning of the northeast wind and unwelcome, but unavoidable, dashing of our paddles." [44]

Before he knew it, Maffitt was in the midst of the blockading fleet, and on the verge of running clear through it, did, in fact, run right between two blockaders at anchor without detection, when he was discovered. The naval guns roared, belching shot and shell at the *Cecile*. The steamer quivered with awful vibration as a missile struck and exploded. A shell had knocked several bales of cotton overboard and wounded two crewmembers. Quickly the fleet began steaming toward Maffitt's vessel from several directions.

One of the terrified passengers ran out of his cabin and clambered up to the bridge where Maffitt was giving orders to his officers on means for escaping the closing net of Union warships. Much aggravated, Maffitt directed one of his quartermasters to take the man below and keep him quiet. "Without ceremony," Maffitt wrote, "he seized the unhappy individual, and as he hurried him to the cabin, menacingly exclaimed, 'Shut up your flytrap, or by the powers of Moll Kelly, I'll hold ye up as a target for the divarsion of them Yankee gunners!' " [45]

Finally, with speed increasing and darkness drawing a curtain over the vessel, Maffitt and his crew outdistanced their pursuers. They were careful to avoid other ships, not knowing when they might run into a Yankee blockader. Maffitt felt that, "Confederates were Ishmaelites upon the broad ocean – the recipients of no man's courtesy." [46]

The next day out was uneventful until late in the afternoon, when another Federal warship was spotted just at the time Maffitt was having the engines overhauled and the fires cleaned. As twilight and the Yankee steamer both were descending on the *Cecile*, Maffitt had the engineer feed coal dust to the fire, causing heavy clouds of sooty vapor to be carried away in a direction opposite to that in which he was heading. The Federal captain, believing in the darkness that he was stalking his prey, followed the coal dust cloud to the west, while the little blockade-runner sped away to the east. [47]

Maffitt said that when they pulled into the port of Nassau, Bahamas early next morning, they were warmly greeted by many, and "by none more vociferously than the sons of Africa. The cargo was promptly landed and the return freight received on board." In short order a fine load of valuable hardware was headed for Dixie, including among other things nine hundred barrels of gunpowder for muskets and artillery. The powder would later find good use in the Confederate Army of the Mississippi, at the bloody battle of Shiloh in April of the same year. [48]

Maffitt's return trip to Wilmington would have its share of danger, though not as hair-raising as on the trip out. As the vessel could cruise at sixteen knots on the open sea, Maffitt was able to outrun any Federal warship that spotted the *Cecile*. Within about two and a half days after leaving Nassau, some 650 miles away, Maffitt steamed into Western Inlet past Fort Caswell, anchoring at the little town of Smithville in the dead of night for some much needed rest. When morning broke, he weighed anchor and proceeded upriver to Wilmington, where he unloaded his valuable cargo that would find its way to civilians and soldiers alike. [49]

During the time of Captain Maffitt's cruise in the *Cecile*, the Yankees were sending an expedition to further assail the North Carolina coast north of

Wilmington, which in the end, would cause the Cape Fear port to become the "main depot of supplies for the Confederacy." [50]

The intent of the expedition would be for a heavy Federal infantry force to occupy the coast, and then move on Goldsboro and Raleigh, to sever the important rail artery of the Wilmington and Weldon Railroad that was ferrying valuable supplies to the Virginia army by way of connections with Richmond. In Raleigh the Yankee troops would link up with the Union army under Don Carlos Buell, who would plow his way through from Tennessee. General Ben Butler was ordered to occupy New Orleans, while W.T. Sherman moved to take Savannah. These movements were expected to divide the Rebel forces sufficiently so the Army of the Potomac could assault and carry Richmond. Command of the North Carolina expedition was entrusted to General Ambrose Burnside, whose name and facial side-whiskers would later become associated with the term "sideburns," and the Navy's commander would be Flag Officer Louis M. Goldsborough. [51]

Confederate General Daniel Harvey Hill, former commandant of the North Carolina Military Institute at Charlotte, and a principal officer in the first land battle of the war at Bethel, Virginia, was charged with defense of the Albemarle and Pamlico Sounds region in the fall of 1861. He was right on target in his assessment of this vital area of North Carolina's northern coast. "Roanoke Island," he wrote his superior in Richmond, " is the key of one-third of North Carolina, and whose occupancy by the enemy would enable him to reach the great railroad from Richmond to New Orleans. Four additional regiments are absolutely indispensable to the protection of this island...I would most earnestly call the attention of the honorable Secretary of War to this island ...The towns of Elizabeth City, Edenton, Plymouth, and Williamston will all be taken should Roanoke be captured or passed." [52]

When General Hill was transferred to Virginia, the Albemarle-Pamlico region of North Carolina came under the supervision of General Benjamin Huger, commander of the Department of Norfolk. As information of the size of Burnside's expedition, some 15,000 troops moving south from Annapolis, Maryland, reached North Carolina, Governor Clark sought to "stir the Confederate secretaries to immediate defensive activity." [53] He wrote to the Secretary of War, the Secretary of the Navy, and to Jefferson Davis, urging immediate reinforcements with veteran, well-armed troops to hold off the Federal onslaught. The conquest of North Carolina's sounds, Clark told them, would be a significant loss to the Confederate States, as well as to North Carolina. If the Federals controlled the sounds inside the Outer Banks, "Norfolk with its navy yard and commanding position" was doomed to fall. "In a letter to Secretary Mallory on January 13, 1862, he demanded that, if the island could not be successfully defended, transportation to relieve the troops should be maintained." [54]

General Henry Wise, former governor of Virginia, was commanding officer of the troops stationed there. He wrote that the island was not only "practically defenseless, but unsupplied with every adequate means of erecting fortifications." He had about 1,500 effective troops to parry the Yankee multitudes about to sweep down upon them, and those men "were undrilled, unpaid, not sufficiently clothed and quartered, and miserably armed." General Wise was to receive no reinforcements other than a battalion that brought his strength up to about 2,500 men. [55]

On Friday morning, February 7, 1862, the thirty Union gunboats of the expeditionary fleet sailed in close to the western side of Roanoke Island, and opened a terrific bombardment on the Rebel defenses, as well as the paltry Confederate fleet of two "old side-wheel steamers and five naval tugboats." Despite the weight of numbers and superiority of ammunition against them, the scant Southern forces gave as good as they got on the first day of the Battle of Roanoke Island. The next day, however, would break their backs. [56]

With no less than 10,000 infantry against about one-fourth that number, Burnside on the 8th advanced up the island to grapple with the Southern troops, who fought gamely and gallantly, though futilely. Valor could not compensate for such overwhelming numbers. Colonel Henry Shaw of the Eight North Carolina Regiment State Troops was in command on the battlefield, General Wise being seriously ill with pleurisy and confined to bed at Nag's Head. Shaw fought his men admirably, until the numbers told and he had to retreat to the northern end of the island where he surrendered. [57]

Roanoke Island had quickly become United States territory. With its control of Albemarle and Currituck Sounds, as well as eight rivers, four major canals, and two railroads (the Petersburg and Norfolk and the Seaboard and Roanoke), Roanoke Island was the key to all the rear defenses of Norfolk. One Confederate naval officer wrote that it "guarded more than four-fifths of Norfolk's supplies of corn, pork and forage and it cut the command of Gen. Huger off from all its most efficient transportation. Its possession by the enemy endangered the existence of Huger's army, threatened the navy yard at Gosport, cut off Norfolk from Richmond, and both from railroad communication with the South Atlantic States. It lodged the enemy in a safe harbor from the storms of Hatteras, gave him a rendezvous and a large and rich range of supplies, and the command of the seaboard from Oregon Inlet to Cape Henry." [58]

Roanoke Island was also uncomfortably close to Wilmington. The *Daily Journal* told its readers on February 12 that the news from Roanoke Island was "certainly discouraging." The paper said further that it "would be folly to deny that a formidable enemy is on our coast, in our Sounds and rivers, or that the same enemy may aim a blow at this point." The paper cautioned its subscribers, however, to remain calm. "It is a duty we owe to ourselves and to the cause in which we are engaged...Let us not in the excitement and irritation inseparable from the first news of our disaster, indulge in any harsh or hasty remarks against each other...let all ill-feeling among ourselves be put aside, and all animosity be reserved for the common enemy." [59]

It would have been difficult for Wilmingtonians to remain calm and collected in the weeks following the Roanoke Island disaster. From that springboard ideally situated at the juncture of Albemarle and Pamlico Sounds, expeditions went forth to seal off a number of important North Carolina ports. On February 10, Elizabeth City, south of the Dismal Swamp Canal leading to Norfolk, was captured. On the 12th, Edenton fell, and on the 20th, Winton was captured and a number of public buildings were burned. [60]

On March 14, the Yankees attacked North Carolina's second most important seaboard town, New Bern, and a savage battle took place there, at which the state's next war governor, Zebulon Vance, commanded the Twenty Sixth North Carolina Infantry. Heavily outnumbered more than two to one, the Rebels were defeated in a vicious battle that lasted about four hours, with the Confederates retreating to Kinston. [61]

North Carolinians were "shocked and angry at the apparently easy conquest of New Bern." Robert E. Lee, currently adviser to the President, told Jeff Davis that more Union troops were headed for North Carolina, and that another "disaster there would be ruinous." [62]

BrigGen Samuel French, C.S.A.

Soon, additional forays "were sent in all directions," and other towns such as Carolina City, Morehead City, Beaufort and Newport were taken over by the bluecoats. [63]

To prevent Burnside's forces from pushing on to Goldsboro, where the Yankees could sever the vital line of the Wilmington & Weldon Railroad, and cause further disaster such as Lee had warned against, additional troops were dispatched to the state to beef up the defenses. Most went to Goldsboro, where they were "constantly drilled and instructed." [64]

There were also changes in the high command in the Tarheel state. These changes were necessary to thwart further Union incursions in the interior of the state or further south along the coast. General R.C. Gatlin was relieved of command of the Department of North Carolina, and in his place was appointed Major General Theophilus H. Holmes, a Sampson County native and North

Carolina's ranking general in the Confederate service. In the Cape Fear region, Brigadier General Samuel G. French assumed command of the District of Wilmington, relieving Brigadier General Joseph Anderson, who had been in charge since October. Anderson was ordered back to his native state, Virginia. These command changes, like the reinforcements, took place in March after the fall of New Bern. [65]

With New Bern gone, as well as the other ports along Albemarle and Pamlico Sounds, and with Hatteras Inlet solidly corked with Union ships, Wilmington was to become even more crucial in the supply network that blockade running fostered. The Federal authorities were to learn this soon.

On March 22, 1862, the U.S. Consul at Liverpool, England notified Washington that: "cargo of the rebel steamer *Annie Childs*, which ran the blockage (sic) at Wilmington and arrived at this port some days ago, was 634 bales of cotton, 788 barrels rosin...and 10 1/2 boxes manufactured tobacco, one box peanuts, and one box, contents unknown. Her consignees at this place, Fraser, Trenholm & Co...She is an American steamer, was called the *North Carolina*, and is said to be (have been) owned, previous to her seizure by the Confederates, by New Yorkers. I understand she is to be loaded with arms and munitions of war and sent back to Wilmington." [66]

Apparently some of the crew of the *Annie Childs* had a streak of disloyalty about them, as the consul continued "they have just left my office." They told the official that some Confederate naval officers had boarded the *Childs* at a place called Smithville, some 20 miles down the river from Wilmington; that it was talked about and understood by all on board that their object in coming was to take command of a vessel which was being built in England for the Southern Confederacy. They further state that it was understood in Wilmington before they left that several war vessels were being built at Liverpool for the South." [67]

The *Oreto* was the vessel referred to as the one to be taken over by the naval officers, and the world was later to hear of her exploits as the *C.S.S. Florida*, to be commanded by the same officer who had taken out the *Cecile* in January past Fort Caswell, Captain John Maffitt. [68]

In the same dispatch, the consul noted his opinion as to the manner in which a number of other vessels would be getting their cargoes to the Confederacy, the method by which most deliveries would be made to Dixie. "It is not unlikely that all of these vessels may land their cargoes at some of the West India ports and run them in upon steamers, rather than incur the risk of running the blockade with sailing vessels." [69]

That running the blockade into Wilmington was becoming more routine resulted from two major factors, in addition to the geographical advantages, as spring came on in the second year of the war. For one thing, there were not that many ships off Cape Fear that flew the Stars and Stripes at this stage of the game. On April 1, 1862, the commander of the North Atlantic

The **CSS Florida,** *formerly the* **Oreto,** *would gain wide fame as a cruiser under the command of daring Captain John Newland Maffitt.*

Blockading Squadron, Flag Officer Louis M. Goldsborough, reported to Secretary of the Navy, Gideon Welles, that there were only six ships off the coast of Wilmington. These six were to cover two inlets and an area of roughly fifty miles in width, owing to the peculiarity of Frying Pan Shoals, the deadly sandbar ridge that jutted some twenty miles out to sea from the tip of the cape. The six ships mentioned were the *Jamestown, Cambridge, Mount Vernon, Monticello, Amanda*, and *Fernandina*. So there was a lot of ocean and not many vessels to watch it. [70]

The second major obstacle for those Yankee ships that could be spared to patrol the Cape Fear were the Rebel forts and batteries that were growing stronger every day. At the end of April, the Federals learned from two Confederate deserters who had been serving at Fort Caswell, that that fort had about six hundred men, and mounted a total of thirty-six guns. "The guns in barbette are thirty in number," wrote a Union naval officer, "six are rifle guns, and look toward the entrance to the harbor, and with these are four VIII-inch columbiads, looking in the same direction. The balance of the guns are light 32 and 24 pounders." [71]

In and around Fort Fisher there were roughly 2,000 men, most of whom were in the vicinity of Camp Wyatt about three miles from the end of Confederate Point. There were supposedly twenty-four guns "in earthwork" at the New Inlet battery positions, the class and caliber being unknown. [72]

Pulling duty at Fort Fisher could be as disagreeable an experience as any duty pulled by any Confederate soldier. J.W. Bone of the Thirtieth North Carolina Troops, Company I, was based at Camp Wyatt from November 1861 through the spring of 1862. His regiment had come across the river from Fort Caswell to relieve the Eighth North Carolina Volunteers then serving at Fisher, when that unit was ordered to duty in South Carolina. Bone wrote that the camp lay "between the Atlantic Ocean and the Cape Fear River, on a strip of land about one mile wide, with Fort Fisher at the end near the inlet, the wind had a fair sweep here and was nearly all the time blowing. The soil was nearly a sandy desert, so our situation here was not a very pleasant one at times. There were two or three sand forts a few miles from the main fort with a few large guns mounted on them." [73]

One of the duties of the infantry was to assist the artillerists with observation of the enemy. Bone related that at Camp Wyatt there was a tall pole sixty or seventy feet high, equipped with steps and attachments so it could be climbed. The pole served a very important and specific purpose. Each morning a soldier would go up to the top of the pole with a spyglass to observe the movements at sea. If just one blockading warship was sighted, he would hang out a white flag on the pole; "if there were two vessels in sight there would be two flags put; if there were three or more there would be a red one put out, so we had some idea of the number of blockade vessels that were watching the inlet." [74]

One morning, one of the Union blockaders ventured in too close to a Rebel battery, which mounted two cannon. "The officer in charge ordered the battery to fire on it, which it did. The vessel returned the fire and sailed off, this being the first time that any of the Regiment had heard a shot from the enemy since its organization. It caused considerable excitement in camp." [75]

Several days later, Bone was detached as a guard and sent down to that fort, where his post of duty was walking up and down the beach for a hundred yards or so. At night, he slept in "the magazine with the ammunition." [76]

During the winter, Bone got sick and was sent home on furlough. He later returned to join the regiment at Camp Wyatt, where the Thirtieth was engaged in drilling and building "winter quarters of sawed lumber large enought (sic) for a company of one hundred to a house, and went into them by companies. We had plenty to eat of almost anything here and grew fat, lazy, and restless." [77]

The Thirtieth remained at Camp Wyatt until March '62, when New Bern having come under attack, it was ordered to move to that place as reinforcement. By the time it reached Wilmington for forwarding, New Bern had fallen, so the regiment remained in the Wilmington area, though not returning to Camp Wyatt.

By the end of May it had left Wilmington, because the commanding officer, Colonel Francis Marion Parker, reported that the "Thirtieth was actively engaged in the battle of Seven Pines on 31 May, 1862." [78]

Though duty was monotony on a "sandy desert" for the average soldier such as Bone, his efforts and those of his comrades were paying off. By the spring of 1862, Fort Fisher had taken on an inverted "L" shape in its configuration. "It consisted of a battery of land defense, a quadrilateral field work," that was more or less the junction point of the land and sea batteries, and which itself was officially dubbed Fort Fisher. Four additional sea batteries ran down Confederate Point south of the quadrilateral work. [79]

By no means impregnable at this time, Fort Fisher was nevertheless impressive enough to convince the captain of the *C.S.S. Nashville* to utilize New Inlet as a protective haven.

The *Nashville* had already had the satisfaction of humiliating the United States Navy once before. On Monday, March 17, in Beaufort harbor, before the fall of Fort Macon to the Federals, the captain of the large American built side-wheel steamer had dashed through the Yankee fleet assembled to participate in reducing the fort.[80] Edward Cavendy, Acting Lieutenant of the U.S. Bark *Gemsbok*, recorded in his ship's log: "At 7:40 PM observed the rebel steamer *Nashville* coming outside Fort Macon; beat to quarters; signalized immediately to *Cambridge*, 'Enemy is coming out;'...The moment the *Nashville* came under our guns, fired at her as quick as we could load; the *Nashville* being now 1 1/4 miles from us, stood out the main ship channel with all speed; being calm, she soon got out of the range of our guns, the *Cambridge* moving slowly to S.E.." [81]

On March 27, ten days after the *Nashville* escaped, Assistant Secretary of the navy Gustavas V. Fox wrote to Flag Officer Louis Goldsborough, commanding the North Atlantic Blockading Squadron. He was in an ugly mood. "I have yours about the *Nashville*. It is a terrible blow to our naval prestige, and will place us all very nearly in the position we were before our victories...This is not blockade...It is a Bull Run to the Navy." [82]

The blockade runner **Nashville**

The Confederates at Fort Macon, who must have realized that their fate was sealed, being virtually surrounded by bluecoats on land and sea, viewed the blockade runner's escape as a great victory. First Lieutenant John Sanders, Company H, Tenth North Carolina Regiment (First Artillery), wrote of the incident: "All the garrison knew that the attempt was to be made, and the parapets of the fort were crowded to witness the experiment. The night was dark and the stillness of death prevailed. The *Nashville* showed no lights as she steamed slowly and noiselessly out of the harbor. When it became morally certain that she had escaped, a yell from three hundred Confederate throats shook the air again and again, and though the distance was too great for those on the Federal ship to hear, the exultant shout was renewed and prolonged." [83]

Now, a month later, the Union Navy was to be mortified again as a result of the *Nashville*'s intrepidity. On April 24, a Thursday, she ran the Wilmington blockade "about 10 a.m. with a large and valuable cargo of arms and munitions of war, passing in through the northern passage, New Inlet, where she grounded, and the rebels, with several tugboats, were busily working until the night of the 25th or morning of the 26th, when they succeeded in getting her into port." [84]

Valuable, indeed, her cargo was, said an officer aboard the *U.S.S. Daylight*, who reported that 60,000 rifles and powder totaling up to forty tons had been brought in by the *Nashville*. "They sent steamers from Wilmington and Smithville to lighten her and succeeded in getting her off on the 26th, when she proceeded to Smithville, where she took in two lighter-loads of cotton and ran the blockade out of the harbor on the 30th of April and went to sea." [85]

This incident raised the hackles of none other than the Secretary of the Navy himself, Gideon Welles. In writing to Flag Officer Goldsborough on June 9, 1862, his dissatisfaction with the whole affair was readily apparent. "The Department is surprised not only at the insufficiency or mismanagement of the blockading force off Wilmington when the rebel steamer *Nashville* ran into and out of that port, but also at the neglect of the commanding officers to report those circumstances promptly." [86]

At this point in the war, it was a genuine slap in the face to Welles and his warship commanders when a steamer ran the blockade. In the months to follow, blockade runs like this would become of such routine nature as to merit little more than brief mention in a ship's log. In the spring of 1862, though, when the Union Navy was flexing its muscles after the coastal victories gained, from Hatteras and Roanoke Island, to Port Royal, South Carolina and even New Orleans, the South's great metropolis, penetration of the blockade brought disgust and quick rebuke. Secretary Welles told Goldsborough: "Officers on blockading duty should be required to report promptly to the flag officer or the Department all matters of importance pertaining to the blockade." He further informed Goldsborough that a report of all the facts and details relating to the

USS Monticello

Nashville were to be reported by all officers commanding vessels off Wilmington at the time the steamer "ran in and out." [87]

Lieutenant D.L. Braine, commanding the *U.S.S. Monticello*, reported on June 15 that when the *Nashville* was discovered, on the afternoon of April 26, the weather had become "squally and thick; wind increased from the northward and eastward...We now stood in at full speed to New Inlet, and at 3:30 p.m. we were near the bar when we discovered a large side-wheel steamer showing English colors lying in Cape Fear River, apparently discharging cargo into tugboats alongside of her. I stood in as close to her as the water would permit." [88]

J.D. Waren, commanding *U.S.S. Victoria*, said he had gone to assist the *Monticello*, but that his efforts had been in vain. On the morning of April 27, "Seeing a steamer aground in the river, I stood in as near as I dared to, and made the steamer inside to be the *Nashville* (as I supposed). I immediately sent a rifled 30-pounder shell at her, but she was too far distant for me to reach her. At 5 p.m. the steamer floated and went up the river." [89]

As further testimony to the Navy' chagrin over the whole affair, a court of inquiry was convened in Philadelphia to investigate the reasons for the escape of the *Nashville* from the Federals' grasp. The court was "of opinion that the part of the coast of North Carolina about Cape Fear is one of the most exposed during the winter and spring months, rendering very difficult and at times almost impossible for a sailing vessel to maintain position, and frequently very dangerous." [90]

The first vessel to spot the *Nashville* was the *Jamestown*, and she had just recently arrived from Hampton Roads without having completed much needed repairs. She did not have guns of sufficient range, either, and her captain had sought help from the *Victoria* and *Monticello*. That the *Nashville* had been able to sit for over a day without either being seen or attempts made to get at her was owing to a lack of specific instructions to ships' captains as to "how to act or to what their attention was to be called, and they were permitted to leave their stations for supplies without being relieved by others." [91]

The court concluded that it was doubtful if "the *Jamestown* and the two steamers were of sufficient force to have made any successful attempt to capture the rebel steamer after she had got off and within the bar, or have effected her destruction, although the *Victoria* was of light draft of water, protected, as the rebel steamer was, by the forts and the armed tugs that had come to her assistance. If it had been possible, it was not deemed advisable to attempt it." [92]

Evidently, then, until the U.S. Navy got some more ships down here in more serviceable condition, there was not much more that was going to be done to plug up the Cape Fear than was done in this case. Even if they did have more blockaders, the protection afforded "by the forts" to blockade runners, as had been afforded to the *Nashville*, was to prove hazardous to Union vessels that ventured too close.

Although there had not been 60,000 rifles on the *Nashville* as the Yankees had thought, the vessel had definitely brought in a valuable cargo. Major Josiah Gorgas, brilliant chief of the Confederate Ordnance Bureau, reported that the *Nashville* had brought in for Confederate troops 6,420 stands of arms. In addition, Gorgas reported that in a little over three months, steamers arriving in Wilmington, Charleston and Savannah brought in a total of 48,510 stands of arms. [93]

The *Nashville*'s run apparently had a lingering effect on Confederate troops as well as on the Yankees. As late as June 12, 1862, S.S. Biddle Jr. was writing to his sister about the blockade runner. His letter offers insight into some of the living conditions on Confederate Point for the average soldier, which could sometimes be fatal, as well as his belief that the *Nashville*'s next entrance would outshine the last.

Biddle advised his sister Rosa that one of their friends, a fellow named Henry, had died the previous night of typhoid fever. He told her they were stationed at Fort Fisher, which he "generally considered a very healthy place. If I could only get enough meat & bread to eat I should be much better satisfied. I have gone several days since I have been here without meat having nothing to eat but dry bread - this occurs only once & awhile. Don't understand me to say that I am grumbling, for I would cheerfully live on bread & water a whole year provided it would secure our independence...Three & four Federal steamers lie near the Fort all the time looking out for the return of the *Nashville*. It is reported that the *Nashville* is going to return accompanied by two iron clad steamers purchased in England for the Confederacy." [94]

Purchasing agents for the Confederate government abroad were hard at work procuring and sending on to Dixie whatever arms, ammo and equipment they could buy or barter for. They intended to have many more successful runs like that of the *Nashville*.

In late June, Louis Heyliger, agent for the Confederate States at Nassau, New Providence, 570 miles southeast of Wilmington, reported to Secretary of War George Randolph, that two steamers would soon be arriving from England. A gentleman representing the pro-Confederate Saul Isaac, Campbell & Company of London, had approached Heyliger about the purchase of certain items on those vessels. "The former has two batteries of eight guns each complete, and the latter a similar cargo. It appears that these guns are from the Vienna Arsenal, and were approved of by Captain Huse. The London parties made a contract to deliver them into the Confederacy at a certain price." [95]

Captain Caleb Huse, purchasing agent for Europe based in London, had already proven himself adept at procuring arms and supplies for the Rebel armies. He had made a trek to Vienna, Austria early in 1862, as Heyliger had reported, where in a matter of days, he had "closed a contract for 100,000 rifles of the latest Austrian pattern, and ten batteries, of six pieces each, of field artillery, with harness complete, ready for service, and a quantity of ammunition, all to be delivered on ship at Hamburg...the arms were delivered, and in due time were shipped to Bermuda from Hamburg.

"I confess to a glow of pride," Huse wrote, "when I saw those sixty pieces of rifled artillery with caissons, field-forges, and battery-wagons complete - some two hundred carriages in all – drawn up in array in the arsenal yard. It was pardonable for a moment to imagine myself in command of a magnificent park of artillery." [96]

Just one month before the *Nashville* made her run into New Inlet under the Yankees' noses, Captain Huse wrote from London to Major Gorgas, his boss, of a contract for rifles from a British supplier: "The rifles of the London Armory Company are so greatly superior to all others that I have made an effort to obtain the control of all that they can make within the next three years. The contract of the company with the British Government is about expiring, and I have requested the managing director not to apply for a renewal of it until I can receive instructions from the War Department, and have also requested him to tender to me a proposal for supplying 50,000." The price for the rifles was to be sixty shillings, or about $15 each. Huse had found the people at the London Armory Company to be, "most honorable and accommodating, and I beg to suggest to the Department the great importance of making such a contract with them as I have proposed, which is similar to one just completing for the British government." [97]

In St. George's, Bermuda, another British island 674 miles east of Wilmington, John T. Bourne served the same capacity as Louis Heyliger in Nassau. A local commission merchant with pro-Southern sympathies, Bourne, like Heyliger, was responsible for cotton coming from Dixie to Bermuda. The cotton was shipped to England to the Confederacy's chief overseas credit banker, Fraser, Trenholm and Company, who saw to it that Caleb Huse's purchases were paid for. [98]

With all the efforts of those Rebels behind the scenes, Wilmington was sure to be the destination of more blockade runners. The U.S. Naval board of inquiry investigating the *Nashville* affair had hardly arrived at its conclusions before another steamer made for the protection of Fort Fisher. At 4:15 a.m. on June 27, 1862, a "large steam propeller, schooner-rigged, and about 1,000 tons burden, was descried under the land about 3 miles from Federal Point batteries." This ship was the *Modern Greece*. Commander William A. Parker, of the *U.S.S. Cambridge*, had "opened on her with a Parrott rifle," when the blockade runner ran up the English flag and beached herself within a half a mile of the Confederate batteries, her crew fleeing the vessel as Parker continued firing on her.

"The atmosphere was hazy," Parker reported, "and the color of the vessel slate, while her stern was toward us, rendering the ship indistinct. In our endeavors to destroy the vessel the fort threw very heavy shots toward us, bursting over our heads and obliging us to haul off.

"The propeller is yet hard and fast upon the beach," Parker continued, "and appears to be full of water and gradually settling down into the sand, and will probably prove a total wreck, while her cargo will be partially secured by the rebels." [99]

The Union officers congratulated themselves for having stopped the blockade runner before she could get into the river and make for Wilmington, but they had also learned to respect and keep some distance from the guns of Fort Fisher. While they had forced the vessel to beach herself, and tried to inflict as much damage as possible, they were obliged to sit off at a respectful distance while the Rebels salvaged much of the cargo, including all kinds of civilian implements, various military equipment, and arms, clothing and liquors. Getting in too close might mean getting blown out of the water.

Commander Parker reported that: "Efforts were made from time to time by the *Cambridge*, the *Monticello*, and the *Stars and Stripes* to destroy the propeller more effectually, and to prevent the enemy from unlading her, by firing upon them, but this was difficult and dangerous work, as the fort has one or more guns of long range and of heavier caliber, apparently, than any of our own guns." [100]

Lieutenant R.S. McCook of the *U.S.S. Stars and Stripes* also bore testimony to the accuracy of the Confederate shore fire: "As soon as we came within range I opened with my rifle guns, making very good firing. I again tried to place the vessel so that we could use the 8-inch guns with effect, without coming in range of the battery. This I found to be impossible, for, before we had reached within 1,800 yards of the steamer, a shot from the battery passed between my main and mizzenmasts and struck the water between our vessels. It was shortly followed by a shell which burst high and abreast of us, throwing pieces all around the *Cambridge*." [101]

Lieutenant McCook stated further that he and Captain Parker felt they could do no further damage to the *Modern Greece* than they had already done, "and that to send our light boats in to burn her, under the fire of two batteries, would only be to insure their destruction, without accomplishing the desired object." [102]

The respect United States Naval officers now displayed for the guns on Confederate Point, was to pale by comparison in the months to follow, when they would come to fear and dread being anywhere near Fort Fisher. The chief responsibility for this rested with her new commandant, who assumed command just one week after the *Modern Greece* ran ashore. He was a twenty-six-year-old cigar smoking Confederate colonel from Norfolk, Virginia, who was to become as widely known and respected abroad as he was in Dixie. He was destined to be one of the South's most successful combat officers in her struggle for independence. His name was William Lamb.

Endnotes to Chapter 2

1. O.R., Series IV, Volume I, p.564
2. Ibid, Volume I, p.577-578
3. Bethel to Sharpsburg, Volume I, p.161
4. Ibid, Volume I, p.154
5. Ibid, Volume I, p.154
6. Foard, Charles H., Map, *A Chart of Wrecks of Vessels Sunk or Captured Near Wilmington, N.C., Circa 1861-1865*, Revised, 1968 (hereinafter Charles Foard map)
7. Bethel to Sharpsburg, Volume I, p.155
8. Scharf, J. Thomas, *History of the Confederate States Navy From Its Organization to the Surrender of Its Last Vessel,* New York, Rogers and Sherwood, 1887, p.369 (hereinafter Scharf, Confederate Navy)
9. Bethel to Sharpsburg, Volume I, p.159
10. Ibid, p.163
11. Ibid, p.163-164
12. Evans, Clement, editor, *Confederate Military History, North Carolina* Volume, Confederate Publishing Company, Atlanta, Georgia, 1899, p.27 (hereinafter referred to as CMH); Bethel to Sharpsburg, Volume I, p.164
13. Bethel to Sharpsburg, Volume I, p.167
14. Johnson, Robert U. and Clarence C. Buel, eds. *Battles and Leaders of the Civil War,* Volume I, p.633 of 4 Volumes, New York, Century Company, 1887 (hereinafter B & L)

15. Porter, David D., *Naval History of the Civil War*, New York, Sherman Publishing Company, 1886, p.47
16. CMH, North Carolina, p.29
17. Daily Journal, September 6, 1861
18. United States Navy Department, *Official Records of the Union and Confederate Navies in the War of the Rebellion,* Volume 6, p.283, of 30 Volumes, Washington, D.C., Government Printing Office, 1897-1901 (hereinafter referred to as ORN)
19. ORN, Volume 6, p.283-284
20. Chronicles of the Cape Fear River, p.5-6
21. Sprunt, James, *Tales of the Cape Fear Blockade,* p.10
22. Clark, Volume V, p.27-28
23. Herring, Ethel and Williams, Carolee, *Fort Caswell In War and Peace,* p.29, Broadfoot's Bookmark, Wendell, North Carolina, 1983 (hereinafter Fort Caswell); Charles Foard map
24. Fort Caswell, p.29
25. Ibid, p.32
26. *Colonel William Lamb Day Booklet*, p.3 (hereinafter Lamb Day Booklet)
27. Ibid, p.3; Daily Journal, April 15, 1861
28. McKoy, Henry B., *Wilmington, N.C. – Do You Remember When?*, p.76-77, Keys Printing Company, Greenville, South Carolina, 1957
29. Lamb Day Booklet, p.3
30. Ibid, p.3
31. Clark, Volume II, p.16-17
32. Clark, Volume II, p.17; Moore, Mark A., *The Wilmington Campaign and the Battles for Fort Fisher,* p.24, Savas Publishing, Mason City, Iowa, 1999, hereinafter Wilmington Campaign
33. Clark, Volume II, p.17
34. Ibid, Volume II, p.17; Lamb Day Booklet, p.3
35. NC Troops, Volume I, p.174; Bethel to Sharpsburg, Volume I, p.185
36. NC Troops, Volume I, p.198, p.218
37. ORN, Volume 6, p.440
38. Ibid, Volume 6, p.468
39. Ibid, Volume 6, p.499
40. Ibid, Volume 6, p.499
41. Ibid, Volume 6, p.499
42. Maffitt, Emma M., *Life and Services of Captain John Newland Maffitt,* p.229, Neale Publishing Company, New York, 1906, (hereinafter Life of Maffitt); "Running of the Blockade. Interesting Narrative of Mr. James Sprunt", Southern Historical Society Papers, Volume XXIV, p.163; Coulter, Confederate States, p.288
43. Life of Maffitt, p.229-230
44. Life of Maffitt, p.230

45. Life of Maffitt, p.231
46. Ibid
47. Ibid, p.232
48. Ibid, p.232, p.236
49. Ibid, p.236
50. Bethel to Sharpsburg, Volume I, p.188
51. Ibid, Volume I, p.190
52. Ibid, Volume I, p.191
53. Ibid, Volume I, p.191
54. Ibid, Volume I, p.193
55. Ibid, Volume I, p.194-195; p.209
56. Ibid, Volume I, p.201-203
57. Ibid, Volume I, p.204-209; Clark, Volume V, p.61-62
58. Scharf, Confederate Navy, p.393
59. Daily Journal, February 12, 1862
60. B & L, Volume I, p.645-647
61. CMH, North Carolina, p.37-41
62. Barrett, Civil War in N.C., p.107
63. CMH, North Carolina, p.41
64. Bethel to Sharpsburg, Volume I, p.305
65. Ibid, Volume I, p.301-303
66. ORN, Volume 7, p.217
67. Ibid, Volume 7, p.217
68. Ibid, p.217; Life of Maffitt, p.238-239
69. ORN, Volume 7, p.217
70. Ibid, Volume 7, p.184
71. Ibid, Volume 7, p.266
72. Ibid, Volume 7, p.266
73. Bone, J.W., *Civil War Reminiscences*, Manuscript dated 1904, North Carolina Department of Archives and History, Raleigh, N.C. (hereinafter Bone Reminiscences)
74. Bone Reminiscences
75. Bone Reminiscences
76. Ibid
77. Ibid
78. Clark, Volume II, p.498
79. Lamb Day booklet, p.3
80. ORN, Volume 7, p.265
81. Ibid, Volume 7, p.138
82. Ibid, Volume 7, p.139
83. Clark, Volume I, p.511
84. ORN, Volume 7, p.266

85. Ibid, Volume 7, p.264
86. Ibid, Volume 7, p.267
87. Ibid, Volume 7, p.267
88. Ibid, Volume 7, p.270
89. Ibid, Volume 7, p.271
90. Ibid, Volume 7, p.272
91. Ibid, Volume 7, p.272-273
92. Ibid, Volume 7, p.273
93. OR, Series IV, Volume II, p.52
94. *Lower Cape Fear Historical Society Bulletin*, Volume X, Number 2, June 1967
95. OR, Series IV, Volume I, p.1175; Bethel to Sharpsburg, Volume I, p.367
96. Huse, Caleb, *The Supplies for the Confederate Army, How They Were Obtained in Europe and How Paid For,* p.26-27, Press of T.R. Marvin & Son, Boston, 1904; OR, Series IV, Volume I, p.1003
97. OR, Series IV, Volume I, p.1004-1005
98. Vandiver, Frank E., *Ploughshares into Swords, Josiah Gorgas and Confederate Ordnance,* p.86-87, University of Texas Press, Austin, 1952; Bethel to Sharpsburg, Volume I, p.367
99. ORN, Volume 7, p.514-515
100. Ibid, Volume 7, p.516
101. Ibid, Volume 7, p.517
102. Ibid, Volume 7, p.518
103. Lamb, William, *Colonel Lamb's Story of Fort Fisher,* Blockade Runner Museum, Carolina Beach, North Carolina, 1966

The land face of Fort Fisher after the final battle in January 1865. You can see the size of the earthworks constructed by Col. Lamb and his men.

Chapter 3

William Lamb and the Guns of Fort Fisher

W illiam Lamb was a capable and enterprising young officer, a good successor to Major John Hedrick, who had commanded the defenses on Confederate Point since late spring of 1861. Born September 7, 1835, Lamb was a native of Norfolk, Virginia, where his father, as mayor, had surrendered the town formally to the occupying Union forces in May 1862. [1]

Lamb's military pursuits had begun early. At the age of fourteen, he left home to enter the Rappahannock Military Academy, where he was required to engage in strenuous manual labor as well as academic studies. Mathematics and military tactics were taught him by William Mahone, who would rise to prominence in Robert E. Lee's Army of Northern Virginia. Young Lamb "was a great student of history and biography, and loved to read about great military heroes." [2]

His historical studies carried on into his adult life, for by the time he was commanding officer at Fort Fisher, he had accumulated over 2,000 volumes in his home library in Norfolk. His knowledge and study of military history and military science would serve him and his new nation well in his assignment. [3]

Lamb had earned a degree in law from William and Mary in Williamsburg, but on returning to Norfolk, decided to enter the newspaper business instead. Joining his father in the cause of the Democratic Party, he strongly championed it as editor of the *Daily Southern Argus* from 1856 to 1861. He had also been a member of the National Democratic Convention, and had served as "Presidential elector on the Breckinridge ticket in 1860." [4]

In 1857 he went north to take a wife, marrying the lovely Sarah Anne Chaffee of Providence, Rhode Island. She was dainty and petite, had hazel eyes, "dark, golden hair", and complexion that reminded her husband of a rose bloom. When the Union forces took over Norfolk, Mrs. Lamb was living there with her three small children, one an infant named Willie. Her father in Rhode Island and her father-in-law, the mayor, insisted that she return to her parents' home for the war. Daisy Lamb, as her family called her, took her children and went north as advised. [5]

Having first served as captain of a Norfolk militia company, William Lamb saw service at Harpers Ferry, Virginia during the John Brown affair. In

Col. William Lamb, C.S.A.

April 1861, his unit was mustered into active duty with other Virginia troops. That summer, the handsome young Virginian was promoted to major, and sent to Wilmington as chief quartermaster for the Cape Fear District. [6]

In May 1862, the same month his father the mayor surrendered Norfolk to the Yankees, he was elected colonel and commanding officer of the Thirty Sixth (Second Artillery) Regiment North Carolina Troops, to serve under the "supervision of Brigadier General Samuel G. French, commanding the district of Cape Fear." The early summer found him commandant of Fort St. Philip (later renamed Fort Anderson), adjacent to Orton Plantation, on the west bank of the Cape Fear River, about halfway between the mouth of the river and Wilmington. On Friday, July 4, 1862, one week after the *Modern Greece* ran aground, Lamb was ordered to relinquish command of Fort St. Philip and to assume command at Fort Fisher. By the time the sun went down on the same day, he had fully inspected the unattached forts and batteries on Confederate Point. [7]

Lamb wrote that the works consisted of a two-gun battery recently erected near the river, called Shepherd's Battery. It was situated on the extreme left of the fort, its rear close to the shore of the Cape Fear. Next, closest to the sea, Lamb said, was "a quadrilateral field work known as Fort Fisher. It was a small work, part of it constructed of perishable sand bags and its longest face was about one hundred yards. Out of its half dozen large guns, only the two eight-inch Columbiads were suitable for seacoast defense. One of the Federal frigates could have cleaned it out with a few broad-sides." Next to Fisher and on its right, Lamb wrote, "facing the sea and opposite the bar, came a very handsome and creditable casemated battery of four eight-inch Columbiads, called after Capt. Meade. It was constructed of turfed sand over a heavy timber framework, the embrasures of palmetto...A one-gun battery stood to the right of this, well out on the seashore. It was called Cumberland's battery and contained a long ranged rifle gun, the only piece of modern ordnance on Confederate Point...To the right and and rear of this and some two hundred yards apart," Lamb continued, "were two batteries, each having two barbette guns of modern caliber, one called Bolles and the other I called Hedrick battery, after the former gallant commander of the Fort. There was besides these batteries a large commissary bomb proof. There were only seventeen guns of respectable caliber, including thirty-two pounders. There was on Zeke's Island a small two-gun battery subsequently washed away by the sea. I thought on assuming command, and experience afterwards demonstrated, that as a defense of New Inlet against a Federal fleet, our works amounted to nothing." [8]

Lamb decided to build a fort of tremendous proportions, one able to withstand the most severe fire the Union Navy could dish out: "I had seen the effect of eleven inch shell, and had read about the force of the fifteen inch, and believed that their penetrating power was well ascertained, and could be provided against. I obtained permission of Maj. Gen. French, who had placed me in command of Confederate Point, to commence such a fortification, although he did not altogether concur with me as to the value of elevated batteries nor the necessity of such unprecedentedly heavy works. Shortly after obtaining permission, I commenced the new Fort Fisher." [9]

One of Lamb's first official acts was to give proper notice to the Yankees, as well as his own garrison, that things would be run differently at Fort Fisher than they had in the past. Shortly after assuming command, Lamb said he "noticed a blockader lying a little over a mile from the bar, not two miles from the work." Asking if the vessel was not abnormally close in, he was told it was not. The colonel responded by saying that the enemy vessel could have fired on "the fort without warning," and he was told that the Yankees sometimes, did, in fact, do just that, driving the men from their work. Lamb told his people it should never happen again. [10]

He hurried a detachment to man the long-range rifled gun in the Cumberland Battery, and ordered them to fire at once on the blockader. "The astonished enemy slipped his cable and retreated as fast as possible, and from that day...no blockader anchored within range of our guns and no working party was ever molested, not even when hundreds were congregated together in constructing the mounds." [11]

Col. Lamb made salvaging the beached blockade runner Modern Greece *one of his first priorities when he assumed command of Fort Fisher.*

Astonished the Unionists were, and not at all accustomed to insolent Rebels taking pot shots at them, unless they were much closer to shore or in pursuit of a blockade runner. Lieutenant D.L. Braine, commanding the *U.S.S. Monticello*, reported that on Friday, July 11, 1862, "whilst lying at anchor in 8 fathoms of water off new inlet, mouth Cape Fear River, Federal Point light-house bearing W.N.W., distant about 3 miles, the rebels opened upon us with a heavy rifled gun. Their first shot struck about 600 yards beyond us. We proceeded to get underway. Whilst doing so they fired two shots; the first passed beyond us about 200 yards, the next about 100 yards. We returned their fire with three shots from the rifled gun, all of which fell short. The steamer *Cambridge*, lying ahead and outside of us, and the steamer *Stars and Stripes*, lying astern and outside of us, also fired at the fort; their shots fell short." Henceforth, Union vessels would keep an even greater distance from Fort Fisher than they had before. [12]

Another significant step the Virginian took on assuming command was to proceed vigorously with salvage operations on the *Modern Greece*. It was tough work. The moribund vessel was already awash with waves curling through her part of her hull, but there were four twelve-pound Whitworth rifled cannon with ammunition down in her hold, and the colonel meant to have them. They were the finest and most advanced artillery pieces of the day, being loaded at the breech, and capable of throwing a shell five miles with deadly accuracy. Lamb went out to the wreck with a party of his soldiers, rigged up tackles, and dragged the cannons and ammo on deck. As the Yankee gunboats began moving into better shelling range, he got the Whitworths loaded on his rowboats, and hurried back to shore under Fort Fisher's protection. [13]

Lamb later reported that with those guns, "we made the U.S. blockading fleet remove their anchorage from two and a half miles to five miles from the fort." Many ships were to be saved with these guns in the months to follow, until they "soon had a reputation throughout the South, and three of them were transferred to other commands, two going to Virginia." [14]

Sergeant Thaddeus Davis of Company I, Thirty Sixth North Carolina Troops, who was a nineteen-year-old boy when he joined the Herring Artillery in the fall of 1861, garrisoned at Fort Johnston on the Old Inlet side of the river near Caswell, could attest to Colonel Lamb's statement about the effectiveness of the Whitworths. He said the artillery pieces "were a terror to the enemy; their range was immense, their accuracy as that of a telescope rifle." [15]

Lieutenant James Myrover of Company B, Starr's Artillery Battery, Thirty Sixth North Carolina Troops, which battery had served the big guns at Fort Fisher since January 1862, bore further testimony to the menace the British rifled cannon were to the Federal gunboats. Myrover said two of the Whitworths taken off the *Modern Greece* were assigned to Starr's Battery, and part of the unit was sent over to Fort Caswell at Old Inlet. He said the guns were "superb breech-loading, rifled steel pieces, carrying a long conical ball, and endowed with a reach and precision of fire in action little short of marvelous." [16]

One evening, the soldiers of Myrover's unit worked all night, diligently preparing masked batteries for their two Whitworths. In the morning, they opened up on the Yankee blockaders that were in range. That day and the next, Starr's Battery fought the Federal ships in an "intensely exciting duel between the sea and land forces, the latter spitting forth its terrible volley of conical projectiles from two clumps of bushes. Again and again the blockaders shifted their position – only to find it apparently impossible to get beyond that deadly range." Several days later, Northern papers confirmed the results of their work, much to the satisfaction of the artillerists. The papers reported that the "Whitworth guns had wrought havoc – the *Miantanomah* having been so badly crippled as to require towing out of the line of fire, while another gunboat was struck no less than three times." [17]

While Colonel Lamb was bringing off the Whitworths from the blockade runner, young William B. Taylor, a Charlotte native who fought with the Charlotte Grays in the first land battle of the war at Bethel, Virginia in June, 1861, now part of the Eleventh North Carolina Troops, described to his mother the regiment's participation in salvage work on the *Modern Greece*. [18] On July 5, he wrote: "I arrived at camp safe; and when I got here, I found companies at Camp Lamb were absent. They were down at Confederate Point unloading a steamer, the *Modern Greece*, which ran aground about half a mile from Fort Fisher. She was a very large steamer. She had twelve thousand rifles aboard of which four thousand were saved, and two hundred tons of powder also, and immense lot of other goods of every description." [19]

Taylor's regiment, the Eleventh North Carolina, had been assigned the role of defending Confederate Point two days prior to the grounding of the

Modern Greece. In Special Order #332 of June 25, 1862, issued by Brigadier General Samuel French, commanding District of the Cape Fear with headquarters in Wilmington, the Eleventh North Carolina under Colonel Collett Leventhorpe was to select a suitable "camping grounds not more than ten miles from Fort Fisher. The camp will be selected with a view to defend Confederate Point in the event of an attack." [20]

This order was issued with a view of nullifying any sort of Federal infantry attack against the batteries of and near Fort Fisher, assuming Union infantry might be landed somewhere up the coast. Infantry like the Eleventh would always be needed here. The heavy artillerists, men of the Thirty Sixth North Carolina command by Colonel Lamb, companies of which were in and about Forts Fisher and Caswell, would of necessity be confined to their big guns in repelling an attack by the Union Navy, which attack would likely come simultaneously with a Union infantry attack.

Some of the soldiers of Colonel Leventhorpe's regiment were evidently tempted by the wealth of goods beached off Fort Fisher inside the *Modern Greece*, and temporarily forgot their duty as guardians and defenders of the coast and the Cause. In General Orders #37, dated August 5, 1862 at Petersburg, Virginia, it was reported that a General Court Martial was held at Wilmington, pursuant to Special Orders #146 of July 8, for the purpose of trying one Captain A.S. Haynes, Eleventh North Carolina Regiment, for "conduct prejudicial to good order and military discipline." [21]

Captain Haynes was accused of ordering and allowing some of the men of I Company, of which he was commander, to open a "box of gloves of the cargo of the British steamer *Modern Greece* and many pair of said gloves to take and carry away and the said gloves to appropriate to their own uses. The same being the property of British subjects. All this at or near Fort Fisher, North Carolina about the 28th of June 1862." [22]

The finding of the court was that Captain Haynes was not guilty of the charges and he was "most honorably acquitted." It is not hard to imagine, however, that there must have been some men in Haynes' Company I who would have warm hands the coming winter thanks to salvage duty on the *Modern Greece.* [23]

Incidents of pilferage of the blockade runners' cargoes were not to be frequent, however, the prime reason being the discipline and integrity of William Lamb as commandant of Fort Fisher. As he would later recall, he "had been sent to Fort Fisher to discipline the garrison against the temptations incident to blockade running." [24]

Much non-military cargo from the *Modern Greece* was salvaged and sold, in addition to the rifles and cannon that the soldiers brought off the vessel. The *Wilmington Daily Journal* of July 1, 1862 advertised an auction sale to be conducted by one Wilkes Morris, the auctioneer, and to be held on Tuesday, 8

July, "at No. 2, Granite Row." The goods for sale were reputed to be "direct from London," and consisted of the "Entire Cargo (900) Tons of Steamship *Modern Greece*." [25]

The newspaper advertisement read: *"This is one of the most valuable cargoes ever imported into the Southern Confederacy, and consists of CASES DRY GOODS; CASKS HARDWARE; CASES BOOTS AND SHOES; BALES BLANKETS; CASES READY MADE CLOTHING; CASES UNDERSHIRTS; BALES SHIRTS; CASES FELT HATS; BAGS PEPPER; BAGS PIMENTO; KEGS BI-CARB. SODA; KEGS SODA ASH; CASES MUSTARD; DRUGS AND MEDICINES; BLACK LEAD; GUNNY BAGS; SACKS SALT; QR. CASKS CHOICE DARK COGNAC BRANDY; QR. CASKS CHOICE PALE COGNAC BRANDY; BASKETS CHAMPAGNE; QR. CASK RED WINE; QR. CASK WHITE WINE; HHDS. CHOICE SCOTH WHISKEY; CASES SANTERINE; CASES CLARET; CASES MARASCHINO; CASES RED SPARKLING BURGUNDY; With various other articles."* [26]

Actually, the *Daily Journal* unknowingly erred in stating that the entire cargo of the steamer was being auctioned off. Many other items, typical of blockade runners' cargoes, crossed the Atlantic in the *Modern Greece*, and remained in the wreckage. Among them were: all kinds of surgical kits and knives, scalpels, tourniquets, bone snips, axes, drill bits, chisels, pipe dies, ratchet drills, various types of files, cross peen machine hammers, handles for awls and rasps, handsaws, hatchets, hoes, ladles, pickaxes, screwdrivers, pipe taps, pipe threaders, crescent wrenches, monkey wrenches, and a hammer wrench. Also in the hold remained Enfield rifles, various types of bayonets, heath knives, Bowie knives, and pocketknives, forks, spoons, table knives, flatirons used in the home or laundry, hinges and horseshoe nails. All in all, the steamer hauled a quite varied and valuable cargo. Fortunately for the Confederates, she had been close to Fort Fisher when run aground. [27]

The sloop *Lizzie* was not so lucky. None of her cargo would ever make it to Wilmington's auction block. On August 1, she was caught where neither Fort Fisher's guns nor the Whitworths would reach. The commander of the U.S. Gunboat *Penobscot* reported capturing the *Lizzie* about twelve to fifteen miles northeast of New Inlet, the vessel having hailed from Nassau, New Providence, and being loaded "with 220 sacks of salt, 1 bale of blankets, 5 boxes of tin, 2 cases of caustic soda, 2 tierces of soda ash, 1 case of enameled cloth, and 2 boxes of arrowroot." The master of the vessel was believed to be a native of North Carolina, though he claimed to be from New Brunswick. [28]

The Yankees obviously preferred to capture such prey as the *Lizzie*, far offshore and out of range of the Rebel guns. They were watching carefully the development of William Lamb's position on the beach near the mouth of the Cape Fear, and they were wary. On August 13, 1862, just one month after Lamb took command at Fort Fisher, Commander James Armstrong, commanding

U.S.S. State of Georgia, reported to Rear Admiral Goldsborough that the Confederates were "very active in strengthening their fortifications, and have on the New Inlet side... rifle guns of great range; they have a well established set of signal flags by day and light by night." [29]

A week later, on August 20, Lieutenant D.L. Braine of the *U.S.S. Monticello* informed the Coast Survey office in Washington that a survey of the bars off New Inlet and Old Inlet would not be a prudent thing to undertake. Such a survey would "be a risky business, as at New Inlet the boats undertaking this business would be within 800 yards of thirty guns, which the enemy, I know, would use with good effect. At the Western Bar they would be distant 1 1/2 miles under a like number of guns." [30]

Braine said there were batteries up and down Federal (Confederate) Point bristling with heavy artillery that ran "nearly to abreast Zeek's Island. . . . This information is based upon my own personal knowledge, together with the information received from contrabands who have run away from this place within the last four months and who have acted as pilots." [31]

Colonel Lamb could verify the statements of Federal officers regarding his fortifications and the efficiency of his signal system. "The perfect code of signals arranged by the fort with blockade runners gave to Fort Fisher the enviable reputation enjoyed by no other sea coast fortification, that while an enemy vessel could not approach without an assault, no friendly vessel was ever fired upon, and none ever displayed a signal without an immediate reply and the setting of the range lights for their entrance." [32]

His garrison was hard at work piling up huge mountains of sand to create a tremendous and powerful citadel, a veritable Gibraltar on the Cape Fear, bristling with heavy artillery and the mobile artillery of the deadly Whitworths. Lamb graphically detailed the heavy works he had his men build, the idea for such a fortress being totally his own. [33]

He wrote: "*The land face commenced about 100 feet from the river with a half-bastion, originally Shepherd's Battery, which I had doubled in strength, and extended with a heavy curtain to a full bastion on the ocean side, where it joined the sea-face. The work was built to withstand the heaviest artillery fire. There was no moat with scarp and counter-scarp, so essential for defense against storming parties, the shifting sands rendering its construction impossible with the material available. The outer slope was twenty feet high from the berme to the top of the parapet, at an angle of 45 degrees, and was sodded with marsh grass, which grew luxuriantly. The parapet was not less than twenty-five feet thick, with an inclination of only one foot. The revetment was five feet nine inches high from the floor of the gun chambers, and these were some twelve feet or more from the interior plane. The guns were all mounted in barbette on Columbiad carriages...Between the gun chambers, containing one or two guns each, there were heavy traverses, exceeding in size*

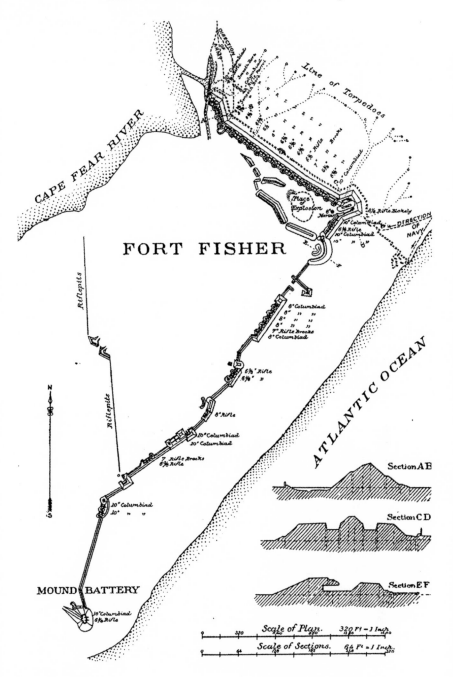

any heretofore constructed, to protect from an enfilading fire. They extended out some twelve feet...and were twelve feet or more in height above the parapet, running back thirty feet or more. The gun chambers were reached from the rear by steps. In each traverse was an alternate magazine or bombproof, the latter ventilated by an air chamber. Passageways penetrated the traverses in the interior of the work forming additional bomb proofs for the reliefs of the guns. " [34]

Colonel Lamb was determined to build a powerful fortress to protect the vital fleet of blockade runners ferrying their cargoes to the embattled Confederacy. He "never ceased to work, sometimes working on Sundays when rumors of an attack reached me, having at times over one thousand men, white and colored, hard at work." [35]

Much backbreaking labor went into the continual moving of sand to create the massive earthworks that were going up at the mouth of the Cape Fear. The process was relatively simple, but tough, grueling work if done for several hours on end. It was a process to be used and repeated in virtually all of the area forts.

Wheelbarrows loaded with sand were "pushed and pulled on gangways...It was very interesting to see two or three hundred wheelbarrows rolling in unison from the points of loading to those of dumping, returning in a circle and passing the loaders who shovel in hand threw sand in the barrows as they passed without stopping. The man with the shovel could get in a shovelful in about every three barrows." [36]

After a number of trips up and down inclines twenty or more feet high, pushing a wheelbarrow full of sand, it would be easy to visualize a Rebel soldier or black laborer being near the point of exhaustion, muscles aching and skin glistening with perspiration. But work they did, day in and day out, making Fort Fisher bigger, more powerful, and more sought after by the blockade runners.

To combat this increased efficiency of Confederate defenses, the Union Navy was still woefully under strength for the task at hand. In September 1862, there were only seven United States vessels off the coast of Wilmington. They were the *U.S.S. State of Georgia, Cambridge, Penobscot, Monticello, Octorara, Mystic,* and the *Daylight.* [37]

As further testimony to the inadequacy of their blockade here, two months after William Lamb's arrival at Fort Fisher, Acting Rear Admiral S.P. Lee, new commander of the North Atlantic Blockading Squadron since Admiral Goldsborough's transfer, wrote to the senior officer off Wilmington to express his consternation over the escape of a blockade runner from New Inlet.

On September 21, 1862, he informed Commander Gustavus Scott: "The Department will be extremely mortified to hear that the *Kate* has run the blockade of Wilmington, out by New Inlet, with a load of cotton, an article now so valuable that a single cargo will purchase a large quantity of arms. It appears that there were three steamers on the blockade off New Inlet at that time. I am informed that these steamers lie at anchor day and night, 5 miles off from the inlet and 2 miles from each other. I hope this is not so; if true, it will easily account for the escape of the *Kate*." Lee apparently did not realize that Lamb's cannoneers made sure the ships stayed at least 5 miles off the inlet. [38]

"Every officer on the blockade," he continued, "loses reputation by these escapes. The senior officer and every commanding officer should feel and act as though his command was subject to censure for every failure to keep the blockade as close as the weather will allow. We may look forward to a time when Wilmington will be ours and this labor cease." [39]

Unfortunately for Admiral Lee and his sailors, the navy would be a long time realizing his dream, and in fact, their toughest work was just beginning. Blockade runners had found a guardian angel on the Cape Fear, and as the summer of 1862 waned into the fall, the greatest activity in this maritime trade into Wilmington was just commencing. Because of Fort Fisher's commandant, the danger for U.S. sailors trying to stop that trade had become increasingly grave.

Gen. Gabriel Rains, C.S.A.

The first true battle between Lamb's artillerists and the Federal navy occurred on Saturday morning, October 11, 1862. Two Yankee warships had on the day before "driven off a working party engaged in leveling the hills" about "four miles below Fort Caswell," reported the *Wilmington Daily Journal* in its October 13 edition. [40]

General Gabriel Rains, who was now district commander, had requested that Colonel Lamb come over from Fort Fisher with "his two long range siege guns belonging to Starr's Fayetteville Battery." The cannon were brought over and set up just off the beach about 400 yards from each other. Somewhere between 9 and 10 a.m. on Saturday morning, while the two unsuspecting blockaders were lying off the beach about two miles, Fort Fisher's "flying artillery" opened up with deadly blasts.

The *Daily Journal* reported that very soon after the guns started banging away, a shell pierced the paddle box of one of the vessels, and she was disabled and "had to be assisted by her consort. Thirty-one shots were fired from the guns, about ten of which took effect, doubtless killing a number of the enemy. The firing surpassed anything for precision that we have heard of on the seacoast. The enemy were so busy in leaving that they did not fire but three times." [41]

The paper further related that the last cannon shot went over the bow of one of the steamers when the vessel was five miles away, with the projectile remaining "in the air about twenty-eight seconds. These siege guns are of wonderful range, throwing further than the best guns the enemy have off this river." Fort Caswell also assisted in the shelling, the paper said. [42]

On board the U.S. Gunboat *Maratanza*, recipient of the worst of the bombardment, blood and debris confirmed the accuracy of the newspaper's report. Senior Officer Gustavus H. Scott wrote to Admiral Lee, who had just three weeks before issued his reprimand over the *Kate*, on the morning of the Rebel attack. He reported that the ship had been hit on the port quarter, where a shell exploded (though he mistakenly thought the guns used were Armstrong rifles), "killing Acting Master's Mate Edward K. Flowers and George Blake, quartermaster, besides seriously wounding Joseph Brink, captain of the after guard, and several others less severely." [43]

Scott went on to say that they straightway got further out to sea, where even at 4 1/2 miles off the beach, a shell passed over his vessel. This proved, Scott said, "that it is no longer safe to lay within 2 1/2 miles, as we have heretofore." [44]

Rear Admiral S.P. Lee himself reported to Gideon Welles on October 27, 1862, that three deserters from Fort Caswell confirmed the growing danger for Union sailors on this part of the North Carolina coast. He said the men told him "the battery which fired on the *Maratanza* on the 11th instant, as I had the honor of informing the Department on the 15th, consisted of two fieldpieces, Whitworth guns, landed from the *Modern Greece*, and brought from Fort Fisher, to which place they were returned on the 15th; that the Rebels are constantly at work enlarging the fort and mounting guns." [45]

At almost the same time of Admiral Lee's report, Colonel Lamb's mule-drawn artillery was at it again. Commander W.H. Macomb of the *U.S.S. Genesee* was cruising off the coast of Oak Island on the morning of October 24, and while trying the range of a 100-pounder Parrott rifle, "the rebels opened fire from two batteries about a quarter of a mile apart, situated on the ridge of the sand hillocks, when we immediately returned their shot from the Parrott and X-inch after pivot guns.

"The shots from the batteries were well directed in line, but nearly all flew over us.

"These are the same batteries which fired on the *Maratanza* and the guns have long ranges.

"The Parrott gun had too much elevation and the shell passed in good line over. (As to) the X-inch, I am unable to tell whether any shell took effect, as one went direct for the batteries and appeared to burst above, some of the fragments of which may have fallen within them." [46]

As the fall of 1862 wore on, blockade running into Wilmington grew brisk, and William Lamb and his artillerists were doing everything in their power to foster it. Less than two weeks after trading salvos with the *U.S.S. Genesee* off Oak Island below Caswell, the Whitworths roared again about two miles south of Masonboro Inlet, some eleven northeast of Fort Fisher.

On Tuesday, November 4, about 8:45 in the morning, J.D. Warren, commanding officer of the *U.S.S. Daylight*, spied a British bark at anchor near Masonboro, when he gave chase and forced the vessel to ground on the beach. He fired on the ship from 9:30 to about 11:00 a.m., even though the blockade runner had hoisted a white flag in surrender, when he ordered three boats manned with well-armed sailors to be dispatched to board the vessel, remove all papers found, and to set her on fire. [47]

The ship was discovered to be the *Sophia*, hailing from Liverpool, England, and "bound from Nassau to Baltimore, with a cargo of salt, saltpeter, soda ash, three brass rifle fieldpieces, gun carriages, truck, etc." Her master told the Yankees that she had already run the Wilmington blockade on two other occasions. [48]

While sailors from the *Daylight* were examining the ship, another gig with sailors from the *U.S.S. Mount Vernon* came ashore to help out. As the afternoon wore on, the surf became heavy and the breakers extremely rough. The result was that the bluejackets, after repeated attempts to get back to their ships, couldn't maneuver their heavy cutters through the crashing waves to the outer edge of the breakers. They were stuck. They were also about to go to a military prison. [49]

The *Daily Journal* told its readers that "information having reached Fort Fisher that some Federals had landed at Masonboro' to destroy an English barque that had grounded, the Colonel took a detachment of the Scotland Neck Cavalry, under Sergt. Baker, and dashed up the beach after the enemy." The Scotland Neck boys were natives of Halifax County, and rode as Company G of the Third North Carolina Cavalry. As twilight was falling, the Rebels came up on the enemy, who surrendered, the paper said, without resistance. [50]

The Yankee gunboats *Daylight* and *Mount Vernon* had, however, offered resistance, keeping up a "constant fire on the woods, on both sides of the boats, to prevent the enemy from molesting our men while they endeavored to launch their boats", reported Lieutenant Trathen of the *Mount Vernon*. Night came on, however, and further efforts were in vain. [51]

As dawn broke the following morning, the two blockaders moved back into position with the idea of bringing off their men. "We then stood in for the beach," said Acting Master Warren of the *Daylight*, "and the enemy opened fire upon us with what appeared to be rifled fieldpieces, overshooting us several times. Not seeing anything of our boats or people, we hauled off again and stood down the coast." Lieutenant Trathen also stated that the Rebs had "erected a battery behind a sand hill and opened fire on us." [52]

The *Daily Journal* confirmed the Union officers' accounts of the loss of one officer and four seamen from the *Mount Vernon*, and two officers and eleven seamen from the *Daylight*, for a total of eighteen men. The newspaper also said "Three splendid barges, besides some Enfield rifles, cutlasses and pistols and a stand of colors, were captured." If the Confederates had had to witness destruction of the British schooner and her valuable supplies of war goods, at least they had made the Federals pay a high price. [53]

One of the captured sailors, Acting Ensign Tom Peakes, reported from his home in Edgartown, Massachusetts, where he was on parole awaiting exchange as a prisoner of war, that for a brief period in their captivity, they

Gen. W.H.C. Whiting, C.S.A.

were concerned about more than just winding up in a Rebel prison. He wrote Gideon Welles on December 2 that they had been captured about eight o'clock at night on November 4 by a company of cavalry, one of infantry and another of artillery, and were "carried to Fort Fisher. The next day after a letter was received by General Rains from citizens of Wilmington requesting him to hang the three officers in his power for firing upon a white flag. A few days after, in passing through Wilmington, the captain of the guard in whose charge we were placed was waited upon with the same request and the same reason assigned, but he refused their modest request." [54]

Peakes readily admitted that his ship, the *U.S.S. Daylight*, had fired on the blockade runner for about an hour, "although she was an unarmed vessel and completely in our power, with a white flag flying, and we could plainly see several men standing upon her cabin deck, which fact was several times reported to our commander, J.D. Warren, to which he replied, 'It is too late now, fire away.' " [55] Fortunately for Ensign Peakes and the other two officers captured, the Confederate authorities had more misgivings about punishing violators of the rules of war, than the Yankees did about breaking the rules.

Just four days after the *Sophia* was destroyed and Ensign Peakes and his companions made the acquaintance of Colonel William Lamb, the Confederate government made a decision that was to prove of much benefit to Lamb and to Wilmington. William Henry Chase Whiting, whose friends called him Chase and who was now a Brigadier General in the Army of Northern Virginia under Robert E. Lee, was reassigned to the Cape Fear defenses, which post he had left after serving a short time in late spring of 1861. In Special Orders #262 of November 8, 1862, Whiting was ordered to Wilmington and charged with "the defense of the Cape Fear River." [56]

Whiting was most comfortable with his area of assignment. "He had been long and successfully engaged, before the war, in the improvement of the navigation of the Cape Fear, and learned to know and esteem her people. He had won, as his bride, one of the noble women of the Cape Fear, Miss Kate D. Walker, daughter of Major John Walker, of Smithville and Wilmington." [57]

A native Mississippian and son of Lieutenant Colonel Levi Whiting of the First Artillery, U.S. Army, who had died at his post in 1853, Whiting had attended the Public High School of Boston between the ages of twelve and fourteen years. Entering Georgetown College, D.C. when he finished school in Boston, he completed the four years' course there in two years, "receiving his diploma with high distinction at the head of his class. It was said of his knowledge of Latin, that he could converse in it with fluency." [58]

At seventeen, Whiting began classes at West Point, where in July 1845, he graduated at the top of his class, with a higher standing than any officer of the army had ever had up to that time. [59]

He was highly regarded at West Point, according to his roommate, Union General Fitz John Porter. His career at the academy "was most exemplary," wrote Porter. "Pure in all his acts; of the strictest integrity, ever kind and gentle and open-hearted to his comrades; free from deception; just in his duty to his service and Academy, and never but kind and just to his comrades, and the cadets under him. These qualities caused him to be loved by his companions, respected by his subordinates, and honored and trusted by his superiors. He was of first-rate ability, as shown in his studies and graduation at the head of his class. So long as he was in the army, he maintained that reputation, and there was great regret that he resigned to take to a different cause and field." [60]

Once he took up arms for the Southern cause, he was at the front of the fight from the start. In his report of the bombardment and capture of Fort Sumter in April 1861, Brigadier General P.G.T. Beauregard had high words of praise for Whiting's contributions to the success of their mission. Major Whiting, with other engineer officer on his staff, had demonstrated "untiring zeal, energy, and gallantry." Also, Whiting had rendered "much assistance, not only as an engineer, in selecting the sites and laying out the channel batteries on Morris Island, but as acting assistant adjutant and inspector general in arranging and stationing the troops on said island." [61]

Right after Sumter fell, Governor John Ellis asked Whiting to come to North Carolina and take over as "Inspector-General in charge of the defences of

North Carolina." Ellis asked the Major to direct particular attention to "Forts Caswell and Johnston, and the mouth of the Cape Fear River, Beaufort harbor and Fort Macon, Ocracoke and the coast generally." [62] Whiting examined the forts and harbors, with particular emphasis on the Cape Fear, and advised for a proper system of defense, which was begun soon after he arrived. It was not easy work, he told his friend and exemplar, P.G.T. Beauregard. "I try to be as cool and patient as you are," he wrote the general, "but it is awful hard work. They are military in South Carolina. Here they are willing enough, but the military has yet to grow." [63]

In the few short weeks Whiting was in Wilmington, before being ordered to the Virginia front to serve under General Joe Johnston, he had the opportunity to see the military in that area grow to a considerable extent, and he must have felt a degree of satisfaction.

By late May he was already in Virginia, having inspected as engineer the vulnerable "fish-in-the-barrel" position of Harpers Ferry, and having advised Johnston what many other officers in the war were to learn. The position was virtually indefensible, and "could not be held against equal numbers, etc." [64]

In the Manassas campaign, Whiting was in charge of the movement of reinforcements from Harpers Ferry to Manassas, and the destruction of the military facilities at the Ferry, all of which he performed with admiration, according to Johnston. Serving as Chief Engineer on the battlefield at Manassas for Johnston, his performance there, in addition to that of his other duties at Harpers Ferry, netted for him the gold wreaths of a Brigadier General in the Confederate Army. [65]

Assigned to command the brigade of the slain South Carolinian Bernard Bee, the new brigadier put his men through the paces with constant and continuous drill. He made them drill "by squad, by company, by regiment, by brigade, by division, or, as the troops called the last, 'neighborhood drill'; thus accustoming the troops to act in concert, and in the presence of each other, so giving them confidence in each other and in their officers. 'Little Billy' as the troops endearingly called him, was indefatigable." [66]

In the Peninsular Campaign and the Seven Days in spring and summer of 1862, first under Joe Johnston, then under Robert E. Lee, Whiting performed with competence in handling two brigades as a division commander. General Gustavus W. Smith, second in command of the army under Joe Johnston, and later appointed commander of the District of North Carolina, was senior to Whiting when he was assigned as chief officer of the Cape Fear defenses. Smith sought higher rank for him. He said that he "repeatedly insisted, that in all fairness, he ought to be promoted to the rank of Major General. The importance of the command he then exercised would more than justify his immediate advancement; and his previous services, as commander of a division in more than one campaign, and upon various battlefields, fully entitled him to this promotion." Promotion in grade, however, was to be delayed until February 1863, some three months after his reassignment to the Cape Fear. [67]

The *Wilmington Daily Journal* applauded the government's decision to transfer Whiting from Virginia. The paper stated that the general would take on his duties "with his accustomed energy."

"The people feel the utmost confidence that all that military skill, determination and valor can effect with the means placed at his disposal will be done, and that, if the invader comes he will meet with a warm reception." [68]

The new district commander, who was to become an encouraging superintendent and strong supporter of the young colonel down at Fort Fisher, wasted no time with his superiors in getting right to the point as to what was needed to make Wilmington secure from the Yankees. On Friday, November 14, 1862, he wrote to Major General Smith in Richmond: "My first and last request will be for troops the instant they are available. The Department is undoubtedly aware of the imminent need for them for the defense of Wilmington. The fever is abating rapidly and there will shortly be no danger to apprehend as to the health of the men." [69]

Wilmington had just gone through one of the worst yellow fever epidemics in the country's history, losing 654 people of 3,000 inhabitants remaining in town in a three months' period of time. "Then it is," the general continued, "that I anticipate trouble from the enemy, who, aware of the undefended condition of this important place, are likely to strike before we can collect our resources." [70]

Whiting said the proximity of Wilmington to the ocean, combined with its distance from the harbor entrances, where sat Fort Fisher on the New Inlet side and Fort Caswell at Old Inlet, made the necessity of a large, mobile force of infantry and artillery critical. "Not less than 10,000 effective men," he said, "should be collected as soon as possible, together with five or six field batteries." [71]

On the same day he wrote to General Smith, the new commander of the Cape Fear District also sent a letter to Secretary of War George Randolph, pointing out with great insight the vast strategic significance that Wilmington already held in the Confederate War effort: "I beg leave to call the attention of the Department to the position of Wilmington and its vital importance in this war. There are now but three great harbors on our coast not in possession of the enemy – Charleston, Mobile, and Wilmington." Even the capture of Charleston, the general wrote, would not be as disastrous a blow as the loss of Mobile or Wilmington, because of their value as arteries of communication via the connecting railroads, and their telegraph connections with Richmond. Should Wilmington fall, for example, and become occupied with Yankee troops, Charleston would be of little value because of its isolation from Richmond. [72]

Mobile was of as great a value as Wilmington, but it was with Wilmington that Whiting had to do. "It is of the last importance to hold the port," he said. "In the fall and winter the blockade is exceedingly difficult, owing to Cape Fear, a dangerous point on the coast, which with its extensive shoals, extends far to seaward between the two entrances to the harbor. The prevalence of southeast weather at the main entrance, while it is very dangerous for vessels outside, forces them to the northward of the Cape and gives easy access to vessels running the blockade. In like manner the northeast gales drive the enemy to shelter to the southward of the Cape and clears the new inlet or upper entrance. The river affords great facilities for building gunboats. Two," he continued, "are already there ready for their iron. Their completion ought not to be left to chance, for either of them would compel most extraordinary preparation on the part of the enemy and undoubtedly enable us to hold the port for a great length of time, and time is much with us now. Once in service and there is nothing to prevent the building of a fleet of similar vessels." Whiting pointed out that extensive salt works, producing 3,000 bushels of salt each day, were along the sound in the vicinity of the river. "This important supply depends entirely on our holding the port. I mention these considerations as worthy of attention, but subordinate to the great strategic importance of the plan in relation to the progress of the war." [73]

General Whiting reiterated to Secretary Randolph what he had told General Smith regarding the nearness of the town to the ocean in an easterly direction, as well as the fact that powerful Fort Fisher was twenty-one miles south, and Fort Caswell was a full twenty-eight miles. They would be of no value, then, in the event of Union attack directly from a landing on the coast by way of Topsail Inlet, for example. It was essential that he have 10,000 effective, mobile infantry, with from four to six batteries of light artillery, so as to be able to hit an attacking force on the beach at its point of landing. [74]

"If this cannot be had," Whiting continued, "we must trust to God in what we have, small as it is, and the blindness of the enemy. Why he neglected this place and struck at New Berne is more than I can tell. I may add that the danger of its reduction is more imminent from the disorders consequent on the pestilence which has desolated the unfortunate city. Preparations have been suspended, the garrison reduced and withdrawn, the workshops deserted, transportation rendered irregular and uncertain, provisions, forage, and supplies exhausted. Unless therefore more speedy measures for re-enforcement and relief be adopted I have great apprehensions of a successful coup de main on the part of the enemy." [75]

Unfortunately, the Confederates could not spare any troops from Virginia at this time, according to General Smith, because of the "pressure of the enemy on the north." [76] Ambrose Burnside, the victor of coastal North Carolina campaigns, now commanded the Union Army of the Potomac, and he was beginning to move into position across the Rappahannock River from Fredericksburg, where he and his men were soon to receive one of the worst defeats for Federal arms in the war. Their numbers were tremendous, however, and Robert E. Lee could spare no man from the ranks for transfer to North Carolina, until the outcome of the campaign was decided. For the time being, the Cape Fear District would have to make do with what it had.

With enterprising and alert officers like William Lamb and Chase Whiting running the show, they would do very well with what they had for some time to come. Their soldiers demonstrated once again the tenacity they had acquired for combating the Union fleet, at almost the same time their general was writing to Richmond requesting more troops.

The *Daily Journal* told its readers on November 18, "Heavy firing was heard here yesterday afternoon. We learn that the blockaders had run a schooner ashore near Moore's Inlet, on the Sound, and a brig ashore near Fort Fisher." [77]

Commander William Parker of the *U.S.S. Cambridge* reported that at 8 a.m. on November 17, he had spied a schooner near Masonboro Inlet, chased her while firing his 30-pound Parrott rifle, and ran the ship ashore. A party of eleven men was dispatched in a boat to fire the schooner, "with instructions (as the surf was high) not to venture too near, and in case of doubt as to reaching the vessel safely to return. The boat, however, was swamped, yet the men...reached the shore and fired the schooner, which is entirely destroyed." [78]

To communicate with and give relief to the sailors whose boat capsized, two other boats with officers were sent out from the *Cambridge*. Acting Master's Mate H.W. Wells "swam ashore with a line", the other officer, Mr. Odiorne, following. At this point, Rebels came suddenly out of nowhere and captured the whole lot of bluejackets on the beach. [79]

The Yanks had been rounded up the by Rebel Rangers under Captain Abram F. Newkirk. The Rangers, also know as Newkirk's Coast Guard, were local boys from New Hanover County, and officially rode as Company A of the Third North Carolina Cavalry.[80] The gray-clad troopers rescued the crew members of the British schooner *J.W. Pindar*, loaded with a cargo of salt, and rode down to the beach, capturing "one Acting Master, two Midshipmen and ten privates. Two Negroes belonging to the schooner having gone to the Yankees were taken at the same time." The privates mentioned in the paper were actually sailors, of course, being in the navy and not the army, and they and their officers were brought before General Whiting as prisoners of war, and forwarded to the North under parole to await exchange. [81]

One of the Union sailors must have had some significant doubts about the side for which he was fighting. While going through Petersburg, Virginia on November 21, Seaman William B. Frost "took the oath of allegiance to the

Confederate Government," presumably to serve under the Stars and Bars, rather than sail under the Stars and Stripes anymore. [82]

As mentioned in the *Daily Journal* story on the *J.W. Pindar* incident, a brig had also been chased and forced to beach near Fort Fisher. Acting Master J.D. Warren of the *U.S.S. Daylight* reported that "we discovered a sail close in under Fort Fisher," shortly after daybreak, the weather at that time being "very foggy." Warren steamed for the vessel at full speed, and the blockade runner "ran for the channel and grounded near the fort. I ran in, manned and armed my two boats...put them in charge of Acting Ensign Brice and Acting Master's Mate Barnett, and sent them in to destroy the vessel if possible, while we went as far as the water would permit and tried to reach her with our rifled 30-pounder, but there was so much sea on that we could not hit her. The boats went in, but could not get to her for the heavy sea running over the bar. The boats were too small for such service.

"The fort and battery on shore opened and kept up a brisk fire on us and the boats all the while, the shot falling but a few yards from us.

"The boats returned and we hauled off out of the range of the fort." [83]

The *Fanny Lewis* was the English flag-flying brig that Warren had run aground at New Inlet. Her commander, a Captain Gardner, along with nine of his crewmembers, drowned while attempting to make it to shore. Two other crewmembers survived. "They were brought off by Midshipmen Moses, and picked crew with the largest garrison boat from Fort Fisher. We presume," reported the *Daily Journal*, "that all the assistance that can be rendered, will be sent down to try and save the vessel and cargo. The weather was very unfavorable yesterday and the chances were bad." [84]

Other blockade runners, more fortunate than the *Pindar* and the *Fanny Lewis*, were observed by the garrison at Fort Fisher in the week following those two having been run aground. On the 24th of November, the fort reported to the *Daily Journal*, "that the schooner *Harkaway*, Captain Sebastian, eleven days from Nassau, with 540 sacks of salt, has arrived safely." The very next day, Fort Fisher sent a message to the paper stating that all was "quiet below. The *Pocotaligo* and *Uncle Ben* went to sea safely last night." [85]

Others were about to join them in their work of supplying the Southern Confederacy. The U.S. consul based in Liverpool wrote to the Navy Department on November 14: "The Confederates and their friends in this country are making rather formidable preparations for operations at sea and to get supplies into Southern ports." Besides the vessels already in West Indies' ports, quite a few others were being built, and others were ready to leave from European ports. "They have recently been buying all the fast vessels – steamers – they can find for sale, and are now in treaty for three of the very fastest and best boats that have been built in England. They are new, all alike, 480 tons each, and built to run between Dover and Calais. They are side-wheel, built in the best possible manner, covered with steel plates instead of iron, and are very fast and of light draft of water, and are wanted to run in with cargoes from Bermuda and Nassau. Two powerful steam rams, iron plated, are building in Thompson's yard in Glasgow. A screw steamer, between 400 and 500 tons, is to be launched by the 20th of this month in Laurie's yard. She is iron screw and is to have a speed of at least 14 knots, and will be ready for sea in fourteen days after launching." [86]

These fast, light draft ships mentioned by the consul, were about to inaugurate a new phase in blockade running activities. It had been sufficiently demonstrated to the blockade running firms, be they Confederate or British, that the old sailing vessels, the schooners, barks, and brigs, were many times too slow to escape from the Federal warships, as was the case with the three ships grounded off the Wilmington coast in November. The swift, new packet boats, paddle wheel steamers or propeller driven screws, built in England and Scotland to run the English Channel and the Irish Sea, and others to be designed along the same lines answered the need.

The first all steel vessels to cross the Atlantic, these new blockade runners were exceedingly fast for their day, and were designed and painted to offer the utmost

Augustus Charles Hobart-Hampden

concealment from Yankee spyglasses on the high sea.[87] Captain C. Augustus Hobart-Hampden, son of the Earl of Buckinghamshire, and Post Captain in the Royal Navy, described the appearance of his fine double-screw steamer, the *Don*, that he took command of in Saint George's Harbor, Bermuda, before steaming westward for Wilmington. [88]

Captain Roberts, as he called himself while running the blockade, said they first of all reduced the "spars to a light pair of lower masts, without any yards across them, the only break in their sharp outline being a small crow's nest on the fore-mast, to be used as a look-out place." The hull sat low, being only about eight feet above the water, and that was painted a dull gray, "to render her as nearly as possible invisible in the night. The boats were lowered square with the gunnels. Coal was taken on board of a nature that never smoked (anthracite); the funnel being what is called 'telescope,' lowered close down to the deck." To reduce the noise level, in the case of an unexpected stop, steam was blown off under water. As an additional precaution, whenever any fowls were brought aboard, no cocks were allowed as part of the cargo, lest they might announce the whereabouts of the blockade-runner to a Yankee cruiser. [89]

One of the first of the former packet line steamers to make for the protection of Fort Fisher was the *Giraffe*, later to be christened the *R.E. Lee*, and commanded by Virginian John Wilkinson. She was built of iron, not steel, but was nevertheless one of the fast, sleek steamers of about six hundred tons, of shallow draft and side-wheeled, and capable of turning up a high rate of speed. She had been employed on the "Glasgow-Belfast packet run for the Alexander Collie Line,' but was now owned by the Confederate States, and commanded by a Confederate captain. Wilkinson could get "thirteen and a half knots from her," which, though not as much as he anticipated, was still faster than most, if not all, of the Yankee ships off New Inlet. [90]

The *Giraffe* carried a most valuable cargo of Enfield rifles, ammunition, uniform cloth, medical supplies, and twenty-six Scottish lithographers, complete with all their necessary equipment, taken aboard ship at Glasgow on orders from Richmond. The Scots had been hired to print money for the Confederacy. [91]

On this night of December 29, 1862, one month after the consul in Liverpool had reported to the U.S. Navy that the *Giraffe* would soon be loading cargo for the South, Wilkinson silently moved about his ship in slippers as he headed for New Inlet and Colonel Lamb's protection.[92] His crewmen knew that any man who intentionally or unintentionally showed a light while passing through the Federal blockaders would be shot instantly. His helmsman had to steer by looking down in a "funnel-like canvas cover put over the binnacle to mask the light that illuminated the compass. There were no lights whatsoever aboard; the fire room hatch, the ventilators, the companionways were masked with tarpaulins and men below sweated in gloomy, coal-gas-reeking misery." [93]

By about 10 o'clock at night the *Giraffe* was within three miles of New Inlet; then she hit a sand bar. She was stuck hard and fast, and Captain Wilkinson could see at least four Yankee cruisers in the dark distance He had to work quickly, and hope for the tide to rise before a Federal shell came crashing through the hull. In the darkness, even though the *Giraffe* was within range of Colonel Lamb's Whitworths and the big guns of Fort Fisher, the artillerists could offer little assistance because they couldn't see that far out at night.

Not taking a chance on the Scottish lithographers so important to the government being captured, Wilkinson sent them into shore in one of his quarter boats, while he and the crew worked with hawsers and anchors to try to swing the ship around into deep water. Finally, with the tide rising, ropes and anchors taut at the right places, and a timely "Full Astern," the ship began to vibrate as paddle wheels bit into the water and she moved off the bar.

Miraculously, no Union vessel reached her, and the blockade runner steamed past Fort Fisher sometime before midnight, and anchored off Smithville. [94]

On the next day, Tuesday, December 30, 1862, Captain Wilkinson steamed up the Cape Fear to Wilmington to discharge his cargo and to take on a load of cotton bound for Nasau. When he arrived at the docks, he quickly observed that the once drowsy town was humming with activity, even though the dread yellow fever epidemic only subsided the month before. [95]

The steam cotton presses, he noted, were running full tilt on the flats across the river, preparing bales for the waiting blockade-runners. Thousands of bales and as many tierces of tobacco awaited loading, along with hundreds of barrels of turpentine, another valuable commodity extracted from the pine trees that covered the eastern section of the state. "More than a dozen blockade runners," Wilkinson noticed, "hung at anchor in the stream or loaded alongside, the cotton stowed almost stack-high on their decks. Some were painted a light buff, the rest a dull gray, and most of them looked fast, capable of getting through to Nassau, Bermuda and Halifax, the main cotton-receiving ports, without much trouble." [96]

How much longer this valuable commerce into and out of Wilmington would continue, was a question of grave concern to W.H.C. Whiting, as the year 1862 drew to a close. He had already made a number of appeals to his superiors to bring his movable infantry forces up to at least 10,000 men, accompanied by six field batteries of artillery. According to field returns in the headquarters of Major General G.W. Smith in Richmond, the District of the Cape Fear was defended by only 174 officers and 2,804 men as of December 10. As of the end of November, these numbers reflected no more than 700 of the infantry Whiting needed, "and about 300 heavy artillery, with two or three companies of Partisan Rangers." In fighting off any kind of Union attack against Wilmington, "the garrisons of Forts Fisher, Caswell, Saint Philip, and other batteries cannot be taken into account. They must man the batteries whether the enemy attack the river or not." There simply were not enough troops for the Yankee attack that was expected any day. [97]

In late November, Whiting had received information from a spy of a large concentration of Federal troops, as many as 20,000, at Roanoke Island, "part of which came from New York and part from the vicinity of Suffolk, intended for an expedition, according to camp talk, against this place...If such an attempt is to be made from there our first intimation of it will probably be from the pickets at Topsail, 22 miles off, too late for efficient support." Whiting continued his dispatch to Smith in Richmond by stating that if the enemy attacked along the "plank road from the Sounds, the garrison of the town and the two sides of the river have no mode of escape. The river and its branches are wide and deep and our water transportation is not sufficient to allow of the escape of even the field batteries." [98]

There was much of value that the Yankees could utilize if they took Wilmington, including ironclad gunboats that were under construction, much machinery, as well as agricultural crops in storage. With his paucity in numbers, totally insufficient to oppose a determined Union expedition, Whiting intended, "unless otherwise ordered, in case of attack in force by land previous to the arrival of the troops estimated as necessary, to destroy all I can, even to burning the city to the ground." [99]

Whiting's fears were well founded. By early December the U.S. Navy Department in Washington had communicated with Admiral S.P. Lee, commanding the North Atlantic Blockading Squadron, about the possibility of an attack on Wilmington. On December 14, Lee wrote to Assistant Secretary Gustavus Fox that he would be willing to make the attempt, but they would need all the ironclad warships they could get. "I am arguing for all the force you can give," Lee said, "more monitors if you can." [100]

"If the ironclads could safely go into New Inlet, thus allowing an inside and outside attack on the works there, Federal Point, the whole force could be used at once and together; but if the former is obliged to enter over the Western Bar, the attack is divided and weakened." [101]

Consideration was given to the *U.S.S. Monitor* and the *U.S.S. Passaic* entering the Cape Fear, but the entrance at New Inlet was too shallow for the heavy ironclads. Commander J.P. Bankhead of the *Monitor* wrote to Admiral Lee that "the New Inlet channel is not, in my opinion, feasible for vessels of the draft of the *Monitor* during the winter months." [102]

The *Monitor* had a draft of ten feet four inches, and the average high tide over the new Inlet bar was nine and one half feet, ten feet in spring tides and six and one half to seven feet at low water. Trying to go over the bar past Fort Fisher and the connecting sea-face batteries, then, was out of the question. It was possible that the ironclads could cross the Western Bar below Fort Caswell, but the likelihood of substantial river obstructions right under the ramparts of the fort, that might snare the gunboats and hold them fast where they could be pounded into submission, made the notion of entering the Cape Fear with the heavy iron ships wishful thinking. [103]

Major General John G. Foster, commanding the Union Army in New Bern, was in charge of the land forces that were to attack Wilmington. Having received notification from Admiral Lee that the ironclads were unable to enter the river, he concluded that further consideration of the expedition should be postponed. In a communication to Lee on the 4th of January 1863, he gave several reasons why the attack would be a deadly gamble, one of the major of them being the frowning parapets and bristling artillery of Fort Fisher.

"I understand," Foster wrote Lee, "that none of the ironclads can, from their draft of water, enter New Inlet. They can not, therefore, obtain – what is so much needed against the earthen batteries of Fort Fisher – a reverse fire upon the guns and gunners on the sea front while the wooden gunboats occupied that front from the outside. The only attack, therefore, that the naval forces can make on Fort Fisher will be from the outside. Against such an attack, however strongly made, the fort is so strongly defended, by means of high and thick earthen parapets and numerous traverses, as well as casemated protections, that the attack in all probability will fail to reduce the work." [104]

Because the naval attack at Fort Fisher would be insufficient to compel all of its garrison to remain at the big guns, thus releasing many of the troops to cooperate in repelling Foster's army moving down from New Bern, the feasibility of an attack on Wilmington was rendered even more doubtful. [105]

Foster was "quite convinced, since learning that the ironclads can not enter New Inlet and cooperate powerfully in that way, by operating on the rear of the defenses on Federal Point, if not even in taking Fort Fisher, which I confidently expected, that my force is too small to undertake the capture of Wilmington and the siege of Fort Fisher upon a single venture." [106]

While the Federals were still pondering what to do, the Confederate authorities were frantic about the likelihood of Union attack at Wilmington. The highest ranking general in the Confederacy, Adjutant and Inspector General Samuel Cooper, on January 8 telegraphed General Beauregard, commanding at Charleston, that he was to send 5,000 of his troops to Wilmington. On the same day, General Whiting wrote to Beauregard to request all the help he could give him. "I have always been of the opinion," Whiting said, "that Wilmington would be attacked before Charleston, if the enemy have any sense. If it is saved, Charleston will not be troubled; if it falls, Charleston will not be long in following, though locally it might hold out for a time. Look at the map. It is for you to decide whether you will risk your troops." [107]

On January 13, Whiting telegraphed Lamb at Fort Fisher, that attack was imminent. "Should you find," he said, "that ironclads are too much for you and succeed in passing, endeavor to save and reserve some of your guns for fire on the wooden ships and transports. You will report by telegraph every hour the progress of events. I do not think ships alone can drive you out, though it is possible that ironclads may be able to dismount your guns. You will, therefore, even if the ironclads pass you, continue to hold the fort as long as you are supplied with provisions...I bid you and your brave garrison Godspeed. Fight as well as you have labored, and I have no fear for the result." [108]

Fortunately for General Whiting and his Cape Fear troops and citizens, the attack on Wilmington was cancelled by the Federals just before the general sent his urgent dispatch to Fort Fisher's young commandant. One of the significant reasons for the expedition being cancelled was the inability of the ironclads to enter New Inlet "to enfilade the strongly built and casemated works on Federal Point". [109] With the army troops under Foster being unable to move on Wilmington and besiege Fort Fisher at the same time, as he had pointed out, the top Union Army commander, General Henry W. Halleck in Washington, had decided to "transfer the troops intended for Wilmington to Port Royal." For the time being, the Yankees would concentrate their efforts in trying to crush the city that gave birth to secession, Charleston. [110]

The respite from attack was used to full advantage by William Lamb and his artillerists. On Friday, the 16th of January, the Rebels snared their biggest catch to date, a Union gunboat. Acting Volunteer Lieutenant Joseph Couthouy, commanding officer of the *U.S.S. Columbia*, wrote to Gideon Welles from the Confederate States Military Prison in Salisbury, North Carolina on January 21, the he and eleven other of his officers were incarcerated there, while twenty-eight of his enlisted men captured with him had been forwarded on to Richmond. He could give no details of the loss of the ship and their capture, but he did say that "from the moment we landed up to the present we have been treated with the greatest courtesy and consideration by every officer who has had us in charge, and that everything has been done which circumstances permitted to alleviate the trials incident to our situation." [111]

The *Daily Journal* told its readers on Saturday, January 17, that on the previous day Colonel Lamb had "captured the U.S. Steamer *Columbia*, commander Couthey (sic), 12 officers and 28 men, ashore at Masonboro Inlet," and that he had "kept off four blockaders that had come up to the *Columbia*'s assistance." The paper said that the ship was a "splendid Iron Steamer, built to run the blockade, and was captured by the *Tuscarora*, on her first trip to Charleston. This is her first cruise as a War Steamer." It was also her last. [112]

In a detailed report written from Boston on May 18, 1863, after his release from prison, Commander Couthouy told Gideon Welles that his ship had run aground on the bar at Masonboro Inlet on the night of January 14. On moving into his station for night blockading duty according to orders, he said that the vessel had unknowingly gotten into the deep water of a narrow gully or swash that carried "up to the very face of the reef, and of which the following day we could clearly distinguish three or four within a mile of our position." Because his leadsman had continued to get good soundings of deep water, over seven fathoms up to the very minute they hit the breakers, they were thumping against the bar in white water "before the action of the propeller could be reversed." [113]

"Every possible exertion was made, with steam and canvas and by lightening her of her coal, to extricate her from her perilous situation," but all efforts were in vain. [114]

By daylight of next morning, January 15, the *Columbia* was stuck hard and fast, with her seams starting to open, and sand silting up under the vessel, rendering it virtually impossible for another ship to try and tow her off. No help was forthcoming from another Union gunboat until afternoon of that day, when the *Columbia* was spotted in distress by the *Penobscot*. About 4 p.m., the *Penobscot* was able to send in boats through the rough swells that were starting to kick up. Their crews hauled off thirty men from the *Columbia* before having to abandon the rescue due to the ferocity of the surf. [115]

As night came on, a fearsome gale blew in, life-threatening in its intensity. "Toward midnight it blew furiously, with torrents of rain and a great surf tumbling in, and the *Penobscot* was herself forced, for her own safety, to get underway and steam to sea." Couthouy told Welles that the surf "broke with great violence" on the *Columbia*'s starboard bow, "forcing (in spite of both anchors being down with 30 fathoms of chain trending to the S.W.) her head gradually round to the eastward, so as to bring her nearly broadside to the rollers and cause her to strike with terrific force along the whole line of her length, and gradually settle on her starboard bilge with her deck facing the sea that began to break over it in a very menacing fashion." [116]

All through the wee hours of the morning of Friday the 16th, the sea broke over the ship with terrible force, until it seemed the *Columbia* would be literally bowled over by the pounding waves. By daylight, the winds had shifted direction, and the vessel lay easier. She also lay an inviting target for William Lamb's artillerists, who jerked on their lanyards as soon as they could see well enough to sight in. [117]

Commander Couthouy said "the rebels opened a sharp and well directed fire with shell on the wreck from two batteries, which we afterwards learned had been mounted with guns brought the day previous from Fort Fisher." Colonel Lamb had brought up four guns to add to the Union sailors' misery, a 30-pound Parrott, a 20-pound Whitworth, and two 6-pound fieldpieces that fired solid shot. The fire of the 6-pounders "all fell short, but the shell from both the others passed directly over the wreck just above our heads, or exploded within a few yards on either side of her." [118]

The Yankee commander decided there was no alternative but surrender, the ship being in a helpless condition, and the Confederate gunners having gotten the range. Couthouy cut the carriages of his six 24-pounder howitzers to pieces, to keep them from drifting to shore intact, dumped his cannon in the sea, and ran up the white flag. The Rebels, however, continued to fire on the wrecked ship, later stating they had not seen the flag, and the Federals hauled down their banner of surrender. [119]

By mid-morning, the *Penobscot* had steamed back into sight, and was soon joined by the *U.S.S. Cambridge* and the *Genesee*, all of which now opened up on Colonel Lamb's battery detachments. The Thirty-Sixth North Carolina artillerists "redoubled their fire on the *Columbia*," and the Yankees ran up the white flag again as a token of surrender. "The rebels persisted in firing upon us for nearly an hour longer," reported Couthouy, "till I sent Acting Ensign Manter ashore in our only remaining boat with a flag of truce to enquire the meaning of their keeping up a fire after our surrender, when they ceased and showed an answering flag of truce, alleging that they had not previously seen our white flag. On the batteries ceasing their fire, the gunboats in the offing ceased theirs also, and soon afterwards the *Penobscot* and *Genesee* steamed away in the direction of New Inlet."

The shot furnace situated along the sea face of the fort was used to super heat the shot fired at the predominantly wooden ships of the Union's blockading fleet.

"At 2:30 p.m.," Couthouy continued, "our boat returned without Mr. Manter, bringing a verbal message from Colonel Lamb, commanding the Whitworth battery, requiring myself and as many of my officers as the boat could take to come on shore immediately and report at his quarters." [120]

At 3 o'clock Couthouy left the ship and formally surrendered to a Colonel Wilson, commanding a Georgia brigade of infantry, whose men were stationed in this vicinity. (Wilson's men were sent to General Whiting's aid in January. By month-end, the Cape Fear District had over 12,000 sorely needed troops.[121]) Couthouy said his men "were courteously treated by Colonel Wilson, who returned our side arms and expressed regret and mortification at the batteries having kept up their fire so long after we showed a white flag." [122]

Darkness fell before all the *Columbia*'s crew could be brought on shore, and on the morning of the 17th, the *Cambridge* came back to engage the Southern batteries, while the *Penobscot* moved in to bombard the wreck of the *Columbia*, not realizing, apparently, that United States sailors were still aboard. "Several shell from the *Penobscot* also struck the beach and exploded within a few feet of where the rest of our men were drawn up, they being apparently mistaken for rebels by those on board the gunboat." Fortunately for the sailors, nobody was hit. [123]

The captured Yankees were taken to Wilmington, where at 2 o'clock in the morning on the 18th they were placed on board a railroad car headed for Goldsboro. On arriving at Goldsboro, the enlisted men were forwarded to prison in Richmond, while Couthouy and his officers were sent to Salisbury, where they remained until March 26. [124]

Their confinement in Salisbury Confederate prison was very lenient, according to Couthouy. He said they had "free range, on parole, of the garrison yard, an enclosure of 15 acres; were comfortably lodged; furnished with fuel 'ad libitum'. Our rations, though insufficient and of a very poor quality of bread and bacon mainly, were the same as those served out to their own men. There was no restraint upon our purchasing outside, and our treatment throughout by all the officers of the garrison was, I feel bound in justice to say, entirely courteous and considerate." [125]

Libby Prison in Richmond was not quite so agreeable. They arrived here on March 28, having left Salisbury on the 26th, and were kept "in close confinement" until their exchange on May 5. [126]

While the bluecoat officers roamed the fifteen acres at Salisbury, William Lamb and company kept busy with their vigilant routine of saving supplies for the Confederacy. Less than two weeks after the *Columbia* came to grief, the commanding officer of the *U.S.S. Cambridge* reported that at daylight on January 31, a steamer was spied inside New Inlet near Fort Fisher, and she was flying the Confederate flag at her mainmast, and the English flag at her foremast. The vessel had run the blockade during the night. Also, that afternoon at 4 o'clock, "Fort Fisher fired a salute of twenty-one guns." [127]

Two weeks later, Commander Ludlow Case of the U.S. Steam Sloop *Iroquois* reported to Rear Admiral Samuel Lee that the Rebels were "working like beavers in adding to the defenses of New Inlet...They have now four casemated batteries west of Fort Fisher completed and a fifth nearly so, each mounting two or three guns, built of heavy framework, and covered deeply with sand and sodded. A steam engine is in use, apparently for the purpose of raising the sand, etc. East of Fort Fisher there are two batteries of three guns each." [128]

The Federal (Confederate) Point lighthouse had been torn down, Case believed, for the purpose of using the materials in the construction of hotshot furnaces for the new batteries.[147] These were heavy brick enclosed ovens or furnaces, in which solid shot was placed until heated red-hot, at which time it was packed down the muzzle of one of the big guns, and fired at the Yankee ships, hopefully setting something on fire.

"The defenses are much more formidable and much more judiciously arranged," Case continued, "on account of detached batteries, than those at the South Bar, Fort Caswell, etc...If a vessel now gets inside of the blockaders she can soon run under cover of the batteries and anchor until the tide serves for crossing the bar." [129]

A week after this report, two blockade runners in one night confirmed its accuracy. On the night of February 20, a steamer was chased by the *U.S.S. Mount Vernon*, which had to halt its pursuit after the fleet-footed vessel "had run under the guns of Fort Fisher." At daylight, the *Mount Vernon* saw the steamer again and gave chase once more, but she quickly got inside of the inlet.

A schooner was spotted as well, and chase was given to within three fourths of a mile of Fort Fisher, "which, together with the batteries around the inlet, replied quite briskly to our firing, many of their shots passing over and falling around us." Almost in defiance, the screw steamer then ran up the English flag while standing in the inlet. [130]

Four days later, the *Wilmington Daily Journal* sarcastically taunted the Union Navy's blockade, which thanks to Colonel Lamb and his sharp-eyed artillerists, was proving to be a genuine embarrassment to the bluecoats. The Journal expressed its acknowledgement "to the Lincoln blockaders, for the great pains they have taken to develop the foreign trade of the port of Wilmington." The paper said the blockade had "been the means of enabling us to see some of the swiftest iron steamers that can be built on the Clyde, a class of vessel we could never have seen while we kept on our trade with New York, Boston, and Philadelphia.

"And these vessels seem to come in and go out with as much certainty as though Uncle Abraham's blockade was not in existence...The 'Union Jack' and the 'Red Cross of St. George' is now quite familiar to our people." [131]

Endnotes to Chapter 3

1. Carse, Robert, *Blockade, the Civil War at Sea*, p.107-108, Rinehart & Company, New York, 1958, hereinafter referred to as Blockade; *Virginian-Pilot* newspaper, Norfolk, Virginia, March 24, 1909
2. Tyler, Lyon G., ed. "Men of Mark in Virginia", p.190, *Ideals of American Life. A Collection of Biographies of the Leading Men of the State*, archives of Norfolk Public Library; and the "Laurentian" of St. Lawrence College, May, 1901, Volume 14, #5, handwritten copy in archives of Sargeant Memorial Room, Norfolk Public Library
3. Thomas, C.M.D., *Letters from the Colonel's Lady: Correspondence of Mrs. William Lamb, written from Fort Fisher, N.C., C.S.A.*, p.55, Charles Towne Preservation Trust, Winnabow, N.C., 1965
4. Blockade, p.107-108
5. Ibid, p.108; William Lamb description of wife, personal papers in author's possession
6. Ibid, p.108; Diary of Colonel William Lamb, October 1, 1861, William Lamb papers, Earl Greg Swem Library, College of William & Mary, Williamsburg, Virginia
7. Clark, Volume II, p.629; Lamb, William, *Colonel Lamb's Story of Fort Fisher*, Blockade Runner Museum, Carolina Beach, North Carolina, 1966, hereinafter Lamb's Story

8.   Lamb's Story, p.1-2
9.   Ibid, p.2
10. Ibid, p.2
11. Ibid
12. ORN, Volume 7, p.567
13. Blockade, p.110
14. Clark, Volume V, p.351
15. N.C. Troops, Volume I, p.300 & 304; Clark, Volume II, p.755
16. N.C. Troops, Volume I, p.198; Clark, Volume IV, p.342-343
17. Clark, Volume IV, p.343
18. William B. Taylor letter to mother, July 5, 1862, typescript copy in author's possession; Bright, Leslie, *The Blockade Runner Modern Greece and Her Cargo*, p.17, Division of Archives & History, N.C. Department of Cultural Resources, Raleigh, N.C., hereinafter Modern Greece
19. Modern Greece, p.17
20. *General Order Book of the Eleventh North Carolina Troops, March 1862-June 1863*, S. Daniels Collection, Charlotte N.C., hereinafter Eleventh N.C. Order Book
21. Eleventh N.C. Order Book
22. Ibid
23. Ibid
24. Lamb, William, "Account of Defense and Fall of Fort Fisher," Southern Historical Society Papers, Volume X, July, 1882, p.361, 52 Volumes, Richmond, Virginia, hereinafter SHSP
25. Daily Journal, July 1, 1862
26. Ibid, July 1, 1862
27. Modern Greece, p.75-152 passim
28. ORN, Volume 7, p.613
29. Ibid, Volume 7, p.645
30. Ibid, Volume 7, p.665
31. Ibid, p.665
32. Clark, Volume II, p.633
33. Lamb's Story, p.2
34. Ibid, p.3-4
35. Ibid, p.2
36. Stick, David, *Bald Head, a History of Smith Island and Cape Fear*, p.45, Broadfoot's Bookmark, Wendell, N.C., 1985
37. ORN, Volume 8, p.71
38. Ibid, Volume 8, p.80
39. Ibid
40. Daily Journal, October 13, 1862
41. Ibid, October 13, 1862
42. Ibid, October 13, 1862

43. ORN, Volume 8, p.127
44. Ibid, Volume 8, p.127
45. Ibid, Volume 8, p.152
46. Ibid, p.179
47. Ibid, p.197-198
48. Ibid, p.194
49. Ibid, p.194-197
50. Clark, Volume II, p.771; Daily Journal, November 13, 1862
51. ORN, Volume 8, p.194
52. ORN, Volume 8, p.194-197
53. Daily Journal, November 13, 1862
54. ORN, Volume 8, p.199
55. Ibid, Volume 8, p.198
56. O.R., Volume XVIII, p.770
57. Denson, Claude B., *An Address Containing a Memoir of the Late Major-General William Henry Chase Whiting*, p.33, Edwards & Broughton, Raleigh, N.C., 1895, hereinafter Denson
58. Denson, p.10-11
59. Denson, p.11
60. Ibid, p.11
61. OR, Volume I, p.34
62. Ibid, Volume I, p.486-487
63. Denson, p.14
64. Denson, p.15
65. Ibid, p.15
66. Ibid, p.16
67. Ibid, p.29-30
68. Daily Journal, November 20, 1862
69. OR, Volume XVIII, p.773
70. Ibid, Volume XVIII, p.773; Chronicles of the Cape Fear River, p.287
71. Ibid, Volume XVIII, p.773
72. Ibid, p.774
73. Ibid, p.774-775
74. Ibid, p.775-776
75. Ibid, p.776
76. Ibid, p.777
77. Daily Journal, November 18, 1862
78. ORN, Volume 8, p.214
79. Ibid, Volume 8, p.214
80. N.C. Troops, Volume II, p.181-182; Daily Journal, November 18 & 20, 1862
81. Daily Journal, November 20, 1862; ORN, Volume 8, p.214-215

82. ORN, Volume 8, p.215
83. Ibid, Volume 8, p.216-217
84. Daily Journal, November 18, 1862
85. ORN, Volume 8, p.260
86. Ibid, Volume 8, p.266
87. Taylor, Thomas, *Running the Blockade: A Personal Narrative of Adventures, Risks, and Escapes During the American Civil War*, p.35, Charles Scribner's Sons, New York, 1896, hereinafter Thomas Taylor; Captain Roberts (C.Augustus Hobart-Hampden), *Never Caught, Personal Adventures Connected With Twelve Successful Trips in Blockade-Running During the American Civil War, 1863-1864,* p.2-3, The Blockade Runner Museum, Carolina Beach, N.C., 1967, hereinafter Never Caught
88. Sprunt, James, *Tales of the Cape Fear Blockade*, p.70, Charles Towne Preservation Trust, Winnabow, N.C., 1960, hereinafter Tales of Cape Fear Blockade
89. Never Caught, p.2-3
90. ORN, Volume 8, p.267; Blockade, p.3-5
91. Blockade, p.3-5
92. Ibid, p.3-5; ORN, Volume 8, p.266
93. Blockade, p.4-5
94. Ibid, p.5-8
95. Ibid, p.9
96. Ibid, p.9-10
97. OR, Volume XVIII, p. 784, 793
98. OR, Volume XVIII, p.783
99. Ibid, p.783
100. ORN, Volume 8, p.298-299
101. Ibid, Volume 8, p.299
102. Ibid, Volume 8, p.327
103. Ibid, p.326-328
104. Ibid, p.399
105. Ibid, p.399
106. Ibid, p.400
107. Ibid, p.830; OR, Volume XVIII, p.826
108. ORN, Volume 8, p.855
109. ORN, Volume 8, p.420, p.574
110. Ibid, Volume 8, p.574-575; Barrett, Civil War in N.C., p.150
111. ORN, Volume 8, p.424-425
112. Daily Journal, January 17, 1863
113. ORN, Volume 8, p.432
114. Ibid, Volume 8, p.432
115. Ibid, p.433

116.Ibid, p.433
117.Ibid, p.433-434
118.Ibid, p.434
119.Ibid, p.434-435
120.Ibid, p.434-435
121.OR, Volume XVIII, p.865
122.ORN, Volume 8, p.435
123.Ibid, Volume 8, p.435
124.Ibid
125.Ibid
126.Ibid, p.435-436
127.Ibid, p.492
128.Ibid, p.525
129.Ibid, p.526
130.Ibid, p.547-548
131.Daily Journal, February 25, 1863

The sea face of Fort Fisher, seen here from inside the fort, stretched for nearly a mile, down to New Inlet. It was anchored on its southern end by the Mound Battery. The heavy guns placed in its traverses were perfectly situated to provide covering fire for blockade runners being pursued by Union warships. All of the sea face of the fort has since disappeared due to erosion.

Chapter 4

"...their rebel flags waving us defiance..."

W
e are all getting into a lame condition," Captain B.F. Sands of the U.S. Steam Sloop *Dacotah*, wrote to Rear Admiral Samuel Lee on March 5, 1863. As senior naval officer commanding off Wilmington, he would know. He said the *Maratanza*'s donkey pump was broken, the *Chocura*'s boiler had sprung a leak, and his own ship's boilers were worn out and the bottom of the hull had sprung a leak; this problem had been "partially remedied by allowing sediment to deposit while repairing at Beaufort." [1]

The condition of the vessels off the Cape Fear was particularly unfortunate, Sands believed, because he thought a Confederate ironclad ram was about to make "its appearance outside of the bar at New Inlet." The ram had been spotted just a few days before at New Inlet, escorting in a large blockade runner that had gotten safely under the guns of Fort Fisher. A drawing of the vessel, which accompanied Sands' report, resembled to a great degree the *C.S.S. Virginia*, that had slugged it out the March before with the U.S.S. *Monitor*. The *Monitor* would be unable to deal with any Rebel ironclads in the

Cape Fear, however. She was at the bottom of the Atlantic off Cape Hatteras, having foundered in a heavy gale on the last day of 1862. [2]

The ironclad Sands referred to was apparently the *C.S.S. North Carolina*. Her keel had been laid early in 1862 at W.B. Beery's shipyard across the river from Wilmington.[3] She may have been testing her engines on a trial run with a skeleton crew when she was spotted at the mouth of the river, but it was doubtful she was ready for combat at this time. According to Flag Officer W.F. Lynch, Commanding Naval Defenses of North Carolina, headquartered in Wilmington, on April 6 "the *North Carolina*, building here, is very nearly ready for her crew, the complement of which is 150 men. The *Raleigh*, is now ready for her iron shield, and can in eight weeks be prepared for service, as far as the material is concerned." Unfortunately, Lynch only had sixty men in all of North Carolina's sounds and rivers to man the gunboats, so even if the two Wilmington ironclads would soon be ready for action, which the bluecoated officers off Fort Fisher greatly dreaded, there would not be enough sailors ready for them. [4]

RAdm Samuel Phillips Lee, U.S.N.

By March 1863, Wilmington was already becoming the favored port of entry for war goods, partly because the blockaders at Charleston had become "too thick there," and to a great extent, because of the proficiency and energy of William Lamb. [5] Major Caleb Huse, working diligently for Dixie in Europe, had purchased and shipped tremendous quantities of war material to the South, much of which came past Fort Fisher. [6]

Colonel Josiah Gorgas, Chief of Confederate Ordnance, wrote to Secretary of War James Seddon in February 1863, that since Major Huse had assumed his duties in London at the beginning of the war, he had procured and shipped to the Confederate States 131,129 small arms, most of which were the superb "long Enfield rifles." He had also shipped one hundred and twenty-nine cannon, consisting of fifty-four 6-pound bronze smoothbores, various howitzers and iron rifles, some of the excellent Blakely rifled guns with 18,680 shells for them, thirty-two Austrian bronze rifled cannon with caissons and almost 11,000 shrapnel shells for them, and various other cannons, artillery harness, shells and fuses.[7]

Cavalry sabers, over 16,000 of them, and 5,392 cavalry saber-belts had been run through the blockade. Over 40,000 gunslings, 34,655 knapsacks, 4,000 canteen straps, 81,406 bayonet scabbards, 357,000 pounds of cannon powder, 94,600 pounds of musket powder, and over 4,000,000 cartridges for small arms were on the list, as well. Additionally, more than 74,000 pairs of boots, 62,025 blankets, 78,520 yards of cloth, 8,675 greatcoats, 8,250 pair of trousers, ninety seven packages of uniform trimmings, forty six sets of armorer's tools, thirty six sets of saddler's tools, ten sets of farrier's tools, 2,000 cartridge bags, 1,013 hundredweight lead, and sixteen flags had been shipped from Europe to the Confederate States, The value of all those goods procured by Major Huse and forwarded through the blockade was almost 819,900 pounds sterling. [8]

He had also purchased and had "in London ready for shipment" as of February 1863, 23,000 rifles that were headed for Nassau, "20,000 scabbards; 2,012,000 cartridges; 3,000,000 percussion-caps; 10,000 pouch tins, prepared for accouterments; 286 ingots tin; —13,750 pair trousers, Quartermaster's Department; 14,250 greatcoats, Quartermaster's Department; 1,804 pair boots, Quartermaster's Department; 4 chests tea, Quartermaster's Department." The value of these commodities awaiting the run through the Yankee blockade was a quarter of a million pounds sterling. [9]

Primed and ready to do all he could to ensure that those supplies got into the Cape Fear safely and intact, was the young Virginia Colonel at Fort Fisher. His daring and expertise with artillery was becoming well known to those engaged in bringing in war goods past the Union gunboats.

One of those who made his acquaintance early in 1863 and came to admire him much was Thomas Taylor. Taylor was a young Englishman who knew blockade running. He probably knew it as well as anybody who ever ran through the Yankee cruisers to strike for the Cape Fear. Because of his frequent activities in this line of work, as supercargo for the Liverpool based Confederate Trading Company, he came to be warm friends with William Lamb, and valued that friendship very much. [10]

Taylor said that Colonel Lamb was most popular with blockade runners, that he was "always on the alert and ever ready to reach a helping hand, he seemed to think no exertion too great to assist their operations, and many a smart vessel did his skill and activity snatch from the very jaws of the blockaders. He came to be regarded by the runners as their guardian angel; and it was no small support in the last trying moments of a run to remember who was in Fort Fisher." [11]

Taylor valued the Virginia Colonel's expertise so highly that he urged his company to give Fort Fisher's commandant something mutually beneficial to the Confederacy and to his employers. Taylor wrote that at his suggestion "my firm subsequently presented him with a battery of six Whitworth guns, of which he was very proud; and good use he made of them in keeping the blockaders at a respectful distance. They were guns with a great range, which many a cruiser found to its cost when venturing too close in chase down the coast. Lamb would gallop them down behind the sandhills, by aid of mules, and open fire upon the enemy before he was aware of his danger." [12]

Maintaining his authority and vigilance on the Wilmington coast in March 1863, Lamb's troops participated in the first use of sea/land coded signals by the Confederacy in assisting a blockade runner to escape the Yankee cruisers. Captain A. Ludlow Case of the U.S.S. Steam Sloop *Iroquois* wrote to Admiral S.P. Lee in late March that on the 2nd of the month the Confederate blockade runner *Cornubia* had run in at New Inlet. The Rebel ship, owned by the Confederate government and not British merchants, had arrived off a prominent point called the Big Hill about twelve miles northeast of New Inlet. Colonel Lamb was informed of the ship's arrival up the coast, and ordered her officers to "be prepared to run in as soon as he could return to the fort and get his guns ready. She was run very close along the breakers by Jim Burroughs (a pilot living on the beach), who reported she ran 5 miles in twenty minutes." [13]

Captain Case's report was mostly accurate, but Confederate Signal Corps Operator Frederick Gregory of Crowells, North Carolina, stationed aboard the *Cornubia* (later renamed the *Lady Davis* in honor of the President's wife), said their pilot for this voyage was C.C. Morse, and that the captain's name was Burroughs. They had taken her out to St. George's, Bermuda, where they had offloaded their cargo of cotton and taken on supplies for the army. When the vessel had gotten to "within fifteen or twenty miles of Fort Fisher, Captain Burroughs sent for me to come on the bridge, and asked if I had my lights ready and if I thought I could send a message ashore, Pilot Morse in the meantime telling me that he would let me know when we were opposite the signal station on land, where a constant watch was kept all night for our signal." Soon, Gregory said, they were off the beach at the signal post, and he was sent on deck with his lights facing land, backed by a screen behind him, and instructed to signal the station. [14]

He used two lights, "a red and a white, covered with a shade in front of the globe to lift up and down, by which we could send messages as we did with the flag on land in the day, and with a torch at night; the red light representing the wave to the right and the white light the wave to the left." [15]

"The officers and sailors," Gregory said, "were highly interested in the movement and crowded around to watch the proceedings. I called but a few times, when I was answered from the shore by a torch. I turned to Captain Burroughs and told him that I had the attention of the land forces and asked what message he wished to send. He replied as follows: 'Colonel Lamb: Steamer *Cornubia*. Protect me. Burroughs.' I got the O.K. for the message from shore, and saw the corps on land call up one station after another and transmit

Deadly accurate fire from rifled cannon like this 12lb Whitworth, of which Fort Fisher had several, kept the Union blockade at a healthy distance.

my message to Fort Fisher miles ahead of us, and afterwards learned that General Whiting was notified by telegraph of the arrival of the *Cornubia* before she crossed the bar that night. When we arrived at the fort, we found Colonel Lamb down on the point with his Whitworth guns ready to protect us if necessary. The success of this attempt gave an impetus to the signal corps, and from that time every steamer that arrived applied to the Government for a signal officer before leaving port." [16]

Not only were the signal lamps and the Whitworths doing their part to facilitate blockade-breakers in this third spring of the war, but Fort Fisher's batteries were becoming more numerous and more formidable as well. On March 10, Commander Ludlow Case reported to Admiral Lee from the *U.S.S. Iroquois* that a large sand tower was in the process of construction on the end of Confederate Point: "It is now, I judge, some 60 feet high, diagonally braced and supported in the rear, and still unfinished. I at first thought it was intended only for a lighthouse, signal, or lookout tower, but now think that guns are to be used in it also, to throw plunging shot on the decks of vessels. The stories are being filled around with sand as they arise, a steam engine being used for that purpose." [17]

Case said that the Confederates were preparing their works at New Inlet with the obvious expectation of "extensive operations." At night, should the Union gunboats have to abandon their positions, it was "tantamount to abandoning them, for they can not be recovered in the day without a fight with four or five forts. The enemy have guns of very long range and never miss an opportunity to let us know it. On the 5th instant, while over 4 miles from the fort, a shot was thrown within a very short distance of this vessel, and the day before three or four near the *State of Georgia*." The Yankee commander said that they were most careful to station themselves just out of range of Fort Fisher, and that when the air was clear, they could "distinctly see the operations of the men at the forts and on the shore, and the movements of vessels in the inlet and river. I judge it to be near 5 miles from the beach." [18]

Paymaster William F. Keeler of the *U.S.S. Florida* could also vouch for the substantial Rebel defenses at New Inlet, almost due east of which his ship was stationed. Keeler was a former Illinois iron works owner and had served as paymaster on the *Monitor*, until she found a watery grave off the Carolina Coast. When the commander of the *Monitor*, John Bankhead, was given command of the *Florida*, he requested that Keeler accompany him to blockading duty off the Wilmington coast. [19]

Keeler wrote his wife, Anna, on March 28 to let her know that the ship had arrived at its post of duty off Wilmington. He did not like what he saw: "To seaward there is nothing but the same wild watery waste very rarely now dotted by the solitary sail of the coaster. In the opposite direction the extended line of white sandy beach stretches far away up & down the coast with its dark background of underbrush broken at intervals with batteries of unknown strength & undefined proportions, their rebel flags waving us defiance while guns of prodigious range bid us stand off." [20]

In company with the *Florida*, trying to intercept blockade-breakers who sought the protection of those "guns of prodigious range," were six other United States warships north of Frying Pan Shoals and off of New Inlet at the end of March. They were the *Iroquois*, the *Mount Vernon*, the *State of Georgia*, the *Arletta*, the *Daylight*, and the *Perry*. Off Old Inlet or the Western Bar, near Fort Caswell, were five other gunboats. They were the *Sacramento*, the *Dacotah*, the *Maratanza*, the *Chocura*, and the *Monticello*. The *Victoria*, the *Matthew Vassar*, and the *William Bacon* cruised off Shallotte Inlet and down to Little River, on the border with South Carolina. Altogether, then, there were fifteen Yankee vessels guarding the sea approaches to the Cape Fear. It still was not enough. [21]

The *Bermuda Royal Gazette* told its readers on March 24 that two days before, the blockade runner "Cornubia" had come into St. George from Wilmington. This was the same ship that several weeks earlier had run past the Yankee blockaders with the help of night signals operated by Frederick Gregory. The *Cornubia* was loaded with "314 bales of cotton, 29 casks of tobacco, and 2 casks of turpentine." The day following the *Cornubia*'s arrival, the British schooner *St. George* also arrived from Wilmington, and she was loaded "with 145 bales of cotton, 160 barrels of rosin, and 65 boxes of tobacco." [22]

It was as tough work for the bluecoated sailors to stop the outgoing traffic from Wilmington as much as it was the incoming, and special precautions and maneuvers were required at night to try to keep the Cape Fear plugged. Rear Admiral Lee reiterated to one officer in mid-April the caution and vigilance required while on night duty, during which time nearly all outgoing runners slipped through the fleet.

"As a general rule," Lee said, "you should not anchor at night, but keep underway, holding your position by turning the propeller and keeping your leads on the bottom to assure you that you are not going ahead or drifting; this requires the most watchful and intelligent attention. At anchor you are liable to be run down, you risk losing your anchor and cable by slipping it, and you are slow to start in chase. It may be sometimes necessary to drop a kedge for a little while, but in this case all should be ready to run it up quickly, and one of the vessels should supply you with extra hands for the night. Care should be taken to keep your fires up; they should not be now high and then low, but be kept bright and even. Great attention to feeding the fires is required and the engineers and firemen should be very vigilant and careful so that the steam may escape gradually and not make a noise. But the steam must be ready. Inform yourself thoroughly regarding the private signals as arranged for communication among the blockaders, and do not repeat the mistake of burning the wrong signal. In chasing, if you have the best speed, you can keep under the stern of the chase and fire until she stops, when signal her surrender and wait for assistance, keeping...in such position that you can not be run over." [23]

Naval vigilance was easy to talk about and order, another thing to enforce. At daybreak of April 23, five days following Admiral Lee's admonishing advice to one of his subordinates, two blockade runners ran into New Inlet past several Union warships. The runners were reported by Rebel prisoners to be the *Merrimac* and the *Eagle*. Commander James Armstrong of the *U.S.S. State of Georgia* reported that one of the vessels "was a long paddle-wheel steamer, two pipes and one mast, painted lead color, and seemed to have a number of men on her deck. She bore the rebel flag." [24]

Armstrong fired on the vessel along with the *Penobscot* and the *Mount Vernon*, but the runner got in past Fort Fisher, while Colonel Lamb's artillerists blasted away at the Union blockaders. Even as the first Rebel ship got safely into New Inlet, firing was heard just up the beach from Fort Fisher, where the *Florida* and *Daylight* were trying to destroy another steamer. Armstrong said he joined the two other ships in their bombardment of the steamer and two batteries of Whitworth guns that were defending her. The vessel had run aground, and Armstrong estimated that at least two hundred to three hundred soldiers were unlading her, with the intention of lightening her cargo to get her off the beach and back in the surf. [25]

While the Yankee commanders of the three vessels discussed what should be their course of action, they apparently inflicting no harm on the blockade runner by their shelling, and unable to land a party of sailors with over two hundred Rebels waiting to give them a warm reception, the British vessel got off the beach and headed for Fort Fisher. "Signal was made to engage her," Armstrong told Admiral Lee, "and all the vessels stood in chase, maintaining a running fire, as she kept on close in with the shore, the English flag flying, until passing safely inside of Fort Fisher, she hoisted the rebel flag, and I was reluctantly compelled to draw off the vessels...The fort fired up the coast, the Whitworth guns passing over us even after we had come out from under the shore." [26]

Commander J.P. Bankhead of the *Florida*, former commanding officer of the *Monitor*, said that all efforts had been made to cut off the steamer after she had gotten afloat, "but her speed and extreme lightness of draft enabled her to reach the protection of Fort Fisher and she succeeded in getting in." [27]

Lieutenant James Trathen of the *Mount Vernon* said that the first vessel had escaped their net due to her superior speed. In the case of the second vessel, not only speed had insured its successful ingress, but the deadly fire of Rebel artillery as well. "At 8 we opened fire on the steamer," he reported, "and a general engagement ensued between the three batteries situated, respectively, 1, 2, and 2 1/2 miles north of Fort Fisher, and Fort Fisher on the one side and on the other the U.S. ships *State of Georgia*, *Florida*, *Penobscot*, and *Mount Vernon*. At 8:20 *Georgia* made signal No. 8; stood inshore to obtain a better range. At 8:45 *State of Georgia* made signal No. 222; ceased firing and stood offshore." [28]

On board the *U.S.S. Florida*, William Keeler was livid with indignation over the escape of the vessel that had gotten off the beach. He said the whole thing had been botched up by "red tape," and adhering to the "rules & regulations of the Navy & the requirements of 'Grandma Gideon' (Welles, Secretary of the Navy) just as 'our prize' was seen to start off for the batteries at the mouth of the river running close in to the beach & parallel with it." [29]

Keeler wrote that the vessel was well on its way to getting into the river before the Union officers ceased their chatter, and decided "it would be best to stop her if possible & opened on her." About thirty naval guns fired on the blockade runner. Keeler told his wife that the ship "glided swiftly & quietly along close in shore all the gun boats abreast of her but taking good care to keep out of reach of the two field pieces...Our shells were bursting over & on all sides of her still she kept steadily along, the English flag flying from her stern...The chase was kept up in this way till our vessels came nearly in range of the batteries at the mouth of the river when we all hauled off." [30]

Keeler was highly disturbed and mortified at what he considered a bungled operation, feeling there was no excuse for the blockade runner to have gotten through their net. [31]

If some of the Yankees were upset with their performance on this occasion, their increasing efforts to stop blockade running traffic were well recognized by the Confederates. Battles with the Federals over their sorely needed supplies were becoming frequent and vicious. Just a month before, in

March, General Whiting had written to Major General Daniel Harvey Hill in Goldsborough, commanding troops in the state, advising him that the Union fleet was getting tough to deal with. "We have now," he wrote, "four British and one Confederate steamer in port daily expecting to leave, and several steamers are expected to arrive. We have had an engagement with the enemy over each one of these vessels, the enemy's sloops of war fiercely attacking the forts while their smaller vessels attempt to cut off the steamers." The *Cornubia* on which Frederick Gregory served as signalman, had just arrived before Whiting's letter, and he said she carried "the most valuable cargo of powder and arms she has yet brought." [32]

To insure that William Lamb's soldiers maintained an edge over the Yankee fleet, General Whiting wrote repeatedly for the War Department to send more big guns. In late February, he asked Secretary Seddon to send him a battery of 20 or 30 pounder Parrott rifles, and also requested him to forward "three 10-inch columbiads and three 7-inch rifles" as quickly as he could. "These guns are absolutely necessary," he said, "to defend the outer harbor, the point of all others we must endeavor to keep." [33]

In March, Seddon responded favorably to Whiting's request, advising him that Colonel T.S. Rhett, inspector of ordnance in Richmond, was forwarding on to him two 10-inch guns, a 4.62- inch rifled gun, as well as a 30-pounder cannon. "Every exertion shall be made," Seddon told him, "as far as the resources of the Ordnance Bureau will allow, to meet the calls for guns necessary for the defense of Wilmington." [34]

By mid-April, whatever heavy cannon had reached the Cape Fear was still inadequate, according to Whiting. In another letter to Seddon on April 15, he renewed his plea for more. He wanted "especially to 8 or 10-inch columbiads and the Brooke rifle. You are aware of the inadequacy of our armament here, and that many guns intended for Wilmington have been diverted to meet what have been required as more pressing necessities elsewhere." [35]

A persistent and energetic officer, Whiting next went directly to Colonel Rhett, whom he addressed as "Chief of Artillery, Richmond, Va." On April 18. He told Rhett that his armament had definitely been improved, but it was still not enough. "I beg that you will do all in your power," he said, "to increase my supply of 8 and 10 inch columbiads and heavy rifles as many as can possibly be sent me, for none will be superfluous at such a point as this. I should be much pleased if you would come down here and assure yourself both of the nature of the problem of defense here and the necessities I have. Both Forts Caswell and Fisher should have Brooke rifles in addition to columbiads. I can make good use of ten or twelve 32-pounder iron bands, many of my 32-pounders being unbanded and therefore not reliable. Please when you send guns to send with them at least 100 rounds." [36]

Whiting was successful in getting more heavy artillery added to Colonel Lamb's positions at Confederate Point, for by the end of April, the Yankees were reporting that guns were "being added to the forts and the general force of the latter is increased weekly." [37] One of the guns added to Fort Fisher had, in fact, been run in on the blockade runner *Merrimac* on the 23rd of April, one of those ships that, to the chagrin of William Keeler, had successfully entered the Cape Fear. Part of the vessel's cargo consisted of three 8-inch Blakely rifles, huge cannon that could fire 130-pound shells almost as far the 12-pound Whitworths. One of the rifles was consigned to the Mississippi River defenses, and one each was slated for Forts Fisher and Caswell. [38]

As well as the addition of more big guns, earthworks continued to rise on the beach like great sand castles, for the purpose of holding and protecting those guns. By mid-April, the large tower on the extreme end of Confederate Point had taken on the appearance of a mound, with an inclined railway running to the top with cars of sand, which were dumped to fill in and around the tower. Sod and brush were used extensively at the base of the mound, to keep the sand from being scattered by high winds.[39] Colonel Lamb wrote, "In the construction of the mound on the extreme right of the seaface, which occupied six months, two inclined railways worked by steam supplemented the labor of men." [40] More obstructions were being sunk off Confederate Point in April as well, to provide additional deterrence to Union ships that might consider chasing a blockade runner into the mouth of the river or try to get into New Inlet and hit Fort Fisher with a reverse fire. [41]

William Lamb's troops were better prepared than ever to fight as spring grew warmer in the third May of the war. With their mobile Whitworths to run up and down the beach at the critical points and times, heavier traverses and sand mounds for protection of more and bigger guns and artillerists as well, there was certain to be a battle anytime a vessel flying the Stars and Stripes got within range.

On May 13, a Wednesday, three days after the death in Virginia of the great Southern warrior, "Stonewall" Jackson, three blockade runners ran past four Yankee warships at daybreak and were discovered only after they had gotten almost inside New Inlet. The *U.S.S. Niphon* tried to stop two of them, but to no avail. "I fired my Parrott gun at them," Commander J.B. Breck reported, "but the shot fell short, and the rebels opened fire on us from their heavy guns on Fort Fisher, but without damage. Finding the steamers had crossed the bar I stood out to report to the senior officer on this station." [42]

One of the steamers, believed to be the *Cornubia*, was paddle-wheeled, long, carried two smokestacks and two light masts, and looked to be painted white. One was a screw steamer with one mast and smokestack, also painted white, and the other was a paddle-wheeler with two masts and one smokestack, but was painted a dark color. [43]

Nine days later, on Friday, May 22, a doctor in blue was killed when his vessel, the *Penobscot*, got too close in pursuit of a blockade breaker off Fort Fisher. Joseph DeHaven, commander of the *Penobscot*, said they spotted a runner at 4 a.m. about 1/4 of a mile off the beach from the fort, and fired on her thirty minutes later, but to no avail, the steamer getting into New Inlet successfully. "Six batteries," DeHaven reported, "together with Fort Fisher, opened a heavy fire upon this vessel, all of the shot, with one exception, falling short or overreaching. At 5 a.m. a shell struck an iron stanchion on the port side, cutting the awning rope, passing through the partners of the mainmast, carrying them all away on the port side, springing one of the deck beams and entering the steerage, seriously wounding Assistant Surgeon Edward A. Pierson and Surgeon's Steward Julius C. Force, who were at their post." At 6:45 a.m. Surgeon Pierson died of his wounds, but his assistant, Julius Force, "was slightly wounded on the scalp at various points," and also suffered dislocation of the left shoulder. [44]

The main sallyport at Fort Caswell.

Colonel Lamb telegraphed to the *Wilmington Daily Journal* before the paper went to press on the 22nd, that the blockade runner which arrived this morning was the *Flora*, commanded by Captain Masters, and fresh in from Nassau "with a valuable cargo...The blockaders made an attack on her but were promptly driven off by the guns of Fort Fisher." [45]

Such regular and repetitive traffic into the river as witnessed by the Union sailors in just a few short days, seemed to confirm what William Keeler told his wife a few weeks before: "how it is on other parts of the coast I do not know but there are goods enough run in here to supply the whole Southern Confederacy. The Secesh boast that Wilmington never had so much trade, & I am inclined to believe them...it is the main inlet through which the rebels get their supplies. After a few weeks' stay here it is no mystery how the rebel armies are so well fed & clothed." [46]

Keeler's assessment was accurate, and his future experiences on board the *Florida* would reinforce his opinions. What he was not able to judge, but naval officers west of Frying Pan Shoals were, was the blockade running activity past Fort Caswell and the Western Bar. Though fewer steamers entered the Cape Fear through this entrance as they did through New Inlet, some chose this route depending on the number of Yankee gunboats off Fort Fisher at particular times. Some came in there if they had first sought to enter Charleston, but were unable to do so because of the tightness of the blockade there. When driven off Charleston, captains would often run north up the coast close to the breakers, instead of detouring far to the east and then back southwest to avoid Frying Pan Shoals and the wide arc of the squadron off Fort Fisher.

Though there were not as many extended batteries west of Caswell as there were north and south of Fisher, the defenses at Old Inlet were formidable

John D. Taylor

and dangerous to Union sailors here, too. Just a few weeks before the advent of spring, a sailor aboard the *U.S.S. Monticello* found out just how dangerous.

Lieutenant Commander D.L. Braine reported to Admiral Lee on February 23, that at daybreak on that day, he had taken the *Monticello* in toward Caswell to fire on a blockade runner, in obedience to orders from Captain B.F. Sands of the *Dacotah*, who reported spying a "two-master single-pipe steamer" near the fort. Braine said he fired on the steamer as ordered. "The fort responded, and at the fifth or sixth shot Acting Master's Mate Henry Baker was mortally wounded, and this morning at 9:30 expired, of which it is my painful duty to inform you." Baker had been struck "in the face, between the eyes, and in the right shoulder, the second piece entering the lungs." Also wounded in the engagement was one "William J. Ferguson, second-class boy," who had been lightly wounded in the back. [47]

Braine later reported their 30-pounder Parrott rifle had been hit with what appeared to be a Whitworth shell, and the wrought-iron band at the breech had been slightly indented. [48]

Captain Sands advised Admiral Lee in Hampton Roads, that with the "recent demonstrations upon this part of the coast by the blockade runners I feel that I have not the force to make it a close blockade. The same may be said of the other side of the reef." [49]

Sands was right; he did not have sufficient force, and he and his subordinates had deadly opposition to deal with on the Western Bar, as demonstrated by the death of Master's Mate Baker. The primary opposition

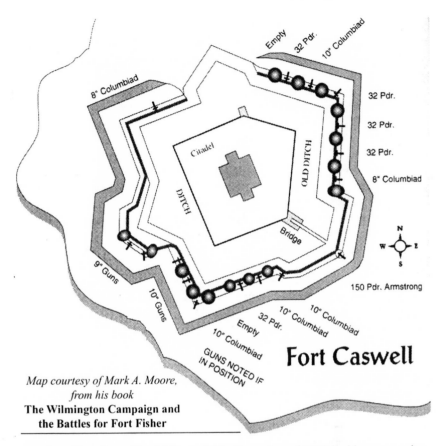

Map courtesy of Mark A. Moore,
from his book
The Wilmington Campaign and
the Battles for Fort Fisher

came from Fort Caswell, which citadel in the spring of 1863 had become quite formidable. [50]

In 1863, Fort Caswell was commanded by Colonel Thomas M. Jones, who was a brother of Captain Pembroke Jones of the Confederate States Navy. Colonel Jones was "associated with the Cape Fear by his marriage with Miss London" of the area.[51] Colonel Jones would become ill of health in the coming months, and in the next year would have to relinquish command. [52]

Second in command at Caswell was a thirty-two year old major of the Thirty-Sixth North Carolina Regiment, John D. Taylor, a native of the Cape Fear. A graduate of the University of North Carolina, class of 1853, he had gone home following graduation to run his father's rice plantation, situated on the west side of the Cape Fear in Brunswick County. Taylor had been a states' rights man before the war, serving in the North Carolina legislature when the Ordinance of Secession was adopted. He had never questioned the right of a state to secede, but thought it should be resorted to only as "the final constitutional remedy." That point had been reached, he felt, when Lincoln called for troops to subjugate the Southern states, "and turned every wavering mind into an ardent supporter of states' rights." [53]

In February 1862, Taylor relinquished the duties of legislator and rice planter to don the Confederate gray of his new country. In that month, he was appointed commanding officer of "Captain John D. Taylor's Company of Heavy Artillery N. C. Volunteers," and he and his outfit were stationed at Fort Johnston. The company soon became Company K of the Thirty-Sixth Regiment North Carolina Troops, at which time Taylor was commissioned Major of the regiment. He went to Fort Fisher for a while, and was later reassigned to second in command at Fort Caswell, Company K and other units of the Thirty-Sixth Regiment being based there. Taylor was a personal friend of General Whiting, and had served as a groomsman in his wedding.[54]

By spring of 1863, Major Taylor, Colonel Jones, and their men at Caswell had transformed the fort into a deadly bastion, compared with its almost dilapidated condition when the war began. Captain Charles Boggs of the *U.S.S. Sacramento* reported on May 14, 1863, that it appeared the Confederates had stopped work on Fort Caswell, evidently because there was not much else that could be done to improve it. "It presents to us," he said, "the appearance of impregnability from assaults by ironclads or land batteries. All the guns of the main work work are casemated; covered with at least two thicknesses of railroad iron, backed with palmetto logs. The original work has been faced with 15 feet of sand. The eastern face of the fort appears to be (even between the casemates) ironclad; and the sand hills for a distance of 2 1/2 miles to the westward of the fort have been plowed up and leveled, leaving no cover for an advance on that side." [55]

Boggs also said information gathered from escaped slaves, as well as observations made from shipboard, seemed to indicate that fortifications were going up on Smith's Island. The "rebels are now throwing up batteries near the light-house on that island," he reported to Admiral Lee, and as the island was believed to be the key of the position "if allowed to perfect their defenses there no human means can dislodge them." [56] As had been proposed back in the winter, when General Whiting's fears of a heavy attack on Wilmington had almost come to fruition, Boggs recommended that Smith Island be occupied by Union troops. The troops could be landed on the east side of the island, protected by gunboats, he said. Once they had secured it, which at this stage would not be too difficult, mortar batteries could be erected near the lighthouse.

The purpose of the mortars would be to bombard Fort Caswell, which "would crush in the casemates, demolish the fort, and cause a surrender. The way would then be open for the ironclads to enter the river, gain the rear of the works on Federal Point north of the shoals, cut off all communications, and force a surrender of that post. This would give us the entire coast of North Carolina, effectually close this port, at all times difficult to, and which never can be effectually blockaded." [57]

This plan to secure the mouth of the Cape Fear never was adopted, partly because much Union effort was being expended in the assaults on Charleston at this time, and later because the Confederates had done just what Boggs feared, perfected their defenses.

If work on Fort Caswell had ceased for the time being, it was going full speed ahead on Confederate Point. The huge slopes of the Mound were being prepared and protected with grass sods, while large parties of men were daily at work on top, preparing the position for guns. Several hundred yards north of Fort Fisher, a new battery opened up by trying out "the range of its guns" on June 3. Work parties were preparing casemates and enlarging another battery, which was not quite a mile south of the northeast corner of Fort Fisher, while other batteries near the head of Myrtle Sound, four and a half miles northeast of Fisher, had been reoccupied. Often, Colonel Lamb's men fired their Whitworths from these batteries, which appeared to be built "all along the beach as far as Masonboro Inlet." [58]

On June 18, the Mound Battery got off its first shot of the war, almost hitting the *U.S.S. Mount Vernon*, while that Yankee gunboat fired at a steamer lying under protection of the Rebel guns. The *U.S.S. State of Georgia* wasn't quite so lucky. On the 17th, the day before the Mound gunners defiantly announced their arrival, the *State of Georgia* was following a lead-colored, side-wheeled blockade runner, when she was struck a shattering blow from a 120-pound Whitworth shell. "It came in over the starboard wheelhouse," reported Commander James Armstrong, "passed through the hurricane deck about 4 feet from starboard rail, splitting and splintering the carline, then struck the main deck about 14 feet forward, abreast the main hatch, passed through the double deck, split and carried away about 2 1/2 feet of a carline, and down, striking the berth deck 8 feet forward, splintering the deck and starting a carline. The shot then rebounded and fell on the berth deck. I regret to say that a landsman was severely and two petty officers slightly wounded by the splinters." [59]

The continuance of such encounters between William Lamb's people and the Yankee sailors was a certainty, given the necessity of supplies for the besieged Confederacy, and the tremendous profits to be reaped by blockade running mercantile firms. Confederate Captain John Wilkinson, commander of the *Robert E. Lee*, former *Giraffe*, estimated that after five trips were made by a runner, the steamer would have paid for itself and would be bringing in a monthly profit of almost $92,000 for the owner of the vessel. Finding competent men to handle the ship was no obstacle, either, as the captain of a private steamer was paid $5,000 per month, the first officer $600, the purser $1,000, and even stewards and cooks received $150. As a Confederate naval officer, Wilkinson refused to work for a Liverpool firm at an exorbitant salary, preferring to command government vessels at his officer's wages. [60]

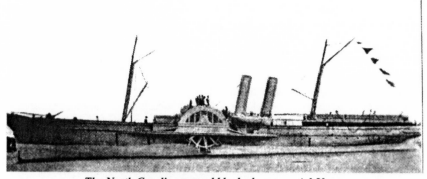

The North Carolina-owned blockade runner Ad-Vance

Most crews of the blockade runners were comprised of Englishmen, Wilkinson said, and the wages brought from shipping out on one made it tough on the British Navy. "The English men-of-war on the West India station found it a difficult matter to prevent their crews from deserting, so great was the temptation offered by the blockade-runners." [61]

One of the most famous of those runners, the North Carolina owned *Ad-Vance*, captained by Commander Thomas Crossan, made her first arrival in the Cape Fear on Friday, the 26th of June, 1863. Her ownership by the state for the furnishing of supplies to soldiers and civilians, was the brainchild of North Carolina's Adjutant General, J.G. Martin. He successfully counseled for such an enterprise with the thirty-two year old governor, Zebulon Vance, former commanding officer of the Twenty-Sixth North Carolina Troops, who succeeded Governor Clark in September 1862. [62]

"The *Ad-Vance* was a first class ship in every respect; she had engines of great power which were very highly finished and her speed was good. With a pressure of twenty pounds to the square inch she easily averaged seventeen knots to the hour and when it was increased to thirty pounds, she reeled off twenty knots without difficulty." The ship was heavy of size and draft, however, and had trouble crossing the Cape Fear shoals, "in consequence of which she could never go out or return with a full cargo either of cotton or supplies." [63]

Originally named the *Lord Clyde*, she was built to run the Irish Sea between Glasgow and Dublin. Commander Crossan, assisted by Governor Vance's financial agent in England, John White, had purchased the ship for North Carolina. "When her elegant saloons and passenger arrangements were cut away, she could carry with ease 800 bales of cotton and a double supply of coal." [64]

North Carolina's sleek vessel was carrying a valuable and much needed cargo when she pulled into the mouth of the Cape Fear on that Friday in late June. In her hold were 203 boxes and bales of uniform material that comprised over 9,500 yards of army cloth and over 6,600 yards of gray flannel.

There were "252 blankets, 400 pairs of shoes, 387 gross of buttons, 500 pounds of thread, 90 sacks of coffee, 21 cases of mill supplies, 2 trusses of mill equipment, 1 case of wire, 4 casks of bleaching powder, 26 boxes and 2 casks of medical supplies, 3 boxes of surgical instruments, 37 kegs of rum 13 boxes of brandy, 2 boxes of stationary." [65]

Governor Vance came to Wilmington as soon as he heard of the arrival of the *Ad-Vance*. On Sunday, June 28, he and some of his friends and dignitaries took one of the river steamers down the Cape Fear to the quarantine station at Fort Anderson, about sixteen miles below the city, where all blockade runners were required to dock for a certain period of time. This was primarily to determine if they were carrying yellow fever, to prevent an epidemic disaster from striking Wilmington again, as had happened the previous summer and fall.

Gov. Zebulon Vance

The Governor and his party spent several hours on board the ship, enjoying the hospitality of her officers, when it was decided to steam up to Wilmington, foregoing the health requirements, the Governor's presence on board presumed to be sufficient for doing so. [66]

No sooner had the *Ad-Vance* docked at the Wilmington wharf, than one of General Whiting's staff officers, a Major Strong, arrived on the scene. He declared in a loud and commanding voice, that no one on board could leave the ship, as it was in violation of quarantine regulations, and must immediately return to the quarantine station downriver. Governor Vance was near the gangway at this time, and distinctly heard Major Strong's imperious and rudely delivered announcement. The Governor was outraged, and with "flashing eyes" he immediately responded to the major. "Do you dare to say, sir, that the Governor of the State shall not leave the deck of his own ship?" Strong's reply was "of such a nature as to add fuel to the flames, and an exciting scene would doubtless have occurred (for the Governor was young then and his blood was hot) had not his friends interposed and persuaded him to retire to the cabin, where, after a while, his equanimity was restored." [67]

P.W. Fanning, who was Chairman of the Board of Commissioners of Navigation, was sent for to settle the discord. He soon arrived and gave his permission for the ship to remain where she was, and for all who desired to leave the vessel to do so. Vance was the first person to exit the ship, respectfully saluting Mr. Fanning as he came down. He then declared in a "ringing voice" for all to hear, "No man is more prompt to obey the civil authority than myself, but I will not be ridden over by epaulettes or bayonets." As the hotheaded young warrior-governor, who just a year ago had been on the blood-soaked Seven Days battlefield with his troops, strode out of sight, the large crowd that had congregated gave him three hearty cheers for his dash, and then added three cheers more for the sleek-looking, flag-bedecked blockade runner. [68]

The *Ad-Vance* slipped out of Wilmington three weeks later, without hindrance from the Yankee blockaders, with a load of cotton bound for Bermuda. When she returned on Monday, August 17, she carried 250 packages of cargo for North Carolina, 150 for the Confederacy, and 25 were consigned to private merchants. The value of North Carolina's cargo was $44,174.40, and consisted of "4,100 pairs of shoes, 6,404 blankets, 9,287 yards of army cloth, 6,210 yards gray flannel, 120 pieces of flannel, 500 pounds of thread, 477 gross of buttons, 10 cases of medicine, 1 cask of medicine, 12 cases of stationery, including ink, wax, pencils, pens, etc., 100 boxes of tin plate, 4 casks of powder, 6 barrels of oil, 1 roll of driving band, 1 case of wire, 2 trusses of web felt." [69]

William H. Oliver, of Newbern, was appointed by Governor Vance to be cotton- purchasing agent for North Carolina. In this capacity, he paid twenty cents a pound for all he could get his hands on, eventually buying 7,000 bales for about $700,000. Much was consigned to run the blockade on the *Ad-Vance*, but not all of it.

A substantial portion of the state purchased cotton was consigned to Saxapahawee Factory, in Alamance County, run by John Newlan & Sons. The cotton was to be fabricated into yarn and cloth. "The cloth was delivered to the Quarter Master for the use of the army, and the yarn was exchanged in Virginia for leather, which was made into shoes." Large amounts of the state purchased cotton not consigned to manufacturing plants was stored in facilities at Graham, North Carolina. [70]

Among the very valuable commodities that the *Ad-Vance* brought in for the state were metal cotton and wool combs, or cards, seven thousand pair of them, and five machines for making cotton cards, with sufficient wire to sustain them for a year. The card machines were set up in a factory owned by a Mr. William Willard, and a tremendous number of pairs of the cards were manufactured and distributed throughout the state. These cards were essential for converting raw cotton and wool into usable material for spinning and weaving. [71]

Two weeks after Governor Vance almost came to blows with Major Strong over the *Ad-Vance*, William Lamb and his artillerists clashed with the Yankees over another blockade runner. The steamer *Kate*, out of London, was driven ashore "twelve miles south of Fort Fisher," on Bald Head Island on Sunday morning, July 12, the *Daily Journal* told its readers in its July 14th edition. [72]

She had been forced to beach about five o'clock in the morning, when the U.S. Gunboat *Penobscot*, commanded by Lt. Commander Joseph DeHaven, a veteran sailor off the Wilmington coast now, had spotted her trying to run into New Inlet, and had chased the ship while firing on her. DeHaven reported she had run aground "with a full head of steam, her officers and crew deserting her. She proved to be the iron steamer *Kate*, Captain Stubbs, a new vessel, of 344 tons, English built, about three months old, and, from her log, bound from Nassau to Charleston with a general cargo." [73]

Because the blockade had become "very strong at Charleston," the *Kate*, like many other vessels recently, was trying to run into Wilmington to deliver her wares. Commander DeHaven dispatched a boat under Acting Master Charles Jack, with the intention of getting her off the beach and securing her for Mr. Lincoln. Her aft was afloat, and it was felt she could be taken off when the tide was in. For several hours they tried, to no avail. By mid-afternoon, Rebel troops were on hand, and the Yankees decided to blow up the *Kate*. Jack reported that he "started a large fire on the starboard side of the vessel near the engines, placing four 20-pound charges of powder close to the fire, thinking that I should have time to leave the vessel before it exploded." [74]

While the bluejackets worked feverishly, William Lamb and his roving Rebel gunners began to arrive on the scene. The *Daily Journal* reported that he "sent about a hundred sharp-shooters via Long Beach, and having sent for the steamer *Congaree*, tried to get a Whitworth gun over, but finally had to carry it via the Light House. The Col. arrived at the main bar about 9 o'clock on Sunday morning, and from that point to Bald Head Beach had to encounter a very severe fire from the blockaders off Caswell, next from both blockading squadrons and lastly from the New Inlet blockaders." [75]

The first troops he brought up, the "sharp-shooters," were from 1st Company I, Thirty-Sixth North Carolina Troops, who came over from Fort Pender at Smithville, being the ones the *Daily Journal* reported moving via Long Beach. Sergeant Thaddeus Davis of Company I, said that his men were "subject to a severe shelling from the fleet," and that Colonel Lamb also had to send Company B of the Fortieth Regiment North Carolina Troops (3rd Regiment Artillery) from Fort Fisher, and Captain Malcom McBryde's Scotch Greys Artillery, later to be named Company E of the Fortieth Regiment, from Fort Caswell. [76]

Davis said the Scotch Greys were first-rate Confederate soldiers from Richmond and Robeson Counties, having in their ranks "many descendants of Highlanders who fought under Lochiel at the fatal battle of Culloden, and who displayed on the sands of Carolina the war-like spirit of their ancestors." There was without question a distinctly Scottish flavor to this company, the first captain's last name being McNair, the present one's McBryde, and the three lieutenants bearing Highland surnames of McArther, McKinnon, and McNair. In addition, the muster rolls showed that 45 of the enlisted men had last names beginning with "Mc" and other Scot surnames such as Davis, Duncan, Douglas, Kennedy, Lewis, Stewart and Southerland were well represented. [77]

These descendants of the fierce Celtic clans were ferried over from Caswell with one of their Whitworths, and in late morning began moving into position behind the sand hills and high chaparral to shell the Yankees trying to destroy the blockade runner. About 11 o'clock the fleet off Old Inlet spotted the Scotch Greys and sharpshooters, and opened up a heavy bombardment on them, hitting and disabling the Whitworth gun carriage, forcing the men to take cover while awaiting reinforcements. [78]

Now more Rebels pitched into the fray, Company B of the Fortieth Regiment from Fort Fisher, a companion regiment to the Thirty-Sixth, coming in at the double-quick with rifles and another Whitworth. They moved rapidly "up the beach under a constant fire from the blockading fleet," which one Union officer said was directed at the woods behind the steamer to "harass and annoy the enemy." The Confederates fought "most handsomely," and drove off four steamers with their deadly British fieldpiece, "when they were enfiladed by the ships off the beach, upon which they came round and drove the Yankees from the stranded ship," driving off the vessels near her as well. [79]

The Confederates were "subjected to a severe fire of grape, canister and shell," but kept up their fire with musketry and Whitworth bolts. Colonel Lamb said that "nearly every shot took effect and the blockaders could not afford to be seriously damaged in the contention over a craft they expected at any moment would be blown up." [80]

The bluejackets thought the *Kate* was heavily damaged "by fire and shell," and that "her cargo, as far as could be judged, a complete loss." This was far from so, however, as Fort Fisher's young commandant boarded the *Kate* after driving the Union gunboats out of range, found the ship was about to blow, and risking life and limb, put out the slow match and threw overboard the powder Mr. Jack had planted. Her cargo was saved and all her machinery removed and sent to Richmond, where it was later to be used in the Confederate ram *Texas*. [81]

While Lamb had his men working diligently to clear the *Kate* of her cargo and machinery down at the end of Smith Island, which he said was about six miles below Fort Fisher (the *Daily Journal* thought it was twelve), his artillerists on Confederate Point were as alert as ever to their opportunities. Just three days after the battle for the *Kate*, Ensign J.B. Breck of the *U.S.S. Niphon* reported being fired on by "a new battery of two heavy guns," which he thought were 100 pound rifles, as he cruised about five miles northeast of Fort Fisher. He also stated there were three additional batteries of small rifled cannon, "and one field battery which is transported along the beach and planted where it is needed." Breck said the batteries had many times fired on the

Niphon as she cruised in 35-40 feet of water, the long-range shells passing over the vessel. [82]

On August 1, a Saturday, a little over two weeks after the initial battle for the *Kate*, another and more severe encounter occurred. By the night of July 31, the Rebels had completely unloaded and gutted the interior of the blockade runner of anything usable. That night, they were also able to get her off the beach, and by early morning of the first of August were towing her with some small boats toward Fort Fisher. Lieutenant James Trathen, commanding the *U.S.S. Mount Vernon*, was ordered to move in and cut her off "or destroy her," along with the help of the *James Adger*. The *Kate*'s commander, Master William Stubbs, said the screw steamer was in a vulnerable position about five miles from Fort Fisher, with the ebb tide going out at this time, and that he had been compelled to anchor, which position he was still in when the Yankees discovered him at daylight. [83]

The *Mount Vernon* began firing on the *Kate* about 7 a.m., and soon after ran in alongside to board her and take possession. William Stubbs and his crew had to get off the blockade runner fast, or else they would wind up in a Yankee prison. The bluecoats shelled the Rebels "furiously," as the men retreated to the beach in their small boats. [84]

If the Federals were making it warm for the blockade runner's crew and assisting Confederate soldiers, the "fire from the rebel batteries at this time was terrific." Lamb's artillerists at the Mound Battery, three miles away, on Zeke's Island two miles away, and "a masked battery of Whitworth flying artillery" only 300 yards away on Smith Island, blasted away at the *Mount Vernon* with fatal accuracy. [85]

First-Class Fireman Edwin H. Peck was "killed by a Whitworth rifle shot, which passed through the side of the vessel into the engine room, cutting both of Peck's legs off." The *Mount Vernon* was hit with other shots as well, mainly from the Whitworth gun and heavy Armstrong rifles. An Armstrong shell "cut away the fore-topmast rigging, and another, also a Whitworth, cut away the fore-gaff; a fifth shot, fired from the Mound battery and apparently from a heavy Armstrong gun, cut away the stock of the port anchor." Many other Secessionist shells struck over and around the Union vessel as they secured the empty blockade runner, and finally towed her out to sea, their dead sailor having paid the price for it. [86]

Two days later, William Stubbs published in the *Daily Journal* a "Card of Thanks" to Colonel Lamb and company, for their exertions in trying to save the *Kate*, so she could run again another day. Stubbs recounted the battle of mid-July, in which Lamb had saved the runner while she sat grounded on "Bald Head Point below Fort Fisher." He then told of how she had finally been taken. "Under the circumstances," he said, "it was impossible for any further assistance to reach us. But I would feel recreant to all gratitude and self-respect were I to withhold the public expression of my sincere thanks for the extreme efforts and vigilance exercised by Col. Lamb, and the officers and men under him, during my misfortune." Stubbs also expressed his appreciation for help rendered him by the Confederate Naval officers and men of the ironclad *North Carolina.* [87]

By the summer of 1863, life on Confederate Point for William Lamb was more than just blockade runners and artillery duels with Union gunboats. His lovely wife "Daisy", a petite beauty with hazel eyes, dark golden hair and rosebloom complexion, had come down with their two oldest children from

Sarah Chaffee "Daisy" Lamb, with her daughter

Providence, Rhode Island, to share his life and his cause to the fullest extent. When she arrived in Wilmington, after having much of her luggage and clothing stolen by Yankee officials when she crossed over into Dixie, she was offered the use of a fine home in town, but declined it. She was even asked to stay at the elegant old plantation home of Orton near Fort Anderson, but declined that as well. Instead, she took up residency in the upper floor of Cape Fear pilot James N. Craig's house, about a mile north of Fort Fisher on the river, Craig's domicile and property being aptly named Craig's Landing. Craig's son, James William, called "Jim Billy" by his friends, was also a pilot, and shipped out on the blockade runners. [88]

While Daisy Lamb lived in Mr. Craig's house, Will, as she called the Colonel, had some of the soldiers of the garrison build her a small cottage on the ocean side of Confederate Point. She was most anxious for it to be built, and on June 30, 1863, wrote her mother in Rhode Island to tell her that she was "at last settled in my little new house and am very comfortable indeed. I wish you could see us. We moved in last Thursday and every thing is finished about us except the little bedroom to be taken off the back porch and the kitchen which is to be built out. I suppose to you just coming from our sweet beautiful home everything would look homely and plain enough but to me who have for the last six months been staying in such poor little places this looks quite charming, it is a dreary situation having no trees about it, but the beautiful view we have of the river nearly compensates for the want of them. —the doors and all the woodwork is Southern pine varnished – a very pretty carved wooden mantle piece painted black and the windows consist of two very larges panes of plait glass, there is also a pane in each of the doors. I have plain white cotton shades to all the windows. —My bed room has a pine bedstead with hair mattress, which when made up neatly with white quilt looks very well. A pine bureau and looking glass above - a pine wash stand, chairs and wardrobe, the children's room has much the same – on my back porch is a store room, or closet which is well filled with tea, coffee, flour – cheeses, preserves – pickles all kinds of sauces, sardines, white and brown sugar, flour &c., &c., our crockery is all white – what little we have, we have some pretty tumblers and wine glasses. —I sent to Bermuda for some bedding we needed but did not send for any table linen I thought we could do without it, and I did not wish to encumber myself with too many things in case we are driven from here in a hurry. —I have a nice little cellar under the back porch a safe and a dining table. We frequently take our meals out there, so you see I am quite comfortably fixed, and really enjoy my little home very much it is so cool and quiet our rooms are high and we keep them clean and fortunately are not infested with fleas like our neighbors though we have a few. — You don't know how much I miss ladies society. I get so tired of seeing nothing or nobody but

The cottage Will and Daisy Lamb lived in, north of Fort Fisher's earthen walls.

men – though I meet some very agreeable ones, there is seldom a week passes that I do not have several gentlemen to dine, one or more at a time.—

"If you enclose your letters to me in an envelope directed to Miss Emma Bashum, St. George, Bermuda, (do not put our address on the envelope – but on the inside) they can not fail to come in that way – she is an old friend of Will's and knows all our Blockade running Captains, do not mention this to any one.

"We are very anxious to hear from Norfolk we have heard that persons there not taking the oath of allegiance to the U.S are to be sent South, and so are expecting Father and Mother to come through, I should hate to have them give up their property there, though would be glad to have them nearer us, if they should have to leave couldn't you and Pa secure some of Will's books – it seems such a pity, there he has over two thousand books – it would be a great loss and I wish you had my bedding and table linen to save for me. The furniture will have to all go I suppose." [89]

Daisy Lamb worked diligently to develop a normal routine for herself and family, despite the adversity of wartime conditions. They usually ate breakfast around seven or eight a.m., Will leaving afterward for Fort Fisher. She had lunch waiting on him when he returned about one p.m. After lunch, she would straighten up around the house, and then sit down for a while to sew, the children playing outside in the meantime. She might read or write for a spell, daydreaming of home with her mother and father, and before long her handsome husband/colonel returned from his duties at the fort to partake of supper with them. After supper, Will would lie down on the sofa, while Daisy read aloud something they both enjoyed. Relaxed by the meal and the presence of family, as well as the exertions of the day's activities, the young wavy-haired officer that Sarah Lamb loved so deeply would drift off to sleep for a much needed rest.

After his nap, Will rode back to the fort for what was usually the last time of the day, returning to tea about 6 or 6:30 p.m. Mail came after tea, and Will and his brother Robert, who was a captain and Assistant Quartermaster of the Thirty-Sixth Regiment, occupied themselves with the newly received correspondence until about 9 o'clock. Daisy would walk on her piazza for exercise during this time, gazing at the stars and "wishing this wicked war was over or I had more patience – then after reading and saying my prayers – I have a search for fleas – and retire." [90]

Daisy told her mother that they frequently had gentlemen for tea as well as dinner. "The Surgeon here is a great friend of mine," she said, "and I am always glad to see him and enjoy my chats with him. Sometimes my neighbors – the females I mean call to see me – but I cannot say their society is very agreeable. We are enlivened considerably when Steamers arrive and I have large packages of presents to overhaul. As I had this morning, a barrel full of good things tea, coffee, white sugar, all kinds of sauces, pickles etc., etc., besides fruit." [91]

She was often lonely, being isolated as she was, living so near the formidable defenses her Confederate husband had erected, but Sarah Lamb's heart was with the Colonel's cause and his men. She often availed herself of the "opportunity to serve the sick and wounded soldiers and sailors." Daisy cared for them deeply, and did all she could to alleviate their suffering, and provide for their comfort. Because of her concern for them, and ministrations to them when needed, the men of the Thirty-Sixth Regiment dubbed their commanding officer's Yankee born, now Southern patriot wife, the "Angel of the Fort." [92]

Shortly after Daisy Lamb and family got settled in to their new home, and a little more than two weeks after the fierce engagement for the blockade runner *Kate*, another severe fight took place, just a few miles north of the Lamb's "Cottage," as they styled it, for yet another Anglo-Rebel steamer. This one was called the *Hebe*.

This vessel was one of the first of the sleek, highly maneuverable double-screw steamers. She initially loaded out from London in the first week of May 1863, carrying many packages of supplies for the Confederate Quartermaster's Department, as well as other cargo for the Navy. The *Hebe* was one of four new double-screws specially purchased for the Confederate War Department by Mr. William Crenshaw, from the British shipbuilding firm of Alexander Collie & Company. The other three ships were scheduled for completion on May 10, June 30, and July 15. Another recently purchased ship was the *Venus*, also loading for sea in the first week of May. [93]

The Confederate States already owned four other blockade runners by the spring of 1863. They were the *Giraffe* or *Robert E. Lee*, which had been brought into Wilmington by Captain Wilkinson, the *Cornubia* or *Lady Davis*, which Signal Corpsman Frederick Gregory had helped bring in with his ship-to-shore lamp messages, the *Eugenie*, and the *Merrimac*. These ships had been purchased by Major Caleb Huse for ferrying the mountains of supplies he had procured for the Ordnance and Medical Departments. The *Merrimac*, however, was captured at sea, "about 40 miles east of Masonboro Inlet," on July 24, with heavy loss tallied against some citizens of Wilmington, who had invested in her cargo of cotton, tobacco and turpentine. Capture of the *Merrimac*, then, reduced the Confederacy's ownership of blockade runners from nine to eight by the end of July. [94]

The *Hebe* was one of those eight, and on Tuesday, August the 18th, she was headed for New Inlet from Bermuda, "with a full cargo of coffee, drugs and medicines, clothing, and a few bales of silk." At 4:45 in the morning, while she was about nine miles northeast of Fort Fisher, making for Colonel Lamb's protective guns, the *Hebe* was spotted by the *U.S.S. Niphon*. Acting Ensign J.B. Breck, commander of the *Niphon*, ordered his men to give chase; the *Hebe* ran for shore, grounded about seven miles north of the fort on the barrier island due east of the head of Myrtle Sound, and the officers and crew escaped to the beach in life boats. [95]

Quickly, Ensign Breck dispatched a boatload of men under Acting Ensign W.W. Crowninshield with orders to board and burn the blockade runner, as there was no hope of getting her off the beach, she being well grounded in only seven feet of water, and also due to a northeast gale blowing a heavy sea. The Yankees found the ship's "engines still in motion," reported Ensign E.H. Dewey of the boarding party, "but the engineer finding no water in the boilers and no means of getting any into them, hauled the fires. We immediately commenced gathering together combustibles in the after cabin and forehold, using bulkheads, furniture, etc. to spread the flames should it become necessary to burn her." [96]

About 5:45 a.m., another cutter under Coxswain John Laroach, with four other seamen, came to render assistance, but their boat was swamped and they had to wade ashore. They were greeted by Confederate cavalry and forced to surrender. About 8 o'clock, more grayback horsemen, about forty of them, came on the scene and took cover behind the sand hills, opening up on the boarding party and the *U.S.S. Niphon* with rapid firing of musketry. These Rebels were soon joined by some of William Lamb's cannoneers, who fired a Whitworth and a Fawcett & Preston rifle at almost point-blank range. Oddly enough, a Whitworth shell never struck the Yankee gunboat in a vulnerable spot, possibly because heavy gale induced swells caused the *Niphon* to pitch and bounce, rendering its hull all the more difficult to hit. Some of the rigging, however, was partly destroyed, and Ensign Breck's vessel had been struck many times with rifle fire. [97]

About 10:30 a.m., Lieutenant William B. Cushing, commanding the *U.S.S. Shokokon*, sent in a boat to help get Crowninshield and his party off the *Hebe*, while Breck sent another cutter in as well. Crowninshield's crew had initially set the *Hebe* on fire about the time the cavalry came on the scene, around 8 o'clock, but their boat was stove in and sunk as they made ready to leave the Rebel ship, so they put out the fires and stayed aboard, waiting for help. Only those who could swim, then, five of the boarding party, leapt from the *Hebe* into the sea, and four of them made it to the *Niphon's* and *Shokokon's* rescue boats. [98]

Cushing now fired on the *Hebe* in her forward section, to warn the other Yankees to get off, which they did, so the *Shokokon* and *Niphon* could destroy her. Cushing reported that after Crowninshield's crew had made it to the beach, "we commenced a heavy fire, that soon riddled her. Twice she was on fire from our shells, and twice the sea extinguished the flames, but just after a shell exploded abaft the smokestack her decks blazed up and continued to burn until she was a wreck. Our fire was kept up at from 100 to 300 yards' range. The rebel artillery was used against us about four hours, but all their shell passed over us and did no injury. The vessel was somewhat marked by musket bullets." [99]

Ensign Breck reported that the *Niphon* shelled the blockade runner for three hours, and that he "saw some men lying on the beach killed." They must have been some of the fifteen sailors listed as missing in action from the *Niphon*'s crew, among them Ensign William Crowninshield, as the only casualty suffered by the Confederates was a Corporal Hall of Braddy's Company C, of the Thirty-Sixth North Carolina. Hall reportedly was hit by a shell fragment, suffering a severe wound in one of his arms. [100]

In addition to losing three boats and fifteen sailors, the Federals lost or expended at least five revolvers, "6 rifles, 9 pistols, 10 cutlasses, 54 32-pounder shell and cartridges, 26 Parrott shell and cartridges, 32 howitzer shell and cartridges, 95 rifle shell and cartridges, 50 revolver cartridges, 10 musket cartridges, 1 battle-ax." They had also had to retreat. [101]

They had likewise failed to accomplish their desired destruction, for salvage work began soon on the *Hebe*. Some of the civilian owners of cargo came down from Wilmington to the beach to engage in that enterprise, and were aided by a portion of the troops of Captain Daniel Munn's 3rd Company of the Thirty-Sixth Regiment, and Lieutenant Henry Benton's Whitworth battery, 2nd Company C of the Thirty-Sixth. Salvaging operations continued until Sunday, August 23, when the Rebels halted to observe the Sabbath. They were not, however, to be allowed that luxury. [102]

Early that morning, about seven o'clock, the Yankee flagship *Minnesota*, with Admiral Samuel Lee aboard, steamed unexpectedly from its normal anchorage, which was generally five miles out when Whitworths were known to be near. She came up within 600 yards of the *Hebe*, while the *U.S.S.*

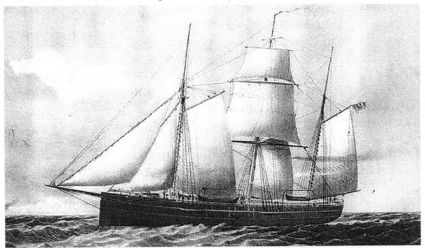

USS Niphon, *on patrol off the Cape Fear*

James Adger steamed to within 300 yards, both vessels firing on the beach and at Captain Munn's detachment of about fifty troops, consisting of Lieutenant Benton's Whitworth gun, and a Fawcett and Preston 4-inch rifled gun. The troops not manning one of the cannon were armed with rifles. [103]

The Federals "commenced a terrific bombardment of the surrounding shore, throwing at one time thirty shells a minute." The Rebels had no prepared battery works in this area as they did further south, and relied on the natural sand dunes and several feet of hastily thrown up earth and sand to protect them from the fast firing monstrous guns that belched 100 and 150 pound shells the size of exploding nail kegs. The *Minnesota* alone carried more guns than were mounted in Fort Fisher, and sound military prudence dictated that Captain Munn, Lieutenant Benton and their men abandon their position and retreat. Instead, Colonel Lamb proudly reported his warriors "defiantly stood their ground and fired on the boat sent by the *James Adger* with a tow line toward the *Hebe*, driving her back, wounding one of the crew." [104]

Boatswain's Mate John Deuchars of the *James Adger* received a flesh wound, as he and some other sailors under Ensign Charles F. Keith tried to come ashore to determine if they could haul the blockade runner back out to sea. The Confederates sprayed the surf with bullets and rifled shells, and the Yankees had to hurry back to their ship.

After their repulse, about 8:30 a.m., the *Minnesota* and *James Adger* "opened a fiercer bombardment of shell, shot, grape and canister, the *Minnesota* discharging broadside after broadside," and the huge missiles began tearing into the Confederates. Private Daniel Holland, just 17 years old when he enlisted the previous month in Captain Munn's Bladen Stars, died instantly when a Parrott shell tore into him. Private Singletary, also of Munn's company, was hit and wounded. Second Lieutenant Benton and Corporal Hockaday of the Whitworth battery were also wounded in the fusillade. [105]

As the bursting shells tore up the sand and sprayed jagged iron splinters in all directions, the Rebels aimed and fired their pieces with coolness and accuracy. At least one bolt hit the *Minnesota*, while others passed directly overhead. The *James Adger* took three shells in her hull, one of the Whitworth bolts cutting braces of the starboard whell, another cutting deck planking over one of the boilers and actually striking the boiler, but doing no damage. Finally, overwhelmed by the bombardment from the two heavy warships, the detachment was forced to retreat with their dead and wounded. The Whitworth was dismounted by a naval shell and so was unmovable, and they buried the Fawcett & Preston rifle in the sand. The *U.S.S. Niphon* moved south down the beach parallel to the retreating Tar Heels, firing at them 172 times with her guns, but none of the Confederates were hit during the escape toward Fort Fisher. [106]

With the Rebels out of the way now, Commander N.B. Harrison of the *Minnesota* commenced a well aimed and deliberate bombardment of the *Hebe*, she being so filled with water as to preclude her being towed out to sea, to insure her boilers and machinery were beyond salvaging for the Confederates. At 10:30 a.m. a launch and four cutters were dispatched to the shore under Fleet Captain Peirce Crosby, who brought off the Whitworth rifle and the Fawcett and Preston gun. The Whitworth carriage was marked "No. 220," and the gun was eight feet ten inches in length, while the Fawcett & Preston rifle was six feet eleven inches long. The Whitworth had been manufactured in Manchester, and the other had been made in Liverpool. The Yankees also found a caisson and limber for the Whitworth, shot and shells, and powder charges. Eighteen shells were found for the Fawcett & Preston piece. Six or seven bales of cloth and blankets, partly damaged by fire, dirt and sea water, were scattered about on the beach, as well as the damaged boats captured from them on the 18th. [107]

During the two to two and a half hour battle, the *Minnesota* expended 162 shot and shell and 1,977 pounds of powder, the *James Adger* 163 shells and 958 pounds of powder, and the *Niphon*, trying to cut off the retreating graycoats, shot away 172 shells and probably about the same amount of powder as the *James Adger*. Altogether, then, the Unionists had burned about two tons of powder while firing nearly 500 shells at fifty Confederates. "A more gallant fight," said William Lamb, "against overwhelming odds was not witnessed during the war." [108]

The woods and homes in the vicinity of the battle "were riddled with shot and shell. Four shot passed through Mr. James Burris' house. The hills around the wreck were furrowed like a ploughed field." [109]

From his headquarters in Wilmington General Whiting wrote Secretary Seddon to inform him of the battle for the *Hebe*. He reported that the Yankees had been initially repulsed by Captain Munn and his troops, but that they had effected a landing about two miles away, and came down on Munn "still gallantly fighting his little guns against the *Minnesota*." The Confederates had been compelled to fall back toward Fort Fisher, losing their artillery in the process. [110]

"The efforts of the enemy to stop our steamers are increasing," Whiting wrote. "Their force is largely increased. I have met with a serious and heavy loss in that Whitworth, a gun that in the hands of the indefatigable Lamb has saved dozens of vessels and millions of money to the Confederate States. I beg that a couple of the Whitworth guns originally saved by him from the *Modern Greece* may be sent here at once. Their long range makes them most suitable for a seaboard position. Could I get them with horses we could save many a vessel that will now be lost to us." [111]

Lamb was definitely in need of another Whitworth on the Confederate Point side of the river, for now he had none. Of the four guns he had pulled out of the hold of the *Modern Greece* the previous summer, he had only been able to retain one on the Fort Fisher side of the Cape Fear. One had gone to Company E of the Fortieth North Carolina stationed at Fort Caswell, and had seen action on Bald Head Island in the fight for the *Kate*. The other two guns had been transferred to the Army of Northern Virginia and had seen action on Oak Ridge at Gettysburg in the first week of July. [112]

Thomas Taylor, the English blockade running agent for the Confederate Trading Company, was as interested as Chase Whiting or William Lamb in having Whitworth guns guard his incoming cargoes. Following the battle for the *Hebe*, Taylor got his Liverpool employers to send Fort Fisher's commander the six new Whitworths, "of which he was very proud; and good use he made of them in keeping the blockaders at a respectful distance. — Lamb would gallop them down behind the sand hills, by aid of mules, and open fire upon the enemy before he was aware of his danger." [113] So while he had lost one Whitworth and a Fawcett & Preston rifle in the fight for the *Hebe*, Fort Fisher's flying artillery more than recouped its loss when the profit-minded British lent a helping hand.

Of more concern to General Whiting than the subject of fieldpieces, though, was the successful landing of two parties of bluecoats in his territory. At the same time Munn and Benton's artillerists were fighting their uneven battle against the three Yankee warships and their landing party, another group of Federals landed north at Topsail and destroyed a salt facility and a schooner, and left with two "artillerymen prisoners." It only confirmed what he had been telling Richmond for months, that he needed more troops in the Wilmington area, particularly since "10,000 of the best troops from this section were sent west to endeavor to save Vicksburg," which was most of those sent to him in January, when Foster's attack on Wilmington was expected daily. [114]

"This is the first time they have landed," Whiting told James Seddon, "but what they have done once they can do again, and doubtless will. There is no day scarcely until the winter gales set in but what they could put 5,000 men on the beach; they can get them from New Berne and Beaufort before I could know it. I only say if they do, they can get either Fort Fisher or the town as they elect, if they set about it at once." [115]

Whiting said that with the tremendous navy and large numbers of troops at their disposal, the Federals could only be successfully repulsed by having enough movable infantry to hammer them when they first hit the shore. "It will not do to let them quietly establish themselves on the islands and approaches, and wait for our re-enforcements, to go through exhausting process of the engineering of siege attack." [116]

Fort Fisher, of course, was being constantly strengthened, but it was designed with the idea of repelling attacks from the sea, not from land. Fisher was essentially "an extensive line of sea-coast batteries connected by covered ways. Its garrison is sufficient to man its guns. The plan of defense here has always been predicated on the support of a movable army, and indeed no other, in my judgment, could be adopted with effect.

"I say now," the general concluded, "that, as far as my opinion in the matter is of value, it is time to commence assembling troops for the defense of Wilmington." [117]

Endnotes to Chapter 4

1. *Official Records of the Union & Confederate Navies*, Volume 8, p.590
2. Ibid, p.338-349
3. Sprunt, Chronicles of the Cape Fear River, p.479
4. O.R.N., Volume 8, p.865
5. Ibid, p.630
6. *Official Records of the Union & Confederate Armies*, Series IV, Vol. II, p.382-384
7. Ibid, p.382
8. Ibid, p.382-383
9. Ibid, p.383
10. Taylor, *Running the Blockade*, p.55 (hereinafter, Running the Blockade); Carse, *Blockade, the Civil War at Sea*, p.34-39 (hereinafter, Blockade)
11. Running the Blockade, p.55-56
12. Ibid, p.56
13. O.R.N., Volume 8, p.630
14. Clark, *Histories of the Several Regiments & Battalions from North Carolina in the Great War, 1861-1865*, Volume V, p.406-407
15. Ibid, p.406
16. Ibid, p.407
17. O.R.N., Volume 8, p.595
18. Ibid, p.595
19. Daly, Robert W. ed. *Aboard the U.S.S. Florida, 1863-1865*, p.xiii, Arno Press, New York, 1980 (hereinafter Aboard the Florida)
20. Ibid, p.11
21. O.R.N., Volume 8, p.700
22. Ibid, p.706
23. Ibid, p.801-802
24. Ibid, p.820
25. Ibid, p.820-821
26. Ibid, p.821
27. Ibid, p.822
28. Ibid, p.823

29. Aboard the Florida, p.27
30. Ibid, p.28
31. Ibid, p.28
32. O.R., Series I, Volume XVIII, p.910-911
33. Ibid, p.892
34. Ibid, p.912
35. Ibid, p.988
36. Ibid, p.1000
37. O.R.N., Volume 8, p.824
38. Aboard the Florida, p.28
39. O.R.N., Volume 8, p.812
40. "Colonel Lamb's Story of Fort Fisher", p.2
41. O.R.N., Volume 8, p.816
42. O.R.N., Volume 9, p.19-20
43. Ibid, p.19
44. Ibid, p.37
45. Daily Journal, May 22, 1863
46. Aboard the Florida, p.23
47. O.R.N., Volume 8, p.560, 563, 570
48. Ibid, p.563
49. Ibid, p.563
50. O.R.N., Volume 9, p.21
51. Chronicles of the Cape Fear River, p.282
52. Ibid, p.282; "Recollections of Colonel John D. Taylor", p.2, North Carolina State Archives, hereinafter Taylor Recollections; *The Wilmington Morning Star*, May 22, 1912
53. Taylor Recollections, p.1
54. Ibid, p.2-4; North Carolina Troops, Volume I, Artillery, p.184, 280, 325
55. O.R.N., Volume 9, p.21
56. Ibid, p.21
57. Ibid, p.21
58. Ibid, p.21
59. Ibid, p.78-79
60. Scharf, *History of the Confederate States Navy,* p.480-481
61. Ibid, p.480-481
62. Hill, *Bethel to Sharpsburg, Volume I*, p.331-334, p.370
63. Clark, Volume V, p.36
64. Ibid, Volume V, p.470-471; "Address Delivered by Governor Z.B. Vance of North Carolina, August 18, 1875", Southern Historical Society Papers, Volume XIV, 1886, p.512
65. Bethel to Sharpsburg, Volume I, p.369
66. Chronicles, p.454; Clark, Volume V, p.359-360
67. Clark, Volume V, p.360; Chronicles, p.454-455

68. Clark, Volume V, p.360-361; North Carolina Troops, Volume VII, p.456-457
69. Bethel to Sharpsburg, Volume I, p.370
70. Oliver, William H., "Blockade Running from Wilmington," Confederate Veteran, Volume III, December 1895, p.361
71. Ibid, p.361
72. Daily Journal, July 14, 1863
73. O.R.N., Volume 9, p.122
74. Ibid, p.120-123
75. Daily Journal, July 14, 1863
76. Clark, Volume II, p.753; North Carolina Troops, Volume I, p.385, 417, 452, 456
77. Clark, Volume II, p.750; North Carolina Troops, Volume I, p.417-425
78. Clark, Volume II, p.750; O.R.N., Volume 9, p.120-122
79. Daily Journal, July 14, 1863; Clark, Volume II, p.748; O.R.N., Volume 9, p.122
80. Daily Journal, July 14, 1863; Clark, Vol. II, p.632
81. Ibid, July 14, 1863; Clark, Volume II, p.632
82. Clark, Volume II, p.632; O.R.N., Volume 9, p.126
83. O.R.N., Volume 9, p.143; Daily Journal, August 3, 1863
84. Ibid, Volume 9, p.143; Daily Journal, August 3, 1863
85. Ibid, Volume 9, p.144
86. Ibid, Volume 9, p.143-144
87. Daily Journal, August 3, 1863
88. Moore, Louis T., "The Heroine of Fort Fisher", Confederate Veteran, Volume XXXVII, July 1929, p.256-257; Chronicles, p.396-406; William Lamb's description of wife, personal papers in author's possession
89. *Letters from the Colonel's Lady*, p.51-55
90. Ibid, p.67-68; North Carolina Troops, Volume I, p.173
91. Ibid, p.68
92. Confederate Veteran, July 1929, p.257
93. O.R., Series IV, Volume II, p.535-537
94. O.R., Series IV, Volume II, p.538; O.R.N., Volume 9, p.131-132; Daily Journal, August 3, 1863
95. O.R.N., Volume 9. p.166-167; Clark, Volume V, p.352; Charles Foard map, June 1968, "A Chart of Wrecks of Vessels Sunk or Captured Near Wilmington, N.C. 1861-1865"
96. Ibid, Volume 9, p.166-167
97. Ibid, Volume 9, p.166-167, p.170-171
98. Ibid, Volume 9, p.166-169
99. Ibid, Volume 9, p.169

100. Ibid, Volume 9, p.167-168; "Hebe Skirmish Centennial and Fort Fisher Visitor Center-Museum Groundbreaking Program", p.3
101. Ibid, Volume 9, p.169
102. Hebe Skirmish program, p.3; Daily Journal, August 24, 1863; North Carolina Troops, Volume I, p.208, 226
103. Daily Journal, Aug. 24, 1863; O.R.N., Volume 9, p.170-171; Clark, Volume V, p.351
104. Ibid, August 24, 1863; O.R.N., Volume 9, p.170; Clark, Volume V, p.351
105. Ibid, August 24, 1863; O.R.N., Volume 9, p.170-172; North Carolina Troops, Volume I, p.207, 212, 217, 226
106. Ibid, August 24, 1863; O.R.N., Volume 9, p.170-172; Clark, Volume V. p.352
107. O.R.N., Volume 9, p.170-171
108. O.R.N., Volume 9, p.170-171; Clark, Volume II, p.633 and Volume V. p.352; Daily Journal, Aug. 24, 1863
109. Daily Journal, August 24, 1863
110. O.R.N., Volume 9, p.173
111. Ibid, Volume 9, p.174
112. Clark, Volume V, p.351; Coddington, *The Gettysburg Campaign, A Study in Command,* p.251, Charles Scribner's Sons, New York, 1968
113. Running the Blockade, p.56; Barrett, *The Civil War in North Carolina,* p.251
114. O.R., Volume XXIX, Part II, p.670-671
115. Ibid, Volume XXIX, Part II, p.671
116. Ibid, Volume XXIX, Part II, p.672
117. Ibid, Volume XXIX, Part II, p.672

"Big" Union School, where Joseph Piram King was enrolled when war broke out.

Chapter 5

"The staid old town of Wilmington was turned topsy-turvy..."

Joe King was just twelve years old in December 1860, the month his father died and South Carolina seceded from the Union. His life as a boy in Wilmington was never the same after that. Just one of the ten thousand people living there when war broke out, the trials and labors of him and his family, mirrored those of many families in this most populous city in the state. [1]

Young Joseph was in his fourth year at the "Union School, a one-room school house on 6th between Church and Nun Streets, taught by one Mr. John Barns" when the secession bells tolled in Raleigh. He was able to "spell and read remarkably well but knew comparatively nothing about mathematics or grammar, having never parsed a sentence in school." It was all the formal education he would ever get. [2]

His four oldest brothers, who in peacetime would be responsible for handling family affairs, and looking after Joe, his mother, sister, and two younger brothers, were all of military age. By mid-summer of 1861, they had enlisted to fight the Yankees, and were gone.[3]

Charles King was twenty when he enlisted as a private in Company D of the Third North Carolina State Troops in May of 1861. During the summer of 1862, while fighting with brothers Isaac and James, also in the Third, in the bloody Seven Days battles outside Richmond, he had become a corporal.

The Old Market House at the foot of Market Street

Shortly before the Battle of Fredericksburg, however, he was demoted to private. Three months after Fredericksburg, in March 1863, he had had a belly full of war, deserted near Port Royal, and in April surrendered to the Federals. He was imprisoned briefly at Old Capitol Prison, but was released on taking the Oath of Allegiance not to take up arms against the United States again. [4]

Brother Isaac Watts enlisted in the same company on the same day with Charles. When he departed for war at the age of twenty-three, Isaac left behind his wife, an infant daughter, and Joe and his other siblings. He was mustered in as a sergeant and a year later was promoted to First Sergeant. In the bloody Battle of Malvern Hill, July 1, 1862, outside Richmond, he was severely wounded in the right shoulder, and had to come back home on furlough to try to recuperate. [5]

Also serving in the Third North Carolina State Troops was nineteen-year-old James Madison King, who joined up in June 1861. In the Maryland Campaign he had been captured at Boonsboro, Maryland two days before the Battle of Sharpsburg while fighting for Major General Daniel Harvey Hill. He was exchanged in November. In the savage battle for Culp's Hill at Gettysburg, James was wounded in action. When the Confederates retreated to Virginia, James was too badly hurt to join the nearly twenty-mile-long wagon train of Rebel wounded winding its way back South in springless wagons and jolting agony.

The seriousness of his wounds may have saved his life, for instead of having to make the grueling journey South that killed many of the wounded, he was captured by the Federals in the field hospital. It was his good fortune to spend about two months in a Federal hospital at Chester, Pennsylvania, where there was sufficient care and medicine to make him well enough to be transferred to Point Lookout, Maryland prison. There he would remain for the next year. [6]

A carpenter in Wilmington and twenty-six years old when he enlisted in July 1861, John Edward, the eldest of the King brothers, joined the famous Wilmington Light Infantry under Captain Henry Savage, which company comprised part of the Eighth Regiment North Carolina Volunteers. John's first duty assignment, in company with the other men of the Eighth, was Confederate Point and Camp Wyatt. Service in Virginia as part of the Eighteenth North Carolina, which the Eighth was redesignated in November 1861, followed. The Eighteenth constituted a part of General Robert E. Lee's Army of Northern Virginia, like the Third, and the bloody engagements of 1862 and 1863 saw the Eighteenth a member of first, Laurence O'B. Branch's Brigade, and after he was killed at Sharpsburg, James H. Lane's Brigade. After Gettysburg, John was promoted to corporal, but feeling the call of the Gospel, he transferred to the Fourteenth Tennessee Infantry as a chaplain in September 1863. [7]

With his brothers gone to war, it remained for young Joe to work to support his family left in Wilmington. They lived in a small house with "four little rooms with a kind of attic of one big room upstairs," situated on the north side of Queen Street "between 6th and 7th Street." [8] Leaving home early in the morning, Joe worked in a slaughterhouse owned by Mr. Thomas H. Johnson, who had a contract with the Confederate government for supplying beef to the Cape Fear area forts, including the Confederate Point garrisons of Fort Fisher and Camp Wyatt.

They also sold meat at several

Joseph Piram King as an old man

stalls in the open air Wilmington Market, located between Front and Water Streets and from which the existing Market Street took its name. On top of the market building was a belfry that rang out the fire alarm for all the town. At the head of the market stairs led to the belfry, and here Mike Cromley, who was an auctioneer partner with Wilkes Morris, an auctioneer of blockade runner cargoes, "would stand and auction off slaves or anything else he had for sale." [9]

Joe's salary was fifty cents per week in cash, plus all the fresh meat his family needed. He could also take home at night trimmings from the slaughtered cattle and sheep, "such as hearts, melts, tails of cattle, beef heads, brains and such like." Having an overabundance of meat and meat trimmings, he sold to neighbors what his family didn't need, gave all his earnings to his mother, and she had soon saved $30.00 from Joe's enterprises, a not inconsiderable sum in 1861. He also bought two hogs from "Uncle John Beasley, one of the colored butchers," and by the time winter of 1861-62 arrived, Joe had "a barrel of fine fat pork for the family." [10]

Because of his age and inexperience, Joe started work as a cleanup boy in the slaughter-house, carrying water for the butchers and sweeping out the blood. He also took the sheep to pasture in the morning and brought them back in the evening in time for slaughter. After several months he was taught how to butcher and dress cattle and sheep, often working until very late at night.

Col. Gaston Meares, C.S.A.

Rising at 3 o'clock in the morning in all kinds of weather, he and his "partner," Jimmie Wells, would hitch their mules to the beef carts and haul the quarter of meat down to the market before dawn. They would go to breakfast, return to the slaughter pen, "chop up heads and feet, boil the oil out and feed the cooked flesh to the hogs, rid the tallow from the entrails, then go home to dinner. We'd sleep an hour or two, then return back to the pen to slaughter more cattle." All in all, it was tough, backbreaking labor for a youngster who turned thirteen in June 1861. [11]

Joe's employer, Mr. Johnson, decided it would be prudent to build a slaughter pen on Confederate Point near Fort Fisher, so as to furnish beef direct to the fort. Joe and Jimmie Wells drove about 30 head of cattle down from Wilmington, a twenty-one mile trip, every week or two, first on foot, then on horseback. They would return to Wilmington the same day, and Joe often fell asleep on his horse riding back to town, being exhausted from the day's labor. [12]

The younger brothers of other Wilmington Confederate soldiers were undoubtedly in similar tough situations as Joseph Piram King, for New Hanover County, with additional men mustered there from several adjoining rural counties, would furnish 4,000 men for service during this war. Companies sent from the Wilmington area were: First Infantry – Company C, Captain J.S.

Hines (commanding), Company E, Captain James A. Wright; Third Infantry – Company D, Captain Edward Savage, Company F, Captain William M. Parsley, Company K, Captain David Williams; Seventh Infantry – Company C, Captain Robert B. McRae; Eighteenth (formerly the Eighth Volunteers) Infantry – Company A, Captain Christian Cornehlson, Company E, Captain John R. Hawes, Company G (Wilmington Light Infantry), Captain Henry R. Savage (formerly Captain William L. DeRosset), Company I, Captain O.P. Meares; Fifty-First Infantry – Company A, Captain John L. Cantwell, Company C, Captain James Robinson, Company E, Captain Willlis H. Pope, Company G, Captain James W. Lippitt, Company H, Captain S.W. Maultsby; Sixty-First Infantry – Company G, Captain J.F. Moore; Sixty-Sixth Infantry – Company K, Captain William C. Freeman; Forty-First Regiment Cavalry – Company A (Rebel Rangers), Captain Abram F. Newkirk; Fifty-Ninth Cavalry – Company C, Captain R.M. McIntire; Second Regiment Artillery (Thirty-Sixth Regiment North Carolina Troops) – Company D, Captain Edward B. Dudley; First Battalion Artillery – Company A, Captain Robert G. Rankin, Company B, Captain Charles D. Ellis, Company C, Captain Alexander MacRae, Company D, Captain James L. McCormack; Fifth Battalion Artillery – Company C, Captain James D. Cumming, Company D, Captain Z.T. Adams; Seventy-Second Junior Reserves – Company D, Captain J.D. Kerr; Seventy-Third Junior Reserves – Company H, First Lieutenant D.J. Byrd; and the Confederate States Navy – 250 men enlisted from the Wilmington area. [13]

Some of Wilmington's finest men wore the gray from the onset, putting the town's families in prideful apprehension of the combat their sons would face to secure Southern independence. Gaston Meares was third son of a distinguished Wilmingtonian, Mr. William B. Meares. Born in 1821, he left for West Point in 1838. Here he studied and drilled until deciding to resign in August 1840. He read law with Governor Swain at Chapel Hill, being admitted to the bar in 1842. In 1844 he moved to southwest Arkansas, opening up shop as an attorney in that frontier state. In 1846, he served as adjutant of Colonel Yell's regiment of Arkansas troops, fought in Mexico, and was elected lieutenant colonel of the regiment. After the Mexican War was over, he returned to family and friends in Wilmington, who presented him with a fine sword in honor of his services to the country. He worked in a commission business for a while in town, then became joint proprietor of a rice plantation on the Brunswick River. In the mid-1850's, Meares moved to New York, where with a Dr. Watson, he established a firm called Watson & Meares.

When North Carolina joined hands with her sisters of the South, however, Gaston Meares came home. He was among the first to buckle on his sword in her defense, Governor Ellis appointing him Colonel of the Third North State Troops on May 16, 1861, to command Joe King's brothers and about 1,000 other men. [14]

Colonel Meares was a handsome man, with sharp features, wavy hair, and a beard without mustache. He "was a man of marked individuality, respected by his superior officers, beloved by his subordinates, and commanded the admiration and confidence of the men of his regiment, for he was always intrepid, and in him they recognized a leader who would lead." [15]

His second in command of the Third North Carolina was Lieutenant Colonel Robert H. Cowan, who was appointed to that rank on the same day Colonel Meares became commanding officer. Cowan was a prominent Wilmingtonian who was active in state politics. He was a gallant gentleman who possessed "charming personality and graceful manners". In April 1862, he left the Third to become colonel of the Eighteenth North Carolina Regiment. [16]

William Lord DeRosset was major of the Third North Carolina, and when Robert Cowan left in April 1862, became lieutenant colonel. DeRosset, a member of "one of the oldest and most prominent families of Wilmington," was the eldest son of six boys of Dr. Armand J. DeRosset. When war erupted in 1861, he was captain and commanding officer of the famous Wilmington Light Infantry. This company, the one John Edward King was part of, was one of the first to occupy Fort Caswell after Fort Sumter and Lincoln's call for troops, and had completed the earthwork on Confederate Point known as Battery Bolles. DeRosset left the Wilmington Light Infantry in May 1861, when he was appointed major in the Third. [17]

Stephen D. Thruston was 28 years old when appointed captain of Company B of the Third North Carolina, in May 1861. He had been in charge of the Smithville Guards in January 1861, when they assisted the Wilmingtonians of the Cape Fear Minute Men in seizing Forts Johnston and Caswell. In the summer of 1862, Thruston was transferred from Company B of the Third, and promoted to major to serve on the field and staff. [18]

The Cape Fear Riflemen had been organized by William M. Parsley in the fall of 1860 and were among the first to occupy Fort Caswell. They became Company F of the Third North Carolina, of which Joe King's brother, James, was a part, in June 1861, and 20-year-old Parsley was appointed captain. His father, O.G. Parsley, bought and paid for uniforms to outfit his son's entire company.

Young Parsley was an excellent officer, one of the finest Wilmington sent to Confederate service. He was most tactful in the discipline of his soldiers. Depending on the time and place, he would act like the youngster he was, and could "enter a wrestling match in camp with all the zest of a schoolboy," at the same time not allowing such off duty antics to preclude proper military decorum when it was called for. In battle, he was exceedingly brave, one of his proud warriors boasted, "kind and considerate towards inferiors in rank, he was at all times thoughtful and careful of his men in every way. I believe all loved him." [19]

John L. Cantwell was a Mexican War veteran. As commanding officer of the Thirtieth Regiment, North Carolina Militia, he had seized Forts Johnston and Caswell in April 1861 upon receiving orders from Governor Ellis to occupy those posts. A native of Charleston, Cantwell had been a cotton broker in Wilmington when war broke out. Waiting several months to join the regular Confederate service, he was 33 years old in December 1861 when he was appointed captain of what was termed Captain John L. Cantwell's Company, North Carolina Volunteers, Wilmington Railroad Guard. The unit was also known as Company A, Wilmington & Weldon Railroad Guards, North Carolina Infantry, and "guarded the bridge over the Roanoke River" in Weldon, and "bridges on the Wilmington & Manchester and Wilmington & Weldon railroads from the South Carolina line to the Roanoke River." [20]

In April 1862, Cantwell was appointed colonel of the Fifty-First North Carolina Troops. Though the unit remained in Wilmington and vicinity for the next several months, he resigned his commission in October for "circumstances of an imperative personal character," and actually reenlisted as a private in Company F of the Third North Carolina, serving under Captain Parsley. [21]

Within a year, he would become a captain in Company F. A striking military figure, albeit not a particularly handsome man, Colonel Cantwell was slender, had a wide, firm mouth, high forehead, and scraggly side-whiskers that grew below his left and right jowls. [22]

Captain Charles P. Bolles was an engineer of wide experience and ability, having worked for the United States in coastal survey for a number of years prior to hostilities. In the first month of war following Fort Sumter, he was assigned to Confederate Point as an engineer, and here he erected the first sand battery protecting New Inlet, known as Battery Bolles. William Lamb would later incorporate the earthwork into the expanded Fort Fisher. After leaving Confederate Point, Bolles worked with the Confederate Engineers for over a year, ultimately being assigned to the Fayetteville Arsenal. As "captain of Company A, Sixth Battalion, Armory Guards," he rendered a most beneficial service to Colonel Lamb's blockade running protection. He made the Whitworth rifle bolts. While Whitworth shells were sometimes imported on the runners, the supply from abroad was inadequate to fill the needs of Fort Fisher and Fort Caswell's flying artillery units. Bolles designed and produced the needed shells. [23]

James Martin Stevenson of Wilmington participated in the initial seizure of Fort Johnston, later being assigned to Fort Caswell as ordnance officer. In October 1861, Governor Clark appointed him commanding officer of a battery styled Captain James M. Stevenson's Company of Artillery, North Carolina Volunteers. In the spring of 1862 they were assigned to the Thirty-Sixth Regiment under Colonel Lamb, and became known as Second Company A of that unit, serving the guns at Fort Caswell, and later at Fisher. In January 1864, he would be promoted to major of the regiment. [24]

Captain Stevenson had two sons who wore Confederate gray. James C. Stevenson as a mere boy served on the blockade runner *Ad-Vance*. When he was fifteen, he enlisted in the same company his father had organized, serving the big guns at Fort Fisher. Dan, his brother, was a Confederate Signal Corpsman on the blockade-runners, working on several different ships. He was fearless when under fire from the Yankee warships, "was a young man of most amiable, generous impulses, and was greatly esteemed by his associates for his many excellent qualities." [25]

James Reilly, a "splendid artillerist," was for two years commanding officer of Company D of the Tenth Regiment North Carolina State Troops, serving in Lee's Army of Northern Virginia. He had been the United States Army sergeant in charge of Fort Johnston in January 1861, when the Cape Fear Minute Men and the Smithville Guards had taken that installation and Caswell against Governor Ellis' orders. When North Carolina seceded, he left the U.S. Army and joined the Tenth. In September 1863, he would be promoted to major of the regiment. [26]

John F.S. Van Bokkelen was a student at Harvard when the thunderhead of war rolled across the country. Smooth-faced and 19 years old, he came home to Wilmington to share in the fight for secession, and was appointed Second Lieutenant, Company D, of the Third North Carolina in May 1861. In April of 1862, he became a First Lieutenant, and in the summer of that year a captain commanding the company, the troops of which almost idolized the young man. Van Bokkelen had "an acute conception of his duties and an indomitable energy in pursuing the line of conduct which a discriminating judgment dictated to him. To him, probably more than to any other officer, was due the high morale which the company attained." [27]

Captain David Williams hailed from the Burgaw district of New Hanover County and was nearly 40 years old when hostilities commenced. Due to his age, the Rebels he commanded in Company K of the Third North Carolina called him "Pap", and friends said he was as brave a soldier as ever buckled on a sword. He was among the first in the Cape Fear region to forsake hearth and home for the battlefield, and "boldly threw himself into the breach and announced his determination to sacrifice, if need be, his all, upon the altar of his country's good." [28]

The commanding officer of Company E, First Regiment North Carolina State Troops, was another Wilmingtonian, James Allan Wright, in his mid-twenties when North Carolina seceded. The son of Dr. Thomas Wright, Captain Wright was regarded as "the most brilliant young man of Wilmington – and of the State," when he joined the army. He was every inch the gentleman, and most popular with all whom knew him. "Sparkling and genial in social intercourse, extremely courteous and respectful to his seniors, a strict observer of all the proprieties of life, he won the respect and esteem of all whom he met." [29]

The families and friends of these Wilmington and New Hanover County soldiers would have a year of conflict to hear and read about before the full shock and tragedy of war was driven home. By the summer of 1862, when Robert E. Lee launched his fierce assaults at the Yankees outside of Richmond in the battles known as the Seven Days, numbers of Wilmington men began coming home for the last time – in coffins.

One of the city's early sacrifices was Captain Wright, of the First Regiment, killed at the Battle of Ellerson's Mill outside Richmond, on June 26, 1862. "There is scarcely a family circle in the South," said the *Daily Journal* on July 1, "from which death has not stricken some gem since this unholy war began; scarcely a community which does not mourn the loss of some valued member, who has sacrificed his life for his country...While leading his Company in a brilliant charge upon a battery which nearly decimated the regiment to which he belonged, Capt. Wright received a ball in his forehead, and died instantly. A noble heart ceased its pulsations, the light of a cultivated mind was quenched, and a brave and chivalrous soul winged its way from earth." [30]

Four days later the paper sorrowfully reported the arrival of the remains of Colonel Gaston Meares, "who fell at the head of his command cheering on his men in the fight of last Tuesday." The bodies of other Wilmington men, Sergeant Major Duncan Moore and First Lieutenant William Wooster, both of the Eighteenth North Carolina, and both killed at Frayser's Farm on June 30, were received in town on July 4. The bodies of all three soldiers were escorted to their homes by Colonel Collett Leventhorpe's Eleventh North Carolina, stationed at Camp Davis outside town, and the Independent Guard of Wilmington, under Captain Burr. Sergeant Major Moore, still a teenager when killed, and Lieutenant Wooster, just 21 when he enlisted, were buried in Oakdale Cemetery at 4 p.m. on July 4 with military honors. Colonel Meares was laid to rest on Saturday the 5th. [31]

Colonel Meares' death was deeply mourned. He had fallen in the bloodbath of Malvern Hill, southeast of Richmond, on the evening of July 1, the same day Joe King's brother, Isaac Watts, had taken a shrapnel wound in the shoulder fighting for Colonel Meares. The Colonel was surveying the Yankee position, studded with artillery lined hub to hub no more than 75 yards away, when he was "struck by the fragment of a shell in the forehead." It was a great loss, a friend grieved, but his death was a glorious one. Colonel Meares had fallen in the "discharge of the highest duty of the citizen," laying down his life on the altar of his country. [32]

"Distinguished for the correctness of his deportment and the purity of his morals, he always commanded the public esteem. In his domestic relations, he was tender and devoted, and was rewarded by unbounded confidence and love. The attachment even of his friends was fraternal in strength. Lawyer, merchant, planter and soldier – he passed through the temptations peculiar to these several vocations with robes unspotted. Honest and just he leaves the recollection of no wrongs to be redressed by his children or avenged by enemies." [33]

On Monday, July 7, the enormity of Wilmington and North Carolina losses in the most savage battles in which their sons had fought so far, became even more evident in the lengthy casualty lists that appeared in the newspaper. In Captain Wright's Company E of the First Regiment, he and 4 others had been killed outright, 13 were wounded, and 7 others were listed as missing in action. In his entire regiment, 50 had been killed, 196 wounded, and 9 were missing.

In addition to the death of Colonel Meares, the Third North Carolina counted 23 more who lost their lives on the battlefield, with 111 others wounded. Captain William Parsley had been severely hurt with a minie ball through the neck, but would recover. Joe King's mother must have read the names with anxiety, hoping her boys, Charles, Isaac, and James, would be spared from the list. Two would escape it, but Sergeant Isaac W. King was the first name that appeared on Company D's casualty roll. They did not know yet, of course, how seriously hurt Isaac was, but he would have to come home to try to mend. He was hit badly in the right shoulder, and would suffer paralysis in the right arm from the wound. [34]

Joe King's oldest brother, John Edward, part of the Wilmington Light Infantry of the Eighteenth Regiment, was involved in the Seven Days battles as well. Like brothers Charles and James, he was spared from wounds in those savage engagements. [35]

New Hanover County's Company C of the Seventh North Carolina State Troops was bloodied in the Seven Days. Four men were killed or mortally wounded, while eighteen others were wounded. [36] Two other Cape Fear companies, the Brunswick Guards (part of the Twentieth North Carolina), and the Brunswick Quicks (the Quicks were part of the Thirtieth North Carolina), suffered heavy losses in the fighting. Twelve men in the Guards were killed, while eighteen were wounded, including Captain John S. Brooks. In the Brunswick Quicks, two soldiers had been killed outright, Lieutenant Ephriam Greer had been wounded in the shoulder or the breast and taken prisoner, while fifteen others had been wounded. Private Abram Danford was seriously hurt; he had been "shot through the jaws, knocking out the back upper teeth of both jaws." [37]

One local citizen had some advice for the area soldiers who had been wounded on the battlefield or were headed home to recuperate, and might be "remote from a physician." In the Tuesday, July 22, 1862 edition of the *Daily Journal*, this advisor stated: "Spirits of Turpentine is death to flies and vermin, besides it is one of our best remedies to check hemorrhage. The impression that it gives pain to fresh wounds is generally false. Should it sting, it is but for a moment. It has soothing, cleansing and healthful effect upon the wounds. If our

The Seamen's Bethel that existed before this one was used as a military hospital.

soldiers were each provided with this article when going into battle, and as soon as wounded would apply it freely to the parts, great suffering from mortification and other concomitants might be saved, and probably many lives."

"Another remedy, is common fresh honey, which is in almost every house in the Southern Confederacy. It is also a styptic, and might well supply the place of lead-water in inflammation or gangrene, and that of iodine in erysipelas. In fact it alleviates the pain in the above diseased wounds perhaps better than any other domestic remedy, and sets up a healthy reaction. Apply it freely to the diseased parts with a mop or feather, then lay on a clean cloth, and change as often as it becomes dry." [38]

To help cope with the suffering of the returning Wilmington wounded, as well as other Southern troops coming through town and headed further South, the ladies of Wilmington banded together in the "Soldiers Aid Society." They were organized and literally commanded by Eliza Lord (Mrs. Armand J.) DeRosset. Mrs. DeRosset was of such excellent administrative ability, that it was said "she ought to have been a General." She was a lady of great heart and sympathy for the sufferings of the troops, and worked diligently to see that food, supplies, and medical attention were provided for them. [39]

Blockade runner Captain John Wilkinson, of the Confederate Navy, was a frequent visitor to Wilmington. He noted that generous contributions were made to Mrs. DeRosset's society by companies and individuals, "and the long tables at the station were spread with delicacies for the sick to be found nowhere else in the Confederacy. The remains of the meals were carried by the ladies to a camp of mere boys – home guards – outside of the town. Some of these children were scarcely able to carry a musket, and were altogether unable to endure the exposure and fatigue of field service; and they suffered fearfully from measles and typhoid fever." [40]

Mrs. DeRosset sought to help them all, having a devout and deeply vested interest in the Southern Cause. Six of her own boys and three sons-in-law wore Confederate gray. Her oldest son was William Lord. Commander of the Wilmington Light Infantry when the state seceded, he had become commanding officer of the Third North Carolina upon the death of Colonel Meares at Malvern Hill. Colonel Meares himself had been one of Mrs. DeRosset's sons-in-law. Armand L. DeRosset was a First Lieutenant in Company H of his brother's regiment. Dr. John DeRosset was Assistant Surgeon at Bellevue Hospital in New York when war broke out. He was offered and refused a commission in a New York regiment, came home, and in the summer of 1862 was a surgeon reporting to "Stonewall" Jackson. Another of Mrs. DeRosset's boys, Louis, was not as physically fit as the others, but nevertheless served in the ordnance and quartermaster departments of the army, for a time seeing duty in Nassau.

In addition to ministering to the sufferings of the wounded and sick troops, Mrs. DeRosset had her female brigade of volunteers assemble each day at City Hall, where they churned out war related articles with sewing machines and needles. Uniforms were pieced together, haversacks were made, and canteen covers were stitched. A Wilmington friend wrote that cartridges "for rifles, and powder bags for the great columbiads were made by hundreds. Canvas bags, to be filled with sand and used on the fortifications, were largely used at Fort Fisher – and much more was in requisition." Mrs. DeRosset was ably assisted by her Vice-President of the Ladies Aid Society, her strong right arm, Mrs. Alfred Martin. Wilmington had a substantial population of German immigrants, and those ladies also gave abundantly of their time and energy. [41]

In addition to the volunteer aid that was generously provided by the citizens of Wilmington, the Richmond government established two Confederate hospitals in town in the spring and summer of 1862. The hospitals were neat, orderly and well supervised, and the patients received good treatment. One of them, General Hospital #4, was situated at the corner of Dock and Front Streets, and was composed of the old Seamen's Home buildings. "Thomas M. Ritenour was surgeon and A.E. Wright and Josh Walker, assistant surgeons. This was one of the largest and best equipped hospitals in the State." The town would need all the medical facilities it could get in the months to come. [42]

Supplemental to the Cape Fear River defense posts of Forts Fisher and Caswell, and Fort St. Philip (or Fort Anderson), halfway upriver on the western

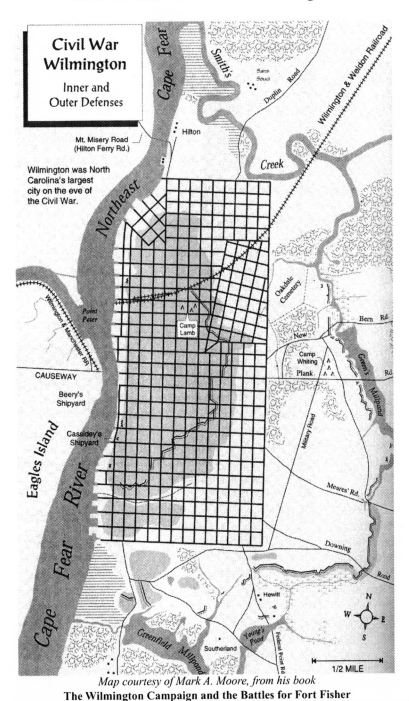

Civil War Wilmington

Inner and Outer Defenses

Wilmington was North Carolina's largest city on the eve of the Civil War.

Map courtesy of Mark A. Moore, from his book
The Wilmington Campaign and the Battles for Fort Fisher

bank, the town itself had substantial earthwork fortifications surrounding it. Second Lieutenant Claudius B. Denson, commanding Company A, Second Regiment Confederate Engineers, stationed at Wrightsville east of town, was responsible for much of the work. Denson was a native of Suffolk County, Virginia, and 23 years old when elected Captain of the Confederate Grays of Duplin County, which became Company E of the Twentieth North Carolina Infantry. He later saw topographical service in Eastern North Carolina and the Cape Fear area, and at the request of Captain Winder, one of the early builders of forts on Confederate Point, he was commissioned Second Lieutenant in the engineers.

Denson's troops, the lieutenant would later recall, planned and oversaw the construction of "many works, including seven batteries on the river, from Sugar Loaf to the city, the redoubts near Wilmington, dams, military bridges and military roads up the coast; also the work shops, the 'Army Navy Yard,' as the establishment for building torpedo-boats was called (these were never fully completed, awaiting machinery which failed to arrive); the preparation of maps and plans; and the construction of pontoons." Denson's officers were so often in the saddle with their multitude of responsibilities that the government furnished each of them with two horses. [43]

Chief responsibility for manning Wilmington's defenses, after the engineers had seen to their erection, rested with the Tenth Battalion North Carolina Heavy Artillery, which was organized in the city in May, 1862. Major Wilton L. Young of Wake County was commanding officer. The battalion was drilled and proficient in both small arms and heavy artillery. Second Lieutenant Charles Powell, the battalion's adjutant, proudly reported most of the soldiers "could name the nomenclature of a Columbiad or Whitworth from knob to tampion, could cut fuses for blank or point blank range, understood the uses of the quadrant and sextant, and drilled with muskets until the index finger of the right hand crooked like a hawk claw, while the barbette carriages on the parapets...mounted field pieces were as play things for them to handle." [44]

Wilmington's defenses consisted of a semi-circle of entrenchments more than three miles around town, and about a mile out from the city limits. The engineers had also skillfully interspersed dams that incorporated various water courses, including streams and ponds, with gauges at the dams to be used as needed in the event of enemy attack. Heavy trenches and traverses were between the military dams, and these contained the big guns. In the city itself were two batteries of ten inch Columbiads with magazines for shells and powder. One battery was situated on a bluff on the northern edge of town, while another was on a bluff on the south side. [45]

The batteries, entrenchments and dams, as well as large government sheds that lined the riverfront, filled with supplies to be shipped to the Confederate armies, were the major posts of duty with which the Tenth

Battalion was entrusted. Lieutenant Powell remembered they were guarded round the clock "with a new guard every day, commanded by a mounted commissioned officer of the day whose duty was to inspect every point twice in twenty-four hours and make written report of the same to headquarters on being relieved. This arduous duty coupled with the exposure to the malarial swamps of the ponds made by the dams, and marshy borders of the river, the yellow fever, the smallpox scourge of 1862-63, the sand flies, mosquitoes and bad water was about as serious and mortal as shrieking shells and the inquisitive minie balls." Many soldiers in the Tenth, Powell recalled, "went down to rise no more till resurrection day," while pulling duty in and around Wilmington. [46]

Some of those Rebels in the Tenth, like hundreds of Wilmington and New Hanover County citizens, were to perish in the town's greatest war disaster, the yellow fever epidemic of the summer and fall of 1862. It came while the city was still burying her dead of the Seven Days, and raged while her men were fighting the Yankees at a picturesque little town in Maryland called Sharpsburg.

Yellow fever plagued the subtropical South for generations. It had struck Wilmington in August 1821, supposedly introduced on a brig called the *John London*, which had shipped out of Havana carrying the disease. Out of a population of 2,500 people at that time, a "large proportion" of Wilmingtonians were stricken and died of the fever in a six week period. In Norfolk, Colonel Lamb's hometown, and Portsmouth, Virginia, the dreaded scourge lasted over three months in 1855, and about one-third of the white people were carried to their graves by it, including at least 45 of the area's doctors. [47]

The true nature and cause of the disease were unknown in 1862, but yellow fever is a deadly virus carried by the Aedes aegypti mosquito. One thing people of the nineteenth century did know, was that once the sickness had been introduced into an area, it spread rapidly. It was also felt that nearness to another person with the disease caused it. That was possible, of course, if an individual were bitten by a mosquito that had come into contact with another yellow fever victim. The mosquito itself, however, without prior human contact, carries the disease.

After being bitten by the insect, an incubation period lasting several days allows time for the virus to multiply in a person's body. Headache, backache, fast rising fever, nausea and vomiting start abruptly. Because the virus destroys liver cells, jaundice or yellowing of the skin and eyes usually occurs, giving rise to the name of the illness. One of the classic signs of yellow fever, at least the latter stage approaching death, is hemorrhaging into mucous membranes and the stomach, resulting in what is called "black vomit." Severity of sickness and fatality is greater in some races than others. Treatment in 1862, as now, consisted of trying to control the fever in the most comfortable manner possible. [48]

The fever was believed to have been brought in on the blockade runner *Kate*, which steamed up to the wharf after a trip from Nassau in late July.

Aboard the vessel were infected crewmembers, and as no quarantine was in effect yet at Fort Anderson, or if it was, it was ignored, and the sick sailors arrived at Wilmington. In the heat of summer, mosquitoes swarmed the riverbank by the tens of thousands, and it was just a matter of time before the infected seamen were bitten, their blood drawn, and the virus passed to someone else. Soon after the *Kate* docked, at least two of her crewmen died of the disease. In the then distraught condition of the people over the casualties of the Seven Days, little attention was paid to the deaths of strangers. [49]

Although some people caught and died from the fever in August, their deaths were not attributed to it, and the incidence at first was sporadic and undetected as the prelude to an epidemic. In fact, the notion "of yellow fever in Wilmington was ridiculed." As time wore on, however, citizens and doctors became suspicious, and individuals' deaths were more closely scrutinized. [50]

The first Wilmingtonian recognized to die of the illness was 36 year old German native by the name of Lewis Swartzman. Swartzman ran a wood and coal business on the river's edge, coincidentally very near the docking point of the *Kate*. Apparently contracting the sickness in mid-to-late August, by the first week of September, Swartzman was burning up with the fever in its last stages. He was already jaundiced and yellow in appearance when Alfred M. Waddell came to visit him.

Waddell was an Orange County native in his late twenties who had set up shop as an attorney and newspaperman in Wilmington. He was not in Confederate service as yet, but the next spring would join the Forty-First North Carolina Troops (Third North Carolina Cavalry), eventually becoming lieutenant colonel of the regiment. In September of 1862, he was on a trip from Richmond to Augusta, and stopped in Wilmington for a few days before heading on to Georgia. He heard about Swartzman being sick and alone, and Waddell decided to pay him a visit:

"I called at his room, sat by his bedside and tried to cheer him, holding his hand in the meantime. I observed that he had a very yellow appearance and supposed he had jaundice. After sitting some time, I bade him good bye, and a few hours later left the city for Augusta. He died with black vomit within forty-eight hours, and his was the first case of the dreadful scourge, or at least it was the first recognized case. My escape was a signal mercy." [51]

Swartzman passed away on Tuesday, the ninth of September. The next morning, on Wednesday the tenth, Reverend John L. Prichard of the First Baptist Church "attended the funeral of a child near Kidder's brick-yard," he wrote to his wife in Richmond, who was visiting relatives there for the summer. On Friday, he visited with three of his parishioners who had gotten sick, and that night at six o'clock one of them died. The next day, Saturday the thirteenth, he "attended E's funeral, and at six attended the funeral of M.S. over the Rail road. And now it began to be rumored that yellow fever was in town," he wrote, "and at a consultation of the doctors, Saturday evening, it was agreed that it was really yellow fever! So I have been in the midst of it without knowing it. Mrs. C's disease is said to have been the same – there have been nearly a dozen cases, and others are reported to day. Many families are leaving." [52]

In an attempt to calm people's fears, the *Daily Journal* told its readers on September 16 that Mayor John Dawson had "made diligent enquiry of all the physicians in town who have been in attendance upon any suspected cases" and had found only five confirmed cases of yellow fever. Official sanitary precautions had been adopted to stop the spread of the disease. James Fulton, editor of the paper, optimistically wrote that he had no "apprehensions personally on the subject of Yellow Fever, as we do not think that there is any likelihood of its becoming epidemic." Wilmington, however, had reached its "sickly season," and there was much moisture and extreme heat about, that should give all people pause for concern. Fulton advised all people who were not in town to stay away for a few weeks, if they could possibly do so. [53]

Dr. James H. Dickson, M.D.

Several days after Fulton's advice, Pastor Prichard inquired of his friend and physician, Dr. James Dickson, what he should do about visiting a man who was known to have the fever. "Well," said the doctor, "I reckon you will have to do as I do. It is like war, we must take our chances. You will have to go and see many during their illness, &c., &c." Prichard did take his chances and decided to stay in town as long as there were sufferers, to do all he could to attend to and minister to them. [54]

Dr. Dickson gave advice to another friend, Alexander Sprunt, who had emigrated with his family from Glasgow, Scotland in the early 1850's. Sprunt had seen yellow fever in South American and the West Indies while engaged in business, and knew well the awful scourge it could be. Dr. Dickson advised his friend to get his family out of town and to keep them out till the fever had permanently ceased.

Sprunt decided to send his family to Duplin County to stay with some relatives. Just before leaving, however, it was feared one of his sons had already caught the fever. The boy had been sick and staying in his room, abnormal behavior, of course, for a young and healthy lad. Sprunt, being somewhat knowledgeable of medicine, told the boy to stick out his tongue. When he did, his father was horrified to see it was yellowish looking, and stated that he had the symptoms of yellow fever. Shame-faced, his son told him he had gotten a yellow tongue and stomachache from having chewed tobacco. The family undoubtedly got a laugh and welcomed relief out of that incident. [55]

As the days of September wore on, the epidemic spread like wildfire. On Monday, September 29, the *Daily Journal*, no longer optimistic, reported that Wilmington was in her "hour of...deepest affliction...No person who has not visited our town since the outbreak of the epidemic can form any estimate of the suffering the people who are compelled to remain here are undergoing." The paper also related the deaths of some of the prominent citizens of town. "Dr. James H. Dickson, a physician of the highest character and standing, died here on Sunday morning of the same disease. Dr. Dickson's death is a great loss to the profession and to the community."

Mr. William Bettencourt, Esq., who was one of the oldest Wilmingtonians, passed away in Clinton, having contracted the illness in town. At Masonboro Sound, Stephen Jewett, cashier at the Bank of Wilmington, also died. Jewett was "a most amiable and estimable gentleman, cabinet-maker by trade", who had settled in Smithville about 1839, and who later operated a school in that community along with his wife. Still later, he had moved to Wilmington after his wife's death, and became cashier of the bank. [56]

To help stem the tide of the disease, which was believed to be borne in the air, barrels of rosin and tar were burned on the sidewalks in front of homes and businesses, in the belief that this would help cleanse the air. John Prichard told his wife that "Hundreds of barrels of rosin have been burnt." Also, lime impregnated with gas had been placed "at nearly all the doors in town," and the whole town reeked of the smell of natural gas. "I know not whether there is any efficacy in this," Prichard said, but "It can do no harm." [57]

In addition to burning the rosin and tar barrels and setting out lime at various places for air purification, Wilmington's Sanitary Committee ordered the wives and children of railroad employees, steamboat workers, and soldiers, to stay away from town during the epidemic. In addition, William H. Lippitt, druggist, was advised that he had to keep his drug store open "during the prevalence of the yellow fever, otherwise steps will be taken to have it kept open by the authorities." [58]

Jonas P. Levy, who had seen and treated much yellow fever in different areas of the world, had some home-style medical advice for people afflicted with the illness. An article in the *Daily Journal* on September 30 presented his view. Levy said that at the first symptoms of the fever, the patient should take a tablespoon full of salt with plenty of water to dissolve it, and an "ordinary dose of castor oil, and swallow it down without delay. Immediately give the patient a hot foot-bath, with a hand full of common salt and one-eighth of a pound of mustard in it. Throw a blanket over him and let him remain in the bath for fifteen minutes. Then take him out and wrap him up in blankets, without wiping him, and lay him in a well-covered bed and ventilated room. Then apply mustard plasters to the abdomen, calves of the legs and soles of the feet." [59]

Levy further recommended that if the first advised cathartic did not seem to operate within an hour, the patient should drink a wineglass of spirits of turpentine mixed with warm soap suds, "molasses and any kind of oil." This was to open up the bowels, which were to be kept open as gently as possible with castor oil. Headache could be relieved, Levy wrote, by cupping the patient on the temples and the back of the neck. Mustard plasters and hot footbaths needed to be applied until the fever had broken.

No food should be given the yellow fever victim until he was completely free of fever, but while treatment was being administered, he could drink lemonade, tartar water, barley water, or take a teaspoonful of sage or arrowroot. The fever would normally break on the seventh, ninth or eleventh day.

Once the fever had been broken, care should be exercised with the diet, or relapse and possible death could occur. Again, no solid food was to be allowed, but chicken broth was acceptable. Levy had experienced "marked success" with his remedies on the Gulf Coast, the coasts of Africa and Brazil, in the Mexican War, and in the Norfolk, Virginia epidemic of 1855 that had been so devastating.

Fortunately for Joe King, he was not to receive this intermittent heating up of the body, while he burned with yellow fever. By late summer of 1862, Mr. Johnson had assigned him to stay at Camp Wyatt north of Fort Fisher, where he was to butcher cattle with the assistance of the soldiers. When he heard about the epidemic spreading so rapidly and terribly in town, he asked Colonel Lamb for a pass to Wilmington to see how is family was doing. He was granted permission, but when he got there, he learned that Isaac, returned home on furlough for his shoulder wound received at Malvern Hill, had taken his wife and little girl, his mother and the other three children to Myrtle Grove Sound, about four miles north of Fort Fisher, to escape the epidemic. The only family member left in town was Joe's grandmother, Eliza Strouse, a Dutch-born lady doctor who refused to leave her patients in the midst of the fever.

Joe returned to Fort Fisher to resume his butchering duties, relieved about his mother and the other children. Then he started worrying about his grandmother, and decided to go back home to see if he could be of any help. Colonel Lamb granted him another pass, but told him as he left, "Young man, don't you bring the yellow fever back down here to these soldiers." Joe again returned to Wilmington, and would never go back to Fort Fisher to butcher beef for the soldiers. [61]

Joe's house was deserted when he got there, but he found his grandmother staying at the residence of her daughter-in-law. As he was talking to her, a young fellow named Johnnie Ellis rushed in on them, crying out "Granny, Mamma is dying." Joe and his grandmother, along with a Mr. Wilder, accompanied Johnnie to his mother's bedside. As Joe "stood in the front door, the dying woman threw up what they called black vomit and quickly passed away." Joe said he smelled a strange odor, as "the wind wafted through the door in which I was standing and I said to myself this may be the time in which to take the yellow fever." [62]

Having caught the fever as he suspected, Joe lay in bed in his old house alone for several days, how many he did not know. He thought his grandmother might have attended to him, but of that he was not sure, because he was unconscious for much of the time, and he knew she was busy with others as well. Not many people were on the streets, except those seeking doctors or medicine. Joe recalled that the "few vehicles that could be seen, were hurriedly carrying out the dead, delivering coffins and carrying other things necessary. I heard that many bodies lay for days unburied at the cemetery." [63]

After several days had transpired, Isaac came to fetch him with a horse and buggy, bundled him up, and carried him down to the sound where the rest of the family was. Joe did not remember much about the trip, because in his delirium it all seemed like a dream, but he did recall that each time the buggy hit a rough place in the road, "it hurt my head and back very much." When they reached the house at the sound, Isaac left Joe in the buggy, and got water, soap, towels and clean clothes from the house. Isaac stripped him naked, it being warm outside, and bathed him completely. Then he bathed him again, Joe said, in "new corn whiskey and gave me some to drink and put clean clothes on me." When Isaac took him inside, their mother, seeing his sickly, yellow appearance, said, "Oh, Joe, you have the yellow jaundice." [64]

For nine days, Joe was confined to bed, while his mother gave him a homemade concoction each day of a "glass containing one teaspoon of pulverized sulfur, the yolk of one egg and about a wine glass full of new corn whiskey...At the end of the ninth day, I walked in the yard and felt good enough to fly. My mother, having never seen a case of yellow fever, thought she had cured me of jaundice." [65]

Joe King was one of the fortunate ones to survive after contracting yellow fever. Hundreds of others were not so lucky. Six-year-old John McCormick died of the fever on September 29, reported the *Daily Journal*. He was the oldest child of a "J. and C. McCormick". On the next day, Joseph Durnin, the primary operator at the telegraph office in town, passed away "in the 25th year of his age." Durnin was a native of the state of Maine and had been working as an operator in Washington when war broke out. "When a decision had to be made between the North and the South," the *Journal* reported, "he at once cast his fate with the Confederacy." He had served as an operator in Alexandria, and then Manassas, before those places fell to Yankee occupation, later relocated to Richmond, and finally to Wilmington. He was "a good and true man, who died here in the flower of his youth," and "he did not pass away unappreciated". [66]

The week of Saturday, September 27 through Friday, October 3 was a deadly one. During that time, 267 new cases of fever were reported by the town's physicians, while 82 Wilmingtonians died of it.

On October 12, William Buford, 42 years old, was listed as a victim of the fever, and on Tuesday, October 14, the distinguished Reverend R.B. Drane, minister of St. James Episcopal Church, passed away at 7 p.m. "This is a loss which will be felt by every member of his church," said the newspaper, "and by the community at large, of which Dr. Drane was a highly respected and useful member." [67]

Oakdale Cemetery was rapidly having its space filled. Mr. Quigley, superintendent of the cemetery, could no longer give a tally of the burials, since he had died of the fever himself on Saturday, October 18. On that same day, fifteen people were interred in Oakdale. The next day, Sunday the 19th, seventeen more were laid to rest. On those same two weekend days, physicians reported sixty-five new cases of yellow fever, and at least twenty additional people died on Sunday who had not yet

Rev. R.B. Drane

been buried. On Monday, October 20, the demand for "coffins, hearses, and other adjuncts of interment" was equal or greater than at any time since the epidemic started. [68]

As the epidemic spread suffering and sorrow, the kind and the caring rallied to help. In addition to Wilmington's own physicians and ministers, Dr. Choppin of General P.G.T. Beauregard's staff in Charleston arrived in late September, as did nurses from that city. A few days later, Reverend Dr. Corcoran and four "Sisters of Mercy" from Charleston came in as well, to lend their assistance. [69]

From all quarters of private and public life, contributions in the form of foodstuffs and money were consigned to Wilmington's Sanitary Committee, to be distributed to the most needy. In the first week of October, Mr. P.K.

Dickinson gave $250, $100 came from the Fayetteville Mills Company, Mr. William Utley sent one barrel of syrup and $50 cash, Colonel Lamb sent $50 from Fort Fisher, Mr. George McDuffie of Warren County sent ten barrels of flour, and the mayor of Goldsboro gave "a quantity of meal, potatoes, bacon, poultry and eggs". Jewish citizens of Wilmington who were staying in Charlotte during the epidemic, "raised over eleven hundred dollars, the money being made up in five minutes, and have bought forty barrels of flour and invested the balance in bacon, for the use of the sick and suffering poor". [70]

The Confederate Hospital, at the corner of Front and Dock streets, was utilized as a medical facility for yellow fever victims, be they civilians or soldiers. In addition, the dispensary connected with the hospital was kept open from nine in the morning until nine at night, to help the families of soldiers and any other people who had need for medicines. A visitor to the hospital on October 21 reported seeing 18 patients there, 9 males and 9 females. Most were doing well, the *Daily Journal* reported, "some few with high fever on, and one, in the female department, apparently hopeless. The black vomit had appeared in its most decided form. This as we were told was the only hopeless case." [71]

The appearance of the hospital was good, the visitor said, the wards were "clean, airy, and comfortable, and the bedding and other things in the purest condition. The attendance seemed to be prompt and judicious." Confederate Surgeon Wragg was in charge, and his assistant in the dispensary, Dr. T.B. Carr, had made certain that there was a "sufficient stock of medicines to compound all prescriptions for some weeks." [72]

For the sick and needy who were unable to provide food for themselves, a public soup house use was opened up on the southeast corner of Front and Dock streets, across from the hospital. A bakery for the purpose of making crackers and bread for the same group was also operated by the Sanitary Committee. [73]

The efforts of many good people to alleviate suffering could only do so much, as the root cause of the virus, the mosquito, would continue to transmit yellow fever until it was sufficiently cold to kill the insect. The tragedy for many New Hanover County residents was the persistence of a typically warm fall in that part of the state, the weather being generally mild in southeastern North Carolina until late December or January, and frost often not occurring until November. All people longed for frost, though they did not connect it with destruction of the mosquito. They did know that somehow the cold eradicated the fever.

On October 20 it was almost sixty degrees at daylight, usually the coldest time of the day. On October 25 the weather was "soft and balmy, with no hope of frost in it," reported the *Daily Journal*. Experience for the last decade indicated that a killing frost could not be expected "before about the 20th of November." The same edition of the paper, now reduced to bulletins every few days due to loss of staff, also reported the direful news of 194 new cases of the fever in the past week, and 111 deaths from it. [74]

One of the late October cases was Reverend John Lamb Prichard. He had been stricken in the midst of burials and funeral services for his friends and flock in the First Baptist Church. On Friday, October 17, he wrote his wife that he had attended Dr. Drane's funeral on Wednesday afternoon. The day before he had been to three funerals, and during the week his own sister had caught yellow fever. On the 18th, he told his wife he could not conceal the truth from her, that he was sick, and that he had headache and backache, which were "true symptoms of fever". [75]

The following day, Rev. Prichard's oldest son, Robert, who had stayed in Wilmington while the rest of the family went to Virginia, wrote his mother that his father had become ill, but that he had been able to hire a nurse. He was "a very good one," Robert said, "a mulatto man, who nursed at Norfolk and Portsmouth." He also told his mother "that Johnnie and Lizzie G. both died yesterday, and while I write, a wagon stands at the door with J's coffin in it." Robert apparently concurred with Mr. Levy's treatment recommended in the *Daily Journal*, for he treated his feverish father with mustard plasters, and "bathed his feet in salt water." [76]

By the 27th of October, Pastor Prichard had become "very yellow," and was gradually sinking under what was to be a prolonged case of the fever. On November 4, Dr. Corcoran, the Catholic priest from Charleston, along with two Sisters of Mercy from that town, paid him a visit. On November 11, he told his son he knew he was dying. [77]

Captain Charles D. Ellis, commanding Company B of the First Battalion North Carolina Heavy Artillery at Fort Strong, on the east side of the Cape Fear below Wilmington, was a church member and close friend of the family, and helped them out in the pastor's final days. He wrote to Mrs. Prichard on November 14 that the end had come. "He left us last night," the captain said, "at half past eleven o'clock, and with a sweet smile on his face, has gone to reap the reward of his works...O, that the Lord may give us grace to bear this heavy loss and say, 'Thy will be done.' " [78]

John Prichard was one of the last to succumb to the deadly illness. The *Daily Journal* reported in its November 17 edition that the epidemic had ceased since the occurrence of frost during the first week of the month. Altogether, at least 1,505 people in the Wilmington area had caught yellow fever. Of that number, at least 654 perished, nearly all of whom died in Wilmington, but some in surrounding counties, and between 15 and 30 in Smithville. Some thought the number could have been higher. Of the dead, 504 were white people, while at least 150 were "colored persons". [79]

Of all the ministers who remained in town during the pestilence, only one, Reverend A. Paul Repiton, lived to tell about it. "He worked unceasingly for the sick and buried the dead. His name is blessed in the annals of Wilmington." [80]

Even as the citizens of Wilmington fell left and right to the yellow jack, their soldiers were falling and bleeding on the hills of western Maryland in their fight for Southern independence. On September 29, the same day Dr. Dickson's and Stephen Jewett's deaths were announced, the Daily Journal ran the casualty report of the Third North Carolina for the Battle of Sharpsburg (Antietam), fought September 17. The report came from Adjutant and First Lieutenant John Van Bokkelen, and was dated September 21, 1862, having been written near Martinsburg, Virginia.

He reported the loss of many good Wilmington men. "While the regiment was going on the battlefield in the evening" of the 16th, he wrote, across Hagerstown Pike from the Dunkard Church, a Yankee artillery shell from across Antietam Creek exploded in the ranks, killing two officers and wounding a corporal. Lieutenant Arthur Speight of Company A had his right leg blown off, Captain David "Pap" Williams of Company K was disemboweled and killed instantly, and Corporal Peter Smith of Company F had his left leg shattered below the knee, all three being hit by the same shellburst. Lieutenant Speight was removed to a house behind Sharpsburg used as a field hospital, where he later expired. He and Captain Williams were both buried in the same grave in the front yard of the house. Colonel DeRosset, commanding officer of the Third, said that Williams was "as brave a man as ever lived...and sleeps in a soldier's grave, with his blanket for a shroud." Corporal Smith's leg was beyond repair, and had to be amputated below the knee. [81]

The real bloodbath of the battle began in earnest at daybreak on the 17th. It would be the bloodiest day in American history. The Wilmingtonians of Companies D and F, with the rest of the regiment slammed into the Yankees "in an open field a little to the south of the famous corn field near the East Woods, and the smooth-bore muskets with the buck and ball cartridges did most excellent service," being no more than 100 yards from the enemy. The regiment fought in the vicinity of the Cornfield "against vast odds for three hours," and was in the midst of "the vortex of the fire," until the ammunition of the living, and the boxes and pockets of the dead had been emptied as well. [82]

Captain Edward Meares, commanding New Hanover County's Company D, was mortally wounded in the side, and buried in the Shepherdstown, Virginia cemetery, across the Potomac from Sharpsburg. He and Lieutenant Speight and Captain Williams were the only officers killed that were brought off the battlefield. Five others, Lieutenants Cowan, Gillespie, Quince, and McNair, and Captain Rhodes, who was shot through the heart and the knee, had to be left where they fell beneath their crimson battleflag, the enemy having possession of that part of the field when the battle ended. [83]

Many others fell to rise no more, the Third North Carolina State Troops losing 330 men killed, wounded and missing out of 520 taken into action. Twenty-four of twenty-seven officers engaged in the battle were either killed or wounded. Colonel William L. DeRosset, having commanded only two months since the death of Colonel Meares, was seriously wounded in the thigh and hip, and would never see field service again. Second Lieutenant Armand L.

DeRosset of Company H, his younger brother, was also wounded. Lieutenant Colonel Stephen D. Thruston, now commanding officer, was himself wounded slightly by a shellburst. In the Wilmington companies, D and F, eight enlisted men were killed, and twenty-three were wounded. [84]

Fortunately for the King family trying to cope with Joe's nearly fatal bout with yellow fever, neither of the two remaining brothers in the Third Regiment, Charles or James, was to be found in Lieutenant Van Bokkelen's list of casualties. The family later learned, however, that the list was incomplete, James Madison having been captured at the Battle of Boonsboro or South Mountain on September 15, two days before Sharpsburg. He would remain a prisoner of the Yankees until November 10, being released about the same time the first frosts of Wilmington's autumn were killing the mosquitoes and eradicating the yellow fever. The eldest King brother, John Edward, in Company G of the Eighteenth North Carolina, was not actively involved in the battle, his unit being part of General A.P. Hill's Division, but his regiment not seeing combat in this battle. [85]

Sergeant Major Thomas Henry McIntire, of Company C of the First North Carolina State Troops, saw many of his New Hanover County friends fall on the field in Maryland. He wrote that in the two New Hanover County companies in the regiment, Company C and Company E, three men had been killed, and forty-six others were either wounded or missing. [86]

With death and mutilation of her sons in uniform added to the losses from yellow fever, Wilmington was a city submerged in suffering and gloom in the fall of 1862. Dr. Thomas F. Wood, an assistant surgeon in the army, wrote that Wilmington was a city whose people had reached a state of exhaustion and anguish. "Panic, distress, mute despair, want", he said, "had fallen upon a population then strained to its utmost, with the bleeding columns of its regiments dyeing the hills of Maryland with their blood, until the whole air was filled with the wail of the widow and the orphan, and the dead could no longer be honored with the last tribute of respect." [87]

The calamities of pestilence and armed combat could not, however, destroy the spirit and energy of a people struggling for their independence. By the end of December, Captain John Wilkinson, having just run past the Yankee fleet off Fort Fisher in the *Giraffe*, later named the *Robert E. Lee*, observed that Wilmington "was fiercely active" with blockade running trade. The steam powered cotton presses on Eagle's Island across the river from town were compressing and baling thousands of pounds of cotton each day for the fleet-footed runners. Also lining the wharves and waiting to be loaded on the Bermuda and Nassau-bound steamers were hundreds of tierces of tobacco and barrels of turpentine. Over a dozen of the sleek, swift blockade runners, painted with marine camouflage of dull gray or buff, hung at anchor in the Cape Fear, or alongside the wharves, where gangs of black stevedores loaded their holds and decks with the precious commodities that were the South's gold for her

Bustling docks never slowed for long once the yellow fever had passed.

foreign purchases. Wartime life and activity, then, were already returning by the end of the year. [88]

The *Daily Journal* proclaimed with great optimism on January 2, 1863, that the "New Year opens brightly for the Confederate arms in the West as well as in the East. Bragg has been giving the enemy 'a little more grape' at Murfreesboro, and the indomitable Semmes, in the *Alabama* or *290* has been on the track of their ocean steamers, rendering them unhappy and perplexed." [89]

The Yankees, the paper said, might soon be forced to negotiate a peace with independence secured for the South. "Bragg and VanDorn and Lee and their brave armies are also smoothing the way. Their mode of negotiating is rough, but it bids fair to be efficient." [90]

From their camps around Port Royal, Virginia in mid-January, the officers of the Third North Carolina Infantry, decimated in the summer campaigns in Virginia and Maryland, issued a tribute of respect for their slain officer comrades, and a clarion call for continued defiance for the invaders, for Wilmingtonians to read and heed. They said the deaths of Colonel Gaston Meares, Captain David Williams, Captain Ed Meares, Lieutenants Cowan, Arthur Speight and five others, were sacrifices of the "lives of ten of a nation's noblest sons, devotees at the shrine of liberty." The officers of the regiment "RESOLVED, That while their deaths have carried sadness to our hearts, we have the consoling reflection that they fell under the banner of freedom, with liberty as a watchword." The resolutions were signed by New Hanover County officers William M. Parsley, as Chairman of the group, and John F.S. Van Bokkelen, Secretary, and were sent to the families of the deceased soldiers, and The Wilmington and Raleigh newspapers for publication. [91]

Life began to settle back to a more normal state by the winter of 1863, despite the threat of invasion by Foster's troops from New Bern, which never came about. The *Daily Journal* was able to refreshingly report in early February that there was "a striking dearth of exciting news." It did comment, however, on the unsanitary conditions of town that might have contributed to the yellow fever epidemic of the fall. "During the last Fall," the paper said, "we had about as much Yellow Fever as any community of our size would care to have in a century. Surely we do not want to have it again." [92]

Cellars in many areas of town, particularly "on Market Street between Front and Second, and in a few cases below Front, are filled with stagnant water nearly all the time, the offensive smell of which, when bailed out or pumped up, at once attracted the attention of the visiting physicians who kindly came to our aid". The paper strongly recommended that cellars and other areas containing standing water should be drained or filled up, as one means of preventing a recurrence of the dread yellow jack. [93]

The Commissioners of the city apparently agreed, for on March 11, they adopted a "health Ordinance for the Town of Wilmington." Citizens were given thirty days from the date of the ordinance to arrange for permanent drainage of any cellars, excavations, or depressions on their property, or else to fill such areas with "sand, gravel or some other imperishable material...to the level of the street or ally next adjacent thereto." People who kept horses, hogs, or cattle within the city were to keep their enclosures clean and dry, and were required to remove any "filth or offal" from those areas beyond the city's limits at least once a week.

Residents were also required to clean their outhouses and privies at least once every two weeks, and "Jamestown or other weeds" were not permitted to grown on a person's lot. People were forbidden to throw or deposit into any drain or gutter, "offal, garbage, filth, manure, feculent matter, corrupt, foul or putrid water or other fluid, or any shells, refuse straw or hay, or kitchen stuff, paper, cloth or any matter of any kind which may be offensive to the smell or injurious to the health on any street, alley, wharf or any public place within the limits of the Town of Wilmington". Violation of any section of the ordinance would result in a $20 fine, and $20 additional fine for each day the violation was not corrected. [94]

Improved sanitary conditions notwithstanding, large numbers of citizens fled the unsettled and dangerous living conditions that were made evident by the yellow fever epidemic, the threat of Yankee invasion, and the turbulence generated by a military garrison and blockade running. Many rented their residences at high prices, which could only be paid by the employees of the shipping firms. The agents of those companies lived in grand style, paying exorbitant prices for hotel and boarding house rooms, sometimes as much as $1,200 per month, "and nearly monopolizing the supplies in the country market." Wilmingtonians who stayed in town by and large "kept themselves much secluded, the ladies rarely being seen upon the more public streets." [95]

Captain John Wilkinson, a frequent visitor to Wilmington while in command of the *R.E. Lee*, and later assigned to duty in the city, noted that the "staid old town of Wilmington was turned 'topsy turvy during the war. Here resorted the speculators from all parts of the South, to attend the weekly auctions of imported cargoes; and the town was infested with rogues and desperadoes, who made a livelihood by robbery and murder. It was unsafe to venture into the suburbs at night, and even in daylight there were frequent conflicts in the public streets, between the crews of the steamers in port and the soldiers stationed in the town, in which knives and pistols would be freely used; and not infrequently a dead body would rise to the surface of the water in one of the docks with marks of violence upon it. The civil authorities were powerless to prevent crime." [96]

Crime was unquestionably a serious problem. In February 1863, Alexander Sprunt's home was broken into twice in a single week. At the end of March, Coroner H.R. Perrin performed an examination on the body of a murdered white man, who had been discovered in Smith's Creek near "the Wilmington & Weldon Railroad, and about a mile from the depot." The man was a stranger, and was "dressed in black broadcloth coat, doeskin pants and cut velvet vest." He was about five feet seven or eight inches in height, had a short goatee and sandy hair. He had been murdered by what appeared to be axe blows to the head and many stab wounds and cuts from a knife to the chest and abdomen.

On the bank of the creek at the murder site were footprints, indications of a struggle, and definite traces of blood, despite the fact it had rained heavily the night before the body was found. The poor fellow had evidently been in the water about 36 hours when his corpse was discovered. At the time of the inquest, there were no clues as to the identity of the suspect or suspects, though robbery was apparently the motive for the crime, the man's pockets having been rifled. [97]

The *Daily Journal*, as early as February 1862, recommended that law-abiding citizens keep a loaded weapon handy, just in case someone tried to assault them or break into their home. Mr. G.J. McRee was lucky he followed the advice, for he had to shoot a man who tried assaulting him in his house. [98]

Probably the largest scale assault on law and order in the city came at the hands of veteran Rebel soldiers, who were accustomed to assaulting far graver odds than they confronted in Wilmington. In September 1863, Hood's Texas Brigade, some of Robert E. Lee's toughest shock troops, under command of General Jerome Robertson, jolted its way south on top of and inside springless railroad boxcars. They were headed for Georgia, to reinforce Braxton Bragg and the Army of Tennessee, which was about to engage William Rosecrans in the bloodbath of Chickamauga.

On September 10 the Texans had arrived in town to change trains. Eleven of them decided to leave military duty and hard-tack behind for a while, and proceeded to get drunk and create "considerable noise and disturbance" at a house down in Paddy's Hollow, a tough part of town on the riverfront situated between the Wilmington & Weldon Railroad Depot and the Farmer's Hotel. [99]

The town guard of three elderly civilians was called out to quell the disturbance, not quite as formidable obstacles as the Yankees the Texans had run into in the Cornfield at Sharpsburg, or on Little Round Top at Gettysburg. It was no contest, really, and the three Wilmingtonians, named Mr. Harker, Mr. Shelly, and Mr. Futrel, were lucky to have gotten away with their lives. Civilians were no match for hell-raising Texas Confederates.

The *Daily Journal* said that Mr. Harker, who was between 50 and 60 years old, received a severe beating. "Futrel got a severe blow on the side of the head from a stick or club, and Shelly was cut with a knife, first, in the side, below the ribs, and secondly in the side higher up, the knife striking against a rib and glancing. Fortunately neither the cavity of the chest nor abdomen was penetrated, and the wounds, although serious are not necessarily dangerous." [100]

The unrepentant Texans apparently found their way back to the brigade, climbed back on the buckboard-like jolting flatcars and boxcars, and continued South toward Georgia, where the western Yankees of the Army of the Cumberland were to give them a warmer reception than Wilmington's town guard. [101]

The morning after the fracas in Paddy's Hollow, the body of a newborn white infant girl was found floating in the Cape Fear. The baby was found near the wharf of the Wilmington & Weldon Railroad. The child had obviously been murdered. "It was wrapped in a new piece of flannel, neatly trimmed with a piece of flannel round its neck, also a rope to which was attached a piece of iron, which proved not sufficient to keep the body down when it swelled and thus became buoyant." No witnesses or additional evidence had been uncovered at the time of the story. [102]

On the same day the article of the dead baby girl was published, a fire took place shortly before noon, "by which some cotton stored near the river and below the Wilmington and Weldon Railroad Depot, was destroyed." Some fires, naturally, were the result of accidents, but others were apparently caused by arson, and some believed Yankee sympathizers were the culprits. One Wilmingtonian suggested to the *Daily Journal* that available male residents be organized into patrols to help supplement the military guards around town, and that they be used to guard the public stores that ran the blockade, such as cotton, as well as the homes and property of Confederate soldiers in the army and civilians who had left for the country. [103]

Despite the trauma of war-time conditions, with its attendant crime, military garrisons and rowdy blockade running crews, soldiers funerals, and the yellow fever epidemic, Wilmingtonians who remained in town could occasionally enjoy a taste of culture and relaxation not found in other cities in the state, or even larger ones in other states.

Wilmington had boasted of a theatrical group since the late eighteenth century, known as the Thalian Association. About 1800, their first building for performances was erected, at a time when the population of the town was about 1,500 people. Even in the early years of the century, the bottom floor of the old Innes Academy at the corner of Third and Princess streets saw amateur actors perform various plays, such as Shakespeare's "Hamlet". [104]

In 1855 the old academy was torn down, and on the same site, a combination city hall and theater was erected. The wing containing the theater was 110 feet by 60 feet, the stage measured 42 feet by 57 feet, the auditorium was 45 feet by 57 feet, and the ceiling was 54 feet high. Thalian Hall, as it came to be known, could seat 950 people, and had 188 gas burners that lighted performances. [105]

Some of the well-known amateur actors who called Wilmington home in the late 1850's were also some of the most prominent and respected citizens of town, and some would perish in the war. Dr. James H. Dickson, who succumbed to yellow fever in September 1862, "appeared frequently upon the stage, and was regarded as an excellent performer." James A. Wright, the same young man who became Captain Wright of the First North Carolina Infantry, and died defending Richmond in June 1862, was one of the youngest members of the Thalian Association. It was said that he would have had a promising career on the stage, had he not been killed. [106]

Shows began about 8 p.m. Prices for seats ranged from 25 cents to 50 cents, depending on the location of the seat. Performances, when they were plays, were normally in two parts, the primary and first one being of a dramatic, tragic, or comic nature, and the secondary one being a shorter and lighter presentation, many times a farce. French Zouaves from the Crimea brought drill and pantomimes to the stage, while the Confederate Minstrels offered singing and dancing that must have had a decidedly Southern patriotic air to it, judging by the group's name. Blind Tom, who was a young and exceptionally talented black pianist, gave outstanding performances in May 1862. [107]

Other diversions were available to Wilmingtonians. One of them was the Wilmington Library Association, also situated in Thalian Hall, which had been formed in 1855 upon acquisition of the books of the Wilmington Mercantile Library Association. For those who wanted to own their books, many volumes were available for purchase from city bookstores. Even in the midst of the yellow fever crisis, residents could find at Kelley's Book Store the poems of Robert Burns, or the works of John Milton or Sir Walter Scott. Charles Dickens' "Nicholas Nickleby", the "Old Curiosity Shop" or "Barnaby Rudge" could also be had. Military related publications, such as "Mahan's Field Fortifications", "Hardee's Infantry Tactics", or "Roberts' Hand Book of

Artillery" also lined the shelves at Kelley's. For Wilmingtonians interested in the latest Southern military songs, Whitaker's Book Store carried them. The "Beauregard Manassas Quickstep", "Dixie Fantasia", Southern Marsailles", "Bonnie Blue Flag with variations", "My Maryland with variations", "The Battle of Bethel Quickstep", and "God will defend the right" were some of the latest popular tunes that were in stock and ready for sale. [108]

There were also two Masonic lodges in town, St. Johns Number One and Concord Chapter Number One. For men who preferred the company of the International Order of Odd Fellows, two lodges were available for their tastes as well. [109]

In addition to the usual saloons where men could wet their whistles, parties could be found, if one associated with or worked for a blockade-running firm, or knew someone who did. Tom Taylor, Colonel Lamb's young English friend who donated Whitworth guns to the Confederate Cause and British profits, found Wilmington to be a town "sadly pinched and war-worn", the people apparently never having enough to eat or drink. When Taylor and his crew on the *Banshee* put in at the docks, invited and uninvited guests flocked to the blockade runner, in hopes of partaking of the food and alcohol known to be aboard.

Taylor was delighted to serve as many as they could. "Men who had been accustomed to live on corn-bread and bacon, and to drink nothing but water, appreciated our delicacies, our bottled beer, good brandy, and, on great occasions, our champagne, warmed their hearts toward us...But we had our reward. If any special favour were asked it was always granted, if possible, to the *Banshee*, and if any push had to be made there was always some one to make it...Whether due to the luncheon parties or not need not be said, but we were within a very few days able to cast off our moorings and drop down the river...with tobacco and laden with cotton – three tiers even on deck." [110]

Parties there were for some, and books, theater, and the other forms of entertainment. It was good there were some diversions from the drudgery and cruelty of war, for fate had dealt a tough hand for Wilmingtonians to play. By and large, people worked very hard just to endure and survive.

Following the King family's return to Wilmington from the sound after the yellow fever ended, Isaac secured "a position as assistant wagon master at the Government stables located in the S.E. corner of 9th and Market Sts.", after his honorable discharge from Confederate service due to his wounds received at Malvern Hill. In the stables were kept hundreds of horses, mules, ambulances and wagons. Isaac got brother Joe a job there as "food master," and it was his responsibility to superintend the feeding of all the animals.

While engaged in this line of work, Joe decided he wanted to try his hand as a crewman on one of the many blockade runners plying the sea-lanes to and from Nassau. He went to General Whiting, who made his headquarters in the DeRosset family home at the corner of 3rd and Market, to seek his permission to ship out on one of the vessels. Whiting was adamantly against it; "you can't get it, we need you here," he said, apparently referring to his position in the Confederate stables. [111]

Not long after, Joe decided to go into the butchering business again, being the enterprising young man he was, and observing the "considerable amount of meat" used by the blockade runners. Isaac joined him in furnishing money to the venture, and they soon had a contract with the "meat firm of Jim Hall and Sellars, in a little wooden shop on the S.W. corner of Front and Princess Sts., who was then furnishing the blockade runners." They were able to get the "highest retail price" for "every butchered animal" they brought to the Hall & Sellars Company, and "furnished them for some time and made a considerable amount of money." [112]

In addition to Confederate government work or the food supply business such as Joe and Isaac King became involved in, some men sought employment with the lucrative blockade running firms, worked for the railroads, or engaged in salt making at the large State Salt Works on Myrtle Grove Sound, about eight miles north of Fort Fisher. There, on the southern end of Masonboro Sound, more than 200 workers lived and operated the huge facility that produced four tons of salt each day, salt that was so essential to the preservation of meat for North Carolina citizens and soldiers. [113]

As well as tending to the normal duties of keeping up a home, women in town could sometimes find work with small industrial companies. Henry Lowe & Company was a stocking factory situated at the foot of Chestnut Street, and used as many as one hundred female workers to fulfill its backlog of orders. The ladies would carry machine knitted upper and lower parts of a stocking home with them to sew together, returning the finished product to the mill. Other women took in dirty clothes from crews of the blockade runners, washing and ironing them for good prices, since employees of the Nassau and Bermuda-based firms could pay for whatever they wanted. Still others rented rooms in their homes to boarders, some charging as much as $500 per week, depending on the number of people in a family. [114]

People desperately needed all the money they could earn in Wilmington, for prices made many commodities almost prohibitive as the war progressed. The cost of a ham went to $50, a barrel of flour rose to $500, as did a pair of boots; $600 was the cost of a suit of clothes, $1,500 was eventually paid for an overcoat, and when you could find it, $100 in Confederate currency was gladly paid for a pound of coffee or tea. [115]

Coffee was the most prized of luxuries and was hard to get, even if Wilmington was the recipient of so much blockade running traffic. The cost alone made it almost out of reach for the average person. Substitute coffee, made of beans, rye, and potatoes, ground together and boiled, and sweetened with sorghum, was widely used in town and country alike.

Near the country home of Alexander Sprunt, where he had moved his family from Wilmington during the yellow fever epidemic, lived two middle-aged spinsters who were as desperate for coffee as anyone else in the Confederacy. When an old man in the neighborhood proposed marriage to one of them, the other sister was irate when her sibling refused his offer. She insisted that her sister had wasted a golden opportunity for both of them, for she said, "Didn't you know he has a bag of coffee in his house?" [116]

As prices and shortages mounted, so, too, did the deaths and maiming of Wilmington's sons on the battlefield. In the First North Carolina State Troops, of which New Hanover's Company E was a part, 32 men were killed, 140 wounded and 27 missing in the Chancellorsville Campaign in April and May, 1863. [117] In the Third North Carolina State Troops, composed of many Wilmington men, 39 soldiers died at Chancellorsville, while 175 were wounded and 17 missing. In Wilmington Captain John Van Bokkelen's Company D, 17 men were wounded, while the captain himself died of wounds the latter part of June. It was with the deepest grief that his death was received by his Wilmington friends in the regiment, as it marched forward to its rendezvous at Gettysburg. [118]

In the Eighteenth North Carolina, of which the Wilmington Light Infantry, the German Volunteers and the Wilmington Rifle Guards comprised three companies, 34 men were killed, 99 were wounded and 21 missing in the battles around Chancellorsville. The German Volunteers, comprised in large part of Wilmingtonians who were native to places such as Wurttemberg, Prussia, Ludwigshafen am Rhein, and who bore surnames such as Vollers, Schulken, Portwig and Schlobohmm, demonstrated with their blood their fealty to the new Southern Fatherland, losing 3 killed or mortally wounded, 11 wounded and 1 captured. The famed Wilmington Light Infantry suffered 3 killed, 5 wounded, and 1 missing. The Wilmington Rifle Guards had 4 soldiers killed or mortally wounded, 1 captured, and 8 wounded in action. [119]

Wilmingtonians had two months to contemplate the carnage of Chancellorsville, before the slaughter of Gettysburg. The three Wilmington companies in the Eighteenth North Carolina participated in the Pettigrew-Pickett assault of July 3, 1863, and the regiment lost 4 men killed in action in the campaign, and 41 wounded. The Third North Carolina suffered fearfully in its assaults on the Yankee breastworks at Culp's Hill on the night of July 2 and early morning of the 3rd. Carrying 300 riflemen into the fight, the Third was able to muster just 77 muskets when the battle ended.

In Company D, 2 soldiers lost their lives and 8 were wounded. In Company F, 9 men were wounded in the company. Among them was Joe King's older brother, James Madison, severely wounded in the leg and thigh. Badly hurt, he was left in a field hospital, captured by the Federals, and later transferred to Point Lookout, Maryland prisoner of war camp. [120]

By late summer of 1863, Wilmingtonians had seen many of their sons killed or mutilated on the field of battle, had suffered tremendous civilian deaths from the yellow fever scourge, and had seen their city turned literally upside-down by military garrison, blockade running, and rampant crime. They had learned as well as any Southerners, better than most, the horrendous suffering and awesome sacrifices to be endured for independence. What they did not know, after more than two years of war, was how much more was to be exacted of them and their gallant defenders, both those in Virginia with Robert E. Lee, and those manning the guns of Fort Fisher below Wilmington, with William Lamb.

Endnotes to Chapter 5

1. Personal Recollections of Joseph Piram King, p.2, Larry Walker collection of great-grandfather's personal papers, hereinafter King recollections; N.C. Historical Review, April 1951, p.122
2. King recollections, p.1-2
3. King recollections, p.1-2
4. NC Troops, Volume III, p.528
5. NC Troops, Volume III, p.528; King recollections, p.3-5; National Archives, Service Record of Isaac W. King, Third North Carolina State Troops, author's collection
6. NC Troops, Volume III, p.549
7. NC Troops, Volume VI, p.295-303, p.378, p.384
8. King recollections, p.1
9. King recollections, p.2
10. King recollections, p.2
11. King recollections, p.3
12. King recollections, p.3
13. Chronicles, p.272-273; NC Troops, Volume II, p.181-182; Clark, Volume II, p.629-630
14. Ashe, *History of North Carolina, Volume II*, p.736; NC Troops, Volume III, p.487; Daily Journal, July 5, 1862
15. Clark, Volume I, p.177; Chronicles, p.296
16. Chronicles, p.299-300; NC Troops, Volume III, p.487
17. NC Troops, Volume III, p.487; Chronicles, p.296-297; William Lamb Day booklet, p.3
18. NC Troops, Volume III, p.501; Chronicles, p.297
19. Chronicles, p.297-298; NC Troops, Volume III, p.543
20. NC Troops, Volume V, p.264; Chronicles, p.300
21. NC Troops, Volume XII, p.258, p.276; Chronicles, p.300
22. NC Troops, Volume III, p.543; Volume XII, back cover

23. Chronicles, p.311
24. Chronicles, p.362; NC Troops, Volume I, p.184-185
25. Chronicles, p.362-363; NC Troops, Volume I, p.195
26. Chronicles, p.359; NC Troops, Volume I, p.74-75
27. Chronicles, p.363-364; NC Troops, Volume III, p.522; Clark, Volume I, p.177
28. Daily Journal, October 7, 1862; Chronicles, p.366; Clark, Volume I, p.228
29. Daily Journal, July 1, 1862; Chronicles, p.367
30. Daily Journal, July 1, 1862; NC Troops, Volume III, p.191
31. Daily Journal, July 5, 1862; NC Troops, Volume VI, p.307, p.401
32. Daily Journal, July 5, 1862; Clark, Volume I, p.183
33. Ibid, July 5, 1862
34. Ibid, July 7, 1862; Chronicles, p.298; Service record of Sergeant Isaac W. King, Third North Carolina State Troops
35. NC Troops, Volume VI, p.296-297, p.384
36. Daily Journal, July 7, 1862
37. Daily Journal, July 7, 1862; NC Troops, Volume VI, p.492; NC Troops, Volume VIII, p.344
38. Daily Journal, July 22, 1862
39. "Patriotic Mrs. Armand J. DeRosset", Confederate Veteran, Volume III (1895), p.218; "North Carolina Women of the Confederacy", Confederate Veteran, Volume XXXVIII (1930), p.420
40. Chronicles, p.414
41. Confederate Veteran, 1895, p.218-219; NC Troops, Volume III, p.566
42. Chronicles, p.356, Clark, Volume IV, p.625-626; Lower Cape Fear Historical Society Bulletin, March, 1968, hereinafter Cape Fear Bulletin
43. Clark, Volume IV, p.426; NC Troops, Volume VI, p.475
44. Clark, Volume IV, p.316-317, p.319; NC Troops, Volume I, p.512, p.523
45. Wilmington Sunday Star-News, Cape Fear Section, March 7, 1976; Clark, Volume IV, p.330
46. Clark, Volume IV, p.330-331
47. Chronicles, p.287; Confederate Veteran, 1931, p.50
48. *The New Encyclopaedia Britannica*, Volume 12, p.832, University of Chicago, Chicago, Illinois, 1987
49. Daily Journal, September 29, 1862; Chronicles, p.286
50. Memoir of Reverend J.L. Prichard, p.138, hereinafter Prichard Memoir; Daily Journal, September 29, 1862
51. Waddell, Some Memories of My Life, p.55; Chronicles, p.286; Cape Fear Bulletin, November 1967; NC Troops, Volume II, p.180, p.825
52. Prichard Memoir, p.146-147; Cape Fear Bulletin, November 1967
53. Daily Journal, September 16, 1862; Chronicles, p.284
54. Prichard Memoir, p.148-151

55. Ashe, *History of North Carolina, Volume II*, p.1234, hereinafter Ashe, Volume II; Chronicles, p.286
56. Daily Journal, September 29, 1862; Chronicles, p.238
57. Prichard Memoir, p.150
58. Daily Journal, September 29, 1862
59. Daily Journal, September 30, 1862
60. Daily Journal, September 30, 1862
61. King recollections, p.3-4
62. King recollections, p.4
63. King recollections, p.4
64. King recollections, p.4
65. King recollections, p.5
66. Daily Journal, October 1 and 7, 1862
67. Daily Journal, October 4 and 15, 1862
68. Daily Journal, October 20, 1862; Memoir of J.L. Prichard, p.159
69. Daily Journal, September 29 and 30, 1862
70. Daily Journal, October 6, 1862
71. Daily Journal, October 20 and 21, 1862
72. Daily Journal, October 21, 1862
73. Daily Journal, October 25 and 27, 1862
74. Daily Journal, October 20 and 25, 1862
75. Prichard Memoir, p.158-159
76. Prichard Memoir, p.161-162
77. Prichard Memoir, p.164-166
78. Prichard Memoir, p.167; NC Troops, Volume I, p.10
79. Daily Journal, November 17, 1862; Ashe, Volume II, p.755
80. Ashe, Volume II, p.755
81. Clark, Volume I, p.225-226, p.228; Daily Journal, September 29, 1862; NC Troops, Volume III, p.553, p.711
82. Clark, Volume I, p.186, p.189, p.225-226
83. Daily Journal, September 29, 1862; NC Troops, Volume III, p.522
84. Clark, Volume I, p.226-227; NC Troops, Volume III, p.487, p.566; Daily Journal, September 29, 1862
85. NC Troops, Volume III, p.549; National Archives Service Record of James Madison King, Third North Carolina State Troops; NC Troops, Volume VI, p.299, p.384
86. Daily Journal, October 3, 1862; NC Troops, Volume III, p.174
87. Chronicles, p.284-285, p.366-367
88. Carse, Blockade, p.9; Wood, Port Town at War, p.154
89. Daily Journal, January 2, 1863
90. Daily Journal, January 2, 1863
91. Daily Journal, January 21, 1863; NC Troops, Volume III, p.483

92. Daily Journal, February 11, 1863
93. Daily Journal, February 11, 1863
94. Daily Journal, May 14, 1863
95. Scharf, Confederate Navy, p.464; Port Town at War, p.141
96. Scharf, Confederate Navy, p.464-465
97. Daily Journal, April 1, 1863; Port Town at War
98. Port Town at War, p.149
99. Daily Journal, September 11, 1863; Tucker, Glenn, *Chickamauga: Bloody Battle in the West*, p.95, Morningside Bookshop, Dayton, Ohio, 1984; Polley, J.B., *Hood's Texas Brigade, Its Marches Its Battles Its Achievements*, p.198-199, Morningside Bookshop, Dayton, Ohio, 1988, hereinafter Hood's Texas Brigade
100. Daily Journal, September 11, 1863
101. Hood's Texas Brigade, p.199-212
102. Daily Journal, September 12, 1863
103. "Port Town at War", p.150; Daily Journal, September 12, 1863
104. Chronicles, p.248-249; North Carolina Historical Review, April 1951, p.119
105. North Carolina Historical Review, April 1951, p.120
106. Chronicles, p.251, p.256
107. "Port Town at War", p.127-128; North Carolina Historical Review, April 1951, p.127
108. Port Town at War, p.128; Daily Journal, October 9, 1862
109. Port Town at War, p.128
110. Thomas Taylor, Running the Blockade, p.65-66
111. King recollections, p.5-6
112. King recollections, p.6
113. Port Town at War, p.139; Salt, That Necessary Article, p.40-41
114. Port Town at War, p.140-142
115. Chronicles, p.288
116. Chronicles, p.288
117. NC Troops, Volume III, p.137, p.194-196, p.199-200
118. NC Troops, Volume III, p.483, p.487, p.522, p.528, p.531; Chronicles p.363-364; Daily Journal, May 25, 1863
119. NC Troops, Volume VI, p.301, p.309-320, p.379-389, p.401-411
120. NC Troops, Volume III, p.544, p.549; NC Troops, Volume VI, p.303; Clark, Volume I, p.195-196; Daily Journal, July 21, 1863

A view of Fort Fisher's land face looking at it from the north. You can make out part of the palisade fence.

Chapter 6

"...this place is quite as important as Vicksburg was."

The necessity here for a very strong movable force," wrote William H.C. Whiting from his office in the DeRosset building at Third and Market Street to his boss, James Seddon, on August 28, 1863, "is daily more apparent, and it should be of all arms. It is hard to say which I need most, infantry, artillery, or cavalry, all are so necessary and so important." Implying to the Secretary of War that loss of the *Hebe* could have been prevented five days before, when Colonel Lamb's mobile Whitworth battery fought so tenaciously against the Yankee warships, the General said: "Two batteries of 10-pounder Parrott guns, so long since applied for, might have saved the *Hebe* with her large and valuable cargo of government stores. I have lost my little Whitworth, which has so often driven off the enemy and saved our steamers, in an unequal contest with a frigate and six steamers. But it is not to save steamers that I want force. It is to make this vital point secure." [1]

With the current paucity of troops at his command, Wilmington was not at all secure in the late summer of 1863. In the entire District of the Cape Fear, including "City and river defenses", the garrisons at Forts Anderson, Caswell and Fisher, and even including troops away at Kenansville, Whiting had at his disposal an effective total of only 3,706 officers and men. An additional 800 soldiers were in the area, but were not considered "effective," due to illness, wounds, or other problems. [2]

With remarkable prescience of what was in store for his department seventeen months in the future, the commander of the Wilmington defenses wrote on August 28 that "the enemy, landing a few thousand men at Masonborough before the movement can be arrested, cuts off the peninsula between the ocean and the Cape Fear River, and the fate of Fort Fisher and the harbor is sealed. I know no place now in the Confederacy where the presence of a large body of veteran troops is more necessary or more important than this...I think now that this place is quite as important as Vicksburg was." [3]

Writing further on September 8, Whiting insisted that Wilmington was extremely vital to the Cause, and hourly becoming more so, since Charleston was effectively bottled up by the formidable Yankee siege investing the place. "The city of Charleston may not be taken," he wrote, "but as a Confederate port it has well nigh ceased to belong to us...As Charleston is closed in the danger increases. If the Department considers this position as worth anything, I beg that troops may be gathered here. At no time in the history of this war has it been entirely stripped, or in so great danger." [4]

Whiting was also specifically worried about Bald Head Island (then known as Smith Island), which Colonel Thomas Jones, commandant of Fort Caswell, had seen reconnoitered by the Yankees on September 6, a Sunday. He reported to Whiting that two boatloads of Union sailors had gone ashore near the cape of the island, and he countered by sending over some of his soldiers from Caswell. By the time the Confederates got there, the Unionists had left. "I am disposed to think," Jones said, "that the enemy is planning to occupy the island before we do, and therefore request permission to keep one of my companies over on Bald Head, or at least a detachment of men and a piece of artillery, until the battery is erected over there." [5]

The general concurred, and on September 8 ordered Lieutenant Colonel B.W. Frobel with Confederate engineers to immediately occupy Bald Head and to begin construction of earthworks and trenches for a fort. New Hanover Captain Robert G. Rankin's Company A of the First Battalion North Carolina Heavy Artillery was ordered there as a defensive force, taking along the mule-drawn Whitworth rifle from Fort Caswell. Captain Rankin had been chairman of Wilmington's Safety Committee prior to the outbreak of hostilities. "At the beginning of the war," his friend James Sprunt wrote, "he was made quartermaster of Wilmington, and was afterwards made captain of the First Battalion, Heavy Artillery." [6]

Major John Hedrick was also ordered to Bald Head to assist in construction of the new fort. "Timber must be immediately secured for bomb-proofs," General Whiting ordered, "and no time must be lost in the construction. Tetes-de-pont should be built to cover the wharves." [7]

To aid in the construction of fortifications on Bald Head, at Fort Fisher, and the many other points in the Cape Fear District, the Bureau of Engineers in Richmond urged Governor Vance to summon black laborers in the state's eastern counties, and send them to Wilmington. Colonel Jeremy Gilmer, head of the bureau, told Zeb Vance that "slave labor is required, and Major General Whiting, commanding in the eastern part of your State, urges that immediate steps be taken to procure it. The works ought to be pressed forward without delay." Gilmer urged Vance to appeal to the patriotism of the planters in the eastern counties, to help ensure "the safety of your principal sea-port...Should any military organization be required for the collection of the requisite number of negroes, at least 1,000, General Whiting can furnish the force." [8]

Additional laborers Whiting would get, but for the present, no more troops would be coming to Wilmington. On September 8, the same day he had ordered the occupation of Bald Head Island, James Seddon wrote to advise him that his concerns for the Cape Fear and the need for more soldiers to protect it, had been presented several times to President Davis and General Lee as well, who had been in consultation with him for several days. "With the limited resources of the Department," the Secretary of War regretfully said, "and the urgent pressure of the enemy's forces at other (for the present) even more vital points, the conclusion has been that no troops beyond those already in North Carolina can be spared for the re-enforcement of Wilmington." [9]

Since no more troops would be coming to Wilmington for the time being, Whiting pushed ahead vigorously with his additional fortifications, both on Bald Head and at other judiciously placed locations, to maximize his insufficient manpower.

Approximately one mile west of Fort Caswell, "near the Old Bug light-house," and at a position commanding the Western Bar entrance to the river, the Rebels were throwing up another heavy sand fortification. The Yankee fleet was powerless to prevent construction, fearing the long-range, well-protected guns at Caswell might blow holes in them. This citadel, known as Fort Campbell, would be completed by the beginning of 1864. When finished, Campbell would mount sixteen guns and two mortars, well protected by high and thick traverses modeled after Fort Fisher. At least four of the big guns would be 10-inch Columbiads, and one would be the powerful 100-pounder Brooke rifle. Major John D. Taylor, second in command at Caswell, was promoted to lieutenant colonel, and assigned to command Fort Campbell. His garrison would consist of Company B of the First Battalion North Carolina Heavy Artillery, and company K, organized by himself in 1862, of the Thirty-Sixth North Carolina Regiment. [10]

Halfway between Caswell and Campbell was a small battery mounting one 10-inch Columbiad, known as Battery Shaw. It served as additional protection to Caswell's western flank, and Campbell's eastern one, as well as providing

Gen. William Dorsey Pender, C.S.A.

additional firepower against Union vessels venturing too close to the Western Bar. [11]

At Smithville, old Fort Johnston had also been turned into a sand and earthwork fortification known as Fort Pender. It was named after North Carolina's fine, young Major General Dorsey Pender, who died of a shrapnel wound to the leg received at Gettysburg. A soldier on duty there in First Company I of the Thirty-Sixth North Carolina, said that his unit had built Pender from the old U.S. installation. When complete, this fort contained seven large and heavy traverses, also modeled after Colonel Lamb's work on Confederate Point, and mounted four of the 10-inch Columbiads. The soldiers also "fortified the town in the rear by a line of breastworks and redoubts from Elizabeth Creek to the Cape Fear river, below deep water point," while at the same time performing the routine chores of drill and picket duty. These Rebels at Fort Pender were good soldiers, having fought the Yankees at Bald Head in July, when they assisted Colonel Lamb in driving away the Federal fleet to save the blockade-runner *Kate*. [12]

As the forts on the western shore of the Cape Fear were being added to and enhanced, much effort was being expended on Bald Head. Hundreds of slaves and Confederate soldiers were hard at work piling up the enormous sand mounds that had proven so effective at absorbing Yankee naval fire. Many of the large palmetto trees growing on the island, some more than twenty inches in diameter and twenty to thirty feet high, were used in the construction, as they had been at Fort Fisher. They were used as revetments on the gun parapets, as well as exterior sheathing to help deflect the huge shells the Union fleet could hurl.

Fort Holmes, as this new bastion on the Cape Fear was named, consisted of more than one and a half miles of twenty foot high sand mounds, casemates, bomb-proofs, protective curtains, and magazines. It was named for one of North Carolina's older, and not so distinguished generals, Major General Theophilus H. Holmes, who had at one time been commanding officer of the Confederate Southern Department of Coastal Defenses. It commenced at Bald Head Point, at the junction of the Cape Fear River and the ocean, ran approximately 800 yards in a northeasterly direction along the ocean, and then angled back due north about 1000 yards to the lighthouse, terminating just

Bald Head Island (or Smith Island) was the site of Fort Holmes at Old Inlet.

south of Light-House Creek. Another heavy curtain ran northeasterly about 1000 yards from the tip of the point to below Light-House Creek, nearly enclosing the entire work in a shape that resembled an uneven triangle. [13]

One of the garrison, Sergeant Thaddeus Davis, previously stationed at Fort Pender, wrote that the men built "Fort Holmes, with twelve guns, on the point, opposite Fort Caswell, and a 6-gun battery on the creek, near the Light House; these were intersected by strong breastworks and redoubts, and we also cleared two roads through the island in order that we might bring into position whenever necessary, the Whitworth and Parrott guns which were principally used to protect blockade-runners while trying to run into port." [14]

To man the stout new fortifications, General Whiting ordered selected companies of heavy artillery units from various regiments to Bald Head Island to form a new unit, specifically organized to defend this vital, center position in the mouth of the river, between Fort Fisher to the northeast, and Fort Caswell to the northwest. The Fortieth Regiment North Carolina Troops, also known as the Third Regiment of North Carolina Artillery, had existed on paper since January 1862. It was assigned as many as fourteen light and heavy artillery batteries in the Cape Fear District at different times between January 1862 and November 1863, when it was officially organized. Up until that time, it had not even had its own regimental commander or field and staff officers, while battery commanders reported directly to the commanding officer of the post to which they were assigned.

Colonel Lamb, for example, was in charge of Captain William Tripp's Company B of the Fortieth Regiment while it served at Fort Fisher. This company had handled one of the Whitworth cannon in July during the battle for the *Kate*, and had helped drive off the Yankee fleet trying to capture her. Company E of the Fortieth, the "Scotch Greys" of Richmond and Robeson Counties, had been an unattached unit manning the guns at Fort Caswell for

Colonel Thomas Jones, when the fight for the *Kate* occurred, and they also had charge of the other Whitworth that was still in the Cape Fear District in the summer. [15]

In November, light artillery batteries still present in the regiment were transferred out, and only heavy batteries constituted the organization. Field officers were elected on December 1, a Tuesday, and Major John Hedrick, one of Wilmington's earliest defenders, being in charge of the seizure of Forts Caswell and Johnston in January 1861, was chosen colonel. George Tait, former captain and commanding officer of the Bladen Artillery Guards, which had served at Fort St. Philip (Fort Anderson) and Fort Fisher, was elected lieutenant colonel. By early 1862, nine companies were stationed at Fort Holmes on Bald Head, with one company, Company F, joining Colonel John Taylor and his other two batteries to serve the guns on Oak Island at Fort Campbell. [16]

If feverish activity was the norm at Bald Head Island and the Western Bar fortifications, it was also proceeding with the usual vigor on Confederate Point. Quite a few slaves were utilized in building fortifications in the fall of 1863. Before Captain Tripp's unit was moved from Fort Fisher to Bald Head, a battery was erected near his quarters, and at least seventy black laborers were hard at work on it. Not all the slaves were content to build fortifications on the Cape Fear, and some occasionally sought freedom. In August, at least two runaways were killed while trying to escape, being caught along the river between Wilmington and Fort Fisher. [17]

Colonel Lamb kept his garrison hard at work on the mounds and batteries, leaving little opportunity for Rebel privates to shirk their responsibility. The men pulled duty on the fortifications every other day, according to Robeson County native Franklin McNeill of Company C, First Battalion North Carolina Heavy Artillery, which had been serving at Fort Fisher since May 1862. The health of the men was good, though, McNeill wrote his father in September 1863. Their diet at Fisher consisted primarily of beef and crackers, so young Franklin, who was eighteen when he enlisted the preceding April, was exceedingly grateful when a parcel arrived from home containing a box of Robeson County potatoes and other food. [18]

McNeill and his comrades continued to do a commendable job building traverses and parapets for William Lamb. One high ranking Union naval officer, writing in the fall of 1863, said that Fort Fisher was an extremely strong fortification, "equal to any in Charleston harbor." Considering the power and resilience of Charleston forts such as Wagner, Sumter, and Moultrie, such an opinion was not to be taken lightly by the Federals.

Part of the fort was casemated, and white refugees had reported "that it is built of palmetto trees 14 feet thick and filled in with sand...I believe it mounts about 20 guns," the officer continued, "most of which are the old-fashioned smoothbore 32-pounders, with perhaps two or three 8-inch rifled guns. Adjoining it is the new Mound fort, built of heavy frame timbers, said to be 70 or 80 feet

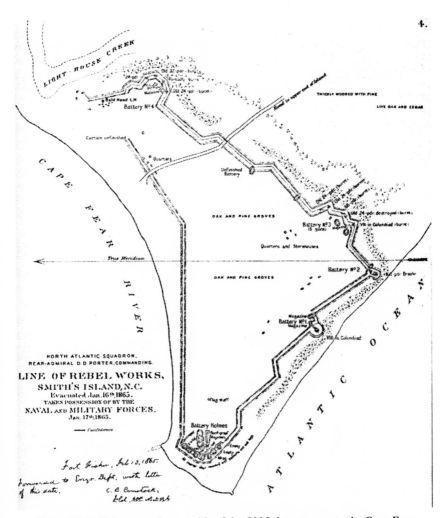

Plan of Fort Holmes, on the east side of the Old Inlet entrance to the Cape Fear.

high and covered with sand to make it bombproof." Two heavy guns mounted on top of the Mound would "fire plunging shot on the decks of ironclads and other vessels."

The Yankee officer continued: "There are six other detached casemated batteries, made bombproof with sand and apparently mounting two heavy guns, each designed to protect the bar and to strengthen Fort Fisher." [19]

If he could not get more troops right now to join Franklin McNeill and his comrades at Fort Fisher, General Whiting was at least pleased to have an old friend join him in late 1863 to assist in the defense of Wilmington. Louis Hebert was a Louisiana born and bred West Point classmate of Whiting's. He started the war as colonel of the Third Louisiana Infantry, and had molded it into one of the crack fighting units in the Trans-Mississippi Confederacy. One of his proud Louisianans said that "he was a strict disciplinarian, punctilious in enforcing a rigid adherence to all orders; as a man, he was genial and kind in manner and conversation...the Colonel became a great favorite with the Regiment." [20]

BrigGen. Louis Hebert, C.S.A.

Hebert was a veteran of the Battles of Wilson's Creek and Elkhorn Tavern (Pea Ridge), as well as the Vicksburg Campaign. In May 1862, Jefferson Davis had made him a Confederate brigadier. He was surrendered with the Army of Vicksburg in July 1863, and in late summer he was a paroled prisoner, along with the rest of the army. President Davis came out to visit and inspect the paroled troops, assembled at Enterprise, Mississippi, and while there told Hebert that his old friend and classmate, William Whiting, had requested that Hebert join him as his second in command of the Cape Fear District. Hebert consented, riding back east on the train with the President. When he reported to Whiting, he was ordered to the mouth of the Cape Fear and given command of the men and works at Forts Fisher, Caswell, Pender, and Holmes. [21]

Fort Fisher and Wilmington saw some interesting people come in and go out in late 1863. James McNeill Whistler was an aspiring artist in London in that year. His mother, Anna Matilda Whistler, was a Wilmingtonian by birth and childhood. In late 1863, having had enough of the war, she took leave of the Confederacy by shipping out on a blockade-runner, eventually joining her son in England. He later painted her portrait, Mrs. Whistler never dreaming that her likeness would become known to the world as "Whistler's Mother." [22]

In early October, Braxton Bragg's Army of Tennessee was besieging the Army of the Cumberland, now entrenched inside Chattanooga, following the barren victory at Chickamauga, Georgia. The high command in Bragg's army was seething with discord and frustration over their commander's failure to capitalize on their battlefield success won at such a terrible price in brave men. To investigate the rumblings and help quell dissension in his western army, Jefferson Davis decided to visit the Army of Tennessee. On October 6,

Davis left Richmond on a circuitous route headed for North Georgia. Wilmington was on that route.

Being on a tight schedule, Davis was limited to a brief visit in Wilmington. He did, however, remain long enough for a personal interview with General Whiting. The President told Whiting to write to Adjutant General Cooper in Richmond for more troops. During the last week of September, the administration, finally responding to Whiting's appeal for movable infantry, had assigned Martin's Brigade of North Carolina troops to his district. Additionally, Clingman's North Carolina Brigade, now at Charleston, was ordered to be on the alert to hurry to Wilmington at a moment's notice. Now, General Cooper should order some artillerists at the forts on the James River to Wilmington, Davis said, since there had been

James MacNeill Whistler

no increase in the number of heavy artillerists in the Cape Fear area since General French had commanded the year before. Additionally, Mr. Davis wanted Cooper to request the Secretary of the Navy, Stephen Mallory, to send down some Marines as well. [23]

Departing Wilmington after his discussions with Whiting, traveling on a special train, the President arrived in Atlanta on October 8. Braxton Bragg met him next morning and accompanied him north to the Chattanooga lines. Davis came back to Wilmington, however, exactly a month later on his return trip to Richmond. Arriving at 7 p.m. on Thursday, November 5, the President was met at the depot of the Wilmington and Manchester Railroad, across the river from town, by General Whiting and his staff, Mayor Dawson, and a committee of citizens. They took the ferry over the river, and as soon as it reached the wharf, "a shout went up that made the welkin ring, and thus escorted by the authorities and accompanied by the people," of which a huge crowd had assembled for the occasion, "President Davis proceeded to the residence of General Whiting, on Market Street below Second." [24]

In a few minutes the President, the general, and the welcoming committee came out on the balcony of the house. Being introduced by Mr. William A. Wright, Jeff Davis gave a patriotic and inspiring speech. He said he hoped Wilmington would forever be free from the tread of the Yankee invader. A reporter for the *Daily Journal* said the President told the people he understood the importance of Wilmington's harbor, "now the only one through which foreign trade was carried on, and he trusted that the valor of her people, assisted by the means which the government would send to her defence would be fully adequate for that purpose."

He had given for the defense of Wilmington one of the ablest soldiers of the Confederacy, General Whiting, "and in case of attack such additions would be made to the garrison in men and arms as would, he believed, enable Wilmington to repulse the foe, however he might come, by land or by sea."

Davis urged all Wilmingtonians to do their duty to the best of their ability during the "present great struggle, the issues of which were on the one hand freedom, independence, prosperity – on the other hand, subjugation, degradation and absolute ruin. The man who could bear arms should do so. The man who could not bear arms, but had wealth, should devote it freely to the support of the soldiers and to taking care of their widows and orphans." [25]

The President had nothing but praise for the gallant soldiers of North Carolina. The state had not been behind any other state in the number of troops sent to the Confederate armies, he said. "In every field, from great Bethel, the first, to Chickamauga, the last, the blood of North Carolinians had been shed and their valor illustrated, and if she had fewer trumpeters than some others to sound her fame, the list of killed and wounded from every battlefield attested her devotion and bore witness to her sacrifices. North Carolina might well be proud of her soldiers in the armies of the Confederacy." [26]

The President echoed the sentiments of most men in the armies when he called for resolve and steady determination. If there were some "who despaired of the Republic," he said, "they were not to be found in the ranks of the army, where all was confidence and determination. Those who complained most, were those who had made the fewest sacrifices, not the soldiers who had made the most.

"In the changing fortunes of war, we may for a time be driven back, but with a resolute purpose and united effort we would regain all that we had lost, and accomplish all that we had proposed. Freed from the shackles imposed upon us by our uncongenial association with a people who had proved themselves to be ten times worse than even he had supposed them to be, the Confederate States would spring forward in a career of happiness and prosperity surpassing the dreams of the most sanguine." [27]

Davis expressed his thanks for the enthusiastic welcome given him, and went inside. A call was then made for General Whiting, but he said "that he could not presume to address the audience after the able and eloquent speech of his Commander-in-chief, President Davis. He could only pledge himself to do all in his power for the defence of Wilmington." [28]

The next morning, Friday, November 6, Davis and Whiting were on a steamer headed down-river to Confederate Point to inspect Fort Fisher and the other positions that protected the entrance to the harbor. Discussing some of the various means by which the government would assist in the defense, the two arrived at the wharf at the end of Confederate Point, where they were met by Colonel Lamb. From there, all rode horseback a mile up the peninsula to the Mound. They climbed the many steps to the top of the sixty-foot high mammoth battery, where the President could get a full view of the Colonel's magnificent fortifications that kept the Yankee ship commanders in awe and at a healthy distance. As soon as they reached the top, and while Davis was scanning the heavy traverses and gun emplacements that stretched for a mile northward, and then across to the river, Lamb, who had had his sea-face guns loaded and manned just for the occasion, gave the order to fire. The giant cannon belched fire and smoke up the beach in a tremendous sequential thunder of twenty-one guns, in honor of the President's visit. The proud young commander of Fort Fisher doubted "whether many of the forts in the South could claim the distinction of having fired such salute." [29]

Afterward, the President, Whiting and Lamb rode northward up the mile long seaface interior of the fort, scrutinizing the huge, man-made sand hills and batteries that protected the Confederacy's lifeline of supplies. Retiring to Lamb's headquarters at the "Pulpit", near the juncture of the seaface and landface that was dubbed the "Northeast Bastion", conversation ranged far and wide. In one discussion, Davis and Whiting gave their opinions about which type of trial each would prefer, should they ever had to appear in court. The President said he preferred "the usual trial by jury, whilst General Whiting preferred the courtmartial." [30]

Another colorful visitor to Fort Fisher in the fall of 1863, and just a few days after Davis had passed through Wilmington the first time, was Reverend Moses D. Hoge, pastor of the Second Presbyterian Church in Richmond. He had enlisted as a chaplain for Camp Lee in one of Richmond's suburbs at the very outset of the war, and had given a sermon to some of D.H. Hill's North Carolinians on the eve of battle. During the war, he was to bring through the blockade literally hundreds of thousands of Bibles, Testaments and parts of Scriptures for Confederate soldiers. In October of 1863, he was a passenger on the third inward bound voyage of the *Ad-Vance*. [31]

Hoge noted in his diary on October 9 his complete enjoyment that day of the trip from Bermuda. "I am now on board the *Ad-Vance* (*Lord Clyde*), about 100 miles from the North Carolina coast. It is 4 o'clock p.m., and I am sitting on the bottom step of the paddle box, from which I can look down directly into the water and see how beautifully it divides before the bow of the steamer, darting through at a noble speed. This is one of the most pleasant days as to temperature I ever felt, clear, coolish, without being cool and something life-giving in the air." [32]

The ship was supposed to pull into New Inlet that night, but the strong current of the Gulf Stream had inadvertently swept the *Ad-Vance* north of her regular course. They first spied land about 9 o'clock that night, but instead of being just north of Fort Fisher, they had actually spotted the lighthouse at Cape Lookout, 80 miles north of the point they intended to strike land. They ran south down the beach the rest of the night, coming within sight of the fort at 8 a.m. on the morning of the 10th, a Saturday.

Dr. Hoge expected they would move out to sea, waiting till dark to try the run in, but to his astonishment, the *Ad-Vance* surged straight ahead for Fort Fisher. There was a valuable cargo in the hold, and the chief officers Colonel Thomas Crossen and Captain Joannes Wiley, intended to risk it now to get the supplies in. The officers of the three Yankee warships off New Inlet this morning were at first startled by the blockade-runner's audacity, but they quickly came about, belching shrapnel, solid shot and shell from their heavy guns.

Tom Taylor, Colonel Lamb's friend and supplier of Whitworth cannon, said that running the blockade was the supreme thrill of his life, and he had experienced many. He had steeplechased, big game hunted, played polo and engaged in pig-sticking, but the exhilaration of dodging Yankee shells while running in on a sleek, fast steamer was the greatest of them all. Now, Dr. Hoge was about to get a sampling of young Taylor's kind of fun. [33]

"It was a scene of intense excitement," Reverend Hoge wrote in his diary on Monday, October 12. "We could see people on the shore, watching the result. We doubted not with utmost interest – the shells were ploughing up the water and tearing up the sand on the shore, bursting over and around us. Two or three of their shells struck the sand just at the edge of the water and directly opposite to us and the wonder was how the balls could get there without passing through us. Colonel C. certainly made a hazardous experiment. Had the mist near the coast not veiled us somewhat from the view of the enemy as we approached, and had he seen us in time to make chase ten minutes sooner, he would have headed us off and driven us ashore, or had one of his shot penetrated our boilers, we would have been blown to fragments. Had we been compelled to take to our boats, we would have still been in great danger, for we would have been under fire perhaps an hour, when the smooth sea made it as easy to fire accurately from the deck as from the walls of a fort." [34]

James Maglenn, Chief Engineer aboard the *Ad-Vance*, saw, too, that the blockade-runner was in tight straits at this time. "By this time their shot were going over us, and when Colonel Lamb's Whitworth guns began their firing upon the fleet, one large steamer, supposed to be the *State of Georgia*, came rapidly towards us, and when in dangerous proximity, was about to turn to bring her broadside guns upon the *Ad-Vance*, but a well-directed shot from a 10-inch Columbiad from the northeast salient of the fort crashed into her bow, when she rapidly backed water and withdrew from the chase, enabling the *Ad-Vance* to get safely in, amid the shouts of the garrison and the cheers of the officers and crew and the waving of handkerchiefs by those on deck of the blockade runner. A number of officers came on board to congratulate us, and Captain Wiley and the Rev. Moses D. Hoge, who was on board bringing in a lot of testaments, Bibles and tracts for the soldiers, sent special thanks to Colonel Lamb and his garrison for their timely aid." [35]

It was a good thing for Confederate soldiers and North Carolina citizens that the *Ad-Vance's* officers had run the risk. There was a valuable cargo in her hold and it was sorely needed, especially with winter close at hand. There were "2,000 pairs of shoes, 1,702 single blankets, 5,040 pairs of hose, 8,638 yards of army cloth, 630 pieces of gray flannel, 960 dozen buckles, 516 dozen buttons, 1,450 yards gunny cloth, 1,161 pairs of cotton cards, 52,536 yards of cotton bagging, 7,329 pounds of rope, 38 bundles of iron, 2 cases of cast steel, 20 reams of paper, 72 dozen of pencils, 84 dozen awls, 1 cask each of borax, emory, and small files, 750,000 water-proof musket caps, 15,696 gun nipples." In conjunction with Dr. Hoge's Scriptural material, these supplies would be of much value to the people and the troops. [36]

Dr. Luke P. Blackburn, M.D.

Another interesting visitor, or more pointedly, a diabolical one, to Fort Fisher in 1863 was a man named Dr. Luke P. Blackburn. Blackburn, a native of Louisville, Kentucky, operated as a Rebel agent in Canada. As a physician years earlier, he had won notoriety in Mississippi and Louisiana for his knowledge and ability at controlling yellow fever. Armed with this knowledge, and aware of the turmoil, death, and devastation that the epidemic wrought on a community, he decided to aid the Confederacy by infecting Northern cities with it.

Going out from Wilmington on a blockade-runner, he had a brief visit with William Lamb at Fort Fisher. He told Lamb he intended to bring in clothing of deceased yellow fever victims from an infected area, say, Nassau or Bermuda, for example, and transport it to Northern town where it could be scattered about among the population to induce sickness. Blackburn did not know, of course, any more than William Lamb or anybody else, that the means of introduction of the illness was the mosquito. Colonel Lamb was indignant, and "revolted at the idea as barbarous." [37]

Undaunted by Lamb's reaction, Blackburn later discussed the subject with the father of Colonel Blanton Duncan. Duncan was a close friend and aid of General Whiting and had served as commanding officer of a Kentucky regiment at Manassas. His father went out on the blockade-runner with Blackburn, after the ship cleared Fort Fisher, and the Kentucky physician discussed his plan with the elder Duncan. [38]

Apparently, Blackburn later put his plan in motion. In the spring and summer of the following year, while yellow fever stalked the Bermuda islands, the Kentucky doctor visited St. George, where he treated patients who died of the illness. One nurse observed him placing woolen shirts on patients to help them sweat, and later returning the soiled shirts to a trunk. Another person noted the odd disappearance of dirty bed linens on which Blackburn's patients had died. An accomplice was later tried and convicted of storing some of the trunks Blackburn planned to ship to Northern cities with the linens and shirts. Some of the trunks actually made it to the North, where they were sold to auctioneers.

Blackburn himself was subsequently arrested in Montreal and tried in a court of law, but insufficient and circumstantial evidence and the lack of violation of any Canadian law resulted in his release. No action was ever taken against him in the United States. [39]

Edward FitzGerald Ross was an English born captain of Austrian cavalry when he visited Colonel Lamb at Fort Fisher in November of 1863. He had been on temporary retirement from active duty when he came to the Confederacy in May 1863. A guest of General Longstreet's staff at the Battle of Gettysburg, Ross was moved by the sacrifices made by Southern soldiers to gain Confederate independence. "There are thousands of men now carrying a musket in the ranks," he wrote, "who before the war were gentlemen of wealth and property, which they are now deprived of – 'it may be for years, or it may be for ever', as one of them said to me; but not one seems to regret it, or would for an instant dream of submission to the North in order to regain what he has lost." [40]

Arriving in Wilmington in the second week of November, Ross was able to obtain lodging with some friends engaged in running the blockade, who were staying "in a fine large house". He paid his respects to General Whiting and visited about town. "Wilmington is at present the most important port of entry in the South," he noted. He saw "about a dozen blockade-running steamers lying at the wharves, loading cotton, and unloading all manner of stores brought from Bermuda and Nassau." Ross was most pleased when he discovered that English newspapers were in abundance in Wilmington, having arrived on the steamers from the British islands. [41]

Soon after he arrived in Wilmington, Colonel Lamb took him down the river to visit Fort Fisher. While going down, they passed three steamers that had run the blockade and were heading for the wharves. They were the *Hansa*, the *Lucy*, and the *Bendigo*, and all exchanged hearty cheers as they passed each other.

Ross was most impressed with Fort Fisher, which he said consisted of "a long line of forts and batteries of all sorts and sizes. The most peculiar one is an artificial hill mounted with two guns, in order to give a plunging fire upon any vessel that may attempt to pass...Although very formidable, the fortifications were still being strengthened, and large numbers of negroes were at work." He particularly noticed that the Federal warships kept a healthy distance, "for if they come within three or fours miles, Colonel Lamb is apt to make targets of them, and his gun practice is very accurate." [42]

Ross' friend and traveling companion, Frank Vizetelly, an affable, red-bearded correspondent and artist for *The Illustrated London News*, agreed with Ross' assessment of Lamb's defenses. "Fort Fisher," he wrote his superiors in London, "is one of the strongest coast defences I have seen, not excepting any of those at Charleston, that have hitherto held an entire iron-clad fleet at bay." [43]

Despite Fisher's great strength, the Yankees were getting better at catching blockade-runners, especially if they were at sea and out of reach of Fisher's powerful guns, or Lamb's mobile Whitworth rifles. November 1863 saw four of the more noted runners caught by the Federals. The *Cornubia* or *Lady Davis*, the Confederate States-owned, 190 foot long iron side-wheel steamer, which had been the first vessel to employ signal messages to run into New Inlet, was headed for Fort Fisher just after midnight on Sunday, November 8. She was spotted by the *U.S.S. James Adger* just off Masonboro Inlet, and the Yankees gave chase.

Captain R.H. Gayle was commanding her on this trip out of Bermuda, her cargo comprising valuable rifles, ammunition, lead and saltpeter. Signal Corpsman Frederick Gregory noticed that the captain had been very sick the day before, and was quite weak. Additionally, Yankee gunboat rockets started going up on all sides of them but the shore, and Union shells were bursting all around them as they drove the vessel at full speed onto the beach, which they struck eleven miles north of New Inlet. All hands took to the land except the captain (who was too feeble to get off), a carpenter, and a seaman. The Yankees chased the crewmen down the beach with small arms and cannon fire, and Gregory and his comrades "dodged about in the bulrushes as best we could and made our way towards the fort." [44]

The next morning, on the 9th of November, the Confederate steamer *Robert E. Lee*, former *Giraffe*, was captured off Cape Lookout flying the Confederate ensign. Having left Bermuda five hours after the *Cornubia*, she was headed for New Inlet with a cargo of 214 large bales and cases of blankets and shoes, "150 cases Austrian rifles, 250 bags saltpeter, 61 barrels salt provisions, 30 pigs lead" and various other commodities. This was a tremendous loss for the Southerners, as she had already run the blockade into Wilmington twenty-one times, had carried out almost 7,000 bales of cotton worth in gold about $2,000,000, and had brought back to the Confederacy cargoes equally as valuable. Significantly, Captain John Wilkinson, who had commanded the vessel since her first run past Fort Fisher the month after the yellow fever ended, had relinquished command just prior to her last cruise. For the first time, the ship was commanded by someone other than a Confederate naval officer. [45]

Also, and perhaps more significantly, the only Confederate government steamer that would be captured during the war while commanded by a Confederate Naval Officer would be the *Cornubia* (*Lady Davis*), officered by Captain Gayle, and he had been ill the day before the ship's capture. One Southern naval officer observed that the Confederates "were skillful seamen, good navigators, gentlemen of standing and character; the cause was their cause, and they were above all the suspicion that could be attached to others less favorably situated." Unlike their British counterparts, they were more concerned with Southern independence than profits, and would take far greater risks with their own safety to insure that supplies got into Wilmington. [46]

Captured the same day as the *Robert E. Lee*, the *Ella and Annie* did not give in to her Yankee captors quite as easily as most of their prizes did. Frank Bonneau was a Charlestonian and a good ship's master, with more nerve than most blockade-runner captains, especially civilian ones. At 5:30 a.m. the morning of the 9th, he was off Masonboro Inlet and eighteen miles north of Fort Fisher's protecting guns, carrying in the hold of the *Ella and Annie* 281 cases of Austrian rifles for the Confederate Army, "480 sacks of salt, 500 sacks saltpeter, 500 barrels of beef," and assorted other goods. [47]

Bonneau's ship was sighted by Master J.B. Breck, commanding *U.S.S. Niphon*, and Breck proceeded to cut him off by moving directly into his path with his gunboat. Undaunted and furious at the Yankees, Bonneau hollered at the bluecoat captain to get out of his way, "telling him he would be afoul of me," and proceeded at full speed to run down the *Niphon* just forward of midships. Breck jerked on the helm to avoid what might have been a fatal collision for the Yankee ship and sailors, and the *Ella and Annie* struck her forward and down her length while "running at great speed." Breck fired a broadside of "grape, canister, and shell," and sent a boarding party of sailors with revolvers and cutlasses leaping over blockade runner's side, firing and slashing wildly, so livid were they at the Rebels' pluck and audacity.[48]

Both cabin boys on the *Ella and Annie* were cut by Union swords, a fireman was shot while coming out of the engine room, and one other fireman had been mortally wounded by grapeshot. There were forty-one shot holes in the blockade-runner's hull. The *U.S.S. Niphon* had her bowsprit and stem broken by the collision, starboard boats destroyed, planks and plates damaged, and decks were leaking badly. She was, in fact, so badly damaged that she would have to be sent to Boston for repairs. Three Federal sailors had been injured in the ramming together of the ships, as well. [49]

Bonneau was to be tried and convicted of piracy in Boston, for ramming a United States naval vessel while engaged in blockade running, and he was sentenced to die. The verdict was set aside, however, by the judge presiding, who was also a Federal admiral. Had he been in Bonneau's place, the judge told the court, he would have done the same thing. [50]

Twelve days after the *Ella and Annie* was taken, one of Thomas Taylor's vessels, the *Banshee*, was captured off Cape Lookout. She had earned her owners 700 percent on their investment in eight previous trips, and also had the distinction of being the first steel vessel to cross the Atlantic. In October, the *Banshee* had brought in an Arabian horse for Jefferson Davis, a present from the Confederate agent in Egypt. As the blockade-runner crept quietly past the Yankee ships, the horse began to neigh, smelling land for the first time in several days. The Union cruisers heard it, and several of them opened on the *Banshee* with their heavy guns. Fortunately, Taylor was close to New Inlet that night as the shrapnel began flying, and was relieved when "our friend Colonel Lamb at Fort Fisher was soon protecting us, playing over our heads with shell." [51]

On Saturday morning of November 21, 1863, she was headed for New Inlet when spotted by the *U.S.S. Grand Gulf* about thirty miles southwest of Cape Lookout. Chased for over twenty miles, she was finally captured after dodging iron from the Yankee ship's 100-pounder Parrott rifle. Tom Taylor was not aboard on this, the *Banshee*'s ninth trip through the blockade. Being assigned to another runner, he would serve his employers and the Confederacy until the close of the war. [52]

Despite the fact that about forty blockade-runners continued to run into Wilmington from Nassau and Bermuda in late 1863, the loss of these four in November, as well as several others during the late summer and fall, was of significant concern to the Richmond authorities. [53]

Five days after the *Banshee*'s capture, November 26, 1863, James Seddon advised Jefferson Davis that Charleston was effectively closed to blockade-runners. The Secretary of War told the President that "the blockade of Wilmington, the port of the Confederacy best adapted for evading the blockade, has been of late more stringent. All the blockading ships of the enemy have been transferred from Charleston, and within the last two months a considerable number of steamers, among them those belonging to the Department, have been captured or destroyed to prevent them falling into the hands of the enemy. While the risk is now certainly increased, still, with the additional steamers which the contracts with the Government or the temptations of private gain has brought into the trade, it is believed the blockade may be evaded so far as to add greatly to our resources needed by the Government. Measures, meantime, are being taken to increase the facilities of entrance into the port by the use of movable batteries of Whitworth guns of long range along the coast and to endanger the safety of the blockading vessels." [54]

Wilmington had become a place of such activity, Seddon continued, that special agents and officers from the War Department had been assigned there to manage the "business of export and import for the Department...It has grown almost a separate branch of administration in the Department, and to be nearly assimilated to a separate bureau." [55]

Ever mindful of Wilmington's vast importance to the Confederacy, Chase Whiting continued to push his subordinates to expand and strengthen their fortifications. On Wednesday, December 30, he wrote Colonel Lamb to suggest the building of an additional fort just adjacent to Battery Gatlin, situated at the south end of Myrtle Grove Sound, about eight miles north of Fort Fisher. "If the enemy design a land attack on this side the river and the fort," he said, "I think a work somewhat similar to Fort Campbell, though not so extensive, can be put up just below Gatlin, inclosed from the Sound to the beach." Heavy traverses were to be erected in the fort to protect the four or five big guns that were to be moved from Fisher and mounted, and a battery of field artillery would be to the west and behind the fort to protect the flank approaches. As with the guns, the labor and soldiers for this position would have to come from Lamb's command, as Whiting's district was still short of sufficient manpower, despite his many entreaties to Richmond since assumption of command thirteen months before. [56]

Even with Martin's Brigade of infantry, assigned to the Cape Fear just before Jefferson Davis' visit to Wilmington back in October, Whiting still only had an effective total of 6,485 officers and men in his command as the year 1864 arrived. Considering the many approaches by land and sea that the Yankees could use to assault Wilmington, it was a woefully inadequate force. Unfortunately, according to General Lee, no reinforcements could be sent to him from the Army of Northern Virginia at this time. To compensate for the lack of troops, he felt that there was "no danger in using the garrisons of the forts to resist a landing or approach at other points to gain time for concentration of troops. I think Martin's brigade and two light batteries sufficient to watch the threatened point." [57]

Had they been permitted, some of the "garrisons of the forts" would have left the Cape Fear District, leaving Whiting with even less men. Sergeant Thaddeus Davis, of Company G, Fortieth North Carolina Troops stationed at Fort Holmes, wrote that after the men had been transferred to Bald Head Island, they sent petitions to General Whiting asking for transfer to field artillery service with the Army of Northern Virginia. In dire straits already from his manpower shortage, and perhaps reflecting on his own unenviable and thankless position, Whiting told his men on Bald Head that "it was a soldier's duty to stay or go where he was ordered, and that we were just where the government wanted us to be." Davis said the men "took the rebuke", and went about their never-ending toil of building sand parapets and traverses to ward off Yankee iron. [58]

Constantly working to get help for Davis and his comrades, Whiting reminded Adjutant and Inspector General Samuel Cooper in a letter on January 12, 1864, that he still had no more troops in his command than did General French in late 1862. With all the additional fortifications, it was essential, Whiting told Cooper, that more men be dispatched to Wilmington. "It must be recollected", Whiting wrote, "that within the past year to defend this place have been erected the powerful works, Forts Campbell, Pender, Holmes, the lines of Smith's Island, besides numerous batteries, great additions to Forts Caswell and Fisher and the advanced works of the latter. Extensive work, considered indispensable, is still in progress". [59]

Yankee sailors could vouch for Whiting's statements about the additional work in progress. One bluecoat aboard a Union blockader off New Inlet wrote home in January that the Rebels were constantly strengthening their fortifications on Confederate Point. He said they could "be seen working at some of the forts, looking from a distance like a swarm of bees, and judging form the way the batteries and earthworks spring up suddenly along the coast, they must work like bees, too, when they go at it." [60]

General Charles Graham, a U.S. brigadier assigned to interview pilots and deserters from the Cape Fear, as well as to make his own observations, agreed with the sailor, reporting in January that Wilmington's defenses were powerful. He reviewed the reinforcing of Fort Caswell with the heavy sand batteries, and spoke of the recent erection of Fort Campbell to the west of Caswell. On Bald Head the Yankees knew a fort had been built. They could see at least four embrasures facing the Atlantic, with "embankments and traverses...of

BrigGen George Burgwyn Anderson, C.S.A.

unusual height and thickness." Fort Pender, which the Federals still called Fort Johnston, was a "strong earthwork, mounting some heavy English guns," located at Smithville.

Fort Fisher, Graham said, was "a formidable work of earth, of extensive proportions, revetted with heavy timber, and having bombproofs sufficient to shelter 2,000 men. It mounts at least thirty guns – some say fifty – most of them facing toward New Inlet, but it likewise has some guns commanding the river, and others the road leading to Wilmington." The Mound Battery was also called the Martello Tower by Graham, and he said it was believed to be sixty feet high, mounting two heavy guns, which was correct. [61]

Fort Fisher's 60 foot-tall Mound Battery, at the southern end of the sea face.

Fort Saint Philip, or Fort Anderson, Colonel Lamb's post before taking command at Fisher, was located at the pre-revolutionary community of Old Brunswick on the west bank of the Cape Fear, and was thirteen miles north of Caswell. The fort was originally named for the old colonial church at Brunswick, Saint Philip's, whose three-foot thick walls, minus roof and floor, stood near the bank of the Cape Fear, as they had since 1740. The installation had later been renamed for Brigadier General George B. Anderson, one of North Carolina's distinguished sons, who had been mortally wounded at Sharpsburg in 1862.

Here, directly across the river from a prominent geographic feature on Confederate Point known as Sugar Loaf, a tremendous sixty foot high natural sand dune, the Cape Fear narrows and the channel comes very close to the riverbank near the fort. This made it ideal for two purposes, first, as the quarantine point for incoming blockade-runners, and second, as the point on the river where obstacles could be placed to impede and snare intruding Yankee vessels that somehow might make it past Forts Fisher, Caswell, Holmes, or Pender. Graham said piles made deadly with iron spikes had been placed all across the river, except for one spot to allow passage of ships. The piles "were firmly bound together by chains, and kept from swagging with the current by heavy anchors. At night a chain is stretched across the opening. No vessels are allowed to pass upward bound before visited and examined." Fort Anderson was reported armed with "quite a number of guns of heavy caliber," possibly as many as thirty. [62]

One of Colonel Lamb's mobile Whitworth batteries was located at Masonborough, and it was believed to be supported by an infantry regiment, which was probably some of General Martin's North Carolinians. "The battery is shifted from point to point", Graham wrote, "as its services are required. Our blockading squadron has been a good deal annoyed by it." [63]

Blockade-runners making land fifteen to twenty-five miles north of New Inlet were adept at evading the Yankee cruisers, the Union officer continued, because of "their light color, exceeding lowness, the noiseless revolutions of their feathering paddles, light draught, and extreme speed". During a chase, if a runner's captain thought they were likely to be captured, they would often beach their craft and "allow the engine to work until she is driven so high on the beach it is almost a work of impossibility to drag her off. On these occasions, as soon as the report of our guns are heard or the signals of the blockade-runners are observed, the light batteries of Whitworth guns are brought down and used." That message was reiterated a few days later in action off Topsail Inlet. [64]

One of the newest vessels in Tom Taylor's fleet of runners owned by the Confederate Trading Company was the *Wild Dayrell*. She was a first class iron side-wheel steamer, "very strong, a perfect sea-boat, and remarkably well engined," according to Taylor. [65]

She left Nassau at 9 p.m. on Friday night, January 29, headed for Wilmington on her second trip in. Her cargo consisted, among other things, of large quantities of army shoes for Lee's infantry, blankets, and writing paper. Before completely clearing the Bahama Islands, she was chased by two of the Nassau line Yankee cruisers. The Union Navy had recently begun assigning blockade chasers to outside duty, roaming the sea lanes between Nassau and Wilmington, and Bermuda and Wilmington, with hopes of intercepting the elusive runners before the North Carolina coast with its attendant fog and forts assisted in their successful ingress. [66]

Thomas Cubbines was captain of the *Wild Dayrell*, to the chagrin of Tom Taylor, because he believed Cubbines suffered from a "want of pluck." As he was somewhat of a favorite of Taylor's employers, however, Taylor did not dismiss him, though he was to regret not doing so. Unsure of his location when he made land on February 1, the mist hanging heavy on the North Carolina coast that morning, Cubbines finished the trip by grounding in the breakers near Topsail Inlet about 9 a.m. on Monday morning.

The 150lb. Armstrong gun was one of the heaviest of Fort Fisher's weapons.

Cubbines ordered the crew to lighten the vessel by throwing overboard cargo and coal, threw out an anchor to try to steady her in the pounding surf, and "had the engines going astern full speed." The blockade-runner, however, would not move off the beach, but "fell more athwart the sea, struck very heavy, and broke her back, I think", Cubbines later reported. [67]

By 11 a.m., the Union Navy arrived, and Cubbines and his crew took to their lifeboats when they spotted a gunboat about four miles away. Lieutenant Commander F.A. Roe of the *U.S.S. Sassacus* came up and fired a few guns to disperse any enemies that might be hovering near," and sent in his men to take possession of the beached British steamer. Hawsers were secured to the *Wild Dayrell*, and they tried to pull her off the beach, but the weather was bad, the tide was falling, and Roe decided to try again next morning. He had no luck then, either, and the *U.S.S. Florida* now came on the scene to join in the efforts to secure the prize. [68]

The *Florida* ran out a hawser as well, and assisted the *Sassacus* in pulling on the *Wild Dayrell*, "when snap went one of the hawsers measuring ten inches in circumference." The afternoon waned, the tide was ebbing, and the Yankee ships moved farther out for the night.

Bright and early on February 3, men from the *Florida* and *Sassacus* boarded the blockade runner and began throwing overboard additional cargo and coal, so as to lighten her even more, and with new hawsers attached, pull her off the beach with the next high tide. William Keeler, still serving as Paymaster on the *Florida*, and among those who boarded the *Wild Dayrell*, was observing the work of the sailors when Colonel Lamb's roving Rebel gunners, having run up the coast after learning of the *Wild Dayrell*'s predicament, greeted them with a warm North Carolina welcome.

Keeler felt and heard the "thud of rifle balls against the iron side of the vessel & the shrill shriek of a Whitworth bolt over our heads gave us the first intimation that there were interested spectators on shore. We could just see the slight puffs of smoke from their guns as they rose from behind the distant sand piles." The sailors from the *Sassacus* abandoned the blockade-runner, but Keeler's men stayed on board, despite the Rebels firing from the far shore across the sound, who "managed to get in a shot now & then notwithstanding our shells were bursting among the sand piles which sheltered them." [70]

While the firing continued, the *Sassacus* tried once more to pull the British steamer into the water, but once again the hawser broke, and as the tide was ebbing, further efforts to secure her were abandoned. Captain Peirce Crosby of the *Florida* decided now to destroy the *Wild Dayrell*, ordering Keeler to permit his men to take all the valuables they could remove quickly, and fire the blockade runner.

Keeler described in a letter to his wife the method of plunder in which his men delighted. Saturnalian destruction was an avocation at which blue-coated sailors and soldiers were peculiarly adept, and the *Florida*'s crew was no exception. Keeler reported barrels, boxes and casks were "smashed open with axes & iron bars, bales of calicoes & blankets ripped open with knives, each one helping himself to what he wanted of the contents, scattering them over the decks, throwing them in the water & crushing them under foot."

Keeler observed a sailor running "across the deck, his arms full of pieces of calico when his eye is caught by an unopened box just thrown out of the hold, down goes the dry goods upon the deck among coal, water, oil and molasses & catching up a heavy hammer he brings it down upon the box with a force which not only crushes in the top but drives it to the bottom through bottles of quinine with which the box is filled. Catching up a bottle – 'damn the medicine' - & in he jumps half up to his knees in quinine, completing the destruction which the hammer had commenced.

"The constant tramp of many feet," Keeler continued, "over all these articles as they are thrown up & scattered about the deck is working them up in one confused, mixed & indistinguishable mass which it is impossible either to imagine or describe. Another party in the cabin are making the plate glass mirrors a target for cut glass tumblers & decanters, the jingle of broken glass mingling with shouts of laughter at a 'splendid shot'." [71]

After this merriment had gone on for a short while, the Yankee sailors abandoned the *Wild Dayrell*, while Lamb's Whitworth gunners and sharpshooters continued firing on the vessel. Keeler and some of his subordinates gathered combustibles in several different places within the ship, and struck their matches at the same time to fire the runner simultaneously. Fortunately for the bluecoats, they got off just as the Rebels had gotten the proper range with their cannon. "Just as we shoved off," Keeler related, "the shrill shriek of a Whitworth bolt mingled with the roar of the flames as the missile passed through the paddle box just over our heads." [72]

As Keeler and the boarding party rowed back to the *Florida*, Commander Crosby ordered his guns, and Lieutenant Commander Roe of the *Sassacus* ordered his to fire into the hull of the burning blockade runner. Soon shells and solid shot were "crashing through the iron hull scattering the fragments & effectually completing the work of destruction." [73]

The graceful but moribund British steamer burned until midnight, while her hull glowed a bright and shimmering red in the pitch darkness. Periodically, a "tongue of flame & a cloud of sparks would occasionally shoot up as the remaining cargo smoldered & burned." [74]

"The poor *Wild Dayrell* deserved a better commander," Tom Taylor wrote, "and consequently a better fate than befell her." Cubbines told his young employer he had run the vessel aground "in order to avoid capture," though he told the readers of the *Daily Journal* the ship had been accidentally grounded, and that the fault lay with the pilot, James Burris.

Burris, a resident of Myrtle Sound, had been a pilot since 1826. Burris scoffed at Thomas Cubbines' accusation that he had lost the vessel, saying he had never been involved in an accident at any time in his career. The captain, he said, was unable to even "tell me whether the steamer was North or South of New Inlet. I was never given charge of the ship, but I gave my advice when we found ourselves befogged on a strange shore, and think, had it been followed, the *Wild Dayrell* would now have been on her return trip to Nassau." Tom Taylor would have agreed. [75]

The Yankees were done with the *Wild Dayrell*, but William Lamb's grayclad cannoneers were not quite done with the Yankees. Given half a chance, they liked to have the last say in an argument, and they sometimes remained in the area of a wrecked blockade-runner for several days, just in case there might be some articles worth salvaging. The *U.S.S. Florida* was to learn this two days after destroying the *Wild Dayrell*.

Shortly after sunrise on Friday, February 5, Commander Crosby steamed up close to the burned out hull, and threw in a few more shots for good measure. Soon there came the eerie, distinct whine of a Whitworth shell in flight, an explosion overhead, and metal splinters spraying over the hurricane deck, where officers and men had gathered to watch the shelling. The Rebels had the range now. Looking up, William Keeler spied a hole in the smokestack about the size of his arm. A shell had been fired from a gun set back a long way from the beach, apparently just waiting for a Union target.

One of the sailors near Keeler was hit "on the breast by a rivet head knocked out of the smoke stack. It penetrated to the ribs & glanced downwards about two inches. Of course we didn't remain long in that position, as nothing was to be gained by staying there a target for their long range guns." [76]

Five days later, Keeler and his comrades found themselves even more vulnerable targets in the fight over the *Fanny and Jenny* at Wrightsville.

The *Fanny and Jenny* was an excellent side-wheel iron steamer, capable of sixteen miles an hour. It was commanded by Captain Louis H. Coxetter of Charleston. Loaded with a cargo of liquor and bacon, and carrying as well a $2500 gold mounted presentation sword for Robert E. Lee, the gift of some English nobility, she left Nassau on Saturday, February 6 at 2:30 in the afternoon. By the night of Tuesday the 9th, she had made land about six miles north of Fort Fisher, but the pilot, Joseph Burris, was not familiar with the coast at that point, and declined to bring her into New Inlet until daylight. Through the night, as the engines were occasionally stopped, the ship drifted northward.

As day broke, the vessel was pointed southward, straight for Colonel Lamb's protecting artillery at Fort Fisher. She never got there, being cut off her course by the *U.S.S. Florida*, and grounding hard and fast on the south end of the beach at Wrightsville Sound, just off Masonboro Inlet.

As the *Florida* sent out boats to board and take possession, Captain Coxetter had his men lower their own boats to flee to safety. As the captain's boat was being lowered, one of the davits broke, spilling Coxetter, his engineers, the purser, and others into the roaring breakers. Many went under and some were drowned, including the Chief Engineer, William Jones, and the First Assistant Engineer, William Morrell, and Coxetter's "colored cabin boy," Charles Lightfoot. The Second Assistant Engineer, John Cowan, who was captured by the Yankees, told his captors that the captain had taken General Lee's sword with him into the lifeboat, the sword had gone to the bottom when the boat dumped out the passengers, and Coxetter was among the drowned. [77]

As a hawser was secured to the vessel by the *Florida*'s boarding party, Captain Crosby ordered Paymaster Keeler to take an additional boarding party and row out to another blockade runner that had been chased aground nearby, this one being called the *Emily*. Keeler never made it. He was standing by the wheelhouse, waiting to walk down into the boat and go out to the *Emily* with his men, when all of a sudden there was a tremendous crash and explosion, and at the exact instant Keeler "received a severe crushing blow in the back."

Fort Fisher's Masonboro based Whitworth gunners, having seen the *Fanny and Jenny* chased ashore, had gotten the range on the first shot. They fired an explosive round through the *Florida*'s paddle-wheelhouse, spraying shards of iron shell and paddlewheels in all directions, some hitting Keeler in the face, but the main wound being in his back.

"For an instant all was black," Keeler wrote his wife Anna, on March 3. "I sank to my feet & should have fallen overboard had I not had hold of the line which surrounds the guard. I knew I was wounded. I put my hand to my back, found my clothes torn away & the flesh raw & bloody & I am free to confess I was frightened...I felt but little pain but I did not know but it was the deadening insensibility which sometimes follows a mortal wound." [78]

The surgeon aboard the *Florida* was standing right by him when the shell struck, and immediately took him below. Fortunately for Keeler, the shrapnel had just missed his spine, but had dug out a furrow of flesh on the left side of his back one inch deep, an inch and a half wide and four inches in length. Huge and painful bruises as big as the palm of a hand were located on either side of the spine. He would suffer intensely for some time to come, but he would live. [79]

The Whitworth cannoneers continued firing, and the *U.S.S. Florida* was hit three more times, while shells were also dropping into the now Yankee held *Fanny and Jenny*, the *Emily*, or passing over and beyond the vessels. Commander Crosby said that the Rebels "had our exact range", and though he ordered the 50-pounder Dahlgren gun fired at them, the Union shells would not reach the Confederates. "The precision of the enemy's fire with those guns is very remarkable," Crosby complimented Lamb's artillerists. But the Whitworths were only part of his concern as the grayjackets began ferrying boatloads of riflemen across Wrightsville Sound to more closely engage the Federals. "Sharpshooters were collecting rapidly behind the sand hills," he said, "and in positions not easily to be dislodged by our fire, except by endangering our own men." Crosby decided the time had arrived to destroy the blockade runners and avoid loss of life, so he ordered them burned. [80]

The Confederate riflemen reached the sand dunes on the beach and fired "a shower of balls" at the Yankees vacating the blockade-runners. Pandemonium and death held full sway on this usually deserted stretch of sand, as the Rebels sprayed musket volleys and lobbed Whitworth shells, flames leaped from the hulls of the stranded steamers, and the bodies of drowned crew members from the *Fanny and Jenny* were cruelly tossed in the raging surf like so many rag dolls.

As the *Florida*'s men got well off shore, they were met by boat crews from another Federal cruiser, the *U.S.S. Cambridge*, who were unwittingly advancing straight into the Confederates, under the delusion they could put out the fires and pull the runners off the shore. The crew of the *Florida*, which had miraculously escaped injury with the exception of Paymaster Keeler, tried to warn the *Cambridge*'s men of the sharpshooters and the Whitworths, but the crew of the approaching ship laughed at them claiming they "knew the vessels could be got off & would shew us how it was done."

"They kept on in spite of our caution," Keeler wrote, "& received a volley from the sharpshooters which wounded every man in the foremost boat – all slightly but one who was shot through the chest. They wasn't long in getting back to their vessel & we saw just 'how it was done'." [81]

The Yankees paid a price for destruction of the *Fanny and Jenny* and *Emily*, but they had the satisfaction of knowing that two more blockade-breakers were put out of commission, and some of the crew members of those vessels would never sail again, as evidenced by their torsos bobbing up and down in the sea or being violently thrown about in the breakers. There was, too, genuine satisfaction that one of those bodies was that of the famous commander of the *Fanny and Jenny*, Louis Coxetter, who in the early days of the war had commanded a Confederate privateer called the *Jeff Davis*, and had been branded by Lincoln as a pirate. William Keeler wrote his wife that Coxetter had gone down with General Lee's ornate sword, and Commander Crosby reported the same to Rear Admiral S.P. Lee. There was no remorse in Lee's report to Gideon Welles, in which he told Welles that the "notorious Captain Coxetter...with the purser, was drowned in endeavoring to reach the shore." [82]

Keeler, Crosby and Lee were all sadly mistaken, however; Louis Coxetter was very much alive, and would sail again as commander of a blockade-runner. His name was first on the list of survivors printed by the *Daily Journal* on Tuesday, February 16. He had obviously gone under and nearly drowned, but had come to the surface and been saved. Some of the crew was rescued "in a sinking and exhausted condition" by one of the other lifeboats, "while others got ashore by clinging to trunks and other articles thrown overboard from the steamer." On the day following the battle for the *Fanny and Jenny*, Coxetter went back to the scene of the carnage and found the body of his cabin boy, Charles Lightfoot, washed up on the beach. He took his corpse across the sound and buried him at Wrightsville. [83]

Coxetter also made a statement to the paper for publication. Apparently, rumors were floating around town that the blockade-runner had been mistaken by Colonel Lamb's gunners for a Yankee blockader, and had been erroneously fired upon and destroyed. The Captain wanted to set the record straight. He stated unequivocally that the *Fanny and Jenny* had not been "fired upon by our batteries until after she had been boarded and taken possession of by the Yankees. She was then opened upon by our people with a Whitworth gun, no doubt sent out by Col. Lamb, the vigilant and indefatigable commandant of Fort Fisher." [84]

More engagements would be occurring between the Rebel gunners and Yankee blockaders, as the Confederates beefed up their stationary defenses and added more mobile artillery units, and as the Unionists gained more warships to patrol the Wilmington coast. By late February of 1864, the U.S. Navy had 25 vessels assigned to duty off the Cape Fear. Eight of these were assigned specifically to blockade New Inlet. Seven were off the Western Bar, while one was off Shallotte Inlet, and one off Little River Inlet. Four were in repair facilities at either Gosport Navy Yard or Baltimore. The other four ships, some of the fastest in the North Atlantic Squadron, were assigned to outside blockade duty,

LtCmdr. William B. Cushing, U.S.N.

two patrolling on the "Bermuda line" route of the blockade-runners, while the other two steamed off Frying Pan Shoals and "on the northern end of the Nassau line." [85]

The commander of one of those blockaders, Lieutenant William B. Cushing, commanding the *U.S.S. Monticello* off the Western Bar, was a brave and reckless young officer. Almost three weeks after the fight over the *Fanny and Jenny* at Wrightsville, Cushing decided to demonstrate his fearlessness, and resolved to capture none other than General Louis Hebert at his Smithville headquarters and to seize any vessels that might be anchored at the town.

On Monday night, February 29 (1864 being a leap year), he took two boats with twenty men, rowed with muffled oars past Fort Caswell, headed north up the river and anchored fifty yards from Fort Pender, directly in front of the town's hotel. Leaving most of the sailors to guard the two cutters, he took two officers and one seaman with him, moving quietly through town. They captured Sam Allen and John Howard, two blacks working in the salt works, and from them obtained directions to Hebert's residential headquarters. [86]

Proceeding to a large white house some two hundred yards away from Fort Pender, the one that General Hebert used and was conveniently unguarded by order of the General himself, Cushing crept in noiselessly. In one of the rooms, Cushing apprehended Captain Kelly, Hebert's chief engineer, and with a revolver to his head, hustled him from the house. Hebert's Adjutant General, Major W.D. Hardeman, hearing the noise and thinking a garrison mutiny was underway, slipped quietly out of the house in his bedclothes and took to the woods.

Learning Hebert had gone to Wilmington earlier that day and remained there, Cushing hurried his party with the captive Confederate captain and the two blacks down to the cutters, and rowed south down the river away from Smithville, undisturbed. [87]

Before Cushing's boats drew even with Fort Caswell, Major Hardeman came to the conclusion that a mutiny was not taking place after all, that Yankees had been the intruders in Hebert's residence. Raphael Greenberg, a native of Bavaria and private in Company A, First Battalion North Carolina Heavy Artillery at Fort Pender, had just settled down for a good night's sleep, when all of a sudden, Hardeman came bursting into the barracks in a panic. Greenberg saw that he was barefooted and almost naked, and was shouting for the "officer of the guard". Waking all those who might have been asleep, Hardeman hollered out, "For God's sake, have every man under arms as soon as possible. The Yankees are upon us. I have seen them and had a very narrow escape from capture. I heard a voice on our front veranda, got up from my bunk, and ran to the window, when all at once a big, strapping fellow pointed his pistol at my head saying, 'Surrender;' but I dropped the window and ran back to Captain Kelly, shouting to him to get up and come along, I had no time to lose, but ran through our back yard to come here. Now, then, bring every man out as soon as possible." [88]

Greenberg heard the long roll beaten, saw rockets fired as alert to the different forts, saw signal lights flashing from Pender to Forts Caswell, Fisher and Holmes, but no Yankees were to be seen or heard. By the time the signals had been passed around the harbor, Cushing and company were "abreast of Fort Caswell", and were never detected or fired upon. At 3:25 a.m. on March 1, his two boats returned to the *Monticello*. All in all, a daring little raid, admitted General Whiting, who complimented the youthful Yankee sailor by saying "the actors deserve great credit". [89]

That afternoon of March 1st, Cushing sent Ensign J.E. Jones in a flag-of-truce boat over to Fort Caswell to pick up a uniform for the captured Captain

Kelly, who still wore only his nightclothes, though Cushing had been kind enough to provide him with dry socks. [90]

Whiting, having been stationed on the Cape Fear for a number of years prior to the war, and being acquainted with other officers who were as well, noted that Cushing was engaged on coast survey duty in Wilmington in 1855 and 1856 with Captain Maffitt, and so knew how to get in and out of the harbor without being detected. "Cushing knew the boat pass," Whiting wrote, "by the east end of Battery Island to Smithville, which could only be known by a pilot or a Coast-Survey man." Whiting wrote to Flag Officer W.F. Lynch, commander of Confederate Naval Forces in Wilmington, to request that armed vessels be strategically stationed at various points in the river to prevent such another episode. Lynch replied that the ironclad *North Carolina*, the steamer *Yadkin*, and tug *Equator* were all nearly complete and ready to move down to the Smithville vicinity for "cruising about occasionally," to prevent such a recurrence of intrusion. [91]

More vessels to patrol the river would naturally be helpful, but what the Department of the Cape Fear really needed, as it had needed all along, was more troops. On the day of Cushing's raid at Smithville, February 29, Whiting's return of soldiers that were "effectively" present for duty, was only 6,690 men. This paucity of manpower, the General had pointed out time and again to Richmond, was grossly inadequate to defend what "has now become the great cotton depot and the entrepot for a very large part of the supplies of the Army of Virginia." [92]

Almost as if in studied prophecy of what Willliam B. Cushing had in mind, on February 28, (the day before the Smithville raid), Whiting wrote to Braxton Bragg in Richmond, where he now sat at the elbow of the President after being relieved in North Georgia. "My great need," he told Bragg, "is to have such an addition to the permanent garrison as to enable me to prevent the works at the mouth of the river from being turned or surprised. I cannot do this as things now are." [93]

Endnotes to Chapter 6

1. O.R., Volume XXIX, Part 2, p.678-679; Recollections of Joseph P. King, p.6
2. Ibid, Part 2, p.691
3. Ibid, Part 2, p.697
4. Ibid, Part 2, p.703
5. Ibid, Part 2, p.705
6. Ibid, Part 2, p.705; Chronicles, p.358-359; NC Troops, Volume I, p.2
7. Ibid, Part 2, p.705
8. Ibid, Part 2, p.635-636
9. Ibid, Part 2, p.703

10. ORN, Volume 9, p.182; Recollections of Colonel John D. Taylor, p.3, N.C. Dept. Archives & History, Raleigh, NC; Atlas to accompany the Official Records, plate 132, hereinafter OR Atlas; NC Troops, Volume I, p.10, p.325

11. OR Atlas, plate 132

12. Clark, Volume II, p.752-753; NC Troops, Volume I, p.300; OR Atlas, plate 132; Freeman, Douglas Southall, *Lee's Lieutenants, A Study in Command,* Volume III, p.193-194, Charles Scribner's Sons, New York, 1944

13. Bald Head, p.43-45; Clark, Volume IV, p.422; Warner, Ezra,*Generals in Gray,* p.141, Louisiana State University Press, 1959; OR Atlas, plate 132

14. Clark, Volume II, p.755

15. NC Troops, Volume I, p.373, p.385-386, p.417; Clark, Volume II, p.748-750

16. NC Troops, Volume I, p.373-374, p.428, p.500-501

17. Honeycutt, Ava L., "Fort Fisher, Malakoff of the South", p. 70-71, Master's Thesis, Duke University, 1963, hereinafter Malakoff of the South

18. Malakoff of the South, p.70-71; NC Troops, Volume I, p.21 & 27

19. RN, Volume 9, p.329

20. Autobiography of General Louis Hebert, p.14, unpublished manuscript, University ofNorth Carolina, hereinafter Louis Hebert; Tunnard, W.H., *A Southern Record. The History of the Third Regiment Louisiana Infantry*, p.28-29, reprint by Morningside Bookshop, Dayton, Ohio, 1988

21. Louis Hebert, p.9-11, p.13-14; O.R., Volume XXIX, Part 2, p.907;

22. Moore, Louis T.,*Stories Old and New of the Cape Fear Region*, p.208, p.233 Wilmington Printing Company, Wilmington, N.C., 1956; Davis, Burke, *Our Incredible Civil War*, p.74, Holt, Rinehart & Winston, New York, 1960

23. McDonough, James L., *Chattanooga – A Death Grip on the Confederacy,* p.34-36, University of Tennessee Press, Knoxville, Tennessee, 1985; O.R., Volume XXIX, Part 2, p.761-762; Daily Journal, October 10, 1863

24. Daily Journal, November 6, 1863

25. Ibid, November 6, 1863

26. Ibid, November 6, 1863

27. Ibid, November 6, 1863

28. Ibid, November 6, 1863

29. Ibid, November 6, 1863; O.R., Volume XXIX, Part 2, p.761-762, 786; S.H.S.P., Volume XXI (1893), p.265

30. S.H.S.P., Volume XXI, p.265

31. "Rev. Moses D. Hoge, Pastor, Chaplain", Confederate Veteran, Volume III (1895), p.66-67; Bethel to Sharpsburg, Volume I, p.370-371

32. Clark, Volume V, p.342

33. Clark, Volume V, p.343-344; Running the Blockade, p.49; Bethel to Sharpsburg, Volume I, p.371, 378

34. Clark, Volume V, p.344
35. Ibid, Volume V, p.337
36. Bethel to Sharpsburg, Volume I, p.371
37. Diary of William Lamb, August 14, 1888; "Civil War Times Illustrated", November, 1974, p.16, hereinafter CWTI
38. Diary of William Lamb, August 14, 1888; Watkins, Mrs. Gipp, "Kentucky in the War Between the States", Confederate Veteran, Volume XXXV (1927), p.464; O.R., Volume II, p.478; O.R., Volume XXIX, Part 2, p.716
39. CWTI, November 1974, p.16-22
40. Ross, Edward FitzGerald, *Cities and Camps of the Confederate States*, p.xiv-xv, p.51, University of Illinois Press, Urbana, 1958, hereinafter Cities and Camps
41. Cities and Camps, p.149-150
42. Ibid, p.150-151
43. Ibid, p. 97, p.150
44. Clark, Volume V, p.407-408; ORN, Volume 9, p.273-275
45. ORN, Volume 9, p.288; Chronicles, p.388; Scharf, Thomas, *History of the Confederate States Navy*, p.481-482, Rogers & Sherwood, New York, 1887, hereinafter Scharf
46. Scharf, p.482; Clark, Volume V, p.408
47. Blockade, Civil War at Sea, p.53; ORN, Volume 9, p.292
48. Blockade, Civil War at Sea, p.54; ORN, Volume 9, p.292
49. Blockade, Civil War at Sea, p.54; ORN, Volume 9, p.292-296
50. Blockade, Civil War at Sea, p.55
51. Running the Blockade, p.35, p.99-100; Gibbons, Tony, *Warships and Naval Battles of the Civil War*, p.156, Gallery Books an imprint of W.H. Smith Publishers, New York, 1989, hereinafter Warships & Naval Battles; Daily Journal, October 17, 1863
52. ORN, Volume 9, p.319, p.323; Running the Blockade, p.84, p.162-163
53. ORN, Volume 9, p.248; p.250-251
54. O.R., Series IV, Volume II, p.1014-1015
55. Ibid, p.1015
56. O.R., Volume XXIX, Part 2, p.896-897
57. O.R., Volume XXIX, Part 2, p.907, p.910
58. Clark, Volume II, p.745, p.754-755
59. O.R., Volume XXXIII, p.1084-1085
60. Daily Journal, February 12, 1864
61. O.R., Volume XXXIII, p.425
62. O.R., Volume XXXIII, p.425-426; Chronicles, p.59; Diary of William Lamb, October 1, 1861; Fonvielle, Chris E. Jr., *Fort Anderson, Battle for Wilmington*, p.15-17, Savas Publishing Company, Mason City, Iowa, 1999; Bethel to Sharpsburg, Volume I, p.185
63. O.R., Volume XXXIII, p.426

64. Ibid, Volume XXXIII, p.426
65. Running the Blockade, p.111; Keeler, Aboard the U.S.S. Florida, p.141
66. Aboard the U.S.S. Florida, p.142; Daily Journal, February 4, 1864
67. Daily Journal, February 4, 1864; Running the Blockade, p.113-114
68. Daily Journal, February 4, 1864; ORN, Volume 9, 438
69. Aboard the U.S.S. Florida, p.141
70. Ibid, p.141-142
71. Ibid, p.143-144
72. Ibid, p.144-145
73. Ibid, p.145; ORN, Volume 9, p.438-439
74. Aboard the U.S.S. Florida, p.146
75. Running the Blockade, p.113; Daily Journal, February 4 & February 6, 1864
76. Aboard the U.S.S. Florida, p.146-147
77. Daily Journal, February 16, 1864; Moore, Louis T., *Stories Old and New of the Cape Fear Region,* p.201, Wilmington Printing Company, Wilmington, N.C., 1956; ORN, Volume 9, p.473-475, p.483
78. Aboard the U.S.S. Florida, p.150; ORN, Volume 9, p.474
79. Aboard the U.S.S. Florida, p.150-151
80. ORN, Volume 9, p.474-475; Aboard the U.S.S. Florida, p.151
81. ORN, Volume 9, p.475; Aboard the U.S.S. Florida, p.151-152
82. Ibid, Volume 9, p.475, p.483; Aboard the U.S.S. Florida, p.152-153
83. Daily Journal, February 16, 1864
84. Daily Journal, February 17, 1864
85. ORN, Volume 9, p.500-501
86. Ibid, p.511-512; Roske, Ralph and Van Doren, Charles, *Lincoln's Commando, The Biography of Commander W.B. Cushing, U.S.N.,* p.9-10, Harper & Brothers, 1957, hereinafter Lincoln's Commando; Daily Journal, June 23, 1864
87. Greenberg, R.G., "A Mysterious Raid", Confederate Veteran, Volume XXVI (1918), p.396; Lincoln's Commando, p.10-12; ORN, Volume 9, p.511
88. Confederate Veteran, Volume XXVI (1918), p.396-397; Lincoln's Commando, p.11-12; NC Troops, Volume I, p.2, p.5; ORN, Volume 9, p.511
89. Confederate Veteran, Volume XXVI (1918), p.397; ORN, Volume 9, p.511-513
90. ORN, Volume 9, p.512-513; Lincoln's Commando, p.13
91. ORN, Volume 9, p.513
92. O.R., Series I, Volume XXXIII, p.1177, p.1202
93. Ibid, Volume XXXIII, p.1200

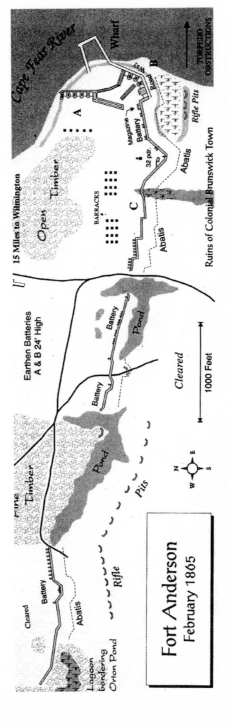

Fort Anderson, just north of Fort Fisher on the Cape Fear River's west bank, was the second largest installation guarding Wilmington. Map courtesy of Mark A. Moore, from his book The Wilmington Campaign and the Battles for Fort Fisher.

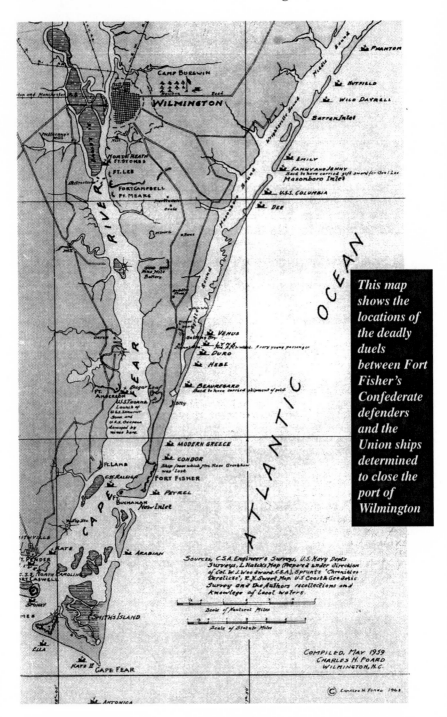

This map shows the locations of the deadly duels between Fort Fisher's Confederate defenders and the Union ships determined to close the port of Wilmington

Chapter 7

"...the port of Wilmington is the only hope of rebeldom..."

C hase Whiting never did have enough soldiers, but the ones he had were good. To make up for their lack of numbers, they relied on the big sand forts on which they were constantly working, and the grit, tenacity, and accuracy of fire in combat for which the Confederate soldier had become known. A week after Cushing's raid on Hebert's headquarters, Whiting's Rebels on Bald Head Island demonstrated just how accurate their fire could be. Artillerists in the Fortieth North Carolina Troops, and those in the Third North Carolina Battalion Light Artillery, based at Fort Holmes, constantly patrolled the beach for stranded blockade-runners or Yankee gunboats. They found an inviting target the first week of March 1864.

The *U.S.S. Peterhoff*, a sleek looking 800-ton, 210-foot-long side wheel steamer, had originally been the yacht of the Emperor of Russia, but had been purchased by a blockade- running company in England. As a runner, she was captured on her first trip out of London bound for Matamoras, Mexico, loaded down with a cargo of medicine and iron bound for the Confederacy. She had been converted to a United States warship, and only recently, on February 20, had been assigned to duty on the North Atlantic Blockading Squadron. It was to be a short assignment. [1]

USS Peterhoff

Perhaps because of his newness to the blockade off Cape Fear, perhaps for some other reason, Acting Volunteer Lieutenant Thomas Pickering, commanding the *Peterhoff*, had anchored close to the east side of Bald Head Island for a couple of days, one Confederate estimating she was no more than two miles off the beach. On Saturday morning, March 6, Lieutenant Colonel George Tait of the Fortieth North Carolina was charged with the responsibility of driving her off, or sinking her.

Directly under Tait on the east side of the island, rolling their guns quietly into place for the best shot, were two batteries of one gun each, but each one deadly. Captain William Badham of Company B, Third Battalion North Carolina Light Artillery, had his men set up their 20-pound Parrott rifle, calculate distance from their position to the Yankee blockader, and wait for orders to fire. First Lieutenant Joseph F. Hellen, of the Fortieth North Carolina, had his men readied to open up with their 12-pound Whitworth.

"At eleven o'clock precisely," recalled one of Hellen's men, the Whitworth roared, and then was heard the distinctive high-pitched, eerie whine of the British shell whirring through the air as it drove for the unsuspecting Yankee ship. "His shot ricocheted once and struck short on second graze about 20 yards. We feel almost certain that this shot penetrated the hull below the water line, a little forward of midship. It must have gone through and through her." [2]

Almost immediately, another Confederate observed, Yankee sailors could be seen running back and forth on deck in a panic, giving "evidence that they were in a fix," and they quickly raised a flag to the foremast, possibly as a signal of distress. Captain Badham now opened up with the deadly Parrott rifle, getting off at least "nine well directed shots, two taking effect," while

Lieutenant Hellen fired five more with the Whitworth, "three of which took effect." [3]

Private Elisha Griggs and five of his comrades in 3rd Company G of the Fortieth Regiment manned the Whitworth rifle. Griggs confirmed the opinion of others when he wrote that they "got range on it and shot a hole clear through it the first fire." Sergeant Thaddeus Davis, one of Griggs' superiors in the same company, recalled that it was "the best shot I witnessed, ever." Davis said that after the *Peterhoff* had been fired on six times by their Whitworth, the ship took off as fast as possible under the altered circumstances, apparently taking on water fast with several holes in her hull, when "she ran out to another blockade ship, and before they could transfer her supplies she sunk." [4]

One Confederate summed up the feelings of all: "The fact of her not returning our fire seems to me pretty good evidence that she was badly hurt, as these fellows never fail to do so when fired upon from the shore. We are very well satisfied," he said, "that we did the work for her, and the boys who worked the guns are a little proud of it." [5]

Curiously, Captain Benjamin Sands, senior U.S. Naval officer off New Inlet, reported that the *Peterhoff* had been sunk in an accidental collision with the *U.S.S. Monticello*, commanded by the young raider, William Cushing. No lives had been lost, and the crew from the *Peterhoff* had all managed to get aboard the *Monticello* before the stricken ship sunk. The *Monticello*, Sands wrote, had been in closer to shore than she should have been, and had run into the *Peterhoff* and sunk her immediately. Blame was placed on Acting Ensign J. Hadfield, who was deck officer at the time of the supposed collision. No blame was attached to Lieutenant Cushing. Strangely, no reports were to be found of either Lieutenant Cushing or Lieutenant Pickering, the commanding officers of the two vessels in question. [6]

Union reports of collision as the cause of the sinking were clearly at variance with Confederate accounts. The Rebels discussed the action in considerable detail, with near precise agreement in terms of participants, number of shots fired, time of the action, the striking of the first round amidships, and the efforts of the *Peterhoff* to stay afloat once she had been hit several times by the Whitworth and Parrott rifles. Considering, too, the inexperience of Lieutenant Pickering, it would be reasonable to understand his being abnormally close to shore, not being fully cognizant of the danger the movable Confederate guns posed. The credibility of the Union accounts appear clouded, too, by the absence of reports of Cushing and Pickering, the commanders of the vessels in question.

At the same time as the sinking of the *Peterhoff*, the high command in Wilmington was having problems of its own. General Whiting and Flag Officer William Lynch, Commanding C.S. Naval Forces in North Carolina, had had their problems since February of 1863. Whiting had at that time requested some of the big guns assigned to the unfinished *C.S.S. North Carolina* and *Raleigh* be temporarily consigned to coastal batteries, where they were desperately needed. Lynch objected to both Secretary of the Navy Stephen Mallory, and also Senator George Davis of Wilmington, at the same time casting aspersions on General Whiting's conduct as commander of the District of the Cape Fear. [7]

The Secretary of the Navy and the War Department sustained General Whiting's request, ignored Lynch's, and the guns were emplaced in the Wilmington coastal defenses. Relations between Whiting and Lynch became exceedingly cold, communication only occurring relative to official business, and until March 1864, tempers simmered beneath the surface. Then they almost exploded in armed collision between the Confederate Army and Navy. [8]

At issue was a government regulation requiring all blockade-runners to carry out a certain portion of Confederate Army cotton in the cargo, and a certain portion for the Navy. The steamers *Alice* and *Hansa* had been out in mid-February without any Navy cotton, with the understanding that they would take out the required amount on their next voyage. On March 6, the same day the *Peterhoff* was sunk, the blockade runners were ordered detained by a Mr. William H. Peters, an agent for the Navy Department, acting on orders of Secretary Mallory. Upon interviewing Peters, Whiting learned of the reason for the action, but was only informed of detention of the *Alice*. Secretary of War James Seddon telegraphed Whiting that the Navy's claim was to be upheld, and Whiting assented to the *Alice* being detained. "No mention was made," Whiting later wrote Seddon, "of steamer *Hansa*." [9]

Hansa left the Wilmington wharf on March 8 to allow another vessel to put in, but Lynch said he thought the ship was trying to get away without the required cotton aboard, and he sent Confederate Marines to board the ship, and ordered it anchored next to the nearly complete and fully gunned *North Carolina* down at Smithville.

Whiting was furious. He branded Lynch's action as "unwarrantable usurpation" of his authority as department commander, the only one truly authorized to grant permission for vessels to come and go in the Cape Fear. Whiting told Seddon that Lynch's contention that the *Hansa* was trying to slip away "is simply absurd, and no one better knows it than Flag Officer Officer Lynch." Whiting said the ship "had not even cleared for sea; had not applied for a pilot's permit; had not asked for the authority from headquarters, without which no vessel is allowed to leave the town even, much less go to sea. If he did not know this he ought to have known it. The orders relative to the port have been published for months in the daily papers." Whiting was positive the Secretary of the Navy would never "have intended for execution in the mode pursued," and Lynch had violated "authority and right by seizing the ship." [10]

Whiting wrote to Lynch that he would "permit no interference with any vessel whatever in this department not belonging to the C.S. Navy by any authority but my own or by orders emanating from the War Department...A guard is ordered upon the *Hansa* and no person will be permitted to approach her without proper authority." [11]

Lynch responded by telling the General he recognized no higher authority to the Secretary of the Navy than the President of the Confederate States. He told Whiting he had ordered Commander Muse, commanding the ironclad *North Carolina*, to keep the *Hansa* near his warship. He had told Muse "not to use force except in the last resort, but if it be necessary to enforce the order, to exercise all the means at his disposal." [12]

Early on the morning of the 9th, Whiting, determined to assert his authority, ordered a contingent of soldiers from Martin's North Carolina brigade to serve as guard and "prevent communication temporarily between the fleet and the shore." He then sent the quartermaster's steamer *Cape Fear* downriver to the *Hansa*, with two companies of the Seventeenth North Carolina Infantry aboard, who ejected the Confederate Marines, "weighed the anchor of the *Hansa*, had her removed to the quartermaster's wharf and moored. There was no collision nor appearance of any, nor did any occur at all," Whiting said, "though after all this the *North Carolina* and *Yadkin* were brought up and placed in a threatening position with all their boats." [13]

Late that night, Chase Whiting received a telegram from Adjutant General Samuel Cooper, which told him to desist "at once from any collision with Captain Lynch or his people." Upon receiving Cooper's order, Whiting at once removed his guard from the *Hansa*, and advised Commander Muse of the *C.S.S. North Carolina* that the blockade runner would not sail without consent of the C.S. Navy. Whiting had made his point about not tolerating usurpation of his authority in Wilmington. [14]

Jefferson Davis was not at all pleased at the spectacle of the Confederate Army and Navy nearly coming to blows and summoned Whiting and Lynch to Richmond. Both officers received reprimands, but were soon on their way back to North Carolina. According to one army officer on duty in Wilmington, Lynch and Whiting "both returned apparently satisfied." The authorities eventually realized a more cooperative naval commander was needed in Wilmington, however, for by the fall of 1864, Lynch had been relieved and replaced by Flag Officer Robert F. Pinckney. [15]

Whiting returned to his Wilmington headquarters about the same time his Rebels at Fort Campbell drove off Yankee blockaders trying to destroy the steamer *Lucy*. The *Lucy*, a "long, low, side-wheel steamer" that resembled the *Ad-Vance*, ran aground on Oak Island approximately five miles east of Lockwood Folly Inlet, and one mile west of the heavy guns of Fort Campbell, at 2 a.m. on Monday, the 14th of March. Captain J.A. Duguid realized, with the "tide making ebb very fast," that he needed to summon some help in the form of gray uniforms and guns as fast as he could get it, no Confederate soldiers being on the immediate scene at that time.

He sent his Mate on shore with dispatches, and ordered him to go seek Colonel Jones' help at Fort Caswell. Jones sent back word for the crew of the *Lucy* to vacate the ship by daylight, and immediately hustled troops and Whitworth guns down the beach to save the vessel, at the same time alerting the garrison at Fort Campbell to be ready to fire at first light, if not already prepared to do so.

At 5:20 the *U.S.S. Aries* opened fire on the *Lucy* and was immediately fired on herself by the big guns in Fort Campbell and the deadly accurate Whitworths. Acting Volunteer Lieutenant Edward Devens, commanding the *Aires*, reported that many shells were "all falling close to us or going over us." By 6:10 a.m., believing that he had hit the *Lucy* at least twice, Devens "deemed it prudent to withdraw, and ran out" to report to his superior officer. Devens was certain the Confederates had fired at least "43 shell at us," and uncomfortably close at that. Captain Duguid said the Federals took off after two Rebel shells hit the *Aires*. [16]

After the Yankees were driven off, the soldiers from Fort Campbell rowed out to the stranded blockade-runner and climbed aboard to put her in a floating condition, so she would be ready once the tide began to come in. They pumped and bailed "the vessel out during the day, on which in a great measure, depended her floating that night." [17]

While the Southern artillerists worked feverishly aboard the *Lucy*, their comrades manning the Whitworths and the heavy guns in Campbell stood by their pieces and kept close watch on the Union squadron as night approached. As evening came on, so did the Yankees. The *Aires* returned with the *U.S.S. State of Georgia*, and both ships commenced firing on the blockade-runner. The Rebels responded immediately. Watching the action from the *Lucy*, Captain Duguid could see as the "Confederate guns opened fire upon them with redoubled vigor." Commander James Madison Frailey of the *U.S.S. Quaker City* said that "in a few minutes a very heavy fire was opened upon both by numerous batteries of greater range, which compelled them to withdraw, without, however, either vessel receiving any injury." [18]

As darkness set in and the Union gunboats retired out of range, the Confederate soldiers and Captain Duguid and his crew were able to get her off the beach, steam eastward past Campbell and Caswell, and head north upriver to Wilmington. The Captain publicly expressed his thanks to "the officers and men for the cordial and willing manner in which they" lent their help. "If it had not been for their punctuality and readiness the Yankees must have destroyed the ship." [19]

Despite such continuing successful engagements with the Union fleet over blockade-runners, the vulnerability of Chase Whiting's command to land assault, about which he had feared and warned his superiors since November 1862, was soundly driven home a month after the fight over the *Lucy*. On the night of April 21, officers and men of the Federal Navy destroyed part of the valuable Masonboro State Salt Works. These works had existed since the spring

The salt works at Masonboro Sound, similar to these, provided a vital commodity.

of 1862, and they had provided much needed salt from the sound for the essential preservation of meat for the populace of the state, as well as for soldiers.

The total area of the operation was extensive, encompassing 220 acres of land in a thin, narrow strip that ran almost three miles inland from Myrtle Grove Sound. The works were situated approximately ten miles north of Fort Fisher, just south of Purviance Creek (also called Cabbage Inlet Creek), and about seven miles southeast of Wilmington.

On this site were pumps, reservoirs for holding water from the sound, wooden sluice gates akin to those in rice fields, and wooden troughs that brought water from the reservoirs to large vats. From the vats, water was then conveyed to large pans that sat on furnaces fed with local pinewood, where the water was boiled off to leave the salt. Some salt was produced by allowing water to sit in a series of shallow ponds, where the sun increasingly evaporated it. The operation was able to produce about 8,500 pounds, or 2 1/2 tons of salt per day, a considerable supply. More than 200 men worked at the site, and dormitories and kitchens provided living and eating quarters. [20]

On Thursday night, April 21, a boat expedition of 102 U.S. Naval officers and sailors commanded by Acting Volunteer Lieutenant J.B. Breck, commander of the *U.S.S. Niphon*, departed from three Union gunboats in gigs and cutters, and rowed into Masonboro Sound by way of the main inlet. Just before 9 p.m., they landed on the mainland "and got in the rear of the works without being discovered, threw out pickets, and commenced the work of destruction." They burned sheds, wagons and harnesses, threw 30-pounder shells into the furnaces and underneath the boilers, and believed they had accomplished "the entire destruction of the State salt works on Masonboro Sound." They also took as prisoners and carried back to their ships sixty of the men engaged in work there. [21]

David Worth, State Salt Commissioner based in Wilmington, reported to Governor Vance that serious damage had indeed been inflicted, but it was not of the magnitude the Yankees thought it was. Worth wrote the Governor the day after the raid, that none of the boiling pans had been damaged, despite the fact that shells had been thrown into the furnaces. "The chief damage done," he said, "was to the steam-pump and engine. They are badly damaged, and it will take some time to repair them and get them in position again. If I could pump water today two-thirds of the works could be run. The blacksmith-shop, wagon-shop, and tools and stables were entirely consumed." [22]

Neither horses nor mules had been injured. "The sheds over the works," the commissioner wrote, "being dampened by the steam from the boiling-pans, burned slowly, and were soon extinguished after departure of the enemy." [23]

What concerned W.H.C. Whiting about the whole affair was not the suspension of salt. He had long considered the works a source of communication between disloyal workers and the Union Navy and was glad to be rid of the operation. "I do not regret it," he wrote Zebulon Vance on April 22. "I consider that the whole affair was done with the complicity and on the information of parties engaged there...The establishment has long been a nuisance, and the circumstantial evidence of their intercourse with the enemy is very strong, and, combined with the known character of many of the conscripts, is sufficient to induce me to remove what the enemy have spared...No more salt-works will be permitted on Masonborough Sound." [24]

Whiting's opinions were not without merit, for the individual who piloted the Union expedition into the sound was one J.H. Pucket, a "refugee" who had been picked up in a small boat with five other men by Lieutenant Breck, the leader of the raid, early in the month. Pucket and two other men, John Sears and John Wheeler, had advised the destruction of the salt works by the Yankees, telling them how lightly defended they were, and that there was only "one battery on the beach between Masonboro Inlet and Fort Fisher." [25]

On the same day as his letter to Vance, Whiting advised his superior, General P.G.T. Beauregard, in Weldon commanding the Department of North Carolina, that the incident further underscored the vulnerability of the Cape Fear to outside attack. With 3,075 men of Martin's North Carolina Brigade away at Weldon when the works were raided, Whiting had only 4,400 men present for duty in his whole command, of which 684 were movable infantry in the Fiftieth North Carolina Troops, the only regiment left him from Martin's brigade. "If your operations will not permit you to leave a brigade with me," he wrote Beauregard, "I beg you will present this to the Department, which has been fully advised of the circumstances of this command. I have not at present sufficient force to perform the heavy garrison duties of the city." [26]

Even so, his men down at Fort Fisher, the key to Wilmington's defenses, maintained an unflinching determination to defend Southern independence. At a meeting held in Fort Fisher on Saturday, April 30, nine days after the Yankee attack on the State Salt Works, members of Company E of the Thirty-Sixth North Carolina Troops issued a call for continued resistance to aggression, and a denunciation for William W. Holden, a Raleigh newspaper editor who was running for governor on a peace platform.

In a series of resolutions, Colonel Lamb's Rebels declared that they had "abiding faith and confidence in our chief executive, President Davis, and that we heartily approve of the course pursued by our present worthy and most able Governor, Z.B. Vance, his untiring efforts to defend the State and the Confederate States, his foresight in providing for the soldiers and their families of his state, entitles him to the thanks and gratitude of all North Carolina soldiers. That we pledge him our hearty support for re-election."

They also denounced "in the most bitter terms, W.W. Holden and his co-adjutors, as alike injurious to the State, Confederate States, and to our cause at large, and that he, by his device and cunning, is seeking to destroy the unity of our army and to sow the seed of discord throughout our ranks by his contaminating influence." Clearly, Fort Fisher's troops, despite Whiting's fears, were committed to fight until peace was won on the battlefield. [27]

Even Flag Officer Lynch, probably to Whiting's surprise, seemed committed to fight in May of 1864. The ironclad *C.S.S. Raleigh*, recently completed in Cassidy's Shipyard in Wilmington, was ready to go out on her first sortie to engage the Yankee fleet, which would also prove to be her last. The armor-plated warship was formidable, being 150 feet long and 32 feet wide. She had a large, sloping casemated gun deck, similar to the Savannah area vessel known as the *C.S.S. Atlanta*, and carried five naval guns. One witness said she had a gun at each end of the casemate roof, with the other three amidships, that could be worked on either the port or starboard side of the ship.

Another observer said the Raleigh looked like a large ship "cut down to the water line, and a house built on and plated. The sides of the house are arched, and having three ports on a side and one in each. She has one smokestack and a small flag post aft. Goes, I think, 6 to 7 knots, and turns very quickly." [28]

Lynch may have been smarting from his altercation with Whiting and the President's reprimand two months previously, and perhaps sought to reassert the Navy's prestige. He may even have genuinely believed the *Raleigh* could sink a few Yankee ships, as the *Virginia* had done in Hampton Roads in March of 1862, and break the Union blockade of Wilmington.

Whatever his specific motive, Lynch steamed down to Fort Fisher with Lieutenant J. Pembroke Jones, formerly executive officer aboard the *Virginia*, now commanding the *Raleigh*, with two small wooden gunboats on the afternoon of Friday, May 6. He revealed his plans to Colonel Lamb to obtain his cooperation and to observe from the parapets with him the positions of the

J. Pembroke Jones, C.S.N.

various Yankee warships. Seven U.S. ships were spied off New Inlet as the sun was setting: *Tuscarora, Britannia, Nansemond, Howquah, Mount Vernon, Kansas,* and *Niphon.* He gave Lamb a note that described the distinguishing signals for his vessels, "a red light above a white one – so that they would not be fired upon by the fort." [29]

About 8 p.m., the range lights were set on the Mount Battery, and the *Raleigh* and her two small escorts, the *Yadkin* and *Equator,* steamed out of New Inlet. William Lamb and some of his officers climbed to the ramparts of Fort Fisher to watch the show. Flying the Confederate Naval Ensign, and steaming at a rate of six to seven knots per hour, the *Raleigh* headed for the Federal fleet.

Coming into New Inlet from Nassau at the same time, was the blockade-runner *Annie,* that had just ridden out a severe hurricane for over forty hours, and nerves aboard were frayed. Pilot James Craig, whose father owned the nearby Cape Fear stop north of Fort Fisher known as Craig's Landing, was bringing the *Annie* in, using the Mound Battery light as a guide, when all of a sudden, the fearsome Rebel warship loomed ahead. Craig was 24 years old this month and an excellent Cape Fear pilot, but he confessed to a friend "we came very near running afoul of the Confederate iron-clad ram *Raleigh* outside of the bar, but, supposing her to be one of the blockaders, got out of her way as quickly as possible." [30]

Acting Volunteer Lieutenant Sam Huse, commanding the *Britannia,* had seen "one of the rebel ironclad rams inside the bar," and had been watching her to see if she would come out. As the *Raleigh* headed straight for his ship, Huse "fired several rockets and fired my 30-pounder Parrott at her, but as he kept on directly after us I ran for the buoy, firing at her with 24-pounder howitzer. She then commenced firing at us; the first shot put out our binnacle lights and next went a little over the starboard paddle box, sounding very like a 100-pounder Parrott shot when it tumbles." [31]

Huse got his ship out of the way as fast as the *Britannia*'s engines could turn, having to change course several times to escape the *Raleigh*'s fire. Finally, after dodging about for some time and getting further offshore, the Yankees had outrun the slow-moving iron monster, and the *Raleigh* hunted for other prey.

She found it about midnight, in the form of the *U.S.S. Nansemond,* Acting Ensign J.H. Porter commanding. One sailor aboard the *Nansemond* said the ironclad was trying to run them down. Porter agreed, saying he had to bring his "helm hard a starboard to prevent collision, and challenged again, which was answered by a steady red light, the vessels now steering directly for us." The *Raleigh* fired at the *Nansemond*, the shell passing "over and near our walking beam," according to Porter. "The vessel at this time not over 500 yards from us; could see the outline of her hull and the white water from her propeller. Fired another shot from the 24-pounder, which was returned, the shot again passing over us."

Porter decided the best thing to do without support from other Federal warships was the same thing Sam Huse of the *Britannia* had done, so he "put on more steam to get out of range." [32]

Second Lieutenant Henry M. Doak of the Confederate States Marine Corps, had been transferred to Wilmington from Savannah in late February 1864. Tonight, with other Marines, he was aboard the *Raleigh* in command of one of the starboard guns, trying to sink Yankee ships that kept running out of range. At one point he was ordered to fire at the next light he saw, on the premise it had to be a Union warship. In the darkness, smoke, and confusion, though, Doak's gun crew fired their next shell into Fort Fisher, and an irate Flag Officer Lynch put him under arrest and hustled him below for the infraction. Pembroke Jones realized the order to fire at the next light seen was a faulty one, however, and he intervened with Lynch to have the Marine Lieutenant restored to his battle station. [33]

2ndLt Henry M. Doak, C.S.M.C.

By this time, about 1 a.m. or so of Saturday, May 7, all was pitch blackness. A bluecoat aboard the *Nansemond* said "we could not see a greater distance than fifty yards off." For the next 3 1/2 hours darkness prevented further action, and *Raleigh* stood offshore nearly five miles waiting for dawn to break, to reengage the Federal fleet. [34]

At 4:25 a.m., Acting Master J.W. Balch, commanding the *U.S.S. Howquah*, spied the ironclad, which he and all the other Yankee officers thought was the *North Carolina*. Balch called his men to battle stations, as the

Raleigh headed for her. As Balch headed his ship offshore to keep the ironclad at a distance, he had his gunners open fire with 30-pound Parrott rifles. A Union sailor saw at least four shells slam into the iron-sheathed casemate, "the shot glancing off her like peas." One of the *Raleigh*'s shells exploded close to the starboard quarter of the *Howquah*, but did no damage.[35]

As the *Howquah* continued moving out, the *Raleigh* followed, "firing from her bow and broadside guns." Now other vessels came on the scene: the *Mount Vernon*, *Fahkee*, *Niphon*, and *Kansas*. *Mount Vernon* opened up with her "100-pounder Parrott rifle and IX-inch guns," while the *Kansas* fired two shells from her 150-pounder rifle, which the commander of the vessel "had the mortification to see turn over and fall short." About 6 a.m., the *Raleigh* fired on the *Howquah* again, sending an 8-inch rifle shell through the smokestack.[36]

Pembroke Jones and William Lynch, aware that the entire fleet off New Inlet was beginning to converge on the *Raleigh* and cognizant that under the circumstances they had done about all the damage they were going to do this day, decided to steam over the bar while the tide was still right. After putting the eight-inch shell through the *Howquah*'s smokestack, then, they headed for Fort Fisher. As the Confederate warship glided back into New Inlet at 7 a.m., Colonel Lamb had his artillerists at nine of the big guns fire a thundering salute of congratulations for their returning naval comrades, who had at least shown their mettle, even if the Yankees had not really been hurt this time.[37]

After the ironclad and her escorts passed the Mound Battery and entered the Cape Fear unscathed, the *Raleigh* ran onto the shoal that was known as the "Rip", a sandbar almost due west of the tip end of Confederate Point. Frantic efforts were made to lighten and get her off, as her heavy iron weight would cause her to literally break apart when the tide went out. It was impossible, however, in such a short period of time to remove guns, ammunition, equipment, etc., from the ship, and transfer it to barges, before the tide did ebb. According to one Wilmingtonian, the "receding tide caused her to hog and break in two, on account of the heavy armor, and becoming a wreck, she subsequently sank and went to pieces."[38]

Confederate Marine Lieutenant Doak was sickened at the loss of the powerful warship, that would have been of tremendous value in defending Wilmington in the months to come. "Owing to careless sounding or a reckless pilot," he wrote, "we ran aground going over the bar – the *Raleigh* and months of labor and thousands of dollars all gone for nothing."[39]

A few weeks later, James Ryder Randall, Baltimore native and composer of the stirring Confederate warsong, "Maryland, My Maryland", who was also secretary to Flag Officer Lynch, was on a trip down the Cape Fear, and spotted the broken hulk of the *Raleigh*. He wrote that the ironclad was about a mile west of the Mound Battery, out in the river. "She was very much sunken at the stern," he said, "lifting her bow considerably. Her sides had been stripped of their armor, the smokestack prostrate, and altogether she had the appearance of a monstrous turtle stranded and forlorn. As we passed, the divers were engaged in removing her boilers and machinery." [40]

A Confederate Naval court of inquiry was held in Wilmington in early June to investigate the causes of the loss of the vessel. The court decided that the *Raleigh*'s loss was not due to "negligence or inattention on the part of anyone on board of her, and every effort was made to save said vessel." The panel of Confederate Naval officers further determined "that the *Raleigh* could have remained outside the bar of Cape Fear River for a few hours with apparent safety, but, in the opinion of the court, it would have been improper; and, in view of all the circumstances, 'her commanding officer was justified in attempting to go back into the harbor when he did.' " [41]

Only two days had passed since the *Raleigh*'s sortie when William B. Cushing wrote to Admiral Lee in Hampton Roads, to express his mortification over a Confederate warship's audacity to go out and attack the United States Navy. Neither he nor any other Federal officer knew at this time that the *Raleigh* was already a wreck. On May 9, Cushing wrote from Beaufort, where he had returned with the *U.S.S. Monticello* after offshore cruising for several weeks. "I feel very badly over the affair, sir," he told the Admiral, "and would have given my life freely to have had the power of showing my high regard for you and the honor of the service by engaging the enemy's vessels. If they are there when I arrive, I shall use the *Monticello* as a ram, and will go over her or to the bottom. If they are inside, I shall send in a written petition to carry the ram by boarding in the harbor." [42]

Admiral Lee was pleased at Cushing's proposal and gave the young Lieutenant his approval to proceed. He was to be furnished with volunteers from the fleet off Wilmington, and these 100 men would accompany him into the harbor to capture or destroy the *Raleigh*. [43]

Before Cushing reconnoitered in June to determine the exact location of the ironclad and decide on the best plan, another Yankee had already learned that the *Raleigh* was severely damaged. Lieutenant J.B. Breck of the *U.S.S. Niphon*, who had destroyed the State Salt Works in April, made a successful fact-finding trip into Masonboro Sound in late May.

On Wednesday night, May 25, Breck took some of his crew in two boats, and "proceeded up Masonboro Sound for the purpose of gaining information as to the enemy's forces and blockade runners at Wilmington." Breck had "weekly communication with the shore," having become acquainted with some secretly Unionist members of the Masonboro Home Guard at the time of his attack on the salt works. [44] One Confederate militia officer, a Second Lieutenant Eli H. Davis of that unit, had even left his home and gone aboard the *Niphon*. He had joined the Yankees "after making arrangement to obtain information from his friends at frequent intervals." [45]

On this night, Breck was told that Colonel Lamb now had 38 heavy guns mounted at Fort Fisher, with 1,000 men to serve them. The rear of Fort Fisher "on the river side is all open and entirely exposed, the road from Wilmington leading directly into the fort on its northwestern side and only 2 guns that will command the road. All cavalry pickets are withdrawn from the beach, two companies, one of South Carolina and one of Georgia cavalry, having left yesterday. The Mound fort is 60 feet high, mounting 2 large guns which can be trained in any direction; also has a small wooden tower built on the top of the Mound, 20 feet high, for a signal light." [46]

One of Lamb's companies of the Thirty-Sixth North Carolina, which was Captain Edward B. Dudley's Company D, was based at what the Unionists

called the Half Moon battery, which was the same as Gatlin's Battery, as designated by the Confederates. [47]

Breck captured four conscripts who were employed at the salt works, where 150 of them were hard at work erecting new facilities on the sound, to replace the wagon-shop, stables and other buildings destroyed in the raid he had made the month before. General Whiting's edict that salt works would no longer be "permitted on Masonborough Sound," had been overruled by his superiors, and repairs were proceeding. [48]

On this Wednesday night, there were nine blockade-runners docked at the wharves in Wilmington, with one of them, the *Alice*, supposedly carrying $1,100,000 in gold to Europe. As for the two ironclads on the river, Breck said that both were "on shore. One of them, the *Raleigh*, is badly injured. Neither is expected to be got off." [49]

Governor Edward B. Dudley, whose son was a captain of the 36th North Carolina.

A month later, Willliam Cushing would confirm firsthand that the *Raleigh* was more than injured and that she would never again go out to molest the United States Navy. Some two months before Cushing's confirmation, a Union Army officer, Brigadier General Innis N. Palmer, commanding the Union District of North Carolina, with headquarters in New Bern, proposed to capture Fort Fisher in a surprise night attack with 1,500 soldiers. The scheme itself was preposterous under the circumstances, but Palmer, a West Point classmate of Stonewall Jackson's who had once served in the Second U.S. Cavalry under Robert E. Lee, had no conception of the strength of William

Lamb's fortifications. Besides, if the plan succeeded, Fort Fisher would be in Union hands, and a mortal blow would be dealt to Confederate blockade running. Even if Fisher was not captured, Palmer believed the Rebels would return some of Whiting's men from Virginia to defend Wilmington, and that would assist Palmer's boss, Major General Benjamin Butler, Union commander of Virginia and North Carolina. [50]

Whiting himself, with most of Martin's North Carolina Brigade, had gone to Petersburg in mid-May to assist General Beauregard in defending Richmond and Petersburg from Butler. A series of bloody battles were fought in what was to become known as the Bermuda Hundred Campaign. [51]

The contemplated attack was ludicrous. Colonel James C. Jourdan, who commanded the sub-district of Beaufort and had made a reconnaissance of New Inlet on June 2, told Commander J.C. Howell of the *U.S.S. Nereus*, that he proposed to "take For Fisher by surprise, and that if he could land 1,500 men on the beach without being discovered, between the hours of 11 p.m. and 1 o'clock a.m., he thought he might succeed." Howell told Jourdan that the most he could land under ideal sea conditions were only 350 men. All the Navy had were "small merchant ship boats," but that large surfboats specially designed for amphibious landing of troops could be had at Fort Monroe, across Hampton Roads from Norfolk. The Colonel told Howell that landing 350 men would not suffice, "that unless he could land one half of his force at once the expedition must be given up." Howell replied that landing "750 men was simply an impossibility." [52]

Commander Howell wrote Rear Admiral Lee that he could "judge as well or better than I what measure of success an attempted surprise of Fort Fisher would have met. I only know that on dark nights the whole beach is alive with signal lights." He told Lee that after discussing the realities of the proposed attack with Howell, Jourdan had "left for Beaufort to concoct some other more feasible scheme for harassing the enemy." [53]

Three surfboats were obtained from Fort Monroe several days later, but they were not sufficient to land enough troops either. When Jourdan tried again "to land in a small boat or to send one to the shore the whole country appeared to be alarmed, and heavy firing with musketry and from the heavy guns at Fort Fisher commenced immediately." William Lamb's Rebels were always ready and waiting anytime Yankees got too close to Fisher, and the ill-conceived assault on Confederate Point was scrapped by June 15. [54]

Eight days later, William Cushing came back. His primary purpose for the expedition, as he had already related to Rear Admiral Lee, was to "attempt the destruction of the ironclad ram *Raleigh,*" after first making a "thorough reconnaissance" of the area. [55]

On Thursday night, June 23, Cushing debarked from the *Monticello,* anchored off the Western Bar, in one of his cutters with two other officers and fifteen sailors. They entered Old Inlet, and, as before, were able to row quietly between Fort Caswell and the Smith Island defenses, heading upriver. Pulling on their oars as noiselessly as possible, the bluejackets glided past Colonel Lamb's batteries on Zeke's Island, nearly being "run down by a steamer," and continued upriver. [56]

When they arrived at Fort Anderson, Rebel soldiers spotted them from the shore, fired at them, and raised an alarm. Immediately, Cushing had his men pull for the opposite shore so as to appear they were headed downriver. When out of sight of Fort Anderson's picket posts, the Yankees reversed their course again, and steered northward for Wilmington. "When within 7 miles from Wilmington," Cushing reported to Admiral Lee, "a good place was selected on the shore, the boat hauled up and into a marsh, and the men stowed along the bank." [57]

As daylight came on, Cushing decided to watch the river for activity, to see if he might capture someone who could provide information and directions. Steamers began gliding up and down the Cape Fear, and Flag Officer Lynch's flagship, the *Yadkin*, passed by within 200 yards of the Yankees. Eight other ships went by during the day, "three of them being fine, large blockade runners." [58]

Soon after dark, Cushing captured two boats containing a group returning to Wilmington who had been out fishing all day. He made them serve as guides. They rowed toward Wilmington as night set in, and three miles below town, the Yankees came up on more Confederate fortifications. They had "found a row of obstructions, consisting of iron pointed spiles, driven in at an angle, and only to be passed by going into the channel left open, about 200 yards from a heavy battery." They were at this point opposite one of the river batteries south of Wilmington on the east bank of the Cape Fear, one that was known as Fort Campbell. Just below Campbell was another battery, known as Fort Meares, which took its name from Wilmington's martyred Colonel Gaston Meares of the Third North Carolina, killed at Malvern Hill. [59]

A little further north of Campbell the Yankees rowed past Fort Lee, and "another line of obstructions, consisting of diamond-shaped crates, filled and supported in position by two rows of spiles, the channel in this instance being within 50 yards of the guns." There was also a third line of obstructions in front of the river battery closest to Wilmington, which was Fort Stokes, approximately two miles south of town. [60]

Cushing had his men pole their way into a swamp known locally as Cypress Swamp, no more than 1 1/2 to 2 miles south of Wilmington, and eventually came upon the road that led south to Fort Fisher, and connected with another further out that ran east to Masonboro Sound. Leaving half of his sailors at the junction of the road that was closest to the swamp, where they stowed their boats, Cushing took the other half of this party two miles out the main road leading from Fort Fisher, and hid.

Just before noon, a soldier on horseback happened by carrying a mailbag from Fort Fisher, and Cushing captured him. He learned from a ration report signed by Colonel Lamb that there were 1,300 men in the fort at this time. As of the 23rd of June, the day Cushing debarked from the *Monticello* on his expedition, Lamb had on hand for his men 19,000 rations of pork or beef, 29,000 rations of flour, 7,000 of hard bread, 39,904 rations of vegetable food, tens of thousands of other assorted food items, and 30,000 rations of soap. [61]

The raiding party, Cushing wrote, "being sadly in need of some grub," was glad to see their commander send one of the sailors, dressed in the captured soldier's coat and hat, to a local store. "He returned with milk, chickens, and eggs, having passed everyone, in and out of service, without suspicion, though conversing with many." [62]

After eating, the Yankees cut the telegraph wires in the area along the road, and then retraced their route to join the other half of the party, along with their prisoners, that remained at the road and swamp junction. Moving back south down the river as night set in, Cushing put some of the prisoners in small boats without oars or sails, "so they could not get ashore in time to injure us." [63]

Continuing downriver, Cushing had one of the prisoners who served as a pilot to take him to the site of the *Raleigh*, where her broken hulk sat on the "Rip", out in the river. He was pleased, he said, to find the vessel was "indeed, destroyed, and nothing now remains of her above water." [64]

As the Yankees drew close to the end of Confederate Point and New Inlet, they captured another boat with a party of six people, four of whom were Rebel soldiers. They learned that a guard boat with 75 Confederates was patrolling the area between the end of the point and Zeke's Island. As they spotted what appeared to be the large boat in question near the battery on the island, three other boats "suddenly shot out from that side, and five more from the other completely blocking up the sole avenue of escape. I immediately put the helm down," Cushing wrote, "but found a large sailboat filled with soldiers to windward and keeping us right in the glimmer of the moon's rays." [65]

It took some quick maneuvering and fast rowing by Cushing's crew to dodge the Confederates who were rapidly closing on them. The sailors turned the boat's head toward the Western Bar, "and by throwing the dark side of the boat toward them were soon lost to view." Cushing said that the Rebels rapidly pursued, "and their whole line dashed off at once to intercept us," when the Federals turned again, and safely made their escape, "before the guns of the forts trained on the channel could be brought to bear upon our unexpected position." [66]

The bluecoats pulled hard on their oars past William Lamb's fortifications, and finally arrived at the *U.S.S. Cherokee* at daybreak, "after an absence from the squadron of two days and three nights." Cushing was proud to report to Rear Admiral Lee that he was "now posted in regard to the city land and water defenses, and everything that it will interest the Department to know." [67]

The U.S. Navy was quite interested, and would make good use of Cushing's detailed information in the next few months. None other than Gideon Welles himself wrote Cushing that the success and boldness of his expedition was "most gratifying to the Department." Medals of honor were awarded to three of the enlisted men who accompanied him, who had shown particular bravery and resolve. [68]

Equally impressed, albeit chagrined and frustrated with the whole affair, was Chase Whiting. Writing from his headquarters in Wilmington on June 27, the day after Cushing returned to the fleet, he admitted to Louis Hebert that the Yankee's exploit was "pretty strong...What do you think can be done? Can you get any help from the navy? I shall have to have a guard for my house in town. He says he was up here three weeks ago. If you have any advice or plan to give me let me hear." [69]

The next day he wrote Hebert again to suggest means "to prevent a repetition of the boat expeditions of the enemy, or at any rate to capture them. Something must be done." [70] Whiting was certain the Yankees would be back again, and he suggested Hebert coordinate search parties "several times a week" with the Confederate Navy, using the *Yadkin* or some other tug "with a well-armed crew" to examine the river at various likely hiding places. "On the west bank, Big Island, Town Creek, and Brunswick River, and perhaps the rice-field ditches, might be examined. You could send a party in a steamer to examine Snow's Marsh and the creek in that vicinity." Whiting would send land parties to search in any area where Federal raiders might be suspected. [71]

"One thing is certain," he told Hebert, "unless some efficient system is carried out our communications and even our small steamers will be in constant danger. The vessels at quarantine also will be in great danger of destruction." He ordered all ships "to come under your guns at Smithville," ordered the guard increased at Fort Anderson, and asked Hebert to coordinate patrols of the river by the Confederate Navy, for that portion of it not covered by land batteries. [72]

On July 4, Whiting wrote to Adjutant and Inspector General Cooper in Richmond, to advise him of the significance of Cushing's raid. "Cushing commands the *Monticello*," Whiting wrote, "and his exploit and information was regarded as so important that he was at once sent with his vessel to report at the North." [73]

He sounded the warning again of Wilmington's vulnerability to attack. Far too much was left to chance, Whiting told Cooper, and "if you hear of disaster it will occur in the manner I have stated, though, for that matter, without a supporting force, there are half a dozen other modes equally possible and against which I am equally powerless...There are too many vital points and it is too open. I think the circumstances warrant the utmost foresight and preparation. Look! The information I received from New York and forwarded, from New Berne and Beaufort to the same effect; preparation of small boats at the North, especially flat bottoms; movement of troops from Foster's command; the two expeditions of Cushing and his immediate departure for the North, especially the present movements of the fleet. If this was like some places still held by us, the taking of which would not materially influence the war, I would not say a word at this crisis. As its commanding officer I would trust to such poor resources as I might command, the people, chance, a storm, what not, and take the consequences; but this is different and every one knows it; still none by myself is aware of the extreme hazard which it now runs, and of which I think it my duty to warn you." [74]

As it so happened, there were discussions going on in Petersburg and Richmond at this same time that would add to Whiting's frustrations and difficulties, and offer further incentive to Union desires to capture Wilmington.

On July 4, the same day as Whiting's letter to Cooper, Commander John Taylor Wood, Confederate States Navy, received orders from Jefferson Davis to proceed from Petersburg, Virginia to Wilmington on a special assignment. Wood was a career naval officer, having served in the U.S. Navy from 1847 until April 1861, when he resigned his commission. His grandfather was the Mexican War hero and later President of the United States, Zachary Taylor, while one of his uncles-in-law was none other than the Confederate President himself. [75]

Though he had been born on the Minnesota frontier to a career army surgeon from Rhode Island and an ardent Unionist, Wood identified more closely with the Taylor side of his lineage. He considered Louisiana his home. When he espoused the Confederate Cause, his father could not abide his sentiments, and the two severed relations with each other. [76]

Wood's Confederate career had been more spectacular than that of his Yankee father. He was aboard the *C.S.S. Virginia* when she fought the battles in Hampton Roads, and he had "organized numerous boat expeditions against the enemy on the Chesapeake Bay and tributary waters." He was in command of "expeditions that captured the U.S. gunboats *Satellite* and *Reliance* in the Rappahannock River, and the *Underwriter* at Newberne, N.C." [77]

Now he planned to embark on the boldest of all his assignments so far. With consent of General Lee and the President, Wood intended to run the blockade of Wilmington with a warship loaded with Rebel soldiers, and land them at Point Lookout, Maryland, the Yankee prison pen that held about 20,000 Confederate prisoners of war at the mouth of the Potomac River. The intention was to hit the beach in an amphibious attack on July 12, "in cooperation with a simultaneous assault from the opposite direction by a detachment of Confederate cavalry under General Bradley T. Johnson." Wood's troops and warship would be carrying extra rifles to arm the prisoners, who, once freed, would join the forces under General Jubal Early in his attack on Washington, D.C.. [78]

Lee ordered Chase Whiting to give Wood two Parrott rifles from the Wilmington defenses to go aboard Wood's vessel, to assist in covering the landing at Point Lookout. With Whiting's assistance, Wood had mustered 800 soldiers and sailors to sail for Maryland by July 9 and telegraphed the President he was ready to go. The next day, however, Davis sent a telegram to Wood calling off the expedition, due to rumors floating around Richmond and the Army of Northern Virginia of the joint expedition to liberate Point Lookout. It was just as well, though, for Bradley Johnson had been recalled by Jubal Early to join him at Silver Spring outside Washington, and the Yankees had sent most of the Confederate prisoners to Elmira, New York before Wood was ready to sail. [79]

As consolation, Wood was given command of a sleek, new Rebel cruiser in Wilmington on July 23, one that was soon to be feared by Yankee ship masters in the North Atlantic, and that was to put Wilmington in focus as a haven for such cruisers. The *C.S.S. Tallahassee* was the former blockade-runner *Atlanta*, launched in March of 1864 on the Thames River near London. She carried three heavy naval guns, was 220 feet long, 24 feet beam, and had a draft of 9 feet. Weighing 700 tons and riding low in the water, she was powered by two propellers that could operate "separately or together," and "by reversing one screw, the ship could turn around on her center." Having a speed of 17 knots when engines were at maximum power, that plus her maneuverability made her far superior to anything the Federals had afloat. [80]

Late at night on Saturday, August 6, Wood steamed past Fort Caswell, seeing five Yankee blockaders and being fired on by two of them. On Thursday the 11th of August, the *Tallahassee* pulled up within 80 miles of Sandy Hook, New York. On that day, Wood burned or scuttled six Yankee merchantmen or pilot boats, while releasing another schooner on bond for $10,000.

Next day, still off the New York coast, Wood scuttled or burned five ships, and bonded another schooner. On this day, August 12, he captured the largest vessel of the cruise, the packet ship *Adriatic*. The New York owned ship of nearly 1,000 tons burden, sailed the London to New York route. There were 170 passengers on board, most of them German emigrants believed to be recruits for the Union Army. When informed the *Adriatic* was to be burned, the Germans were terrified with the belief that they were to be left on board when the ship was consigned to the flames. Some time elapsed before Wood was able to convince them that Southerners were not quite as inhumane as they thought, and the bonded bark *Suliote* took the Germans, as well as the passengers of the other vessels burned, to the nearest port. [81]

On the 13th, Wood "ran eastward, around Georges Banks, to the coast of Maine," where he cruised and captured schooners and fishing vessels for the next five days. Running low on coal, the *Tallahassee* was forced to run into Halifax, Nova Scotia to replenish her stock, arriving there on August 18. Wood

CSS Tallahassee

encountered some difficulty with the authorities there, even though the Canadians were required to observe British neutrality laws. [82]

The next night, Friday the 19th, Wood steamed out of Halifax and headed for Wilmington, being permitted to take out only enough coal as would allow him to return directly to his homeport. By the time the *Tallahassee* arrived off the Cape Fear on the night of August 25, Wood had burned and scuttled 26 vessels, bonded 5, and released 2, for a total of 33. [83]

A minor engagement with the fleet occurred as Wood ran along the breakers just off Fort Fisher. Acting Volunteer Lieutenant Sam Huse of the *U.S.S. Britannia*, reported that he chased and fired on the *Tallahassee* "until she was close under Fort Fisher, in white water, the breakers being between us and her. She fired one shrapnel at us, which burst close aboard, cutting our starboard paddle box a little. The Mound also fired at us, and the stranger being past Fort Fisher, we hauled off into 5 1/2 fathoms." [84]

Wood pulled the *Tallahassee* into New Inlet and anchored under the protection of William Lamb's guns. Early next morning, August 26, he raised the Second National Confederate flag on board, which was the large, white banner with the square battleflag in the top left corner, or canton. Lieutenant J.B. Breck of the *U.S.S. Niphon* saw *Tallahassee* resting at anchor near Fort fisher. He observed that the cruiser was "a large screw steamer, painted light lead color, and apparently carrying three guns – two abaft and one forward; two smokestacks near together, small foremast, and had a white rebel ensign flying at her flagstaff...At 6:30 Fort Fisher fired a salute, which was returned by the rebel steamer." Soon after, Wood steamed up the Cape Fear to Wilmington. [85]

Reaction to the *Tallahassee*'s raid varied. Even before the cruiser returned to Wilmington, U.S. Secretary of the Navy Gideon Welles had been well alerted as to the destruction of schooners and fishing vessels off the New York and New England coasts. On August 23, he was already advising Rear Admiral Lee in Beaufort to be on the lookout for the raider. He wrote that "the

Tallahassee, formerly *Atlanta*, is now at sea, and has inflicted serious injury on our commerce...Increased vigilance should be exercised and every precaution adopted." [86]

Some Southerners praised the raid as vindication for the loss of Mobile Bay and the sinking of the cruiser *Alabama* off the coast of France, both defeats having occurred this summer. Some were glad to see revenge exacted for the barbarities and cruelties inflicted on the Southern people by vandals in Union blue. [87]

Those charged with the defense of Wilmington, however, were not so pleased, for they knew it would only heighten the Union high command's interest in seeing Wilmington attacked. On August 31, Chase Whiting wrote to his superior and friend, General P.G.T. Beauregard, in Petersburg, warning him again, as he had done so many others so many times, of the impending fall of Wilmington if more troops were not sent there. He emphasized, too, "that a very material change has taken place as to the immunity of this port from attack. Since the fitting out of the *Tallahassee* and her expedition, extensive destruction of the enemy's commerce, and return to this port, their fleet has been much increased and many earnest appeals are made by the Northern press to shut up this port. If we continue to send out privateers certainly the only port of refuge for them now in the world ought to be made secure beyond peradventure." [88]

Robert E. Lee was convinced Whiting's concerns were merited. He wrote to James Seddon on September 22, that since the *Tallahassee* had returned to Wilmington from her cruise, "the enemy's fleet of blockaders off that coast has been very much increased, and the dangers of running the blockade rendered much greater. The question arises whether it is of more importance to us to obtain supplies through that port or to prey upon the enemy's commerce by privateers sent from thence." Lee suggested to the Secretary of War that Charleston be considered as an alternative base of operations for privateers, and that Wilmington be kept "open as long as possible as a port of entry" for blockade-runners. [89]

The Union Secretary of the Navy soon substantiated Confederate concerns. In little more than a week after the *Tallahassee* returned from her cruise, Welles had convinced the War Department it was time to attack. Pressured by New England shipping and fishing interests, Welles used the cruiser's raid to help him achieve the Union Navy's long hoped for operation – an attack on Fort Fisher and Wilmington by a joint operation of the army and navy.

On September 5, he wrote to Rear Admiral David Farragut, who had recently taken Mobile Bay, to offer him command of the navy's part in the operation. "Lieutenant General Grant," he said, "has recently given the subject his attention, and thinks an army force can be spared and ready to move by the

1st day of October." Farragut would decline for health reasons, but henceforth, the Union Navy's primary objective would be preparations for attacking and closing the Cape Fear River to Confederate commerce and warships. The *Tallahassee*'s cruise had given significant impetus to this forthcoming campaign. [90]

While planning for the expedition commenced in earnest, blockade running continued unabated, keeping frustration high for the line officers on duty. Captain O.S. Glisson, commander of the New Inlet Division, wrote to Rear

Sec. of the Navy Gideon Welles

Admiral Lee from the *U.S.S. Santiago de Cuba* on September 6, of "another side-wheel steamer, with two pipes and one mast," passing into New Inlet. He was convinced that nothing would stop blockade running except an attack. "The taking of Fort Fisher is perfectly feasible with 20,000 men, and the port of Wilmington is the only hope of rebeldom." He then predicted with remarkable prescience, that he was "convinced that if this port is taken the rebellion will not last three months." [91]

Until it was taken, Confederate and British cargo ships would keep running in on a regular basis, adding to Federal frustrations. One of those vessels, newly completed and ready to start her career as one of the finest of the blockade-runners, was named for the young commandant of Fort Fisher. The *Colonel Lamb*, launched from the shipyard of Jones, Quiggin & Company in Liverpool in late May 1864, was a "splendid paddle steam ship, constructed of steel," and was "the largest steel merchant ship" ever built for the trade. She was 281 feet long, 36 feet of beam, and between 15 and 17 feet depth of hold, drawing about 8 feet of water when loaded down with cargo. One of the very fastest ships afloat, she could steam at almost 17 knots, or 19 miles per hour. [92]

United States Consul Thomas Dudley, stationed in Liverpool, reported in September that the *Colonel Lamb* was "one of the largest and best built steamers that has been constructed in this country for running the blockade...I regard her as a very superior steamer." [93]

Superior she was in every way. The ship's First Officer, Charlestonian Joseph F. Torrent, who was thirty years old this fall, said that "there was no Yankee warship that could run her down." He wrote that Captain Thomas Lockwood, a North Carolinian, had a special tactic for bringing the *Colonel*

CSS Colonel Lamb

Lamb in on a run. Arriving off Charleston on her first voyage, "the Captain decided to give the blockading fleet a chase. So he ventured up close enough to let them get a good view of his craft. Finally some of the fleet started north and some south, as though they intended to cut him off from shore. Then he headed straight out for sea, but very slowly. Then almost the entire fleet started in hot pursuit. He led them a merry chase until dark, when he put out lights, made a big swing to the north, ran around them and sailed into Charleston." [94]

The *Colonel Lamb* stayed in Charleston for just a couple of days, long enough to discharge the inbound cargo, and to take on the outbound cargo headed for Nassau. Getting out of Charleston proved simple enough, but by the time the blockade-runner was about to clear the outer cordon of Yankee warships, some 30-40 miles off the coast, the *Colonel Lamb* was spotted. "Captain Lockwood was equal to the occasion," said Torrent, "for, as soon as he observed the fog rising, he put on all steam and proceeded out to sea, keeping the firing ships in as straight a line behind him as possible. Several of the fleet gave chase, but in less than an hour all they could see to shoot at was a streak of black smoke, which was out of reach of their guns." [95]

The *Colonel Lamb* made it safely to Nassau. Cargoes were exchanged with a British vessel, and ten days after departing Charleston, the blockade-runner was headed back to the Confederacy, bound for Wilmington this time. "Arriving off the bar there in daylight," Torrent reported, "we employed the same tactics as at Charleston, leading the blockading fleet off its base, then going around it and running into Wilmington at night." She had no trouble outrunning any vessel the Federals could bring against her. [96]

Another blockade-runner that normally had no trouble outrunning the Yankees, North Carolina's *Ad-Vance*, was finally caught as the Yankees began their preliminary discussions on the assault against Wilmington. Steaming out of the Cape Fear past Fort Fisher on Friday, September 9 with a cargo of 410 bales of cotton and some turpentine, the ship was compelled to burn North Carolina bituminous, black-smoking coal, having given up her superior English anthracite coal to supply the cruiser *Tallahassee*. It proved her undoing as a blockade-runner. [97]

The *Ad-Vance*'s Chief Engineer, James Maglenn, said she was sailing for Halifax, and that all the remaining good coal had been used up in dodging the Yankee blockaders off Fort Fisher. They had been successful at avoiding capture that night, but next morning, the 10th, the *U.S.S. Santiago de Cuba*, commanded by New Inlet Division commander Captain O.S. Glisson, spotted the telltale black smoke. "We were using Chatham, or Egypt coal," wrote Maglenn, "which was very inferior; in fact nothing but slate or the cropping of the mine. Our good coal at Wilmington was taken for the Confederate cruisers, which accounts for our capture." [98]

The *Santiago de Cuba* gave chase to the black smoke, and two hours later had gotten sufficiently close to realize a blockade-runner was the source. The Yankees continued the chase all afternoon, drawing every closer to the *Ad-Vance*, while the "steaming qualities of the coal were against" the Rebel runner. Maglenn said they hoped to be able to elude the Yankee warship when night set in, but "in our present condition, she was too fast for us and was able to throw some shot over us some time before sundown, which caused us to stop the ship and surrender." [99]

General Whiting, in a letter to Robert E. Lee on September 24, blamed the loss of the valuable runner entirely on John Taylor Wood's August raid off the Yankee coast. "The expedition of the *Tallahassee* has greatly increased the danger to this place. It has doubled the number of the enemy off this coast and the efficiency of the blockade; it has made your reception of supplies very precarious; it has attracted the attention of the enemy here, flushed with their success at Mobile; it has caused the loss of the fine steamer *Ad-Vance*, the fastest and best of the trade, in consequence of the latter being obliged to transfer all her fine English coal to the *Tallahassee*, and take North Carolina coal instead, and brought the whole pressure of the Northern press to bear upon the speedy capture of this place." [100]

As if to confirm Whiting's allegations of increased efficiency of the blockade, the next night the blockade-runner *Lynx* was destroyed off Fort Fisher as she tried to run out, not however, without the Yankees paying a price for her.

The *Lynx* was a side-wheel, double smoke-stacked runner, commanded by one of the best in the trade, Captain E.C. Reed, formerly commanding officer of the Confederate cruiser *Sumter*. The *Lynx* was headed for Nassau, and one of the passengers on board was the sister-in-law of Colonel William L. DeRosset of the Third North Carolina, Mrs. Louis H. DeRosset. Her husband, the Colonel's younger brother, served in the Confederate Ordnance and Quartermaster Departments, and was stationed in Nassau. This summer, while yellow fever stalked the Bahamas, Louis contracted it, and his young wife decided to go to him and nurse him through the illness. She also took along their infant daughter. [101]

Shortly after 7 p.m. on Sunday, September 25, Captain Reed steamed the *Lynx* out of New Inlet below Fort Fisher, racing to escape a cordon of Federal warships that quickly began to close on him. The *U.S.S. Niphon*, under Acting Master Edmund Kemble, saw the runner first. Kemble gave chase immediately, and opened with his port battery "several broadsides, nearly every shot taking effect in the sides of the steamer." The *Lynx*, however, despite the damage, ran past the *Niphon*, which "continued firing at her and throwing up rockets until she was sighted by the blockaders to the northward." [102]

Volunteer Lieutenant John MacDiarmid, in command of the *U.S.S. Governor Buckingham*, near the *Niphon*, saw the firing of the heavy guns and rockets thrown skyward, and took up the firing and chase of the *Lynx* as well. MacDiarmid said they got so close to the "long, side-wheel steamer," that at least two of his shells struck the *Lynx*, and "I fired all the charges from my revolver at the men on her bridge." [103]

Next to sight and severely damage the *Lynx* was the *U.S.S. Howquah*, commanded by Acting Volunteer Lieutenant J.W. Balch. Balch reported that he was able to steam up to within 100 yards of the blockade-runner, though she was outrunning the *Howquah*, opening up with "the starboard battery two percussion shells from the 30-pounder rifles, one of them striking the paddle box and the other forward of the paddle box. The explosion of the shells illuminated the ship so that we could plainly see the parts of the paddle box and ship flying in all directions." [104]

Destruction and near certain death reigned on the *Lynx*. Mrs. De Rosset wrote that "broadside upon broadside, volley upon volley, was poured upon us. The captain put me in the wheelhouse for safety. I had scarcely taken my seat when a ball passed three inches above my head, wounding the man at the wheel next to me; a large piece of the wheelhouse knocked me violently on the head. I flew to the cabin and took my baby in my arms, and immediately another ball passed through the cabin. We came so near one of the enemy's boats that they fired a round of musketry and demanded surrender." [105]

While this action was action was occurring about 1 1/2 miles northeast of Fort Fisher, Lamb's artillerists jerked on the lanyards of their heavy seacoast guns in support of the *Lynx*. Lieutenant Balch of the *Howquah* wrote that "shot and shell were fired at us from the shore batteries, and also a continued fire from our own vessels, coming from a southeast direction, shot and shell passing over and near us. At 7:20 p.m. one 30-pounder percussion shell struck the main rail on the starboard bow," the shell cutting into the carriage of a 30-pounder rifle of the ship's starboard battery, killing and wounding some of the gun crew. "This shell in its passage struck Patrick Bagley, ordinary seaman, taking off his right leg and killing him almost instantly; also slightly wounded Martin Glynn, landsman, Thomas Judge, landsman, William Roach, landsman, and George Stevens, coxswain." [106]

As the *Howquah* was about two miles northeast of Fort Fisher at the time she was hit, with the starboard side facing the *Buckingham*'s fire, it was almost certainly a Union shell that killed and wounded the sailors. Had one of Fort Fisher's shells hit the *Howquah*, it would have entered at the stern or port side of the ship, headed in a northeasterly direction. The shell that killed Seaman Bagley came from the southeast, where the *Buckingham* was located. [107]

By this time, the *Lynx* was mortally hurt and headed for the protection of the beach in a sinking condition. Mrs. DeRosset said she "stayed in the cabin until I could no longer keep the baby out of the water," and then she headed topside. The sea was extremely rough, and the breakers echoed deafening roars as the *Lynx* was driven aground, slamming all on board hard to the deck when the keel rammed into the sand. Lifeboats were lowered into the crashing breakers, "the sea dashing over the bulwarks and drenching the sailors to the point of strangulation." Mrs. DeRosset watched for the right moment to jump into the boat, all the while the boat tossing in the surf, and pounding into the side of the ship. She jumped into the boat, while "the baby, wrapped in a blanket, was tossed from the deck to her mother ten feet below, and then the fight for a landing began". [108]

Admiring the spunky young mother's actions, the crew forgot their own imminent danger, "and inspired with courage by the brave lady's example, joined in three hearty cheers as she disappeared in the darkness towards the shore." The *Lynx* was set afire, and the crew was able to make a safe landing. "Soaking wet, without food or drink, they remained on the beach until a message could reach Colonel Lamb at Fort Fisher, five miles distant, whence an ambulance was sent to carry the passengers twenty miles up to Wilmington." [109]

Shot through with holes and moribund on the beach just east of Battery Gatlin, the *Lynx* burned to her destruction off Myrtle Grove Sound during the night, testimonial to the increasing tightness of the blockade. [110]

Tom Taylor, William Lamb's good friend, knew only too well how stringent the blockade was becoming, with the additional Yankee gunboats concentrated there. Four nights after Mrs. DeRosset's harrowing experience aboard the *Lynx*, Taylor almost lost his life in the closest call he was to experience as a blockade-runner.

Steaming out of Hamilton, Bermuda on Tuesday, September 27, the young Englishman was in charge of a cargo of supplies aboard the newest ship in his company's fleet, the *Night Hawk*. She was a first-rate blockade-runner, Taylor wrote, being a "new side-wheel steamer of some 600 tons gross, rigged as a fore and aft schooner, with two funnels, 220 feet long, 21 1/2 feet beam, and 11 feet in depth; a capital boat for the work, fast, strong, of light draught, and a splendid sea-boat – a great merit in a blockade-runner that sometimes has to be forced in all weathers." Taylor said she "passed an unusually lively night off Fort Fisher on her first attempt." [111]

Taylor's pilot knew little about the Old Inlet entrance, so Taylor decided they would go in by New Inlet, which he himself knew exceedingly well, and "where at all events, we should have the advantage of our good friend Lamb to protect us". [112]

About 11:15 p.m. on the 29th of September, the *Night Hawk* was in the midst of the blockading fleet and driving for New Inlet, when she was spotted by several Yankee vessels that fired on her. The pilot veered from the course Taylor gave him to follow, and grounded the ship on the bar just east of Fort Fisher. The *U.S.S. Niphon*, under command of Acting Master Edmund Kemble, spotted the *Night Hawk*, and after firing on her, sent a cutter with armed crew to board and secure her as a prize. Acting Ensign E.N. Semon left the gunboat with some sailors, and while rowing over to board the blockade-runner, they fired several volleys of musketry at the *Night Hawk*'s crew, some of who were fleeing in the ship's dinghy. One of the bullets wounded Tom Taylor in the thigh, and two others of the runner's crew, all three of whom were still on board. [113]

Though no one on the *Night Hawk* resisted the Union sailors as they clambered aboard, Ensign Semon and his men "acted more like maniacs than sane men," Taylor later recalled. He said they continued firing revolvers and swinging cutlasses at the *Night Hawk*'s men. Taylor said he "stood in front of the men on the poop and said that we surrendered, but all the reply I received from the lieutenant commanding was, 'Oh, you surrender, do you?'... accompanied by a string of the choicest Yankee oaths and sundry reflections upon my parentage; whereupon he fired his revolver twice point blank at me not two yards distant; it was a miracle he did not kill me, as I heard the bullets whiz past my head." [114]

Taylor was outraged at this violation of civilized warfare, and he remonstrated vigorously with Semon for firing upon unarmed and unresisting men. The Yankee cooled off somewhat, and desisted from his unnecessary violence. The Federals then began loading the *Night Hawk*'s crew into their cutter to take back to the *Niphon*, and finding they could not get the ship off the bar, set the blockade-runner on fire to destroy her. As the fire began to blaze "merrily," a sly Irishman, one of Taylor's firemen, lied and sang out loud for the Yankees to hear, "Begorra, we shall all be in the air in a minute, the ship is full of gunpowder!" The Yankee sailors immediately high-tailed it for their boats, Taylor said, "threatening to leave their officers behind if they did not come along." Taylor and 18 others were left behind, some of who had already escaped from the *Night Hawk*. [115]

Willliam Lamb also helped to motivate the Yankees to leave. His sentinels, having heard the musketry offshore, surmised the runner had gone aground and was being attacked. They alerted Lamb, and he "immediately lighted her up by means of rockets and shelled right and left of her. At the first rocket," the *Daily Journal* reported, "the enemy took fright and skedaddled, leaving more than half the officers and crew to take care of themselves." [116]

Taylor and the few men left on deck were unable to contain the fire, so they abandoned the *Night Hawk* and headed for shore. The Union gunboats had opened fire on the blockade-runner when they saw their own men depart. Taylor recalled that "Lamb's great shells hurtling over our heads, and those from the blockading fleet bursting all around us, formed a weird picture. In spite of the hail of shot and shell and the dangers of the boiling surf, we reached the shore in safety, wet through, and glad I was in my state of exhaustion from loss of blood and fatigue to be welcomed by Lamb's orderly officer." [117]

Taylor was sure the *Night Hawk* was done for, but Fort Fisher's commandant called on his men to put out the fire on board, and quickly got several boatloads from the garrison. The *Daily Journal* reported that "the gallant soldiers boarded the steamer admidships, and with all the available buckets, commenced to fight the flames. It was not very long before the fire was got under". By the time Taylor had gotten his thigh wound dressed at the fort's hospital, rested a short spell, and gone back down to the beach, the fire was under control. Before noon of the next day, it was completely out. [118]

Taylor telegraphed from Fort Fisher to the resident agent of the Confederate Trading Company in Wilmington, his employer, to send down some help. The agent sent "down about 300 negroes to assist in bailing and pumping," and he "set them to work at once." The next night, his company's *Banshee No. 2* ran through the blockade, and he put the 53 men and engineers to work to get the *Night Hawk* off the sand bar and into the Cape Fear River. [119]

They were assisted in their efforts by the grounding of another blockade-runner just one hundred yards away, the steamer *Condor*. Using the wreck of the *Condor* to secure cables with which to haul the *Night Hawk* off the bar, Taylor said they were able, after several days of tedious winching and pulling, to get the steamer "afloat in a gut between the bank and the shore." When high tide came in, Taylor said, "we steamed under our own steam gaily up the river to Wilmington." [120]

While the wreck of the *Condor* meant renewed life for Taylor's *Night Hawk*, it also represented death for one of the Confederacy's most colorful women. The *Condor* had been chased aground by the *Niphon* just before dawn on Saturday, October 1, and aboard her was Mrs. Rose O'Neal Greenhow, former Washington resident and Confederate spy who had supplied valuable information of Union troops movements to General Beauregard before First Manassas. She was arrested a month after the battle, detained by Federal authorities in her Washington home, and later Old Capitol Prison. In June 1862, she was released with the understanding that she would not venture north of the Potomac for the duration of the war. [121]

Arriving in Richmond soon after her release, she was given a $2500 check by Judah P. Benjamin, Secretary of State, as a reward for her service to the

Confederacy. In August of 1863, "Rebel Rose" made the acquaintance of General Whiting when she shipped out on the blockade-runner *Phantom* past Fort Fisher. She wound up in London, where she secured a publisher for her book titled *My Imprisonment and the First Year of Abolition Rule at Washington*, which was published in November 1863. Rose traveled for months between England and France, trying to win support and recognition for the Confederacy. By early fall of 1864, she was returning to the South aboard the *Condor*. [122]

At 4 a.m. on October 1, Acting Master Edmund Kemble of the *U.S.S.*

Niphon, the same ship that nearly destroyed Tom Taylor's steamer the night before, spotted the *Condor* running into New Inlet, "when said steamer ran on Federal Shoals near the wreck of the *Night Hawk*." Kemble moved in close to shell the blockade-runner, but Fort Fisher's "batteries opened fire upon me with shot and shell, falling in close proximity to us," he reported, "and daylight coming on rapidly, I deemed it prudent to stand offshore. I much regret not being able to destroy the steamer, but the safety of this vessel demanded that I should forego the pleasure of doing so until the coming night." [123]

Tragically, Rose Greenhow did not know the Yankees would be driven off, and the *Condor* spared from Federal guns and capture of passengers or crew. She was terrified of being captured and imprisoned again, and insisted that

Rebel spy Rose O'Neal Greenhow and her daughter

Captain Hewett, commanding the *Condor*, dispatch a lifeboat to take her to shore. Hewett relented, had a boat manned to take her in, but the boat capsized in the heavy breakers, and she drowned. Daisy Lamb and some of Fort Fisher's garrison helped pull the two sailors from the surf who had been manning the lifeboat, and they related the sad story of Rose's death. [124]

At the first light of dawn, Colonel Lamb had some of his men search the beach for Mrs. Greenhow's body, but it was Tom Taylor who found it. "A remarkably handsome woman, she was, with features which showed much character. Although one cannot altogether admire the profession of a spy, still there was no doubt that she imagined herself in following such a profession to be serving her country in the only way open to her." [125]

Colonel Lamb gave his wife custody of the body, to clean and care for it, and examine "the fatally heavy tangle of the black dress and petticoats. Dispatches were sewn in one of the petticoats, and in the hem of another, a bag that contained more than two thousand dollars in gold sovereigns." [126]

Lamb sent a detail of soldiers to accompany Mrs. Greenhow's remains to Wilmington, and they did so in company with Thomas Taylor, who took charge of getting the dead heroine's body upriver aboard a steamer. [127]

When the vessel docked in Wilmington, hundreds of ladies of the town lined the wharf in admiration. The Soldiers' Aid Society took charge of Mrs. Greenhow's funeral and initially had her remains lie in state in the chapel of government Hospital #4, also known as the Seaman's Bethel. One who saw her there said that the scene was "solemn and imposing."

There were wax lights and flowers around the casket, "in crosses, garlands, and bouquets, scattered over it." Many visitors, women, children and soldiers, came to pay their "last tribute of respect to the departed heroine. On the bier, draped with a magnificent Confederate flag, lay the body, so unchanged as to look like a calm sleeper, while above all rose the tall ebony crucifix – emblem of the faith she embraced in happier hours". [128]

At 2 p.m. the following day, Sunday, October 2, the casket was taken to St. Thomas Catholic Church for the

Mrs. Greenhow's tombstone in Oakdale Cemetery.

funeral, where Father Corcoran delivered a "touching tribute to the heroism and patriotic devotion of the deceased." The Confederate flag-draped casket was then borne to Oakdale Cemetery, followed by a large crowd of people.

"A beautiful spot on a grassy slope...was chosen for her resting place," a correspondent for the *Daily Journal* reported in the October 17 edition of the paper. He said that torrential rain had fallen much of the day, "but as the coffin was being lowered into the grave, the sun burst forth in the brightest majesty, and a rainbow of the most vivid color spanned the horizon. Let us accept the omen, not only for her, the quiet sleeper, who after many storms and a tumultuous and checkered life, came to peace and rest at last, but also for our beloved country, over which we trust the rainbow of hope will ere long shine with brightest dyes." [129]

There was to be no rainbow of hope for the future, however, for Wilmington or the Confederate States. The skies were darkening, and heavy thunderclouds were looming on the horizon. On October 22, five days after Rose Greenhow's funeral was reported, the *Daily Journal* editorialized that the "Hour of Trial" had arrived. "What has been so long threatened and so much talked about seems to have come at last. The long deferred attack on Wilmington would appear to be at hand. We have good reason to believe, from information received, that an attack is imminent – may be looked for any day. The fleet is assembling both at Fortress Monroe and Beaufort harbor, N.C...It is expected that all the men who remain will bear their full part in defending their homes, and in repelling the invaders of our soil." [130]

Endnotes to Chapter 7

1. Daily Journal, March 11, 1864; Warships & Naval Battles, p.154; ORN, Volume 9, p.498
2. Daily Journal, March 17, 1864; ORN, Volume 9, p.535; N.C. Troops, Volume I, p.347, p.374, p.479
3. Ibid, March 11, 1864
4. "History & War Record of Elisha Griggs, 40th N.C. Troops", unpublished manuscript in author's collection; Clark, Volume II, p.755; N.C. Troops, Volume I, p.456-457
5. Daily Journal, March 17,1864
6. ORN, Volume 9, p.535-536
7. "Lower Cape Fear Historical Society Bulletin, February 1992, p.1-2, Wilmington, N.C., hereinafter Cape Fear Bulletin; O.R., Volume XXXIII, p.1223
8. Cape Fear Bulletin, February 1992, p.3
9. Ibid, February 1992, p.3; O.R., Volume XXXIII, p.1219
10. O.R., Volume XXXIII, p.1220
11. Ibid, p.1220
12. Ibid, p.1224
13. Ibid, p.1221; Cape Fear Bulletin, February 1992, p.4; Donnelly, Ralph W., *The Confederate States Marine Corps: The Rebel Leathernecks*, p.106, White Mane Publishing Company, Shippensburg, Pennsylvania, 1989, hereinafter Rebel Leathernecks
14. O.R., Volume XXXIII, p.1221-1222, p.1228
15. Cape Fear Bulletin, February 1992, p.4; Chronicles, p.487
16. Daily Journal, March 22, 1864; ORN, Volume 9, p.551-552
17. Daily Journal, March 22, 1864
18. Ibid, March 22, 1864; ORN, Volume 9, p.551

19. Ibid, March 22, 1864
20. ORN, Volume 9, p.675-677; Williams, Isabel M. & McEachern, Leora H., *Salt, That Necessaray Article*, p.p.37-42, Louis T. Moore Memorial Fund, Wilmington, N.C. 1973; William Lamb Day booklet, covermap; Russell, Ann, *Wilmington - A Pictorial History*, p.40, Donning Company Publishers, Norfolk, Virginia, 1981, hereinafter Wilmington Pictorial History
21. ORN, Volume 9, p.675-676
22. O.R., Volume XXXIII, p.1304
23. Ibid, Volume XXXIII, p.1304
24. Ibid, Volume XXXIII, p.1303-1304
25. ORN, Volume 9, p.674
26. Ibid, Volume 9, p.677-678; O.R., Volume XXXIII, p.1292, p.1300
27. Daily Journal, May 5, 1864; Ashe, Samuel A., *History of North Carolina in Two Volumes, Volume II, from 1783 to 1925*, p.841-844, p.878-881, Edwards & Broughton Printing Company, Raleigh, N.C., 1925, hereinafter Ashe
28. ORN, Volume 10, p.24; Warships & Naval Battles, p.45, p.54-55; Chronicles, p.480-481; Daily Journal, May 25, 1864
29. Chronicles, p.480-481; Signal note from Flag Officer Lynch to Colonel William Lamb, May 6, 1864, papers of William Lamb, author's collection; "Captain John Pembroke Jones," Confederate Veteran, Volume XVIII, (1910), p.341
30. Chronicles, p.397-398, p.400-401, p.481; ORN, Volume 10, p.21, p.24
31. ORN, Volume 10, p.21-22
32. Ibid, Volume 10, p.22-23
33. Rebel Leathernecks, p.105-107
34. Daily Journal, May 25, 1864; ORN, Volume 10, p.20
35. Daily Journal, May 25, 1864; ORN, Volume 10, p.21
36. ORN, Volume 10, p.20-21, p.18
37. Ibid, Volume 10, p.21; Chronicles, p.481, p.483
38. Chronicles, p.412, p.481-482
39. Rebel Leathernecks, p.107
40. "Lower Cape Fear Historical Society Bulletin", May 1978, p.1-3
41. ORN, Volume 10, p.24-25
42. Ibid, Volume 10, p.39-40
43. Ibid, Volume 10, p.57
44. Ibid, Volume 10, p.93-94
45. Ibid, Volume 9, p.678; Bradley, Stephen E., editor, *North Carolina Confederate Militia Officers Roster, As Contained in the Adjutant-General's Officers Roster,* p.57, Broadfoot Publishing, Wilmington, N.C., 1992, hereinafter Confederate Militia Roster
46. ORN, Volume 10, p.93

47. Ibid, Volume 10, p.93; Daily Journal, May 10, 1864; N.C. Troops, Volume I, p.236-237
48. Ibid, Volume 10, p.93-94; O.R., Volume XXXIII, p.1304; O.R., Volume XL, Part II, p.715
49. Ibid, Volume 10, p.93-94
50. Ibid, Volume 10, p.203; O.R., Volume XXXVI, Part III, p.374-375, p.425, p.597-598; Warner, Ezra, *Generals in Blue*, p.357-358, Louisiana State University Press, Baton Rouge, 1964
51. Schiller, Herbert M., M.D., *The Bermuda Hundred Campaign*, p.164-165, Morningside House Inc., Dayton, Ohio, 1988; O.R., Volume XXXVI, Part II, p.256-259
52. ORN, Volume 10, p.126; Honeycutt, Ava L., "Fort Fisher, Malakoff of the South", p.124, unpublished Master's thesis, Duke University, Durham, N.C., 1963
53. ORN, Volume 10, p.126
54. O.R., Volume XL, Part II, p.85
55. ORN, Volume 10, p.202
56. Ibid, Volume 10, p.202
57. Ibid
58. Ibid
59. Ibid; Chronicles, p.412 map
60. Ibid; Chronicles, p.412 map
61. Ibid, Volume 10, p.202-205; Chronicles p.412 map
62. Ibid, Volume 10, p.203
63. Ibid
64. Ibid
65. Ibid
66. Ibid, Volume 10, p.203-204
67. Ibid, Volume 10, p.204
68. Ibid
69. O.R., Volume XL, Part II, p.695
70. O.R., Volume XL, Part II, p.700
71. Ibid, Volume XL, Part II, p.700
72. Ibid, Part II, p.700-701
73. Ibid, Part II, p.715
74. Ibid, Part II, p.716
75. Shingleton, Royce G., *John Taylor Wood, Sea Ghost of the Confederacy*, p.2-4, p.16, p.116-117, University of Georgia Press, Athens, Ga. 1979, hereinafter John Taylor Wood; Strode, Hudson, *Jefferson Davis, Tragic Hero, The Last Twenty-Five Years, 1864-1889*, p.185, Harcourt, Brace & World Inc., New York, 1964
76. John Taylor Wood, p.4, p.17-19

77. Scharf, History of the Confederate Navy, p.806
78. John Taylor Wood, p.116-117
79. John Taylor Wood, p.117-118
80. Ibid, p.119-120
81. Ibid, p.124-125, p.130; ORN, Volume 3, p.701-703
82. ORN, Volume 3, p.702-704
83. ORN, Volume 3, p.702-704
84. ORN, Volume 3, p.173
85. Ibid, Volume 3, p.174; John Taylor Wood, p.141
86. ORN, Volume 10, p.386
87. John Taylor Wood, p.141-142
88. O.R., Volume XLII, Part II, p.1212
89. O.R., Volume LI, Part II, p.1040-1041
90. ORN, Volume 10, p.430; Reed, Rowena, *Combined Operations in the Civil War*, p.331, Naval Institute Press, Annapolis, Maryland, 1978, hereinafter Combined Operations; Barrett, Civil War in North Carolina, p.262
91. ORN, Volume 10, p.433
92. Daily Journal, July 6, 1864; Chronicles, p.452
93. ORN, Volume 10, p.439
94. Torrent, Captain Joseph F., "With the Blockade Runners," Confederate Veteran, Volume XXXIII, June 1925, p.209
95. Ibid, Volume XXXIII, June 1925, p.209
96. Ibid, Volume XXXIII, June 1925, p.209
97. ORN, Volume 10, p.453; Clark, Volume V, p.337
98. ORN, Volume 10, p.453; Clark, Volume V, p.337-338
99. ORN, Volume 10, p.453, Clark, Volume V, p.338
100. O.R., Volume XLII, Part II, p.1281
101. Chronicles, p.294, p.398, p.450; ORN, Volume 10, p.479; Stories Old and New of the Cape Fear, p.164
102. ORN, Volume 10, p.481; Chronicles, p.450
103. ORN, Volume 10, p.480-481
104. Ibid, Volume 10, p.479
105. Chronicles, p.450
106. ORN, Volume 10, p.479
107. ORN, Volume 10, p.479-481
108. Chronicles, p.451
109. Chronicles, p.451
110. ORN, Volume 10, p.481
111. Running the Blockade, p.116-118; ORN, Volume 10, p.498
112. Running the Blockade, p.118
113. Running the Blockade, p.118-119; ORN, Volume 10, p.493, p.498

114. Running the Blockade, p.120-121
115. Running the Blockade, p.121-122; ORN, Volume 10, p.493
116. Daily Journal, October 12, 1864
117. Running the Blockade, p.122-123
118. Ibid, p.123-124; Daily Journal, October 12, 1864
119. Ibid, p.124-125
120. Ibid, p.125
121. Ross, Ishbel, *Rebel Rose, Life of Rose O'Neal Greenhow, Confederate Spy*, p.113-116, p.135, p.180-182, p.195, p.233, Harper & Brothers Publishers, New York, 1954, hereinafter Rebel Rose; ORN, Volume 10, p.531
122. Rebel Rose, p.237, p.248, p.255, p.266-268; Blockade, The Civil War at Sea, p.156, p.159
123. ORN, Volume 10, p.532, p.552
124. Chronicles, p.489; Blockade, The Civil War at Sea, p.160
125. Running the Blockade, p.128-129
126. Blockade, The Civil War at Sea, p.160; Chronicles, p.490
127. Blockade, The Civil War at Sea, p.161; Running the Blockade, p.129; Daily Journal, October 17, 1864
128. Daily Journal, October 17, 1864; Chronicles, p.490
129. Daily Journal, October 17, 1864, Daily Journal, October 22, 1864

The exterior of Fort Fisher's land face after the second battle in January 1865. The line at Sugar Loaf was supposed to secure the fort's northern, or land, flank. Note the huge unexploded cannonball in the middle foreground.

Chapter 8

"Bragg is going to Wilmington. Good-bye Wilmington!"

Your letter in relation to the defense of Wilmington has been received," Zebulon Vance wrote to Robert E. Lee on September 5, 1864, a month before Rose Greenhow's funeral. General Lee had written to him at the end of August, that "our chief reliance for the protection of Wilmington must be placed upon the reserves and local troops of the State." The Governor advised General Lee that he would do all in his power to aid the militia, but that there were only two full regiments, the Thirty-Sixth and the Fortieth North Carolina, and Young's Battalion, totaling about 2,600 effective troops, with which to defend the entrance to the Cape Fear. He advised replacing them with veteran troops who had experienced severe combat, even though Chase Whiting's men were "well-drilled and disciplined." The experiences "at Mobile and elsewhere have demonstrated their inefficiency to hold their own under the fierce cannonade of the enemy's fleet."

Additionally, Vance preferred that P.G.T. Beauregard be given overall command at Wilmington, partly because of his solid defense of Charleston, and also because General Whiting had experienced some command problems during the Bermuda Hundred Campaign in Virginia the preceding May. Lee forwarded Vance's letter to Jefferson Davis, with his endorsement that Beauregard be placed in "command of Wilmington or Charleston, whichever may be attacked." [1]

Criticism of Whiting's performance at the Battle of Drewry's Bluff, halfway between Richmond and Petersburg, fought May 16 along the Richmond and Petersburg Railroad, concerned his failure to attack the rear of Ben Butler's Army of the James, while Beauregard attacked in front. Having taken position at Port Walthall Junction the morning of May 16, in accordance with Beauregard's orders to advance in the "direction of heaviest firing," Whiting waited to hear the firing that Beauregard would commence, but it never came.

Despite the fact that a severe battle was being fought between Beauregard's troops and Butler's men just seven miles north of Whiting's position,

an "acoustic window" kept the battle from being heard, and kept Whiting's troops out of action. This natural phenomenon, caused by variances in terrain, temperature and humidity, prevented the crashing sounds of battle from being heard at relatively close distances, and had taken place at the battles of Perryville, Kentucky, Iuka, Mississippi, and even at Chancellorsville, to name a few. [2]

One officer serving under Whiting alleged his use of alcohol as the reason for his inaction at Drewry's Bluff, while still another said his problem had been in honoring a pledge to General Beauregard not to drink anything during the campaign. Whiting had also been ill when ordered to Virginia from Wilmington, and went several days without sleep after arriving in Petersburg, which severely drained his physical and mental capacities. The primary reason, however, for his failure to act in concert with Beauregard's attack on May 16, was likely as he stated,

Gen. P.G.T. Beauregard, C.S.A.

because he did not hear the battle going on to the north, and was to advance only when he did hear such action. [3]

Whatever the cause of his inaction on the Drewry's Bluff battlefield, a cloud of doubt hung over him for the remainder of the war. This was the reason both Vance and Lee wanted someone else commanding at Wilmington when the expected Union attack was finally launched.

In recommending Beauregard to supersede Whiting, General Lee unwittingly helped bring about the appointment of the Confederacy's most solid failure as a general officer, Braxton Bragg, to command of the

Wilmington defenses. His appointment would ultimately prove fatal to Whiting, Fort Fisher, and Wilmington itself. Jefferson Davis was not about to appoint Beauregard as commander of the Cape Fear District. Since the close of the campaign of First Manassas, Davis had exhibited personal hostility to Beauregard and to his sometimes grandiose plans of operations. The attempted intervention of Beauregard's political friends to intercede on his behalf with the President only seemed to exacerbate Davis's animosity toward the Creole general. [4]

Bypassing Lee's suggestion of Beauregard, the President wrote to Braxton Bragg, his military adviser and counsel, on Saturday, October 15. Davis told Bragg the "condition and threatening aspect of affairs in the District of the Cape Fear River renders it, in my judgment, desirable that you should exercise immediate command over the troops and defenses of Wilmington and its approaches. For this purpose you will temporarily leave your office here in charge of one or more of the members of your staff and proceed to Wilmington to assume for the time being the command above indicated." [5]

In giving Bragg this position, he was obviously counting on his performance on the Cape Fear being an improvement over his performance with the Army of Tennessee. It was a significant gamble to take with the most important port left in the South. In the fall of 1864, no general officer in the Confederate States was as vilified by public, press, or soldiers for his past performances as Braxton Bragg.

At the Battle of Shiloh, on April 6, 1862, he had squandered the lives of Southern troops in repeated ineffective assaults against the Yankee

Gen. Braxton Bragg, C.S.A.

strongpoint known as the "Hornets' Nest," when that position could have been, and later was, flanked and turned. In the Kentucky campaign in 1862, Bragg failed to bring all his available troops together to drive the Federals out of that state and advance into Ohio. Had this been properly done, instead of having 16,000 men to face the Yankees at Perryville, Bragg would have had about 50,000. And since the 16,000 he had on the field actually defeated the 20,000 Union troops they engaged, there is little doubt the outcome of the campaign could have been something other than Confederate retreat from Kentucky. [6]

Several months later, in the great Battle of Murfreesboro of December 31, 1862 – January 2, 1863, Bragg botched an initially successful attack and sacrificed his men in a suicidal charge on the last day of battle. Plagued with self-doubt and vacillation, he retreated to Tullahoma, Tennessee, partly as a result of high command wrangling among his subordinates and in spite of his soldiers' belief that they had won the battle. [7]

Allowing himself to be maneuvered out of Middle Tennessee and then Chattanooga in the summer of 1863, Bragg struck back at his antagonist William Rosecrans and his Army of the Cumberland in September at a sluggish stream in North Georgia called Chickamauga. With the help of James Longstreet and part of his corps from the Army of Northern Virginia, the soldiers of the Army of Tennessee achieved a smashing victory in the second bloodiest battle of the war, on September 19 and 20, driving the Yankees back into their base of Chattanooga. The Confederate troops were victorious despite the incompetence of their commander. Bragg seemed not to realize they had won one of the South's greatest victories, which very well might have secured Confederate independence, had the battle been properly followed up. The results, however, were not consummated. Bragg decided to besiege the Union army in Chattanooga instead of crushing it when he had the opportunity, and time and reinforcements were on their side, not his. Chickamauga became a barren and bloody Pyrrhic victory. [8]

The barren results of Chickamauga and Bragg's incompetence were driven home two months later, in November 1863. In the Battle of Missionary Ridge, just east of Chattanooga, the improperly placed infantry and artillery of the Army of Tennessee were outmaneuvered and outfought by George Thomas' Army of the Cumberland, and the Confederates were driven from a seemingly impregnable position, underscoring Bragg's inability to command an army in the field. He submitted his resignation as commander of the Army of Tennessee, and President Davis accepted it, later bringing him to Richmond as military adviser to himself. [9]

For all these failures and missed opportunities, Bragg was rightly criticized by virtually everyone, except Jeff Davis. Davis never forgot a friend, and many years before, Bragg had sided with General Zachary Taylor in some dispute he had with General Winfield Scott. As Taylor was Davis' father-in-law, Davis was eternally grateful to Bragg, despite the fact he and Bragg had had serious disagreement in the 1850's, when Davis was Secretary of War under Franklin Pierce. As one staff officer under General Whiting wrote, "he seemed determined to sustain Bragg at all events, though the feeling throughout the whole army, and, in fact, the South, was against that general." [10]

Apparently hearing of Davis' order to Bragg, the Charlottesville, Virginia *Chronicle* sarcastically reported in its paper toward the end of October, "We suspect that General Bragg is going to Wilmington. Good bye, Wilmington." A few days later, on the 26th, the *Richmond Enquirer* repeated the biting comment, and the editor of the *Daily Journal* in Wilmington was outraged. "While legitimate criticism of the conduct of public men is the right, and often the duty, of the press," the *Journal* stated, "it by no means follows that there can be either justification or excuse for making that the cover of vulgar malice or unreasonable prejudice. The flippant style, 'Good bye, Wilmington,' of the writer, shows him not only deficient in the cultivated form of expression, but also unappreciative of the peril of a town in a sister State, if he really believed what he wrote."

Trying to encourage confidence in its readers as to Bragg's abilities, and negate the criticism in the Virginia papers for the man who would now be chief architect of military defense for Wilmington, the *Daily Journal* counseled "General Bragg is in his native State, and we believe justly enjoys the confidence of her people. They know him to be well qualified for his place, and unselfishly devoted to the cause, and they are willing to trust their safety in his hands, with a confident feeling that Wilmington will not be lost by any deficiency on his part." [11]

In the months to come, the optimism of the *Daily Journal* would prove to be a hollow prediction. In fact, on October 25, six days before the paper's editorial defense of Bragg, the dour-looking general with the depressive disposition, heavy eyebrows, salt and pepper beard and frowning stare, reported to Jefferson Davis and Robert E. Lee that he had already conducted "a hasty inspection of all the defensive works for the protection of this harbor." Although he confirmed that the forts and works were "now prepared to oppose a powerful resistance to any naval attack, and will hold any considerable land force in check for a considerable time, if the garrisons will do their duty," Bragg also implicitly revealed what would be his course of action three months later, that would eventuate in the loss of Fort Fisher and Wilmington.

Should the Yankees "make a descent with a land force on the peninsula," Confederate Point that is, "above Fort Fisher, intrench across it, and thus control the river...the harbor is lost." The position could "only be recovered by means much greater than would suffice to hold it." Confirming his ignorance of the significance of Wilmington to the Confederacy, Bragg left it to Lee's discretion whether "the importance of the harbor is such as to justify the withdrawal of means from other points, also endangered." Bragg agreed with Whiting, whose appearance, he said, "does not indicate recent dissipation," referring to rumors of his drinking, that "a movable force of good troops will be necessary" to prevent the Federals from securing a solid position north of Fort Fisher. It was clear from the tone of his communication to Davis and Lee, that if the Yankees were successful in their efforts to intrench on Confederate Point, he did not think the harbor could be held, the implication being that it would eventually be abandoned. [12]

That the test was soon to come was quickly becoming evident. The day before Bragg's letter to Lee and Davis, William Lamb noted in his diary on October 24, that information had been "received which leads to the belief that Wilmington is to be attacked by the enemy. Commodore Porter to command the fleet which is said to include the armored ships, *Ironsides* & *Dictator*. Genl. Braxton Bragg has assumed command of the defences of Wilmington & its approaches. Maj. Genl. Whiting will be second in command. Only five blockaders off here during today." The same day as Bragg's communique, October 25, Secretary of War James Seddon telegraphed Bragg that reliable information had been received from scouts that 25 large war vessels, "including several monitors, to have been a day or two since at Fortress Monroe, declared in conversation of officers to be intended for attack on Wilmington, and expected to sail to-day." [13]

Headquarters in Wilmington also advised Colonel Lamb of an anonymous letter stating that his men were expected to spike their guns, "cut telegraph wires and pilot the enemy to the city. This was conveyed to me confidentially, but I repudiated it so far as my garrison was concerned, having implicit faith in their loyalty". [14]

Fort Fisher's 32lb seacoast guns packed a big punch.

Lamb was bitterly disappointed by the assignment of Bragg to supersede Whiting, whom he greatly admired, though Whiting was still retained as second in command. He and his men "felt that no one was so capable of defending the Cape Fear as the brilliant officer who had given so much of his time and ability for its defence. When a few days after, a Virginia paper announced, 'Braxton Bragg has been ordered to Wilmington, good-bye Wilmington,' to many, it seemed as prophetic as the wizard's warning to Lochiel on the eve of the battle of Culloden." [15]

Confederate Engineer and Second Lieutenant C.B. Denson echoed Lamb's emotions, stating, "the troops were thunderstruck at the news that Gen. Braxton Bragg had assumed command at Wilmington." Denson "found the feeling of melancholy foreboding at this change to be universal." [16]

Lamb would not, however, be downcast at the change of command, and he and his men, at the direction and encouragement of Chase Whiting, went to work with a will preparing for the expected Union attack. On Wednesday, October 26, his men began installing, about fifty feet out from the base of Fort Fisher's landface works, a "heavy palisade of sharpened logs nine feet high, pierced for musketry, and laid out as to have an enfilading fire on the center, where there was a redoubt guarding a sally port, from which two Napoleons were run out as occasion required."

The next day, Thursday the 27th, his soldiers mounted two additional heavy guns on the seaface of the fort. One was a 32-pounder, and the other was an 8-inch Columbiad. In his diary for Thursday, he also noted that the new heavy battery his men had constructed at the Rip, just inside New Inlet and at the tip end of Confederate Point, "is to be commanded by a Navy officer with a naval garrison and is to be called Battery Buchanan." [17]

Buchanan was nearly complete, and on November 6 General Whiting wrote to Flag Officer Robert F. Pinckney, commanding naval forces in North Carolina, that "the time has come for your naval force to occupy, in part at least, the battery commanding the Eastern Rip, which I propose to turn over to you. I beg that until it is completed entirely you will give instructions to your officers and men not to interfere in any way with the working parties engaged in finishing the defenses or with their officers." [18]

At the present time, there were three 10-pounder Columbiads mounted, and Whiting suggested that the naval detachment assigned to the fort, named for the "gallant hero of Mobile," Admiral Franklin Buchanan, accustom themselves with their quarters and position, and practice with their artillery. Whiting apologized to Pinckney for the battery and quarters not yet being completed, but told him that "with the great pressure upon me now for labor at so many important points I am compelled to place first the new battery in condition to be fought with effect and to wait awhile before putting up all the conveniences which you will require."

Whiting emphasized to Pinckney that Buchanan occupied one of the most important points in the system of defense for the Cape Fear, and "must be held at all hazards and to the last extremity...I understand that the enemy are covering their wooden ships with chain armor. This is very formidable and effective, and may enable many of them, unless obstructed, to pass the forts of the army. You will have the defense of a narrow and difficult pass and one of the last importance as regards the harbor. The command will be exclusively

Battery Buchanan in 1865

naval, as much so as if the defensive force was in a ship-of-war at anchor off the Rip." [19]

The pickets covering Battery Buchanan would come from Colonel Lamb's garrison. They were completing the massive fortification. An additional redoubt would later be added, bringing the total at the site to four heavy guns. A wharf had been constructed nearby for large steamers. Buchanan was extremely formidable, much larger than the Mound Battery at the south end of Fort Fisher. Buchanan was "a citadel to which an overpowered garrison might retreat and with proper transportation might be carried off at night, and to which reinforcements could be safely sent under the cover of darkness." [20]

Over the next several weeks, Whiting came from Wilmington frequently to visit with and give directions to Fort Fisher's commander for

Sugar Loaf

improving the already powerful defenses on Confederate Point. The two rode horseback over the area north of Fisher, Whiting "selecting points for batteries and covered ways, so as to keep up communication after the arrival of the enemy, between the fort and the entrenched camp," which Lamb began constructing at Sugar Loaf. Whiting pointed out to his friend and young subordinate, "where the enemy would land on the beach beyond the range of our guns, and...had prepared ample shelter for troops to seriously retard if not prevent a landing." [21]

All the preparations the Confederates could make would be needed. By late October, fifty-one year old U.S. Admiral David Dixon Porter, a full-bearded, combat hardened professional in dark blue uniform with bright gold trim, was ready to attack Fort Fisher. Having taken command of the North Atlantic Blockading Squadron on October 12, Porter was ambitious, arrogant, and not averse to stretching the truth to his own benefit. He was a crack naval officer, though, and came from a long line of sailors. His greatest contribution to the war effort so far had been the much needed close support and naval assistance of his Mississippi Squadron in helping Ulysses Grant capture Vicksburg in the summer of 1863. [22]

Now, some fifteen months after Vicksburg's fall to the Union, Porter had assembled a huge fleet at Hampton Roads, Virginia, for the planned assault on the Cape Fear defenses. "There was a great variety of vessels," Porter wrote, "as every class in the Navy was represented, from the lofty frigate down to the fragile steamer taken from the merchant service; but all mounted good guns." [23]

There were about one hundred ships of war from several different squadrons, and Porter put the sailors and their commanders through a regular system of drilling with masts, yards and sails, as well as gunnery practice. "Immense quantities of shells were fired away, for the commanding officers of the ships were given 'carte blanche' in this respect, the Admiral believing that it would be an ultimate saving in time of battle." [24]

While the U.S. Navy drilled and prepared to sail against Confederate Point, Ulysses Grant dragged his feet. As early as September, Grant had considered sending 6,000 to 10,000 soldiers from Ben Butler's Army of the James, bottled up at Bermuda Hundred outside Richmond, to cooperate with the Navy, but he was unsure of the full significance of Wilmington, the strength of its defenses, or the timing of the attack. He had even appointed one of Butler's subordinates, General Godfrey Weitzel, a corps commander in the Army of the James, as commanding officer of the army troops in the upcoming expedition. A twenty-nine year old West Pointer and chief engineer officer of the Army of the James, Weitzel had performed well in the operations against New Orleans and Port Hudson, Louisiana, and was respected and well-liked by Grant. He told Weitzel that "this is another Mobile affair. The navy will run in some vessels up the Cape Fear

RAdm David Dixon Porter

River, and I advise you to land your troops on a position across the peninsula, and then Fort Fisher will fall exactly as Fort Morgan did." [25]

When it became apparent that the press, North and South, had gotten wind of the expedition and broadcast their information as the *Daily Journal* had done, he decided to cancel the sending of troops for the time being. He told the rotund Massachusetts political general Butler, nicknamed "Spoons" and "Beast" by Southerners for his knack at stealing Southern silverware and insulting women, that "he would not have anything to do with it, to use his exact phrase, because he could not afford an army for a siege, and he supposed the purpose for which the fleet was getting ready was so far known to everybody that there could be no surprise." [26]

In the interim, as the army lagged and Porter continued drilling his sailors in Hampton Roads, a novel idea came to the Yankee high command.

***Porter's powdership,** the* USS Louisiana.

Though Butler would claim credit for the plan, and Porter would later let him, the idea of a floating bomb in the form of an exploding ship came about. A vessel was to be loaded with several hundred tons of gunpowder, run aground near Fort Fisher and exploded, hopefully destroying earthworks, killing soldiers and dismounting guns. The idea may actually have originated with the Admiral himself. [27]

While Porter was readying his fleet in October, news was received in the United States of a massive explosion in the Thames River. Between the town of Erith and Woolwich, England, two barges loaded with large quantities of gunpowder exploded, triggering sympathetic explosions on shore in two powder magazines, killing eight or nine people, and producing shock waves felt fifteen miles away in London. Butler later claimed to have heard the news and broached the idea of a powder vessel at Fort Fisher to Abraham Lincoln and Assistant Secretary of the navy Gustavus V. Fox. Lincoln was cool to the idea, but Fox was all for it. On November 16, Fox telegraphed Porter in Hampton Roads to find "any shaky steamer that will carry 300 tons. It will save time. Otherwise I will get a blockade runner. We will go on with this. General Butler left this evening and will cooperate." [28]

Grant was not impressed with the idea, especially after the army's chief engineer studied the plan and rendered a negative opinion. Sixty-six year old Brigadier General Richard Delafield, whose military service had spanned fifty years, examined the proposal, and was candid in his appraisal. "I consider," Delafield reported, "that the explosion of a vessel load of gunpowder at the nearest point it can approach Fort Caswell or Fort Fisher can produce no useful result toward the reduction of those works, and that no such vessels as are proposed to be so loaded can be navigated and placed at the nearest points to these forts, provided the fort is garrisoned and its guns are served with hollow projectiles and hot shot." [29]

The army had little more to do with the scheme after that, other than Grant's agreeing to furnish the requisite number of troops when he decided the time was right. Porter, however, became more than enthusiastic over the potential results and saw to it everything needed to help insure success was furnished. Writing to Commander Alexander C. Rhind, who volunteered to take charge of the enterprise, the admiral told him: "I have studied this matter very fairly and impartially...I do not anticipate such a dreadful earthquake as some suppose will take place (destroying everything), nor do I think the effect will in any way be mild.

"I take a mean between the two, and think the effect of the explosion will be simply very severe, stunning men at a distance of three or four hundred yards, demoralizing them completely, and making them unable to stand for any length of time a fire from the ships. I think that the concussion will tumble magazines that are built on framework, and that the famous Mound will be among the things that were, and the guns buried beneath the ruins.

"I think that houses in Wilmington and Smithville will tumble to the ground and much demoralize the people, and I think if the Rebels fight after the explosion they have more in them than I give them credit for.

"I expect more good to our cause from a success in this instance than from an advance of all of the armies in the field. If we succeed it is a mere matter of who has the most powder, and as I believe it is generally conceded that we are better supplied than the rebels, we can blow them into submission. The names of those connected with the expedition will be famous for all time to come." [30]

Clearly, Porter thought the powder boat and the navy would play the decisive role in victory on the Cape Fear. For the mission, he assigned an old, worn out, flat bottom steamer, the *U.S.S. Louisiana*, as the sacrificial vessel. She was to be loaded with 300 tons of gunpowder, her superstructure modified to resemble a blockade runner, and a crew of sailors who had volunteered for "death or glory, honor and promotion," serving under Commander Rhind, would run her in close to Fort Fisher, and blow her up. [31]

The difficulty for the experts planning the explosion, which was to occur instantaneously for the entire cargo of powder to obtain the "maximum shock wave effect," was how to have it occur at a precise time and allow the crew to get off the ship and out of harm's way before it blew. They decided on a system called the Gomez fuse, which burned at an extremely rapid rate of one mile in four seconds. Using clocks set for the same time in several locations throughout the powder cargo, the clocks would set off a small amount of powder, "into which were wired all the Gomez fuses. When this small amount of powder exploded all the fuses would be lit." As additional insurance, five different candles containing Gomez fuses were distributed in the cargo, any one of which could trigger the explosion. As guarantee against the ship falling into

Confederate hands, a fire of pine knots and waste cotton was to be set by the crew immediately before departing the *Louisiana*, which would eventually trigger the explosion if all else failed. [32]

While work proceeded with the powder boat and Yankee planning for the expedition, Whiting and Lamb prepared for a fight, apparently with little direction or input from Braxton Bragg. On Sunday, November 6, Colonel Lamb had a visit from General Hebert, and the two of them rode over an area General Whiting had selected for additional earthworks to be built, studying "the lines around Sugar Loaf and the proposed site of advanced work at Battery Gatlin." Gatlin was the small bastion situated on a sand spit east of Myrtle Grove sound some five miles north of Fort Fisher, and about one and a half miles east of Sugar Loaf. It was armed with a 6.4 inch 32-pounder rifled cannon, and had protected blockade-runners headed for Fort Fisher and New Inlet for some time. [33]

On the next day, November 7, General Whiting and his aide, Captain Strong, came down from Wilmington to meet Lamb at Sugar Loaf, and the three of them rode over to Battery Gatlin, where Lamb pointed out to Whiting the difficulty of putting up a larger advanced work right on the beach. Whiting agreed it should go west of Myrtle Sound, on the mainland. There was to be a covered road running parallel to the beach and connecting with the redoubt, and another road would connect "the advanced work with Sugar Loaf." [34]

As additional protection from the fire of the heavy naval guns, beginning fifty yards north of Fort Fisher, "the river bank was high enough to form a perfect defence from the fleet at sea...This natural protection from the fleet extended for some miles up the river until it reached the camp" at the Sugar Loaf position. [35]

The substantial cover afforded to infantry by the riverbank was augmented by numerous man-made and natural barriers. Battery Holland was a half mile north of the landface of Fort Fisher, and from there for over four miles north to Myrtle Sound, "were a series of batteries, curtains and sand hills," that gave superb protection to troops. A mile below the sound, 600-800 yards west of the beach, and extending one and a half miles south in the direction of Fisher, was a heavy infantry curtain, situated mostly in woods and scrub to conceal the position and located where it was expected the Yankee infantry would hit the beach. The left of these earthworks were anchored on a pond several hundred yards wide, and the right of the line was about one-half mile north of Battery Anderson, which mounted a 20-pounder rifle nicknamed "Long Tom," that later exploded when being fired. All these positions, between Fort Fisher and the fortified lines at Sugar Loaf and Myrtle Sound, were connected one with the other by the River Road to Wilmington and man-made military roads, to facilitate movement of troops, artillery, and supplies. [36]

According to the studied opinions of Lamb, Whiting, P.G.T. Beauregard, and even James Longstreet, man and nature had "combined to make a landing of troops from beyond the close range of Fort Fisher "to the head of the sound impossible in the face of a few thousand determined troops," who would have the option of shuttling on their interior lines "from point to point behind the works and hills unobserved by the enemy." [37]

The history of naval bombardment on land positions during this war, and all previous wars, had demonstrated the inaccuracy and inefficiency of cannon fire from ships trying to hit and reduce works and enemy positions, even when great quantities of powder and projectiles were expended. The Yankee fleet during the day would have great difficulty firing over the heads of Federal troops to appreciably damage the Confederate infantry without risk of killing their own men. Those bluecoats who did land, if properly opposed by vigorous assaults from behind fortifications, should be either destroyed or captured. [38]

On Wednesday, November 9, Governor Vance, Bragg and Whiting met Lamb at Sugar Loaf. They rode over and inspected the earthworks from that area down to Fort Fisher. Lamb recorded in his diary that the "Governor was very much pleased with my works." They then took a boat over to tour Forts Caswell, Holmes, and Campbell, Lamb regarding Holmes as the only strong position of the three. [39]

Zebulon Vance, writing to Jefferson Davis on his return to Raleigh, sounded the same call Chase Whiting had been sounding since November 1862, when he was assigned to Wilmington. Advising Davis he had just returned from an inspection of the fortifications on Confederate Point and the west bank of the Cape Fear, he told the President he found "them all in excellent condition." He said "there seems to be nothing wanting but troops." Unless Confederate Point was strengthened by at least two brigades of veteran infantry, he regarded the capture of Wilmington as inevitable. He requested that Robert E. Lee "spare a few veterans as a nucleus for the raw troops defending Wilmington, notwithstanding the great pressure on his lines." [40]

Lee responded that Richmond was currently besieged by an army three times the number of his, and for the time being, no army was attacking Wilmington. When it was determined Wilmington was about to be attacked, reinforcements could then be sent to meet the threat. [41]

In the midst of preparations to meet the Federals, Bragg was ordered by Jefferson Davis to Augusta, Georgia on Tuesday, November 22. William T. Sherman, who had destroyed and left the city of Atlanta, was advancing on Savannah with about 60,000 troops by late November. The Confederates opposing him, under Lieutenant General William J. Hardee, former commandant of cadets at West Point and veteran corps commander in the Army of Tennessee, needed all the help they could get. [42]

The already thin garrison of Fort Fisher, chiefly comprised of the Thirty-Sixth North Carolina Troops, was reduced even further, five of the ten companies being ordered to accompany Bragg to Georgia. Major James M.

254 - *Rebel Gibraltar: Fort Fisher and Wilmington, C.S.A.*

Stevenson was assigned to command the battalion of artillerists, which also included five companies of the Fortieth North Carolina Troops, who were primarily stationed at Fort Holmes on Smith's Island. On the very eve of battle with tremendous odds to contend with, Fort Fisher's garrison numbered no more than 500 men. [43]

On Thursday, November 24, two days after William Lamb was forced to reduce his garrison by half, one of the saddest events in his military career occurred. He had to execute two deserters. Neither of them had deserted from his command, but "when captured, their companies were stationed at Fort Fisher," and it was his "painful duty to see the sentences of the courts-martial enforced." [44]

Dempsey Watts was a 37-year-old private in Company E of Lamb's Thirty-Sixth North Carolina Troops. A native of Horry County, South Carolina, he was married and had been a farmer when he enlisted. Vincent Allen was a 38-year-old private in Company D of the Thirteenth Battalion North Carolina Light Artillery, which most recently had been stationed at Battery Gatlin on the sand spit east of Myrtle Sound, five miles north of Fisher. He was also a farmer, married, and hailed from Gaston County, North Carolina. Lamb believed "the condition of their families at home" had probably caused desertion from their posts, and both men "died fearlessly." [45]

Shortly before noon on that Thursday, the garrison was assembled in two long lines facing the condemned, who rode to the execution site on their coffins, "the band playing the dead march." Chaplain Luther McKinnon prayed for the men, who declined to give any remarks of their own, except to request they not be tied to the stakes. Nine rifle bearing soldiers faced each of the two as they knelt down and were blindfolded, the ordnance sergeant having loaded the weapons with one blank cartridge, so that no soldier of the detail would be certain he fired a bullet when the time came.

"Both men were cool," Lamb recorded in his diary, "Watts as calm as if he had been on parade, the last thing he did before being bandaged, was to turn & look at Allen & adjust his arms & hands like his. Allen stood during the Chaplain's prayer & seemed a little effected but as if in prayer; he was praying while shot." [46]

Allen was killed instantly, but Watts was only mortally wounded, crying out pitifully, "Lord have mercy on me." Lamb then ordered his reserve rifle guard of four men up "to within two paces of him & he rec'd two shots through the head, & died." Following the executions, the garrison was marched in column around the bodies of the deserters, underscoring the severity of the offense and punishment. [47]

Down in Georgia, Wilmington's defenders performed admirably, helping Hardee fight Sherman's massive forces. One news account told of a battle fourteen miles outside Savannah called Harrison's Old Field. Major Stevenson was in command of his companies of the Thirty-Sixth North

Carolina, the Fortieth North Carolina, parts of the Fiftieth North Carolina and Tenth North Carolina Battalion. Hardee had not planned for them to become engaged in a regular battle, but to hold the Yankees back until an orderly retreat could be conducted into Savannah. The order to pull out, however, did not reach Stevenson in time, and his men were cut off by two Federal brigades.

"Major Stevenson," one of his soldiers recalled, "seems to have known the country better than General Hardee's informant, and made his escape with all his men, except thirteen killed. He also brought off all his wounded, his artillery and wagons, and that same night marched into Savannah and reported in person to General Hardee, by whom he was warmly received and highly complimented." [48]

The loss of any of the Cape Fear troops was serious, considering the small numbers and the soon to come Yankee attack. William Lamb wrote in his diary of "the sad tidings that Capt. Melvin of Co. J had been killed in Georgia, or S.C., also heard that Capt. Charley Whitehurst who was formerly under me Comd. of Co. J of 40th N.C. Rgt. had been mortally wounded & that Maj. Young of the battalion recently at Sugar Loaf had been killed." [49]

On November 30, learning of Bragg's transfer to Georgia with troops from the Cape Fear, Grant decided the time for attack had come. He sent a telegram to Ben Butler advising him to get the expedition moving. "I have files of Savannah and Augusta papers by Colonel Mulford," he wrote, "from which I gather that Bragg has gone to Georgia, taking with him, I judge, most of the forces from about Wilmington. It is, therefore, important that Weitzel should get off during his absence; and if successful in effecting a landing he may, by a bold dash, succeed in capturing Wilmington. Make all the arrangements for his departure so that the navy may not be detained one moment for the army." [50]

It was a good thing for the Yankees that, at long last, something was finally going to be done "to close to the enemy the port of Wilmington." At nearly the same time as Grant's dispatches to proceed with the expedition, George A. Trenholm, Confederate Secretary of the Treasury, was preparing a report for Jefferson Davis, advising of the tremendous success of blockade running during the past year, the vast majority of imports having arrived in Wilmington. From November 1, 1863 to October 25, 1864, blockade runners had brought in 1,490,000 pounds of lead, 1,850,000 pounds of saltpeter, 6,200,000 pounds of meat, 408,000 pounds of coffee, 420,000 pairs of boots and shoes, 292,000 blankets, and 136,832 rifles, carbines or muskets. [51]

In addition, and despite the increasing stringency of the blockade under David Porter, from October 31 to December 6, twenty-eight more blockade-runners arrived in Wilmington. These ships bore such varied cargoes as 222 cases of rifles for the Ordnance Department shipped from Bermuda, 1,270 cases of preserved meat for the Commissary Department, also out of Bermuda, 7 bundles of vises and 13 anvils for the Quartermaster Department, shipped from Nassau, and hundreds of tons of other supplies of every description necessary for prosecution of a war. The Confederate States, it seemed, would be supplied indefinitely if Wilmington remained open to commerce. [52]

On December 7, the U.S. Army began to move at the prodding of Grant, who worried the troops under Bragg would return to Wilmington before the Yankees hit. He urged Butler to get the movement underway with or without the powder boat that had become David Porter's pet project. About 7,000 troops from the Army of the James, under overall command of Major General Godfrey Weitzel, commanding the Twenty-Fifth Army Corps, were assigned for the expedition.

Two divisions of infantry totaling 6,500 men, in addition to two batteries of artillery and fifty cavalry would comprise Weitzel's force. Brigadier

MajGen. Godfrey Weitzel, U.S. Army

General Adelbert Ames' Second Division, Twenty-Fourth Corps, was the primary unit chosen for the landing and assault. Ames was a 29-year-old native of Maine, who in his early youth had been a sailor on a clipper ship. He married a daughter of Ben Butler. An 1861 graduate of West Point, he had served in the army in Virginia since First Manassas, where he was badly wounded, later winning the Congressional Medal for his service there. [53]

Charles J. Paine, brigadier general of the First Division, Twenty-Fifth Corps of black troops with white officers, was commander of the supporting division. Boston born to a family of wealth and a Harvard educated lawyer, the 31-year-old Paine had commanded black soldiers since October 1862 when he became colonel of the Second Louisiana (U.S.), recruited in New Orleans. He served competently with those troops under Nathaniel Banks in the Port Hudson campaign the following spring and summer of 1863. [54]

Marching their men to a staging area at Bermuda Hundred on the James River, Ames and Paine embarked the troops on army transport ships and sailed down to Fort Monroe at Hampton Roads, where they waited for the navy for several days. David Porter advising Ben Butler the navy would be ready to sail south on the 13th of December, Butler ordered the transports to sail north initially, to deceive Confederate spies and scouts as to their destination.

BrigGen. Charles Paine, U.S. Army

Reaching Mathias Point on the Potomac River the middle of the night, the army vessels reversed course to the south, left Cape Henry the afternoon of the 14th, and arrived on Thursday night, the 15th of December, off Masonboro Inlet. The agreed-on rendezvous point with Porter's fleet was sufficiently far from land not to be seen by the Confederates on shore. [55]

The next day, Friday December 16, 29-year-old Sergeant Major Edward K. Wightman, of Company C, Third New York Volunteer Infantry, of Newton Martin Curtis' brigade, Ames' division, wrote to his brother from the army transport *Weybosset*, while the fleet lay off Masonboro Inlet. Wightman assumed they were "about to enter the Mason (borough) Inlet, which will land us within eight miles of Wilmington." [56]

"The passage around the Cape was not rough for the season," he wrote, "and the men suffered only from close quarters and seasickness. Five hundred soldiers are crowded on the *Weybosset*. Part are on the decks, part between, and part of them are half smothered in the lower hold, where they remain day and night making their bed on the coal. Coffee is made for them twice a day by steam, a caskful at a time. This, together with raw pork and hardtack, constitutes their rations. In the early part of the voyage, however, we had some codfish, which the boys called 'Lincoln trout,' and a few rations of dried herring, which they have christened, 'Lincoln's sardines.'

"The appearance of the fleet at night when the vessels sail abreast and each steamer displays three lights, red, white, and blue, is magnificent." [57]

BrigGen. Adlebert Ames, U.S. Army

Wightman did not think the expedition would be ordered to capture Wilmington, as he judged the force too small for such an assignment. Because they had brought with them numerous entrenching tools, he noted, "the general opinion is that we are to feel the strength of the enemy, take everything which can be taken, and then select a position and fortify it." [58]

They would be several more days, however, before feeling "the strength of the enemy." Porter and the U.S. Navy were nowhere around, except for the usual blockading vessels. They were holed up in Beaufort, North Carolina. Only 185 tons of gunpowder had been loaded on the *U.S.S. Louisiana* in Virginia, and David Porter expected to have 235 tons packed on board for the explosion near Fort Fisher, so he put into Beaufort Harbor to take on more. It took longer than expected, and delayed the rendezvous with Butler's transports. Butler stated that they waited "there Friday, Saturday, and Sunday." It was an unfortunate delay, as the wind was calm and the sea extremely smooth and conducive to landing troops. The water was, in fact, so lake-like and easy, that the goggle-eyed Massachusetts general actually let his gig down and "took a row for pleasure. There was not wind enough to fill the sail of a yawl boat that was let down." [59]

Porter finally showed up on Sunday night, the 18th, after the Army of the James had been waiting aboard ships for three days. Now he informed Butler he was sending the powder vessel in toward Fort Fisher right away. He planned to move in with the fleet "the moment the explosion takes place and open fire with some of the vessels at night to prevent the enemy repairing damages if he has any." [60]

Colonel Cyrus Comstock, Ulysses Grant's Chief Engineer, who had been assigned to Ben Butler to help superintend the Army of the James' land assault on Fisher, noted in his diary on December 18 that Porter planned to send in the powder boat despite the fact that the weather was worsening. By the evening of the 18th, "a stiff run & rough water" indicated to Comstock, Godfrey Weitzel and Butler, that the opportunity for landing troops the next day to follow up the explosion of the powder boat was slim to none. "Now it looks like bad weather after losing three fine days" the Colonel further noted in his December 18 entry.

Butler dispatched Comstock and Weitzel to Porter's flagship, the *Malvern*, to advise against sending in the powder-laden *Louisiana*. "For whatever damage that explosion might do the enemy would have time to repair, and, as we could not land, the advantage of the powder vessel would be lost entirely. As all of us would have to stand off during the northeasterly gale" that was clearly coming, it was only reasonable to wait for weather that would accommodate the landing of troops. [61]

Porter agreed, and the experiment was called off till the weather improved. That, too, would be several more days in coming. A powerful gale was coming in from the northeast. Comstock noted in his diary the next day that it was "pretty rough all day," and the storm continued for the better part of the week. [62]

On Tuesday, December 20, Colonel Lamb was awakened at the "Cottage" north of Fort Fisher and advised that "the enemy's fleet were off the fort." Lamb went outside and saw five of the usual blockading vessels offshore, as well as twenty-five other warships, "including several frigates further out, nearly all hull down." He got Daisy to pack some of the belongings and take the children across the river to Orton Plantation for safety, went back to the fort, and "got everything in readiness for a fight." He initially thought Porter's ships would attack at high tide around noontime, but as the gale was still blowing hard, he rightfully concluded the storm "interfered with their operations." [63]

Since the army transports had only taken on ten days supply of coal and water on the 7th and 8th of December before leaving Virginia, it was necessary for them to put into Beaufort to replenish, especially since it was unclear how long the gale would continue. In the meantime, the delay in attack was proving favorable to the defenders of Wilmington. [64]

On the afternoon of the 18th, as the wind and waves began to pick up off Fort Fisher, Robert E. Lee reported to Secretary of War James Seddon, that he had received word (belatedly as it turned out) of the Yankee fleet heading for Wilmington. That night, he ordered Major General Robert Hoke's Division of four veteran infantry brigades relieved from the lines outside Richmond

MajGen. Robert Hoke, C.S.A.

and sent to Wilmington. With most of the Cape Fear defenses severely stripped of troops sent to the aid of Savannah under Bragg, who himself had returned but without the troops, it was none too soon. On the same day Lee ordered Hoke's Division sent south, Chase Whiting telegraphed Seddon that the Cape Fear troops "ordered away cannot return; if not helped, the forts may be turned and the city goes. The reduced garrisons are not able to hold this extended position without support." [65]

Of Hoke's four brigades, only two would arrive in time to be present on the field during the Union attack, Johnson Hagood's South Carolinians, and William Kirkland's North Carolinians, and only Kirkland's would fire any shots at the bluecoats. General Hagood reported the movement took place under the worst possible conditions. "The troops were saturated with the freezing rain on the march to Richmond," he wrote, "and they were loaded on freight cars without seats or fires – the men so crowded as to preclude individual motion. The rain began to be accompanied by a high wind, and lying motionless in their wet garments, the men were whistled along on the train the balance of the day and all night. At daylight we arrived at Danville. The suffering was intense. One poor fellow, of the Seventh battalion, was found dead from the exposure, and a dozen others had to be borne from the cars to the wayside hospital." [66]

First Lieutenant George M. Rose, Adjutant of the Sixty-Sixth North Carolina Troops of Kirkland's Brigade, echoed Hagood's account of the harrowing trip south. After marching and standing around for hours in wet freezing temperatures to board the trains, they "were placed on and in box cars and flat cars, and the train made its way slowly from Richmond to Danville amid snow, sleet and rain, and the severest bitter cold we had ever experienced. There was no opportunity to have fires, no way to keep ourselves warm and the train worked its way along, the men frequently having to get off and run alongside of it to keep themselves warm." [67]

As Hoke's Division headed south for Wilmington, a detachment of twenty-nine sailors from the Confederate cruiser *C.S.S. Chickamauga* were temporarily assigned to man two naval guns taken off the sunken *C.S.S. Raleigh*, that had been mounted in the Columbiad Battery on the seaface of Fort Fisher. Midshipman Clarence Cary wrote that they were assigned to "man two seven-inch Brooke rifled and banded guns which...had been mounted in a partially completed battery on the sea-face of the fort; the navy men being desired in this instance, because the soldiers did not understand the tackling and management of the pieces." These sailors would be under command of First Lieutenant F.M. Roby of the Confederate Navy, who would report to Colonel Lamb. [68]

While the gale continued and Butler's transports remained at Beaufort, Lamb received more reinforcements after the sailors from the *Chickamauga* came in. 110 men of the Fortieth North Carolina, two companies of the Tenth North Carolina, one company of the Thirteenth North Carolina Battalion, and 140 boys of the Seventh Battalion North Carolina Junior Reserves, arrived on December 23. They were all sorely needed, since only 425 men constituted Lamb's entire garrison prior to the arrival of the sailors or additional soldiers. [69]

By Friday, December 23, David Porter believed the gale had sufficiently subsided to allow the powder boat to be taken in and exploded. He ordered Commander A.C. Rhind to move the vessel to shore that night, "the explosion to take place at 2 a.m., or as near to that as possible," Captain Haswell C. Clarke, one of Ben Butler's staff officers, had been dispatched to Porter from Beaufort. He advised the Admiral that the army was expected to be back off Masonboro Sound by the night of December 24, to enable the troops to land on Christmas Day. Porter told Clarke he would not be waiting on the Army of the James, that the powder boat was being exploded, and the navy would be attacking. Due to continued adverse weather off Beaufort, Butler did not receive the message from Clarke until the *Louisiana* was already destroyed. [70]

The night of the 23rd was sufficiently dark to enable the *Louisiana* to steam toward the fort without detection by Confederate sentries. Being towed most of the way by the *U.S.S. Wilderness*, the *Louisiana* was released about 11:30 p.m., and Alexander Rhind steered the vessel in under its own power until he and his officers believed they were about 300 yards from the beach, but which the Confederates later estimated to be no closer than 1,200 yards.

When the *Louisiana* dropped anchor, the crew was ordered overboard into a small cutter. Rhind and his executive officer, Lieutenant Samuel W. Preston, moved quickly around the ship to prime the ignition that would cause the vessel to blow. The Gomez fuzing system was activated at 11:50 p.m., with the clocks set for an hour and a half, about 1:20 a.m., before explosion was to occur. If the clocks failed, then candles judiciously placed in the powder were supposed to trigger the blast by 1:35 a.m. As final insurance, a supplemental fire from debris was built to keep the Rebels off the ship, and ultimately produce detonation.

They were finished with their task, in the cutter, and back to the *Wilderness* by midnight. Because of life-threatening concussions and shock waves expected as a result of the blast, the *Wilderness* steamed at full speed away from the shore, to join the rest of the fleet twelve miles out. [71]

The fireworks anticipated for 1:20 a.m. from the Gomez system did not occur. Then the backup explosion to be triggered by the candles failed to materialize at 1:35 a.m., by which time the *Louisiana* was ablaze from stem to stern. The fires set by Rhind and Porter as a last resort had spread the length of the ship, and at 1:40 a.m., the *Louisiana* came apart in four separate, distinct blasts of reverberating concussion and flame. They were followed by many smaller blasts as ignited powder bags exploded after being blown into the air. [72]

The Fourth Battalion North Carolina Junior Reserves, commanded by Major J.M. Reece and camped up the beach north of the fort that night, were the troops closest to the explosions. The concussions jolted them awake, bouncing them around "like popcorn in a popper" and out of their blankets, the boys scared out of their wits, but otherwise unhurt. William Lamb had observed from Fisher's ramparts the *Louisiana* burning offshore before the vessel blew. He had thought it might be the blockade runner *Agnes Fry* out of Nassau, that had run aground about a mile from the fort and set herself afire. Lamb had just laid down in his quarters, when he felt "a gentle rocking of the small brick house (formerly the light keeper's)," that was immediately followed by an explosion, which he believed sounded like the "report of a ten-inch Columbiad." [73]

The tremendous concussion convinced Lamb that it was not a blockade-runner but a Federal warship, whose magazine had blown after the fire reached the hold. "I telegraphed General Whiting, at Wilmington, of the explosion, and retired to rest...The vessel was doubtless afloat when the explosion occurred, or the result might have been very serious. The shock was distinctly felt in Wilmington." [74]

Yankee sailors who witnessed the blasts twelve miles offshore, expected severe vibrations to rock their vessels, and braced themselves for the shock. Fifteen seconds later, the slight rattling of masts, minor trembling of ships, and a few broken windows, was about the extent of damage done to the Federal fleet. Commander Rhind, having observed from afar the series of disjointed explosions rather than the hoped for single massive one, turned to one of his officers with obvious disgust that was shared by others, and glumly remarked, "There's a fizzle." [75]

Indeed, no damage of any kind had been inflicted on Fort Fisher. The *Daily Journal* said that the Yankee's notion of "exploding a powder vessel way out at sea, a thousand yards from the fort, was a rich one. It really did no harm to the Fort nor to anything in it. The thing would have been complete if they had deployed two or three hundred Chinese gongs 'to fright the souls of timorous adversaries'." [76]

The problem, in addition to the ship's distance from shore, was the improper fuzing of the powder. Of the 215 tons on board the vessel, only 30 tons had been properly fuzed. Commander Rhind reported to David Porter that 185 tons of powder had already been loaded on the vessel by the time it was entrusted to him, none had been fuzed for explosion, and there was no way to break out the cargo loaded to do so. Rhind and his young executive officer, Lieutenant Preston, supervised loading of the other 30 tons on arrival at Beaufort, and they had placed the Gomez fuzes in that portion. The whole other 185 tons had had no fuzes run through it at all.

"Had the Gomez fuze been circulated, as it should have been," he told Porter, "through the cargo of the hold or berth deck, the effect of the explosion would doubtless have been increased.

"As to my impression of the results and the effect produced," it was Rhind's opinion, "that owing to the want of confinement and insufficient fuzing of the mass, that much of the powder was blown away before ignition and its effect lost." [77]

Porter, the optimistic proponent of the experiment, was forced to admit that no injury had been sustained by the fort, "nor were any of the wooden huts, about a half mile off, thrown down; but on looking at the massive structures built of sandbags, it could scarcely be expected to move them by such a process. That could only be done by continued hammering with shot and shell," he concluded. [78]

"Saturday, December 24th," William Lamb wrote, "was one of those perfect winter days that are occasionally experienced in the latitude of the Cape Fear. The gale, which had backed around from the northeast to the southwest, had subsided the day before, and was followed by a dead calm. The air was balmy for winter, and the sun shone with almost Indian summer warmth, and the deep blue sea was as calm as a lake and broke lazily on the bar and beach.

"A grander sight than the approach of Porter's formidable armada towards the fort was never witnessed on our coast," Lamb recalled. "With the rising sun out of old ocean there came upon the horizon one after another, the vessels of the fleet, the grand frigates leading the van, followed by the iron-clads. More than fifty men-of-war headed for the Confederate stronghold. At 9 o'clock the men were beat to quarters, and silently the detachments stood by their guns. On the vessels came, growing larger and more imposing as the distance lessened between them and the resolute men who had rallied to defend their homes. The *Minnesota, Colorado,* and *Wabash* came on, floating fortresses, each mounting more guns than all the batteries on the land, and the two first combined carrying more shot and shell than all the magazines in the fort contained. From the left salient to the mound Fort Fisher had forty-four guns, and not over 3,600 shot and shell, exclusive of grape and shrapnel." [79]

Lamb ordered that no guns were to be fired until the 10-inch Columbiad at the "Pulpit", as headquarters was known, was fired, and that each gun bearing on a Union warship was to fire every thirty minutes. Should any Yankee ship try to cross the bar, then "every gun bearing on it should be fired as rapidly as accuracy would permit, the smooth bores at richochette." [80]

Commodore Willliam Radford was in charge of the Federal ironclad division consisting of the *New Ironsides*, of which he was in immediate command, and the monitors *Monadnock, Canonicus,* and *Mahopac.* Under orders to commence the battle for Porter's fleet, the ironclads steamed slowly toward the beach, and when positioned 1,200 to 1,500 yards north of Fort Fisher, opened fire at 12:40 p.m., the *New Ironsides* starboard battery belching a huge 11-inch shell toward William Lamb's defenders. The young colonel saw a white puff of smoke, heard a heavy boom, "and over our heads came an eleven inch shell, which I saw distinctly in its passage towards our flag staff, past which it exploded harmlessly with a sharp report." [81]

Twenty-three year old Captain Samuel B. Hunter of Halifax County, commanding Company F in Lamb's Thirty-Sixty North Carolina Regiment, had a never-to-be-forgotten view of the 64-warship fleet in his position in the Northeast Bastion of Fisher. "The engagement commenced at 12.40 p.m.," the young captain reported. The *Ironsides* took the lead, followed by the other monitors. "In regular order after these a large number of heavy frigates, carrying from forty to fifty guns each, formed in order of battle, some halting in the rear of the *Ironsides*, others passing to the left of her until they extended past the direction of the bar. The *Ironsides* took position about one mile and a half from the fort and in nearly an eastern direction from the northeast corner; the iron-clad monitors about the same distance, but a little farther to the northward. The first shot fired by the enemy was from the Ironsides, as she took position first and was nearer at that time to the fort than the rest. Soon after the bombardment commenced in earnest, shot and shell, shrapnel, &c., flying thick as hail, but perhaps a little hotter." [82]

According to Captain Hunter, Fort Fisher "remained silent for thirty minutes, when the signal gun therefrom was fired from the pulpit (a 10-inch) at the nearest frigate in." After Lamb ordered one of the big Columbiads to be fired on an approaching warship, the giant gun boomed, and a heavy shot "went bowling along, richochetted, and bounded through the smoke-stack of the *Susquehanna*." [83]

Lieutenant Commander Thomas O. Selfridge, commanding the *U.S.S. Huron*, had a ringside seat of the heavy bombardment of the fort. "It was a magnificent sight to see these frigates fairly engaged, and one never to be forgotten. Their sides seemed a sheet of flame, and the roar of their guns like a mighty thunderbolt...Nothing could withstand such a storm of shot and shell as was now poured into this fort. The enemy took refuge in their bombproofs, replying sullenly with an occasional gun." [84]

As Lamb's artillerists were under orders to fire only every thirty minutes to conserve ammunition, it seemed to Selfridge and other Yankee officers that the fort's reply to the heavy shelling was sporadic and piecemeal. Midshipman Clarence Cary, one of the young naval officers in Fisher's Columbiad Battery on the seaface, did not see it that way. He described it as "a lively, rattling interchange of fire opened between the hundreds of guns of the fleet and the fifty odd pieces perched on the sand mounds of the fortress. What with the continuous roar of the firing, and the scarcely frequent reports of bursting shell, the aggregate noise was not unlike that of a rolling, volleying, long sustained thunder storm." [85]

Eighteen-year-old U.S. Ensign Robley Evans, Virginia born and raised whose brother served on the staff of Robert E. Lee, could have told Thomas Selfridge that Fort Fisher was firing back, sometimes with precision. Serving aboard the *U.S.S. Powhatan*, Evans was ordered aloft by his commanding officer, Commodore James Schenck, to try and locate some guns in Fort Fisher that "were annoying him."

Evans climbed up in the ship's rigging near the top, took out a piece of hardtack from the pocket of his blue jacket to munch on, and scanned the fort through field glasses for the guns. Clenching the hardtack between his teeth, Evans spied Rebel gunners aiming a cannon at the *Powhatan*. "There was a puff of smoke," Evans said, "something like a lamp-post crossed the field of the glass, and a moment after the rigging was cut four feet below me, and I swung into the mast. I at once thought of my hard-tack, but it was gone, and I never found even a crumb of it. I am sure that I swallowed it whole." Visibly shaken, Evans was ordered down from the perch from which he had almost been blown, to take his position as officer "in charge of the after division of guns." [86]

William Lamb observed from his headquarters post at the Pulpit, some 200 yards north of Midshipman Cary's position, that much of the Federal Navy's powder and shells were being wasted on the garrison flag in the center of the fort's parade ground, which was slightly south of the landface batteries and about 300 yards east of the marshes that grew along the bank of the Cape Fear. Many of the shells were harmlessly arcing over the fort, and exploding in tall geysers of water in the river.

Other Yankee missiles were obliterating about half of the wooden quarters of the garrison and setting them on fire, along with the troops' overcoats and blankets, and casks of tar and pitch situated nearby. Clarence Cary watched with humane sympathy as some of the screaming projectiles blasted apart and set afire wooden stables some 200 yards behind his Columbiad Battery, the terrified horses inside breaking free to gallop up and down the interior of the fort. As the animals dashed helter-skelter in wide-eyed fright, flying shrapnel from the heavy iron bolts destroyed them one by one, until all were dead. [87]

Despite his youth, eighteen-year-old Bladen County native George Washington Benson, a private in Company H of Lamb's Thirty-Sixth North Carolina, was assigned to operate one of the landface cannons. He said that the Yankees "had the biggest fleet ever assembled on the Atlantic Coast." Their shells, as Benson later described the battle, "came over in swarms – little shells the size of beer bottles to great bombs the size of wash pots...I fired my six-inch gun. It operated by a friction device. You stood on your toes with your mouth open, otherwise it would knock you silly and jar your teeth out. Guns fired from all over the fort." [88]

One of the first Confederate casualties was a seaman with the naval detachment manning part of the Columbiad Battery. "Early in the day," one of the sailors wrote, "he found his left leg spinning away from him across the sand plain before a bursting shell. Later, other mishaps here and there occurred, and in the afternoon a shell burst in the battery of gun No. 1, which sent a five pound fragment through the shoulder of a sailor, and at the same moment bestowed a crack on the knee to the officer in charge." [89]

One Rebel defender was intrigued by the various types of projectiles hurled at Fisher, that in the estimation of David Porter, were rocketing into the earthworks, sand, and river at the rate of 115 shells per minute. Their explosions sprayed hot, jagged chunks of iron in all directions, blanketing Fort Fisher with a hailstorm of deadly flying metal. "These were of all sorts and sizes," Midshipman Cary recalled, "from the big fifteen-inch spherical shot or shell, and the 100-pounder rifled Parrotts, down through the list, and the whiz or whistle of each variety seemed to strike a different and more vicious note. Occasionally a spherical shell, after it had passed safely by, and was nearly spent, exploded with its base turned towards the battery, the result being to toss its bottom-end back among the unprotected gunners." [90]

Not all casualties and concern were inside the fort. Despite the more than 10 to 1 advantage in ordnance enjoyed by the Federals, Lamb's artillerists were following orders, and firing methodically about every 30 minutes, when they had a Yankee warship sighted in. As Robley Evans could attest, sometimes their aim was precise. The men of the *U.S.S. Mackinaw* discovered it was, too.

In position one mile east of the Northeast Bastion, the *Mackinaw* was firing her guns at Fisher, when "at 2:25 p.m. a 150-pounder rifle shot struck the vessel at the water line," the huge iron bolt boring through the forward bunker and perforating the port boiler, which sprayed scalding steam and water all over the fire room and a nearby gun. Sailors John Smith, James Sullivan, John Kerner, Michael Burns, Thomas McBride, Cornelius Kirby, and Samuel Smith were all burned, John Smith and James Sulllivan being severely scalded. In addition, three Marines manning one of the guns, Paul Lientard, Nicholas Miller, and James McDermott, were scalded by the spraying steam. [91]

Thirty-five minutes later, the *U.S.S. Yantic*, also a mile out and slightly northeast of Fisher, was firing her guns and "doing good execution," according to her commanding officer, T.C. Harris, when at 3 p.m., their 100-pounder Parrott rifle burst. Two sailors were mortally wounded, and three others slightly wounded. Edward Winnemore, acting ensign and officer commanding the division, had his right leg "blown off at the knee" and the lower third of his thigh crushed. James Horton, boatswain's mate and captain of the gun, had his "right foot, leg, and thigh" crushed by the explosion, and both men died before the day ended. Richard Husted, Theodore Vannata and Robert Adelton suffered contusions and burns, but would recover. [92]

At virtually the same time as the unfortunate accident aboard the *Yantic*, another of the 100-pounder Parrotts exploded near the muzzle on the *U.S.S. Quaker City*. According to the log of Commander William F. Spicer, the gun "burst about 4 feet from face, a large piece landing on deck, slightly wounding George F. Locke." [93]

Lamb's artillerists had a hard time seeing their targets. There was a dead calm in the air, the Colonel noted, causing "the smoke to hang around the hulls of the vessels, so enveloping them as to prevent the effect of the shots our gunners were allowed to fire from being seen." Fortunately, the "thousands of shot and shell" hurled at the fort for the first two hours of bombardment had produced no casualties he was aware of, with the possible exception of the sailors in the Columbiad Battery, who may have been wounded about the time the garrison flag was shot down. [94]

Commodore Joseph Lanman, commanding the big frigate, *U.S.S. Minnesota*, one mile out and firing briskly on the Northeast Bastion reported seeing the "rebel flag shot away" at 3:15 p.m.. Lamb saw that the shaft was "so split and shivered" it was useless to attempt to raise another flag on it. He sent word to Captain Daniel Munn, who had fought so ferociously for the blockade runner *Hebe* in August of 1863, to raise the Confederate flag at the Mound Battery.

The halyards on the Mound flagstaff had gotten unreeved, so a volunteer was called for to climb the staff and fasten the flag. Private Christopher Columbus "Kit" Bland, a resident of the small fishing village of Calabash, North Carolina, near the South Carolina line, was nineteen when he enlisted in July of 1864 in Company K of Lamb's Thirty-Sixth North Carolina, serving the big guns at Fort Campbell. Now he stepped forward at Captain Munn's call, and shinnying up the pole as the awesome fleet continued to pour its fire, secured the ensign to the masthead.

"At once a terrific fire was poured on the mound," Lamb observed, "and the lower end of the flag having been cut loose, again, that heroic soldier repeated the daring act, amid the cheers of the garrison, and securely fastened the flag where it floated in triumph." The Colonel watched with admiration as Kit Bland descended the pole for the second time, a nearly fatal shell whizzing past his head to brush his hair. [95]

Even as Lamb watched Bland raise the flag on the Mound, he was running to the extreme left of the leftmost salient, Shepherd's Battery, with a company battle flag. Two hours of naval bombardment had convinced him the armada would concentrate its fire on the fort's flags, and he "wanted to put it where it would do the most good by causing the least harm." [96]

At the same time Fisher's garrison flag was shot down, more United States sailors were dying from their own guns. Captain Charles Steedman, commanding the *U.S.S. Ticonderoga* one mile due east of Lamb's headquarters, sadly reported the killing and wounding of part of his crew. At 3:15 p.m., the *Ticonderoga*'s 100-pounder Parrott, like that of the *Yantic*, exploded into fragments, "wounding Acting Volunteer Lieutenant L.G. Vassallo (at the time coolly sighting the gun) and killing 8 men." Ten other men were wounded in addition to Vassallo. [97]

Nine of the men had been those serving the Parrott rifle, while the other ten had been operating the "No. 1 IX-inch gun." The sailors killed were John Hill, James McCormick, Ludwig Wiltz, Charles Stites, James Duffy, James McMillen, James Ward and William Sinton, a young "Second-class boy." [98]

Despite the gruesome loss, William Shipman, captain of another gun near the Parrott rifle, immediately shouted encouragement to his shipmates to stay at their work. "Go ahead, boys," he screamed amidst the carnage of dismembered bodies and deafening roar of the bombardment, "this is only the fortune of war!" Shipman and his fellow sailors continued loading, firing, swabbing, loading and firing again. [99]

The Confederate naval detachment in Columbiad Battery was enduring the screeching bombardment by "crouching in comparative safety under the sand mounds", during the lulls between firing the Brooke rifles.

During one of those respites, the sailors decided they would all feel better after a good drink of liquor. As one of the men was raising the bottle to take the first swig before passing it around, an exploding Yankee shell blew a piece of shrapnel at the man, literally knocking the bottle out of his hands, and wounding him in the process. The other sailors were not overly sympathetic under the circumstances.

Sometime after the liquor became a casualty, a teenage courier was seen running at full speed in the fort's interior, headed for the Columbiad Battery and cover from the rain of flying metal splinters. "Before the lad reached it, however, an exploding fifteen-inch shell intervened," Clarence Cary wrote, and blew the young fellow to shreds. There was hardly enough left of him "to bury in the little hole they hastily scraped out of the sand for that purpose." [100]

Casualties were mounting, too, aboard the Federal vessels. The *U.S.S. Wabash* was a mile due east of the Northeast Bastion and firing on that position. During the engagement that afternoon, Peter Campbell received a severe wound to the left shoulder, and William Howard a severe wound to the right thigh, from incoming shellfire from the fort. Three other sailors were slightly wounded. [101]

Still another 100-pounder Parrott exploded aboard the *U.S.S. Juniata*. Naval Lieutenant D.D. Wemple died when he was eviscerated and had both legs pulverized by the blast. Marine Second Lieutenant Jones Pile died from wounds to the head, left arm, and shoulder, and his mangled corpse was catapulted overboard by the explosion. Theodore Abos and Henry Payne had extensive bone fractures and abdominal wounds that caused their deaths from blood loss and shock, and young James Ennels, a "first-class boy," died after his shattered left leg and thigh were amputated. Eight other crewmen were wounded, some severely. [102]

Watching the bombardment with "very powerful glasses" from Orton Plantation across the river, Daisy Lamb wrote her parents that it was "an awful but magnificent sight." Despite her Rhode Island upbringing, she remained Rebel to the core since coming to Fort Fisher. "I kept up very bravely," she said, "(for you know I am brave, and would, if I thought I could, whip Porter and Butler myself), until the last gun had ceased and it began to get dark and still." During the afternoon, "in the midst of the roaring and awful thundering," her little boy Dick came to her with a touching request. " 'Mamma, I want to pray to God for my papa'. He knelt down and said his little earnest prayer; then jumped up, exclaiming and dancing about; 'Oh, sister, I am so glad! I am so glad! Now God will keep care of my papa'." [103]

Lieutenant Commander William G. Temple was in command of the *U.S.S. Pontoosuc*, one mile northeast of the landface of the fort and firing his IX-inch guns directly at Shepherd's Battery on the far left, near the Cape Fear. In midafternoon, a shell from a 6-1/2 inch rifled gun, possibly one operated by

George Benson, came screaming through the side of the *Pontoosuc*, punched "through the iron bulkhead of the engine room and the starboard steerage and mess lockers," bored through the berth deck, and penetrated "the paymaster's store room, where it exploded," very near the bulkhead of the shell room, setting the ship on fire. Fortunately, the crew was able to bring the fire under control, no serious damage was done, and no one was hurt, in what could easily have been a fatal shot for the *Pontoosuc*. [104]

The big frigate *U.S.S. Colorado*, one mile out and hurling nearly 1,600 projectiles that afternoon at the Northeast Bastion, was hit at least four times by shells from Fisher. Shots were received in the gangway area, bow, masts and deck planks, according to Commodore H.K. Thatcher's report. No serious damages were sustained, but sailor Edmund Prebel was slightly wounded. [105]

Though casualties were not heavy inside Fisher, some were naturally sustained as the afternoon wore on. In addition to the severely wounded Seaman J.F. Higgins, whose leg was shot off early in the engagement, First Sergeant J.M. Benson of Company B, Thirty-Sixth North Carolina, received a concussion and contusion of the brain. Private Benjamin Merritt of Company F, Thirty-Sixth North Carolina, was severely wounded in the left arm, necessitating amputation. Private Charles Cherry, also of Company F, was wounded in both legs, with the right leg having to be amputated. "Up in the bomb-proof," one of Fisher's defenders recalled, "in the angle formed by the meeting of the land and sea faces of the fort, the surgeons were busily at work over the stream of wounded which trickled in to them during the day." [106]

Brigadier General William W. Kirkland's Brigade, the lead unit of Robert Hoke's Division, had arrived in Wilmington at midnight of the 23rd. Thirty-one years old, Kirkland was a native of Hillsboro, North Carolina, and had been a Marine Corps Second Lieutenant in the days before the war. A highly skilled and thrice-wounded combat veteran of the Army of Northern Virginia, he also had the distinction of serving as chief of staff to General Patrick R. Cleburne of the Army of Tennessee, during the bloody battle of Murfreesboro, Tennessee, December 1862 and January 1863. [107]

About 1,300 effective troops were in Kirkland's Brigade, consisting of the Seventeenth, Forty-Second and 100 men of the Sixty-Sixth North Carolina infantry regiments. Resting the brigade in town for the night, by daybreak of the 24th Kirkland had his men hustling south from Wilmington, headed for Sugar Loaf. Riding in advance, Kirkland arrived there about 1 p.m., shortly after Porter's fleet had commenced bombarding Fort Fisher. He found Colonel J.K, Connally with "1,200 men of the Junior and Senior Reserves; Lieutenant Colonel John P. Read, of the artillery, with Southerland's battery, a Whitworth of Paris' battery, and 32-pounder gun in position at Battery Gatlin." Kirkland assumed command over all the troops there, and his own command finally arrived at 4:30 p.m. [108]

Riding down to the beach after his arrival, he had observed the "large fleet of heavy steam frigates, corvettes, gun-boats, ironclads, and transports in line of battle stretching from opposite Gatlin to Fisher." Colonel Connally had placed a company in the fortifications near Gatlin as support for the "artillery near Burriss' house and a corporal with gun detachment to work the 32-pounder in Gatlin." Burriss' house was between the newly extended Sugar Loaf earthworks and the south end of Myrtle Grove Sound.

When Kirkland's Brigade came up, he dispatched Major David S. Davis of the Sixty-Sixth North Carolina to the earthworks near Battery Gatlin and Burris' house "to prevent a landing there." The Forty-Second North Carolina was hurried down to fortifications about a mile south, that were the "prolongation of the sea front of the Sugar Loaf works," and Colonel John E. Brown, commanding the regiment, was ordered to intrench, and "if possible to stretch his line to Burris' to connect with Major Davis." Company A of the Forty-Second, with about 80 men under Captain Jacob H. Koonts, was ordered down to Battery Anderson "to repel the enemy if they attempted to land there." The Seventeenth North Carolina, Lieutenant Colonel Thomas H. Sharp commanding, "was directed to go down the road toward Fisher and Anderson and support Koonts." [109]

Shortly after posting Sharp and the Seventeenth, Kirkland received "an order from Major General Whiting to send the Junior Reserves and 500 men of my brigade into Fort Fisher. I sent the former and the Seventeenth Regiment." Whiting had come down from Wilmington and arrived in the fort about 4:30 p.m., during the thickest of the action. With only 900 men in the fort at the time, he knew more would be needed for the Yankee infantry assault that was bound to come. [110]

Whiting had been given no assignment by Braxton Bragg, though it should have been his right and duty to "have commanded the supporting troops" he had been calling for since November of 1862. He determined to go to Fisher and share its fate with Lamb and his men. Upon his arrival, the colonel offered to relinquish command, but Whiting declined to "take away the glory of the defence from the brave Lamb, but declared he would counsel him, and fight as a volunteer." [111]

Whiting's Chief of Ordnance, Major Benjamin Sloan, said that Whiting's troops "almost worshipped him," due to his kindness and unselfishness. His refusal to assume command of Fort Fisher from Lamb, which he had every right to do as his superior, was evidence of that. His coolness and bravery under fire, some would call recklessness, inspired his men. First Lieutenant Exum L. Hunter of Halifax County, like his captain, Samuel B. Hunter of Company F in the Thirty-Sixth North Carolina, was with his artillerists in the Northeast Bastion of Fisher. He saw General Whiting strolling on the rampart of their position while smoking his pipe, observing the

Yankee ships and bombardment, as shells screamed in and exploded all around.

"I saw him stand with folded arms," Hunter said, "smiling upon a four hundred pound shell, as it stood smoking and spinning like a billiard ball on the sand, not twenty feet away, until it burst, and then move quietly away...I saw him fight, and saw him pray, and he was all that a general should be in battle. He was the best equipped man in the Confederate States to defend the port of Wilmington, and his relief by Bragg brought gloom over the entire command." [112]

One mile out, and slightly southeast of Fisher's hospital bombproof, the *U.S.S. Osceola* was firing briskly on the fort's seaface batteries. At 4:50 p.m., shortly after Whiting's arrival in the fort, the ship "received a X-inch solid shot about 3 feet below the water line, which passed through the side – through the sandbags placed to protect the boiler, and into the starboard boiler, passing into No. 4 furnace." Six men were scalded from the steam spewing from the boiler, two of them severely. The ship continued firing on the fort until the incoming seawater nearly reached the fires, when Commander J.M.B. Clitz decided to "move out of line and made signal 'Disabled'." Water was "gaining very rapidly, extinguishing the fires underneath the port boiler," when Clitz signaled that the ship was in a sinking condition. Reaching the outer line of reserve vessels, he had a boat lowered, and crewmen were able to partially stop the leak. [113]

At 5:10 p.m., the *U.S.S. Quaker City*, that had suffered a muzzle burst of its 100-pounder Parrott two hours before, received a shot from the Mound Battery. Though it did no significant damage, the shell hit the vessel on its starboard bow and penetrated the planking. At 5:30, Porter's fleet ceased firing, and moved off for the night to a "safe anchorage." About the same time, Ben Butler arrived from Beaufort with a few of his army transports, the rest of which would be down by morning, Christmas Day, for landing of the troops. [114]

With his penchant for stretching the truth to his own advantage, Porter wrote to Gideon Welles that within an hour and fifteen minutes after the fleet had commenced its bombardment of Fisher, "not a shot came from the fort." He said "such a torrent of missiles were falling into and bursting over it that it was impossible for anything human to stand it. Finding that the batteries were silenced completely, I directed the ships to keep up a moderate fire in hopes of attracting the attention of the transports and bringing them in. At sunset General Butler came in in his flagship with a few transports, the rest not having arrived from Beaufort." [115]

William Lamb was surprised the fleet had not attempted to cross the bar, run past the fort's guns, and move into the Cape Fear to take Fisher in reverse. Lamb did "not regard the battle as seriously begun until the American navy, with its accustomed dash attempted the passage of the fort." This was the primary reason he had rigidly ordered his men to fire no more than every thirty minutes, to conserve the maximum amount of ammunition to resist the expected crossing of the bar. During the afternoon, his artillerists had fired only 672 shot and shell, in response to at least 10,000 thrown at them. "It was this deliberation," Lamb said, "which gave the fleet the false idea that they had silenced our guns, and the fact that on this day I took care to fire the last shot as they were withdrawing, did not disabuse their minds of this erroneous idea." [116]

According to General Whiting, Lamb's men "served their guns with great deliberation and coolness" that day, and he was justly proud of them and their young commander. A total of only 23 men had been wounded, one of them mortally, despite the intensity of the bombardment. The Yankees had "destroyed about one-half of the garrison's quarters, disabled 3 gun carriages, tore up large quantities of the earth-works, splintered some of the revetments, but did not injure a single bomb-proof or endanger any magazine. The greatest penetration noticed" of any of the naval shells "was not over five feet perpendicularly." [117]

Blowhard though he was, Porter must have been aware, as Whiting and Lamb were, of the minimal damage inflicted on the fort, otherwise he would not have been so reluctant to press what he claimed was a decided advantage. As evidence, Ben Butler asked General Weitzel and Colonel Comstock "to urge upon Admiral Porter to run by the fort into Cape Fear River." Porter, though, said he could not do it "because there was not enough water," meaning his vessels had too deep a draft for New Inlet. This statement was absurd, as four of the gunboats were captured blockade runners. These ships had often steamed past Fort Fisher, such as the famous *U.S.S. Ad-Vance*, formerly the pride of North Carolina's war governor. "Yet Porter reported," Ben Butler later wrote, "that the navy could not run in there because they had no light draft vessels." [118]

Butler further recalled that even Admiral Farragut "had never taken a fort except by running by and cutting it off from all prospect of re-enforcement (as at Fort Jackson and Fort Morgan), and that no casemated fort had been silenced by naval fire during the war." Porter broached an additional caveat "that he should probably lose a boat by torpedoes if he attempted to run by. He was reminded that the army might lose 500 men by the assault, and that his boat would not weigh in the balance even in a money point of view for a moment with the lives of the men." Porter would not budge, however, contradicting with inaction, his boasts of the silencing of Fort Fisher's guns. [119]

Wilmingtonians were acutely aware of the Christmas Eve attack on Confederate Point. The roar of artillery easily carried the twenty miles upriver, lending a somber backdrop of thunder and worry to normal routines. Joe King, the teenager whom Colonel Lamb had ordered to stay away from the fort during the 1862 yellow fever epidemic, and who had nearly died from it, said that there "was at this time a good deal of confusion and consternation among the people in this city...In the last days of 1864, we could distinctly hear, day and night, the roar of cannons bombarding Fort Fisher. I remember my sweetheart Eliza J. King and I as waiters (wedding attendants), at the wedding of Joe Daymon and Senie Hobbs, that during the ceremony, we could hear the constant booming of cannons from that fort. The next morning Daymon was summoned to appear at the fort." [120]

At 6 p.m., thirty minutes after Porter's fleet withdrew, Colonel Lamb sent a dispatch to Wilmington, advising the results of the day's battle. "The enemy's fleet," he wrote, "consisting of over 50 vessels, including 2 monitors, several armed vessels, and a large proportion of heavily armed frigates and sloops of war, commenced a furious bombardment of Fort Fisher at 20 minutes to one o'clock, which they kept up until 5 1/2 P.M., when they withdrew. No part of the work was greatly injured. Casualties 23 wounded, one mortally, 3 severely, 19 slightly.

"The officers, soldiers and seamen, all did their whole duty. As the enemy attempted no passage of the bar and staid out at long range – with the exception of the ironclads – I fired very slowly and deliberately. I am unable to know what damage was done them, but I am certain the injury inflicted upon them far exceeds the injury their bombardment did us. Our Heavenly Father has protected my garrison this day, and I feel that he will sustain us in defending our homes from the invaders." [121]

Endnotes to Chapter 8

1. O.R., Volume XLII, Part II, p.1206-1207, p.1235; Schiller, Herbert M., M.D., *The Bermuda Hundred Campaign, "Operations on the South Side of the James River, Virginia, May, 1864"*, p.275-283, Morningside House Inc., Dayton, Ohio, 1988, hereinafter Bermuda Hundred Campaign

2. O.R., Volume XXXVI, Part II, p.256-257; Bermuda Hundred Campaign, p.275-276

3. Bermuda Hundred Campaign, p.276-285

4. Battles & Leaders, Volume I, p.219-226

5. O.R., Volume XLII, Part III, p.1149

6. Sword, Wiley, *Shiloh, Bloody April*, p.234-307, Morningside House Inc., Dayton, Ohio, 1983; Battles & Leaders, Volume III, p.1-25

7. Cozzens, Peter, *No Better Place to Die, The Battle of Stones River*, p.109-143, p.177-218, University of Illinois Press, Urbana and Chicago, 1990

8. Tucker, Glenn, *Chickamauga, Bloody Battle in the West*, p.376-393, Morningside House Inc., Dayton, Ohio, 1984

9. Cozzens, Peter, *The Shipwreck of Their Hopes, The Battles for Chattanooga*, p.320-369, p.385-398, University of Illinois Press, Urbana and Chicago, 1994

10. Chronicles, p.491-492; Noe, Kenneth W., *Perryville, This Grand Havoc of Battle*, p.17, University Press of Kentucky, Lexington, 2001

11. Daily Journal, October 31, 1864

12 O.R., Volume XLII, Part III, p.1171-1172

13. Diary of Willliam Lamb, October 24, 1864, hereinafter Lamb Diary; O.R., Volume XLII, Part III, p.1172

14. Lamb, William, "Fort Fisher – The Battles Fought There in 1864 and '65", Southern Historical Society Papers, Volume XXI, p.266, hereinafter SHSP

15. Ibid, Volume XXI, p.266

16. Denson, C.B., *An Address Containing a Memoir of the Late Major-General William Henry Chase Whiting*, p.37, Edwards & Broughton Printing Company, Raleigh, North Carolina, 1895

17. SHSP, Volume XXI, p.263, p.266; Lamb Diary, October 26-27, 1864

18. O.R., Volume XLII, Part III, p.1203-1204

19. Ibid, Volume XLII, Part III, p.1204; SHSP, Volume XXI, p.262

20. Ibid, Volume XLII, Part III, p.1204; SHSP, Volume XXI, p.262

21. SHSP, Volume XXI, p.266

22. Gragg, Rod, *Confederate Goliath, The Battle of Fort Fisher*, p.31, Harper Collins Publishers, New York, 1991, hereinafter Confederate Goliath; Bearss, Edwin, *The Campaign for Vicksburg, Volume I – Vicksburg is the Key*, p.479, Morningside House Inc., Dayton, Ohio, 1985

23. Porter, David D., *The Naval History of the Civil War*, p.684, Sherman Publishing Company, New York, 1886, hereinafter Porter Naval History

24. Porter Naval History, p.684

25. Price, Charles and Sturgill, Claude, "Shock and Assault in the First Battle of Fort Fisher", *The North Carolina Historical Review*, 1970, p.26, Raleigh, hereinafter Shock and Assault; Confederate Goliath, p.35; Grant, U.S. *Personal Memoirs of U.S. Grant,* p.485, World Publishing Company, Cleveland, Ohio, 1952, hereinafter Memoirs of Grant

26. Butler, Benjamin F., *Butler's Book*, p.774, A.M. Thayer & Co., Boston, 1892, hereinafter Butler's Book; Moore, Mark A., *Moore's Historical Guide to The Wilmington Campaign and the Battles for Fort Fisher*, p.14-15, Savas Publishing Company, Mason City, Iowa, 1999, hereinafter The Wilmington Campaign; Confederate Goliath, p.37-39

27. Butler's Book, p.775-776; Reed, Rowena, *Combined Operations in the Civil War*, p.435, Naval Institute Press, Annapolis, Maryland, 1978, hereinafter Combined Operations; ORN, Volume XI, p.68, p.79

28. Butler's Book, p.775; ORN, Volume XI, p.68, p.213

29. ORN, Volume XI, p.210; Shock and Assault, p.30; Warner, Generals in Blue, p.117-118

30. ORN, Volume XI, p.222-223

31. Ibid, Volume XI, p.79; Shock and Assault, p.30-31

32. Shock and Assault, p.30-31

33. William Lamb Diary, November 3 and 6, 1864; The Wilmington Campaign, p.22

34. SHSP, Volume X, p.352

35. SHSP, Volume X, p.352

36. Ibid, Volume X, p.352; The Wilmington Campaign, p.22; Lamb Diary, December 17, 1864

37. Ibid, Volume X, p.352

38. Ibid, Volume X, p.352-353; Combined Operations, p.269, p.275, p.296; O.R., Volume XLII, Part I, p.986

39. Lamb Diary, November 9, 1864

40. O.R., Volume XLII, Part III, p.1214

41. O.R., Volume XLII, Part III, p.1215

42. O.R., Volume XLII, Part III, p.1225; Warner, General in Gray, p.124; Scaife, William R., *The March to the Sea*, p.19, McNaughton & Gunn Inc., Saline, Michigan, 1993

43. Clark, Volume II, p.634-635, p.756-757; SHSP, Volume XXI, p.267; Lamb Diary, November 22, 1864

44. SHSP, Volume XXI, p.266

45. SHSP, Volume XXI, p.265-266; Lamb Diary, November 24, 1864; NC Troops, Volume I, p.255, p.576-577

46. Lamb Diary, November 24, 1864; SHSP, Volume XXI, p.265

47. Lamb Diary, November 24, 1864

48. Clark, Volume II, p.634

49. Lamb Diary, December 11, 1864

50. Butler's Book, p.780, Appendix p.63; O.R., Volume XLVI, Part I, p.41

51. O.R., Volume XLVI, Part I, p.41; O.R., Series IV, Volume III, p.953-958

52. O.R., Series IV, Volume III, p.955-958; Porter Naval History, p.685-686

53. O.R., Volume XLII, Part I, p.985; Butler's Book, p.781, Appendix p.63; Generals in Blue, p.5-6

54. Confederate Goliath, p.36; Generals in Blue, p.354-355

55. O.R., Volume XLII, Part I, p.966-967, p.985; Butler's Book, p.785-787

56. Longacre, Edward G. editor, *From Antietam to Fort Fisher: The Civil War Letters of Edward K. Wightman, 1862-1865*, p.16, p.220, p.235, Associated University Presses, Cranbury, New Jersey, 1985, hereinafter Antietam to Fort Fisher

57. Antietam to Fort Fisher, p.220

58. Antietam to Fort Fisher, p.220-221

59. Butler's Book, p.787; ORN, Volume 11, p.224, p.230

60. ORN, Volume 11, p.224

61. Sumner, Merlin E., editor, *The Diary of Cyrus B. Comstock*, p.5-6, p.298, Morningside House Inc., 1987, hereinafter Comstock Diary; Butler's Book, p.788, Appendix p.68

62. Comstock Diary, p.298
63. Lamb Diary, December 20, 1864
64. O.R., Volume XLII, Part I, p.965; Butler's Book, p.789
65. O.R., Volume XLII, Part III, p.1278-1281; Clark, Volume III, p.691-692
66. Hagood, Johnson, *Memoirs of the War of Secession*, p.315-317, The State Company, Columbia, South Carolina, 1910, hereinafter War of Secession; The Wilmington Campaign, p.27
67. Clark, Volume III, p.692
68. Lamb Diary, December 21, 1864; O.R., Volume XLII, Part III, p.1255-1256; ORN, Volume 11, p.373-374; Scharf, p.422
69. The Wilmington Campaign, p.33
70. ORN, Volume 11, p.225; Butler's Book, p.790; Shock and Assault, p.33
71. Shock and Assault, p.34-35; ORN, Volume e11, p.226-227; O.R., Volume XLII, Part I, p.979
72. Shock and Assault, p.35; ORN, Volume 11, p.226-227
73. Gragg, Rod, "Fort Fisher: The Confederate Goliath, 1862-1864", p.109, Master's Thesis, University of South Carolina, Columbia, 1979; Clark, Volume IV, p.38, p.46-47; SHSP, Volume XXI, p.268-269
74. SHSP, Volume XXI, p.269
75. Shock and Assault, p.36
76. Daily Journal, January 6, 1865
77. ORN, Volume 11, p.230; O.R., Volume XLII, Part I, p.979
78. ORN, Volume 11, p.263
79. SHSP, Volume XXI, p.269-270
80. Ibid, Volume XXI, p.270
81. ORN, Volume 11, p.275-278; SHSP, Volume XXI, p.270
82. O.R., Volume XLII, Part I, p.1015; N.C. Troops, Volume I, p.257; The Wilmington Campaign, p.21, p.30-31
83. O.R., Volume XLII, Part I, p.1015; SHSP, Volume XXI, p.270
84. Battles & Leaders, Volume IV, p.657
85. Scharf, p.424
86. Evans, Robley D., *A Sailor's Log: Recollections of Forty Years of Naval Life*, p.1-9, p.60, p.75, p.80, D. Appleton Company, New York, 1901, hereinafter Sailor's Log; ORN, Volume 11, p.306
87. The Wilmington Campaign, p.12, p.30; SHSP, Volume XXI, p.270-271; O.R., Volume XLII, Part I, p.1004; Scharf, p.424-425
88. "Charlotte News", Charlotte, North Carolina, January 15, 1944; N.C. Troops, Volume I, p.290-291; The Wilmington Campaign, p.30-31
89. Scharf, p.424
90. Scharf, p.424; ORN, Volume 11, p.256
91. ORN, Volume 11, map p.245, p.319
92. ORN, Volume 11, p.312-313

93. Ibid, Volume 11, p.331
94. SHSP, Volume XXI, p.270-271
95. SHSP, Volume XXI, p.271; ORN, Volume 11, p.298; Ashe, History of North Carolina, p.940; N.C. Troops, Volume I, p.325, p.327
96. SHSP, Volume XXI, p.271; The Wilmington Campaign, p.30-31
97. ORN, Volume 11, map p.245, p.328-329
98. ORN, Volume 11, p.329
99. ORN, Volume 11, p.328
100. Scharf, p.424
101. ORN, Volume 11, p.308
102. ORN, Volume 11, p.322
103. Letters from the Colonel's Lady, p.84-85
104. ORN, Volume 11, map p.245, p.285-286
105. Ibid, map p.245, p.293-296
106. Lamb Diary, December 24, 1864; N.C. Troops, Volume I, p.259, p.265; Scharf, p.424-425
107. O.R., Volume XLII, Part I, p.1020; Generals in Gray, p.171-172
108. O.R., Volume XLII, Part I, p.1020-1021, p.1023, p.1026
109. O.R., Volume XLII, Part I, p.1020-1021; Clark, Volume II, p.2; Clark, Volume III, p.689; N.C. Troops, Volume X, p.190, p.194; The Wilmington Campaign, p.22-23
110. O.R., Volume XLII, Part I, p.1021; The Wilmington Campaign, p.23, p.33; Lamb Diary, December 24, 1864
111. SHSP, Volume XXVI, p.163
112. SHSP, Volume XXVI, p.164; Chronicles, p.484; N.C. Troops, Volume I, p.257; The Wilmington Campaign, p.30-31
113. ORN, Volume 11, map p.245, p.336-337
114. ORN, Volume 11, p.256, p.331; SHSP, Volume XXI, p.271
115. ORN, Volume 11, p.256
116. SHSP, Volume XXI, p.271-272
117. O.R., Volume XLII, Part I, p.994, p.1004
118. Butler's Book, p.791
119. O.R., Volume XLII, Part I, p.967
120. Recollections of Joseph P. King
121. Daily Journal, December 27, 1864

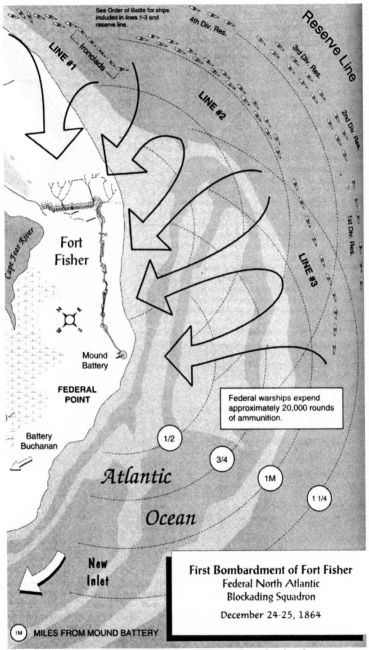

Map courtesy of Mark A. Moore, from his book
The Wilmington Campaign and the Battles for Fort Fisher

Chapter 9

"I am not going to evacuate... this place so long as a man is left to stand to his gun."

General Whiting estimated, as did Colonel Lamb, that about 10,000 projectiles had been hurled at Fort Fisher the afternoon of Christmas Eve. He asserted that the "rapidity and weight of fire was extraordinary," but noted that the fleet's rate of fire was 40 to 50 shells per minute, and not the 115 each minute as David Porter related. To help repel potential infantry attacks during the night, Whiting ordered Kirkland to send about 500 reinforcements from the Seventeenth North Carolina into the fort. The garrison made preparations for the action that was to come on Christmas Day. [1]

Edward Wightman of the Third New York scanned the horizon toward Fort Fisher from aboard the transport steamer *Weybosset*. He wrote that December 25th dawned with a cloudy sky and tranquil sea, "disturbed only by a gentle swell." The soft quiet of the morning contrasted starkly with the man-made thunder of the previous day. "There was no wind blowing, and the beach was only three miles distant. Everything seemed to favor our enterprise, and the troops, who had been eighteen days embarked (long enough to visit Europe and return) were eager to land." [2]

About 10 a.m., "the fleet advanced again in single line toward the fort, led by the *Ironsides*," noted William Lamb. About 10:30, the naval vessels, with the addition of another ironclad, the *U.S.S. Saugus*, which arrived during the night, and several more wooden steamers, "recommenced an incessant bombardment, if possible more noisy and furious than that of the preceding day." [3]

General Kirkland also observed warships moving into position to shell the woods and beach near Battery Gatlin, and noted that transports were with them as well. He was convinced "that a landing would be attempted at Gatlin." He directed Lieutenant Colonel John Read, in charge of the artillery at and near Gatlin, "to put his guns in position and annoy them as much as he could. A furious bombardment against Fisher and along the beach from that fort to Gatlin was now commenced." [4]

Alfred M. Waddell was attending Sunday worship service at St. James Episcopal Church in Wilmington that morning. A large congregation was assembled, comprised mostly of women in mourning for dead soldiers, whose facial expressions spoke of worry and anxiety for the men on Confederate Point, many of whom were relatives and friends.

Waddell said that the "thunder of the guns, distinctly audible and shaking the atmosphere like jelly, had been irregular until the Litany was read, when from the beginning of that solemn service to its conclusion almost simultaneously the responses of the congregation and the roar of broadsides united. 'From battle and murder, and from sudden death,' read the minister, 'Good Lord, deliver us,' prayed the congregation, and, simultaneously 'Boom – boom – boom,' answered the guns until the situation was almost intolerable. It was an experience never to be forgotten." [5]

Midshipman Clarence Cary, continuing to man one of the naval guns in the Columbiad Battery, recalled the "same hammering from the ships, and the same sullen and slow response from the fort, characterized the proceedings of the second day's work during the morning hours." Sometime after noon, the Confederate naval detachment received its first casualties of the day. The men "were engaged in firing gun No. 1, and just as a shell burst over the battery, severely wounding Lieut. Dornin of the navy, who was standing near, the piece itself exploded with terrific force. This heavy gun, weighing about 15,000 pounds," blew apart in several directions. "When the officers at the rear struggled to their feet...and whether they were knocked down by concussion or astonishment they never knew...a strange sight presented itself."

Clarence Cary observed that one man was lying dead, "with his arms stretched out toward them and his skull blown off, while another appeared twisted in a knot over a piece of iron band lapped across his stomach. Others were more or less hurt, and one man was leaping about the battery like a lunatic, crying out that he was on fire. He could scarcely be comforted, even when on stripping off his shirt he was found only to be tattooed by grains of powder and sand blown into his back and shoulders." An hour and a half later, the second gun in the Columbiad battery exploded, injuring some of the crew, but no one was killed. [6]

The bombardment of the fleet was terrific. As Edward Wightman watched the cannonade from his vantage point just off the coast, he could not imagine anything worse. "The belching of a volcano with accompanying explosions may suggest a corresponding idea. The din was deafening. Above the fort the countless flashes and puffs of smoke from bursting shells spoke for the accuracy of our guns while occasionally columns of sand heaved high in the air suggested that possibly the casements were not so safe and cozy after all. 'I'd rather Johnny'd be where them eggs is breaking than me,' was the sententious remark of a philosophic who stood with his hands in his pockets on the deck of the *Weybosset*." The soldier's comrades rolled their chewing tobacco in their mouths, and responded together, "Them's my sentiments." [7]

Lamb ordered his men to fire even slower and more deliberately Christmas Day than on the day before. "The temptation to concentrate the whole of the available fire of the fort on a single frigate and drive her out and destroy her was very great," he said, "as I found that the garrison were disappointed at having no such trophy for the first day's engagement, but I had a limited supply of ammunition and did not know when it could be replenished." On Christmas Eve he had shot away almost one-sixth of his ammunition, trying to keep the mens' morale up by permitting an occasional shot at the Yankees. Not knowing the duration of the fleet's attack, or when the Federal army would attempt its land assault, the young colonel was forced to conserve his munitions. [8]

Despite that conservation, Fort Fisher's gunners still scored hits on the Union vessels. The big frigate *Minnesota*, one mile out and northeast of Lamb's headquarters at the Pulpit, was struck by a shell below the water line shortly after one p.m. Later, she was hit amidships. The *Juniata*, which had lost so heavily on Christmas Eve from the bursting of the 100-pounder Parrott rifle, was hit again on the 25th. A shell slammed into the side of the vessel on the berth deck, spraying splinters and wounding William Gillam, a coal heaver, David Conner, captain's cook, and George H. Carpenter, a landsman. The surgeon, Albert Gorgas, reported that all the wounds were slight and the men were "likely to do well." [9]

The big warship *Wabash*, which carried forty-six heavy guns, or almost the same number as were in Fort Fisher itself, commenced firing on the Rebels at 1:50 p.m., according to Captain Melancton Smith. He soon discovered that Lamb's artillerists were "making severe practice on the ship, and therefore gradually increased the number of guns in use until entire starboard battery was engaged deliberately and accurately." Three men were wounded as a result of shellfire, John Farley, a landsman, Peter Carberry, ordinary seaman, and James Collins, seaman. [10]

The *U.S.S. Mackinaw* began its firing on the Mound Battery at 12:40 p.m.. An hour later, its "after 100-pounder Parrott rifle burst, instantly killing Acting Ensign John S. Griscom, officer of the gun." Severely wounded was Joseph

Heard, an ordinary seaman and captain of the gun. The *Mackinaw* later dispatched three boats equipped with grapnels for the purpose of dragging for torpedoes. [11]

Approaching 2 p.m., Confederates several miles up the beach from Fort Fisher spied Federal army transports lowering yawls and gigs to begin the landing of infantry. Brevet Brigadier General Newton Martin Curtis, a handsome 29-year-old New Yorker sporting a long, thick full beard, had been badly wounded in action during the Peninsular Campaign in May 1862. As regimental commander of the One Hundred Forty-Second New York Infantry, he was temporary commander now of the First Brigade of Adelbert Ames' Second Division, Twenty-Fourth Army Corps. He was also commanding officer of 450 men of the One Hundred Forty-Second New York and 50 more of the One Hundred Twelfth New York, as their cutters and gigs plowed their way through the salt spray and breakers, headed for the beach on Confederate Point, some three and one half miles north of Fisher, halfway between Battery Gatlin and Battery Anderson. [12]

Sergeant Ed Wightman, observing the amphibious landing from aboard the *Weybosset*, saw that "five hundred men, Brg. Gen. Curtis commanding our brigade, were making for the beach in yawl boats, arranged in line of battle. We watched them anxiously. Before they touched shore, the men were over the sides of the boats waist deep in water and were actually deploying at skirmishing and advancing at a double quick ere they had reached dry land. A rousing cheer – a stentorian Christmas cheer – went up from the whole fleet." [13]

Curtis' men "effected a landing about 2 p.m. on the beach...without any opposition from the enemy", he reported. His statement of landing unopposed underscored the fears of many Confederates two months before, that the unresourceful Braxton Bragg, once combat operations commenced, would be remiss in his defense of Wilmington. Curtis first deployed one company of the One Hundred Forty-Second New York to his right, "as a protection to my rear," sent another company of the same regiment fronting toward Fort Fisher, and began to move down the beach. A Federal soldier aboard ship described his advancing comrades as running "with their heels toward us and their front to the enemy while, more rapidly than I can write, a solid line of battle formed close behind and followed on." [14]

Confederate General Kirkland was reconnoitering the advanced earthworks near Battery Anderson as Curtis' troops were hitting the beach. Late Christmas Eve, he had sent Captain Jacob Koonts of Davidson County, with about 80 men in his Company A of the Forty-Second North Carolina, to Anderson "with orders to repel the enemy if they attempted to land there." As the Yankee fleet was pummeling Rebel positions, Koonts' North Carolinians received their fair share of the pounding.

Lieutenant Samuel Huse of the *U.S.S. Britannia*, reported that his vessel was anchored just 250 yards off the beach, directly opposite "Flag Pond Hill battery," as the Federals called Anderson, and was firing point-blank at the battery and the soldiers. "I opened and continued a rapid fire with 24-pounder howitzers," he wrote. Just as Martin Curtis' first boatload of Federal infantry hit the shore, three-fourths of a mile north of Anderson, Koonts' troops began waving a white flag of surrender. Huse immediately ordered firing to cease, dispatched Acting Ensign W.H. Bryant with a boat of sailors to take possession, and shortly after 2:30 p.m., the Stars and Stripes were flying over Battery Anderson to the accompaniment of "a deafening cheer from the fleet" as the Union ensign was raised. Between 70 and 80 Confederates, including Captain Koonts, were taken prisoner and sent aboard the *Santiago de Cuba*, to be taken to prison camps up North. General Curtis wrote that when he and his men arrived

Gen. Newton M. Curtis, U.S. Army

at Anderson, "I found it in full possession of the navy." [15]

Accompanying William Kirkland in scouting the battleground between the fortified lines and the beach, was his 24-year-old Assistant Adjutant General, Captain Charles G. Elliott of Elizabeth City, North Carolina. Elliott also happened to be the builder of the Confederate ironclad *C.S.S. Albemarle.* Successful in helping the Rebels recapture Plymouth, North Carolina in the spring, the *Albemarle* had been sunk in a raid in October 1864 by none other than William B. Cushing, current commander of the *U.S.S. Malvern*, the flagship of David Porter.

Some of the troops assigned to Kirkland were Senior Reserves 45 to 50 years old, and Elliott thought it was sad that men their age had to endure the trials of combat. "It was pitiful," he wrote, "to see some of those gray-haired patriots dead in the woods, killed by shells from the fleet. Among those who carried a musket there was Mr. William Pettigrew, brother of the heroic General," who had died in the Gettysburg Campaign.

Federal reinforcements in the Second Brigade of Adelbert Ames' divison were hitting the beach as Curtis' troops were moving south on Battery Anderson. When it became clear the Yankees had indeed landed, Kirkland ordered the Seventeenth and Forty-Second North Carolina Troops "forward to the edge of the woods which skirted the shore and deployed both regiments as skirmishers." [16]

Coming up with his men near Battery Anderson after Koonts' company surrendered, Kirkland deployed Captain Thomas J. Norman's Company G of the Seventeenth North Carolina as skirmishers, and ordered Colonel Thomas H. Sharp to move up the rest of his regiment and attack the

Yankees under Ames deploying on the beach. Upon closer examination, Kirkland realized many more Federals were in his front than he had first thought, so he was forced to deploy Sharp's entire regiment as skirmishers. "Even with this extended order of battle," Kirkland reported, "there was an interval of at least a mile between the Seventeenth and Forty-second Regiments. As well as I could judge, I considered the force now on the beach at least three brigades, and others landing all the while. As soon as Sharp's line was deployed I ordered the advance."

Norman's company was in advance and soon came upon the Yankees. His men fired several volleys, and some Federals were seen to fall. "Sharp pressed close upon and drove their skirmish line back upon their main body, which was covered by the guns of at least thirty men of war lying broadside to the beach. It would have been madness to have advanced farther," and Kirkland was fearful the enemy would land troops at Gatlin and secure the Wilmington road, which was guarded by only one infantry regiment, the Sixty-Sixth North Carolina, and several artillery batteries.

Captain Elliott, under Kirkland's orders, "rode down the line and told the men to keep up the fire upon the enemy and cheer as much as they could, but if they were hard pressed to fall back from pine to pine in the direction of Wilmington, and not let the enemy cut us off." [17]

North of the skirmishing between Kirkland's troops and Ames' Federals, Lieutenant Colonel John P.W. Read was in command of the artillery manning Batteries Gatlin and Ramseur, and the Sugar Loaf lines west of there. He had placed several of his guns in "an excellent position almost entirely protected from the enemy's shot and ordered a 6 and 12-pounder Whitworth to open upon the enemy's fleet. The position of these five guns completely commanded Fort Gatlin in the rear as well as the coast and the ford." Despite strong, heavy earthworks, and accurate and powerful guns, Colonel Read was unable to compel his men, mainly New Hanover County boys of the Wilmington Horse Artillery, Company I of the Tenth North Carolina Troops, to stay at their posts and engage the fleet. Many of them were cowed into inaction by the ferocity of the fleet's bombardment. "The 32-pounder at Fort Gatlin never fired a shot, neither am I aware of the 6-pounder Whitworth having been used," the colonel wrote.

Read was soon out of action from shrapnel that cost him his left arm, and his subordinate, Captain Thomas J. Southerland of the Tenth North Carolina, eventually pulled his men back to the Sugar Loaf defenses when he perceived the Yankees were about to outflank him. It was a significant source of regret to Colonel Read. "Experience on former occasions convinces me beyond a doubt," he reported, "that the enemy could have been repulsed with great slaughter, the range being not over 700 or 800 yards and the natural protections almost perfect." [18]

As Curtis and his 500 men moved down the beach past Anderson, headed for William Lamb's fort, they were accompanied by Godfrey Weitzel, whom Grant had actually put in command of the army expedition, but whose authority had been usurped by Butler. The additional troops under Ames, a total of 1800 more, had landed, were skirmishing with Kirkland's Confederates, and fanned out to secure the beachhead, as the generals with their reconnaissance in force moved south toward the main goal. Ames took Bell's Brigade with him and followed Curtis toward Fisher. A party of the One Hundred Forty-Second New York was sent across the narrow peninsula to the Cape Fear, where they found and cut the telegraph wires that ran down the River Road from Wilmington to the fort. Curtis' protective skirmish line now extended across the full width of Confederate Point from the beach to the river, facing north toward Wilmington. [19]

When within about 800 yards of Fort Fisher, Wietzel stopped to study with field glasses the fortifications. He did not like what he saw. "I counted seventeen guns in position bearing up the beach," he reported, "and between each pair of guns there was a traverse so thick and so high above the parapet that I have no doubt they were all bomb-proofs. A stockade ran from the northeast angle of the counterscarps of the work to the water's edge on the seaside. I saw plainly that the work had not been materially injured by the heavy and very accurate shell fire of the navy, and having a distinct and vivid recollection of the bombardment of Fort Jackson, of Vicksburg, of Charleston, and of Fort Wagner, in all of which instances an enormous and well-directed shell fire had done but little damage, and having a distinct and vivid recollection of the two unsuccessful assaults on Fort Wagner, both of which were made under four times more favorable circumstances than those under which we were placed, I returned, as directed, to the major-general commanding; found him on the gun-boat *Chamberlain* within easy range and good view of the work, and frankly reported to him that it would be butchery to order an assault on that work under the circumstances." [20]

Ben Butler was reluctant to order an assault after Weitzel's report, but also reluctant to call off the attack. He asked Colonel Comstock, Grant's engineer, to study the fort himself, and return with his recommendation. [21]

While the Union infantry was skirmishing and moving south down Confederate Point, Porter's fleet continued pounding Fort Fisher and the woods and fortifications north of there. Additionally, Lieutenant Commander William B. Cushing was ordered by Porter "to sound and buoy out a channel, if he could find one," while Commander John Guest, commanding the *U.S.S. Iosco*, was to "drag for torpedoes and be ready to run in by the buoys when ordered."

Cushing's soundings determined that a "narrow and crooked channel was partly made out and buoyed, but running so close to the upper forts that boats could not work there." William Lamb reported that "a heavy fire was...directed against them and they were promptly driven out." [22]

Shortly after, additional boats were dispatched to "sound the Carolina shoals, south of the mound," in what Lamb described as a "gallant attempt...by a number of barges." Lieutenant Commander W.T. Truxtun, commanding the *U.S.S. Tacony*, reported that some of his sailors were assigned this duty, the result being that shellfire from Battery Buchanan and the Mound sunk one of his cutters, killed one sailor and wounded another. Twenty-six-year-old Henry Sands, an "ordinary seaman," had both of his legs "shot away at the knee joint," probably by a "24 or 32 pound Whitworth shot," while engaged in "sounding and dragging the channel in front of the fortifications," while twenty-five-year-old Joseph Riley, quartermaster, received two shrapnel wounds in his "left gluteal region." Young Sands expired from his mortal wounds about 6 p.m. [23]

Aboard the *Powhatan*, Robley Evans observed that Rebel gunners were dropping their shells ever closer to his ship. "There was a wreck of a blockade runner," Evans said, "between us and the battery at which we were to fire, and it was soon evident that this had been used as a target and the range was well known. One or two shots were fired in line with it, each one coming closer to us, and then they struck us with a ten-inch shot. Four more followed, each one striking nearly in the same place, on the bends forward of the starboard wheel, and going through on to the berth deck."

Then the shells began passing over the ship, and Evans suspected the gunners in the fort were unable to see the splashing of the shots, thinking the *Powhatan* was being hit. "If they had not changed their range when they did," Evans remembered, "they would have sunk us in an hour. As it was, we hauled out at sundown pretty well hammered, and leaking so that we had to shift all our guns to port in order to stop the shot holes." [25]

The fleet continued to take hits as the troops under Curtis and Weitzel drew close to Fisher. Commodore H.K. Thatcher, commanding the *U.S.S. Colorado*, "perceived the near approach of the advanced skirmishers of our army force, which had landed late in the day, when our fire ceased for nearly thirty minutes, and was only resumed after we had been hulled several times by a vicious gun which appeared to be fired from the N.E. angle of Fort Fisher. We then reopened heavily, but more to the left than we had previously fired, to avoid annoying our own troops who were seen approaching the forts." During the action, Thatcher said the *Colorado* had one sailor killed and five others wounded. [26]

Between 3:30 and 4 p.m., Chase Whiting, in his role as advisor and counsel to Lamb, sent the following dispatch by telegraph to Bragg in Wilmington: "A large body of the enemy have landed near the fort, deploying as skirmishers. May be able to carry me by storm. Do the best I can. All behaving well. Order supports to attack." At 4 p.m., Whiting's aide-de-camp, Major Strong, who was in charge of the telegraph, "reported all communications gone," the result of Martin Curtis' squad of the One Hundred Forty-Second New York having cut the wires to Wilmington. No response was received from Bragg. [27]

By 4:30 p.m., Curtis had pushed his "main line of skirmishers forward to within 150 paces of Fort Fisher, capturing in their advance an outwork of the fort, containing a large gun which was spiked, as it could not be removed, and completely isolating the fort from the city." Lamb saw Curtis' sharpshooters fire on his gunners "from the old quarters across the causeway," at the same time killing a young courier, Private Amos Jones, and capturing his horse. Lamb had "two pieces of artillery run out of the sally port, and a few discharges of canister stopped the annoyance." By the time Curtis' skirmishers began firing on Fisher, Lamb's "effective force had been increased to 921 regulars and 450 junior reserves, total 1,371." [28]

About the time skirmishing commenced, First Lieutenant W.H. Walling of the One Hundred Forty-Second New York, was able to creep through a jagged opening in the log stockade blasted by the fleet's fire near Battery Shepherd. He was after a Confederate flag. Lamb had placed a company flag there, and "it was carried away and thrown off the parapet by an enfilading shot from the navy." Walling retrieved the flag and took it back to his regiment. [29]

At 5:30 p.m. an overwhelming fire from the fleet began on the landface and palisade. The rate of fire was "130 shot and shell per minute." Lamb ordered his troops "to protect themselves behind the traverses, and removed all extra men from the chambers, with the order, the moment the firing stopped to rally to the ramparts without further orders."

"Just as the naval fire ceased," Lamb continued, "the guns were manned, and I opened with grape and canister, and as it was becoming too dark to see the advance from the ramparts, threw 800 men and boys behind the palisades, which had been scarcely injured. I never shall forget the gallant youths whom I rallied that night to meet the enemy. I had ordered all to man the parapets as soon as the naval fire ceased, as I supposed it would be followed by an assault. I thought the junior reserves were coming up too slowly, and I called out rather impatiently, 'Don't be cowards, boys,' when one manly little officer rushed over the work, followed by his companions, shouting, 'We are no cowards, Colonel,' and manned the palisades. I ordered them not to fire until the enemy were within a few feet of the palisades". [30]

Accompanying the boys was Major James Reilly, commanding the Tenth North Carolina, and commander of the landface batteries of the fort. General Whiting said Reilly, "with his battalion, who had served the guns on the curtain during the entire action, poured with the reserves, cheering, over the parapet and through the sally-port and manned the line of palisades. The enemy had occupied the redoubt (an unfinished outwork) and advanced in to the post garden." As Reilly advanced with the troops, Colonel Robert Tansill, on Whiting's staff, was ordered to temporary command of the landface batteries. [31]

Lamb was confident that hitting the Yankees at the palisade was the best way to defend the fort against their infantry. Those Federals who might "reach it would easily be captured or repulsed," he believed. The Colonel had his light and heavy land guns manned, "with orders to fire grape and canister whenever they saw an advance in force, and the operators stood ready upon my order to explode some of the sub-terra torpedoes."

Lamb directed the operations of his officers and men while standing on the "parapet to the left of the centre sally port." The fleet had now ceased firing, except for an occasional shell fired from one of the ironclads. [32]

On the Federal skirmish line closest to the fort, some 75 yards away, ten Union soldiers were wounded by the shelling of the fleet. Lieutenant Walling noted that when the naval fire ceased, "the parapet was lined with troops" that Lamb had hustled to the ramparts and down to the palisades. The Union sharpshooters fired wild and inaccurately high shots at the fort in the darkness. Cyrus Comstock, on orders from Butler to reconnoiter the fort, was 500 yards north of the landface with General Curtis. Curtis initially and mistakenly believed he could take the fort with fifty men, and Comstock told him he ought to try it if he thought he could. Once the fleet halted its bombardment, however, both officers quickly saw that Fisher "opened heavily with artillery & musketry." [33]

Some of the most tenacious of Lamb's defenders firing at Curtis' troops were those boys of the Fourth, Seventh and Eight Battalions of Junior Reserves. A brave band of lads, they were all just 17 and 18 years old, including their officers. Initially assigned to help defend Fort Holmes on Bald Head Island, they had been unable to obtain the boat they needed to cross New Inlet from the wharf at Battery Buchanan, so Lamb had ordered them to reinforce Fisher. This was in the morning just before the fleet commenced its shelling.

Junior Reserve Captain John Hinsdale had seen combat serving on the staffs of Generals Dorsey Pender and Johnston Pettigrew in the Army of Northern Virginia, and even Theophilus Holmes in the Trans-Mississippi. Now he was in a fight for his home state, and said that all were terrified at the prospect of crossing the unprotected mile of ground between Buchanan and Fisher. The distance between the two was "a clear, open beach, upon which a partridge could not hide himself, over which they must pass in full view of the fleet. As soon as the march began the fleet poured upon the command a terrific discharge of shot and shell. The first one killed at Fort Fisher was Private Davis, of French's Battalion," the Seventh, "of Juniors, who on this march was cut in two by a large shell." The same shell severely wounded another private. Hinsdale said the inaccurate fire "of the fleet saved the boys from utter destruction" on their "perilous march" to get to Fisher.

The boys' eyes met a "scene of desolation." In addition to the barracks and stables being destroyed, "the interior of the fort was honeycombed by holes in the ground large enough to bury an ox team made by the huge shells from the fleet." Most of the boys were able to take cover in the crowded bombproofs under the traverses, but about 200 of them were taken by Major J.M. Reece to the protection of the earthworks at Camp Wyatt, three miles north of the fort.

The gunboats "discovered their presence there and enfiladed the trenches with a terrific fire." First Lieutenant F.M. Hamlin of the Fourth Battalion, "a brave young subaltern," urged Reece to move the troops to the beach of the river, and there "they spent the day listening to the music of the great guns of the fleet and watching the great shells as they passed over them into the river." Hamlin said they remained in that position "until the small-arms were heard at the fort." [34]

Alongside Lamb's other troops, those boys still in the fort, excited and nervous in the presence of the enemy, "kept up a fusillade" of bullets spraying in the direction of the Yankees. "One little fellow from Columbus County...being too small to shoot over the parapet, mounted a cannon and fired from there as coolly as if he were shooting squirrels, until he fell wounded." The heavy volume of musketry and cannon fire exceeded anything the Federals had envisioned. [35]

Second Division commander Adelbert Ames saw that the Confederate troops, "which during the day had to seek shelter, now boldly manned their guns." Ben Butler, observing the twilight action from aboard the army transport *Chamberlain* a few hundred yards offshore from the fort, said that when the naval fire ceased, "the guns of the fort were fully manned, and a sharp fire of musketry, grape, and canister swept the plain over which the column must have advanced." [36]

Butler gave the order to retire. He had learned from prisoners that Kirkland and Hagood's Brigades had come down from Richmond, in his view giving the Confederates a force in his rear greater than the number of Federals who had landed. Additionally, "the weather assumed a threatening aspect. The surf began to roll in so that the landing became difficult." Coupled with Godfrey Weitzel's combat experienced opinion that an assault on Fisher had no prospect of success, which coincided with his own, he decided he would not sacrifice his troops without purpose. "Not so strong a work as Fort Fisher had been taken by assault during this war," Butler said, "and I had to guide me the experience of Port Hudson, with its slaughtered thousands in the repulsed assault, and the double assault of Fort Wagner, where thousands were sacrificed in an attempt to take a work less strong than Fisher after it had been subjected to a more continued and fully as severe fire; and in neither of the instances I have mentioned had the assaulting force in its rear, as I had, an army of the enemy larger than itself. I therefore ordered that no assault should be made, and that the troops should re-embark." Ames wholeheartedly agreed. "Had the attack been made it would have failed," he said. [37]

In a mix-up of orders typical of the confusion of combat, Martin Curtis was initially informed by messenger to withdraw his brigade, so he pulled back his "line of skirmishers to the outwork," Battery Holland, "some one-third of a mile from the fort, the enemy firing sharply after us with musketry and canister."

Then he was told by Ames to advance back to Fisher, Ames at that point not having received the order to disengage. Finally, Curtis was told to remove his troops from in front of Fisher, and return to the point of embarkation. [38]

During the movements back and forth, some of his troops in the One Hundred Seventeenth New York captured two light artillery pieces, and 236 men from all three of the North Carolina Junior Reserves battalions. Lieutenant Hamlin reported that he had asked Major Reece to move the troops from the beach along the river back to a position closer to the fort prior to darkness. Reece decided not to do so, however, as he feared it was still too dangerous to move the men while the fleet was still firing. As night fell, they moved south toward Fisher until they reached Craig's Landing, about two thirds of a mile north of the fort. Here they learned the Yankees were nearby, and some of the officers requested Reece to throw out a line of skirmishers. He refused to do so, however, his apprehensions concerning combat apparently getting the best of him. Reece went out on his own, found a Union captain of the One Hundred Seventeenth New York, and surrendered his command without letting his men fire a shot.

Lieutenant Hamlin, commanding the rearguard, would have no part of surrender. "I then determined," he said, "to make my escape the best way I could, and came out to the rear and did not see a Yankee anywhere. I arrived at this camp (Sugar Loaf) about 9 o'clock at night and reported to General Kirkland." [39]

As Martin Curtis was withdrawing his troops from in front of Fisher, the weather grew increasingly ugly. Sergeant Ed Wightman, back aboard the *Weybosset* after an aborted attempt at landing with a boatload of his company, observed the re-embarkation with a soldier's concern for his comrades. He believed the attack on Fisher had been called off at least partly because "the wind had changed to the northeast and the surf was boiling."

"The command came too late," Wightman wrote. "Many boats were swamped and dashed in pieces on the sands. A part only succeeded in getting away, and the remainder, including two thirds of our regiment, were left to defend themselves as best they might during the night." [40]

Curtis had his men up to the beach for re-embarkation by 8:30 p.m., most of the other commands having already left and gotten back aboard the army transports. The young general reported he was only able to get off part of his command that night, "owing to the roughness of the sea, and with the remainder," about 700 troops, "remained on shore." Ben Butler confirmed Curtis' opinion of the sea's tempest. "The gale was increasing," he said, "and by ten o'clock the sea got so high that I could get off no more men that night with my utmost efforts. In the morning my vessel was rolling so that no man not a sailor could stand on deck, and it was impossible for the navy to come in or open fire upon the fort even if they had had ammunition." [41]

Butler actually thought the troops might be landed again when the storm subsided. Should it become necessary "to effect a landing again, we could do it any day, in a smooth sea, in two hours without the loss of a man. I thought it a greatly less risk waiting with the men on board the transports than to attempt to get them on shore and have them intrench there during the night in the coming storm." Admiral Porter himself, however, insured that a new landing would not take place very soon. Porter told Butler he had exhausted his ammunition, and must return to Beaufort to replenish it.

"As it took him four days," Butler said, "to put in his ammunition at a time when I supposed his vessels were already nearly full, I thought it would take him quite as long to fill them when they were quite empty. Now Beaufort was some seventy miles off, and as it would take him at least four days to go there and back, he would be absent certainly a week." [42]

All Christmas night and through the wee hours of Monday, December 26th, Whiting, Lamb and his garrison were on high alert, expectant and prepared for any assault. Whiting sent a dispatch at 9 p.m. Christmas via steamship to General Louis Hebert at Smithville. "We are in great straits," he told Hebert. "Enemy have landed, reported in force. Prisoners state we will be attacked to-night by three divisions. Send all the men you can raise by Clarendon," the steamer, "to Confederate Point to re-enforce us, if possible with boats to land them." Hebert forwarded the dispatch to Bragg's headquarters in Wilmington, commenting that he was sending four companies, which he did not expect to reach Fort Fisher that night. He also stated there was a strong wind blowing out of the southwest, and that it was very dark and raining. [43]

Unaware of the fleet's paucity of ammunition, or of the re-embarkation of most of the 3,500 Federal troops that had landed in the afternoon, Lamb's primary concern was that the Yankees would launch an attack in the rear, "between the mound and battery Buchanan, where a thousand sailors and marines" could land with little opposition at that time. At 3 a.m. on the 26th, a report came that just such a landing was taking place, and Lamb dispatched "Major Reilly, with two companies, to repulse them, following shortly after in person with a third company to reinforce him." That the attack did not materialize, Lamb attributed to the "heavy rain and windstorm" that "had arisen at midnight." [44]

Whiting noted the anticipated landing must have been a false alarm, but the pickets had reported the advance of some of the fleet "outside the bar," and that the "channel batteries opened a very heavy fire of grape and musketry." The general said the men "showed great spirit and discipline, though much worn by the two days' action and exposed to very severe weather." William Lamb concurred with his friend the general. "During the night," he said, "the rain fell in torrents, wetting the troops and their arms, but it did not dampen their spirits nor interfere with their efficiency." [45]

Dawn of the 26th was foggy and dark. Porter's vessels were now about four miles off the beach. Scouts patrolling north from the fort reported Curtis' troops intrenching in the vicinity of Battery Anderson, and some were seen "not over 1,400 yards from the curtain." Fresh graves were discovered on the beach, an indication that some Federals had been killed last night, and an officer's sword, small arms and accoutrements were found scattered in front of the landface. The garrison "went to work at repairs and replacing guns with hearty good will." [46]

The fleet's expected paucity of ammunition, a heavy surf that prevented Union reinforcements from coming ashore, and a thick fog persisting through the day, rendering bombardment from the ships inaccurate and diffuse. It was an ideal opportunity for Bragg to attack Curtis. By Monday afternoon he was finally at Sugar Loaf headquarters, learning from reconnaissance reports that about 500 Yankees were on the beach, "concentrated in and about Battery Anderson." He also knew he had present for duty at Sugar Loaf approximately 3,400 troops, or nearly seven times the number of Federals between him and Fort Fisher. They were primarily of Hoke's Division, and included men of Kirkland's, Hagood's and Connally's brigades, Second South Carolina Cavalry, and Paris' and Southerland's batteries of artillery. Seventeen hundred more troops, Bragg learned, would be arriving in Wilmington and forwarded to Sugar Loaf the night of the 26th. [47]

A dispatch from Bragg's Wilmington headquarters to Whiting, dated just before midnight Christmas, must have given Whiting some indication of Bragg's lack of resolve to attack the Yankees or fight for Wilmington. "Should it become necessary," Bragg's dispatch read, "to evacuate Fort Fisher, Forts Holmes, Caswell, and Campbell must be abandoned also. A sufficient force from them will be left to hold Fort Anderson and prevent the enemy from ascending the river. The balance will march to the city." [48]

Chase Whiting's response was immediate and unequivocal, underscoring his two years' experienced opinion of the importance to the Confederacy of Wilmington and the forts defending it. Receiving the order at noontime Monday, he replied almost insubordinately. "General Bragg: Major Parker's dispatch of yesterday just received. I am not going to evacuate or give up this place so long as a man is left to stand to his gun. Will instruct General Hebert. We can only be taken by being overpowered." His final three one-syllable words admonished his defeatist-minded superior. "Press their rear," he scolded. [49]

But Bragg did not press their rear. Instead, Bragg permitted the day to pass without assaulting the Yankee lines. Hoke's troops were ordered to "build a line of breastworks from the top of Sugar Loaf Hill diagonally across the strip of land between it and the ocean and in the direction" of Battery Gatlin on the beach. They were to hold fast in their intrenchments, with the possibility of attacking on the 27th. [50]

Tuesday the 27th, however, would pass without attack. General Whiting noted that the day dawned clear and bright, and the fleet was observed to be "three to five miles off, some ten or twelve transports being very close in near Battery Anderson, with a large number of small boats plying to and fro. Several vessels were engaged in shelling the woods." Whiting said they could see a "considerable force" of men on the beach, but were unsure "whether they were landing or embarking troops." At least six hours transpired as the Yankees removed their troops. At noontime, Bragg and Robert Hoke arrived at Fort Fisher, and "examined the work and the movements of the enemy," instead of attacking him. [51]

General Curtis reported that by 2 p.m. of that afternoon, "through the exertions of the navy, I succeeded in re-embarking the whole of my command." He made no mention of any assault on his lines by the Rebels, for none was made.

Whiting, disgusted with his superior's performance, told Lamb "that but for the supineness of General Bragg, the 3,500 men who were landed would have been captured on Christmas night, and it is incomprehensible why he should have allowed the 700 demoralized troops who were forced to remain on the beach on the night of the 26th of December to escape unmolested." Bragg "had the force and the position," Whiting said. Lamb fully agreed. [52]

As if to underscore the significance of the Yankee repulse, even if tinged with less than complete results, the blockade runner *Wild Rover* ran through Porter's fleet the same evening Curtis' men reembarked. At 7 a.m. the morning of the 28th, the blockade-runner *Banshee #2* also sped swiftly through the Union frigates, while four gunboats in sight of "the main body of the fleet" fired on and sought to intercept her. Lamb "opened on them with the Whitworth, but they kept far out of range." [53]

What the runners were hauling was much needed food and other supplies for the Army of Northern Virginia. In early December, young Thomas Taylor, Lamb's good friend of the Liverpool based Confederate Trading Company, whose vessels and blockade running offices still operated in Nassau, was on business in Richmond. There he had an interview with Confederate Commissary General Lucius Northrop. Taylor said Northrop told him "that Lee's army was in terrible straits, and had in fact rations only for about thirty days. He asked me if I could help him; I said I would do my best, and after some negotiations he undertook to pay me a profit of 350 percent upon any provision and meat I could bring in within the next three weeks!"

Taylor was as good as his word, and wrote to his superiors in Liverpool of the running in past the Union fleet. He told his bosses they should "be proud of their two vessels (*Banshee* and *Wild Rover*) both running through that immense fleet and getting safely in. The *Banshee* was out in front of them all for half an hour after daylight, as we were rather late and could not get up to the bar before." Lamb and his men cheered for the *Banshee*, and told Taylor it was a grand sight to watch the little blockade runner dashing through "in front of the whole fleet.

They sent some vessels in to pepper us, but every shot missed, and we got in safely. Porter's fleet left that evening, and I think they have given up the attack for a time." [54]

Taylor also reported he had gotten "the last of the Whitworths in, and they are now at the Fort." The Confederates were "very hard up for food in the field, but the *Banshee* has this time 600 barrels of pork and 1500 boxes of meat – enough to feed Lee's army for a month." [55]

As the Yankees sailed north, both sides tallied their losses. Official count of the casualties of the garrison, consisting of the Confederate Navy detachment, various companies of artillery in the Thirty-Sixth North Carolina Regiment, Fortieth North Carolina, Tenth North Carolina, and Thirteenth North Carolina, and almost 600 men in the Fourth, Seventh and Eighth Battalions North Carolina Junior Reserves, was 3 killed and 59 wounded for both days of combat. Hoke's Division, consisting primarily of the Twenty-Seventh, Forty-Second, and Sixty-Sixth North Carolina Infantry of Kirkland's Brigade, and troops outside Fisher subject to Kirkland's orders comprising other companies of the Fourth, Seventh and Eight Battalions Junior Reserves, and Eighth North Carolina Senior Reserves, lost 5 men killed, 16 wounded, and 307 missing or captured. Most of the captured were the boys surrendered by Major Reece of the Junior Reserves. The total Confederate casualties, then, were 390 men. [56]

Union army casualties were from Curtis' One Hundred Forty-Second New York Infantry. They consisted of one man drowned in the surf upon reembarkation, two others killed in action, either by the fire of the fleet or combat on the evening of December 25, underscoring Lamb's report of new graves on the beach, eleven wounded, mostly from fire of the fleet, and one captured. Total army casualties, then, were twelve.

The majority of the Federal killed and wounded were sailors, resulting mostly from bursting of the Parrott rifles aboard ship, but some from the return fire of Fort Fisher and Battery Buchanan. In Porter's fleet, 20 men were killed and 63 wounded, for a combined total of 83 sailors or marines. [57]

General satisfaction over the results of the just completed campaign was pervasive in the Confederate ranks. General Whiting, in his official report to Bragg, wanted it clearly "understood that in no sense did I assume the command of Colonel Lamb. I was a witness, simply confining my action to observation and advice, and to our communications, and it is as a witness that I report."

His praise for the young colonel was unstinted. While first giving recognition to the Lord of Hosts for intervening in their hour of need, Whiting said that the "gallant and successful resistance, humanly speaking, is due to the untiring energy, the dauntless resolution, and brilliant courage of Col. William Lamb, of the Thirty-sixth North Carolina, devotedly supported by men that know him and will fight for him anywhere. His thorough knowledge of the post, its approaches, the skill displayed in his constructions, and his remarkable practical resources have brought their best fruit in the confidence of his men and his commanders, and there only remains that his services should be suitably acknowledged." [58]

Still, there was a caveat Whiting felt compelled to insert reporting to his superior. The landing of the Yankees, he said, "was effected precisely at the point so often indicated in my reports to the War Department as the true point of attack," which not only demonstrated the value of heavy works in the Sugar Loaf area, but underscored his appeals over the last two years for a strong supporting force of infantry to man those works, as well as a strong garrison for the fort. He correctly surmised that the withdrawal of troops from Wilmington was known to the Federals, and was one reason for their attack at this time.

Despite the powerful works and resistance of Fisher itself, the General continued, "the delay due to the heavy weather of Wednesday and Thursday after arrival of the fleet was its salvation, the small number of artillerymen then present being totally inadequate to so extensive a line." With that delay, they were enabled to throw in the Junior Reserves as well as some regular troops garrisoned at other forts, and allowed time for part of Hoke's Division to arrive from Virginia to lend support from the Sugar Loaf-Battery Gatlin to Battery Anderson and infantry curtain lines set back from the beach.

The appearance of Fisher's garrison, ready and able to repel Union assault when the navy ceased its bombardment, as well as "the advance of Hoke's division completed their discomfiture." Whiting warned though, that weather delays and Yankee blunders could not be counted on in the future, and he trusted "the lesson will not be lost." [59]

Louis Hebert, immediate subordinate to Whiting and overall commander of the forts at the mouth of the river, was less reserved in his report of the defense. After making a complete inspection of Fort Fisher, he was convinced that "the bombardment was probably the most terrific the world ever saw, and yet the fort is as fit to fight now as before. A few guns, a few carriages, a patching up of sods. And Fort Fisher will not show signs that it was attacked. The result is that it is now known that earth-works can resist the powerful U.S. Navy."

Hebert said all who were present at the fort during the battle, which he was not, since Whiting had ordered him to remain at his Smithville headquarters and funnel reinforcements, commended the "conduct of officers and men." He could not praise specific individuals, since he was not there, with the exception of one. "I will only name Colonel Lamb," he said, "who has been the immediate constructor of the fort, who has for many months been preparing it for the awful trial. No one doubted that he would fight his fort with intelligence, with gallantry, and to the last. He has not disappointed any one." [60]

Around noontime of Wednesday, January 4, General Bragg and members of his staff, as well as a reporter for the *Wilmington Daily Journal*, accompanied Ladies of the Soldiers' Aid Society aboard ship down the Cape Fear to the fort. The reporter saw that the fort showed significant signs of the fleet's bombardment. "Deep holes are dug in the parapets and many of the traverses are marked and scarred." Some of the soldiers were working at repair of quarters, while others had been loading wagons with pieces of shrapnel and shells the navy had hurled at Fisher.

This itself was risky business. Two days before the group's visit, Lamb's ordnance sergeant Montgomery Long was "instantly killed by the explosion of a shell through accident," and a "Negro teamster" who had been helping him, was also "killed at the same time." [61]

"The outside and top of the ramparts," the journalist reported, "and in many places of the traverses, looked as though rooted by gigantic hogs; none of this rooting, however, seemed to do more than roughen the surface. The great masses of the Fort everywhere remained perfectly intact," with only two guns dismounted by the enemy, two dismounted by recoil, and the Brooke guns that had burst. [62]

The purpose of the ladies' visit was to offer thanks for the victory over the Federals, and tender them a fine New Year's dinner. The garrison was formed up on three sides of a square, with the ladies forming the fourth side. The spokesman for the women, Major Strange of Bragg's staff, expressed to the men the heartfelt thanks and "congratulations of those whose homes had been saved by their gallantry – between whom and the ruthless invader they had stood like a wall of fire."

To Colonel Lamb, their thanks were especially due. "They had relied upon his skill – his coolness and his undaunted courage. They had felt that while he and his brave men stood between them and the enemy, Wilmington was safe, and their reliance was not in vain." Lamb responded by thanking the ladies for their kindness, and told them they had accomplished what the enemy had not. "They had surprised the garrison," the Colonel said, "and taken the fort by storm." Lamb said the victory achieved was due to the blessing of Providence in providing him with such fine men, and promised them their homes would continue to be protected by the garrison. [63]

If congratulations and accolades were the order of the day among Confederates, recrimination and accusations, mostly targeted at Ben Butler, were rampant in the Union ranks. One Yankee soldier wrote his brother that all the troops were disgusted. Everyone, he said, believed that Fort Fisher was ripe for capture, and that "Butler prevented them from taking it. The men were close up to the embrasures, and all the rebel guns were silenced when the retreat was ordered." [64]

David Dixon Porter would become Butler's most vocal critic of all. Writing Navy Secretary Gideon Welles on December 27, even as Curtis' 700 men remained on the beach, he was quick to begin political maneuvering and laying blame for the expedition's failure on someone other than himself or the navy. He told Welles that the fort's guns had been silenced, and that Fisher had been "so blown up, burst up, and torn up that the people inside had no intention of fighting any longer. Had the army made a show of surrounding it, it would have been ours, but nothing of the kind was done...There never was a fort that invited soldiers to walk in and take possession more plainly than Fort Fisher." [65]

This, of course, as the army commanders had clearly determined from personal reconnaissance and combat, was preposterous, only two guns having been dismounted on the landface, and Lamb's troops firing heavily with musketry, grape and canister once the fleet's bombardment lifted. Not only Butler, but Adelbert Ames and Godfrey Wetzel both believed that, "it would be murder to order an attack on that work with that force." And Grant's engineer, Lieutenant Colonel Comstock, who had also seen Fisher with his own eyes, wrote to his boss, "an assault of the work in its uninjured condition, with sixteen or seventeen heavy guns sweeping the ground over which the assault would be made, was deemed impracticable, and the troops were re-embarked." [66]

"I feel ashamed," Porter continued in his diatribe to Welles two days later, "that men calling themselves soldiers should have left this place so ingloriously; it was, however, nothing more than I expected when General Butler mixed himself up in this expedition." Stating plainly that he considered Butler incompetent, that all the army had to do was "take possession of the panic-stricken garrison," he then moved to the subject of the powder boat scheme, which had proven as dismal a failure as the naval bombardment.

True it was that Butler may have originated the proposal for the explosion, yet Porter had enthusiastically endorsed the idea, and staunchly promoted it with subordinates and superiors. It had been a naval affair from start to finish, and it was the U.S. Navy that had furnished the boat, the powder, the crew, and the method to explode it. Yet Porter, realizing the experiment would prove to be the subject of military jokes as well as a possible court of inquiry, sought early on to distance himself from responsibility. He told Welles in his December 29 letter, that "Butler only came here to reap the credit of this affair, supposing that the explosion would sweep the works off from the face of the earth." [67]

Porter's subordinates took their cue from the admiral, and quickly came to endorse his criticism of the experiment and Butler. Executive Officer of the big frigate *Minnesota*, Lieutenant Commander James Parker later admitted that, "we all believed in it (the powder boat) from the Admiral down, but when it proved so laughable a failure we, of the Navy, laid its paternity upon General Butler." [68]

Parker's commanding officer, Commodore Joseph Lanman, told Porter that the *Minnesota*'s shells fell "like a perfect hailstorm upon Fort Fisher, and that the firing was of the most excellent effect." He said he would never had had "the slightest doubt of the flag of the Union being hoisted at daylight upon the well-battered fort." [69]

Echoing Lanman's opinion and confirming both of the officers' ignorance of Fisher's strength, Captain James Alden, commanding the big 26 gun *U.S.S. Brooklyn*, stated confidently, "the rebels, I am satisfied, considered from the moment that our troops obtained a footing on the shore that the work (battered as it was) was untenable, and were merely waiting for someone to come and take it...I am satisfied that if our troops had not been stopped in their triumphal march toward Fort Fisher, they would have been in it before dark, and in quiet possession without firing a shot." [70]

Porter was sufficiently certain of his many subordinate officers' endorsements, to advise Welles that the "ships did their work so beautifully that you will hear of but one opinion expressed by lookers-on." On December 31, in another letter advising of his intention to remain in Carolina waters until more troops could be dispatched, possibly from Sherman, Porter's ego revealed why he was so quick to heap criticism on Butler. "I intend to write my share of the history of this rebellion and place it on record where future historians can have access to it." [71]

U.S. Grant was obviously disgusted over results of the campaign when he wrote to Abraham Lincoln the night of December 28, but he was more circumspect than Porter and his officers as to who was at fault. "The Wilmington expedition has proven a gross and culpable failure. Many of the troops are now back here. Delays and free talk of the object of the expedition enabled the enemy to move troops to Wilmington to defeat it...Who is to blame I hope will be known." [72]

Four days later, having received a full report from his engineer and aide-de-camp Cyrus Comstock, Grant wrote to Secretary of War Edwin M. Stanton, that the failure of the campaign "was the result of delays by the navy. I do not say unavoidable, for I know nothing of the cause." He assured Stanton that on this first day of 1865, having learned Porter was still holding on with his fleet off Wilmington, preparations were "now going on to get troops back to the mouth of Cape Fear River as soon as possible. The enemy may by that time have withdrawn Hoke's division, which went from here to Wilmington." [73]

Grant also advised Porter to maintain his position off the Cape Fear, that he would resend troops as soon as possible, "with an increased force and without the former commander." Grant, like many Union officers, intensely disliked Ben Butler. Even though Butler would be exonerated for the Fort Fisher repulse by the Congressional Committee on the Conduct of the War, the non-military watchdog that investigated military debacles, Grant would use the occasion to get rid of him. "The enemy should be lulled into all the security possible," he told Porter, "in hopes he will send back here or against Sherman the re-enforcements sent to defend Wilmington." [74]

Accordingly, to conceal the nature of the new expedition and deceive Confederate spies, Grant's "Special Orders No. 2" said nothing about Wilmington. "Eight thousand infantry and two batteries of artillery," the first paragraph read, "without horses, will be got in immediate readiness to embark on transports, with orders to report to Maj. Gen. W.T. Sherman, at Savannah, Ga." [75]

It was ironic and probably not coincidental, that in Grant's deceptive orders, Sherman and Savannah were mentioned as the recipients of the expeditionary troops. By the end of December, Sherman had captured Savannah, and was poised for an invasion of the Carolinas. Grant had reluctantly agreed to give his top lieutenant free rein to move north, cut a swath through South and then North Carolina, and join him to defeat Lee. Wilmington, therefore, took on a whole new meaning in Grant's perspective, as a base of supplies for his second largest army of the Union. Sherman himself said that he preferred "Wilmington, as a live place, over Charleston, which is dead and unimportant when its railroad communications are broken." [76]

Wilmington was the most logical point from which Sherman could draw his supplies, once he got into North Carolina. The Cape Fear could be navigated all the way to Fayetteville, one hundred miles northwest of

Wilmington. This water line, "plus the railway from New Berne to Goldsborough would prove sufficient." [77]

To command the renewed expedition, Grant chose Brevet Major General Alfred H. Terry. Terry was a solid, dependable officer, even if his war record had so far been unspectacular. A full-bearded and handsome 37 year old native of Hartford, Connecticut, he had studied law at Yale and become clerk of court in New Haven in the 1850's. When war broke out, he fought in the Battle of First Manassas as

MajGen Alfred H. Terry, U.S. Army

colonel of the Second Connecticut Militia Regiment. As commanding officer of the Seventh Connecticut, he served in the capture of Port Royal, South Carolina and the siege and capture of Fort Pulaski, Georgia. He was serving in combat operations against Charleston in 1863, when he was transferred to command of the Tenth Corps of Butler's Army of the James. In 1864, his troops fought Robert E. Lee's veterans in various battles outside Richmond and Petersburg. [78]

Most of the soldiers, 6,600 of 8,000 infantry, were the same as those Butler had taken in December. They were the Second Division of the Twenty-Fourth Corps under Adelbert Ames, consisting of Brigadier General Curtis' First Brigade, the Second Brigade of 20-year-old Colonel Galusha Pennypacker, who would become a general before his 21st birthday, and the Third Brigade of Colonel Louis Bell. As before, Brigadier General Charles

Paine's Third Division of the Twenty-Fifth Corps, consisting of the Second Brigade of U.S. Colored Troops under Colonel John Ames, and the Third Brigade of U.S. Colored Troops under Colonel Elias Wright, would be on the expedition. The additional 1,400 infantry consisted of the Second Brigade, First Division of the Twenty-Fourth Corps, commanded by Colonel Joseph Abbott. Three companies of the First Connecticut Heavy Artillery, the Sixteenth New York Light Artillery, Battery E of the Third U.S. Artillery, and two companies of the Fifteenth New York Engineers would make up the balance of the army's troops. [79]

The troops were embarked at Bermuda Landing on the James River on 4th and 5th of January, and by the night of the 5th, all the transports were collected in Hampton Roads, ready to move south. On the trip down the James, Grant told Terry for the first time the true destination of the expedition, and presented him with formal orders drafted two days before. [80]

The orders, dated January 3rd, were quite specific as to the object of the campaign. They offered no opportunity for abandoning the coast above Fort Fisher, once a landing had been achieved. "The expedition intrusted to your command," Grant's instructions read, "has been fitted out to renew the attempt to capture Fort Fisher, N.C., and Wilmington ultimately, if the fort falls...It is exceedingly desirable that the most complete understanding should exist between yourself and the naval commander...The first object to be attained is to get a firm position on the spit of land on which Fort Fisher is built, from which you can operate against that fort. You want to look to the practicability of receiving your supplies, and to defending yourself against superior forces sent against you by any of the avenues left open to the enemy. If such a position can be obtained the siege of Fort Fisher will not be abandoned until its reduction is accomplished or another plan of campaign is ordered from these headquarters." [81]

In addition to his troops, accompanying General Terry as his Assistant Adjutant General was his 33-year-old brother, Captain Adrian Terry. The captain, like his brother, was a veteran of the several campaigns since Fort Pulaski, Georgia, and would insure that a meticulous record was kept of the expedition. [82]

To assist with intelligence deception, Porter told Grant that he would "have the report spread that the troops are to co-operate with Sherman in the attack on Charleston...I propose (if it is possible) that you send every man you can spare here, with intrenching tools, and fifteen 30-pounders". [83]

One Union soldier reported from aboard the army transport *Atlantic*, that his quarters were far improved over those of the first trip, "as we have more room and better ventilation. My quarters are in the after cabin. The men are able to get their pork half boiled." At 4 a.m. on the morning of January 6, the transports bearing approximately 10,000 Federal troops, infantry, artillery, and engineers, commenced steaming out of Hampton Roads, headed for their rendezvous with Porter off Beaufort, North Carolina. [84]

William Lamb's garrison was anything but idle, as the Yankees made preparations to hit them again. "We have been hard at work all day repairing damages," the colonel's December 28 diary entry read. General Whiting said the men were "hard at work repairing damages and strengthening the position." The last day of 1864 two more 12-pound Whitworth rifled cannon were presented to Lamb from Thomas Taylor, part of the cargo brought in on the blockade runner *Banshee*. In addition, four carriages for guns arrived to replace others destroyed during the naval bombardment. [85]

In the week following Taylor's successful run in on the *Banshee*, he traveled back to Richmond, meeting with various officials in regard to supplying the army. He did not like what he saw and heard. "I never saw things look so gloomy, and I think spring will finish them unless they make a change for the better...if Wilmington goes Lee has to evacuate Richmond and retire into Tennessee. He told me the other day, that if they did not keep Wilmington he could not save Richmond." [86]

Whiting requested Bragg to authorize, at Whiting's discretion, the use of Hoke's Division for various duty details, "outpost guards to Masonborough, the sounds, and Virginia Creek." This was part of the proper role for supporting troops outside the forts, and since the reserves and home guards had been sent home, the Cape Fear District was strapped for soldiers again. Hoke's men were available, and should be used as needed, especially for duty on the coast.

Bragg's response was prompt. "Hoke's division is held for a special purpose, and it is not deemed advisable to use it as indicated. It is supposed that all the duties proposed can be performed by the senior reserves, the artillery and cavalry." That same day, December 31st, Bragg ordered Hoke to bring Kirkland and Hagood's brigades up to Wilmington to join the other two brigades of Colquitt and Clingman. Their troops were in bivouac at Camp Whiting, two miles out the plank road from downtown, and along the western bank of Green's Millpond. [87]

Kirkland's Assistant Adjutant General, Captain Charles Elliott, said Bragg did not expect "a renewal of the attack on Fort Fisher." Though it was only known by a handful of officers, Bragg wanted the division back in Wilmington to make preparations for a new assault on New Bern, to try to capture that town from the Federals. "We marched," Elliott wrote, "with colors flying and bands playing, into the city, and were enthusiastically received by the people as their victorious defenders." [88]

Disgusted with his role as supernumerary to an incompetent, Whiting wrote directly to Secretary of War James Seddon in Richmond on January 1. Unlike Bragg, he was certain another attack would be made on Wilmington, probably very soon. "It can scarcely be possible," he told Seddon, "that after such extraordinary preparations the enemy has altogether abandoned, or even long postponed, his designs upon this port on account of the repulse of the 24th and 25th of December...The enemy landed at the point which I have so often indicated to you as the one of several they would be likely to try; that is, to occupy the neck above Confederate Point, which for many miles is very narrow, and attempt either to carry Fort Fisher or to establish themselves. That they have not succeeded on this occasion is solely owing to the manifest favor of Providence." The General reiterated, with the just finished campaign as evidence, what he had been telling the War Department since November of 1862. He told Seddon it was a fact that the Federals had landed "in large force unmolested on Sunday and re-embarked on Tuesday. This fact well illustrates what I have so often urged, that if we desire to hold this place let us have a suitable garrison here and some force, at least, in support." Essentially going over Bragg's head, Whiting was appealing to Seddon to authorize his use of Hoke's troops as they were intended to be used. [89]

Robert F. Hoke, one of Lee's crack division commanders from Lincolnton, North Carolina, and the South's youngest major general when so appointed at age 26 the previous April, knew exactly what Whiting was talking about. Combat experienced since Big Bethel in June of 1861, he was a skillful, bulldog warrior who had fought stoutly for Lee since the Seven Days, was severely wounded at Chancellorsville, and thereby missed Gettysburg. He was, in fact, so highly regarded by the great Virginian, Lee, with the concurrence of President Davis, decided in the fall of 1864 that Hoke would be his replacement, should he die, or become incapacitated.

His presence north of Fort Fisher was unquestionably one of the prime factors that impelled Butler to abandon the campaign in December. Hoke, the exemplar of a battlefield tactician, was acutely aware his division had been sent from Virginia expressly to support the defenses on Confederate Point, not to sit in bivouac on the edge of Wilmington, or go on a wild goose chase to New Bern. He protested Bragg's directive, but to no avail. He would go where his superior ordered him. [90]

Second Lieutenant A.A. McKethan of Company B, Fifty-First North Carolina Troops, Thomas Clingman's Brigade, was encamped with the rest of Hoke's Division east of town, and was surprised they were not down on Confederate Point as a supporting force. "Why we should have been stopped in Wilmington, thirty miles from Fort Fisher," he could not understand, he wrote. [91]

George Rose, Adjutant of the Sixty-Sixth North Carolina of Kirkland's Brigade, said the officers he knew in Hoke's Division thought they were in the wrong place. Most believed they should have been "allowed to remain at Sugar Loaf and not have been carried to Wilmington," for the purpose of parades, but should have been within supporting distance of Fort Fisher. [92]

First Lieutenant George H. Moffett, Adjutant of the Twenty-Fifth South Carolina, and staff officer for Johnson Hagood's Brigade, wrote his wife on January 2 from his bivouac outside town. "It seems strange to me," he told Liz, "that this Div. should be kept here idle when they might be employed to advantage in so many other places. It is to be hoped that our generals have good reason for so doing." [93]

William Lamb was almost as disgusted with Braxton Bragg as Chase Whiting. "Although it was known that the fleet would return, General Bragg withdrew the supporting army from Sugar Loaf and marched it to a camp" outside Wilmington. Despite his dissatisfaction, he continued to work with a will to improve his fort's defenses. In addition to repairing ramparts and traverses, he made requisitions for artillery and rifle ammunition. Particular emphasis was placed on the need for hand grenades, which would be especially useful in the event of close combat with infantry on the parapets and traverses. Marine torpedoes to be placed where the big ironclads had anchored during the first battle, were requested as well. Unfortunately, none of these items were to be available anytime soon. [94]

On January 4, the same day as the visit of the Ladies Soldiers' Aid Society, Fisher's garrison mounted a 32-pounder on the landface. The next day, they laid "off a new face to Battery Buchanan," and mounted a 24-pounder cannon. Over the next several days, Lamb would receive two new Brooke rifles, mounting one of them on the landface, and would mount two big 8-inch Columbiads in the Columbiad Battery, to replace the Brooke rifles destroyed during the Christmas attack. Whiting also sent Lamb additional palisades for reinforcing the landface defenses as well as Battery Buchanan, and ordered the installation of a submarine telegraph line, to "start from the left of the land front at any convenient traverse, and go straight over the shoals to Battery Lamb, or a convenient point just above the battery not exposed to the effect of fire directed on that work." [95]

Whiting also called on Zebulon Vance to help with the labor shortage, an acute problem at this stage of the game, when shoring up defenses or building new fortifications was essential. "We must not let our last place go for want of work;" he wrote the young governor on January 4, "still less, because we have foiled the enemy's first effort, must we fold our arms and say enough has been done...An enrolled corps of 1,200 to 1,500 free negroes, properly organized into companies according to regulations, entitled to furlough at proper times, fed, clothed, paid, &, retained in service, would relieve the people of the State of all use of their slaves for the defense here." [96]

On Sunday, January 8, Robert E. Lee wrote Secretary of War Seddon from his Petersburg headquarters, that various information sources pointed to a renewal of the attack on Wilmington, and they knew the commanding officer of the army was General Alfred Terry. Lee further advised the Secretary he had already notified Braxton Bragg, and that he was "endeavoring to ascertain the strength of the land force." Bragg replied to Lee on the 9th, advising him that the same report had reached him from Beaufort, "but nothing has yet appeared off here." [97]

Based on Bragg's knowledge of the second Yankee assault on the way, Whiting's January 8 memorandum to him should have seemed especially appropriate. "I think it not at all unlikely," Whiting told his superior, "that a renewal of the attack on Wilmington will be made very soon. It is hardly possible that the enemy will put up with such a failure as the last. I should keep one good brigade and a battery at Sugar Loaf, and send at least a regiment, and a strong one, if not a brigade, to Piney Point...I hope that on any renewal of an attempt to land, the enemy will not be allowed to do so without opposition. [98]

Bragg, however, had other plans for Robert Hoke's men. In addition to his projected attack on New Bern, Bragg decided these veterans of Lee should participate in a division review, instead of being down on Confederate Point. Some of his admirers in town had given the general a new uniform, and he proudly sported it on January 12. Lieutenant McKethan of the Fifty-First North Carolina said the review was held "for the benefit of a large number from the city, and after marching and countermarching for the greater portion of the day, we returned to our quarters for rest." Their rest was very brief. [99]

That evening, William Lamb, scanning the northeastern horizon with his field glasses from the ramparts of Fort Fisher, saw the ominous sight. He telegraphed Wilmington headquarters of the presence of "a number of signal-lights being shown northeast and southeast; they are not the blockade signals, but the old fleet signals." By 10 o'clock that night, the number of lights had increased, and more than thirty vessels were clearly in view, headed for the fort. The Yankees were back, and Lamb was furious. "The fort was not even advised of the approach of the fleet, but its arrival was reported from Fort Fisher to headquarters." [100]

Lamb dispatched one of his couriers to the "Cottage" to tell Daisy to pack quickly, and be ready to leave with the children and nurse at a moment's notice. He sent a garrison barge to Craig's Landing near their little home, to stand ready to transport his family across the river. After midnight, he rode to the house to bid them goodbye, but found the place eerily dark and quiet. The courier had delivered the message, but Daisy "had been so undisturbed by the news, that she had fallen asleep and no preparations for a retreat had been made." Lamb immediately awakened her and the children, helped her hastily gather a few personal belongings, and hustled them down to the landing to catch the barge. [101]

As word spread rapidly through Wilmington that the fleet had returned, Bragg finally decided it was time to heed Whiting's advice, even as the band of Hoke's Division was in town serenading the citizens, and officers and men were paying evening visits. Late that night, he advised Whiting he had ordered Hoke to send a brigade "to the vicinity of Sugar Loaf, for the purpose of throwing up a line of works on the beach between the head of the sound and Fort Fisher." Now, incredibly, when the Federals were poised to strike, Bragg came to the conclusion more earthworks on the beach would be of benefit! [102]

The Yankees were indeed back again, though the weather, as before, had been a stumbling block to their progress. Having left Hampton Roads early on the morning of January 6, with the unit commanders on each vessel receiving sealed orders to rendezvous at a point 25 miles off Beaufort, the army transports ran into trouble that afternoon. Alfred Terry reported that a "severe storm arose, which so much impeded our progress that it was not until the morning of the 8th that my own vessel arrived at the rendezvous; all the others, excepting the flag-ship of General Paine, were still behind." Leaving Paine to assemble the other transports as they arrived at the rendezvous, Terry ordered his vessel, the *McClellan*, to steam into Beaufort so he could confer with Admiral Porter. [103]

The weather continued foul for several more days, but Terry's brother Adrian noted that the general and the admiral made the most of the enforced delay. "General Terry and the Admiral had several conferences," he wrote, "in which they exchanged views and information and discussed the difficult problem before them, arriving at a perfect understanding as to the work to be performed by each part of the combined expedition, so far as could then be done." [104]

One thing Porter made crystal clear to Terry during their series of meetings, was his staunch opposition "to run a portion of his fleet past the forts into Cape Fear River," as Grant had hoped he could do. Even if there were a successful landing of troops, it was deemed "too dangerous an undertaking on account of the shallowness and intricacy of the channel," as well as the likelihood of sunken obstructions or marine torpedoes. That idea was "necessarily abandoned." [105]

By morning tide of Thursday, January 12, the transports that had been forced to enter Beaufort for repairs or re-coaling, as well as Porter's heavy fleet, steamed out, met the other transports at the rendezvous, and all headed south for Fort Fisher. Since they arrived off the coast after dark, Porter decided the disembarkation of troops should not commence until the next morning, due to the hazards of a nighttime amphibious landing. [106]

On the eve of battle, Edward Wightman, aboard the army transport *Atlantic* with Curtis' Brigade offshore near Fort Fisher, wrote to his brother in New York. He speculated on various aspects of the upcoming attack. The troops were obviously ignorant of any details of the orders, or even knew Alfred Terry was in command. "Our second attempt, it is rumored, is to be made in a different direction from the first. Although Gens. Ames and Curtis are both with us, no one knows anything positive; but it is believed that the troops, to the number of 15,000 will be landed tomorrow morning at Gainsboro Inlet, to march direct to the City of Wilmington. I am ignorant as to who commands the expedition. It is said that Gen. Hancock has a division of his new corps here and will lead us." [107]

As the night wore on, William Lamb prepared his garrison for the storm that portended thunder and lightning with the coming dawn. "I began at once to put my works in order for action", he wrote. "I had but 800 men - the 36th North Carolina - at least 100 of whom were not fit for duty." Early on the morning of the 13th, Whiting telegraphed Lamb, "be on your guard...I will be with you, either inside or out. Keep the same orders about firing tomorrow, and a good lookout to-night." [108]

To insure targets of importance were hit by the fleet's big shells, Porter issued precise orders to his ship commanders. This time they would aim specifically for Fort Fisher's guns and traverses. "Fire deliberately," he told his subordinates. "Fill the vessels up with every shell they can carry, and fire to dismount the guns and knock away the traverses. The angle near the ships has heavy casemates; knock it away. Concentrate fire always on one point. With guns disabled the fort will soon be ours...Commanders are directed to strictly enjoin upon their officers and men never to fire at the flag or pole, but to pick out the guns."

When the traverses were the targets, the shells were to be timed to burst in the earthwork itself. "The object is to lodge the shell in the parapets, and tear away the traverses under which the bombproofs are located. A shell now and then exploding over a gun en barbette may have good effect, but there is nothing like lodging the shell before it explodes."

Once the range had been obtained on any target, the division officer was required to log the proper "distance marked on the sight, so that he will not forget it." This was to insure continued accuracy of fire, once battle smoke had become too thick to clearly observe onshore targets. [109]

Porter also wanted sailors and marines to participate in the assault on Fisher's ramparts with the army. Each ship's commander was ordered to detail men who could be spared from manning the deck guns, to comprise a landing party totaling 2,000 men. The sailors would be "armed with cutlasses, well sharpened, and with revolvers." When signal was made to commence the assault, the sailors in landing boats would hit the beach, and "board the fort on the run in a seaman-like way." The marines would form to the rear of the charging sailors, covering them with musket volleys directed over their heads at the fort's garrison. As the infantry assaulted the landface, the navy would attack the seaface. "Two thousand active men from the fleet will carry the day," the admiral boasted. [110]

Robley Evans, aboard the *Powhatan*, said that volunteers were called for to participate in the attack, and "it was gratifying to see the officers and men come forward, almost in a body for a job they knew would be a desperate one. So many volunteered that finally a detail had to be made from each ship, and there were many sorely disappointed ones when the names were published." As Evans was officer of the deck when the order was received, he wrote his name first on the list of volunteers. [111]

At 5 a.m. of the 13th, the vessels designated Battle Line No.1, comprising thirteen warships commanded by Captain James Alden, of the *Brooklyn*, got underway from their offshore anchorage, and headed for the beach about four miles north of Fort Fisher. The army transports were with them and protected by Alden's battleline. While moving north past Battery Anderson, and approximately 800 yards offshore, they began shelling the woods around 7:20 a.m. Anchoring off Battery Gatlin, the frigates continued the shore bombardment for the next several hours.

Ensign Robley Evans, U.S. Navy

One totally unexpected consequence of the shelling was to drive several hundred head of cattle to the beach. These terrified bovines had apparently been driven down from Wilmington to feed the garrison. Breaking loose from whatever corral restrained them as big naval shells started exploding in the woods all around them, they "rushed wildly to the beach and delivered themselves over, opportune food for the army." [112]

As the shelling continued, the army vessels moved toward the shore, when about 8 a.m., "a swarm of boats from the navy," about 200 of them, surrounded the transports, ready to receive the several thousand infantry gathered aboard the decks. The "disembarkation of men, provisions, tools, and ammunition simultaneously commenced." Despite heavy surf that was still running, the weather was otherwise favorable for landing. The soldiers, more than 8,000 of them, were laden "with three days' rations in their haversacks and forty rounds of ammunition" in their cartridge boxes. [113]

The sailors in the gigs and launches slowly pulled away from the transports, and rowed as rapidly as possible with their heavy cargoes of men and equipment. Pulling through the breakers to hit the beach, they began landing the troops on the eastern shore of Myrtle Sound near Battery Gatlin, about one mile north of Butler's December landing site, and approximately one half mile east and across the sound from William Kirkland's infantry, who were just beginning to file into the extended Sugar Loaf entrenchments. General Curtis wrote that "officers, men, provisions in haversacks, and ammunition in boxes were thoroughly soaked." [114]

"Where is Hoke?" William Lamb frantically appealed to headquarters in Wilmington. "The Yankees are landing a heavy force. I should have a regiment of veterans before sundown." Hoke was just arriving himself, as Kirkland's men and a detachment of the Second South Carolina Cavalry observed the Federals coming ashore. With their numbers, observation was about all they could do. Hagood's, Clingman's, and Colquitt's Brigades, heading south from Wilmington, were not yet up to help Kirkland repulse the Yankees, if indeed, that could be done at all, while the fleet continued its pounding of the shore. [115]

Bragg's directive to Hoke the night before to carry a brigade down and erect earthworks between the sound and Fort Fisher was classic Braxton Bragg, another case of too little, too late. Hoke's veterans were inured to the heavy labor required for constructing fortifications. Had those 6,400 soldiers been employed from December 27 to January 12 in building a heavy, bombproof-laced, timber reinforced network of earthworks, from the head of Myrtle Sound down Confederate Point, strengthening the infantry curtain Lamb's people had already built, the result would have been powerful works able to endure the fleet's shelling, which was diffused in this area anyway.

All Lee's men were master builders of stout fieldworks in short order, able to withstand the bombardment of heavy siege artillery and huge stationary mortars that hurled projectiles heavier than the navy's. Their sophisticated forts, trenches, redoubts, and bombproofs on the Richmond-Petersburg line, many thrown up hurriedly, confirmed that fact. With such earthworks and all of Hoke's crack veterans in place to man them, the Yankees would now be reeling from heavy casualties as they landed, fleet or no fleet. This was precisely what Chase Whiting had been telling his superiors for the past two years.

Second Lieutenant Augustus McKethan of the Fifty-First North Carolina was convinced he and his comrades should have been down there to repel the Federals. "Had General Hoke and his division been put in supporting distance of Fisher," he wrote, "the enemy could not have made their landing." Adjutant George Rose of the Sixty-Sixth North Carolina wholeheartedly agreed. "If Hoke's division had been where, it seemed to the officers, it ought to have been, this landing of troops could never have been made," he said. [116]

Captain Elliott of Kirkland's Brigade, wrote that the men had taken vessels down to Sugar Loaf in the wee hours before dawn. When they began filing into the entrenchments west of Myrtle Sound, they saw that "Terry had landed his forces without opposition, and we began skirmishing with them at once." [117]

Kirkland's men were skirmishing with Abbott's Brigade of infantry. They were the first of Terry's troops to land, and as soon as companies could be formed, they began firing volleys of musketry across Myrtle Sound at Kirkland's troops in the extended Sugar Loaf trenches. Some of Abbott's units were hustled off the beach from near the abandoned Battery Gatlin, even as the other Federal troops continued to land, and the fleet's thunder continued to boom over their heads at the Rebels. Terry ordered him to demonstrate toward Wilmington, which he did, in an effort to deceive the Confederates into thinking the attack would be directed at Wilmington. [118]

The ruse worked. Though Hoke had been ordered to repulse the enemy landing, by the time he arrived to confer with Kirkland, the landing was an ongoing and accomplished fact. The water of Myrtle Sound and the swampy ground in the area was a topographic obstacle to attack, as well as the tremendous shelling of the fleet. At this point in the action, Hoke felt he had no option but to reinforce his position with further intrenchments, and be prepared to repulse attacks of the enemy toward Wilmington. [119]

While Terry's men were landing, Porter's ironclads and monitors, led by the *New Ironsides*, moved into position just over one-half mile off the Northeast Bastion. As William Lamb's gunners opened up first on the heavy iron frigates, the bombardment of Fort Fisher commenced in earnest. The colonel reported that "soon there rained upon fort and beach a storm of shot and shell which caused both earth and sea to tremble." [120]

Major Willliam Saunders, Chief of Artillery for the several Cape Fear forts, was sent to Fisher by General Hebert to report to Lamb. He observed that Porter's ironclads were more methodical about their fire than in the previous attack. "Their firing was slow and deliberate," he noted, "and directed upon the land face of the fort, evidently with a view to dismounting our guns and breaking down the palisades in front of the work. Our guns, under my immediate command, replied steadily and with accuracy." [121]

George Benson, still serving one of the 6-inch landface guns in the Thirty-Sixth North Carolina, had been on guard duty the night before, and seen the flickering lights at sea mark the return of the fleet. Just 18 years old, he and the other privates in Fort Fisher knew instinctively the Yankees would be coming back, even if Braxton Bragg did not. "We were expecting them," he said. "Up the beach they were making a landing," while inside Fisher, there were ear-splitting concussions, flying metal shards of all sizes, and pandemonium. "Then the buildings in the fort, inside of the great sand walls, began to burn. The whole place filled with fire and smoke and explosions and wounded men." Benson was struck on the knee with a piece of shrapnel while in the traverse manning the gun, "but it was so well spent that it only tore my trousers. One of those huge bombs fell close to me and I thought I was a goner, but a soldier doused its fuse in a sponge tub and it did not explode." [122]

During the height of the bombardment, Chase Whiting and his staff arrived in the fort, having landed at Battery Buchanan and walking more than a mile to reach the interior. Lamb was unaware "of their approach until the general came to me on the works and remarked, 'Lamb, my boy, I have come to share your fate. You and your garrison are to be sacrificed.' " The colonel was thunderstruck at Whiting's comment, and optimistically responded, "Don't say so, General; we shall certainly whip the enemy again." Whiting told him, however, that as he was leaving Wilmington, "Bragg was hastily removing his stores and ammunition, and was looking for a place to fall back upon." Lamb offered Whiting command of the fort, "but he refused, saying he would counsel with me, but would leave me to conduct the defense." [123]

Endnotes to Chapter 9

1. O.R., Volume XLII, Part I, p.994, p.1021; ORN, Volume 11, p.256
2. Antietam to Fort Fisher, p.222-223
3. O.R., Volume XLII, Part I, p.1004; ORN, Volume 11, p.275
4. O.R., Volume XLII, Part I, p.1021
5. Waddell, Some Memories of My Life, p.57-58
6. Scharf, Confederate Navy, p.425; O.R., Volume XLII, Part I, p.995
7. Antietam to Fort Fisher, p.223-224
8. S.H.S.P., Volume XXI, p.273
9. ORN, Volume 11, map p.245, p.304, p.322
10. Ibid, Volume 11, p.307-308
11. Ibid, Volume 11, p.319
12. O.R., Volume XLII, Part I, p.982; Generals in Blue, p.106-107; The Wilmington Campaign, p.22-23
13. Antietam to Fort Fisher, p.224
14. O.R., Volume XLII, Part I, p.982; Antietam to Fort Fisher, p.224
15. O.R., Volume XLII, Part I, p.982, p.1021; ORN, Volume 11, p.351-352; N.C. Troops, Volume X, p.190, p.194
16. Clark, Volume IV, p.527-528, p.539-540; N.C. Troops, Volume VI, p.204; p.254; O.R., Volume XLII, Part I, p.980-981, p.1021; ORN, Volume 11, p.252-254, p.384; Battles & Leaders, Volume IV, p.634-640
17. Clark, Volume IV, p.540; O.R., Volume XLII, Part 1, p.981, p.1021-1022
18. O.R., Volume IV, Part I, p.1023-1024; Clark, Volume I, p.582; N.C. Troops, Volume I, p.149
19. O.R., Volume XLII, Part I, p.982-983, p.985-986; The Wilmington Campaign, p.23-25
20. Ibid, Volume XLII, Part I, p.986

21. Butler's Book, p.794, Appendix, p.72-73
22. ORN, Volume 11, p.258, p.330; S.H.S.P., Volume XXI, p.272
23. ORN, Volume 11, p.334-335; S.H.S.P., Volume XXI, p.272; The Wilmington Campaign, p.23
24. ORN, Volume 11, p.319
25. A Sailor's Log, p.81
26. ORN, Volume 11, p.295-296
27. O.R., Volume XLII, Part I, p.994, p.998
28. O.R., Volume XLII, Part I, p.982-983; S.H.S.P., Volume XXI, p.273; The Wilmington Campaign, p.25
29. O.R., Volume XLII, Part I, p.976; S.H.S.P., Volume XXI, p.276
30. S.H.S.P., Volume XXI, p.274
31. O.R., Volume XLII, Part I, p.995, p.1113; The Wilmington Campaign, p.31
32. S.H.S.P., Volume XXI, p.274
33. O.R., Volume XLII, Part I, p.968, p.976, p.983; S.H.S.P., Volume XXI, p.274; Diary of Cyrus Comstock, p.299
34. Clark, Volume IV, p.35-38, p.40-41, p.45-49; O.R., Volume XLII, Part I, p.1025
35. S.H.S.P., Volume XXI, p.274; Clark, Volume IV, p.49
36. O.R., Volume XLII, Part I, p.968-969, p.981
37. O.R., Volume XLII, Part I, p.968, p.981
38. O.R., Volume XLII, Part I, p.981, p.983; The Wilmington Campaign, p.24
39. O.R., Volume XLII, Part I, p.983, p.1025
40. Antietam to Fort Fisher, p.224-225
41. O.R., Volume XLII, Part I, p.983; Butler's Book, p.797
42. Butler's Book, p.797
43. S.H.S.P., Volume XXI, p.275; O.R., Volume XLII, Part III, p.1308
44. S.H.S.P., Volume XXI, p.275
45. O.R., Volume XLII, Part I, p.995, p.1005
46. Ibid, p.995, p.1005
47. O.R., Volume XLII, Part III, p.1313-1314, p.1318
48. O.R., Volume XLII, Part III, p.1307
49. O.R., Volume XLII, Part III, p.1312
50. Clark, Volume III, p.693; O.R., Volume XLII, Part I, p.1022, Part III, p.1313, p.1316
51. O.R., Volume XLII, Part I, p.995-996
52. O.R., Volume XLII, Part I, p.980; S.H.S.P., Volume XXI, p.275-276
53. Ibid, p.996; Running the Blockade, p.139-141
54. Running the Blockade, p.139-141; Generals in Gray, p.225
55. Running the Blockade, p.137
56. O.R., Volume XLII, Part I, p.1001; The Wilmington Campaign, p.33
57. O.R., Volume XLII, Part I, p.985; The Wilmington Campaign, p.33
58. Ibid, p.996-998

59. Ibid, p.996
60. Ibid, p.1000-1001
61. Daily Journal, January 6, 1865; William Lamb Diary, January 2, 1865
62. Daily Journal, January 6, 1865
63. Daily Journal, January 6, 1865; Clark, Volume II, p.646-647
64. Antietam to Fort Fisher, p.226
65. ORN, Volume 11, p.261-262
66. Butler's Book, Appendix p.73; O.R., Volume XLVI, Part II, p.4
67. ORN, Volume 11, p.264
68. ORN, Volume 11, p.300; *Papers of the Military Historical Society of Massachusetts, Volume IX, Operations on the Atlantic Coast 1861-1865, Virginia 1862, 1864, Vicksburg*, p.393, Reprint of 1912 edition, Broadfoot Publishing Company, Wilmington, North Carolina, 1989
69. ORN, Volume 11, p.302
70. Ibid, p.317-318
71. Ibid, p.264, p.266
72. O.R., Volume XLII, Part III, p.1087
73. O.R., Volume XLVI, Part I, p.43, Part II, p.3; O.R., Volume XLII, Part III, p.1101
74. O.R., Volume XLII, Part III, p.1098-1099, p.1100-1101; Butler's Book, p.820-822; Foote, Shelby, *The Civil War a Narrative, Red River to Appomattox*, p.739-740, Random House Inc., New York, 1974
75. O.R., Volume XLVI, Part II, p.11
76. O.R., volume XLIV, p.798; Reed, Rowena, *Combined Operations in the Civil War*, p.356-357, Naval Institute Press, Annapolis, Maryland, 1977, hereinafter Combined Operations; Memoirs of Grant, p.513-516
77. Combined Operations, p.357
78. Generals in Blue, p.497
79. O.R., Volume XLVI, Part I, p.394-395, p.403-404; Generals in Blue, p.365-366
80. O.R., Volume XLVI, Part I, p.395; Terry, Adrian, "Wilmington and Fort Fisher", p.39, unpublished manuscript in Adrian Terry papers of Terry Family Collection, Yale University Library, New Haven, Connecticut, hereinafter Adrian Terry account
81. O.R., Volume XLVI, Part II, p.25
82. Adrian Terry account, biographical sketch following p.39; O.R., Volume XLVI, Part I, p.168
83. O.R., Volume XLVI, Part II, p.20
84. Antietam to Fort Fisher, p.227; Adrian Terry account, p.43; Wilmington Campaign, p.37
85. Lamb Diary, December 28 & December 30, 1864; Running the Blockade, p.137; O.R., Volume XLII, Part III, p.1346

86. Running the Blockade, p.137
87. O.R., Volume XLII, Part III, p.1359-1360, p.1362; Wilmington Campaign, p.2
88. S.H.S.P., Volume XXIII, p.167
89. O.R., Volume XLVI, Part II, p.1000-1001
90. Generals in Gray, p.140; Barefoot, Daniel W., *General Robert F. Hoke: Lee's Modest Warrior*, p.150, p.250, p.360-365, John Blair Publishing, Winston Salem, North Carolina, 1996, hereinafter Robert F. Hoke; Barrett, Civil War in North Carolina, p.271
91. Clark, Volume III, p.205, p.215
92. Clark, Volume III, p.685, p.694
93. War of Secession, p.286; Moffett, George, letter to wife Liz, January 2, 1865, Moffett family papers, South Carolina Historical Society, Charleston
94. S.H.S.P., Volume XXI, p.276
95. William Lamb Diary, January 4 – January 12, 1865; O.R., Volume XLVI, Part II, p.1012-1013
96. O.R., Volume XLVI, Part II, p.1014-1015
97. O.R., Volume XLVI, Part II, p.1023
98. O.R., Volume XLVI, Part II, p.1024
99. Clark, Volume III, p.215; Chronicles, p.492-493
100. O.R., Volume XLVI, Part II, p.1043; S.H.S.P., Volume XXI, p.276
101. S.H.S.P., Volume XX, p.303-304
102. O.R., Volume XLVI, Part II, p.1043; Chronicles, p.492
103. O.R., Volume XLVI, Part I, p.395; Adrian Terry account, p.43-44
104. Adrian Terry account, p.44
105. Adrian Terry account, p.44-45
106. O.R., Volume XLVI, Part I, p.395-396
107. Antietam to Fort Fisher, p.227
108. Battles & Leaders, Volume IV, p.647; O.R, Volume XLVI, Part II, p.1047
109. ORN, Volume 11, p.426-427
110. ORN, Volume 11, p.427
111. A Sailor's Log, p.84
112. ORN, Volume 11, p.468; Ammen, Daniel, *The Navy in the Civil War: The Atlantic Coast*, p.230, Charles Scribner's Sons, New York, 1883, hereinafter The Atlantic Coast; The Wilmington Campaign, p.37
113. Adrian Terry account, p.46; O.R., Volume XLVI, Part I, p.396; Wilmington Campaign, p.37-39
114. The Wilmington Campaign, p.36-37; Adrian Terry account, p.46; "The Capture of Fort Fisher", by Brevet Major General Newton Martin Curtis, p.306, in Civil War Papers of the State of Massachusetts, Military Order

of the Loyal Legion of the United States, Volume I, 1900, hereinafter The Capture of Fort Fisher; Robert F. Hoke, p.253

115. O.R., Volume XLVI, Part II, p.1047; Robert F. Hoke, p.253-254; The Wilmington Campaign, p.36-37

116. Clark, Volume III, p.215, p.694; N.C. Troops, Volume XII, p.289

117. Elliott, Captain Charles G., "Kirkland's Brigade, Hoke's Division, 1864-'65", S.H.S.P., Volume XXIII, p.167-168

118. S.H.S.P., Volume XXIII, p.168; Adrian Terry account, p.1; The Wilmington Campaign, p.37

119. Robert F. Hoke; The Wilmington Campaign, p.37

120. ORN, Volume 11, p.461; S.H.S.P., Volume XXI, p.277

121. O.R., Volume XLVI, Part I, p.437

122. "The Charlotte News", January 15, 1944, Charlotte, North Carolina

123. Battles & Leaders, Volume IV, p.647

124. O.R., Volume XLVI, Part II, p.

"Bloody Gate," which opened on to the road to Wilmington, and Shepherd's Battery, next to it. It was here that Federal troops first breached the walls of Fort Fisher, and where some of the worst fighting took place in the second battle.

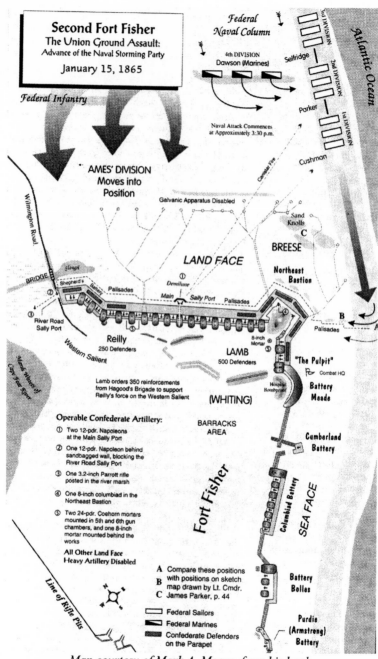

Map courtesy of Mark A. Moore, from his book
The Wilmington Campaign and the Battles for Fort Fisher

Chapter 10

"...officers on both sides were loading and firing with their men..."

A round noontime, fifty to sixty sailors and marines were ordered up from Battery Buchanan to reinforce Lamb's gunners on the landface. Robert Watson, a sailor who had formerly served aboard the ironclad *C.S.S. Savannah*, was one of that contingent. He noted in his diary that day the men had to double quick all the way to Fort Fisher, with "the shell bursting around us in large numbers," but doing them no harm. "We manned three guns and commenced firing at 1 PM. The Yankees had been firing on the fort all day with 3 monitors and the *Ironsides*." [1]

Augustus Buell, a Union artillerist awaiting debarkation from one of the Federal transports, was awestruck at the fleet's heavy pounding of Fisher. "I cannot describe," he said, "the discharges of those 13 and 15-inch Rodman guns of the monitors, or the explosion of their great shells in the air over the fort or among its traverses. To me it seemed like firing meteors out of volcanoes." Buell watched the action of the big monitors through his field glasses. As the sailors in them made ready to reload their pieces, the iron turrets turned in the opposite direction of the fort to protect the men doing the loading. "I could distinctly see the big rammer staves come out of the ports," he wrote. "Then they would wheel round on a line with the fort, there would be two puffs of blue smoke about the size of a

Admiral Porter's fleet bombards Fort Fisher a second time in January 1865.

thunder cloud in June, and then I could see the big shell make a black streak through the air with a tail of white smoke behind it – and then would come over the water, not the quick bark of a field gun, but a slow, quivering, overpowering roar like an earthquake, and then, away among the Rebel traverses, there would be another huge ball of mingled smoke and flame as big as a meeting house." [2]

Despite the more accurate shelling, Lamb's men stayed at their posts enduring heavier casualties, the Colonel ordering the "same slow and deliberate firing" as in December. Robley Evans, aboard the *U.S.S. Powhatan*, was impressed with the Confederates' tenacity. "They stood up and fought their guns most gallantly," he said, "and would not be driven into the bombproofs." [3]

As the cannoneers manfully loaded, fired, swabbed, and reloaded their guns, while big chunks of iron sprayed around and even through some of them, their so-called support force continued to mark time. "The enemy, apparently, is preparing to attack me," Robert Hoke wired headquarters in Wilmington, as Abbott's brigade skirmished with Kirkland's men in the Sugar Loaf line, while the troops of Hagood, Colquitt, and Clingman began to file into the trenches. The infantry in Abbott's Sixth Connecticut, Seventh Connecticut, Third New Hampshire and Seventh New Hampshire regiments, and the continuous shelling of the navy, convinced Hoke he had better stay put, at least for now. It was just what Alfred Terry wanted, and Chase Whiting feared. [4]

After getting his 8,000 effective troops ashore by 3 p.m. (some returns showed he had nearly 9,000), Terry said his initial objective was to secure "a strong defensive line across the peninsula, from the Cape Fear River to the sea, facing Wilmington, so as to protect our rear from attack while we should be engaged in operating against Fisher." Engineer maps indicated the area of landing, five miles north of Fisher, would be a satisfactory place to intrench his northern protective line, with the head of Myrtle Sound, the southern extremity of Masonboro Sound, serving to anchor the right flank.

With the Federals in control of the beach east of the sound, Masonboro Inlet, several miles to the north, could be used by vessels to bring in supplies and reinforcements "in quiet water there." It was quickly determined, however, that for a considerable distance north of the head of Myrtle Sound, the water was "so shallow as to offer no obstacle to the passage of troops at low tide." The Rebels, then, could attack across Myrtle Sound, if they took the notion. [5] Determining to move further south with the bulk of his force, while Abbott remained near Hoke's line to build numerous campfires and "hold his position until daybreak and then retreat unless previously driven back by the enemy," Paine's division and two of Ames' brigades moved out. Captain Benjamin F. Sands, commanding the *U.S.S. Fort Jackson*, was ordered to move his warship "in closer to cover the skirmishers...close to the beach, shelling it in advance of the army." He said "the troops on shore could be seen advancing as we steamed down to our position, a beautiful sight being presented by that mass of 'boys in blue' who covered the beach, following our first line of gunboats." [6]

As the infantry moved closer to Fisher, much of the balance of the fleet came to anchor near the ironclads, and added their broadsides to the heavy pounding of the fort. Robert Watson noted in his diary that about 4 p.m. the other warships joined in, and bombarded their positions with a "terrific fire until dark." He further recorded that "none of our men were hurt except Lieut. Hudgins who was slightly wounded in the mouth with a fragment of shell and several of us were knocked down with sand bags. We were all nearly buried in sand several times. This was caused by shell bursting in the sand. Whenever one would strike near us in the sand it would throw the sand over us by the cart load." [7]

Two miles south of the landing and about three north of Fisher, the infantry stopped as night was setting in, in an area where the maps indicated the presence of a large pond, "occupying nearly one-third of the width of the peninsula," which could be used to help protect the line. It was found, however, that the pond was really a large sand flat, covered with water in rainy weather, but at this time dry. Terry ordered Paine to extend his division to the river, anyway, to determine if the position could be utilized. [8]

"As the sun went down, and the shadows fell over the water," a Union sailor aboard the *U.S.S. Mohican* wrote, "the spectacle was truly grand; the smoke rose and partially drifted off, permitting glimpses now and then of the earthwork, and the fitful yet incessant gleams from the hundreds of shells bursting on or beyond the parapet illuminated, like lightning flashes, the clouds above and the smoke of battle beneath." The wooden ships withdrew by 6 p.m., while the ironclads kept up a slow and methodical fire on Fisher. [9]

As the bluecoats sloshed their way through marshy ground toward the Cape Fear, and the pounding from the ironclads went on, Lamb's reinforcements were coming into the embattled fort. Sergeant Thaddeus Davis of Third Company G, Fortieth North Carolina (Third Regiment Artillery), said his company, and Companies D, E, and K of the Fortieth, "arrived at Confederate Point about dark" on the steamer *Pettaway*, having to wade ashore in water waist deep "to reach the beach." They came over from Fort Holmes as the ironclads continued their shelling, and were assigned to guns on the landface, as well as positions on the palisade fence. [10]

Arriving from Fort Caswell was Company D of the First Battalion North Carolina Heavy Artillery, under command of Captain James L. McCormic. Sergeant Thomas McNeill said the men "landed near Battery Buchanan after dark that night," and by order of Colonel Lamb, were hustled to the land face, where an infantry assault was anticipated. McNeill recalled the company "double-quicked to its position near the west end of the land face, but the enemy did not then approach." [11]

More troops, two companies of the Tenth North Carolina (First Artillery), under Major James Reilly, and one company of the Thirteenth Battalion North Carolina Light Artillery under Captain Zachariah T. Adams, would be coming in through the night. Company C of the Third Battalion North Carolina Light Artillery under Captain John M. Sutton, had remained in Fisher after reinforcing the garrison in December. Altogether, 700 more troops would augment Lamb's Thirty-Sixth North Carolina through the night hours, raising his troop strength to 1,500. [12]

As reinforcements were arriving, General Whiting fired off another demanding message to Bragg, asking him to explain the inaction on the north end of Confederate Point. At 8 p.m. he communicated from Fisher, "Enemy are on the beach, where they have been all day. Why are they not attacked? Our casualties about forty, after a furious bombardment. I have ordered troops from the other posts. Our submarine cable and telegraph cut by shell." With the telegraph lines severed, and signal flags at Battery Buchanan undiscernible at Battery Lamb across the river, due to the dust and smoke of battle, messages would be slow getting out. Henceforth, signalmen would have to row across the mouth of the river to Smithville, Louis Hebert's headquarters, and telegraph messages to Wilmington and Sugar Loaf from there. It was an additional hindrance the Confederates could ill afford. [13]

As Whiting vented his anger at his superior, Captain Sands, aboard the *Fort Jackson*, watched with admiration the continuing bombardment of Fort Fisher by the ironclad division, the wooden frigates having withdrawn for the night. "When they opened fire," he wrote, "it seemed to rain shells, and as the night drew over the scene its veil of darkness, it seemed one grand pyrotechnic display as the guns flashed brightly and shells exploded in the air...the ironclads kept up a regular fire at intervals to keep them stirred up in the fort." [14]

When Charles Paine's infantry finally reached the river about 9 p.m., the line Alfred Terry wanted constructed was found to be impractical in this

Gen. Charles Paine's U.S. Colored Troops

area. The ground was too marshy, and "illy adapted to the construction of works, and the distance was found to be too great to be properly defended by the troops which could be spared from the direct attack upon the fort." The ground further south was reconnoitered, and found to be better suited for construction of earthworks. The troops were withdrawn and established on the new line, some two miles north of Fisher, by 2 a.m. of the 14th. The right flank, facing north toward Hoke's position, was anchored on Battery Anderson.

"Tools were immediately brought up," General Terry wrote, "and intrenchments were commenced; at 8 o'clock a good breast-work, reaching from the river to the sea and partially covered by abatis had been constructed and was in a defensible condition. It was much improved afterward, but from this time our foothold on the peninsula was secured. Early in the morning of the 14th the landing of the artillery was commenced." [15]

All through the night and early morning, the monitors continued their pounding of the fort. The ironclads, William Lamb related, "bowled their eleven and fifteen-inch shells along its parapet, scattering shrapnel in the darkness." Meals could not be prepared, and even the dead could not be buried without risk of further casualties. The landface guns were being systematically destroyed and dismounted, as the fleet concentrated its fire on those positions, in preparation for the infantry assault that was to come. [16]

As Terry's northern line was being completed Saturday morning, "the troops of General Ames' division were withdrawn from the line," and Paine's division and Abbott's brigade, under Paine's command, were left to defend it. Abbott reported a quiet night had been spent in Hoke's front, and that a few captured Confederate pickets confirmed Hoke had 6,000 to 7,000 troops on hand. [17]

As Ames' division moved south toward the fort, Curtis' brigade was detached from it, so far as taking orders from Ames was concerned, to receive orders directly from General Terry. At least Martin Curtis later claimed that to be the case, though Terry's official report to U.S. Grant stated clearly that General Ames "commanded all the troops engaged," and said nothing of Curtis reporting directly to him. The motive for the detachment, Curtis alleged, was Adelbert Ames' vindictiveness toward Curtis. When the expedition had left Hampton Roads, Ames had literally missed the boat, the army transport *Atlantic*, and had been several days catching up to his division at its rendezvous off Beaufort. Curtis had reluctantly been forced to take command of the vessel, being senior officer onboard, and had done all in his power to communicate the circumstances to the division commander through Ames' staff officers.

Obviously embarrassed at being absent when he should have been present with his division, when Ames finally showed up on the *Atlantic*, he apparently sought to deflect criticism of himself at Curtis' expense. He accused Curtis of "sailing with his division for the purpose of commanding it," and was offensive and abrasive with his subordinate, who had followed that which military protocol required. Curtis hotly protested such inflammatory language and accusations, demanding a retraction from Ames. For the remainder of the expedition, the two engaged in verbal interchange only on the "strictest requirements of official duty." [18]

As the troops headed for William Lamb's defenses, Ames asked Terry not to assign Curtis to any special duty, and said he would not be held responsible for Curtis' actions. According to Curtis, Terry told Ames he would assume responsibility for Curtis, saying " 'I have known General Curtis for nearly two years, and have perfect confidence in his ability and fidelity. I will relieve him from your command, and direct him to report to me for orders.' " Terry, said Curtis, then advised him he would thenceforth receive orders directly from him. Again, there is no mention of such command change in Terry's official report, nor in the detailed account of his brother Adrian. [19]

Early that morning, as Terry's northern line was in the process of completion, Bragg and Hoke pushed their pickets forward to reconnoiter, not realizing the Federals had extended across the point and fortified. The Second South Carolina Cavalry was supposed to be on watch between the Sugar Loaf lines and Fort Fisher, to keep Bragg apprised of movements and to maintain patrols between the fort and the enemy. They failed miserably.

Bragg wrote that he and his men advanced on the left in the direction of the beach, while Hoke moved on the right toward the river. Bragg said Hoke found the enemy had extended across the peninsula and was strongly entrenched, between Hoke's troops and Fort Fisher. "Not a word," Bragg said, "had been heard from our cavalry, and they had evidently withdrawn from their position in the night and did not themselves know what had occurred, for they fired on Hoke and his staff, who got in front of them in reconnoitering."

Bragg was mortified, and ordered Hoke to dislodge the Yankees, "if it was at all practicable. Hoke and his brigadiers," Bragg said, "made a close reconnaissance and expressed to me the opinion that their troops were unequal to the task. I moved forward with them and made a close examination, confirmed their opinion, and after a conference decided not to attack...We could not have succeeded without defeating double our number behind entrenchments, whilst at the same time exposed to a raking fire from their fleet." Failure of an attack, Bragg said, would not only have insured the fall of Fisher, but Wilmington and the state itself. [20]

Not surprised at Bragg's continued bungling, Lamb would write that Hoke's infantry, not cavalry, should have been hard on the heels of the Yankees that night, when they could not have been covered by the fire of the fleet. "Cavalry on the beach at night to watch the enemy!" Lamb said disgustedly. "A reconnaissance that an officer could have made on foot within an hour. To those familiar with the Carolina sea coast at night," Lamb wrote, "and how a man on horseback looms up like a dromedary in the desert, it will not be surprising that these horsemarines, not wishing to become targets for the Federal sharpshooters, followed the example of General Bragg and his army, and retired for the night." [21]

Early Saturday morning, Robert Watson and his fellow sailors were assembled behind Fisher's landface. They had been up all night in anticipation of an infantry attack, firing their "guns every 15 minutes along the beach with canister," and were temporarily returning to their naval quarters for some much needed rest. They "fell in and marched back to Battery Buchanan," Watson noted in his diary. They marched, he said, "in quick time and got a drink of whiskey on arrival, got breakfast and turned in and just as I fell asleep we were ordered to fall in and go back to Fort Fisher."

They had to run a gauntlet of naval fire all the way back to the landface. "The Yankees saw us," Watson wrote, "for they shelled us furiously all the way but did us no injury. We got through safe and manned the same guns we had yesterday. I was at a...Brooke rifle and made some excellent shots." [22]

At 11:45 that morning, distressingly aware that the Federal noose was tightening, Chase Whiting telegraphed Bragg from Louis Hebert's headquarters in Smithville, being unable to do so from Fisher with the wires now severed. He told the district commander the fleet would not be able to cross the bar to run past Fisher, as the tide was now outgoing, and would not be incoming until that night. "Sooner you attack the enemy the better," he chided Bragg.

Upon his arrival back at Fisher, Whiting got the dire news from Bragg that the Yankees had extended across the peninsula, something over two miles above Fisher on the river. "Hoke is now moving on him," Bragg told Whiting. Whiting responded promptly that he had received news of the enemy extending to the riverbank. "This they never should have been allowed to do," Whiting admonished Bragg with complete disregard for rank, "and if they are permitted to remain there the reduction of Fort Fisher is but a question of tine. This has been notified heretofore frequently both to yourself and to the Department. I will hold this place till the last extremities; but unless you drive that land force from its position I cannot answer for the security of this harbor. The fire," Whiting told him, "has been and continues to be exceedingly heavy, surpassing not so much its volume as in its extraordinary condition even the fire of Christmas. The garrison is in good spirits and condition." [23]

Bragg's response to Whiting's criticism was to order 1,000 infantry from Hoke's Division to reinforce Fisher, while at the same time ordering the six companies sent in by Hebert the night before, to report to Gander Hall Landing, near Sugar Loaf, to reinforce Hoke. He considered those six companies "less reliable troops" than the ones he was sending in. Bragg's notion that he would send 1,000 infantry to Fort Fisher, while at the same time removing troops from Fisher to reinforce Sugar Loaf, which was not even threatened, was ludicrous. It was one more indication of how out of touch he was from reality. He even wired Whiting that he believed the reinforcements sent to Fisher "will render your position impregnable against assault." [24]

How impregnable Fisher would be after the pounding it was taking from the navy was questionable. One Union sailor aboard the *U.S.S. Fort Jackson*, whose vessel was employed in landing the Federal artillery, confirmed Whiting's estimate of the heavy, accurate firing: "Our fleet and the iron-clads were doing some beautiful marksmanship, landing their shells between and in the enemy's traverses, throwing up clouds of sand and driving the rebels from their guns. I saw several alight near a gun, between a couple of traverses, and the men kept on loading their gun and were training it on the fleet, when another shell exploded right over them and cleaned them away entirely, that gun not being fired afterwards." [25]

By early afternoon, Martin Curtis' brigade was at Battery Holland, 500 to 600 yards north of the west end of Fisher's landface. On the way down, they had captured a Confederate steamer at Craig's Landing on the Cape Fear, about one mile north of the fort. The *Isaac Wells*, loaded with forage and ammunition, had been sent down to resupply Lamb's garrison.

Braxton Bragg, in his clouded misunderstanding of the battle situation, was not even aware that Craig's had been in Union hands for several hours. Clear, visual observation of "everything transpiring on the beach," the river road, or in the fort, could have been had by Bragg or his subordinates with field glasses across the Cape Fear, or in one of the steamers at his disposal. Such observation would have made it evident that the proper place to send the vessel was Battery Buchanan, and at night, so as not to be detected by the fleet. Instead, Bragg sent the vessel to a position in enemy hands in broad daylight.

Lamb ordered one of his cannon crew to fire a shot near the transport to warn her off, but she kept on to Craig's to become the prize of Terry's infantry. The Confederate warship *Chickamauga*, patrolling the river and looking for Yankees to shoot at, had already inflicted casualties on Curtis' Brigade. Lamb reported that the *Chickamauga*, seeing the "stupid surrender" of the supply ship, fired into the stern-wheeler and sunk her, a 30-pound Parrott shell hulling her below the water line. [26]

Battery Holland, the redoubt situated on Howard's Hill, was an ideal location for the Yankees to secure. Adrian Terry said this position "overlooked the ground between it and the main work and commanded the best general view of Fort Fisher." From here in mid-afternoon, General Terry, Cyrus Comstock, Martin Curtis, and two staff officers headed south a couple of hundred yards even closer to the fort, wading through river rushes and hugging sand dunes, to study in detail the massive work with "their powerful field glasses." Terry's up-close, personal reconnaissance under the very guns of his enemy, contrasted starkly with the fumbling, armchair generalship of Bragg.

Their observations revealed that the fleet's pounding had been of significantly more value this time than the last. "The reconnaissance showed," Chief Engineer Comstock wrote, "that the palisading in front of the work had been seriously injured by the navy fire. Only nine guns could be seen on the land front where sixteen had been counted on Christmas day. The steady though not rapid fire of the navy prevented the enemy from using either artillery or musketry on the reconnoitering party. It seemed probable that troops could be got up within 200 yards of the work without serious loss." [27]

Agreeing with Comstock's observations, Terry turned to Curtis and asked him if he thought the three brigades of Ames' Division could take the fort. Curtis said he believed they could, "if the dispositions were properly made, and if the Navy should support the troops from start to finish." Terry told him, so said Curtis, "that in case an assault is made you will make it. I will see Admiral Porter this evening, and we will then decide what course to pursue." [28]

Leaving Curtis with his brigade to maintain the line at Battery Holland, as well as a skirmish line in the area of the just completed reconnaissance, he returned to his headquarters at the northern defensive line. He told his Assistant Adjutant General brother, Adrian, that he was now headed for Porter's flagship for a conference. "If he will cooperate in the way I shall propose, I will assault the work tomorrow afternoon," he told Adrian.

Adrian was a great admirer of his brother. He wrote that the general's nature was "such that, as had been shown on many previous occasions, he would take great personal risks in examining into the feasibility of a projected attack upon the enemy, before assuming the responsibility of sending his gallant comrades against an obstacle which might be insurmountable...His careful observation of the work of the navy," Terry wrote, "in the Department of the South, had given him firm belief in its ability to accomplish great things, and while he knew that it could not knock away earthworks, he was confident that it could knock down palisades, disable guns, and drive the garrison to the cover of their bombproofs. His observation of the effect already produced upon Fort Fisher by the naval fire confirmed that belief, and upon it was based his determination to assault if the Admiral would cooperate in the way that he desired." [29]

Hugging a sand dune on the skirmish line, Curtis further surveyed the ground in front of the fort's parapet, and decided to have breastworks thrown up in front of the western end of Fisher to cover the soldiers prior to assault. The marshy ground in front of the western half was an obstacle, but it was lower terrain than the ground further to the east. Also, the western end of the fort was higher than the eastern end, and therefore made it easier to get under the plane of fire from the garrison, thus affording greater protection from that fire.

As darkness came on, Curtis sent out a skirmish line "deployed at five paces, the front rank carrying muskets, the rear shovels, and advanced to the place selected for the first line." With their shovels, the men in the rear threw up a sufficient amount of sand to cover a man in the prone position, while at the same time the men with rifles moved forward twenty paces. "In the drift sand," Curtis said, "the work was quickly done." Now the soldier with the shovel advanced and handed it to the picket, took that man's musket, moved out twenty paces himself, and the former picket went to work throwing up sand in his front.

By this method, Curtis was able to have four lines of breastworks built, the last one "being under the plane of fire" from the fort. New squads of men connected these "Gopher Holes," as the soldiers dubbed them. "About one hundred and seventy-five yards from the parapet," Curtis said, "a higher and heavier breastwork was thrown up to protect a party of sharpshooters; and forty men, selected on account of their skill as marksmen, were immediately sent to occupy it." The sharpshooters were charged with killing any Confederates who appeared on the parapets to load the cannon. [30]

Curtis' sharpshooters would merely reinforce the merciless pounding of the fleet, which continued without letup into the night hours. Inside Fort Fisher, Cape Fear District Chief of Artillery Major William Saunders grimly attested to the results of the fire. "During this day," he wrote, "the enemy dismounted all of our guns on the land face, with the exception of one 8-inch columbiad, three 32-pounders (smooth-bores), and one 30-pounder Parrott. These, however, kept a steady fire...The enemy's fire was very effective, killing and wounding many of our men." Colonel Lamb concurred, saying that anytime his men fired on Curtis' approaching line, "it drew upon the gunners the fury of the fleet." Two hundred men were killed or wounded in the first two days of combat, and no more than "three or four of my land guns were serviceable." [31]

General Terry and Colonel Comstock arrived on Porter's flagship, the *Malvern*, during the night. Porter was eager to discuss the next day's battle plan with Terry. Terry advised Porter of their detailed reconnaissance, and of his decision to attack the landface along the western end of the fort, "providing the navy would co-operate as he wished it to do." Porter was more than enthusiastic, and told the general that his "ships should go in early and fire rapidly through the day until the time for the assault came off." Porter thought the time agreed upon was 2 p.m., though the army commander said it was 3 p.m., so there was some misunderstanding over the exact time. The admiral told Terry he was assigning 1,600 sailors and 400 marines, as previously discussed with his fleet subordinates, to participate in the assault with the army.

The sailors would, in naval parlance, "board the sea face, while the troops assaulted the land side." The men were to be armed with revolvers and swords, with some carrying carbines or Sharps rifles. The marines, also armed with rifles, would cover the naval assault from rifle pits they would dig in the sand.

Porter considered Alfred Terry his "beau ideal of a soldier and a general." There was cordial cooperation between the two, and they established a system of army based wig-wag signals that would allow them to communicate with each other as often as needed, "though nearly a mile apart and amidst the din of battle." [32]

At William Lamb's request, Chase Whiting communicated to Bragg that evening to attack the Yankees from the north under cover of darkness, when the navy could not cooperate with accurate fire. Lamb would be ready with ten companies taken from the fort, and hit Curtis' men at the same time from the south. With his troops and the 6,000 or more in Hoke's Division, Lamb believed the Confederates would have about the same numbers as the Federals, and they would be ground between upper and nether millstones. He felt "we could capture a portion or the whole of the force, or at least demoralize it." Though no response was forthcoming from Bragg, Lamb still believed he would respond to his plea for action.

Captain Daniel Patterson's Clarendon Guards, Company H of the Thirty-Sixth North Carolina, moved out of the fort about 9 p.m. as skirmishers under Lamb. They advanced beyond the palisade fence and the range of the fleet's fire, to feel out the enemy. "We found none on the sea-shore within half a mile," Lamb said, "but on the river-shore they were occupying the redoubt, where their skirmishers extended toward the left of the fort. Some of them fired on us, but we remained there awaiting a message from Bragg, or the sound of his guns from the north, but in vain, and before daylight we retired to the fort." [33]

Returning to headquarters on the northern defensive line after his conference with Porter, Alfred Terry assured himself that the guns of his light batteries were all on shore and in position on his left flank adjacent to the river, where the fleet was least able to protect the army. He spent nearly all the rest of the night in working out the details of the attack that was fast approaching.

Sunday, January the 15th dawned bright and cold. "At 8 a.m.," Terry reported, "all of the vessels, except a division left to aid in the defense of our northern line, moved into position, and a fire, magnificent alike for its power and accuracy, was opened." Terry summoned Adelbert Ames and the commanding officers of his three brigades, Curtis, Galusha Pennypacker, and Louis Bell. Advising them he had decided their division was definitely the one to make the assault, he explained the order of battle.

First, one hundred picked sharpshooters armed with breech-loading rifles, one hundred rounds of ammunition and a shovel, under the command of Lieutenant Colonel Samuel M. Zent of the Thirteenth Indiana Infantry, were to be posted in the area of Battery Holland early in the afternoon. Sixty of these soldiers were to be from the Thirteenth Indiana, while the other forty were from Curtis' brigade, already at the front near the fort.

Secondly, the Second and Third Brigades of Pennypacker and Bell were ordered to move up "until they reached the end of the woods about half a mile from the fort and there form line." The Third Brigade was to be in a proper interval behind the Second, while the First Brigade of Curtis, "as the others approached should also form line in front of the 2nd Brigade."

Thirdly, Curtis' First Brigade would move "up to the outwork," the Second behind the First and the Third behind the Second, maintaining their proper intervals.

Fourthly, the sharpshooters would now "advance in skirmishing order at the run until they arrived within 150 yards of the fort when each man should dig a pit in the sand for his own protection." Once he had dug what in later wars would be called a "foxhole," he was to be ready to fire at any Confederate showing himself on the parapet, paying special attention to artillerists. [34]

Finally, once the sharpshooters were firmly in position, Curtis' First Brigade would advance to the rifle pits thrown up by his picket line the night before, with the Second Brigade of Pennypacker moving up to the position just vacated by Curtis. The Third Brigade of Bell would then advance to Pennypacker's former line.

All preparations for assault were to be completed before 3 p.m., so that when the signal for attack was given, there would be four lines of troops in front of Fisher ready to hit it. The sharpshooters would be 150-175 yards from it, Curtis' brigade some 100 yards behind them, Pennypacker's men 250 yards behind Curtis, and Bell's brigade 250 yards in rear of Pennypacker.

Terry's command center would be at Battery Holland. From here, he could easily communicate with Porter through their signal officers. Since it was so close to Fisher, he could clearly discern every movement of his soldiers until they had gotten on the ramparts of the fort, and maintain communication with them afterward as the fight progressed. At the same time, he would be able to stay in touch with his rear defensive line under General Paine.

When all brigades were in position, Adelbert Ames would report the fact to Terry, who would then signal Porter, whose vessels would still be bombarding Fisher. If the naval contingent of sailors and marines were ready to assault, the fire of the fleet would then be "diverted from the points of attack to other parts of the work," mainly along the seaface of the fort. [35]

As Curtis' troops were the lead brigade, Terry asked him how he intended to form his men for the assault. Curtis told him he "wished to charge in line, brigade front, make successive advances from one rifle pit to the next, the final rush not to be made until we were as near the fort as we could get without drawing the infantry fire, and that our movements in this particular would be governed by the action of the enemy in coming to the parapet." They would advance gradually at first, hopscotching forward from one set of trenches to the next, as the fire of the fleet suppressed the garrison's musketry and forced them to hunker down behind the parapets.

Ultimately, Curtis told Terry, "the final rush will be made when you see me rise in the middle of the line and hear me call aloud. Soon after you will see the First Brigade go through the stockade and up the parapet; then send Pennypacker's brigade." Terry responded by telling Curtis when he saw his men on the parapets of the fort, he would "feel certain of success. A lodgment there assures victory." [36]

Aboard the *U.S.S. Powhatan*, Robley Evans eagerly awaited the chance to attack Fort Fisher as part of the naval contingent. "January 15th proved a beautiful day for our work," he said, "with a smooth beach for our landing. At early daylight the whole fleet opened on the fort, and poured shells in on it at a fearful rate."

Evans' enthusiasm may have been somewhat tempered by an incident that occurred a few hours before. One of the sailors on the *Powhatan*, Seaman James Flannigan, had approached Evans on the night of the 14th with a small box. He asked Evans if he would, "be kind enough to take charge of this box for me – it has some little trinkets in it – and give it to my sister in Philadelphia?" When Evans asked him why he didn't give it to her himself, he replied, "I am going ashore with you tomorrow, and will be killed." Evans tried to assure him there was slight chance of that, that it took many bullets fired from an enemy to kill a man in battle. Flannigan, however, was convinced of his fate. He "seemed to regard it as a matter of course," and displayed no fear over what he believed to be his coming death. [37]

About 10 a.m., Lieutenant John Bartlett of the *U.S.S. Susquehanna* wrote, the signal went out to the fleet from the admiral's flagship to "Arm and away all boats," and for the naval contingent to assemble for duty on the beach. "In a few moments," he said, "the whole place was alive with hundreds of boats pulling for the shore." Bartlett was in command of one of the two boats from the *Susquehanna*, with Lieutenant Commander F.B. Blake in charge of the other, fifty sailors and eighteen marines being rowed ashore from their ship. [38]

Lieutenant Commander Thomas O. Selfridge, commander of the *U.S.S. Huron* and heading for the beach with some of his shipmates, noted that from "thirty-five of the sixty ships of the fleet boats shoved off, making, with their flags flying as they pulled toward the beach in line abreast, a most spirited scene. The general order of Admiral Porter required that the assaulting column of sailors should be armed with cutlasses and pistols." [39]

Robley Evans and his men left the *Powhatan* accompanied by cheers from their shipmates. As they were pulling for shore, Evans noted, a cannon shot "struck the stroke oar of my boat, cut it in two, and sent the handle spinning across my stomach with such force that I thought I was broken in two." He sustained no injury, however, other than a bruised stomach, and he and his men landed safely. [40]

LtCmdr Kidder Breese, U.S. Navy

A total of 1,600 sailors and 400 marines landed about one and a half miles north of Fisher. Thomas Selfridge noted that they were a "heterogeneous assembly," with companies of 200 or more men from the largest frigates, down to squads of no more than 20 men from some of the smaller gunboats. Confined for months aboard vessels, most of the men did not know officers or sailors from other ships, they "had never drilled together, and their arms, the old-fashioned cutlass and pistol, were hardly the weapons to cope with the rifles and bayonets of the enemy. Sailor-like, however, they looked upon the landing in the light of a lark." [41]

Overall command of the fleet's force was given to Lieutenant Commander Kidder R. Breese. Three divisions, comprised of the men from the "corresponding division squadrons of the fleet," were formed from the 1,600 sailors. The first division was commanded by Lieutenant Commander Charles H. Cushman of the *U.S.S. Wabash*, the second division was under Lieutenant Commander James Parker, Executive Officer of the *U.S.S. Minnesota*, and the third division was under Thomas Selfridge. The 400 U.S. Marines comprised a fourth division or line of battle, and were commanded by Marine Captain Lucien L. Dawson.

Flag Lieutenant Samuel Preston was a handsome and talented young officer serving on Porter's staff. Breese said he was among "the bravest of the brave." He was sent forward with a force of about 350 sailors carrying shovels and picks, "and threw up within 600 yards of the fort a well-protected breastwork, and from that gradually advanced to within 200 yards a succession of rifle pits." Those rifle pits, which connected westward opposite the palisade fence with General Curtis' infantry skirmishers, were quickly occupied by about 50 marines under Second Lieutenant Louis E. Fagan. [42]

Captain Dawson was prodded several times by Breese to quickly bring up the balance of the marines, some 365 men. Against his better military judgment, Dawson, "had to move off without time to equalize the companies, to number them off for facing and marching; to select sergeants to replace officers, or post the guides of a single company or platoon."

Dawson sent his marines across the point and out in front of the sailors. Breese pointed out to him some of the intrenchments Samuel Preston had had his party throw up "toward the main bastion of Fort Fisher, which were dug and being completed under cover of the fire of the fleet." Dawson's men were ordered "to advance to those that were finished, and as soon as those nearest the fort were completed to occupy them, and when the assault was made that I should keep up a full fire, when the sailors would rush by me, and when well past, the marines would follow them into the fort." In the event of a repulse, then, the assaulting party would have cover and a rallying point. It was a sound plan, could it have been followed. [43]

Inside Fort Fisher, carnage and death reigned supreme, as Lamb and his battle-weary men prepared to resist the assault soon to be launched. "The sea was smooth," Lamb recalled, "and the

Capt. Lucien Dawson, U.S.M.C.

navy having become accurate from practice, by noon had destroyed every gun on that face (land) except one Columbiad, which was somewhat protected by the angle formed by the northeast salient. The palisade had been practically destroyed as a defensive line and was so torn up that it actually afforded cover for the assailants. The harvest of wounded and dead was hourly increasing, and at that time I had not 1,200 effective men to defend the long line of works." [44]

Major William Saunders estimated the fleet was bringing to bear at least 300 guns against them. "Its effect was terrible," he wrote, "the works being torn to pieces and every gun on the land face (except one 8-inch columbiad) dismounted." General Whiting, echoing Major Saunders and Colonel Lamb, said, "the fire of the fleet reached a pitch of fury to which no language can do justice. It was concentrated on the land front and fort. In a short time nearly every gun was dismounted or disabled, and the garrison suffered severely from the fire." [45]

In spite of the hailstorm of iron that rained down on them, Lamb ordered the crews of two Napoleon guns at the sally port and one other at the River Road entrance on the left, next to Shepherd's Battery, to fire on the advancing skirmishers of Curtis' Brigade. His men obeyed the orders without flinching, but several of them were quickly killed and wounded. As he observed the gradually approaching column of sailors and marines along the beach, he ordered the remaining gun on the landface and two guns at the Mound Battery opened on them. [46]

Robley Evans said the naval column, after forming up in their several divisions, advanced to within about 1,200 yards of the fort, "where we halted and waited the signal to charge, which was to be the blowing of the steam whistle on the flagship, repeated by other vessels of the fleet." The heavy shells Lamb's men were firing at them, "generally struck short of us, and would then ricochet down the level beach, jumping along for all the world like rabbits." To minimize casualties, the officers marched the column toward the water, to seek the protection offered by the slope of the beach. [47]

Johnny Barltett, with his company of sailors on the beach, said several marines in front of the column were wounded by Fisher's big guns. He said they all laid down in the sand so as to make as small a target "as possible, and waited patiently for the time to come for the assault. While we were here the fleet was hard at work, keeping up a terrific bombardment on the fort. We had a grand chance to see it. It was a most magnificent sight."

As they moved closer to the fort, Lamb's riflemen began firing on them at long range. To be protected from musketry, Bartlett said, some threw up sand in front of themselves, using their hands as they lay on the beach. They were uncomfortably near Fort Fisher for another reason. The fleet was, "firing directly over our heads, which was far from pleasant, as some of them fell short and right among us, wounding several." [48]

Shortly after noontime, part of the 1,000 reinforcements Bragg had dispatched from Hagood's Brigade, now under Colonel Robert Graham of the Twenty-First South Carolina, Hagood being on leave in South Carolina, landed at Battery Buchanan. Some of Porter's warships bombarding the seaface batteries, observing the disembarking, redirected their fire to the steamer and the troops. Only two regiments, the Eleventh and Twenty-Fifth South Carolina, made it to shore, the majority remaining on board ship, as the steamer *Sampson* beat a hasty retreat. Graham, who had been unable to land with the men, sent a telegram to Bragg from Smithville at 1 p.m.: "As instructed by you about four hundred of my men landed at Fisher. The rest were prevented by the fire of the enemy. I will go there tonight unless otherwise instructed." [49]

North of Fisher's landface, Martin Curtis and some of his New Yorkers observed with field glasses the reinforcements coming ashore at Buchanan about two miles south. This fact was reported at General Terry's headquarters. Both he and Cyrus Comstock believed the assault would now be more hazardous, and thought of telling each other the attack should be cancelled. Neither did, however, and kept it to themselves. [50]

William Lamb was furious. Instead of having 1,000 more troops to add to his 1,200 effectives, he only got 350. "Never was there a more stupid blunder," Lamb recalled with indignation, "committed by a commanding general. If this fresh brigade had been sent to this point the night before, they could have reached the fort unobserved, could have been protected until needed, and could have easily repulsed the assault by the army on our left; but landed in view of the fleet they had to double quick over an open beach to the mound under a heavy fire." When the 350 South Carolinians finally reached the fort, they were winded, demoralized and without organization. Lamb ordered them into a bombproof to catch their breath.

Lamb's headquarters, the Pulpit battery 100 yards south of the Northeast Salient, gave him the best view of the fort and the enemy approaches by "sea and land." Around 2:30 p.m., as Lamb was coming back from inspection of another battery position, one of his lookouts called out to him, "Colonel, the enemy are about to charge." General Whiting was nearby, and Lamb asked him to have another telegram sent to Bragg right away.

Whiting got off a dispatch to be telegraphed from Smithville that was as pointed and demanding as any could be. "The enemy are about to assault," he said, "they outnumber us heavily. We are just manning our parapets. Fleet have extended down the sea front side and are firing very heavily. Enemy on the beach in front of us in very heavy force, not more than 700 yards from us. Nearly all land guns disabled. Attack! Attack! It is all I can say, and all you can do." [51]

Lamb now hurried down behind the landface and passed through the bombproof galleries. He knew the fleet's bombardment would soon stop, so he ordered more sharpshooters to the parapets to pick off Yankee officers. He also ordered battery commanders to double-quick their troops to the parapets as soon as the naval fire ceased, and "drive the assailants back."

About 200 yards from the landface was a system of 20-inch shells and boiler-iron cylinders buried underground, wired for use as torpedoes or land mines. Three sets of double wires connected the torpedoes with batteries in the fort, and other wires connected the devices one to the other, so that some or all could be detonated as the operator chose. Lamb decided to wait for detonation until the assaulting troops were at the base of the fort's walls, "believing it would enable us to kill or capture their first line, while destroying and demoralizing their supports." Unknown to Lamb, the heavy naval fire had severed the detonation wires, and the torpedoes would be of no value. [52]

As he waited for General Terry's troops to move into final position, Fleet Captain Breese commanding the naval contingent, ordered the marines under Captain Dawson to move down to the shelf of the beach, "that there was splendid cover on the beach". Dawson was quite puzzled at this order. It contradicted the previous one to advance to rifle pits near the fort, so his men could serve as sharpshooters for the sailors as they charged, following them inside the works if successful, covering them on their retreat if unsuccessful. Dawson asked the courier delivering Breese's order if there might be some mistake, the sailor replied "No," and Dawson promptly moved his men to the beach, where they laid down abreast of the second division of sailors, and awaited further word. While lying there, Dawson received no orders as to what the marines were now supposed to do. [53]

By 3:20 p.m., preparations for attack were completed by Terry's troops. Ames' division was ready. The men were now in four successive battle lines, waiting for the signal. Colonel Zent's sharpshooters were the first line, 175 yards out from Fisher. Curtis' brigade was next, 225 yards out, Pennypacker's beyond Curtis, 450 yards out. Bell's brigade, the last battle line, was 650 yards out and around Battery Holland. The total number of troops set to charge the ramparts was approximately 4,200. With the additional 2,000 sailors and marines, more than 6,000 men, or roughly four times the number of effective troops now inside Fisher, some 1,500, were ready to attack. [54]

Curtis' men having now approached within easy musket range, Lamb ordered some of his troops on the west end of the landface to hustle from their bombproofs, man the palisade fence, and commence firing, even as the fleet continued its pounding. Sergeant Thomas McNeill of Company D, First Battalion North Carolina Heavy Artillery, had observed the day before the 15-inch naval shells knocking off trunnions, "breaking off great pieces of the Columbiad muzzles, wrecking gun carriages, and often bespattering the walls of the gun chambers with the blood and brains of the men of the detachments," as the Confederates coolly worked their big guns.

Now, as they ran from the galleries to man the palisade, the fleet turned its "whole fire on the land face to cover the assault and drive the men to shelter." The fury of the bombardment was like nothing any army had ever been subjected to before. "All the land face now looked as if wrapped in flame and smoke," McNeill said, "the screaming, exploding shells tearing the earthwork, making holes in the traverses, and in all the history of war it is doubtful if a more infernal fire ever fell upon a fort." McNeill's company was rushed to the sallyport west of Shepherd's Battery, to support the 30-35 men of Captain Kinchen Braddy's Second Company C, Thirty-Sixth North Carolina, who were manning a Napoleon gun and a Parrott rifle. [55]

On the 14th, Braddy had been ordered by Lamb to take half of his company to the gate at the far left, and defend the position along with Lieutenant Charles Latham's men, detached from Adam's Battery, which was manning the guns at the main sallyport. Latham and his men were supposed to operate the Napoleon and Parrott rifle, but they refused to leave their bombproof, making it necessary for Braddy's troops to man the fieldpieces, once the Yankee infantry charged. They could use all the help they could get. "I was in perfect ignorance of the dispositions of the other forces", Braddy recalled, "or the assignments of commanders of the different parts of the fort." Until Company D of the First Battalion North Carolina Artillery showed up, he had not seen an officer since being assigned to his position at the gate. Although Braddy later learned Major James Reilly had been assigned to command of the leftmost defenses, he had not seen him up to this point. "I never saw him," he said, "I have heard he was in a bombproof near us." [56]

At 3:25 p.m., Alfred Terry had his signalman communicate to David Porter that the time for attack had arrived, and for the fleet to switch its direction of fire to the seaface. Within minutes, the shrill steam whistles of the big ships pierced the afternoon air with loud, warning blasts as the bombardment temporarily stopped, for the ships to readjust their targeting of the batteries facing the beach. "It was," William Lamb wrote, "a soul-stirring signal both to the besiegers and the besieged." [57]

Captain Kinchen Braddy, C.S.A.

Lamb ordered his aid, Captain Charles Blocker, to have the South Carolinians immediately leave the bombproofs to reinforce Captain Braddy and the other troops manning the palisade on the left. At the same time, Lamb "rallied to the right of the land face some 500 of the garrison, placing the larger portion of them on top of the parapet of and adjoining the northeast salient. Initially, only a few officers and about 40 of the South Carolina troops responded to Lamb's orders, leaving a total of no more than 300 men on the left end of the landface to resist Ames' division. [58]

The first attack, however, was not to come from the infantry. It was to come from the navy. Captain Dawson, lying in the sand with his marines beside the second division of sailors, remembered Admiral Porter telling his men they were to be guided by the movements of the army, and that Terry's infantry was, "to be seen going in over the northwest parapet of the fort before we were to move to assault the sea face."

"The army had not yet assaulted," recalled Robley Evans, also prone on the beach, when all at once, Kidder Breese stood up at the head of his men, and yelled, "Charge! Charge!"

U.S. Marines and sailors charge the Northeast Bastion.

The bluejackets and marines jumped up in mass, cheering so loudly "that no order could either be heard or passed." The men raced along the beach, and as they drew nearer to Fisher, bullets, grape and canister began to tear into their tightly compacted ranks, Lamb's soldiers firing methodically from the military crest of the traverses and parapets. Men screamed and toppled over, clutching their chests or abdomens, while others witnessed war's sickening spectacle of their comrades' heads, arms and legs being torn from their torsos by spraying shards of iron.

Johnny Bartlett saw that they were advancing into a "murderous fire of musketry, with now and then a round of grape and canister." Men "were dropping all around me," he wrote. James Flannigan, who had told Robley Evans the night before he would be killed, fell with a bullet through his heart almost as soon as the advance started. [59]

"Under the shower of bullets," Evans recalled, "the marines broke before reaching the rifle pits that had been dug for them, and did not appear again as an organization in the assault." Most of the marines mixed in with the sailors and continued the charge, however. Some 500 yards from the fort the mass of men dropped down in the sand, "like a row of falling bricks," each man flat on his stomach. The officers rallied their troops, and they started forward again, only to hit the sand again at 300 yards from Fisher. "Again we rallied them," Evans said, "and once more started to the front under a perfect hail of lead, with men dropping rapidly in every direction."

They were so close to the fort now that they could hear the Rebel yells, and the Confederates hollering and cursing at them. Chase Whiting and William Lamb were both at the Northeast Bastion, inspiring and calling on their men to shoot down the Yankees. "Volley after volley was poured into their faltering ranks by cool, determined men," said the young colonel. Seeing Lamb, "gallantly standing out on the parapet," Evans took careful aim at him with his revolver, fired, and missed.

Just as he fired, a rifle ball burning across his chest above the heart spun him around, and blood immediately began to ooze from the hole in his blue jacket. It was only a surface wound, however, not penetrating the chest, and Evans continued on with his company. "As we approached the remains of the stockade," Evans remembered, "I was aware that one particular sharpshooter was shooting at me, and when we were a hundred yards away he hit me in the left leg, about three inches below the knee." The crushing impact of the heavy minie ball slammed him flat on his face in the sand. When he had somewhat recovered from the blow, Evans took a silk handkerchief from his pocket to stanch the flow of blood, and hobbled forward in his crippled condition. [60]

As the sailors and marines drew closer to Fisher, they began stumbling over the wires that led to the torpedoes, now useless in the sand. Evans' wounded leg felt numb, but he was still able to use it. Making it to the palisade fence, he intended to lead his company through the shell torn logs and up the sides of the fort. "I managed to get through the stockade with seven others, when my sharpshooter friend sent a bullet through my right knee, and I realized that my chance of going was settled. I tried to stand up, but it was no use; my legs would not hold me, and besides this I was bleeding dreadfully, and I knew that was a matter which had to be looked to."

Evans heard someone say that the men were retreating. As he looked back, Evans said he "saw our men breaking from the rear of the columns and retreating. All the officers, in their anxiety to be the first into the fort, had advanced to the heads of the columns, leaving no one to steady the men in behind; and it was in this way we were defeated, by the men breaking from the rear." [61]

Also at the palisade in front of the Northeast Bastion was Johnny Bartlett. "Sailors and officers were dropping all around me," he said. Both Lieutenants Porter and Preston, close friends and classmates at Annapolis, and two of the bright young stars in David Porter's entourage, were shot down and killed near Bartlett. Benjamin Porter, waving the admiral's standard as he charged, was shot through the chest. Sam Preston was shot in the left thigh or groin area, and the wound severed the femoral artery. Another classmate and friend, Lieutenant Roswell H. Lamson, saw him fall and saw one of the sailors stop to assist him. That man was also shot and fell on Preston. Some one pulled the sailor off, and Preston "turned over on his back and soon expired."

Lamson himself was then shot in the left arm and shoulder and collapsed from exhaustion and blood loss. Men were falling so fast around him "that every formation was instantly broken," much of the confusion ensuing, he said, because so many of the leading officers had been killed and wounded. [62]

Thomas Selfridge said that the bluejackets were packed, "like sheep in a pen, while the enemy were crowding the ramparts not forty yards away, and shooting into them as fast as they could fire." The sailors had only their pistols to reply, and, "against veteran soldiers armed with rifles and bayonets," it was pitiful reply. Some of the men did get through the palisade, but those who did were shot down.

"Flesh and blood could not long endure being killed in this slaughter-pen," Selfridge recalled with sadness," and the rear of the sailors broke, followed by the whole body, in spite of all efforts to rally them. It was certainly mortifying," he said, after advancing all that distance, "to have the whole force retreat down the beach." "Our men fell back," Lieutenant Lamson said, "taking many wounded with them, but leaving the ground covered with the dead, dying, and wounded." [63]

Left with the other wounded who had fallen at the base of the fort, Robley Evans fended for himself the best he could. After being shot in the right knee, he pulled out another of the half dozen silk handkerchiefs he had brought along, as if in anticipation of being shot and needing them as tourniquets. As he was tying the handkerchief around his knee and thigh, the Confederate who shot him continued in his effort to kill him, cursing Evans as he aimed. Evans was hit again, the minie ball taking off the end of one of his toes and wrenching his ankle. The pain was intense, and now Evans was enraged at his opponent.

The Virginia Yankee rolled over in the sand, cursing his antagonist. As another soldier handed the Rebel a loaded musket, Evans fired his revolver at the man's chest. Evans said he knew he would "kill him if I shot at him, but had not intended to do so until he shot me in the toe. My bullet went a little high, striking the poor chap in the throat and passing out at the back of his neck. He staggered around, after dropping his gun, and finally pitched over the parapet and rolled down near me, where he lay dead. I could see his feet as they projected over a pile of sand, and from their position knew that he had fought his last fight."

One of the marines from the *Powhatan*, a Private Wasmouth, spied Evans through the shattered palisade, ran through it, and dragged the young ensign to relative safety. Soon, however, shells from the fleet began dropping uncomfortably close again, sending "great chunks of mud and pieces of log flying in all directions." Wasmouth dragged Evans another 50 yards further away from the fort, dropping him into a large shell crater, where he was protected from Confederate fire. Evans warned the marine to take cover himself, but Wasmouth told him, the "bullet has not been made that will kill me." As Evans drifted almost asleep from wounds and fatigue, he heard the distinctive thud of a bullet impacting flesh. Looking around, he saw Wasmouth holding his neck as he turned round and round, "the blood spurting out in a steady stream." The bullet had severed his jugular vein, and the marine dropped to the edge of the surf, where he bled to death on the wet sand. [64]

As the naval attack on the Northeast Bastion was breaking apart, the army was hitting the western end of the fort. Martin Curtis had been carefully watching the Confederates on the ramparts as the navy halted, then switched its fire from the landface to the sea batteries. When they "seemed determined to remain on the parapet the final rush was made." Curtis rose up in the middle of his line and yelled "forward!" The soldiers of the One Hundred Seventeenth, Third, One Hundred Forty-Second and One Hundred Twelfth New York Regiments, 225 yards north of Fisher and spread in that order from west to east, from the River Road to the sallyport centered in the landface, rose up and moved out.

The men had been ordered to get up on the run, keeping low for the first 15-20 yards, refraining from cheering or yelling to save their breath for the final dash up the sides of the fort. The first volley fired by the defenders did little damage, passing over the heads of most of the Yankees. Had the troops been formed and marched forward in the usual ponderous maneuvers typical of earlier battles, "many in the line would have been shot down before a start was made," Curtis said. [65]

Even though the initial volley missed its mark, those following did not, and soldiers in blue crumpled to the sand screaming as rebel bullets found their targets. Sergeant Thomas McNeill, standing at the palisade near the River Road, said his men in D Company of the First Battalion North Carolina Heavy Artillery, poured a "destructive fire" on the enemy. Simultaneously, the artillery at the gate under Captain Braddy fired into Curtis' right flank, and the battery in the sallyport of the landface sprayed hot iron into the left flank. Soon, Braddy's artillerists were shot down by Union sharpshooters, but musketry did cause Curtis' men to veer left away from the road, while some sought cover in the marsh slough and under the bridge that crossed the slough north of the western end. Some of the Yankees got stuck in the marshy ground, becoming easy targets for Confederate riflemen. [66]

Private Zachariah Fulmore was in Sergeant McNeill's company, "occupying the space on both sides of the Napoleon." He said they "successfully repulsed every charge made by Curtis' brigade in front, and compelled the charging columns to abandon this usually traveled but unprotected entrance to the fort and to go off to the right, to climb the high parapets in order to get into the fort, some fifty yards to the right and back of us." [67]

To reach the base of the parapets, the Federals had to first get through the heavy palisade. Though the fleet's shelling had shivered the log fence close to the beach, not near as many openings had been knocked through on the western end. One hundred of Curtis' troops were armed with axes as well as rifles, to hack openings through the logs. The work was done under what Curtis described as a "galling fire," from the Confederates.

Among the first men through the fence was Captain A.G. Lawrence, aide-de-camp to Adelbert Ames. Colonel Rufus Daggett of the One Hundred

Seventeenth New York, who took command of Curtis' Brigade later in the day, wrote that Curtis had received his orders to charge "from General Ames, through Captain Lawrence." Just as he stepped through one of the openings in the palisade, he extended his hand to receive a guidon he intended to plant on the parapet of the fort. At that instant, "a shell exploded near him, taking off his left arm and seriously injuring his throat." Soon afterward, he was also shot in the right arm. Borne to the rear bleeding profusely, his fight for Fort Fisher was over. [68]

As musketry from the palisade near Shepherd's Battery scattered Federals off the Wilmington Road, a Parrott rifle close to the river's edge discharged its rounds at the bridge crossing the slough. Some of the Yankees who sought cover under the bridge did not find much to protect them, the planks having been pulled up by the garrison, while others hustled to the base of the parapets. The commander of the One Hundred Twelfth New York, Colonel John F. Smith, fell with a mortal wound, as his regiment on Curtis' left flank began to crowd to the right, while men of the rightmost regiments crowded to the left. [69]

The Yankees who survived the gauntlet of fire and made it to the fort's exterior base, began massing in the ditch formed by the excavation of sand used in building the fort. In this ditch at the base of the western parapet, the Federals found some safety from the Confederate rifles and cannon as they caught their breath. There was a major flaw in the defense of the left, one that exacerbated the already small number of troops available. Unlike the troops under Lamb and Whiting at the Northeast Bastion, who decimated the naval contingent by firing on the attackers from the crest of their parapets, the men on the western end had not been ordered to the crest. Instead, their officers permitted them to wait for the Federals within the gun revetments, the sandbags and timber reinforced walls serving as infantry breastworks. Unfortunately, by the time the bluecoats got within musket range they would be right on top of the Confederates, and large numbers of them would be swarming all over the few defenders. [70]

Thomas McNeill saw that the Federals had penetrated the palisade, scores were advancing up the parapet, while some of their officers carried the battleflags of their regiments. Now, McNeill said, "desperate struggle succeeded almost hand-to-hand, some of Company D to the left of the sallyport clubbing their muskets and fighting with the width of the palisade only between them and the enemy. But to the right of the sallyport and on that angle of the fort, the enemy in this assault got possession of the exterior slope, a lodgment was effected, the parapet gained, and the men were surrounded." Many prisoners were taken at the palisade, while some retreated down the interior of the fort to continue fighting between other traverses, or pulled back to trenches in rear of the landface to continue firing across the parade ground. Lying dead in the sand was the company commander, Captain James L. McCormic. [71]

Federal infantry storm "Bloody Gate" by Shepherd's Battery

Kinchen Braddy, in the midst of the heavy firing, had dispatched two men from their position to find reinforcements and a senior officer. When neither returned, he went himself. Just as he got past the "first angle" at the third traverse, he was fired upon by some of the South Carolina troops who had finally rallied to fight, believing he and some of the men around him were Yankees. Two men on either side of him were "shot down and killed." [72]

Sergeant Major Edward Wightman of the Third New York had written his family on January 12, the day before the infantry landed on the beach, while still aboard the transport *Atlantic*. He enviously complimented them on the fine Christmas he heard they had had last month, and reminded all, "that I long to rejoin you and resume my place in your midst." Now, as bullets were whistling around him and his comrades in Curtis' Brigade, he was in the front of the regiment as it crested the first mound of Shepherd's Battery. Suddenly, a minie ball bored through the right side of his chest, and Wightman fell dead on Fort Fisher's sand. [73]

William Lamb said his troops "poured a destructive fire on the assailants as they reached the parapet, and the enemy fell thick and fast in their front, but they were too few to load and fire in time to stop the ever increasing column, and soon the assailants were firing down upon them." Some of Lamb's bravest officers and soldiers were on the western end of the fort, "but the fatal mistake of the commander was fighting from behind the revetment instead of from the top of the parapet, as ordered." If the men had been on top of the parapet, "they could have used their bayonets or clubbed their guns, and thus delayed a lodgment until reinforcements came." [74]

Curtis' troops began pouring over the crest in large numbers just as Lamb, Whiting, and their soldiers at the Northeast Bastion were cheering and cursing the fleeing mob of sailors and marines. "As our shouts of triumph went up at the retreat of the naval forces," Lamb wrote, he was amazed to see Federal troops and Union battleflags waving on the western end. Whiting saw them too, and calling on the men around him, led them in a charge to drive the Yankees out. [75]

To make a reconnaissance of the Union position, Lamb found it necessary to go outside the fort. Rushing through the sallyport, he "witnessed a fierce hand to hand conflict for the possession of the fourth gun chamber from the left bastion. The men, led by the fearless Whiting, had driven the standard-bearer from the top of the traverse and the enemy from the parapet in front." One of the gun chambers had been recovered from the Federals with "great slaughter," and the "contestants were savagely firing into each others faces and in some cases clubbing with their guns, being too close to load and fire." [76]

In the melee, Chase Whiting reported, he was shot and fell "severely wounded, two balls in my right leg, about 4 P.M." Kinchen Braddy, still looking for Colonel Lamb or a senior officer to solicit help from, saw the general fall, and "ran to him." Whiting told Braddy he was seriously wounded. The artillery captain told the general that, "everything was confusion and the S.C. troops were killing more of our men than the Yankees," as they continued to mistakenly fire on garrison troops. Whiting told him, "Captain for God's sake try and stop it." Braddy tried to get the South Carolinians to stop firing on their own men and come to the relief of his troops, "but they payed no attention to me." [77]

As Union infantry continued to pour in around Shepherd's Battery, Battery Buchanan and the Mound Battery pounded the position with grape and canister, "killing and wounding friend and foe alike," according to Colonel Lamb and Captain Braddy. Forty-one-year-old Private John S. Cooper, one of Braddy's "best men was killed by a shell from the Mound battery." [78]

Seeing many of his troops shot down or surrounded and captured, Lamb hurried back inside the fort at the sallyport, and ordered Captain Adams to continue firing his Napoleons at the Federals as they rushed forward. Rallying his men, he "placed them behind every cover that could be found, and poured at close range a deadlier fire into the flank of the enemy occupying the gun chambers and traverses than they were able to deliver upon my men from the left salient." [79]

Many of the Yankees battling Lamb's men now were troops of the Second Brigade of Ames' division, commanded by one of the youngest colonels in the army's history, Pennsylvanian Galusha Pennypacker. Enlisting at the age of 16, he was a captain and company commander soon after his 17th birthday. Now 20 years old, he was a brigade commander of four veteran regiments bloodied in the battles for Battery Wagner at Charleston in 1863, and one new regiment. The Forty-Eighth New York and Seventy-Sixth Pennsylvania had both suffered heavy casualties fighting for the resilient sand fort on Morris Island, while the Ninety-Seventh Pennsylvania and Forty-Seventh New York, involved in siege operations, had experienced fewer losses. The Two Hundred Third Pennsylvania was just four months old, and had served briefly in the Richmond Campaign.

Ames sent Pennypacker's troops forward as soon as it was clear that Curtis had obtained a foothold on the western end. Pennypacker's men "came on like an avalanche," overlapping the right of Curtis' line. Alfred Terry said they "drove the enemy from the heavy palisading which extended from the west end of the land face to the river, capturing a considerable number of prisoners." Charging up the outer wall of Shepherd's Battery leading his men, the 20 year old colonel picked up and waved the fallen flag of the Ninety-Seventh Pennsylvania after its color bearer was shot down. Over the deafening roar of battle he yelled to his subordinate, 25 year old Colonel John W. Moore, commander of the Two Hundred Third Pennsylvania, "Moore, I want you to take notice that this is the flag of my old regiment." [80]

Shortly after boasting to Moore, and just as he was "planting his colors on the third traverse," Pennypacker felt the crushing blow of a bullet through the hip that exited his back, the force slamming him down to the sand. He appeared to be mortally wounded, and was carried to the rear. Colonel Moore, on the second traverse, "waving his colors and commanding his men to follow,"

Col. Galusha Pennypacker, U.S. Army

was also shot through the body. Bleeding to death, he admonished his men to continue charging the Rebels, yelling, "No, boys, I am not killed...keep on and give them hell." But he was killed, and expired on the sand mound soon after his valiant fighting message. [81]

As Pennypacker was borne to the rear for medical aid, he was met by one of Terry's staff officers, who extended to the young colonel his deepest sympathy. Pennypacker responded, "I know I cannot live with such a wound, but I want you to tell the general that when I fell the two leading flags on those ramparts were those of the 97th and 203rd Pennsylvania, two of my regiments." [82]

Despite the loss of a significant part of the fort and several hundred troops already killed, disabled or captured, William Lamb said the Confederates "were still undaunted, and seemed determined to recover the captured salient and gun chambers." They had retaken one of those gun chambers just before Whiting was shot and taken to the hospital at the Pulpit. The Confederates, the

Colonel said, had actually become the assailants, with the superior numbered Yankees going on the defensive.

As the tide of battle seemed to turn in favor of the outnumbered defenders, Porter's fleet came once more to the aid of the army. The bombardment, which had been confined to the seaface during the land attacks, was now resumed on the landface, "and with deadly precision," Lamb somberly noted. The gunboats "drove in our two Napoleons, killing and wounding nearly all the men at these guns, which had been doing effective service at the entrance to the sallyport." The gun chamber recovered by Whiting's charge was swept clear of defenders, and the huge naval shells sprayed death-dealing iron shards throughout the interior of the fort. Additionally, Lamb's troops soon had to contend with even more Yankee infantry. [83]

Fifteen minutes after Pennypacker's men hit the fort, accompanied by Adelbert Ames and his staff, Alfred Terry ordered Louis Bell's Third Brigade to follow into Fisher. A highly regarded lawyer before the war, the 27-year-old colonel was the son of a former New Hampshire governor, and father of a 4-year-old daughter and 6-week-old son he had never seen. His men of the Thirteenth Indiana, Fourth New Hampshire, One Hundred Fifteenth New York and One Hundred Sixty-Ninth New York charged down the Wilmington Road, the planks of the bridge crossing the slough at Shepherd's Battery having been replaced by Pennypacker's troops.

As Bell was about to cross the bridge, a minie ball slammed through his chest and out his lower back, slamming him to the ground mortally wounded. Refusing to be carried to the rear at first, he waited until he could see the colors of the Fourth New Hampshire, his former regiment, planted on the parapet of Fisher. Bell would expire early next morning. [84]

Most of Bell's brigade charged around the far end of the western salient, adding the weight of numbers to those Federals already fighting on the parade ground in rear of the parapet. Lamb said the Yankees "moved slowly and cautiously, apparently in column of companies and in close order. I met it with an effective infantry fire, my men using the remains of an old work as a breastwork, and taking advantage of every object that would offer cover, for we were now greatly outnumbered." Indeed, once Bell's troops got inside Fisher, there were over 4,000 Union infantry fighting around the western salient, either on the parade ground, traverses, walls or revetments. Combined with the fire of the big guns from Battery Buchanan, Lamb's men stopped the Yankees in their tracks, "when a quick advance would have overwhelmed us." [85]

Lamb now rushed to one of the seaface batteries to have those guns turned on the Federals inside the fort, encouraging the men at the Mound to continue doing the same. He brought back from the seaface every available man who could be spared from the guns. When he returned to the landface, he witnessed the viciousness of the continuing battle. "As the men would fall," he said, "others would take their places. It was a soldiers fight at that point, for there could be no organization; the officers on both sides were loading and firing with their men. If there ever was a longer or more desperate hand-to-hand fight during the war, I have never heard of it."

Lamb threw into the fight another 100 men he had brought from the seaface, giving him possibly 300-500 troops on the landface, if that many (no Confederate officer seemed to know for sure at this point in the fight), with which to oppose about ten times that number. The colonel ran through the bombproofs, begging his sick and wounded soldiers to come out and help repel the Yankees. He was sickened at the carnage he saw on the ramparts. "Great cannon broken in two, their carriages wrecked, and among their ruins the mutilated bodies of my dead and dying comrades." As he rallied his men for

one more supreme effort with the rifle and bayonet, the Federals not only having stopped their forward assault, but some close to the river actually beginning to entrench, he hoped for the sound of firing from the north. That would indicate relief action on the part of Braxton Bragg and Robert Hoke. His hopes were in vain. [86]

Captain Charles Elliott said their troops in Kirkland's Brigade and those in Clingman's Brigade were ordered out from the Sugar Loaf lines to attack Paine's division and Abbott's brigade in Terry's northern trenches. The Confederates drove in the Yankee skirmishers, took their rifle-pits, and the Rebels'

Col. Louis Bell, U.S. Army

musketry was making the main Federal line keep their heads down behind the earthworks. "When we all expected the order to charge," Elliott wrote, "a courier came to Hoke from Bragg, ordering him to withdraw to Sugar Loaf. My recollection is that we confidently expected to run over the troops in our front and drive them in confusion upon Terry's attacking column." A division of Porter's warships was off the beach, firing on the Confederates, and, according to Elliott, Hoke concurred with Bragg that his force was insufficient for taking the Union position, "with the fleet on their flank." Elliott personally believed "our charge would have been successful, because the troops in front were blacks." [87]

Second Lieutenant Wilson Lamb of the Seventeenth North Carolina, commanding skirmishers on the left of Kirkland's Brigade as they advanced, said their effort was only partially successful, because several Yankee gunboats lay close to shore and "opened a terrible enfilading fire," as soon as they saw the Confederates on the open beach. The advance proved more successful closer to the river, where the undergrowth and pines offered cover and protection, just as Lamb said it would. He recalled the "calm and heroic bearing of the modest and gallant Hoke, who withdrew from the reconnaissance with two bullet holes through his coat." He also believed the attack could have carried the Union position, because there were now no more than 2,500 black troops defending a mile long line, Abbott's brigade having just moved south to reinforce Fisher. [88]

Lieutenant Commander John H. Upshur, commanding ironically the former and famous North Carolina blockade-runner *Ad-Vance*, now the *U.S.S. Ad-Vance*, and in charge of eight other gunboats protecting Terry's northern line, said the Rebel advance moved out about 4 p.m. He "observed skirmishing between our pickets and those of the enemy close at hand, several of the balls passing over and near us, and killing a soldier near our boats. I suspected the enemy had moved down the peninsula in force to surprise or to create a diversion from the assault. Immediately went to quarters, followed by the other vessels, and began shelling the woods and cover in front of our intrenchments. Our firing was a success, eliciting cheers from our troops as the shell fell among the enemy, driving him off in haste." [89]

Colonel John W. Ames, commanding the Fourth, Sixth, Thirtieth and Thirty-Ninth U.S. Colored Troops, was in charge of the picket line for Paine's division, which extended "from the ocean on the right over to the river-bank, thence down the river-bank to the picket-line of General Ames' division." By mid-afternoon, inspecting his line, he had walked down as far as Terry's headquarters at Battery Holland, just as the army assault commenced. "Somewhere about four o'clock in the afternoon, when the obstinate fight looked dubious," and it appeared to him that "the assault at the fort had slackened to a stand-still, and the exhausted men were losing heart", Ames heard firing from the north. He knew it had to be Hoke's expected attack, and he hurried back to his proper post.

Running ankle deep through sand up the Wilmington Road, now littered with grapeshot, shrapnel and bullets, he anxiously approached the rear of the Federal lines, not knowing what to expect. As he got closer, the firing slackened and then stopped, giving him some reassurance. Soon, "coming upon the idle groups of Negro soldiers lolling about the rear of their unscathed breastworks, I knew, at last, that General Hoke had made no impression on them." A few picket posts had been taken, but were soon recovered, and no damage had been inflicted on the line. [90]

As Hoke's Divison was pulling back, William Lamb continued to round up men in preparation for the assault he believed would rout Ames'division from the fort. Helping him was Kinchen Braddy, who in his search for other officers had finally bumped into Lamb after Whiting was carried to the hospital. Braddy still had not seen Major Reilly, the supposed overall commander of the left. Braddy asked the Colonel what they should do. Lamb shouted above the din of battle, "get me some men, I want to drive those Yankees out of the fort," and Braddy hustled off to bring up additional troops for the purpose. [91]

Meanwhile, with Union minie balls hissing through the air, striking sand and soldiers, Lamb "passed quickly down the rear of the line, and asked officers and men if they would follow me. They all responded fearlessly that they would." Feeling the time had arrived and he now had enough men for the charge, Lamb decided he could wait no longer. The Yankees were only a hundred feet from his position. Giving the command to "charge bayonets," Lamb jumped up on the breastwork, brandished his sword, and roared to his men, "forward, double quick, march!" Immediately, a rifle bullet pierced his gray coat, drove into his hip, and slammed him to his knees, bleeding profusely. Lieutenant Daniel R. Perry, commanding Company B of the Thirty-Sixth North Carolina fell mortally wounded at Lamb's side. Perry had commanded the upper oceanside batteries during the Christmas attack. [92]

Charging into a heavy volley of musketry from many hundreds of rifles, the Confederates "wavered and fell back behind the breastworks," as more crumpled to the ground. In considerable pain, Lamb turned to Captain Daniel Munn, who had fought so stoutly for the blockade-runner *Hebe* back in August 1863, and told him to "keep the enemy in check," that as soon as he had gotten his wound bandaged, he would be back to resume command. While his men were carrying him to the hospital, Lamb grew progressively weaker from heavy bleeding, and came to the realization that his command of Fort Fisher was over.

It was about 4:30 p.m. when Lamb was hit, and he soon joined General Whiting in the hospital bombproof at the Pulpit. Whiting was "suffering uncomplainingly from his wounds," Lamb said, and told him that Bragg had completely ignored his presence in the fort and the messages he had sent to him. Whiting would report that the wounding of both himself and Lamb "had a perceptible effect upon the men, and no doubt hastened greatly the result." [93]

As Lamb was getting situated at the hospital, Union reinforcements were headed for Fisher to supplement Ames' division, now stalled and trading musket volleys with the fort's outnumbered defenders. Cyrus Comstock noted in his diary that "after 2 hours fighting...our men have got half the front & stop – stories come of short ammunition – two brigade commanders mortally wounded...and the commands disgraced & with severe loss cannot be got to go forward. Everything is doubtful, & if the enemy were to make a vigorous attempt they would drive us from all the traverses."

Comstock urged Terry to bring Abbott's brigade down from Paine's line even as Hoke's demonstration was in progress. Terry agreed, and ordered Paine to have Abbott bring his brigade down and report to him at once, while at the same time requesting the remnants of the naval contingent to move up to reinforce Paine. Abbott's 1,500 troops, armed with repeating rifles, moved out, while William B. Cushing, temporarily in command of the decimated and disorganized sailors and marines, rounded up the scattered forces and moved north to report to Paine. [94]

Major Reilly, being next in command, soon reported to Lamb, and assured the Colonel he would continue the battle "as long as it was possible." The prospects for success were bleak. Reilly recalled that "the command devolved on me, and under the circumstances, I was placed in a very disagreeable situation, but I assumed it with all its responsibility and with a small number of brave men."

Leaving Lamb and Whiting in the hospital bombproof, he hurried to the parade ground where he met Captain Braddy for the first time, and took stock of his forces in the open area behind the sallyport. Heavy casualties among officers and men, and the mass confusion of point-blank, hand-to-hand combat had taken its toll. Reilly was only able to muster about 150 men behind the landface at this time, around 5 to 5:30 p.m., as the sun began to set over the horizon. Despite the odds against them, Reilly said the soldiers displayed "considerable enthusiasm and determination," and "showed plainly that they meant business." [95]

Additionally, to bolster their resolve, several hundred Confederates still blazed away at the enemy from the uncaptured traverses on the landface and Northeast Bastion. From the seaface batteries and Battery Buchanan, occasional, heavy shells still wreaked havoc in the bluecoated ranks. One of the Yankees critically wounded as Reilly was rounding up men to counterattack, was Martin Curtis.

As he mounted a sand dune or magazine "for the purpose of looking into the angle of the bastion I intended to attack," he was "struck and disabled by two fragments of a shell, one destroying the left eye, and the other carrying away a portion of the bone at the base of the brain. I was unconscious for several hours," he later said. His men dragged him off the field to the rear, thinking he was dead. A key officer in the planning and early stages of the attack, Curtis' presence would be sorely missed. All three of Ames' brigade commanders, Bell, Pennypacker and Curtis had been mortally or severely wounded. [96]

Adelbert Ames said that now "brigade and regimental formations were impossible. What was accomplished was through the heroic efforts of small bodies of officers and men." As the sun was sinking "to the horizon," Ames wrote, "the ardor of the assault abated. Our advance was but slow. Ten of my officers had been killed, 47 wounded, and about 500 men were killed and wounded. Among the killed was one brigade commander, the other two were wounded and disabled. I now requested Terry to join me in the fort." It was a propitious time for a Rebel counterattack. [97]

Some of the troops Reilly had been able to assemble were of Hagood's Brigade, and he had the colorbearer of one of the South Carolina battleflags stand by him as a rallying point. Calling on the soldiers to attack, he advanced on Ames' three disorganized brigades, his 150 men a bold display of defiance in the face of overwhelming odds. As they moved forward, the Yankees poured a fusillade of bullets into their ranks, and dozens of Confederates screamed in agony as they fell to the sand clutching wounds, or crumpled in silence with the rattle of death in their throats.

Under "such a fire, our men began to waver and fall back, and by the time I reached near the angle of the work, I had not sixty men with me. The balance who was not killed or wounded took shelter behind the traverses and in the sallyport. In this last effort to expel the enemy, I lost heavily and that brave and gallant soldier who carried the colors was killed by my side. His loss created some confusion in the attack and I was compelled to fall back but without apparent confusion, to the...main magazine where I reformed and kept up as heavy and as destructive a fire on the enemy as my small command would admit of." [98]

Reilly's men who retreated to the sallyport found only temporary refuge. Martin Curtis later wrote that "Captain R.D. Morehouse, 142nd New York volunteers, in charge of a party, captured a large number of Confederates in the sally-port, from which they had energetically opposed the advance of our forces on the floor of the fort; but our progress on the parapet rendered their position untenable, and by a skillful movement, he captured them before they could retire to other defences." [99]

Kinchen Braddy and Major Reilly did not view their capture in the same light as the Federals. Braddy said from their position behind the main magazine, they saw a white flag being displayed "just around first angle from our position and Maj. Riley (sic) ordered me to go and see what it meant. We thought some Yankees had surrendered."

As the Confederates held their fire, Braddy placed on his swordtip a white handkerchief Major Reilly gave him, and advanced with Second Lieutenant James Owen of his company. Getting within a few yards of the men displaying the white flag, he realized it was Confederates, not Federals. Soon, Yankees did appear, very close and advancing. Braddy jerked the handkerchief from his sword, and hollered for his men to fire, as he and Lieutenant Owen raced back to their position. They stopped the Yankees in their tracks. Braddy later learned the troops were part of Second Company I, Thirty-Sixth North Carolina, and were surrendered by their commander, Captain John T. Melvin.

Braddy, Reilly and their soldiers were livid. Braddy said the surrender was "inexcusable," as the men surrendering had a clear avenue from their bombproof position to the rear of the troops under Reilly. Reilly said he had his men pour a constant and heavy fire on the Federals. It kept the Yankees off balance, and remaining behind their earthworks. His "men fought with more determination than ever, and my gallant troops were greatly incensed at the dastardly conduct of their comrades." [100]

As darkness settled in, Abbott's 1,500 troops arrived at Battery Holland and reported to General Terry. He ordered the brigade to move immediately into the fort and report to Adelbert Ames. Terry told Abbott and a staff officer of Ames who was with them, that the brigade was to "go in fresh while the enemy were nearly exhausted and finish the work."

When Abbott reported to Ames, the firing between the two sides was still heavy, "but no forward movement against the enemy was being made, and a part of the troops were employed in intrenching the position that they had gained." Instead of sending Abbott's troops forward immediately to renew the attack, well armed with their Spencer repeaters, Ames employed them in digging. The Sixth Connecticut Volunteers was set to work "expanding and thickening the breastwork," that the Second Division had been constructing from the traverses to the river. The Seventh Connecticut was told to do likewise, from the eighth traverse to the river. The Third New Hampshire was the only regiment ordered to the front line to fire on the Confederates, while the Seventh New Hampshire was halted at the sallyport to await orders.

Having heard no increase in the sound of firing from Fisher after sending Abbott's Brigade in, Alfred Terry, accompanied by Cyrus Comstock, decided to join Ames, who claimed to have sought his commander's presence anyway. Prior to leaving headquarters, Terry ordered Paine to dispatch one of his best regiments as even further support. Colonel Albert M. Blackman moved out of the northern trenches with his Twenty-Seventh U.S. Colored Troops, and headed for Fisher.

When Terry entered the fort, he saw that Ames' division was "sadly disorganized as the heavy loss of officers, especially brigade and regimental commanders had thrown the machinery out of gear. Brigades, regiments and even companies were badly mixed and cohesive aggressive action could not be obtained from them as matters stood." The soldiers were ready to fight and prepared to hold the ground they had wrested from the enemy, but "this was all that could be expected from them." [101]

Ames told Terry he wanted to continue the intrenching, and hold on until morning before attacking further. Terry was not willing to permit this, knowing the garrison had to have sustained heavy losses, and must be nearly exhausted. Waiting would only give the Rebels time to rest, refit, bring in reinforcements, or evacuate the fort. And Terry wanted the fort and garrison.

So shot up was Ames' Second Division, Terry gave consideration to relieving it with Paine's, but the time consumed in extricating one division engaged in combat, to replace it with another several miles away, would have been substantial, and the idea was rejected. Colonel Comstock proposed using Abbott's brigade for the purpose for which it had originally been dispatched from the northern line, "the task of assaulting and carrying those traverses on the landface of the work which were still held by the garrison." Comstock suggested the brigade be divided "into squads of 100 men, that the first squad have for their task to take the next traverse & that it must be done no matter what loss & thus their work is ours – 2nd squad shall take the next and so on." [102]

The assailants and defenders continued to trade volleys of musketry, neither side gaining ground. The strength of the outnumbered garrison was waning under the continuous fire of Yankee infantry and the fleet, which maintained occasional fire into the Confederate positions.

Around 8 p.m., Colonel Lamb's aide, Captain Charles H. Blocker, came to him to advise the ammunition supply was virtually exhausted. He told Lamb that "Chaplain McKinnon and others had gathered all from the dead and wounded and distributed it; that the enemy had possession of nearly all the land face, and it was impossible to hold out much longer." Captain Blocker recommended that it was time to surrender, saying further combat "would be a useless sacrifice of life. "I replied," Lamb said, "that while I lived I would not surrender, as Bragg would surely come to our rescue in time to save us." When Whiting heard Lamb's statement, he told the young colonel that should he die, "he would assume command and would not surrender." [103]

Adrian Terry wrote that "it was just after moonrise, about 9 p.m., before everything was ready to renew the attack." At this time, the Third New Hampshire was on the ramparts nearest to the Confederates, with the Seventh Connecticut to the right of them on the parade ground to assist and help cover their right flank "in the projected charge along the parapet." The Seventh New Hampshire and Sixth Connecticut were drawn up inside the fort to support the two lead regiments and follow up whatever advantage might be gained by them.

Captain William H. Trickey, in command of the Third New Hampshire, selected twenty men from his regiment to lead the assault. These troops had to "crawl through bomb-proofs and traverses, clambering over the dead, wounded and dying – literally piled upon one another," to arrive at the traverse closest to the enemy. It is around 9 p.m. when they open fire with their seven shot Spencer repeaters, driving the rebels from the traverse in their immediate front. "Thinking we could go farther," Trickey wrote, "we charged and took the next two, with a like result. After taking the third traverse, having met with considerable resistance, I did not deem it prudent to go farther with so few men, and opened a vigorous fire upon the enemy, who was rallying for the recapture of the traverses." [104]

Incredibly, after some six hours of savage combat with rifles, clubbed muskets and bare knuckles against overwhelming odds, and in spite of their paucity of manpower and ammunition, the Confederate soldiers left in Fisher still fought ferociously as the end came clearly in view. The infantry action, of course, had only begun after three days and two nights of the most tremendous bombardment in world history. Captain George F. Towle of General Terry's staff, said the Confederates fought stubbornly until long after dark. "Never did soldiers display more desperate bravery and brilliant valor," he wrote. [105]

As the Rebels stopped Trickey's Third New Hampshire in its tracks, the bluecoats in the Seventh New Hampshire clambered across the parapet around the third traverse to the outside of the fort, and "pushed rapidly along between the palisades and the foot of the exterior slope of the fort." The attention of the Confederates being focused on the fight raging on the ramparts and traverses, the Seventh New Hampshire was able to navigate around the flank and rear of the enemy. "They reached the north-east bastion unobserved, enveloped it by passing around the salient, reached the sea-face of the bastion, which had been badly battered by the naval fire, drove the enemy from the parapet, and poured a heavy fire into the interior of the work." [106]

Lieutenant Colonel Augustus W. Rollins, commanding the Seventh New Hampshire, wrote that when he reached the Northeast Bastion, he formed his regiment for attack up the same slopes the sailors and marines had intended to capture, but from which they had been slaughtered. Rollins ordered his men to charge, capturing the last three traverses. They "then pushed on by right flank and by so doing cut off the angle of the fort, moved to the right, and by a rapid and determined advance captured the remaining traverses and batteries of the fort proper, with about 350 prisoners, including one field officer and several line officers." [107]

The Confederates were caught off guard by the flank attack, those not captured being forced to retreat south along the seaface, while at the same time, Kinchen Braddy said, "all our small arm ammunition had been expended." Major Reilly considered the defense his men had made one of the finest of the war. "It was from traverse to traverse, from traverse to the main magazine, from that to the breastwork where the last and most determined stand was made," and they did not pull out until they had been hit on front and flank simultaneously with superior numbers. [108]

Reilly had Whiting and Lamb carried on stretchers from the Pulpit hospital to Battery Buchanan, where it was intended a final defense could be made. Even if the position could not be held more than 2-3 hours, it was believed that a stout enough fight could be made so that substantial numbers of troops could retreat across the river by boat, before the Federals captured them. Reilly expected Captain Robert Chapman, C.S. Navy, commanding Buchanan, "had everything in readiness to render what assistance he could," for Buchanan had suffered no damage and the garrison had not been injured.

Lamb recalled that when they left the hospital, "the men were fighting over the adjoining traverse, and the spent balls fell like hail-stones around us. The remnant of the garrison then fell back in an orderly retreat along the sea face, the rear guard keeping the enemy engaged as they advanced slowly and cautiously in the darkness as far as the Mound Battery, where they halted." Some of the men were cut off from the main body of troops, and had to elude the Yankees by crossing over at the marshes along the river, or hugging the seashore until they could make their escape unseen across the peninsula. [109]

Major Reilly "was confident Chapman was still in the battery for I thought him too good a soldier to abandon us, for we were sailing in the same ship and let us all go down together." But Reilly was wrong. Late that afternoon, Robert Watson noted in his journal, he and his fellow Confederate sailors in Battery Buchanan could see that the Yankees had made a lodgment on the western end of Fisher. They decided then and there that the fort was lost. Captain Chapman had the men mustered and the roll called. Watson said Chapman then "informed us that the fort was lost and that it was useless for him to keep us here to be taken prisoners or slaughtered, that we could fight the battery for some time and probably do the enemy some damage but that we could not hold it for any length of time."

Chapman ordered the sailors into the boats, and they "had to wade out to them" up to their waists in water. As they started to pull away, Chapman ordered them to stand fast and await further orders. Watson said Buchanan then "opened fire on the left of Fort Fisher with one 11 inch and one 10 inch gun, the other two guns would not bear. Continued shelling until 8 PM. At 10 PM we were ordered to go across the river to Battery Lamb. We were very glad to leave for we were nearly frozen as our clothes were wet and it was a very cold night. The shells were bursting very near us all the time." [110]

When Reilly and his small rearguard of troops arrived at Buchanan, almost all of Chapman's command was gone, the cannon unserviceable due to being spiked, and there were about 600 officers and men in a "perfectly disorganized" condition. Three-fourths of the troops had no weapons, and there was no way to obtain any. Reilly knew there was only one thing left to do – surrender. [111]

Hard on the heels of the retreating troops were the Federals. Two of Abbott's regiments, the Seventh New Hampshire and the Sixth Connecticut, covered on their right flank by the Twenty-Seventh U.S. Colored Troops, moved southwest from the Mound Battery in battle formation, headed for Buchanan. The moon by now had risen high in the clear night sky, James Reilly wrote, and it was "as bright as day" on the open ground between the Mound and Buchanan. Had the big guns been serviceable, Reilly said the Union infantry would have been easy targets for the "shell and canister," fired "on them as they advanced down the sandy plain." He believed they could at the very least have fought off the Union attacks until most of the men were evacuated by boats furnished by General Hebert from across the river. But that was not to be. [112]

At virtually the same time Reilly, Major James Hill of Whiting's staff and Captain A.C. Van Benthuysen of the Confederate Marines were moving out of Buchanan with a white flag to surrender, a new arrival came in, compliments of Braxton Bragg. Alfred H. Colquitt, one of Robert Hoke's brigade commanders, accompanied by three young aides, had been sent by Bragg to assume command of Fort Fisher, Bragg later inferring he believed Whiting had lost all sense of rationale.

Colquitt and his party landed about 500 yards north of Buchanan, and from several black and white men in a "shanty" nearby, learned that Fisher had been taken. Discounting this information, he headed towards Buchanan, when he ran into Captain Daniel Munn with 12-15 unarmed troops. The "captain informed me," Colquitt wrote, "that the fort was evacuated; that he had just come from it, and that General Whiting and Colonel Lamb were already at Battery Buchanan."

Arriving at the battery, Colquitt was escorted to Lamb. He said he "found the colonel prostrate with a wound, which he thought, however, was not severe. In answer to my inquiry whether anything more could be done, he replied that a fresh brigade might then retake the fort." Colquitt told him there was "no brigade with me, and wished to know of him the condition of the men who had escaped." Lamb confirmed that the troops were in a disorganized condition, but so was the enemy. Lamb further asked Colquitt "to carry General Whiting to a place of safety, as he came a volunteer to the fort. Just then," Lamb said, "the near approach of the enemy was reported and Colquitt made a precipitate retreat." As the rightmost companies of the Twenty-Seventh U.S. Colored Troops passed within "thirty to forty yards," of Colquitt and his aides, they narrowly escaped to their rowboat and shoved off across the river to Battery Lamb. From there, sometime around midnight, Colquitt telegraphed to Bragg confirmation of the fall of Fort Fisher. [113]

Lamb recalled the incident as another in a long list of insults to Chase Whiting, and further example of Bragg's detachment from reality. Bragg had actually ordered Whiting to report to him that afternoon, even as the Yankees made ready for the land assault, informing him that Colquitt had been assigned to relieve him. The notion of Bragg's "removing a gifted, brilliant and courageous hero," Lamb recalled, "whose men loved him, and would follow him into the jaws of death, and supplanting him with a Georgia militia General, unknown to the garrison, was an act in keeping with the whole of General Bragg's conduct of the defence of Wilmington." [114]

As Colquitt headed across the river, out on the sandy ground north of Buchanan, Major Reilly and the other two officers waited somberly with their white flag of surrender. Soon, the dark forms of the enemy loomed into view under the bright moonlight. Captain Lewis Moore, adjutant of the Seventh Connecticut Infantry, came forward to speak to the Confederate officers. Reilly "offered his sword in surrender," and requested of the captain that his defenseless troops not be fired upon. Soon, Colonels Abbott and Blackman arrived with their regiments, and they were escorted into Battery Buchanan by Major Hill. Alfred Terry, who personally supervised the pursuit from the Mound, came upon the scene shortly after, and accepted the surrender. [115]

Some fifteen minutes before formal acceptance of the surrender, Union troops were cheering and yelling wildly from the ramparts and parade ground, fully aware they had won one of the great victories of the war. At the same time, the fleet, having been signaled from the parapets that the fort was taken, was sending up rockets and flares by the thousands in celebration, while the yells of the sailors offshore were clearly heard on land. The scene in the moonlit night, wrote William Lamb, was one of a "grand pyrotechnic display of the fleet over the capture." [116]

Captain Charles Elliott of Kirkland's Brigade said the men in Hoke's Division watched dejectedly at the Yankee victory celebration. The sight was sad, indeed, Elliott wrote, "when the rockets from the ships and display of colored lights and blowing of whistles announced the surrender of the fort. I felt that all had not been done to save it." Adjutant George Rose of the Sixty-Sixth North Carolina Troops, wrote that "the scene was brilliant; rockets and roman candles were thrown in every direction from the gunboats in its front, and the soldiers of Hoke's Division had to grind their teeth and bear the humiliation of not having 'been there' to prevent the fall of Fisher, and to listen in silence to the shouts and huzzas of the enemy over their victory." [117]

One Union sailor said that, "thousands of rockets and colored lights went up from the fleet which were reflected again and again in the mirror-like water." Another wrote that the air was filled with loud racket, "men hurrahing, steam whistles screaming. Rockets, the air was alive with rockets of all colors." Confederate Point was once again Federal Point, and Fort Fisher was now a seacoast bastion of the Union. [118]

Endnotes to Chapter 10

1. S.H.S.P., Volume XXI, p.277; O.R., Volume XLVI, Part I, p.435; Still, William N., ed., "The Yankees Were Landing Below Us: The Journal of Robert Watson, C.S.N.", Civil War Times Illustrated, April 1976, p.12, p.15, hereinafter Journal of Robert Watson
2. The Wilmington Campaign, p.40, p.192
3. A Sailor's Log, p.85; S.H.S.P., Volume XXI, p.277-278
4. O.R., Volume XLVI, Part II, p.1048; Battles & Leaders, Volume IV, p.661; Terry, Adrian, "Capture of Fort Fisher", p.1, unpublished manuscript, Terry family papers, Yale University Library, New Haven, Connecticut, hereinafter Terry's Capture of Fort Fisher
5. O.R., Volume XLVI, Part I, p.396, p.403
6. O.R., Volume XLVI, Part I, p.396-397; Terry's Capture of Fort Fisher, p.1; ORN, Volume 11, p.547; Sands, Benjamin, *From Reefer to Rear-Admiral*, p.262, Frederick A. Stokes Company, New York, 1899, hereinafter Reefer to Rear Admiral

7.   Ammen, Daniel, *Campaigns of the Civil War, The Atlantic Coast*, p.230, Broadfoot Publishing Company, Wilmington, North Carolina, 1989, hereinafter The Atlantic Coast; Journal of Robert Watson, p.15

8.   O.R., Volume XLVI, p.397

9.   The Atlantic Coast, p.230

10. Clark, Volume II, p.759-760; NC Troops, Volume I, p.456

11. Clark, Volume IV, p.303, p.308; NC Troops, Volume I, p.31, p.36

12. Battles & Leaders, Volume IV, p.661; NC Troops, Volume I, p.358-359, p.576-577; S.H.S.P., Volume XXI, p.277

13. OR., Volume XLVI, Part II, p.1048; Fonvielle, Chris, *The Wilmington Campaign, Last Rays of Departing Hope,* p.217, Savas Publishing Company, Campbell, California, 1997, hereinafter Last Rays

14. Reefer to Rear Admiral, p.263

15. O.R., Volume XLVI, Part I, p.397

16. S.H.S.P., Volume XXI, p.277-278

17. Curtis, N. Martin, "The Capture of Fort Fisher", *War of the Rebellion: Addresses Delivered Before the Military Order of the Loyal Legion of the United States, Commandery of Massachusetts,* p.306-307, Boston, 1900, hereinafter Martin Curtis account of Fort Fisher; Terry's Capture of Fort Fisher, p.1

18. Martin Curtis account of Fort Fisher, p.304-306; O.R., Volume XLVI, Part I, p.399

19. Martin Curtis account of Fort Fisher, p.307

20. S.H.S.P., Volume I, p.346-347

21. S.H.S.P., Volume I, p.354

22. Journal of Robert Watson, p.15

23. O.R., Volume XLVI, Part II, p.1056

24. O.R., Volume XLVI, Part II, p.1056-1057; S.H.S.P., Volume I, p.347

25. Reefer to Rear Admiral, p.263; ORN, Volume 11, p.547

26. Martin Curtis account of Fort Fisher, p.307-308; S.H.S.P., Volume XXI, p.278; Moore, The Wilmington Campaign, p.38-39; Towle, G.F., "Terry's Fort Fisher Expedition", Our Living and Our Dead, Volume III, July to December, 1875, p.472, Raleigh, North Carolina, hereinafter Towle, Terry's Expedition

27. Terry, Wilmington and Fort Fisher, p.52-54; O.R., Volume XLVI, p.407; Martin Curtis account of Fort Fisher, p.307-308

28. Martin Curtis account of Fort Fisher, p.308

29. Wilmington and Fort Fisher, p.55-56

30. Martin Curtis account of Fort Fisher, p.309

31. O.R., Volume XLVI, Part I, p.437; S.H.S.P., Volume XXI, p.278

32. ORN, Volume 11, p.433-434, p.438-439; O.R., Volume XLVI, Part I, p.397

33. Battles & Leaders, Volume IV, p.649; S.H.S.P., Volume XXI, p.278; S.H.S.P., Volume X, p.356; NC Troops, Volume I, p.290

34. Terry's Capture of Fort Fisher, p.3-4; Wilmington and Fort Fisher, p.58-60; O.R., Volume XLVI, Part I, p.398; Wilmington Campaign, p.41, p.161

35. Terry's Capture of Fort Fisher, p.4-6; O.R., Volume XLVI, Part I, p.397

36. Martin Curtis account of Fort Fisher, p.310-311

37. A Sailor's Log, p.86-87; ORN, Volume 11, p.532

38. ORN, Volume 11, p.527

39. ORN, Volume 11, p.476

40. A Sailor's Log, p.87

41. Battles & Leaders, Volume IV, p.659; A Sailor's Log, p.87

42. ORN, Volume 11, p.446-449; Wilmington Campaign, p.41-43; Battles & Leaders, Volume IV, p.659

43. ORN, Volume 11, p.576

44. S.H.S.P., Volume XXI, p.279

45. O.R., Volume XLVI, Part I, p.437-439

46. S.H.S.P., Volume XXI, p.279

47. A Sailor's Log, p.87-88

48. ORN, Volume 11, p.527

49. S.H.S.P., Volume XXI, p.279; S.H.S.P., Volume X, p.357; Wilmington Campaign, p.41, p.157

50. Comstock Diary, p.302

51. S.H.S.P., p.279-280

52. S.H.S.P., p.280; O.R., Volume XLVI, Part II, p.215

53. ORN, Volume 11, p.576

54. Wilmington and Fort Fisher, p.61; Wilmington Campaign, p.43, p.48-49

55. Clark, Volume IV, p.309-310; NC Troops, Volume I, p.36; Wilmington Campaign, p.48; Kinchen Braddy letter to Z.T. Fulmore, March 25, 1901, N.C. Department Archives and History, Raleigh, North Carolina, hereinafter Kinchen Braddy letter

56. Kinchen Braddy letter

57. O.R., Volume XLVI, Part I, p.398; S.H.S.P. Volume XXI, p.280

58. S.H.S.P., Volume XXI, p.280; S.H.S.P., Volume X, p.366

59. S.H.S.P., Volume XXI, p.280-281; ORN, Volume 11, p.576-577; A Sailor's Log, p.86-89; Wilmington Campaign, p.42-43

60. A Sailor's Log, p.89-90; S.H.S.P., Volume XXI, p.281

61. A Sailor's Log, p.89-90

62. ORN, Volume 11, p.450, p.527; Wilmington Campaign, p.46

63. Battles & Leaders, Volume IV, p.660; ORN, Volume 11, p.450

64. A Sailor's Log, p.91-92; ORN, Volume 11, p.533

65. Martin Curtis account of Fort Fisher, p.313

66. Clark, Volume IV, p.303, p.309-310

67. S.H.S.P., Volume XXI, p.283; NC Troops, Volume I, p.33
68. Martin Curtis account of Fort Fisher, p.312-313; O.R., Volume XLVI, Part I, p.417-418; Wilmington Campaign, p.50; "The Capture of Fort Fisher, January 15, 1865 by Brigadier and Brevet Major-General Adelbert Ames", read before the Society December 3, 1895, *Papers of the Military Historical Society of Massachusetts*, Volume IX, p.402-403, hereinafter Massachusetts Military Papers
69. Wilmington Campaign, p.50
70. Wilmington Campaign, p.50; Kinchen Braddy letter; S.H.S.P., Volume XXI, p.284
71. Clark, Volume IV, p.310; NC Troops, Volume I, p.31; Last Rays, p.271
72. Kinchen Braddy letter
73. Antietam to Fort Fisher, p.228-229, p.241
74. S.H.S.P., Volume XXI, p.284
75. Ibid, Volume XXI, p.281
76. Ibid, Volume XXI, p.281
77. S.H.S.P., Volume XXVI, p.174; Kinchen Braddy letter
78. S.H.S.P., Volume XXI, p.282; Kinchen Braddy letter; NC Troops, Volume I, p.228
79. S.H.S.P., Volume XXI, p.282
80. Wilmington Campaign, p.51-52; Generals in Blue, p.365-366; O.R., Volume XLVI, Part I, p.398-399
81. O.R., Volume XLVI, Part I, p.419-420; Wilmington Campaign, p.52
82. Wilmington and Fort Fisher, note following p.64
83. S.H.S.P., Volume XXI, p.285
84. Last Rays, p.274-275; Wilmington Campaign, p.52-53
85. Wilmington Campaign, p.52-53; S.H.S.P., Volume XXI, p.285
86. S.H.S.P., Volume XXI, p.285-286
87. S.H.S.P., Volume XXIII, p.168
88. Clark, Volume II, p.10
89. ORN, Volume 11, p.568-569
90. "A Yankee Account of the Battle at Fort Fisher", Our Living and Our Dead, Volume I, September 1874 – February 1875, p.319-321, p.324-325; Last Rays, p.277-279; Wilmington Campaign, p.161
91. S.H.S.P., Volume XXI, p.286; Kinchen Braddy letter
92. S.H.S.P., Volume XXI, p.286; O.R., Volume XLII, Part I, p.1013; Wilmington Campaign, p.55
93. Ibid, Volume XXI, p.286-287; O.R., Volume XLVI, Part I, p.440
94. Comstock Diary, p.303-304; Wilmington and Fort Fisher, p.67-68; ORN, Volume 11, p.560
95. Major James Reilly's account of Battle of Fort Fisher, DeRossett Papers, N.C. Department of Archives and History, Raleigh, North Carolina,

hereinafter Major Reilly's account; Kinchen Braddy letter; Martin Curtis account of Fort Fisher, p.319

96. O.R., Volume XLVI, Part I, p.415; Journal of Robert Watson, CWTI, April 1976, p.16; Martin Curtis account of Fort Fisher, p.319
97. Massachusetts Military Papers, p.405-406
98. Major Reilly's account; Kinchen Braddy letter; S.H.S.P., Volume XXI, p.287
99. Martin Curtis account of Fort Fisher, p.317
100. Kinchen Braddy letter; Major Reilly's account; NC Troops, Volume I, p.226, p.313
101. Adrian Terry, Wilmington and Fort Fisher, p.67-70; Wilmington Campaign, p.162
102. Adrian Terry, Wilmington and Fort Fisher, p.71; Comstock Diary, p.304
103. Adrian Terry, Wilmington and Fort Fisher, p.71; S.H.S.P., Volume XXI, p.287; NC Troops, Volume I, p.173
104. Terry, Wilmington and Fort Fisher, p.71-72; Wilmington Campaign, p.57-58; O.R., Volume XLVI, Part I, p.413
105. Towle, Terry's Expedition
106. Wilmington and Fort Fisher, p.72
107. O.R., Volume XLVI, Part I, p.414-415
108. Kinchen Braddy letter; Major Reilly's account
109. Major Reilly's account; S.H.S.P., Volume XXI, p.288
110. Major Reilly's account; Journal of Robert Watson, p.16
111. Major Reilly's account
112. Wilmington Campaign, p.58-59; Major Reilly's accout
113. O.R., Volume XLVI, Part I, p.442-443; S.H.S.P., Volume XXI, p.288-289; Wilmington Campaign, p.59-61; S.H.S.P., Volume X, p.358-359
114. S.H.S.P., Volume X, p.358-359
115. Wilmington Campaign, p.59-60; O.R., Volume XLVI, Part I, p.410; Wilmington and Fort Fisher, p.74
116. Wilmington Campaign, p.61; S.H.S.P., Volume XXI, p.288
117. S.H.S.P., Volume XXIII, p.168; Clark, Volume III, p.694
118. Wilmington Campaign, p.61

A sketch of the capture of Fort Fisher by an eyewitness of the battle.

Fort Fisher's 4th gun emplacement after the battle

Chapter 11
"...we slowly fell back to Wilmington..."

Fort Fisher was a bloody, gruesome shambles, as the first streaks of light rose on Monday morning, January the 16th. The stench of blood and sulfurous black powder hung heavy in the clear, cold morning air. Everywhere, individually and in heaps, were the dead and wounded, blue and gray, mingled together. Scattered about were "fragments of shells, dismounted guns, splintered carriages, earthworks ploughed in furrows, devastation, ruin, death in every attitude and every form." One Union sailor observed clothing, caps, "bayonets, swords, muskets, rifles, scattered, battered, blood-stained." Men were lying about in all postures, "mangled in the head and body, with brains out, but with perfect features, covered with sand and grimed with powder."

James J. Cleer, a Yankee tar from the *U.S.S. Maratanza*, was milling around the fort out of curiosity, and a desire to do a little "pillaging."

"I never saw such a sight in all my life," he wrote his mother and father. There were "soldiers and sailors laying around me dead, some with arms and legs and heads off." Corpses were strewn all over the ramparts, traverses, and sides and bases of the huge sand mounds. They were scattered about and bunched in mangled, bloody piles on the parade ground and in the trenches Ames' men had been digging after getting a foothold in the fort. They were lying face up or face down, some with no faces at all, in dirty pools of water tinged red with their life's blood. [1]

Most of the dismembered bodies were the result of the heavy shells, some from Fisher's light artillery. In addition to the unremitting barrage of the fleet, that killed mostly Confederates, once the Union infantry broke through on the western end, the concentrated fire of the Mound Battery, Columbiad Battery and Battery Buchanan had decimated the ranks of the Yankees, but also killed Rebels. Mens' heads, arms and legs were blown off, abdomens eviscerated, torsos cut in two, while some soldiers were literally blown to bits and would show up on casualty lists as "missing." The grim harvest of battle, said a Union officer, was something "we lose sight of when the pride, pomp and circumstances of Glorious war are mentioned." [2]

Casualties on both sides were obviously heavy, given the nature of the three day bombardment that had been unequalled in the history of warfare, and the savage nature of the close quarters combat that was waged for more than six hours.

In a January 20 report to U.S. Grant, Alfred Terry stated they had captured "96 officers and 1,164 enlisted men unhurt, and 8 officers and 278 enlisted men wounded." The total of 1,546 enemy troops alive as of January 20, meant that 354 of William Lamb's 1,900 soldiers had been killed in action. This 19 percent combat deaths for the total number engaged, ranked Fort Fisher as one of the highest, if not the highest, percentage-wise, for Confederates killed in action, of any battle in the war. Deaths among the wounded in the days ahead would increase the total from 354 to 550, according to some Confederate records. This total, which made an incredible 29 percent deaths for troops engaged, would far surpass any other battle of the war. [3]

Among the roughly 8,000 effective Union army troops, Terry reported the loss of "12 officers and 107 enlisted men killed, and 45 officers and 495 enlisted men wounded." This total of 659 troops was later increased by some estimates to 184 killed, 749 wounded and 22 missing, for a total of 955 Federal soldiers. The U.S. Navy had suffered 82 killed, 269 wounded and 35 missing, for a total of 386 sailors and marines. Many of the missing on both sides were men who had been obliterated by the heavy shells. [4]

Before the tallying of casualties had been completed, more were added in a freakish, deadly explosion that occurred about 9 o'clock on the morning of the 16th, while some were catching their first daylight glimpses of the death and destruction of the battle. "My large reserve magazine," Colonel Lamb wrote, "which my ordnance officer, Captain J.C. Little, informed me contained some 13,000 pounds of powder, blew up, killing and wounding more than a hundred of the enemy and some of my own wounded officers and men. It was an artificial mound, covered with luxuriant turf, a most inviting bivouac for wearied soldiers." Many men of the One Hundred Sixty-Ninth New York, of Louis Bell's Third Brigade, were resting and sleeping on its surface, while some of Lamb's wounded were inside the magazine galleries for warmth. Colonel Bell himself had expired before sunrise from his chest wound.

The magazine explosion could be heard miles away in Wilmington.

Lieutenant Colonel Samuel Zent of the Thirteenth Indiana, who had commanded the sharpshooters during the assault, was in charge of guarding the fort's magazines after its capture. He had posted three men at the entrance to each of thirty-one magazines situated along the inside base of the traverses and bombproofs. The large reserve magazine, however, had not been pointed out to him, and he was not aware that it was such. But the men of the One Hundred Sixty-Ninth New York, along with the One Hundred Fifteenth New York and Fourth New Hampshire, who were right there, should have determined the contents of the interior and taken proper precautions.

Several soldiers, who were "seen with lights searching for plunder in the main magazine," just as James Cleer was doing, were observed going into the structure. Some "ten or fifteen minutes" later, a tremendous concussion rocked the whole northern end of Fisher. A massive explosion of 6 1/2 tons of powder catapulted sand, turf, bodies, rifles, bayonets, cartridge belts, and splintered timbers several hundred feet into the air. When the debris settled, the result was a macabre and open mass grave of disfigured bodies and parts of bodies. Some initially thought the Confederates might have been responsible, but it was soon determined "that the explosion was the result of carelessness on the part of persons," unknown, but who were Federals. Some estimates put the total dead from the blast, Union and Confederate, at about 200 men. [5]

The unwounded prisoners of the battle were marched under guard outside of the fort after its fall, and "placed on the beach, cold, wet, and hungry, sentinels closely guarding us," wrote William R. Greer of the Twenty-Fifth South Carolina. He and his comrades witnessed the rocket display of the fleet the night of the 15th, and then the "heavy explosion in the magazine" the next morning.

"The weather was clear but quite cold," Greer, said, "but we were ordered to wade knee deep in the surf and were then hauled in launches, and after boarding a tug," were loaded into a slow moving vessel that took ten days to get to Jersey City. [6]

All of Adelbert Ames' brigade commanders had been severely wounded, and all were expected to die. Colonel Louis Bell, expiring before sunrise of the 16th, was the only one that would. Newton Martin Curtis had lost his left eye, and had pieces of the back of his skull blown off. But he would recover, as would young Galusha Pennypacker. Suffering intensely from his wounds at a field hospital at the fort, Pennypacker was visited the morning of the 16th by General Terry. Terry, who called Pennypacker the "real hero of Fort Fisher," told him he was to be rewarded with appointment to the rank of Brevet Brigadier General, making him, at the age of 20, the youngest general officer in U.S. history. [7]

Colonel Lamb and General Whiting were carried from Battery Buchanan back to the fort's hospital at the Pulpit. From there, they were transported north, Lamb to Fort Monroe, to begin recuperation in Virginia near his Norfolk home, and Whiting to Governor's Island in New York harbor. [8]

The Confederates began evacuating the Old Inlet defenses prior to dawn on January 16. Troops in the Fortieth North Carolina at Fort Holmes abandoned their works on Bald Head Island, while men at Forts Caswell and Campbell, on Oak Island, were ordered to pull back as well. Bragg had dictated that the new line of defense would be the Fort Anderson – Sugar Loaf line. Lieutenant William Calder, Adjutant of the First Battalion North Carolina Heavy Artillery at Fort Caswell, recorded in his diary that at 2 a.m. on the morning of the 16th, Colonel Charles Simonton woke him up "to prepare for immediate evacuation. Everything was busy and confusion."

Site of the magazine after the blast

Calder wrote that the men heard the tremendous explosion of the magazine at Fisher later that morning. "At 7 a.m.," he recorded, "troops marched out from Caswell & Campbell & pursued their way down the beach. It was with sad hearts and & unwilling footsteps that we left behind us these powerful works where we had spent so many pleasant hours, erected at such a cost of time money & labor. The commanding officer of each remained behind with a detach. of men to blow up the works & destroy everything." [9]

At 1:30 on the morning of January 17, the magazines at Campbell and Caswell were exploded, guns were spiked, buildings were set on fire, and "the works were completely demolished...The Yankees made a banner capture in Forts Caswell & Campbell," Calder wrote. [10]

On the 18th, David Porter sent William Cushing to the Old Inlet area to reconnoiter. Cushing raised the Stars and Stripes at the ruined Fort Caswell, then moved up to Fort Pender at Smithville, where the mayor of the town surrendered his community to the Union.

Control of both inlets gave the Yankees a base for further operations against Wilmington, and as one of the prime objectives of the campaign, sealed off the port from ingress of foreign goods on blockade runners. Over the next few days, several Wilmington bound runners would be captured by Porter's fleet, Union naval officers forcing Cape Fear pilots with their existing harbor lights and signals to lure unsuspecting runners into capture. [11]

On Thursday the 19th, Lieutenant Calder noted in his diary that he and the men of the First Battalion Heavy Artillery arrived at Fort Anderson, where they bivouacked "alongside the road." Rain began to fall in the afternoon. [12]

The high command in Richmond told Bragg that Wilmington, somehow, must be held, to preclude its being used as a base for William Sherman's advancing army, and at the very least until government supplies could be removed. There was also an ironclad, *C.S.S. Wilmington*, under construction on Eagles Island, and it was hoped that vessel could be finished to help thwart Porter's expected advance up the river.

Bragg, therefore, ordered Wilmington's defenses significantly strengthened, using both soldiers and slaves to increase the works, something that should have been done on the Sugar Loaf – Confederate Point line between the first and second assault on Fort Fisher. More torpedoes were set out in the river channel, and derelict vessels were sunk south of Eagles Island to increase obstructions in the river. Despite his renewed efforts, river obstacles and increased earthworks, however, Bragg was only able to count 7,600 men to man the defenses. [13]

Three brigades and three artillery batteries of Hoke's Division still manned the trenches on the Sugar Loaf line, some 4,400 troops. Hagood's Brigade of the division was at Fort Anderson, where it had been since the botched effort to reinforce Fort Fisher. With the arrival of the refugee troops from Bald Head, Caswell, Campbell, Battery Shaw and Fort Pender, the total number of Confederates at Anderson was about 2,300 troops, for the time being under command of General Hebert.

Despite his generally competent command of the lower Cape Fear in 1863 and 1864, some Rebels felt that Hebert had conducted an inept withdrawal following the loss of Fort Fisher. There were those who believed valuable supplies and equipment had been destroyed and lost that should have been removed to Fort Anderson, and some thought Hebert was drunk during the withdrawal. For the time being, however, he was in command at Anderson. [14]

On January 20, Braxton Bragg had his adjutant general, Archer Anderson, advise Hebert that if the "enemy's gunboats should pass Fort Anderson there will be no necessity for its immediate evacuation; but you will have to be vigilant and take care, by means of your scouts and cavalry, that their infantry does not move around or land above you." Should Union troops pass around the western flank of the fort in numbers to make it untenable, Hebert was directed to pull back to the line along Town Creek, several miles upriver. Bragg further advised him that unless the "necessity is immediate to save your command, you will not give up your present position without further orders from these headquarters." [15]

Hebert responded that he would "act in accordance" with the directions from headquarters. Noting that part of the Yankee fleet was off Battery Lamb, downriver from Anderson, he reported the addition of two more vessels the night of the 20th. They were apparently two of the blockade runners that had been lured into the river and captured. "We judged so," Hebert said, "from the fact that one had a Confederate flag, another an English flag, with the U.S. flag flying over them." [16]

Upriver from Anderson and the Sugar Loaf line, Bragg ordered additional breastworks erected from Fort Meares along the river (so named for Colonel Gaston Meares of the Third North Carolina, killed at Malvern Hill in 1862), eastward toward Masonboro Sound, to be anchored on Hewlett's Creek. West of the Cape Fear, a new line of works were to be built just north of Town Creek, which as Hebert was ordered, would be his fallback position in the event Anderson fell.

Bragg ordered military property and valuable supplies removed from the city, much of which was sent to Raleigh. Anticipating possible evacuation, he ordered surveys and repair work done on the Duplin Road, which ran north out of town to cross the Northeast Cape Fear River. Such preparations were obviously observed by the people in Wilmington, who believed Bragg would soon be giving up the city without a fight. Criticism of this officer justifiably began to be voiced. [17]

The *Wilmington Daily Journal*, which had come to Bragg's defense in October, when the Virginia editorials predicted dire consequences, lamented the loss of Fort Fisher in its January 17th edition. "God only knows why our outer defences were taken," the paper said, and why "heroic men like Whiting,

Lamb, and others are prisoners." The paper said they had "lost many good and true friends; we may lose many more. We fear that they were sacrificed."

The paper went on to say that it was evident "there is a strong excitement against Gen. Bragg. There can be no doubt either, that Gen. Bragg has attached to him the prestige of bad luck. Unfortunately he always has that prestige. Permanent bad luck means permanent bad management, somewhere. A man with this prestige ought not to have been sent here.

"It is not our part," the *Daily Journal* continued, "to give advice to our citizens. There are so many that, under any circumstances, cannot leave, while there are so many that, under any circumstances, must leave, that no single rule could apply to all. Every man's conscience must be his own judge." [18]

Robert Hoke, commanding the Sugar Loaf line, would give no counsel to defeatism, nor would his men. Following a January 19th demonstration against his line that was vigorously repulsed, he wrote the next day to Bragg's headquarters. "The enemy retired to their intrenched camp last night...Two deserters came in this morning, but gave very little information. They state that the move was only a reconnoiter. I do not think they will make an advance until Sherman's movements are more fully developed...If the governor would collect a force for the protection of Wilmington we would be able then to move against Terry." [19]

Adjutant George Rose of the Sixty-Sixth North Carolina wrote that the soldiers continued to strengthen the Sugar Loaf lines. They became conditioned to living "amidst sand and dust and on unsifted corn meal and spoiled Nassau bacon until life became almost unendurable, but the spirit of the troops never flagged; they were always willing to do their full duty, and always glad to see the enemy in their front. Almost every day there would be fighting upon the skirmish line."

The Yankee gunboats shelled the lines almost every day, Rose said. The men could see the heavy projectiles leave the cannon mouths and come hurtling toward their positions. Undaunted, Rose remembered, the Confederates risked injury or death "in claiming the parts of the shells when they had burst, so as to make rings and other ornaments out of the brass parts connected therewith. As soon as the missile burst you would see men running in every direction toward the place for the purpose of finding the broken parts. We here buried ourselves literally under the ground, and the shelling had little or no effect upon us." These veterans of Hoke were eager to engage the enemy, even if their commanding general in Wilmington was not. [20]

As the weather turned cold and rainy in the latter part of January, discipline and morale of the troops was not as good at Fort Anderson under Louis Hebert, as it was at Sugar Loaf. On January 25, Bragg sent an order to Lieutenant Colonel George T. Gordon, former Assistant Inspector General for the captured General Whiting, to proceed to Fort Anderson, thoroughly inspect the command there, and report on its condition. Citizens in the area had

Today Ft. Anderson is one of our best preserved Civil War forts, as seen in this photo from 1964.

complained of "drunkenness, straggling, plundering, and demoralization of every sort, which will require your attention. Even the commanding officer, General Hebert, is represented as being himself compromised." Gordon was ordered to study and observe the entire situation there, the posting of troops, cavalry and outposts, and prepare a detailed report of what he found. [21]

The following day, Colonel Gordon reported that he had inspected the earthworks "from Fort Anderson to Orton Pond. It is thoroughly repaired but bad in design. The other line has not yet been commenced. The works of the fort are being strengthened; only sixty shovels in use." [22]

Though Gordon's report did not mention Hebert, discussions at headquarters in Wilmington must have, because on the 28th, Hebert was relieved of command at Anderson, and appointed chief engineer of the Department of North Carolina. At the same time, Johnson Hagood was given command of the fort, following his return from furlough in South Carolina.

Nearly half the troops in Anderson were part of his brigade anyhow. There were 925 enlisted men of his regiments there, and "the fragments of the garrisons...converted into infantry, and brigaded under Colonel Hedrick. Fortieth North Carolina. These numbered," Hagood said, "805 enlisted for duty. In addition, there was Moseley's and Bradham's light batteries, together 132 enlisted for duty, and 152 enlisted mounted men of the Second South Carolina cavalry." Hagood tallied slightly over 2,000 enlisted, and with officers, "about 2,300." [23]

At the same time Fort Anderson was getting a new commandant, the Federal command structure was also changing. By the end of January, Ulysses Grant had determined Wilmington was of vital importance to William T. Sherman's upcoming Campaign of the Carolinas. His 60,000 veteran troops were ready to leave Savannah, and cut a swath through first South Carolina, and then the Old North State. Grant had agreed to Sherman's proposal to link up with the Army of the Potomac in Virginia, by marching his battle hardened men through the Carolinas in a campaign of destruction and plunder akin to the one recently completed in Georgia, which had culminated in the occupation of Savannah in December. [24]

Grant intended to insure that his old friend and subordinate would have a secure supply base in North Carolina. The hub of the base was to be the harbor of Wilmington, and Grant wanted to have the city in Union hands by the time Sherman arrived in the state. [25]

Traveling south from Virginia, Grant was accompanied by the Assistant Secretary of the Navy, Gustavus Fox. Also with them was Major General John Schofield, whose Yankee Westerners had decimated John Bell Hoods' Army of Tennessee in the bloody trenches of Franklin, Tennessee in November 1864, two weeks prior to Hood's final destruction at Nashville. On the evening of January 28, he, Schofield and Fox met with David Dixon Porter and Alfred Terry aboard Porter's flagship, the *Malvern.*

Grant explained Sherman's upcoming campaign, stating that the city of Goldsboro, North Carolina was the final destination for Sherman's troops. Goldsboro was important because it was the junction of two railroads – the Wilmington & Weldon, and the Atlantic & North Carolina. The first came north out of Wilmington, and the second came westward out of

Gen. Johnson Hagood, C.S.A.

New Bern. In Goldsboro, Sherman's ragged veterans could be supplied or sent additional troops by rail from New Bern or Wilmington or both.

The initial step in securing a base of supply at Goldsboro was to take and hold Wilmington. Grant assumed correctly that the rail lines running out of town were still operating. Those running from New Bern into the interior of the state needed substantial repairs, and Grant decided that a rapid seizure of Wilmington could secure the railroad facilities for the Federals. Hopefully it could be done before the Rebels had time to destroy them. [26]

During the meeting aboard the *Malvern*, both Porter and Terry advised the landing of infantry at Smithville, with an advance on Wilmington up the west bank of the Cape Fear. Fort Anderson would naturally have to be taken, but there would be far more room for the maneuvering of troops on the mainland west bank than on the narrow peninsula of Federal Point. Porter's fleet would add its weight with the gunboats, while Alfred Terry's men would keep heavy pressure on the rest of Hoke's Division along the Sugar Loaf line. [27]

Grant approved of the suggested plan. Alfred Terry, however, the victor of Fort Fisher, would be a subordinate officer in the forthcoming drive on Wilmington. Grant wanted one of his proven western commanders in charge. Having returned to City Point, Virginia, his headquarters during the Richmond-Petersburg Campaign, Grant ordered Schofield on January 31 to assume command of the newly recreated Department of North Carolina.

He told Schofield he would be subject to Sherman's orders, but for the time being, until Sherman was in the vicinity, would take orders directly from Grant. Schofield was to assume command of all troops in North Carolina, with his communications designated as originating from the "Headquarters Army of the Ohio."

"Your headquarters will be in the field," Grant told him, "and with the portion of the army where you feel yourself most needed. In the first move you will go to Cape Fear River. Your movements are intended as co-operative with Sherman through the States of South and North Carolina. The first point to be attained is to secure Wilmington. Goldsborough will then be your objective point, moving either from Wilmington or New Berne, or both, as you deem best." [28]

Schofield had 21,000 soldiers in his Twenty-Third Corps of the Army of the Ohio, a substantial number that were being transferred to the Cape Fear to bolster Terry's forces. The first of those, some 4,500 men in the Third Division of Major General Jacob Cox, an Ohioan, left Alexandria, Virginia on army transports on February 4, and came ashore on Federal Point on a cold and rainy Wednesday, February 8. General Hagood at Fort Anderson reported to headquarters at 5:30 that evening that there were six "large steam transports lying outside near Battery Holland all day. Think they are landing troops." The balance of Cox's division landed on the 10th.

Even before Cox arrived, Terry received reinforcements from some of his own command left in Virginia during the Fort Fisher expedition, which raised his troop strength to 9,000 men. General Hagood reported from Fort Anderson on February 7, "enemy landing troops at Buchanan from transports in the inlet and outside, brought to Buchanan in tugs. They had guns, knapsacks, &c.; wagons hauling up baggage. They were discovered when fog lifted at 12 o'clock." Hagood said his signal operator observed the landing of about 1,200 men. They marched through Fort Fisher to Camp Wyatt, where a considerable number of new tents had recently been pitched. [29]

On Thursday the 9th, Schofield decided to attack Hoke's Sugar Loaf lines, before moving over the river to take Fort Anderson. All of the Twenty-Third Corps was not yet on hand, just Cox's division, giving the Yankees a total of 13,500 men with which to make the assault. Making it hot for Hoke just might prevent him from sending reinforcements to Fort Anderson, and it just might open the door to Wilmington.

Writing to David Porter from Fort Fisher that same day, Schofield requested the admiral's help. "It will greatly facilitate the operations," he told Porter, "to have for a short time previous to the advance a strong fire from the gun-boats upon the right of the enemy's lines, viz, immediately opposite Fort Anderson. Possibly the effect of this may be so great as to enable the troops to take possession of Sugar Loaf Hill, and thus obviate the necessity of the proposed operations west of the river."

Schofield also asked Porter to have the fleet east of Federal Point fire on the left of Hoke's line to keep the Confederates pinned down in that sector, though he did not believe much damage would be done, due to the extreme distance and the intervening woods. He hoped to make the attack on the 10th or 11th, if the navy could be ready. "If this movement results in a decided success," Schofield told him, "which I do not count upon, I will push for Wilmington at once. If not, I will then be prepared to transfer troops to the west bank of the river, and threaten in like manner Fort Anderson and the adjacent line, preparatory to the more extended movement to turn the enemy's position." [30]

If the Confederates could not be ousted from their earthworks, Schofield told his army commanders Terry and Cox, then "the troops will be intrenched near enough to the enemy to threaten his position and maintain a skirmish line in close proximity to the enemy's works. At the same time our own line will be kept as much out of the enemy's view as practicable." [31]

MajGen John Schofield, U.S.A.

As if to underscore the folly of the Confederate high command at this critical juncture, the day after Schofield's dispatches to Porter, Terry and Cox, Bragg left Wilmington February 10 on the train bound for Richmond. Davis had been requesting his presence there to discuss some insignificant "technicalities" in his staff organization, and though Bragg had tried to convince him now was not the time, the Confederate President was insistent. Bragg left, and ordered General Hoke to assume command of the Department of North Carolina in his absence. [32]

Early in the morning of Saturday the 11th, Lieutenant William Calder observed from Fort Anderson, the Union gunboats began to bombard Hoke's position. "The shelling was more rapid than ever," he recorded in his diary. "It is known that the enemy have landed additional forces on Confederate Point & this shelling may be preparatory to an assault upon Hoke's lines. The vessels in the river shelled the Sugar Loaf at varying range...About 11 a.m. the shelling ceased on the other side & a heavy infantry fire could be heard which continued until night."

Calder also noted the firing of Porter's vessels on Fort Anderson from a distance. "The guns in the fort having driven off the wooden vessels, the monitor *Montauk* came up within 1 1/2 miles of the fort and opened fire. She continued to fire 15 and 11 inch shells until night. She was struck several times by our shots but of course received no damage as our heaviest guns were 32 pdrs. She fired with the utmost regularity one shot in seven minutes."

Anderson's soldiers had to hug the breastworks and traverses when they were not working the guns, and three men in the fort were wounded during the day's shelling. Calder estimated the Yankees threw 140 shells into the fort that day. [33]

MajGen Jacob Cox, U.S.A.

By late morning, as Calder noted in his diary, the rattle of musketry was reverberating across Federal Point. The Union infantry that launched Schofield's reconnaissance in force was from left to right across the peninsula and facing north toward Hoke's Division: Colonel Elias Wright's brigade of U.S. Colored Troops of Charles Paine's division, Adelbert Ames' division that had been so bloodied on January 15th, Colonel John Ames' brigade of U.S. Colored Troops, Paine's division, and Joseph Abbott's brigade that had captured the easternmost landface traverses and the Northeast Bastion on the night of January 15th. General Terry was in direct command of the assault troops, giving orders from a buggy in the rear due to illness. Jacob Cox's division moved up about a mile in rear of the charging lines as support, in the event of a breakthrough. John Schofield, as new commander of the department, was in overall command of the operation. [34]

Adelbert Ames ordered Abbott's brigade to "advance up the beach and press the outposts of the enemy near the head of Myrtle Sound." He therefore threw out the Third New Hampshire, under Captain William Trickey, at 10:00 a.m. as skirmishers, "and advanced rapidly upon the enemy's outposts. These posts consisted of about 100 men, partly in a heavy earth-work, partly in rifle-pits, on the left of the enemy's line."

Trickey was warned the Confederates might have reoccupied Battery Gatlin, and that in crossing the head of Myrtle Sound, the enemy would then be on his right flank. Gatlin, however, was found to be unmanned, so his regiment moved forward in the direction of Kirkland's Brigade manning the center of the Sugar Loaf line. Captain J.H. Edgerly, who had captured the garrison flag at the Mound Battery, was in command of Trickey's skirmishers, and Edgerly determined the Rebels were in some force behind rifle pits in front of the main line.

Not wishing to remain in an exposed position so close to the enemy works, "and having entire confidence in the men," Trickey decided to charge the rifle pits. Within "perhaps three minutes we had possession of the work," Trickey wrote, "and sixty-four prisoners, which was nearly the number our line consisted of."

Abbott's entire brigade now came up, and Trickey's men were ordered to advance once more. As they moved across an open field they were met with a severe fire from the Rebel line, so the Yankees quickly ran to cover in the edge of some woods some sixty yards from the enemy works. "Here the undergrowth and swamp," Trickey said, "rendered it impossible for a farther advance with anything like concert or safety. I therefore halted and reported circumstances. The position was looked over by staff officers of General Abbott and General Ames. It was, I believe, decided that a farther advance with a skirmish line was impracticable." [35]

The black troops of Wright's and John Ames' brigades advanced vigorously on Hoke's line. These men had seen significant action in Virginia in the summer and fall of 1864, including the bloody Union debacle known as the Battle of the Crater, where many of their comrades had been killed and wounded. Now they were once again assaulting veterans of Lee's army, Hoke's Division of crack combat troops with much experience under fire, who had proven time and again they could hold a fixed position against heavy odds. Some of their picket posts and skirmishers might be overrun, but their main line would not be. George Rose of the Sixty-Sixth North Carolina recalled that an attack "in considerable force was made upon us by a negro regiment in command of white officers. The fact of seeing those negro troops in front of us exasperated the men and they fought with great gallantry and easily repulsed the attack made upon us." [36]

General Paine wrote that the Fourth U.S. Colored Troops had been deployed as skirmishers, and they "drove the enemy very handsomely from his intrenched picket-line into his main works. The division constructed a line of works at this point and occupied them." Heavy firing between the lines continued until about four o'clock in the afternoon, by which time Alfred Terry had decided Hoke's position could not be carried. Paine's division lost "2 commissioned officers and 14 men killed, and 7 commissioned officers and 69 men wounded." Their loss in this attack would constitute almost fifty percent of the total Union loss of some 200 men "from February 11 to the capture of Wilmington." [37]

Adelbert Ames' division had significant problems getting into action. Being in the left-center of the advancing line of battle, they were forced to navigate some of the same swampy ground they had bypassed in January, when they were seeking good defensive terrain facing north. That boggy ground had forced them then to move about a mile further south, where their right flank had been anchored on Battery Anderson. Though the soldiers endured heavy fire from Colquitt's Georgia Brigade and field artillery, they were not as heavily engaged as Paine's Division or Abbott's Brigade. [38]

Firing along the lines ceased by darkness, except for the occasional picket firing that always occurred when the armies were so close together. On this Saturday night, they were quite close, somewhere between 500 and 900 yards apart. John Schofield was satisfied with the result of the day's action, reporting that his men were "intrenched in a new position, close enough to the enemy's line to compel him to hold the latter in force." [39]

That same evening, now Brevet Brigadier General Cyrus Comstock made a proposition to Schofield. He advised taking bridging pontoons north about eight miles up the narrow strip of sand between the ocean and Myrtle Sound. The pontoons would be towed by naval vessels to the point selected, while 8,000 infantry would march across the pontoon bridge to debouch in Hoke's rear. It was a good plan, but the fickle winter weather that prevails on the North Carolina coast at this time of year intervened.

Comstock recorded in his diary on February 12, the night the movement was ordered, that "the wind shifted from S.W. to N.N.E. & blew a gale. Gen. S(chofield) decided it was too rough. I was willing to try it; but it was lucky I did not, for every pontoon would have been lost." [40]

General Cox's division was to be the advance force. He said they moved after darkness up the beach, when the wind was "blowing a gale from the northeast, as searching and cold a blast as I ever felt." Cox said they marched in silence for the first hour, guiding the troops by the line of the surf. "The moon rises," Cox wrote, "just as we are passing the enemy's picket fires and in full view of them, the low sand beach not covering us from their view. The sand driving with the wind cuts like a knife and adds much to the unpleasantness of the night. The enemy take no notice of us, as we are out of musket range and the sound intervening between us. We march about four miles, when we get orders recalling us. No reason given for the change, so I suspect that the boats could not be put around on account of the surf." [41]

Over the next two days, Cox noted in his journal, "the raw, cold weather continues." An attempt was renewed to bring pontoons up the narrow beach east of Myrtle Sound, and Cox's division marched north from their camps once more on the 14th. This time, the troops got about two miles beyond Battery Gatlin, or Half-Moon Battery, as the Federals called it. Only 18 of the heavy pontoons, however, could be gotten up, and they could see Confederates on the opposite side on the lookout, campfires burning, and apparently tracking the progress of the Yankees. It soon became evident they would not get up sufficient pontoons to bridge the sound or ferry men over, and Schofield called off the operation for the second time in two days. "The delay of the pontoons," Cox noted, "was owing to the impossibility of dragging a heavy loaded truck in the soft sand with scant teams." [42]

Schofield now realized his efforts should be directed to the west bank of the Cape Fear, where, he said, "I would not have to contend with the difficulties of both land and sea." From February 14 through 16, Cox's entire division, consisting of Colonel Oscar Sterl's First Brigade, Colonel John Casement's Second Brigade, and Colonel Thomas Henderson's Third Brigade, was ferried across the river to Smithville. Additionally, the Second Brigade of Colonel Orlando Moore, of the Second Division of Schofield's Twenty-Third Army Corps, was sent across as well. [43]

At 8 o'clock in the morning, February 17, Cox moved his four brigades and Battery D of the First Ohio Light Artillery north from Smithville on the west bank of the Cape Fear. They were headed for Fort Anderson, slightly over one mile directly across the river from Sugar Loaf.

The fort at this time was large, with heavy batteries, traverses and curtains similar to Fort Fisher. Part of the fort encompassed the ruins of old St. Philip's Church, which served the colonial community of Brunswick Town. The primary batteries facing the river channel, which ran close by the shore and was laced with torpedoes, resembled in size and strength those of the land face of Fort Fisher. In the gun emplacements were mounted nine large seacoast cannon, 32-pounder rifles and smoothbores. A Whitworth battery was situated between the river batteries and the ruins of the old church. Other light batteries faced south as well.

The similarity to Fort Fisher was not coincidental. William Lamb was commandant here from late 1861 until being ordered to Fisher in July 1862. Additionally, many of the other officers and engineers who wound up at Fisher originally were stationed at Anderson. The fort's right flank was protected by a small lagoon that ran out to Orton Pond, of the same name as the large and still operating plantation built by "King" Roger Moore in the early 1700's. The pond itself was an ideal anchor for Anderson's right flank, running southwest beyond the fort for approximately five miles, and bordered by marsh, swamps, boggy ground, and alligators all around.

With the heavy gun emplacements on Fort Anderson's southern and eastern batteries, as well as light artillery pieces facing south, a frontal assault at Anderson would be costly to the Federals. But with the large body of water that anchored its right, the Yankees must navigate a considerable distance, some 15 miles, to debouch in the Confederate rear. [44]

Cox ran into Thomas Lipscomb's Second South Carolina Cavalry some three miles north of Smithville, and a running skirmish commenced that would last all day. To retard the Federal advance, the Rebel troopers set the woods on fire on either side of the Wilmington Road, and felled trees across it as well.

The shelling of Fort Anderson by Federal warships, including the ironclad **Montauk.**

William Calder recorded in his diary that picket firing had commenced around noontime. "Men ordered in the trenches," he wrote, "& everything made ready for a fight. The monitor & 7 steamers came up & shelled the fort until night. The monitor was repeatedly struck. The enemy," he remembered, "continued to press forward until night when their line was about 1 1/2 miles from the works." [45]

Johnson Hagood said that his mounted troops and infantry pickets skirmished with Cox's troops as they advanced up the road to Anderson. "The monitor engaged at 1,000 yards, and the gunboats out of range of our 32 pdrs. Firing commenced at 1:30 p.m. and continued till sunset; 170 shell were thrown into the fort; one man was wounded, and no damage done to the work. Forty-seven (47) shot were thrown by the fort at the monitor, of which several struck, doing no apparent damage." Hagood said their Whitworth 12-pounder fired several shells at the gunboats, but its ammunition was soon spent, and the fieldpiece was withdrawn to the bridge at Lower Town Creek, to await resupply from Wilmington. Only 30 rounds for the deadly cannon were later obtained, but they arrived too late to be of service at Fort Anderson. [46]

Lieutenant Calder remembered that at dark "the firing ceased & all was quiet during the night. Slept comfortably in a shanty near the lines on a pile of pine straw." Cox's men also bedded down to await the morning's renewed action. The general was satisfied with the day's progress. They had advanced a total of ten miles that day, and were now "within two miles of Fort Anderson." [47]

Promptly at 7 a.m., Cox's 6,000 infantry moved forward, "driving back the enemy and establishing a line of investments on the south side of the fort," where heavy skirmishing ensued. Fort Anderson now opened up with its artillery all along the line, while Porter's fleet joined the action. William Calder said the "monitor came within half a mile of the fort. The fire was tremendous & the fall & bursting of immense shells almost continuous." [48]

As the shelling of Porter's fleet and the return fire of the fort saluted the morning sun, the *Daily Journal* reported that Saturday morning what it knew of the situation. With Braxton Bragg in Richmond, and headquarters in town giving no information on the military condition downriver, speculation in Wilmington was rampant. It said that rumors had been heard that Fort Anderson had fallen, "or been evacuated yesterday evening – This is not so, for the enemy kept up their firing nearly all night, which would not have been the case had the fort fallen into their hands."

The paper advised its readers that there were reports of a Union force landed on the west side of the river, with Fort Anderson being attacked by infantry. Guns were booming, the paper said, even as the article was being written. The paper was certain that the Confederate flag still flew over Anderson, and that readers should not be overly alarmed at rumors.

"The newspapers are not perfect," the *Journal* confessed, "but we think that, upon the whole, the dailies of this place will be found much more reliable than street rumor, or the tales of the 'reliable gentleman'." [49]

Jacob Cox observed that Fort Anderson was going to be a tough nut to crack, if his men were forced to make a frontal assault. "The ground in front of the works," he said, "was entirely open for 200 or 300 yards, and the breastworks themselves were well made, covered with abatis, and commanded by the artillery fire of the fort. The enemy also opened a brisk artillery fire from a battery in position near the right – our left – of their line."

Schofield came to the front to reconnoiter himself. What he saw must have reminded him of the strong position he had commanded at the Battle of Franklin, Tennessee the preceding November, where John Bell Hood had bled his gallant army white in almost suicidal frontal attacks. He decided not to do the same with his men.

He ordered two brigades to intrench in the treeline on the edge of the open ground fronting the fort, "reaching from Orton Pond to the river." When that line was completed, the two other brigades and battery of artillery would move to the southwest down the Brunswick Road, cross the head of Orton Pond, outflank Anderson, and drive down on the rear of the Confederates. The entire distance was believed to be about 25 miles.

Moore's and Henderson's brigades were selected to hold the ground in front, while Casement's and Sterl's brigades were picked for the flanking maneuver, with Cox accompanying them. At this point, Adelbert Ames' division, which had also been ferried across the river, Paine's troops holding Hoke's Division in check on the Sugar Loaf line, would then join Cox to add sledge-hammer weight to the flank attack.

By 2 p.m. Casement and Sterl were on their way, and after a six mile march, reached the head of the pond. A narrow causeway crossed a creek bordered by a 100 yard marsh. Some videttes of Lipscomb's Second South Carolina Cavalry were encountered, and fighting broke out. The far bank of the marsh "was found to be occupied by a considerable detachment, occupying several detached trenches on the rising ground commanding" the road. A sharp skirmish ensued for 30 minutes, and the causeway was captured, the cavalry retreating north. Ames'division came up around 9 p.m., and the entire force camped for the night. [50]

Johnson Hagood learned at 10 p.m. from dispatches Lipscomb had sent, from the "examination of prisoners and deserters," and from scouting reports, "that the force on his right and rear was large and of the three arms, and that Lipscomb's force was entirely too few to check it." Hagood determined that "an evacuation was necessary to save his command."

Around 1 a.m. on the 19th, Hagood telegraphed Hoke of his perilous situation. "To this General Hoke replied: 'Dispatch received...What do you think best?' General Hagood replied: 'I think this place ought to be evacuated and the movement commenced in half an hour.' This last dispatch was sent at 2:05 a.m., and at 2:48 a.m. the reply was received from General Hoke ordering the evacuation and the taking up of a line behind Town Creek."

The movement commenced immediately, and the retreating forces marched out along the Orton causeway. "As soon as the infantry and heavy artillerists had crossed the Orton canal," Hagood recalled, "orders were sent to the infantry pickets in the pits ahead of the entrenchments to withdraw. It was in the early dawn when this last move was commenced, and almost simultaneously with it the enemy advanced with a heavy skirmish line at double quick, followed closely by a line of battle." Some 50 or 60 of the Rebel pickets were captured by these advanced elements of the Federal line of battle, as the Confederates evacuated Fort Anderson with minimal loss. [51]

February 19 was not a good day for Robert Hoke, commander of all forces in the Wilmington area. Hagood's withdrawal from Fort Anderson had significant consequences. As Yankee warships could now move unfettered almost the entire length of the river, Hoke's position at Sugar Loaf was untenable. Both his rear and his right flank were now exposed to naval fire. He retreated up the east bank of the Cape Fear to a point that was opposite to and northeast of Town Creek. [52]

Hoke's men filed into the already constructed earthworks some three miles south of town that ran east from Battery Meares on the river, to Hewlett's Creek that fed into Masonboro Sound. Most of the division went into position in the area near the river batteries and across Forks Road, some two miles inland from the Cape Fear.

As the Confederates moved closer to Wilmington, the Yankees followed hard on their heels. Cox's troops moved up to Town Creek in mid-afternoon of the 19th, while General Terry's men followed up Hoke's pullback on Federal Point Road. David Dixon Porter took his fleet upriver to keep abreast of the infantry forces, and Schofield set up his headquarters on board the hospital vessel *S.R. Spaulding.* [53]

Hagood's position at Town Creek was about six miles north of Fort Anderson, also on the west bank. The creek was forty to fifty yards in width, with crossings at two bridges several miles apart, an "upper" bridge and a "lower" bridge. Though Hagood made his headquarters at the upper bridge, some nine miles by road from the lower, his troops were situated on the north bank of the lower bridge crossing, where some earthworks had been erected.

The high ground, unfortunately, was on the southern bank. A dispatch to headquarters reflected his opinion of the strength of the position. "This place needs much work if it is to be held for any length of time." After personally examining several miles of the creek, he telegraphed Hoke that afternoon what proved to be a forecast of things to come. "From my observation it can be crossed almost anywhere that sufficient troops are not stationed," and he certainly did not have enough troops, as evidenced by his retreat from the powerfully built Fort Anderson. [54]

Daylight of the 20th saw large numbers of Yankees in front of the lower bridge. Jacob Cox ordered Henderson to "push his skirmish line in as close to the creek as possible and to make such demonstrations as would keep the enemy's attention fastened upon the crossing at the bridge." At the same time, he ordered Casement to take charge of his and Sterl's brigade, take a small flatboat discovered during the night, proceed down the creek to find a crossing well beyond the Rebel pickets, and ferry over the brigades to the north. The result would be smashing into Hagood on his left flank and rear with overwhelming force. [55]

William Calder saw the Confederate skirmishers on the creek-banks receive fire from Federals at long range. "Everyone repaired to the breastworks," he said. "Groups of the enemy could be seen on the opposite hills abt. one mile off. Our artillery opened upon them, causing them to scatter. In a few moments," Calder observed, "they returned the fire with rifle guns & it was now our time to scatter. From this time the sharpshooting became brisk & animated, enlivened by occasional sharp duels between the arty. on either side." [56]

All the while, as Henderson's Brigade pressed the front, Casement and Sterl crossed their men to the north bank using the one small scow, a slow and tedious operation. Hagood's left had been anchored in rice fields and swamp, and so the Confederates did not concern themselves with that part of the field.

"This fact enabled us," Jacob Cox reported, "to cross the two brigades without the movement being observed by the rebels. Meanwhile Henderson's skirmishers gradually advanced by alternate lines, each group digging a small rifle-pit at each successive advance till they had approached within very close musket range of the enemy's works, and were enabled to prevent the rebels from showing themselves above the parapet."

Cox then ordered Colonel Orlando Moore to cross his brigade behind the other two, with Cox now joining all three brigades to unite them on the north bank. Sterl & Casement now marched southwest to engage the Eleventh, Twenty-First, Twenty-Fifth and Twenty-Seventh South Carolina Troops of Hagood's Brigade. Colonel Charles Simonton of the Twenty-Fifth South Carolina was in command of these troops, and he had formed them "in a line of breast-works, partially completed, facing to the rear." Moore took his brigade further north and then west, in the expectation of cutting off Hagood's other units in their retreat from the field. [57]

"In the afternoon," William Calder recorded in his diary, "the arty. was gradually withdrawn & sent to the left of the lines where the enemy was making heavy demonstrations. They landed," Calder thought, "in our rear from the river. It soon became evident that we should have to evacuate. About 4 p.m. orders were received to retreat as soon as possible...a hurried flight from the trenches followed. The men were rallied & formed on the road. In the meantime Hagood's S. Carolinians were fighting fiercely on the river & holding the enemy in check." [58]

Late in the afternoon, Hagood sent a dispatch to headquarters. "I am now evacuating," he said. "Enemy are turning my flank and are pushing me too strong. Am obliged to do so." [59]

William V. Izlar was a sergeant in the Edisto Rifles of the Twenty-Fifth South Carolina Infantry. He recalled they skirmished with the Yankees most of the day until near sunset, when the Federals charged their small force, and the South Carolinians were overwhelmed. On the skirmish line two hundred yards to the right of the main battleline, the firing had stopped so abruptly that Izlar concluded the Confederates had been captured. He was convinced of it when he saw some of his own officers quietly conversing with the Yankees.

He decided not to surrender without first making an effort to escape, and some of the men of his company of skirmishers decided to do the same. They worked their way through swampy ground, waist deep in water. When they reached a hill on the "opposite side in safety" at the point they expected to be clear of Federals, they emerged from the marshy bog to reach the road to Wilmington. They walked right into the middle of a brigade of Yankees. "One of them in a very jollifying manner," Izlar remembered, "called out: 'Hello, Johnnie, how deep have you been in!' I tried to hide my mortification and disgust and replied: 'Just so deep,' at the same time indicating with my hand the height around my waist reached by the water. I felt terribly chagrined at this denouement to plans, but quiet submission was the only alternative." [60]

Of Hagood's already reduced brigade engaged in the fight with Cox's three flanking brigades, 20 men were reported killed in action, while 330 men and officers were captured or missing, including the wounded. For those lucky enough to get away from the field, the retreat was a trying experience. William Calder wrote that they began a "hurried" march to get away and head north for Wilmington. "The road was in terrible condition. Mud & water up to our knees. After a most fatiguing march, we reached town at 11 p.m." [61]

As Cox's troops were preparing to charge the South Carolinians in late afternoon, Charles Paine's division of U.S. Colored Troops was preparing to do the same against Hoke's men in the Forks Road entrenchments. Paine said he "came upon an earth-work well manned and showing artillery." He deployed the Fifth Regiment of Colonel Elias Wright's Third Brigade on the right of the line as skirmishers, and John Ames' Second Brigade on the left. Terry's troops under Adelbert Ames were in reserve, while Abbott's brigade was to the rear of Ames. [62]

The Confederates waiting on them were regiments of Clingman's Brigade, the Eighth, Thirty-First, Fifty-First, and Sixty-First North Carolina Infantry, under command of Colonel William Devane. Captain William H.S. Burgwyn, Assistant Adjutant General of the brigade, said that the men "seemed to appreciate the importance of the duty they were called upon to perform," the last defense of Wilmington and the rear of the army. Veterans of the battles of Fort Wagner at Charleston, and Drewry's Bluff and Cold Harbor in Virginia, they were assisted by the six guns and men of Southerland's Wilmington Horse Artillery, which straddled the road itself. [63]

Paine sent his men forward about 3 p.m. "The enemy's fire along our whole front," he said, "was found to be that of a single rank or a little more, and his artillery fire was from six or seven guns." The Yankees got within 150 yards of Clingman's trenches, before musketry, canister and swampy ground stopped them in their tracks. The Rebel fire was hot, and Paine reported that his "loss was 1 officer and 1 man killed, and 3 officers and 48 men wounded, including Col. E. Wright, the commander of the Third Brigade." Paine's losses, combined with those suffered in the February 11th attack on the Sugar Loaf lines would give his division of Colored Troops the distinction of sustaining 73 percent of the Union army's casualties "from February 11 to the capture of Wilmington." [64]

It was clear to Alfred Terry and Charles Paine that the Rebels would not be driven from their position, at least not with the numbers of troops at hand. One of the soldiers who made the attack remarked that "General Terry ordered (us) to charge...and we done it, but we were unable to take the works." Paine reported that a "line of intrenchments was then thrown up covering the position of my division on the south side of the telegraph road." [65]

As Clingman's Brigade was skirmishing with Paine's troops, artillerists in the river batteries three miles below Wilmington were dueling with Porter's gunboats. At the confluence of the Brunswick and Cape Fear Rivers and opposite the south end of Eagles Island, were four small river forts, Batteries Meares, Campbell, Lee and Davis, all of which the Federals called

Fort Strong. There were 15 heavy seacoast guns mounted in these batteries, and they overlooked a network of pilings, sunken ships, trees with branches sticking out of the water, chains and other obstructions that blocked the channel. It was the last river defense to prevent enemy vessels from pulling up to the wharves of Wilmington.

In command of the batteries was 52-year-old Colonel Peter C. Gaillard. A South Carolinian and West Pointer with three years U.S. Army service in the antebellum days, he had played a key role in the repulse of the Federals outside Charleston at the Battle of Secessionville in June of 1862. He had also been a participant in the bloody, successful defense of Battery Wagner in July 1863, where he had lost one of his hands. [66]

His cannoneers were good shots, as the Yankees discovered. Some of the men were Confederate sailors, such as Robert Watson, who with his Battery Buchanan comrades, after evacuating that post and leaving the defenders of Fort Fisher to be captured, had marched up to Wilmington for orders and assignments. Officers at the navy yard sent them down to Battery Campbell, next to Battery Meares. Campbell was a fort that mounted "1 eight inch smooth bore, 1 eighteen pounder, 1 twenty-four, and 2 thirty-two pounders, all smooth bore. The qrs. are old leaky shanties," Watson recalled, "not half room enough for us, 6 of us slept out doors." [67]

Some of Gaillard's artillerists were also members of Company C, Sixty-Eighth North Carolina Troops. Fourth Sergeant W.T. Caho said his company was "assigned to duty at some obstructions on the Cape Fear river a few miles below Wilmington, then known as Batteries or Forts Lee, Davis, Campbell and Meares. While here the company performed duty as heavy artillerists and infantry," and also furnished details "for train guards" and the river steamers. [68]

Robert Watson stood by his gun at Battery Campbell as nine of Porter's gunboats came up and stood off the batteries late morning of the 20th. At 3 p.m., the same time as Paine's troops were going forward against Hoke at the Forks Road trenches, the Union vessels opened up. "Our Parrot gun opened on them in return," Watson recorded, "it being the only gun that would bear on them. The third shell the Yankees threw came very near killing me and several more." Watson said they had reinforced their position with many sandbags, which saved their lives, even though they "were buried in sand. Several shell exploded near our gun and one struck the platform and tore it all to pieces. Ceased fire at dark and we worked nearly all night repairing damages with sand bags. Very cold." [69]

U.S. Naval Assistant Surgeon Stephen C. Bartlett was serving aboard the *U.S.S. Lenapee*, one of the ships bombarding the river batteries. Writing home to his parents in Connecticut on the evening of the 20th, he told them that fighting had been going on all afternoon. "The enemy have a casemated iron Fort and with a continual firing today we have not been able to silence it. The

Rebs keep up a regular fire. The *U S S Sassacus* and the *Lenapee* are in advance. The *Sassacus* has been struck and is leaking badly tonight. We have not been injured yet although shell have struck all around us, and I really believe that a shell came within two feet of me and burst just over the side of us. I assure you I dipped my head as well as others who were near me for you have no idea what an ugly scream they give. The Rebs have set the woods on fire and the river is well lit up." [70]

Bartlett told his parents that after the battle with the river forts, the Confederates then released about 100 torpedoes, made of wood and containing 100 pounds of powder, which floated down the river into the middle of the Union fleet. Admiral Porter reported that one of them exploded under a boat belonging to the *U.S.S. Shawmut.* Seaman James Cobb was killed, Seaman James Hayes drowned, and Acting Ensign W.B. Trufant was "severely wounded", while Seaman Martin Wall was "slightly wounded."

Porter also said that one of the torpedoes blew the wheelhouse of the *Osceola* to "pieces, and knocked down her bulkheads inboard, but there was no damage to the hull." Some of the torpedoes were gathered up with the ships' torpedo nets, while others next morning began to harvest more with "fishing nets across the river." [71]

Early on the morning of Tuesday, February 21, the last day of Confederate Wilmington, Lipscomb's South Carolina troopers burned the trestle of the Wilmington & Manchester Railroad connecting the city to the west. They also destroyed other bridges and pontoons across the Brunswick River and on Eagles Island. Jacob Cox's men were fast approaching from the battlefield of Town Creek, southwest of town. [72]

Returning to Wilmington on this day from his Richmond trip, Bragg could see that there was no alternative to abandoning the city. He wired army headquarters in Richmond, "I find all our troops on this side Cape Fear. The enemy in force on the west, and our communications south cut. We are greatly outnumbered. General Schofield in command with two corps." Later, he advised Robert E. Lee that with one corps confronting Hoke to the south of town, and another just to the west of the Cape Fear, he had no choice. "This compels me to cross the Northeast River or they will be in my rear tomorrow. Our small forces renders it impossible to make any serious stand." [73]

William Calder, after a good night's sleep following the weary march from Town Creek battlefield with the rest of Hagood's forces, was busy that morning with his duties as Adjutant, First Battalion North Carolina Troops, preparing for evacuation of the city. In the afternoon, he was calling on old friends to bid them goodbye. "I think this has been one of the saddest days of my life," he recorded in his diary. "I never had such a hard thing to do as leave all my old friends & the home where my childhood's days were spent. I procured a horse in the afternoon & rode over the town for the last time." [74]

That afternoon, after his engineers repaired one of the bridges and secured some of the pontoons the Rebels failed to destroy, Jacob Cox sent the Sixteenth Kentucky Infantry of Oscar Sterl's brigade across the causeway that traversed Eagles Island. They chased Confederate pickets down the causeway, and began to approach Wilmington from across the mile and a half wide island. The causeway was the only dry approach to the river's edge, as the island was mostly a huge marsh and swampy bog, teeming with wildlife and alligators.

As the Kentuckians, now joined by the Sixty-Fifth Illinois, got about halfway across the island, they were met by artillery fire from Captain Abner Moseley's Sampson Battery. These North Carolinians had seen action at Fort Anderson and Town Creek, and were now banging away with two guns situated on Market Street near the riverfront, and on either side of the Market House itself. One soldier was killed and several others wounded, while the others instinctively dove for cover in the marshy ground on either side of the causeway. [75]

Joe King heard the whir and explosion of the shells close by. He and some of his teenage friends, "William Bryant, Dick Steljes, Joe Kirkham and others," not wishing to be conscripted by Bragg's retreating army, and knowing the days of the Confederacy were numbered, had taken shad boats up Alligator Creek to hide on Eagles Island. Peering from their boats across the marshes, they saw some parts of town were already in flames, as military stores were being burned and destroyed. King said that "Van Bucklan's turpentine still, with a vast amount of rosin and turpentine," was burning out of control, and "made a most horrifying sight."

King recalled that "our forces had planted a cannon at the foot of Market Street to resist the oncoming Yankees on the causeway coming through Brunswick. We were near enough that day, lying in the rushes, to see some of the Yankee forces advancing from Brunswick on the causeway. We actually heard the cannon balls from Wilmington strike the mud and we saw the Yankee soldiers retreating back across the bridge." [76]

Jacob Cox ordered up rifled fieldpieces, Battery D of the First Ohio Light Artillery, to counter the Confederate fire, while his infantry began to entrench on either side of the causeway in the marsh. Numbers of shells began to crash into buildings in Wilmington, several hitting the Market House, and adding to the fear and pandemonium among the civilians. Moseley was ordered to cease firing, lest the Yankee artillery destroy the town and kill men, women and children alike. When the Confederates stopped, so too did the Federals. [77]

For the balance of the afternoon and evening, Cox employed his men in gathering materials for repairing the destroyed bridge. He, like Joe King and his friends in their shad boats, watched the burning of naval stores and cotton in town, clear indications the Confederates would be evacuating Wilmington, probably tomorrow, Wednesday the 22nd, George Washington's birthday. [78]

Johnson Hagood had sent his infantry to reinforce Hoke's troops, who continued to engage in heavy skirmishing with the Federals all day. He was in command of the town during its last hours as a military post. Hundreds of Union prisoners had been unwisely sent to Wilmington, adding to the logistical problems, and they were marched out before the Confederate troops, headed for the Northeast Cape Fear River nine miles north. From there they would catch trains. In addition to the destruction of ships and various military stores that could not be taken, others were given to the troops. As the soldiers began to pull out of town, they were handed shoes, clothing and other items from quartermaster stocks "which could not be got off by rail." That night, Hagood said, "guards were stationed with rigid orders to put down all pillage that might be attempted by the most summary measures." [79]

Word was quietly passed to the soldiers to leave their posts early in the morning. It was galling to some. Charles Elliott of Kirkland's Brigade remembered bitterly that though they had fought gallantly against Terry's Yankees over the several weeks since Fort Fisher, holding their own against heavy odds, "we slowly fell back to Wilmington." He said that their "retreat through the city was gloomy indeed, for we had many strong personal friends among its kind and hospitable people." [80]

Robert Watson recorded in his dairy that the sailors at Battery Campbell were roused at 1 a.m. They were ordered to take everything they could carry, and to be quiet about it. They waited for marching orders for an hour in a hollow about 400 yards from the battery. "It was bitter cold," he wrote, "and I thought that my feet would freeze. Started and marched through the city of Wilmington, not a word spoken for the Yankees were very close to us, in fact we afterwards found out that they were in the city when we passed through, but we went through the back part of the city and they were in the city front. Marched without resting till 10 AM when we rested for one hour then started and crossed a pontoon bridge at N.E. River." [81]

Jacob Cox recorded in his journal their entry into Wilmington Wednesday morning without Confederate opposition. He wrote that since it was Washington's birthday, the Federals hailed the event as a "good omen. The enemy has retreated up the line of the Goldsborough road...General Terry, being on the same side of the river, marches through in pursuit of Hoke. My troops are put in camp around the town, and I assume command of the place." [82]

Upon his arrival in town, John Schofield got off a dispatch to the general commanding all Union armies, to present him with the news. Sent from his new "Headquarters Department of North Carolina, Wilmington, February 22, 1865," Schofield greeted U.S. Grant at his headquarters in City Point, Virginia with this message: "General: I have the satisfaction of announcing the capture of Wilmington." [83]

Mrs. Katherine Douglas DeRosset Meares, a native Wilmingtonian, had lost much in this war. One brother, a seventeen-year-old private, had died in it. Her oldest brother, Colonel William L. DeRosset of the Third North Carolina Troops, had suffered severe wounds in the Battle of Sharpsburg, where he was almost killed. Her husband, Colonel Gaston Meares, commander of the Third North Carolina before her brother William, lay in his grave, a victim of the bloody battle at Malvern Hill in July 1862.

The Confederate widow was bitter at Wilmington's fall. "Darkness and gloom cover us as a pall," she wrote to her parents, who had fled town for the interior of the state. "These immense fires on each side of the town were fearful. Contrary winds blew the dense black smoke of both directly toward the town, and when the heavy black clouds met in the center, it seemed as if a dark, oppressive girdle (typical of our future) encompassed the town." [84]

In beautiful Oakdale, where her slain husband had rested these two and a half years, a lovely headstone was to be erected at his grave. It was fairly tall, and in the shape of the cross of his Christian faith. The inscription it bore might well be an epitaph for this city of his birth, now shattered and broken, that the dead warrior fought for, to protect from invasion. It would read poignantly, "A Martyr To The Cause of Southern Independence." [85]

Endnotes to Chapter 11

1. Barrett, Civil War in North Carolina, p.279; Wilmington Campaign, p.62; Cleer, James J. Papers, letter to Father & Mother, January 17, 1865, Manuscript Department, William R. Perkins Library, Duke University, Durham, North Carolina
2. Civil War in North Carolina, p.279
3. O.R., Volume XLVI, Part I, p.401; Confederate Soldier Memorial & Mass grave of Confederate dead from Fort Fisher, Oakdale Cemetery, Wilmington
4. O.R., Volume XLVI, Part I, p.396; Battles & Leaders, Volume IV, p.661-662
5. S.H.S.P., Volume XXI, p.289; O.R., Volume XLVI, Part I, p.426-431; Wilmington Campaign, p.72; Last Rays of Departing Hope, p.303-304
6. Greer, William R., "Recollections of a Private Soldier of the Army of the Confederate States," p.25-26, Manuscript Department, William Perkins Library, Duke University, Durham, North Carolina
7. Wilmington Campaign, p.72; Martin Curtis account of Fort Fisher, p. 319; Generals in Blue, p.366
8. Wilmington Campaign, p.73
9. Wilmington Campaign, p.89; Calder, William, First Battalion N.C. Heavy Artillery, Diary of January 15 & 16, 1865, William Perkins Library, Duke University, Durham, North Carolina, hereinafter Calder Diary
10. Calder Diary, January 17, 1865
11. Wilmington Campaign, p.89; Fonvielle, Chris E. Jr., *Fort Anderson: Battle for Wilmington*, p.32-33, Savas Publishing Company, Mason City, Iowa, 1999, hereinafter Fort Anderson

12. Calder Diary, January 19, 1865
13. Wilmington Campaign, p.89-90
14. Fort Anderson, p.32
15. O.R., Volume XLVI, Part II, p.1117
16. O.R., Volume XLVI, Part II, p.1116-1117, p.1120
17. Wilmington Campaign, p.91, p.132
18. Wilmington Daily Journal, January 17, 1865
19. O.R., Volume XLVI, Part II, p.1115; Wilmington Campaign, p.90
20. Clark, Volume III, p.694-695
21. O.R., Volume XLVI, Part II, p.1137; Fort Anderson, p. 33-34; Wilmington Campaign, p.57
22. O.R., Volume XLVI, Part II, p.1142
23. O.R., Volume XLVI, Part II, p.1160; Hagood, War of Secession, p.334-335
24. Wilmington Campaign, p.93; O.R., Volume XLVII, Part I, p.17-19
25. Wilmington Campaign, p.93
26. Wilmington Campaign, p.93
27. Wilmington Campaign, p.93
28. O.R., Volume XLVII, Part II, p.189-190
29. Wilmington Campaign, p.94-95; O.R., Volume XLVII, Part II, p.1119, p.1139; Generals in Blue, p.97
30. O.R., Volume XLVII, Part II, p.371
31. O.R., Volume XLVII, Part II, p.384-385
32. Wilmington Campaign, p.95; O.R., Volume XLVII, Part II, p.1138
33. Calder Diary, February 11, 1865
34. Wilmington Campaign, p.96-97; O.R., Volume XLVII, Part I, p.910, p.921-923
35. O.R., Volume XLVII, Part I, p.921-923
36. Clark, Volume III p.695; Wilmington Campaign, p.96-97
37. O.R., Volume XLVII, Part I, p.911, p.925; Wilmington Campaign, p.97
38. Wilmington Campaign, p.96
39. O.R., Volume XLVII, Part I, p.910, p.927; Wilmington Campaign, p.97
40. Comstock Diary, p.309; Barrett, Civil War in North Carolina, p.281; O.R., Volume XLVII, Part I, p.928
41. O.R., Volume XLVII, Part I, p.928
42. O.R., Volume XLVII, Part I, p.928-929
43. O.R., Volume XLVII, Part I, p.910; Wilmington Campaign, p.102-103
44. O.R., Volume XLVII, Part I, p.929; Wilmington Campaign, p.102-107; Chronicles, p.57
45. O.R., Volume XLVII, Part I, p.929; Wilmington Campaign, p.103; Calder Diary, February 17, 1865
46. War of Secession, p.335-336
47. Calder Diary, February 17, 1865; O.R., Volume XLVII, Part I, p.929

48. O.R., Volume XLVII, Part I, p.929; Calder Diary, February 18, 1865; Wilmington Campaign, p.107
49. Wilmington Daily Journal, February 18, 1865
50. O.R., Volume XLVII, Part I, p.960-961
51. War of Secession, p.338-339
52. Barefoot, General Robert F. Hoke, p.273; Wilmington Campaign, p.116-117
53. Wilmington Campaign, p.116-117
54. War of Secession, p.340-342; O.R., Volume XLVII, Part II, p.1228
55. War of Secession, p.343; O.R., Volume XLVII, Part I, p.961-962
56. Calder Diary, February 20, 1865
57. O.R., Volume XLVII, Part I, p.962; Wilmington Campaign, p.124; War of Secession, p.343
58. Calder Diary, February 20, 1865
59. O.R., Volume XLVII, Part II p.1236
60. Izlar, Willliam V., *A Sketch of the War Record of the Edisto Rifles, 1861-1865*, p.115-117, The State Company, Columbia, South Carolina, 1914
61. Calder Diary, February 20, 1865; War of Secession, p.347
62. O.R., Volume XLVII, Part I, p.925; Wilmington Campaign, p.120
63. Last Rays, p.395-397; Clark, Volume IV, p.481, p.498
64. O.R., Volume XLVII, Part I, p.911, p.925; Wilmington Campaign, p.121
65. Last Rays, p.398; O.R., Volume XLVII, Part I, p.925
66. Last Rays, p.389; Bradshaw, Timothy E., *Battery Wagner: The Siege, The Men Who Fought, and the Casualties*, p.45, Palmetto Historical Works, Columbia, South Carolina, 1993; ORN, Volume 12, p.56; Wilmington Campaign, p.123
67. Robert Watson Journal, p.16-17
68. Clark, Volume III, p.725-726
69. Robert Watson Journal, p.18
70. Murray, Paul and Stephen R. Bartlett, eds., "The Letters of Stephen Chaulker Bartlett Aboard the U.S.S. 'Lenapee,' January to August 1865." *North Carolina Historical Review,* p.78-79, January 1956, hereinafter Bartlett letters
71. Bartlett letters, p.79; ORN, Volume 12, p.44-45
72. O.R., Volume XLVII, Part I, p.963; Wilmington Campaign, p.128
73. O.R., Volume XLVII, Part II, p.1241-1242
74. Calder Diary, February 20 and 21, 1865
75. O.R., Volume XLVII, Part I, p.963
76. Personal Recollections of Joseph P. King, p.7
77. O.R., Volume XLVII, Part I, p.963; Last Rays, p.417-418; Wilmington Campaign, p.128
78. O.R., Volume XLVII, Part I, p.963

79. War of Secession, p.348; Wilmington Campaign, p.128
80. S.H.S.P., Volume XXIII, p.169
81. Robert Watson Journal, p.18
82. O.R., Volume XLVII, Part II, p.930
83. O.R., Volume XLVII, Part II, p.535
84. Chronicles, p.292-294; Cape Fear Special section of "Wilmington Sunday Star-News," March 7, 1976, p.21
85. Gravestone of Colonel Gaston Meares, Oakdale Cemetery, Wilmington

Epilogue

A month before the fall of Wilmington, official finger-pointing for the loss of Fort Fisher, linchpin of all Wilmington's defenses, began. On January 18, three days after Fisher's fall, General Whiting, suffering from his leg wound in the hospital at the fort, dictated the first of two official reports to Robert E. Lee. Whiting gave full credit to the Federals for the unprecedented attack. "On Sunday," he told General Lee, "the fire of the fleet reached a pitch of fury to which no language can do justice. It was concentrated on the land front and fort. In a short time nearly every gun was dismounted or disabled, and the garrison suffered severely from the fire." He next spoke of the heavy columns of the enemy making a lodgment on the western end of the landface, and the garrison fighting tenaciously to hold the traverses until they were overwhelmed by superior numbers.

Then, obviously seething with rage as he got to the heart of the matter, he emphasized to Lee that Fort Fisher "has fallen in precisely the manner indicated so often by myself, and to which your attention has been so frequently called, and in the presence of the ample force provided by you to meet the contingency...I think that the result might have been avoided, and Fort Fisher still held, if the commanding general had have done his duty. I charge him with this loss."

On February 19, three days before Wilmington fell, and while now a prisoner in Fort Columbus Hospital on Governor's Island in New York harbor, Whiting presented Lee with additional details of the battle in a follow-up report. Then he returned to Bragg's conduct. Whiting told Lee he had gone into "the fort with the conviction that it was to be sacrificed, for the last I heard General Bragg say was to point out a line to fall back on if Fort Fisher fell. In all his career of failure and defeat from Pensacola out, there has been no such chance missed, and no such stupendous disaster."

Indignant as he completed his report, he demanded of Lee, "in justice to the country, to the army, and to myself, that the course of this officer be investigated...I do not know what he was sent to Wilmington for. I had hoped that I was considered competent...My proper place," he continued, "was in command of the troops you sent to support the defense; then I should not now be a prisoner, and an effort at least would have been made to save a harbor on which I had expended for two years all the labor and skill I had." [1]

Whiting's grave marker in Oakdale Cemetery

In a letter to his good friend Blanton Duncan on March 2, eight days before his death from the soldier's most common illness in that war, diarrhea, Chase Whiting was even more blunt in his vilification of Bragg. "That I am here," he told Duncan, "and that Wilmington and Fisher are gone, is due wholly and solely to the incompetency, the imbecility and the pusillanimity of Braxton Bragg, who was sent to spy upon and supersede me about two weeks (months?) before the attack. He could have taken every one of the enemy, but he was afraid." [2]

Following his death, Whiting received a respectful and honorable funeral service in New York, with several Union officers serving as pallbearers. Initially buried in Brooklyn's Greenwood Cemetery, his remains were removed to Oakdale in Wilmington in 1900, where he rests today beside his wife, a daughter of the Cape Fear. [3]

The end came quickly for the Confederacy after Fort Fisher and Wilmington were captured, as a Union naval officer had predicted in late summer of 1864. On September 6, Captain O.S. Glisson, commanding the New Inlet Division, had written to Admiral S.P. Lee he was "convinced that if this port is taken the rebellion will not last three months." It was an accurate prophecy, based on his observation of the massive quantities of supplies incoming on the many blockade runners, successfully guarded by Fisher and her dependent batteries and forts. Fort Fisher fell on January 15; Lee surrendered the Army of Northern Virginia, the South's most successful force, on April 9 at Appomattox Courthouse, Virginia. [4]

Unlike Chase Whiting, the close friend he so greatly admired, William Lamb would live to see the end of Southern independence, and eventually, the rebirth of the South. He would have much to do with economic revitalization himself, particularly in his hometown of Norfolk, where he served as mayor like his father and grandfather, and curried business with British merchants with whom he had dealt during the war. Lamb, like some other business minded former Confederates, eventually embraced the Republican Party as another means of promoting development and free enterprise in the South. As a result, he met General Newton Martin Curtis at a national convention. The two former enemies became close personal friends, visiting each other often and Fort Fisher during reunions and other visits to Wilmington.

William Lamb at age 70

Lamb wrote various articles concerning the defense of Fort Fisher for the *Southern Historical Society Papers* and *Battles and Leaders of the Civil War, Volume IV*. He also gave speeches in Wilmington and other places on the same subject as well, agreeing fully with the assessment of General Whiting relative to the conduct, or misconduct, of Braxton Bragg, in the battle for the fort.

In one such speech, delivered February 4, 1896, before the Military Historical Society of Massachusetts, he concluded with emotional and personal reflections of the 31 years that had transpired since the fall of his fort. He confessed to the old soldiers that as he lay on the sand badly wounded at Battery Buchanan, he lost all faith in the belief that "God defends the right. But I have lived to learn," Lamb told them, "that He doeth all things well and that it was decreed in Heaven that this great country of ours should be one and inseparable; and while I love the cause for which I fought, believing it was a reserved right, not incompatible with my oath to support the Constitution of the United States, and while my heart will be as cold as death can make it, when I cease to revere the memory of the brave comrades who fell in battle by my side, yet I believe that it is all for the best, and have transferred that allegiance, which I was taught was first due to my native State, Virginia, to the United

Sisterhood of States. And henceforth and forever, their flag shall be my flag, their people my people, and until I am gathered to my fathers, I shall do all in my power for their safety, honor and welfare." [5]

Lamb's beloved wife Daisy died in March 1892. Lamb was heartbroken, and involved himself more in veterans' affairs, public service and various new businesses, several of which failed. When he passed away of age and ill health on March 23, 1909, he was living with one of his daughters, and in dire financial straits. He and his Yankee-born, Confederate heroine, Daisy, lie side by side in Elmwood Cemetery in Norfolk. [6]

Major General Alfred Terry received the accolades of the public and the Congress for his capture of Fort Fisher. Better still, he was awarded with a brigadier general's commission in the Regular U.S. Army. The year following the war, he was transferred west as commanding officer of the Department of Dakota. The historical event for which he would become best known had nothing to do with Fort Fisher. It had to do with a strong willed and vainglorious subordinate named George Armstrong Custer.

In 1876, Terry was in command of a number of cavalry regiments in the field, seeking out hostile Indians to fight. Custer was leading one of Terry's regiments, the Seventh U.S. Cavalry. Custer found hostile Indians, lots of them. Thousands of Sioux and Cheyenne warriors attacked his immediate battalion (1/3 of the Seventh Cavalry) on June 25, 1876, virtually wiping them out at the Battle of the Little Big Horn. The public was outraged, and much controversy was generated by this military debacle on the plains, some saying Custer had exceeded or violated orders. Terry was forever after associated with this calamitous event.

Alfred H. Terry retired to New Haven, Connecticut in 1888 as a major general, the first non-academy graduate to attain such rank in quite a few years. Suffering from declining health the last few years of his life, he died on December 16, 1890, and was buried in the Grove Street Cemetery in New Haven. [7]

General Newton Martin Curtis recovered from his grievous wound, one so mortal looking a coffin had been ordered for him, when he revived enough to show signs of life. He left the army in 1866 and moved to Ogdensburg, New York. As previously stated, he and Colonel Lamb became good friends, visiting one another and making trips to Fort Fisher on occasion, especially during reunions of the survivors of the battle. From 1891 to 1897, he served his district in the U.S. House of Representatives.

In the mid-to-late 1890's, after General Terry's death, Curtis became embroiled in a controversy with Adelbert Ames over responsibility for the failure of the December 1864 expedition against Fort Fisher, and responsibility for the success of the January 1865 expedition. Curtis alleged that he had not only been under the direct command of General Terry and not Ames in January 1865, but that Ames' contribution to victory had not been that significant.

In rebuttals delivered over the years on several occasions, Ames defended his father in law, Ben Butler. Butler's decision to abandon the first expedition due to ineffective naval fire failing to knock out the landface guns had been a sound one. General Godfrey Weitzel, a courageous officer with much experience storming fixed positions, had clearly seen with his own eyes the slaughter pen for Union troops that Fort Fisher would be if an assault was launched against the virtually intact positions of the landface. It would have been "butchery to order an assault on that work under the circumstances," he had reported at the time. Both General Whiting and Colonel Lamb agreed. [8]

Ames also defended himself, with the words of General Terry. He simply reiterated verbatim, the statement Terry made to U.S. Grant in his official report, compiled just 10 days after the battle. "Of General Ames," Terry had written Grant from Fort Fisher, "I have already spoken in a letter recommending his promotion. He commanded all the troops engaged, and was constantly under fire. His great coolness, good judgment, and skill were never more conspicuous than in this assault."

And one would hardly think Ames would have complimented Martin Curtis for his role in the attack, had Curtis actually been removed from his command due to a personality clash. But in his January 16 report, written the day after the fort fell, Ames said that General Curtis, "commanding First Brigade, was prominent throughout the day for his bravery, coolness, and judgment. His services cannot be over-estimated." Ames further pointed to the report of Colonel Rufus Daggett, One Hundred and Seventeenth New York Infantry, commanding the First Brigade after the battle was over. Colonel Daggett's official report, written January 17, 1865, states that at "about 3 p.m. (General Curtis having received orders to that effect from General Ames, through Captain Lawrence) the brigade advanced to the charge, obliquing to the right." [9]

The rift apparently was never healed between Curtis and Ames. An accomplished historian with his Civil War study of *From Bull Run to Chancellorsville*, Curtis died in New York City on January 8, 1910. He was buried in Ogdensburg. [10]

Ames had a checkered career as a corrupt Reconstruction governor in Mississippi. He resigned to avoid impeachment, after whites regained control of the state, and left Mississippi in 1876. He served briefly at a training camp in the Spanish-American War as a brigadier general of volunteers. At the age of ninety-seven, on April 13, 1933, Ames died at his home in Ormond, Florida, the last surviving full-rank general on either side of the war. He not only outlived his nemesis, Martin Curtis, but unlike most of his contemporaries, lived to see radio, automobiles, and airplanes. [11]

Admiral David Dixon Porter, one of the great naval commanders in American history, was one of the prime contributors to Union victory at Fort Fisher and Wilmington. Of all his campaigns, it was probably second only to

Vicksburg in terms of strategic importance, for its particular time in the war. His star was definitely in the ascendancy as the war drew to a close. Despite that, his temperament and personality would not allow for humility or graciousness. If Grant had benefited from Porter's help in the Vicksburg and Fort Fisher-Wilmington Campaigns, Porter had certainly benefited from Grant's.

It was axiomatic that the navy alone could not capture Fort Fisher. It could only destroy the guns and other defenses in the fort to permit army troops to attack. Infantry assault was essential to the securing and holding of any position. Despite Porter's understanding of that, he still felt the need to continually lay blame for his own mistakes at others' feet, and criticize someone when silence would have been wiser.

He wrote privately to Gideon Welles that Grant had tried to deny the Navy its proper share of the glory of Fort Fisher, and said Grant would sacrifice a friend to protect himself. Porter apparently believed such statements to his boss would be of benefit to him. Years later, when Grant was President, one of Porter's enemies discovered the letter and showed it to Grant. Their relationship after that was only of an official one, and certainly must have been icy.

Porter was a competent and efficient superintendent at the Naval Academy at Annapolis. He wrote a detailed history of the Navy's part in the war, called *The Naval History of the Civil War*, which was published in 1886. That, too, like his opinions, reports and letters, had to be taken with a grain of salt. He reiterated in his history, for example, the absurd notion that Fort Fisher was ready for the taking in December 1864, and had it not been for Butler being there, it would have been taken. "The abandonment of the expedition by General Butler with his army," he wrote in his book, "created the greatest indignation on the part of the Navy, who had seen the prize so nearly within their reach." Forever the finger-pointer, Porter would never concede the Navy, and by implication, he, had failed on that expedition. Porter died on February 13, 1891, and is buried in Arlington National Cemetery. [12]

The eighteen-year-old Virginia Yankee, Robley Evans, was critically wounded when he arrived at Norfolk Navy Yard. He was so badly shot in the legs that the doctors at the Naval Hospital decided to amputate both of them. He told one of the surgeons that he had rather die with both legs, than to be a young man with none. When the doctor was insistent about the operation, Evans pulled his pistol from under his pillow. "I told him," Evans wrote years later, "that there were six loads in it, and that if he or any one else entered my door with anything that looked like a case of instruments I meant to begin shooting, and that he might rest perfectly sure that I would kill six before they cut my legs off." The doctors dismissed the idea of amputation, and Evans eventually healed. [13]

Staying in the navy, in the 1880's he was one of the primary proponents of all steel warships. In October 1895, he was given command of America's first truly modern battleship, the *U.S.S. Indiana*, "the heaviest armed and armoured ship in the world," at the time she was commissioned, Evans said. With such vessels as these, the U.S. Navy had no difficulty defeating the Spanish fleet in the Spanish-American War. By the turn of the century, Evans was a rear admiral. He died January 3, 1912, and is buried in Arlington. [14]

Braxton Bragg proceeded north from Wilmington with Hoke's Division and the other area troops after withdrawing from the city. He linked up the next month with General Joseph E. Johnston, who was charged by Robert E. Lee with assembling a hodge-podge of troops from various commands into one cohesive force to strike William T. Sherman. On March 15 at Smithfield, North Carolina, Johnston formed what was officially called the Army of the South. It was comprised of four distinct forces from different armies that had not served together. Here Hoke's Division received reinforcements, a brigade of several North Carolina Junior Reserve regiments, mostly teenage boys who had not seen combat.

Bragg was one of many high-ranking generals present on the field at the Battle of Bentonville four days later, and as on most other battlefields where he had been present, he thwarted potential Confederate success. He called on Joe Johnston to reinforce Hoke when Hoke did not need support, delaying the main Confederate attack, and reducing the force of the attack by one fourth of its full strength. The Left Wing of Sherman's army was roundly pummeled, but it was not defeated and driven off the field, when it might have been. "This movement," Wade Hampton the great South Carolinian wrote years later, "was in my judgment the only mistake committed on our part during the fight." Joe Johnston himself later confirmed that responding to Bragg's plea for reinforcements was a mistake. [15]

Seemingly devoted to the Southern Cause, many times a sound stategist in planning campaigns, Bragg was seldom able to achieve on the battlefield the victory his country needed. The one great victory his army did attain with the help of Lee's troops, Chickamauga, was squandered by Bragg's failure to follow it up by crushing the Union army. Then came the disaster of Missionary Ridge, and more disgrace. Then came Fort Fisher, and finally Bentonville.

After the war, Bragg moved to Alabama to work as the state's chief engineer. He later moved to Galveston, Texas, where on September 27, 1876, he fell dead as he walked down the street with a friend. He is buried in the Confederate section, Magnolia Cemetery, in Mobile, Alabama. [16] The largest military post in the country, Fort Bragg, North Carolina, is named in his honor.

General Robert F. Hoke, one of North Carolina's finest sons, came home to work and rebuild his battered state and Southland. "Once the great war was over, it was over forever for Hoke," wrote his biographer, Daniel Barefoot. He never wrote his memoirs, and would not write or even talk of the war. His overwhelming modesty was one of his many sterling traits as a man of character.

Hoke shunned public office, but firmly believed economic development of the South was desperately needed to bring her out of the depths of war's devastation. He involved himself in iron manufacturing, and especially encouraged and became manager of several railroad companies in the 1870's and 1880's. He was particularly instrumental in the development and management of the Georgia, Carolina, and Northern Railway Company, that ran from Monroe, North Carolina to Atlanta. It eventually became one of the prime components of the Seaboard Airline System, a company name and business that provided thousands of Southerners with jobs well into the Twentieth Century. Admired and revered by people of all ages and stations, as was his great commander, Robert E. Lee, General Hoke even looked like Lee in his later years. This warrior gentleman died from the effects of diabetes on July

Pvt. George Benson, C.S.A., at age 94

3, 1912. He is buried in Oakwood Cemetery in Raleigh. [17]

Eighteen-year-old Private George W. Benson, of Company H, William Lamb's Thirty-Sixth North Carolina Troops, was sent to Point Lookout, Maryland prison camp, along with many of his comrades captured in Fort Fisher. "They kept me there for five months," he recalled on November 3, 1940, his 94th birthday, "from January in '65 till June in '65. There were 26,000 of us up there."

Benson remembered that the "Yankees ate well, all right, but we didn't. A little slab of meat big as three of your fingers at 8 o'clock, and a half of a small loaf of bread at 11. At 2 they gave us some soup. They called it vegetable soup. Sometimes they did put some potato peelings in it. I got sick. Everybody did." Benson said he was "sick all over" by the time they let him out of prison, disease had loosened all of his teeth, and he weighed only 75 pounds.

When he got home to Bladen County, North Carolina, he got married and raised 10 children. He was a farmer and a carpenter, and register of deeds in Bladen County. Moving to Charlotte years later, he worked for over 30 years as a ticket agent with the Southern Railroad, retiring at the age of 89. In the 1940's, he was honored by the ladies of the United Daughters of the

Confederacy as the last Confederate
Veteran in Mecklenburg County. When he
died on June 14, 1948 at the age of 101, he
was also the last survivor of William
Lamb's regiment, or any Confederate
regiment, that fought at Fort Fisher.

When Mr. Benson passed away, he
was survived by 58 descendants, children,
grandchildren, great grandchildren, and
great great grandchildren. One of his great
great grandsons, Mr. Rusty Lewis, has been
a friend of the author since the year after
George Benson died. He is buried in
Newell Presbyterian Church Cemetery,
Charlotte, with a headstone at his resting
place which reads, "He Was the Last
Veteran of the Garrison of Fort Fisher N.C.,
the Gibraltar of the Confederacy." [18]

Benson's Charlotte grave marker

When Joe King and his friends
emerged from the marsh creek where they
had been hiding for two days as the
Federals took possession of Wilmington,
they "saw many ships flying the Stars and Stripes. We then knew that the
Yankees had the city," he recalled. Martial law had already been established,
and the city was relatively quiet, except for the unloading of ships at the
wharves. "Our people in general settled down to the inevitable issue," he said.
"However, we were grieved in our hearts for the cause that we had lost and
suffered so much to maintain. Amidst this disorganized and confused state,
nothing remained for us to do but to cast about for some way of support." Like
most Wilmingtonians, he and his family went to work.

Joe King married his childhood sweetheart, Eliza, in 1866, and in a
few years, became pastor of the Second Baptist Church on Sixth Street. In the
late 1870's, while still a Baptist preacher, he embraced the doctrines of the
Advent Christians. That doctrine, called conditional immortality as Joe
explained it, meant the recognition that people are unconscious in death, and
remain so until the Second Coming of Christ, at which time judgment takes
place. For this, he was tried for heresy and expelled by the Eastern Baptist
Association in 1880. In time, he became one of the most recognized and
esteemed Advent Christian ministers in the South.

During his ministry through the years, he was drawn to the suffering of
the sick and the poor. Because medical care was limited and primitive in those
days, he decided to study medicine on his own, becoming proficient at treating
the sick and injured, and in delivering babies, hundreds of them. He treated

black and white alike, seldom charging a penny for his services. The "love and esteem I have from hundreds of patients today," he said in 1926, "is more than enough pay in these my old days." [19]

When his family celebrated his 98th birthday in Wilmington, on June 20, 1946, Reverend Joseph P. King had 4 living children, 48 grandchildren, 62 great grandchildren, and 8 great great grandchildren. [20] My Grandpa King died on January 7, 1948 at 99 1/2 years of age, and is buried in Bellevue Cemetery.

For years after the war, Fort Fisher was visited by the old veterans, North and South, who had fought there. Around the turn of the century, the Fort Fisher Survivors Association, comprised of men from both sides, tried to get Congress to appropriate funds for a national battlefield park. They were not interested, and over the years the fort fell into ruins, weeds and scrub growth covering the old mounds and ramparts.

In the 1920's, the Army Corps of Engineers extracted tons of natural rock bed, called "coquina rock," offshore of the fort, to use in the building of Highway 421. The result was the almost immediate onset of beach erosion. By the late 1930's, much of the fort had been washed away by the Atlantic. During World War II, Fort Fisher became an antiaircraft training base, an auxiliary facility of the Camp Davis-Holly Ridge complex 50 miles north. An airstrip was built through the landface mounds, obliterating several of them, and much of Battery Buchanan was destroyed during construction of facilities on the base.

Ten years after World War II ended, Robert Harrill, the "Fort Fisher Hermit," took up residence in one of the old ammunition bunkers along the sea, near the current state aquarium. He had dropped out of society, leaving a family behind, and enjoyed the natural surroundings of the sea and the shore. He gained a local reputation as something of a philosopher, and thousands of visitors came to see him and hear his pearls of wisdom about life. Harrill died under mysterious circumstances in 1972, but visitors still make pilgrimages to his old bunker-home. [21]

As the decades went by, the Atlantic continued to bore its way through the peninsula, threatening to make an island of the southern end of Federal Point where the fort and the aquarium sit, or wipe it away entirely. Finally, in the late 1990's, a massive rock revetment was built along the beach adjacent to the fort's remains, to halt erosion. As of this date, it seems to be having a positive effect.

The state, which began creating a battlefield historic site in the late 1950's to early 1960's, has in recent years begun restoring the remaining mounds. They have rebuilt a palisade fence similar to the one Colonel Lamb erected in the fall of 1864, and have installed walking trails and historical plaques throughout the area. Fortunately, the area of the fort that witnessed some of the bloodiest fighting during the first several hours of battle, still remains. Despite the loss of so much of the fort to the sea over the last 70 odd years, Fort Fisher State Historic Site, with its museum, walking trails and historical markers, is one of the finest and most educational of all North Carolina's historic sites to visit and learn. For those with family connections to its history, it is also a gripping and emotional journey into one's heritage.

Endnotes to Epilogue

1. O.R., Volume XLVI, Part I, p.439-440; Confederate Goliath, p.251
2. Denson, C.B., "William Henry Chase Whiting, Major General C.S. Army," S.H.S.P., Volume XXVI, (1898), p.173
3. Confederate Goliath, p.252-253
4. ORN, Volume 10, p.433
5. Confederate Goliath, p.269-271; Massachusetts Military Historical Papers, p.384-385
6. Confederate Goliath, p.271-272
7. Generals in Blue, p.109-110, p.497-498; Confederate Goliath, p.254-255
8. Confederate Goliath, p.170-174, p.265-268; Martin Curtis account of Fort Fisher, p.307; Massachusetts Military Historical Papers, p.396-400, p.402-407, p.409-415; O.R., Volume XLII, Part I, p.986; Generals in Blue, p.106-107
9. Massachusetts Military Historical Papers, p.403-409; O.R., Volume XLVI, Part I, p.394, p.399, p.415-416, p.418
10. Generals in Blue, p.107; Confederate Goliath, p.267
11. Generals in Blue, p.5-6
12. Confederate Goliath, p.255-257; Porter, Naval History of the Civil War, p.700-701
13. A Sailor's Log, p.101-106
14. A Sailor's Log, p.230, p.393, p.440-459; Confederate Goliath, p.262
15. Bradley, Mark L., *Last Stand in the Carolinas, The Battle of Bentonville,* p.137-139, p.178-181, Savas Woodbury Publishers, Campbell, California, 1996; Battles & Leaders, Volume IV, p.703-704
16. Generals in Gray, p.30-31
17. General Robert F. Hoke, p.x-xi, p.169, p.335-340, p.344, p.352-355
18. Charlotte News, November 3, 1940; Charlotte News, June 15, 1948; Hoar, Jay S., *The South's Last Boys in Gray, A Epic Prose Elegy,* p.526-557, Bowling Green State University Popular Press, Bowling Green, Ohio, 1986
19. Recollections of Joseph Piram King, p.7-8, p.12-14, p.16-17; Chronicles, p.639; "The Ministry of Joseph P. King", p.1-9, p.11, Unpublished recollections of the ministry of Reverend Joseph P. King of the First Advent Christian Church, Wilmington, author's collection; Russell, Anne and Marjorie Megivern, with Kevin Coughlin, *North Carolina Portraits of*

Faith, a pictorial history of religions, p.180, p.186-187, Donning Company Publishers, Norfolk/Virginia Beach, Virginia, 1986

20. *The Wilmington News*, June 20, 1946
21. Confederate Goliath, p.272-274; Wilmington Campaign, p.180-183

Appendix:
Confederate and Union Forces at the Second Battle of Fort Fisher
January 13 - 15, 1865
(from Battles & Leaders of the Civil War, Vol. IV*)*

CONFEDERATE STATES ARMY
General Braxton Bragg (department commander)
Major General William H.C. Whiting (district commander)
Brigadier General Louis Hebert (Defenses, Mouth of Cape Fear River)
GARRISON OF FORT FISHER
Colonel William Lamb, Major James M. Stevenson (ill), Major James Reilly
10th North Carolina Artillery (1st Artillery) Major James Reilly (2 companies)
Company F, Captain E.D. Walsh
Company K, Captain William Shaw
36th North Carolina Troops (2nd Artillery), Major James M. Stevenson (ill),
Captain Daniel Munn (10 companies)
Company A, Captain R.J. Murphy
Company B, Captain Daniel Munn
Company C, Captain K.J. Braddy
Company D, Captain E.B. Dudley
Company E, Captain O.H. Powell
Company F, Lieutenant E.L. Hunter
Company G. Captain William Swain
Company H, Captain Daniel Patterson
Company I, Captain J.F. Melvin
Company K, Captain William F. Brooks
40th North Carolina Troops (3rd Artillery) (4 companies)
Company D, Captain James L. Lane
Company E, Captain M.H. McBryde
Company G, Captain George C. Buchan
Company K, Captain D.J. Clarke
1st North Carolina Artillery Battalion
Company D, Captain James L. McCormic
3rd North Carolina Artillery Battalion
Company C, Captain John M. Sutton
13th North Carolina Artillery Battalion
Company D, Captain Z.T. Adams
Naval Detachment

Captain A.C. Van Benthuysen

BATTERY BUCHANAN
Captain R.F. Chapman, Confederate States Navy

HOKE'S DIVISION (Sugar Loaf Defenses)
Major General Robert F. Hoke
Clingman's Brigade, Brigadier General Thomas L. Clingman
8th North Carolina State Troops
31st North Carolina Troops
51th North Carolina Troops
61st North Carolina Troops
Colquitt's Brigade, Brigadier General Alfred H. Colquitt
6th Georgia Infantry
19th Georgia Infantry
23rd Georgia Infantry
27th Georgia Infantry
28th Georgia Infantry
Hagood's Brigade, Brigadier General Johnson Hagood
11th South Carolina Regiment Infantry
21st South Carolina Regiment Infantry
25th South Carolina Regiment Infantry
27th South Carolina Regiment Infantry
7th South Carolina Battalion Infantry
Kirkland's Brigade, Brigadier General William W. Kirkland
17th North Carolina Troops
42nd North Carolina Troops
50th North Carolina Troops
66th North Carolina Troops
Cavalry, Colonel Thomas J. Lipscomb
2nd South Carolina Cavalry

UNITED STATES ARMY
Major General Alfred H. Terry
TWENTY-FOURTH ARMY CORPS
SECOND DIVISION, Brigadier General Adelbert Ames
First Brigade, Brevet Brigadier General N. Martin Curtis, Major Ezra L. Walrath
3rd New York
112th New York
117th New York
142nd New York

Second Brigade, Colonel Galusha Pennypacker, Major Oliver P. Harding

      47th New York
      48th New York
      76th Pennsylvania
      97th Pennsylvania
      203rd Pennsylvania

Third Brigade, Colonel Louis Bell, Colonel Alonzo Alden

      13th Indiana
      4th New Hampshire
      115th New York
      169th New York

Second Brigade, First Division (temporarily attached to Second Division), Colonel Joseph C. Abbott

      6th Connecticut
      7th Connecticut
      3rd New Hampshire
      7th New Hampshire
      16th New York Heavy Artillery (detachment)

TWENTY-FIFTH ARMY CORPS

THIRD DIVISION, Brigadier General Charles J. Paine

Second Brigade, Colonel John W. Ames

      4th U.S. Colored Troops
      6th U.S. Colored Troops
      30th U.S. Colored Troops
      39th U.S. Colored Troops

Third Brigade, Colonel Elias Wright

      1st U.S. Colored Troops
      5th U.S. Colored Troops
      10th U.S. Colored Troops
      27th U.S. Colored Troops
      37th U.S. Colored Troops

Artillery

      1st Connecticut Heavy Artillery, Companies B, G. and L
      16th Battery New York Light Artillery
      3rd United States Artillery, Battery E

Engineers

      15th New York, Companies A and I

**UNITED STATES NAVY AT FORT FISHER,
DECEMBER 1864 AND JANUARY 1865
NORTH ATLANTIC SQUADRON**
Rear Admiral David D. Porter, Commanding

Lieutenant Commander K.R. Breese, Fleet Captain
FIRST DIVISION, Commodore Henry K. Thatcher
SECOND DIVISION, Commodore Joseph Lanman
THIRD DIVISION, Commodore James Findlay Schenck
FOURTH DIVISION, Commodore S.W. Godon
IRONCLAD DIVISION, Commodore William Radford
VESSELS:
Flagship – *Malvern*
Ironclads – *Canonicus, Mahopac, Monadnock, New Ironsides, Saugus*
Screw Frigates – *Colorado, Minnesota, Wabash*
Side-Wheel Steamers (1st Class) – *Powhatan, Susquehanna*
Screw Sloops – *Brooklyn, Juniata, Mohican, Shenandoah, Ticonderoga, Tuscarora*
Screw Gun-Vessels – *Kansas, Maumee, Nyack, Pequo*t, *Yantic*
Screw Gunboats – *Chippewa, Huron, Seneca, Unadilla*
Double-Enders – *Iosco, Mackinaw, Maratanza, Osceola, Pawtuxet, Pontoosuc, Sassacus, Tacony*
Miscellaneous Vessels – *Fort Jackson, Monticello, Nereus, Quaker City, Rhode Island, Santiago de Cuba, Vanderbilt*
Powder Vessel – *Louisiana*
Reserve – *Ad-Vance, Alabama, Britannia, Cherokee, Emma, Gettysburg, Governor Buckingham, Howquah, Keystone State, Lilian, Little Ada, Moccasin, Nansemond, Tristram Shandy, Wilderness*
In the second attack on Fort Fisher, the fleet was composed of the same vessels, with the exception of the *Nyack, Keystone State,* and *Quaker City*. The following additions were also made to the fleet: *Montgomery, R.R. Cuyler, Aries, Eolus, Fort Donelson* and *Republic*

Armament of the Fleet
In the first attack on Fort Fisher, the total number of shipboard guns available for use was 619. In the second attack, the total number of guns was 627.

Bibliography

• *"A Yankee Account of the Battle at Fort Fisher"*, **Our Living and Our Dead**, Volume I, September 1874 – February 1875
• Abernathy, Thomas P., **The South in the New Nation, 1789-1819, Volume IV of A History Of the South**, Louisiana State University Press, Baton Rouge, 1961
• *"Address Delivered by Governor Z.B. Vance of North Carolina, August 18, 1875"*, **Southern Historical Society Papers**, Volume XIV, 1886, of 52 Volumes, Richmond, Virginia
• Ammen, Daniel, **The Navy in the Civil War: the Atlantic Coast**, Charles Scribner's Sons, New York, 1883
• Ames, Adelbert, Brevet Major General, *"The Capture of Fort Fisher, January 15, 1865"*, read before the Society December 3, 1895, **Papers of the Military Historical Society of Massachusetts**, Volume IX, published by the Society, 1912
• Ashe, Samuel A., **History of North Carolina, Volume II, from 1783 to 1925**, Edwards & Broughton Printing Company, Raleigh, 1925
• Baird, Nancy D., *"The Yellow Fever Plot"*, *"Civil War Times Illustrated"*, November 1974
• Barefoot, Daniel W., **General Robert F. Hoke, Lee's Modest Warrior**, John Blair Publishing, Winston Salem, North Carolina, 1996
• Barrett, John G., **The Civil War in North Carolina**, University of North Carolina Press, Chapel Hill, 1963
• Bearss, Edwin, **The Campaign for Vicksburg, Volume I – Vicksburg is the Key**, Morningside House, Dayton Ohio, 1985
• Beauregard, General G.T., *"The First Battle of Bull Run"*, **Battles and Leaders of the Civil War**, Volume I of Four Volumes, Edited by Robert U. Johnson and Clarence C. Buel, Century Company, New York, 1887
• Bone, J.W., *"Civil War Reminiscences"*, Manuscript dated 1904, North Carolina Department of Archives and History, Raleigh
• Braddy, Kinchen, letter to Z.T. Fulmore, March 25, 1901, North Carolina Department of Archives and History, Raleigh
• Bradley, Mark L., **Last Stand in the Carolinas, The Battle of Bentonville**, Savas Woodbury Publishers, Campbell, California, 1996
• Bradley, Stephen E., editor, **North Carolina Confederate Militia Officers Roster, As Contained in the Adjutant-General's Officers Roster**, Broadfoot Publishing, Wilmington, North Carolina, 1992
• Bright, Leslie, **The Blockade Runner Modern Greece and Her Cargo**, Division of Archives and History, North Carolina Department of Cultural Resources, Raleigh, 1977

• Bradshaw, Timothy E., **Battery Wagner: The Siege, The Men Who Fought, and the Casualties,** Palmetto Historical Works, Columbia, South Carolina, 1993

• Burgwyn, Captain W.H.S., *"Clingman's Brigade"*, from **Histories of the Several Regiments and Battalions from North Carolina in the Great War, 1861-'65,** Volume IV of Five Volumes, Edited by Walter Clark, Nash Brothers Book and Job Printers, Goldsboro, North Carolina, 1901

• Burnside, General A.E., "The Burnside Expedition", from **Battles and Leaders of the Civil War,** Volume I, Edited by Robert U. Johnson and Clarence C. Buel

• Busbee, Lieutenant F.H., *"Junior Reserves' Brigade"*, from **Histories of the Several Regiments and Battalions from North Carolina in the Great War, 1861-'65,** Volume IV, Edited by Walter Clark

• Butler, Benjamin F. **Butler's Book,** A.M. Thayer & Company, Boston, 1892

• Calder, William, First Battalion N.C. Heavy Artillery, Diary of January – February, 1865, William Perkins Library, Duke University, Durham, North Carolina

• Cantwell, Colonel John L., *"Capture of Forts Before the War"*, from **Histories of the Several Regiments and Battalions from North Carolina in the Great War, 1861-'65,** Volume V, Edited by Walter Clark

• *"Captain John Pembroke Jones"*, **Confederate Veteran,** Volume XVIII (1910), Nashville, Tennessee

• Captains Cowan, John and J.I. Metts, "Third Regiment", from **Histories of the Several Regiments and Battalions from North Carolina in the Great War, 1861-'65,** Volume I, Edited by Walter Clark

• Carse, Robert, **Blockade, the Civil War at Sea,** Rinehart & Company, New York, 1958

• *"Charlotte News"*, Charlotte, North Carolina, articles related to George W. Benson, last Confederate soldier of Fort Fisher, November 3, 1940, January 15, 1944, and June 15, 1948

• Cleer, James J. Papers, *"Letter to Father & Mother, January 17, 1865"*, Manuscript Department, William R. Perkins Library, Duke University, Durham, North Carolina

• Coddington, Edwin B., **The Gettysburg Campaign, A Study in Command,** Charles Scribner's Sons, New York, 1968

• *"Colonel William Lamb Day Booklet"*, Carolina Printing Company, Wilmington, North Carolina, 1962

• Confederate Soldier Memorial and mass grave historical inscription for Confederate dead from Battle of Fort Fisher, Oakdale Cemetery, Wilmington, North Carolina

• Coulter, E. Merton, **The Confederate States of America, Volume VII of A History of the South,** Louisiana State University Press, Baton Rouge, 1950

• Cozzens, Peter, **No Better Place to Die, The Battle of Stones River,** University of Illinois Press, Urbana and Chicago, 1990

• Cozzens, Peter, **The Shipwreck of Their Hopes, The Battles for Chattanooga,** University of Illinois Press, 1994

• Craven, Avery, **The Growth of Southern Nationalism, 1848-1861, Volume VI of A History of the South,** Louisiana State University Press, Baton Rouge, 1953

• Curtis, Newton Martin, Brevet Major General, "The Capture of Fort Fisher", from **Civil War Papers of the State of Massachusetts, Military Order of the Loyal Legion of the United States,** Volume I, 1900

• Daley, Robert W., editor, **Aboard the U.S.S. Florida, 1863-1865,** p.xiii, Arno Press, New York, 1980

• Davis, Burke, **Our Incredible Civil War,** Holt, Rinehart & Winston, New York, 1960

• Davis, Jefferson, **The Rise and Fall of the Confederate Government, Volume I,** reprint by Thomas Yoseloff Publisher, Cranbury, New Jersey, 1958

• Davis, Sergeant T.C., *"Fortieth Regiment (Third Artillery)",* from **Histories of the Several Regiments and Battalions from North Carolina in the Great War, 1861-'65,** Volume II, Edited by Walter Clark

• Denson, Claude B., **An Address Containing a Memoir of the Late Major-General William Henry Chase Whiting,** Edwards & Broughton, Raleigh, North Carolina, 1895

• Denson, Captain Claude B., *"The Corps of Engineers",* from **Histories of the Several Regiments and Battalions from North Carolina in the Great War, 1861-'65,** Volume IV, Edited by Walter Clark

• Denson, C.B., *"William Henry Chase Whiting, Major-General, C.S. Army",* from **Southern Historical Society Papers,** Volume XXVI, 1898

• DeRosset, Colonel William L., article to *Wilmington Messenger,* October 1906, in North Carolina Department Archives & History, Raleigh

• DeRosset, Colonel William L., "Third Regiment", from **Histories of the Several Regiments and Battalions from North Carolina in the Great War, 1861-'65,** Volume I, Edited by Walter Clark

• Donnelly, Ralph W., **The Confederate States Marine Corps: The Rebel Leathernecks,** White Mane Publishing Company, Shippensburg, Pennsylvania, 1989

• Dowdey, Clifford, **The Land They Fought For, The Story of the South as the Confederacy, 1832-1865,** Doubleday & Company, Garden City, New York, 1955

• Elliott, Captain Charles G., *"Kirkland's Brigade, Hoke's Division, 1864-'65",* from **Southern Historical Society Papers,** Volume XXIII of fifty-two volumes, Richmond, Virginia

• Elliott, Captain Charles G., *"Martin-Kirkland Brigade"*, from **Histories of the Several Regiments and Battalions from North Carolina in the Great War, 1861-'65,** Volume IV, Edited by Walter Clark

• Evans, Clement, editor, **Confederate Military History, North Carolina,** Confederate Publishing Company, Atlanta, Georgia, 1899

• Evans, Robley D., **A Sailor's Log: Recollections of Forty Years of Naval Life,** D. Appleton Company, New York, 1901

• Foard, Charles H., Map – *"A Chart of Wrecks of Vessels Sunk or Captured Near Wilmington, N.C., Circa 1861-1865"*, Revised, 1968

• Fonvielle, Chris E. Jr., **Fort Anderson, Battle for Wilmington,** Savas Publishing Company, Mason City, Iowa, 1999

• Fonvielle, Chris E. Jr., **The Wilmington Campaign: Last Rays of Departing Hope,** Savas Publishing Company, Campbell, California, 1997

• Foote, Shelby, **The Civil War, A Narrative, Fort Sumter to Perryville,** Random House, New York, 1958

• Foote, Shelby, **The Civil War, A Narrative, Red River to Appomattox,** Random House, New York, 1974

• Freeman, Douglas Southall, **Lee's Lieutenants, A Study in Command,** Volume III of Three Volumes, Charles Scribner's Sons, New York, 1944

• General Order Book of the Eleventh North Carolina Troops, March 1862-June 1863, Daniels Collection, Charlotte, North Carolina

• Gibbons, Tony, **Warships and Naval Battles of the Civil War,** W.H. Smith Publishers, New York, 1989

• Gragg, Rod, **Confederate Goliath, The Battle of Fort Fisher,** HarperCollins Publishers, New York, 1991

• Gragg, Rod, *"Fort Fisher: The Confederate Goliath, 1862-1864"*, Master's Thesis, University of South Carolina, Columbia, 1979

• Grant, U.S., **Personal Memoirs of U.S. Grant,** World Publishing Company, Cleveland, 1952

• Greenberg, R.G., *"A Mysterious Raid"*, **Confederate Veteran,** Volume XXVI, 1918

• Greer, William R., *"Recollections of a Private Soldier of the Army of the Confederate States"*, Manuscript Department, William R. Perkins Library, Duke University, Durham

• Griggs, Elisha, *"History & War Record of Elisha Griggs, 40th N.C. Troops"*, unpublished manuscript, copy in author's collection

• Hagood, Johnson, **Memoirs of the War of Secession,** The State Company, Columbia, South Carolina, 1910

• *"Hebe Skirmish Centennial and Fort Fisher Visitor Center-Museum Groundbreaking Program"*, Commercial Printing and Mailing Company, Wilmington, North Carolina, 1963

• Hebert, Louis, *"Autobiography of General Louis Hebert"*, unpublished manuscript, Southern Historical Collection, University of North Carolina, Chapel Hill
• Herring, Ethel and Williams, Carolee, **Fort Caswell In War and Peace,** Broadfoot's Bookmark, Wendell, North Carolina, 1983
• Hill, Daniel H., **Bethel to Sharpsburg – A History of North Carolina in the War Between The States,**Volume I of Two volumes, The North Carolina Historical Commission, Edwards & Broughton Company, Raleigh, 1926
• Hinsdale, Colonel John W., *"Seventy-Second Regiment (Third Junior Reserves)"*, from **Histories of the Several Regiments and Battalions from North Carolina in the Great War, 1861-'65,** Volume IV, Edited by Walter Clark
• Hoar, Jay S., **The South's Last Boys in Gray, An Epic Prose Elegy,** Bowling Green State University Popular Press, Bowling Green, Ohio, 1986
• Hoge, Rev. Dr. Moses D., *"Running the Blockade"*, from **Histories of the Several Regiments And Battalions from North Carolina in the Great War, 1861-'65,** Volume V, Edited by Walter Clark
• Honeycutt, Ava L., *Fort Fisher, Malakoff of the South*, Master's Thesis, Duke University, Durham, 1963
• Hufham, Rev. J.D., **Memoir of Rev. John L. Prichard, Late Pastor of the First Baptist Church, Wilmington, N.C.,** Hufham and Hughes Publishers, Raleigh, 1867
• Huse, Caleb, **The Supplies for the Confederate Army, How They Were Obtained in Europe and How Paid For,** T.R. Marvin & Son, Boston, 1904
• Izlar, William V., **A Sketch of the War Record of the Edisto Rifles, 1861-1865,** The State Company, Columbia, South Carolina, 1914
• King, Isaac W., National Archives service record of First Sergeant Isaac W. King, Third North Carolina State Troops, author's collection
• King, James M., National Archives service record of James Madison King, Third North Carolina State Troops, author's collection
• King, Joseph P., *"Personal Recollections of Joseph Piram King"*, author's collection of great-grandfather's papers
• King, Joseph P., *"The Ministry of Joseph P. King"*, First Advent Christian Church, Wilmington, author's collection of great-grandfather's papers
• Lamb, William, "Account of Defense and Fall of Fort Fisher", from **Southern Historical Society Papers,** Volume X, 1882
• Lamb, William, **Colonel Lamb's Story of Fort Fisher,** Blockade Runner Museum, Carolina Beach, North Carolina, 1966
• Lamb, William, Description of wife, personal papers of Colonel Lamb in author's collection
• Lamb, William, *"Diary of Colonel William Lamb"*, Lamb papers, Earl Greg Swem Library, College of William and Mary, Williamsburg, Virginia

• Lamb, William, *"Defence of Fort Fisher, North Carolina"*, read before the Society February 4, 1896, **Papers of the Military Historical Society of Massachusetts,** Volume IX

• Lamb, William, *"Defense of Fort Fisher"*, from **Battles and Leaders of the Civil War,** Volume I , Edited by Robert U. Johnson and Clarence C. Buel

• Lamb, William, *"Fight With Blockaders"*, from **Histories of the Several Regiments and Battalions from North Carolina in the Great War, 1861-'65,** Volume V, Edited by Walter Clark

• Lamb, William, *"Fort Fisher – The Battles Fought There in 1864 and '65"*, from **Southern Historical Society Papers,** Volume XXI, 1893

• Lamb, William, *"The Heroine of Confederate Point"*, from **Southern Historical Society Papers,** Volume XX, 1892

• Lamb, William, *"Thirty-Sixth Regiment"*, from **Histories of the Several Regiments and Battalions from North Carolina in the Great War, 1861-'65,** Volume II, Edited by Walter Clark

• Lamb, Lieutenant Wilson G., "Seventeenth Regiment", from **Histories of the Several Regiments and Battalions from North Carolina in the Great War, 1861-'65,** Volume II, Edited by Walter Clark

• *"Laurentian"* of St. Lawrence College, May 1901, Volume 14, #5, handwritten copy in archives Sargeant Memorial Room, Norfolk Public Library

• Longacre, Edward G., Editor, **From Antietam to Fort Fisher: The Civil War Letters of Edward K. Wightman, 1862-1865,** Associated University Presses, Cranbury, New Jersey, 1985

• Lossing, Benson J., *"The First Attack on Fort Fisher"*, **Annals of the War,** Facsimile reprint of 1878 edition, Morningside House, Dayton, Ohio, 1988

• *"Lower Cape Fear Historical Society Bulletin"*, June 1967, Wilmington, North Carolina

• *"Lower Cape Fear Historical Society Bulletin"*, March 1968

• *"Lower Cape Fear Historical Society Bulletin"*, May 1978

• *"Lower Cape Fear Historical Society Bulletin"*, February 1992

• Lynch, Flag Officer William F., C.S.N., Signal note from Lynch to Colonel William Lamb, May 6, 1864, papers of Colonel Lamb in author's collection

• Maffitt, Emma M., **Life and Services of John Newland Maffitt,** Neale Publishing Company, New York, 1906

• Maglenn, James, Chief Engineer, *"The Steamer Ad-Vance"*, from **Histories of the Several Regiments and Battalions from North Carolina in the Great War, 1861-'65,** Volume V, Edited by Walter Clark

• Manarin, Louis, **North Carolina Troops 1861-1865, A Roster,** Volume I of Fifteen Volumes, North Carolina Division of Archives and History, Raleigh, 1966

• McDonough, James L., **Chattanooga – A Death Grip on the Confederacy,** University of Tennessee Press, Knoxville, 1985

• McKethan, Lieutenant A.A., *"Fifty-First Regiment"*, from **Histories of the Several Regiments and Battalions from North Carolina in the Great War, 1861-'65,** Volume III, Edited by Walter Clark

• McKoy, Henry B., **Wilmington, N.C. – Do You Remember When?,** Keys Printing Company, Greenville, South Carolina

• McNeill, Sergeant T.A., *"Ninth Battalion (First Heavy Artillery)"*, from **Histories of the Several Regiments and Battalions from North Carolina in the Great War, 1861-'65,** Volume IV, Edited by Walter Clark

• Meares, Gaston, Gravestone memorial inscription of Colonel Gaston Meares, Oakdale Cemetery, Wilmington

• Moffett, George, *"Letter to wife Liz, January 2, 1865"*, Moffett family papers, South Carolina Historical Society, Charleston

• Moore, Louis T. **Stories Old and New of the Cape Fear Region,** Wilmington Printing Company, Wilmington, North Carolina, 1956

• Moore, Louis T., *"The Heroine of Fort Fisher"*, **Confederate Veteran,** Volume XXXVII, July 1929

• Moore, Mark A., **The Wilmington Campaign and the Battles for Fort Fisher,** Savas Publishing, Mason City, Iowa, 1999

• Murray, Paul and Stephen R. Bartlett, editors, *The Letters of Stephen Chaulker Bartlett Aboard the U.S.S. 'Lenapee', January to August 1865"*, from **North Carolina Historical Review,** Raleigh, January 1956

• Myrover, Lieutenant J.H., *"Thirteenth Battalion (Starr's Battalion Artillery)"*, from **Histories of the Several Regiments and Battalions from North Carolina in the Great War, 1861-'65,** Volume IV, Edited by Walter Clark

• *"North Carolina Women of the Confederacy"*, **Confederate Veteran,** Volume XXXVIII, November 1930

• Noe, Kenneth W., **Perryville, This Grand Havoc of Battle,** University Press of Kentucky, Lexington, 2001

• **Official Records of the Union and Confederate Navies in the War of the Rebellion,** 30 Volumes, Government Printing Office, Washington, D.C., 1897-1901

• Osterweis, Rollin G., *"The Idea of Southern Nationalism"*, from **The Causes of the American Civil War,** D.C. Heath and Company, Lexington, Massachusetts, 1961

• Oliver, William H., *"Blockade Running from Wilmington"*, **Confederate Veteran,** Volume III, December 1895

• **Papers of the Military Historical Society of Massachusetts, Volume IX, Operations on the Atlantic Coast 1861-1865, Virginia 1862, 1864,** published by the Society, 1912, reprint Edition Broadfoot Publishing Company, Wilmington, North Carolina, 1989

• *"Patriotic Mrs. Armand J. DeRosset"*, **Confederate Veteran,** Volume III, July 1895

• Phillips, Ulrich B., **American Negro Slavery,** Louisiana State University Press, Baton Rouge, 1966 reprint of 1918 edition
• Polley, J.B., **Hood's Texas Brigade, Its Marches Its Battles Its Achievements,** Morningside Bookshop, Dayton, Ohio, 1988
• Porter, Admiral David D., **Naval History of the Civil War,** Sherman Publishing Company New York, 1886
• Powell, Adjutant C.S., "Tenth Battalion (Second Heavy Artillery)", from **Histories of the Several Regiments and Battalions from North Carolina in the Great War, 1861-'65,**Volume IV, Edited by Walter Clark
• Price, Charles and Sturgill, Claude, *"Shock and Assault in the First Battle of Fort Fisher",* **The North Carolina Historical Review,** January 1970, Raleigh
• Reed, Rowena, **Combined Operations in the Civil War,** Naval Institute Press, Annapolis, Maryland, 1978
• Reilly, James, *"Major James Reilly's account of Battle of Fort Fisher",* unpublished manuscript in DeRosset Papers, North Carolina Department of Archives and History, Raleigh
• *"Rev. Moses D. Hoge, Pastor, Chaplain",* **Confederate Veteran,** Volume III, March 1895
• Roberts, Captain, (C. Augustus Hobart-Hampden), **Never Caught, Personal Adventures Connected With Twelve Successful Trips in Blockade-Running During the American Civil War, 1863-1864,** The Blockade Runner Museum, Carolina Beach, North Carolina, 1967
• Rose, George M., Adjutant, "Sixty-Sixth Regiment", from **Histories of the Several Regiments and Battalions from North Carolina in the Great War, 1861-'65,** Volume III, Edited by Walter Clark
• Roske, Ralph and Van Doren, Charles, **Lincoln's Commando, The Biography of Commander W.B. Cushing, U.S.N.,** Harper & Brothers, New York, 1957
• Ross, Edward FitzGerald, **Cities and Camps of the Confederate States,** reprint, University of Illinois Press, Urbana, 1958
• Ross, Ishbel, **Rebel Rose, Life of Rose O'Neal Greenhow, Confederate Spy,** Harper & Brothers Publishers, New York, 1954
• *"Running the Blockade. Interesting Narrative of Mr. James Sprunt",* from **Southern Historical Society Papers,** Volume XXIV, 1896
• Russell, Anne and Megivern, Marjorie, with Kevin Coughlin, **North Carolina Portraits of Faith, a pictorial history of religions,** Donning Company Publishers, Norfolk/Virginia Beach, Virginia, 1986
• Russell, Anne, **Wilmington – A Pictorial History,** Donning Company Publishers, Norfolk/Virginia Beach, Virginia, 1981
• Sanders, Lieutenant J.W., "Tenth Regiment", from **Histories of the Several Regiments and Battalions from North Carolina in the Great War, 1861-'65,** Volume I, Edited by Walter Clark

• Sands, Benjamin, **From Reefer to Rear-Admiral,**Frederick A. Stokes Company, New York, 1899
• Scaife, William R., **The March to the Sea,** McNaughton & Gunn Inc., Saline, Michigan, 1993
• Scharf, J. Thomas, **History of the Confederate States Navy From Its Organization to the Surrender of Its Last Vessel,** Rogers and Sherwood, New York, 1887
• Schiller, Herbert M., M.D., **The Bermuda Hundred Campaign,** *"Operations on the South Side of the James River, Virginia, May 1864"*, Morningside House, Dayton, Ohio, 1988
• Selfridge, Captain Thomas O. Jr., *"The Navy at Fort Fisher"*, from **Battles and Leaders of the Civil War,** Volume IV, Edited by Robert U. Johnson and Clarence C. Buel
• Shingleton, Royce G., **John Taylor Wood, Sea Ghost of the Confederacy,** University of Georgia Press, Athens, Georgia, 1979
• Sitterson, J.C., **The Secession Movement in North Carolina,** University of North Carolina Press, Chapel Hill, 1939
• Sprunt, James, **Chronicles of the Cape Fear River, 1660-1916,** Edwards & Broughton Printing Company, Raleigh, North Carolina, 1916
• Sprunt, James, **Tales of the Cape Fear Blockade,** Charles Towne Preservation Trust, Winnabow, North Carolina, 1960
• Sprunt, James, Purser, "Blockade Running", from **Histories of the Several Regiments and Battalions from North Carolina in the Great War, 1861-'65,** Volume V, Edited by Walter Clark
• Stick, David, **Bald Head, a History of Smith Island and Cape Fear,** Broadfoot's Bookmark, Wendell, North Carolina, 1985
• Still, William N., Editor, *"The Yankees Were Landing Below Us: The Journal of Robert Watson, C.S.N."*, Civil War Times Illustrated, April 1976
• Strode, Hudson, **Jefferson Davis, Tragic Hero, The Last Twenty-Five Years, 1864-1889,** Harcourt, Brace & World Inc., New York, 1964
• Sumner, Merlin E., Editor, **The Diary of Cyrus B. Comstock,** Morningside House, Dayton, Ohio, 1987
• Sword, Wiley, **Shiloh, Bloody April,** Morningside House, Dayton, Ohio, 1983
• Taylor, John D., *"Recollections of Colonel John D. Taylor"*, unpublished manuscript in North Carolina Department of Archives and History, Raleigh
• Taylor, Thomas, **Running the Blockade: A Personal Narrative of Adventures, Risks, and Escapes During the American Civil War,** Charles Scribner's Sons, New York, 1896
• Taylor, William B., Eleventh North Carolina Troops, *"Letter to mother, July 5, 1862"*, typescript copy in author's collection

• Terry, Captain Adrian, *"Capture of Fort Fisher"*, unpublished manuscript in Terry family papers, Terry Collection, Yale University Library, New Haven, Connecticut

• Terry, Captain Adrian, *"Wilmington and Fort Fisher"*, unpublished manuscript in Terry family papers, Terry Collection, Yale University Library, New Haven

• **The New Encyclopaedia Britannica,** Volume 12, University of Chicago, Chicago, Illinois, 1987

• Thomas, C.M.D., **Letters from the Colonel's Lady: Correspondence of Mrs. William Lamb, Written from Fort Fisher, N.C., C.S.A.,** Charles Towne Preservation Trust, Winnabow, North Carolina, 1965

• Torrent, Captain Joseph F., *"With the Blockade Runners"*, **Confederate Veteran,** Volume XXXIII, June 1925

• Towle, G.F., *"Terry's Fort Fisher Expedition"* from **Our Living and Our Dead,** Volume III, July to December, 1875, Raleigh

• Tredwell, Adam, Paymaster, "North Carolina Navy", from **Histories of the Several Regiments and Battalions from North Carolina in the Great War, 1861-'65,** Volume V, Edited by Walter Clark

• Tucker, Glenn, **Chickamauga: Bloody Battle in the West,** Morningside Bookshop, Dayton, Ohio, 1984

• Tunnard, W.H., **A Southern Record. The History of the Third Regiment Louisiana Infantry,** Morningside Bookshop, Dayton, Ohio, 1988

• Tyler, Lyon G., Editor, *"Men of Mark in Virginia"*, **Ideals of American Life. A Collection of Biographies of the Leading Men of the State,** archives of Sargeant Memorial Room, Norfolk Public Library, Norfolk, Virginia

• Vance, Governor Z.B., "North Carolina's Record", from **Histories of the Several Regiments and Battalions from North Carolina in the Great War, 1861-'65,** Volume V, Edited by Walter Clark

• Vandiver, Frank E., **Ploughshares into Swords, Josiah Gorgas and Confederate Ordnance,** University of Texas Press, Austin, 1952

• *Virginian-Pilot* newspaper, March 24, 1909, Norfolk, Virginia

• Waddell, Alfred M., **Some Memories of My Life,** Edwards & Broughton Printing, Raleigh, North Carolina, 1908

• **War of the Rebellion, A Compilation of the Official Records of the Union and Confederate Armies,** 70 Volumes in 128 Parts, U.S. War Department, Government Printing Office, Washington, D.C., 1880-1901

• Warner, Ezra, **Generals in Blue,** Louisiana State University Press, Baton Rouge, 1964

• Warner, Ezra, **Generals in Gray,** Louisiana State University Press, Baton Rouge, 1959

• Watkins, Mrs.Gipp, *"Kentucky in the War Between the States"*, **Confederate Veteran,** Volume XXXV, December 1927

• White, John, Commissioner, *"North Carolina's Financial Operations in England"*, from**Histories of the Several Regiments and Battalions from North Carolina in the Great War, 1861-'65,** Volume V, Edited by Walter Clark
• Williams, Isabel M. & McEachern, Lleora H., **Salt, That Necessary Article,** Louis T. Moore Memorial Fund, Wilmington, North Carolina, 1973
• *Wilmington Daily Journal*, November 1860 – February 1865, Wilmington, North Carolina
• *Wilmington Morning Star*, May 22, 1912, Wilmington, North Carolina
• *Wilmington News*, June 20, 1946, Wilmington, North Carolina
• *Wilmington Sunday Star-News, Cape Fear Section*, March 7, 1976, Wilmington, North Carolina
• Wood, Richard E., *Port Town at War: Wilmington, North Carolina 1860-1865*, Unpublished Doctoral Dissertation at Florida State University, 1976

Index

Rip, the, sandbar off Confederate Point, p.214, 247-248

River Road, p.252, 285, 332, 339-340, 344, 346

Roanoke Island, NC, Federal capture of, p.41-43

Robert E. Lee (former Giraffe), blockade-runner, p.109, 155, 183

Roby, 1st Lt., F.M., p.260

Roe, Cmdr. F.A., p.190-191

Rollins, Lt.Col. Augustus, p.352

Rose, 1st Lt. George M., p.260, 302, 308, 355, 367, 373

Ross, Capt. E. FitzGerald, p.182-183

Sacramento, U.S.S., p.100

Saint George's, Bermuda, p.51-52, 117

Saint Philip's Church, p.375

Salisbury Confederate prison, NC, p.84, 87

Sampson, transport steamer, p.332

Sanders, John, p.48

Sands, Capt. Benjamin F., p.95-96, 106, 205, 319-320

Sands, Henry, p.286

Santiago de Cuba, U.S.S., p.227

Sassacus, U.S.S., p.190-191, 382-383

Saunders, Maj. William, p.309, 326, 331

Savannah, GA, p.253-255, 369

Schenck, Commodore James, p.264

Schofield, Maj.Gen John, captures Wilmington, p.385; operations against defenses of Wilmington, p.371-385; replaces Alfred Terry as commander U.S. Army forces, p.369-370

Scotch Boys, p.36

Scotch Greys, p.113

Scott, Comdr. Gustavus, p.68-70

Second Brigade, First Division, Twenty-Fourth Corps, p.300

Second Brigade, Second Division, Twenty-Fourth Corps, p.299, 328, 342

Second Brigade, U.S. Colored Troops, Twenty-Fifth Corps, p.300

Second Division, Twenty-Fifth Corps, p.256, 289

Second Division, Twenty-Fourth Corps, p.350

Seddon, James A. (C.S. Secretary of War), p.96, 103, 123-124, 185, 246, 259, 302-303

Selfridge, Lt.Cmdr. Thomas O., p.29, 264, 329-330, 338

Sharp, Lt.Col. Thomas H., p.270, 283-284

Sharpsburg (Antietam), MD, battle of, p.154-155, 385

Shaw, Col. Henry, p.42

Shawmut, U.S.S., p.383

Shepherd's Battery, Fort Fisher, p.60, 267-268, 287, 332, 334, 340, 342-343

Sherman, Maj.Gen. William T., p.253, 298-299, 365, 368-369

Shiloh, TN, battle of, p.243

Shipman, William, p.267

Shokokon, U.S.S., p.120

Signal Corps, Confederate, use of on blockade-runners, p.98-99, 189

Simonton, Col. Charles, p.364, 380

Sinton, William, p.267

Sloan, Maj. Benjamin, p.270

Smith, Col. John F., p.340

Smith's Island (Bald Head Island), p.32, 108, 112-115, 170-175, 186, 203-205, 288, 364-365

Smithville Guards, p.7

Smithville (Southport), NC, p.6, 10, 40, 44, 48, 195-197, 206, 220, 251, 295, 320, 323, 332, 365, 375

Soldiers Aid Society, Wilmington, p.141142, 233, 295-296

Sophia, blockade-runner, p.71

South Carolina, secession from Union, p.6

South Carolina Troops: 2nd Cavalry, p.292, 308, 322, 368, 375; 7th Bn., p.260; 11th, p.332, 380; 21st, p.332, 380; 25th, p.302, 332, 363, 380

Sprunt, Alexander, p.147-148

Stanton, Edwin M. (U.S. Secretary of War), p.298

Starr's Battery, p.63, 69

Stars and Stripes, U.S.S., p.52

State of Georgia, U.S.S., p.100, 109

Steljes, Dick, p.384

Sterl, Col. Oscar (and Sterl's Brigade), p.375, 377-380, 383

Stevenson, Maj. James M., p.137, 253-255

Illustrations

collection

Chapter 8:

- **Interior land face**, FFSHS
- **Gen. P.G.T. Beauregard**, LC
- **Gen. Braxton Bragg**, LC
- **Ft. Fisher's 32lb. seacoast gun**, Jack E. Fryar, Jr.
- **Battery Buchanan**, FFSHS
- **Sugar Loaf**, author's collection
- **RAdm. David Dixon Porter**, NA
- *USS Louisiana*, FFSHS
- **MajGen. Robert Hoke**, NCDAH
- **MajGen. Godfrey Weitzel**, NA
- **BrigGen. Charles Paine**, NA
- **BrigGen. Adelbert Ames**, LC

Chapter 9:

- **Gen. Newton Martin Curtis**, LC
- **MajGen. Alfred Terry**, NA
- **Ensign Robley Evans**, *A Sailor's Log*
- **"Bloody Gate,"** FFSHS

Chapter 10:

- **Bombardment of Fort Fisher**, FFSHS
- **U.S. Colored Troops**, NA
- **LtCmdr. Kidder Breese**, FFSHS
- **Capt. Lucien Dawson**, NA
- **Capt. Kinchen Braddy**, NCDAH
- *Assault on the North East Basation*, FFSHS
- **Storming Bloody Gate**, *Frank Leslie's Illustrated News*
- **Col. Galusha Pennypacker**, NA
- **Col. Louis Bell**, NA

Chapter 11:

- *Capture of Fort Fisher*, courtesy North Carolina Collection, UNC-Chapel Hill
- **4th gun emplacement**, FFSHS
- **The magazine explosion**, FFSHS
- **Site of magazine explosion**, FFSHS
- **Fort Anderson 1964**, NCDAH
- **Gen. Johnson Hagood**, NA
- **MajGen. John Schofield**, LC
- **MajGen. Jacob Cox**, LC
- **Shelling of Fort Anderson**, BT/FASHS

Epilogue:

- **Whiting's grave**, author's collection
- **William Lamb as an old man**, FFSHS

- **Pvt. George Benson**, courtesy Doris Lewis
- **Benson's grave marker**, author's collection

- *Author's Picture courtesy of Brad Bush*

About The Author...

James Laurence Walker, Jr. is a 59-year-old native of Wilmington who now lives in Charlotte, North Carolina. A Marine Corps veteran of Vietnam, he is a graduate of UNC-Charlotte with a degree in history. Walker has been a student of the War Between the States all of his life, and a reenactor since 1976. He is a member of the 30th North Carolina Troops, Company K (Reactivated), the Piedmont (Charlotte) Civil War Roundtable, and the Sergeant Aaron L. DeArmond Chapter, Robert E. Lee Confederate Heritage Association. Larry Walker has spoken to schools and various history groups in the two Carolinas and Virginia for over thirty years, on topics ranging from Fort Fisher to Confederate regimental battleflags. Since 1976, he has supervised the fund-raising and erection of eleven Confederate monuments, one World War II monument, and five Confederate soldier headstones, including that of George Benson, the last survivor of Fort Fisher. His initial research and writing on Fort Fisher and Wilmington began in the 1980s. For almost forty years, he has studied and hiked nearly all the battlegrounds of consequence in the war, be they in Virginia or Louisiana, Maryland or Missouri. Walker credits his life-long passion for Civil War history to his family's military heritage, and the numerous monuments erected all across the South by the women, past and present, of the United Daughters of the Confederacy. He is a retired credit manager of Clariant Corp., and lives in Charlotte with his wife, Janice. Their son, Shawn, daughter Kelly Burton and her husband, Anthony Burton, live nearby.

Printed in the United States
200681BV00003B/83/A